⚖ NOLO Products & Services

➡️ **Books & Software**

Get in-depth information. Nolo publishes hundreds of great books and software programs for consumers and business owners. Order a copy—or download an ebook version instantly—at Nolo.com.

➡️ **Legal Encyclopedia**

Free at Nolo.com. Here are more than 1,400 free articles and answers to common questions about everyday legal issues including wills, bankruptcy, small business formation, divorce, patents, employment and much more.

➡️ **Plain-English Legal Dictionary**

Free at Nolo.com. Stumped by jargon? Look it up in America's most up-to-date source for definitions of legal terms.

➡️ **Online Legal Documents**

Create documents at your computer. Go to Nolo.com to make a will or living trust, form an LLC or corporation or obtain a trademark or provisional patent. For simpler matters, download one of our hundreds of high-quality legal forms, including bills of sale, promissory notes, nondisclosure agreements and many more.

➡️ **Lawyer Directory**

Find an attorney at Nolo.com. Nolo's consumer-friendly lawyer directory provides in-depth profiles of lawyers all over America. From fees and experience to legal philosophy, education and special expertise, you'll find all the information you need to pick the right lawyer. Every lawyer listed has pledged to work diligently and respectfully with clients.

➡️ **Free Legal Updates**

Keep up to date. Check for free updates at Nolo.com. Under "Products," find this book and click "Legal Updates." You can also sign up for our free e-newsletters at Nolo.com/newsletters.

6th Edition

The Manager's Legal Handbook

Amy DelPo, J.D.

Lisa Guerin, J.D.

SIXTH EDITION	JANUARY 2012
Cover & Book Design	SUSAN PUTNEY
Proofreading	ROBERT WELLS
Index	VICTORIA BAKER
Printing	BANG PRINTING

DelPo, Amy, 1967–
   The manager's legal handbook / by Amy DelPo and Lisa Guerin. — 6th ed.
      p. cm.
   Includes index.
   Summary: "Explains how to handle employment issues that come up every day, including the hiring process, compensation and hours, discrimination and harassment, privacy rights, types of leave, working with independent contractors, and firing and layoffs."—Provided by publisher.
   ISBN 978-1-4133-1638-4 (pbk.) — ISBN 978-1-4133-1660-5 (epub e-book)
   1. Labor laws and legislation—United States—Popular works. 2. Labor contract—United States—Popular works. 3. Employee rights—United States—Popular works. 4. Executives—United States—Handbooks, manuals, etc. I. Guerin, Lisa, 1964– II. Title.
   KF3455.G84 2011
   344.7301—dc23

                                        2011023253

Please note

We believe accurate, plain-English legal information should help you solve many of your own legal problems. But this text is not a substitute for personalized advice from a knowledgeable lawyer. If you want the help of a trained professional—and we'll always point out situations in which we think that's a good idea—consult an attorney licensed to practice in your state.

Acknowledgments

The authors would like to thank:

On the first edition, our wonderful editor, Shannon Miehe, whose sense of humor, organizational skills, lightning-fast speed, and careful editing made working on this book a pleasure.

On subsequent editions, our editor and friend, Stephanie Bornstein, who helped transform the book into a must-have legal guide for managers.

Mary Randolph, Jake Warner, and Janet Portman, all of whom helped us figure out how to organize this material—and how to avoid the dreaded "scope creep."

Ella Hirst, Alayna Schroeder, and Drew Wheaton for meticulously researching and compiling the state charts.

Stan Jacobsen, for his research help and ever-positive attitude.

John M. True, III, formerly of Leonard Carder, LLP, in Oakland, California, for writing some of the privacy material and helping out with the information on unions.

Philip Monrad, also of Leonard Carder, for his generous help with the unions chapter.

Table of Contents

Navigating the Maze of Employment Law

Some managers learn the hard way that good intentions aren't enough. In these days of burgeoning employment laws, regulations, and lawsuits, successfully and safely managing workers (employees and independent contractors alike) requires a whole lot more than just following your instincts. Lawmakers and courts have created a complicated web of dos and don'ts that covers the entire spectrum of workplace issues, from hiring and firing to discrimination and harassment. If you are a supervisor, manager, or human resources specialist, you've got to learn how to navigate this legal maze or risk serious trouble for your company and yourself.

Fortunately, learning what you need to know to manage workers on a daily basis doesn't have to be time-consuming, difficult, or even unpleasant. This book distills these complicated issues down to the basics, providing the most important information you need to know when you walk into your workplace every day.

How to Use This Book

This book gives you the information you need to deal with many common workplace concerns and issues. Each chapter focuses on a specific employment law topic—such as hiring, compensation and hours, privacy in the workplace, and so on—and breaks that subject down into the issues managers are most likely to face.

Of course, every company is different and every manager has different areas of responsibility and expertise. Although this book explains the legal rules that apply to managers and companies alike, not every manager will have the authority to make ultimate decisions on matters of policy or serious personnel matters, such as firing and layoffs. We provide this information to give you some legal background that will help you understand your role in the process, as your company defines it.

Each chapter includes:

- **Frequently Asked Questions (FAQs).** We introduce you to the chapter topic through quick answers to questions that managers and employers commonly face.
- **Articles.** We break down the chapter's topic into a series of separate articles, so that you can get right to the information you need. That way, you can focus only on the rules that apply to the situation at hand without having to wade through an entire book looking for your answer.
- **50-State Charts.** We provide you with a summary of information on your state's legal requirements where necessary, in addition to the federal law covered in the chapter.
- **Lessons From the Real World.** Learn from the failures and victories of companies that have been taken to court by their employees.
- **Legal Dos and Don'ts.** We provide a handful of strategies to follow—and traps to avoid—as you implement the information in each chapter.
- **Test Your Knowledge.** Find out how well you understand each topic by taking our quiz at the end of each chapter.

You can read through the entire book at once, pick and choose among chapters of special interest to your company, or use the book as a desk reference by consulting particular articles as issues come up. No matter how you use the book, the basic information we provide will help answer your most common employment questions.

Additional Resources

Although most managers will rarely need more information than what we provide here, you might occasionally have a problem that requires you to seek additional help. We alert you to those potential trouble spots and point you toward resources that can give you the extra information you need.

The appendix (at the end of the book) contains a list of resources you can consult for more information. These resources include:

- Contact information for the federal agencies that enforce federal workplace laws, including the Equal Employment Opportunity Commission (EEOC), the Occupational Safety and Health Administration (OSHA), the Department of Labor (DOL), and the Federal Trade Commission (FTC).
- Contact information for the state agencies that enforce state workplace laws, including a list of state departments of labor and state fair employment offices.
- A list of Internet resources, including government agencies and private organizations whose websites provide helpful information about the topics we cover here.
- A list of Nolo's employment and human resources titles, including books that will help you investigate workplace problems, evaluate employee performance, create legally sound independent contractor agreements, draft an employee handbook, and much more.

Get Updates and More Online

When there are important changes to the information in this book, we'll post updates online, on a page dedicated to this book: **www.nolo.com/back-of-book/ELBA6.html**. You'll find other useful information there, too, including author blogs, podcasts, and videos.

Hiring

H iring can be a tough task for managers. It's challenging enough to find the right hire for the job, with the skills, attitude, personality, and other important qualities to be a success at your company. When you add legal concerns to the mix, hiring can seem like a truly daunting responsibility.

But you cannot ignore your legal obligations when hiring new employees. Federal and state employment laws reach beyond current employees; many also protect those who apply for jobs by, for example, prohibiting discriminatory job postings, putting limits on the information you can gather in a background check, or outlawing certain kinds of applicant screening tests. What's more, the things you say and do during the hiring process could come back to haunt you and your company later, particularly if an employee claims that you offered a job contract or promised job security.

The good news is that following sensible and careful hiring practices will keep your company out of immediate legal trouble, help you find the most qualified employees, and— by screening out problem employees from the get-go—help prevent management headaches and possible lawsuits down the road.

This chapter explains the legal ins and outs of hiring, including practical advice on how to find, interview, and seal the deal with your lucky new hire.

Frequently Asked Questions About Hiring

Do I have to advertise open positions?

No. Although federal, state, and local governments typically have to post openings, private companies don't. Nonetheless, there are some very good reasons to advertise:

- You can choose from a larger pool of applicants, which increases your odds of finding a great person for the job.
- You avoid unintentional discrimination. (For example, if you rely solely on word of mouth when looking for applicants and you only know people of your race or ethnicity, then your hiring process may be discriminatory.)
- You can avoid the appearance of nepotism or favoritism. If you hire your friends, family members, or neighbors to come work for you, the employees who currently report to you may think you'll play favorites. By posting open positions and choosing your hires from a broad range of applicants, you can show your reports that you hire—and manage—on merit alone. (For advice on effective and legal job advertisements, see "Advertisements," below.)

Frequently Asked Questions About Hiring (cont'd)

Are there questions I cannot ask during a job interview?

Yes. For example, you may not ask whether an applicant has a disability, what country an applicant comes from, and, in some states, whether an applicant has ever been arrested. (To learn what questions you can and cannot ask an applicant during an interview, see "Interviews," below.)

Are there things I shouldn't say when I'm trying to convince a really strong applicant to take a job?

Absolutely. Although you'll be tempted to sell your company during a job interview with a hot prospect, don't overdo it. If you exaggerate—or out-and-out lie—about the position, the company's future, or other important facts, and the applicant takes the job based on your statements, that employee can sue the company if your statements turn out to be false. (For more information on statements to avoid when hiring, see "Making Promises," below.)

Can I ask whether an applicant has a disability?

No. The Americans with Disabilities Act (ADA) prohibits you from asking whether an applicant has a disability. Instead, you should focus your interview questions on the applicant's abilities—for example, you may ask whether and how an applicant would perform each essential job function. If you know that an applicant has a disability (because it is obvious or the applicant has told you about it), you may ask whether the applicant will need an accommodation to perform the job. (For more on avoiding disability discrimination when hiring, see "Applicants With Disabilities," below.)

Can I ask every applicant to take a lie detector test?

No. The Employee Polygraph Protection Act (EPPA) prohibits lie detector tests by all but a few types of employers—those that provide certain types of security services or manufacture pharmaceuticals, for example. (For more information on what tests you can—and can't—ask applicants to take, see "Testing Applicants," below.)

Can I run background checks on applicants?

It depends on the information you plan to collect. You can check information that is relevant to the job for which you are hiring. However, state and federal laws restrict you from gathering or using certain types of records. If you are considering running a background check, you should ask applicants to consent to the check in advance, in writing. (See "Background Checks," below, for more information.)

Frequently Asked Questions About Hiring (cont'd)

Can I hire teenagers to do clerical work?

Generally, yes. Teenagers who are at least 16 years old may work unlimited hours in any profession that the government has not deemed hazardous. You can also hire younger teens, although the law restricts how many hours they may work and the types of jobs they may do. (For more information, see "Young Workers," below.)

If I want to offer someone a job, do I have to do it in writing?

There is no law that governs how you offer someone a job. You can do it in person, over the phone, or with a formal letter. However, you should probably send written offer letters just to make sure potential hires understand exactly what you are offering. Offer letters aren't without their pitfalls, however, so be careful what you write. (To learn more, see "Offer Letters," below.)

When I hire someone, should I use a written contract?

It depends on the circumstances. The law does not require you to use a written employment contract and, for the most part, you probably won't want to. However, there may be times when writing a contract is a good idea, such as when you want the employee to make a long-term commitment to the company. (To learn about when you should and should not use an employment contract, see "Written Employment Contracts," below.)

What forms or paperwork do new employees have to complete?

In addition to paperwork your company requires—such as signing an acknowledgment form for the employee handbook, completing benefits registration forms, or naming someone to call in case of emergency—you should also ask employees to complete the following documents:

- IRS Form W-4, *Withholding Allowance Certificate*. Employees use this form to tell you how many allowances they are claiming for tax purposes and, therefore, how much you should withhold from their paychecks.
- USCIS Form I-9, *Employee Eligibility Verification*. You and the employee each complete a portion of this form to verify that the employee is eligible to work in the United States.
- New Hire Reporting Form. The new hire reporting program requires employers to report basic identifying information on all new employees to a state agency, to be used to locate parents who owe child support.

(For more on these requirements, see "Checklist: First-Day Paperwork," below.)

Advertisements

Although most "help wanted" ads contain only a handful of words, using the wrong words can land your company in legal trouble. Any job requirement that discriminates against applicants based on a characteristic protected by law (for example, race or gender) violates federal law and the laws of many states. (To learn which characteristics are protected by federal and state law, see Chapter 3.)

Some off-limits topics are obvious: Most managers know that an ad can't state "only white males need apply." But companies can get into trouble by posting an ad that discriminates on a more subtle level, even if they don't intend to.

For example, let's say you want to hire a technician for your company's information systems department. Almost all of the technician's day would be spent at a computer. On occasion, however, technicians at your company have to install new equipment, which might require them to carry computers, monitors, printers, and so on. Should you write an ad saying that you are looking for someone who can lift at least 50 pounds? Well, that kind of requirement would screen out applicants with certain disabilities, as well as disproportionate numbers of women. Because the lifting is only occasional and could be accomplished by other means—using machinery, for example—including such a requirement in your ad could be discriminatory.

Similarly, watch for words or descriptions that imply you have a discriminatory preference. For example, let's say you are looking for a sales representative. If you use the term, "salesman" in your ad, it implies that you are only looking for men—and therefore that you would discriminate against female applicants. The same precaution applies to terms like "handyman" or "waiter."

So what can you say? If you follow two basic rules, you should steer clear of trouble:

- **Focus on the essential functions of the job.** In other words, advertise only for the skills or characteristics that the job absolutely requires. For example, if you are looking for someone to proofread magazine articles, you probably don't need someone with a college science degree unless your magazine is a professional scientific journal. If there is an up-to-date job description for the position, you can use it to focus the ad appropriately.
- **Pay attention to the literal meaning of the words you use.** This is particularly important with the suffix "-man"—as in "salesman," "repairman," and so on (try "salesperson" and "general repair person" instead), or gendered positions such as "waiter" (use "server" or "wait staff" instead). It is also important to be cautious when using words that refer to age. For example, if you want someone who is energetic, has a lot of fresh ideas, and is up-to-date on current trends, you might want to shorthand that in your ad by stating that you're "looking for worker with a youthful attitude." But if you do, you are expressing an age preference, which is discriminatory and illegal.

Interviews

The spontaneous and unpredictable nature of the job interview makes it rife with traps, even for managers with the best of intentions. Well-meaning, innocent comments could be construed by an applicant as prejudicial or used as the basis of a discrimination lawsuit.

For example, let's say an applicant speaks with an accent you've never heard before. You might be curious about where the applicant is from. However, if you ask about the applicant's national origin, and the applicant doesn't get the job, your question could become part of a discrimination claim against your company.

On the other hand, you don't want to get so hung up on every word you say that you defeat the purpose of the interview: to learn about the applicant's skills and experience so you can choose the best-qualified candidate for the position.

Here are some tips that will help you stay out of legal trouble while also getting the information you need to make the right choice:

- **Don't ask about any characteristic that the law prohibits you from considering in making your decision.** (To learn about these protected characteristics, see Chapter 3.) For example, you can't base your hiring decisions on an applicant's religious beliefs or race, so you shouldn't be asking about those things in your interviews. In "Preemployment Inquiries," at the end of this chapter, we give you some ideas on how to get information while staying within the bounds of the federal law.

- **Respect the applicant's privacy.** Although federal law does not require you to do so, many state laws and rules of etiquette do. For example, asking applicants in California about their sexual fantasies (yes, that actually happened in a real life case) violates their state-protected right to privacy. (For more information on privacy in the workplace, see Chapter 6.)

- **If an applicant raises a delicate subject, it's usually best to skirt the issue.** Unless the topic is directly related to the position— for example, the applicant reveals that he or she has a disability and will need an accommodation to perform the job— politely steer the conversation in another direction. Although it might seem a bit awkward, you'll be better off in the long run if you don't take the applicant's comments as an invitation to start a long conversation about, for example, relationship troubles or political beliefs.

- **Ask open-ended questions to get the candidate talking.** There's a big difference between a closed question—such as "How many supervisory positions have you held?"—and an open one—such as "Tell me about your most recent experience supervising others." The more open your questions, the more you invite the candidate to talk. This will not only give you the factual information you need to make a decision, but will also let you see how well applicants express themselves, think on their feet, and so on.

- **Ask behavioral questions, if possible.** It can be tough to find out whether applicants have important, yet somewhat intangible qualifications, such as problem-solving skills or the ability to work well as part of a team. If you just come out and ask, all but the most dim-witted applicants are going to know the correct answer. ("Are you good at solving problems?" "You bet!") On the other hand, if you ask about specific instances in which the applicant had to use that skill, you're more likely to get a helpful response. To find out about a candidate's problem-solving skills, for example, you could say, "Tell me about a problem you recently faced in your current position and how you handled it."

- **Focus on what the job really requires.** Use the job description for the position (if you have one) to script some interview questions that will help you find out whether the applicant has the necessary skills and experience. If you don't have a job description, create a list of the essential tasks the employee you hire will have to perform, then craft questions that will help you figure out whether the applicant can meet these requirements. Remember, the law absolutely allows you to ask questions that directly relate to the requirements of the job you are trying to fill.

- **Cover similar ground with each applicant.** You can't ask exactly the same questions of each applicant, nor should you. After all, you don't want to miss the opportunity an interview offers to ask follow-up questions spontaneously or delve more deeply into particular topics. On the other hand, you should try to cover the same basic topics and general questions with each applicant. This will help you compare candidates when it's time to choose your hire; it will also help you avoid claims of discrimination by applicants who don't get the job.

Making Promises

A common mistake managers make during hiring is to exaggerate about the prospects of the business ("We're expanding like wildfire —those stock options will be worth millions in no time!") or about the security of the job ("As long as you do good work, you won't lose your job"). Lots of companies and managers embellish when they're trying to sell an especially desirable applicant on a job. No harm in that, right?

Wrong. If you tell a prospective employee something about a job, you'd better be able to back it up. If the employee takes the job in part because of what you said, then that employee may be allowed to sue if your promises or statements later prove false. Courts sometimes decide that a promise or statement you make to a prospective employee turns into a contract if the employee accepts the job offer because of what you said. If the position doesn't live up to your statements, your company has broken the contract and might have to pay damages to the employee.

It's easy to avoid making inflated promises if you follow one simple rule: Tell the truth. After all, job applicants are trying to figure out whether the job will fit with their career goals, skills, and lives outside the workplace. They deserve to know the truth so they can make the right decision.

This strategy will not only keep you out of legal trouble, but also increase your chances of finding an employee who is right for the job and for your business. No one wants a disgruntled employee on the payroll. If you've told the applicant the truth and he or she still wants the job, then you've probably found a good fit.

Here are a few rules that will help you avoid common promise pitfalls:

- **Don't make predictions about your company's financial future.** Even if you honestly believe that your company is headed for the Fortune 500, keep your optimism to yourself. If the applicant asks about the company's prospects, stick to the facts. If you make any statements about what the future might bring, clearly identify them as hopes, not predictions. For example, you might say, "Our business has continued to grow despite the economic downturn, and w're hoping that trend will continue," but you shouldn't say, "We'll be the industry leader by this time next year."

- **Don't estimate the future value of stock options.** Let's face it: You simply can't know what your company's stock options will be worth in the future. It's fine to explain the stock option program to applicants and to tell them that you hope the options will be valuable,

but don't say things like, "When these options vest, we'll all be millionaires!"

- **Don't say anything that might limit your right to make personnel decisions in the future.** If you tell an applicant that your company fires workers only for poor performance, this will limit your ability to terminate that person for any other reason—such as personality conflicts or economic downturns—if he or she accepts the job. Similarly, if you promise pay increases at regular intervals, the employee could hold you to that promise, even if the flagging economy or the employee's performance don't warrant a raise.

- **If layoffs are likely, say so.** If your company is considering staff reductions and there is even a remote chance that the applicant you are interviewing might lose that new job as a result, disclose this before the applicant accepts the job. Otherwise, you may find your company slapped with a lawsuit, especially if the employee left a secure job elsewhere to come work for your company. Of course, this strategy might make it difficult to find new employees, but it really isn't fair (or legal) to hire people on false pretenses.

- **Be accurate in describing the position.** Don't exaggerate to land an applicant, and don't play bait and switch by offering an applicant one job, then placing him or her in another. It may not matter much to you who does what, but it will matter a lot to the employee. An employee who accepts the position based on statements that turn out to be false may have grounds for a lawsuit.

Lessons From the Real World

A California company paid the price for intensely recruiting an employee with promises it couldn't keep. Rykoff-Sexton, Inc., promised Andrew Lazar job security, significant pay increases, an eventual executive position, and a bright future with a company that was financially strong. Lazar took the bait and left a lucrative job in New York City, his home of 40 years.

Although Lazar excelled in his new job, the pay increases and bonuses never came. Eventually, Rykoff fired Lazar because of a "reorganization."

Lazar sued and won. He argued to the California Supreme Court that Rykoff should have to keep the promises it used to recruit him, and the court agreed. The court decided that Rykoff's broken promises amounted to fraud because it knew the promises were untrue when it made them.

Lazar v. Rykoff-Sexton, Inc., 12 Cal.4th 631 (1996).

Applicants With Disabilities

Of all the antidiscrimination laws, perhaps none confuses managers more than the Americans with Disabilities Act (ADA), 42 U.S.C. §§ 12101–12213, especially when it

comes to hiring. Managers want to find out if the person they hire can actually perform the job but often aren't sure how to explore this issue without running afoul of the law. (For information on how the ADA applies to employees, see "Disability" in Chapter 3.)

If you remember one simple rule, you'll be in good shape: You can ask candidates about their abilities, but not about their disabilities. This means that you can ask how an applicant plans to perform each function of the job, but you cannot ask whether the applicant has any disabilities that will prevent him or her from performing each function of the job.

One way to ensure that you stay within the rules is to attach a detailed job description to the application or describe the job duties to applicants during the job interview. Then ask how the applicant plans to perform the job. This approach gives applicants an opportunity to talk about their qualifications and strengths. It also gives them a chance to let you know whether they might need reasonable accommodations to do the job.

If you choose to ask applicants how they would perform the job duties, you should ask these questions of all applicants. Don't single out those you suspect may have a disability. If an applicant has a "known" disability—a disability that the applicant has disclosed or that is obvious (for example, if the applicant uses a wheelchair)—of a type that makes it reasonable to believe the applicant might not be able to perform the job's functions, the employer may ask how the applicant would perform those functions or whether the applicant would need an accommodation to do so.

Generally, you may not ask an applicant questions, on an application or during a job interview, that are likely to require the applicant to reveal a disability. The Equal Employment Opportunity Commission (EEOC), the federal agency that interprets and enforces the ADA, gives the following examples of questions you should not ask:

- Do you have a disability that would interfere with your ability to do the job?
- How many days were you sick last year?
- Have you ever filed for workers' compensation? Have you ever been injured on the job?
- Have you ever been treated for mental health problems?
- What prescription drugs are you currently taking?

You may ask questions like these:

- Can you perform all of the functions of this job?
- How would you perform each of the job functions?
- What certifications and licenses do you hold?
- Tell me about your education and work history.
- Can you meet the attendance requirements of this job?

If you have no reason to believe that the applicant has a disability, you may not ask whether the applicant will need an accommodation to perform the job. If, however, you know that the applicant has a disability—because it is obvious, for example, or the applicant has told you about it—you may ask about accommodations.

Testing Applicants

Many companies like to use preemployment tests as a way to screen out applicants who are not suitable for a job. These tests include skills tests, aptitude tests, psychological tests, personality tests, honesty tests, medical tests, and drug tests.

Although you are allowed to do some testing of applicants, both state and federal law impose numerous restrictions on what you can do. Because these restrictions are often vague and open to contradictory interpretations, you should use only tests that are absolutely necessary. You should also consider consulting with a lawyer before administering the test to make sure that it will pass legal muster in your state.

Avoiding Disability Discrimination

For all tests—including those described below—you must take care to avoid discriminating against applicants who are protected by the Americans with Disabilities Act (ADA). (For information on the ADA, see Chapter 3.) To ensure that a test does not unfairly screen out people with disabilities, it must accurately measure people's skills, not their disabilities. For example:

- Avoid testing mental, sensory, manual, or speaking skills unless they are job-related. For example, even though a typing test is a manual test that will screen out people who have particular impairments, it is acceptable if you are filling a job for a typist. However, if the job could be done using voice-activated software, you should make that option available for the test, too.

- Accommodate people with disabilities by giving them a test that is "disability neutral" whenever possible. For example, if you are giving a written test to applicants for a sales position to test their knowledge of sales techniques, you can offer to read the test to a blind applicant. This is a reasonable accommodation because sight is not required for the job, but it is required to take the test.

Skills Tests

Skills tests range from something as simple as a typing test to something as complicated as an architectural drafting test. Generally speaking, these tests are legal as long as they genuinely test a skill necessary to perform the job, don't violate the ADA (see above), and don't unfairly exclude anyone based on a protected characteristic.

Aptitude, Psychological, and Personality Tests

Some companies use written tests—often in a multiple choice format—to learn about an applicant's general abilities, personality, and/ or work style. However, using these tests leaves you vulnerable to various types of lawsuits. For example:

- A multiple-choice aptitude test may discriminate against minority applicants or female applicants because it really reflects test-taking ability rather than actual job skills. (Studies have shown

that some aptitude tests are biased against women and minority test-takers.)

- A personality test can be even riskier. Such a test may invade a person's privacy by inquiring into topics that are personal in nature, such as sexual preferences or religious beliefs. (Many states specifically protect a person's right to privacy—even from inquiries by employers.) In addition, these tests can lead to a discrimination lawsuit. For example, if you decide not to hire someone based on his or her answers to questions dealing with religious issues, the applicant could argue that you discriminated based on his or her religion. (For more about discrimination, see Chapter 3.)

- Psychological and personality tests are treated like medical tests (see below) when they ask for answers that would indicate whether the applicant has a mental disorder or impairment. If they do, they will be governed by the Americans with Disabilities Act (ADA) and all of its restrictions. (For more on hiring and the ADA, see "Applicants With Disabilities," above.)

If you decide to use one of these types of tests, proceed with extreme caution. Make sure that the test has been screened scientifically for validity and that it genuinely correlates to necessary job skills. Review the test carefully for any questions that may intrude into an applicant's privacy. And, depending on the complexity and purpose of the test you use, your company may need to hire an expert to interpret the results.

Lessons From the Real World

Rent-A-Center, Inc., a company that offers furniture and other household goods on a rent-to-own basis, required applicants for certain management positions to take the Minnesota Multiphasic Personality Inventory test (MMPI), answering questions such as:

- I see things or animals or people around me that others do not see.
- My soul sometimes leaves my body.
- At times I have fits of laughing and crying that I cannot control.
- I have a habit of counting things that are not important such as bulbs on electric signs, and so forth.

Applicants who were required to take the test sued, arguing (among other things) that the test violated the ADA because it was a medical examination designed to reveal mental impairments. Although the trial court rejected this argument, the federal Court of Appeals agreed with the applicants. Rent-A-Center stopped using the MMPI, and was ordered to destroy all test results in its possession; it also had to pay the plaintiff class's attorney fees.

Karraker v. Rent-A-Center, 492 F.3d 896 (7th Cir. 2007); *Karraker v. Rent-A-Center*, 411 F.3d 831 (7th Cir. 2005).

Lie Detector and Honesty Tests

The federal Employee Polygraph Protection Act, 29 U.S.C. §§ 2001 and following, generally prohibits employers from requiring applicants to take a lie detector test or from asking applicants about the results of previous lie detector tests. The law contains a few narrowly defined exceptions for certain types of employers, including those that provide armored car, alarm, or guard services, and those that manufacture, distribute, or dispense pharmaceuticals.

Even though no federal law specifically outlaws written honesty tests, these tests sometimes violate federal and state laws that protect against discrimination and violations of privacy. Plus, the tests can be unreliable.

Some states have adopted their own rules about polygraph tests—and some of these rules are even stricter than the federal law. To find out what your state requires, see "Employee Polygraph Examination Laws," at the end of this chapter.

Medical Tests

Medical testing is tricky. To avoid violating the Americans with Disabilities Act, you shouldn't ask for an applicant's medical history or conduct any medical exam before you make a job offer.

However, once you decide to offer the applicant a job, you can make the offer conditional on the applicant passing a medical exam. You must require the exam for all entering employees doing the same job. If you only require people whom you believe or know to have disabilities to take the exam, you will be violating the Americans with Disabilities Act. If the exam screens out disproportionately large numbers of applicants with disabilities, you may administer it only if it is job-related and correlates to necessary job skills.

The Genetic Information Nondiscrimination Act (GINA) prohibits employers from requesting or requiring that applicants provide genetic information, including through genetic tests. Even though the ADA allows employers to require a post-offer medical exam, as described above, that exam may not include genetic testing, nor may it include the collection of family medical history. Employers must tell its health care providers not to collect genetic information as part of any employment-related medical exam. If an employer discovers that a health care provider is nonetheless requesting this information, it must take reasonable steps to put a stop to it by, for example, no longer using that provider.

Drug Tests

The laws on drug testing vary widely from state to state. Some states allow these tests only for jobs involving public safety; some states allow them only for drivers; some states allow them for any occupation; some states don't allow them at all. Consult "State Drug and Alcohol Testing Laws," at the end of this chapter, for information on your state's rules.

Background Checks

When you are making hiring decisions, you might need a bit more information than applicants provide. After all, some folks—surveys estimate between 30% and 40% of applicants—give false or incomplete information in employment applications. And workers probably don't want you to know certain facts about their past that might disqualify them from getting a job. Generally, it's good policy to do a little checking before making a job offer.

However, you do not have an unfettered right to dig into applicants' personal affairs. Workers have a right to privacy in certain personal matters, a right they can enforce by suing your company if you pry too deeply. How can you avoid crossing this line? Here are a few tips to keep in mind:

- **Make sure your inquiries are related to the job.** If you decide to do a background check, stick to information that is relevant to the job for which you are considering the worker. For example, if you are hiring a security guard who will carry a weapon and be responsible for large amounts of cash, you might reasonably check for past criminal convictions.
- **Ask for consent.** You are on safest legal ground if you ask the applicant, in writing, to consent to a background check. Explain clearly what you plan to check and how you will gather information. This gives applicants a chance to take themselves out of the running if there are things

they don't want you to know. It also prevents applicants from later claiming invasion of privacy. If an applicant refuses to consent to a reasonable request for information, you may legally decide not to consider that applicant for the position.

- **Be reasonable.** Managers can get their employers into legal trouble if they engage in background check overkill. You will not need to perform an extensive background check on every applicant. Even if you decide to check, you probably won't need to get into excessive detail for every position. If you find yourself questioning neighbors, ordering credit checks, and performing exhaustive searches of public records every time you hire a clerk or counterperson, you need to scale your efforts back.

In addition to these general considerations, specific rules apply to certain types of information:

- **School records.** Under federal law and the law of some states, educational records—including transcripts, recommendations, and financial information—are confidential. Because of these laws, most schools will not release records without the consent of the student. And some schools will only release records directly to the student.
- **Credit reports.** Under the Fair Credit Reporting Act (FCRA), 15 U.S.C. § 1681, employers must get written consent to check an applicant's credit report. Many companies routinely include a request for such consent along with their employment applications. If you decide not to hire or promote someone based on information in the credit report, you must provide a copy of the report and let the applicant know how to challenge the report under the FCRA. Some states have more stringent rules limiting the use of credit reports; some prohibit employers from considering credit reports in making hiring decisions period. (See "Running Credit Checks," below, for more information.).

- **Bankruptcies.** Federal law prohibits discriminating against applicants because they have filed for bankruptcy. This means that you cannot decide not to hire someone simply because he or she has declared bankruptcy in the past.
- **Criminal records.** The law varies from state to state on whether, and to what extent, a private employer may consider an applicant's criminal history in making hiring decisions. Some states don't allow you to ask about arrests (as opposed to convictions), convictions that occurred well in the past, juvenile crimes, or sealed records. Some states allow you to consider convictions only if the crimes are relevant to the job. And some states allow you to consider criminal history only for certain positions: nurses, child care workers, private detectives, and other jobs requiring licenses, for example. Because of this variation among the states, you should consult with a lawyer or do further legal research on the law of your state before digging into an applicant's criminal past.

- **Workers' compensation records.** You may consider information contained in the public record from a workers' compensation appeal in making a job decision only if the applicant's injury might interfere with his or her ability to perform required duties.

- **Other medical records.** Under the Americans with Disabilities Act, you may inquire about an applicant's ability to perform specific job duties only; you may not request medical records. Companies cannot make job decisions (on hiring or promotion, for example) based on an applicant's disability, as long as the employee can do the job, with or without a reasonable accommodation. Employers also can't discriminate on the

Lessons From the Real World

After a handful of interviews and long-distance communications, including half a dozen phone calls and 20 email exchanges, Microsoft's Associate General Counsel, Michele Gammer, offered Mitchell Schley a job as a senior attorney. The offer letter, which Schley signed and returned, said that the job was at will, and that his employment was contingent on the successful completion of a background and reference check, among other things.

Gammer encouraged Schley to give notice to his current employer, recommended a real estate agent, and helped facilitate his purchase of a home in Washington from someone she knew. (Schley lived in New Jersey when he accepted the job.) After Schley put down a deposit of $30,000 on the new home, put his New Jersey home on the market, and began to relocate, Gammer told him that his start date would have to be delayed while the company investigated a felony charge that came up in his background check. Schley told Gammer

that the charge was frivolous and the complaint had been dropped; he also sent Gammer documents supporting his claims. A few days later, Gammer again contacted Schley to tell him that Microsoft was revoking the job offer. Schley had to immediately resell the home he purchased in Washington and was out of work for two years afterwards. He sued Microsoft.

The court threw out Schley's claim that Microsoft broke an employment contract, because the job was to be at will. Because Microsoft had reserved the right to fire him at any time, the company had the legal right to revoke the offer. However, the court allowed Schley to bring his claim of promissory estoppel: Because he was promised the job and was encouraged to quit his job and buy a new home based on that promise, Microsoft might be legally liable for the damages he suffered as a result.

Schley v. Microsoft, Civ. No. 08-3589 (D. New Jersey, 2008).

basis of genetic information. Nor may they request or require that applicants provide such information. Some states also have laws protecting the confidentiality of medical records.

- **Records of military service.** Members and former members of the armed forces have a right to privacy in their service records. These records may be released only under limited circumstances, and consent is generally required. However, the military may disclose name, rank, salary, duty assignments, awards, and duty status without the member's consent.
- **Driving records.** You should check the driving record of any employee whose job will require large amounts of driving (delivery persons or bus drivers, for example). These records are available, sometimes for a small fee, from the state's motor vehicles department.

Running Credit Checks

If an employer checks credit reports when hiring employees, it must follow the legal rules set out in the federal Fair Credit Reporting Act (FCRA). The FCRA requires employers to:

- get the applicant's consent before pulling the report
- give the applicant a warning (along with a copy of the report received) if the employer plans to reject the applicant on the basis of the report, and
- give the applicant an official adverse action notice if the employer does not hire him or her because of the contents of the report.

State Law Restrictions

The economic downturn of the last few years —and the resulting damage to credit reports and scores—have led many politicians to reconsider whether it's really appropriate for employers to use credit reports in making hiring decisions. At least four states (Hawaii, Illinois, Oregon, and Washington) have passed laws prohibiting employers from pulling credit reports and/or using them to make hiring or other job decisions in most circumstances. According to the National Conference of State Legislatures (NCSL), about 20 states are currently considering similar legislation. To find out whether your state is among them, go to the NCSL's detailed chart at www.ncsl.org.

If your state prohibits you from checking applicants' credit reports or using their credit histories in your hiring decisions, you can't do it. Even though the federal FCRA allows employers to consider credit reports, state laws that are more protective of employee rights trump the federal law.

Following the FCRA

If your state allows you to consider an applicant's credit report in the hiring process, and you plan to do so, you must abide by the FCRA by getting the applicant's consent, warning the applicant if you plan to reject him or her based on the report, and giving the applicant a final notice if you ultimately follow through with those plans.

The purpose of these rules is to ensure the accuracy of credit reports by letting consumers know when these reports are checked, whether the reports include disqualifying information, and how consumers can challenge incorrect entries. Investigations by public interest groups reveal that one-quarter to one-third of all credit reports include significant errors. Given these numbers—and how often credit reports are consulted by lenders, employers, and landlords—it makes sense that the law builds in a few consumer protections.

Get Written Consent

Before you request an applicant's credit report, you must notify the applicant that you plan to do so and get the applicant's written authorization. This notice and authorization must be set forth in a separate document that doesn't include other information. In other words, it can't be a section of your employment application.

Send a Pre-Adverse-Action Disclosure

Once you get the report, you may decide not to hire the applicant based on something in the report. In this situation, you must first send the applicant a notice stating that you plan to take this "adverse action" (deciding not to hire him or her). With your notice, you must include two documents: (1) a copy of the credit report, and (2) a copy of a notice from the Federal Trade Commission entitled "A Summary of Your Rights Under the Fair Credit Reporting Act," which tells the applicant how to challenge any incorrect information in the report, among other things.

(The credit reporting agency that sent you the report should also give you a copy of the FTC's Summary of Rights; if it doesn't, you can find a copy at the FTC's website, www.ftc.gov.)

Send an Adverse Action Notice

Once you have made a final decision not to hire the applicant based on information contained in the credit report, you must send the applicant another document called an "adverse action notice." This notice explains that you are not hiring the applicant and provides some information on the applicant's rights, including the right to dispute the accuracy of the report and the right to obtain an additional copy.

Young Workers

Many jobs around an office and in a business are perfect for younger workers. For example, if you need someone to photocopy documents for an hour or two a day, a high school student who comes in after school might be just what you are looking for. The student gets experience and extra pocket money, and your company gets someone who is willing to work just a few hours a week on the cheap.

The history of child labor in this country isn't quite so benign, however. Children once worked long hours in hazardous jobs—such as manufacturing and mining—for very little money. They didn't attend school, and they often suffered serious—even fatal—health problems.

To protect child workers, the federal and state governments passed laws regulating the type of work children can do, the number of hours they can work, and the types of businesses that can employ them.

Before you hire any worker younger than 18, you should check both federal and state law. We describe the federal law here. To find out about your state child labor law, contact your state department of labor.

The Fair Labor Standards Act (FLSA), 29 U.S.C. §§ 2201 and following, is the federal law that governs child labor. Virtually all employees and businesses must follow the FLSA, although a handful of businesses, including small farms, are not required to. To find out about exceptions to FLSA requirements, refer to the website of the U.S. Department of Labor—the federal agency that enforces the FLSA—at www.dol.gov.

Hazardous Jobs

According to the U.S. Department of Labor, workers younger than 18 may never perform the following types of hazardous jobs (some exceptions are made for apprentices and students):

- manufacturing or storing explosives
- being an outside helper on a motor vehicle
- coal or other mining
- logging and sawmilling
- anything involving power-driven, wood-working machines
- anything involving exposure to radioactive substances and ionizing radiations
- anything involving power-driven hoisting equipment
- anything involving power-driven metal-forming, punching, and shearing machines
- meat packing or processing (including anything involving power-driven meat slicing machines)

- anything involving power-driven bakery machines
- anything involving power-driven paper products machines
- manufacturing brick, tile, and related products
- anything involving power-driven circular saws, band saws, and guillotine shears
- wrecking, demolition, and shipbreaking operations
- roofing and work performed on or near roofs, including installing or working on antennas and rooftop appliances, and
- excavation operations.

Special rules apply to jobs that involve driving. As noted above, employees younger than 18 may not work as outside helpers on a vehicle. Employees who are not yet 17 also may not drive on public roads as part of their jobs. An employee who is at least 17 may drive on public roads as part of a job only if all of the following are true:

- The driving takes place during daylight hours only.
- The minor has a valid state driver's license for the type of driving involved.
- The minor has completed a driver education course and has no moving violations.
- The vehicle weighs no more than 6,000 pounds.
- The vehicle is equipped with seat belts (and the employer has told employees to use them when driving).
- The driving is only occasional and incidental to the job, defined as taking up no more than a third of the workday and 20% of the minor's total weekly hours.

Even if all of the above conditions are met, a 17-year-old is legally prohibited from driving:
- a towing vehicle
- any vehicle other than a car or truck
- route deliveries or sales
- to transport property, goods, or passengers for hire
- to make urgent, time-sensitive deliveries (including pizza)
- with more than three passengers, even if they are also employees
- beyond a 30-mile radius from the workplace, or
- more than two trips per day to deliver goods to customers or to transport passengers (other than other employees).

Agricultural Jobs

If you own or operate a farm or other type of agricultural business, the following child labor rules apply to you:
- You may hire a worker who is 16 years or older for any work, whether hazardous or not, for unlimited hours.
- You may hire a worker who is 14 or 15 years old for any nonhazardous work outside of school hours.
- You may hire a worker who is 12 or 13 years old for any nonhazardous work outside of school hours if the child's parents work on the same farm or if you have their written consent.
- You may hire a worker who is ten or 11 years old if you've been granted a waiver by the U.S. Department of Labor to employ the youngster as a hand-harvest laborer for no more than eight weeks in any calendar year.

- If you own or operate the farm, you can hire your own children to do any kind of work on the farm, regardless of their ages.

Nonagricultural Jobs

If you seek to hire a youngster for work that is nonagricultural, the following rules apply:
- You may hire a worker who is 18 years or older for any job, hazardous or not, for unlimited hours.
- A worker who will do job-related driving on public roads must be at least 17 years old, must have a valid driver's license, and must not have any moving violations.
- You may hire a worker who is 16 or 17 years old for any nonhazardous job, for unlimited hours.
- You may hire a worker who is 14 or 15 years old outside school hours in various nonmanufacturing, nonmining, and nonhazardous jobs, but some restrictions apply. The teen cannot work more than three hours on a school day, 18 hours in a school week, eight hours on a nonschool day, or 40 hours in a nonschool week. Also, the work cannot begin before 7 a.m. or end after 7 p.m., except from June 1 through Labor Day, when evening hours are extended to 9 p.m.

Offer Letters

When it comes to offer letters, keep them short and sweet. The same rules that apply to job interviews apply to offer letters: Stick to the facts and don't make promises you can't keep. Applicants might some day try to turn an offer letter into a contract that sets the terms and conditions of the job or limits your company's right to fire or discipline them.

Avoid using language that makes promises or assurances about the employment relationship. For example, if you tell the applicant "We look forward to a long and happy relationship with you" or "We think you have a bright future at this company," the applicant might assume that you're offering more than the normal "at-will" employment—and that you won't end the employment relationship without a good reason. If you want to fire the employee in the future, these words might come back to haunt you.

Similarly, don't specify job duties, benefits, pay schedules, vacation/sick leave, or any other benefit you might want to change in the future. The employee might argue that your letter created a contract and try to hold the company to it.

So what can you say? You might want to:

- congratulate the applicant
- confirm the job title
- name the applicant's supervisor
- state the starting salary, and
- establish a start date.

In addition, if you haven't or won't offer the applicant a written contract for employment (the vast majority of employees don't have written employment contracts), confirm in writing that employment is at will, meaning that there is no employment contract and you can fire the employee at any time for any reason that isn't illegal.

For more about written employment contracts, see "Written Employment Contracts," below. For more about at-will employment, see "At-Will Employment" in Chapter 4.

Written Employment Contracts

A written employment contract is a document that an employer and an employee sign, setting forth the terms of their relationship with each other. In addition to clearly describing what the employee is going to do for the employer (the job) and what the employer is going to do for the employee (the salary), the contract can address many other issues, including:

- the duration of the job (for example, one year, two years, or indefinitely)
- the specifics of the employee's responsibilities
- the employee's benefits (for example, health insurance, vacation leave, or disability leave)
- grounds for termination
- limitations on the employee's ability to compete with your company once the employee leaves
- protection of company trade secrets and client lists
- who will own the employee's work product (for example, if the employee writes books or invents gadgets for your company), and
- a method for resolving any disputes between the employee and the company.

Written employment contracts have distinct advantages and disadvantages that you should consider carefully before committing your company.

Advantages

Employment contracts can make sense if you want or need to control the employee's ability to quit. For example, if the employee is a high-level manager or executive, or if the employee is especially valuable to the company (such as the administrator who is the organizational backbone of the office), then a contract can protect the company against the sudden, unexpected loss of the employee. It can lock the employee into a specific term (for example, two years), or it can require the employee to provide enough notice to allow your company to find and train a suitable replacement.

Employment contracts can also protect your company if the employee will learn or have access to confidential and sensitive business information. You can insert confidentiality clauses into the contract that prevent the employee from disclosing this information or using it for personal gain. (For more on this topic, see "Nondisclosure Agreements" in Chapter 10.)

Similarly, a contract can prevent employees from competing against your company after they move on to other pursuits, at least in some states. (For more on this topic, see "Noncompete Agreements" in Chapter 10.)

Sometimes, you can use an employment contract as a way to entice a highly skilled individual to accept a job offer. Job security and beneficial terms often sweeten the deal enough for a highly desirable applicant who is on the fence to join your team.

Finally, an employment contract can give the company greater control over the employee. If you specify the standards for the employee's performance and grounds for termination, you may have an easier time terminating an employee who doesn't live up to those standards.

Disadvantages

An employment contract is a two-way street: Just as the contract requires the worker to stay for a certain period of time, it limits your company's right to fire the worker for the same period. Your company won't have the ability to alter the terms of the employment as its business needs change. To alter the terms, you'll have to renegotiate the contract and offer the employee some new benefit in exchange for the alteration to make the new agreement binding. And, no matter what you offer, the employee is free to reject any proposed new terms. These factors can make the renegotiation process time-consuming and complicated.

For example, let's say you sign a two-year contract with a new employee. If, six months later, you decide you don't need the employee after all, you can't terminate the relationship. If you do, you will set your company up for a breach of contract lawsuit. Similarly, if you promised benefits in the contract, the company can't stop paying for them before the term is up without breaching the contract and risking a lawsuit.

Another disadvantage of employment contracts is that they always contain an unwritten obligation, imposed by law, to deal fairly with the employee. In legal terms, this is called the "covenant of good faith and fair dealing." If you treat an employee with whom you have signed a contract in a way that seems unfair, your company may end up in court.

Checklist: First-Day Paperwork

When your new hire shows up on the first day of work, there will be lots to do, including plenty of forms to be completed. Use this checklist to make sure you don't forget any important paperwork. (Of course, your company may not use every form on this list—or may have come up with additional paperwork of its own—so make sure you modify this checklist if necessary.)

Required Government Paperwork

☐ USCIS Form I-9, *Employment Eligibility Verification.* The federal government requires employers to complete this form verifying that new hires are eligible to work in the United States. Get more information at www.uscis.gov.

☐ IRS Form W-4, *Withholding Allowance Certificate.* New employees use this form to tell your company how much income tax to withhold from their paychecks. Go to www.irs.gov for information.

☐ New hire reporting information. Employers must provide information on new employees to a state agency, which uses it to find parents who owe child support. For information on your state's requirements, go to www.acf.hhs.gov, and select "Employer Info" under the "Working with ACF" tab.

Company Forms

☐ Signed offer letter or employment contract.

☐ Employee handbook acknowledgment form (see Chapter 4).

☐ Acknowledgment of company email policy (see Chapter 6).

☐ Benefits paperwork, such as enrollment forms.

☐ Emergency contact information.

☐ Acknowledgment of receiving company property, such as a cell phone, car, or laptop computer to be used off-site.

Legal Dos and Don'ts: Hiring

Do:

- **Focus on the essential elements of the job.** You can avoid problems with antidiscrimination and privacy laws by remembering your hiring goal: to find an applicant who can do the job well. Keeping your eyes on this prize will stop you from delving into an applicant's personal affairs, religious beliefs, medical conditions, or other forbidden topics.
- **Use written contracts sparingly.** A written contract is a great way to seal the deal with a stellar applicant whom you want to retain. It's also a fast track to the courthouse if used with an employee whom you might have to fire or lay off.
- **Put your offer in writing.** No law requires you to use written offer letters, but they're an easy and effective way to make sure the applicant knows exactly what the job entails. And if you are offering an at-will position, an offer letter spelling that out will help you document your intentions.

Don't:

- **Shade the truth.** Always be honest when dealing with job applicants. Someone who accepts a job based on your false statements about the job can ask a court to hold the company to your promises—or to pay for your misrepresentations.
- **Get too personal.** Privacy laws differ from state to state, but you'll always be on shaky legal ground if you delve into an applicant's personal life.
- **Test unless you really need to—and you've cleared the test with a lawyer.** The law of testing is changing all the time, which makes it a ripe source of lawsuits for invasion of privacy, disability discrimination, and more. The good news is that the vast majority of companies can make sound hiring decisions without resorting to testing.

Test Your Knowledge

Questions

1. You should ask every applicant exactly the same questions when interviewing for a position. ☐ True ☐ False

2. You may ask applicants with disablilities whether and how they could perform the essential functions of the position. ☐ True ☐ False

3. It's best to ask only about verifiable facts during an interview, such as where an applicant works or what positions he or she has held. ☐ True ☐ False

4. You can make promises to an applicant during the hiring process, as long as employees at your company have to sign an at-will agreement. ☐ True ☐ False

5. If an applicant brings up his or her religion, it's okay to ask questions and state your opinions about it. ☐ True ☐ False

6. A company can require all applicants to take a personality test. ☐ True ☐ False

7. You have the right to look at an applicant's credit report when making hiring decisions. ☐ True ☐ False

8. It's a good idea to send an offer letter to successful applicants. ☐ True ☐ False

9. A company should never offer applicants a written employment contract. ☐ True ☐ False

10. Antidiscrimination laws and other workplace restrictions apply only to employees, not to job applicants. ☐ True ☐ False

Answers

1. False. Although you should cover the same basic ground with every applicant, you shouldn't script the entire interview. Otherwise, you'll miss opportunities to follow up on issues applicants raise and delve more deeply into areas of interest or concern.

2. True. Although there are some limits on what you can ask about disabilities, you are entitled to find out whether the applicant can do the job.

3. False. You should certainly find out what positions an applicant has held, but the most informative questions are open-ended queries that invite the applicant to talk about his or her experience and skills.

4. False. An at-will agreement is not a silver bullet, especially if an applicant left a good position to come to work for your company based on your false statements. If you entice someone with promises that won't come true, you will have an unhappy employee—and perhaps a lawsuit—on your hands.

5. False. Even if an employee brings up a delicate topic, it's best to simply move on. If you get into a discussion and say something that the employee finds distasteful or biased, the fact that the employee raised the issue in the first place won't save you from a discrimination claim.

6. The answer depends on the test, how it's administered, what it measures, and what you use it for. Courts have found that some personality tests are unnecessarily invasive and violate applicants' rights.

7. It depends; some states prohibit employers from using an applicant's credit report in making hiring decisions. In states that allow it, federal law requires employers to get the applicant's consent, in writing, before running a credit check.

8. True. You can use the offer letter to set forth the basic terms of the job and let future employees know that they will be working at will, if that's your company's policy.

9. False. Written employment contracts should be the exception rather than the rule, but there are circumstances when it makes sense to use one.

10. False. Antidiscrimination laws apply to every stage of the employment relationship, including "help wanted" ads, applications, interviews, and actually selecting your new hire.

Preemployment Inquiries

Subject	Lawful Preemployment Inquiries	Unlawful or Risky Preemployment Inquiries
Name	Applicant's full name Have you ever worked for this company under a different name? Is any additional information relative to a different name necessary to check work record? If yes, explain.	Original name of an applicant whose name has been changed by court order or otherwise Applicant's maiden name
Address or duration of residence	How long have you been a resident of this state or city?	Do you rent or own?
Birthplace	None	Birthplace of applicant Birthplace of applicant's parents, spouse, or other close relatives Requirement that applicant submit birth certificate, naturalization, or baptismal record
Age	Are you 18 years old or older? This question may be asked only for the purpose of determining whether applicants are of legal age for employment.	How old are you? What is your date of birth?
Religion or creed	None	Inquiry into an applicant's religious denomination, religious affiliations, church, parish, pastor, or religious holidays observed
Race or color	None	Complexion or color of skin Inquiry regarding applicant's race
Photograph	None	Any requirement for a photograph prior to hire
Height	None	Inquiry regarding applicant's height (unless you have a legitimate business reason)
Weight	None	Inquiry regarding applicant's weight (unless you have a legitimate business reason)
Marital status	Is your spouse employed by this employer?	Requirement that an applicant provide any information regarding marital status or children Are you single or married? Do you have any children? Is your spouse employed? What is your spouse's name?
Gender	None	Mr., Miss, Mrs., or an inquiry regarding gender; inquiry as to ability or plans to reproduce or advocacy of any form of birth control
Disability	These [provide applicant with list] are the essential functions of the job. How would you perform them?	Inquiries regarding an individual's physical or mental condition that are not directly related to the requirements of a specific job

Preemployment Inquiries (cont'd)

Subject	Lawful Preemployment Inquiries	Unlawful or Risky Preemployment Inquiries
Citizenship	Are you legally authorized to work in the United States on a full-time basis?	Questions about subjects below are unlawful, but the applicant may be required to reveal some of this information as part of the federal I-9 process: • Country of citizenship • Whether an applicant is naturalized or a native-born citizen; the date when the applicant acquired citizenship • Requirement that an applicant produce naturalization papers or first papers • Whether applicant's parents or spouse are naturalized or native-born citizens of the United States, and, if so, the date when such parent or spouse acquired citizenship
National origin	Inquiry into language applicant speaks and writes fluently	Inquiry into applicant's lineage, ancestry, national origin, descent, parentage, or nationality, unless part of the federal I-9 process in determining employment eligibility Nationality of applicant's parents or spouse Inquiry into how applicant acquired ability to read, write, or speak a foreign language
Education	Inquiry into the academic, vocational, or professional education of an applicant and public and private schools attended	
Experience	Inquiry into work experience Inquiry into countries applicant has visited	
Arrests	Have you ever been convicted of a crime? Are there any felony charges pending against you?	Inquiry regarding arrests that did not result in conviction (except for law enforcement agencies)
Relatives	Names of applicant's relatives already employed by this company	Address of any relative of applicant, other than address (within the United States) of applicant's father and mother, husband or wife, and minor dependent children
Notice in case of emergency	Name and address of person to be notified in case of accident or emergency	Name and address of nearest relative to be notified in case of accident or emergency
Organizations	Inquiry into the organizations of which an applicant is a member, excluding organizations the name or character of which indicates the race, color, religion, national origin, or ancestry of its members	List all clubs, societies, and lodges to which the applicant belongs
Personal finance	None	Inquiries about financial problems, such as garnishment or bankruptcy

Employee Polygraph Examination Laws

ALASKA
Alaska Stat. § 23.10.037

Employers covered: All

What's prohibited: Employer may not suggest, request, or require that employee or applicant take a lie detector test.

CALIFORNIA
Cal. Lab. Code § 432.2

Employers covered: All

What's prohibited: Employer may not demand or require that employee or applicant take a lie detector test.

What's allowed: Employer may request a test, if applicant is advised in writing of legal right to refuse to take it.

CONNECTICUT
Conn. Gen. Stat. Ann. § 31-51g

Employers covered: All, including employment agencies

What's prohibited: Employer may not request or require that employee or applicant take a lie detector test.

DELAWARE
Del. Code Ann. tit. 19, § 704

Employers covered: All

What's prohibited: Employer may not suggest, request, or require that employee or applicant take a lie detector test in order to obtain or continue employment.

DISTRICT OF COLUMBIA
D.C. Code Ann. §§ 32-901 to 32-903

Employers covered: All

What's prohibited: Employer may not administer, have administered, use, or accept the results of any polygraph examination.

HAWAII
Haw. Rev. Stat. § 378-26.5

Employers covered: All

What's prohibited: Employer may not require employee or applicant to take lie detector test.

What's allowed: Employer may request test if current or prospective employee is told, orally and in writing, that refusing to take test will not result in being fired or hurt chances of getting job.

IDAHO
Idaho Code § 44-903

Employers covered: All

What's prohibited: Employer may not require an employee or applicant to take a lie detector test.

ILLINOIS
225 Ill. Comp. Stat. § 430/14.1

Employers covered: All

What's prohibited: Unless directly related to employment, examination may not include questions about:
- political, religious, or labor-related beliefs, affiliations, or lawful activities
- beliefs or opinions on racial matters, or
- sexual preferences or activity.

IOWA
Iowa Code § 730.4

Employers covered: All

What's prohibited: Employer may not request, require, administer, or attempt or threaten to administer a lie detector test; may not request or require that employee or applicant sign waiver of any action prohibited by this law.

Employee Polygraph Examination Laws (cont'd)

MAINE

Me. Rev. Stat. Ann. tit. 32, § 7166

Employers covered: All

What's prohibited: Employer may not request, require, suggest, or administer a lie detector test.

What's allowed: Employee may voluntarily request a test if these conditions are met:
- results cannot be used against employee
- employer must give employee a copy of the law when employee requests test, and
- test must be recorded or employee's witness must be present during the test, or both.

MARYLAND

Md. Code Ann. [Lab. & Empl.] § 3-702

Employers covered: All

What's prohibited: Employer may not require or demand that employee or applicant take a lie detector test.

What's required: All employment applications must include specified notice that no person can be required to take a lie detector test as a condition of obtaining or continuing employment and must include space for applicant to sign and acknowledge notice.

MASSACHUSETTS

Mass. Gen. Laws ch. 149, § 19B

Employers covered: All

What's prohibited: Employer may not request, require, or administer a lie detector test.

What's required: All employment applications must include specified notice that it is unlawful to require a lie detector test as a condition of obtaining or continuing employment.

MICHIGAN

Mich. Comp. Laws §§ 37.203, 338.1719

Employers covered: All

What's prohibited: Employer may not request, require, administer, or attempt or threaten to administer a lie detector test; may not request or require that employee or applicant sign waiver of any action prohibited by this law.

What's allowed: Employee may voluntarily request a test if these conditions are met:
- before taking test employee is given copy of the law
- employee is given copies of test results and reports
- no questions asked about sexual practices; marital relationship; or political, religious, or labor or union affiliations, unless questions are relevant to areas under examination, and
- examiner informs employee:
  - of all questions that will be asked
  - of right to accept, refuse, or stop test at any time
  - that employee is not required to answer questions or give information, and
  - that information volunteered could be used against employee or made available to employer, unless otherwise agreed to in writing.

MINNESOTA

Minn. Stat. Ann. §§ 181.75, 181.76

Employers covered: All

What's prohibited: Employer may not directly or indirectly solicit or require an applicant or employee to take a lie detector test.

What's allowed: Employee may request a test, but only if employer informs employee that test is voluntary. Results of voluntary test may be given only to those authorized by employee.

Employee Polygraph Examination Laws (cont'd)

MONTANA

Mont. Code Ann. § 39-2-304

What's prohibited: Employer may not require an employee or applicant to take a lie detector test.

NEBRASKA

Neb. Rev. Stat. § 81-1932

Employers covered: All

What's prohibited: Employer may not require an employee or applicant to take a lie detector test.

What's allowed: Employer may request that test be taken, but only if these conditions are met:

- No questions are asked about sexual practices; marital relationship; or political, religious, or labor or union affiliations.
- An examinee is given written and oral notice that test is voluntary and may be discontinued at any time.
- An examinee signs a form stating that test is being taken voluntarily.
- Prospective employees are asked only job-related questions and are not singled out for testing in a discriminatory manner.
- An employee is requested to take test only in connection with a specific investigation.
- Results of a test are not the sole reason for terminating employment.
- All questions and responses are kept on file by the employer for at least one year.

NEVADA

Nev. Rev. Stat. Ann. §§ 613.480 to 613.510

Employers covered: All

Exceptions: Manufacturers or distributors of controlled substances; providers or designers of security systems and other security personnel; ongoing investigation

What's prohibited: Employer may not directly or indirectly require, request, suggest, or cause a lie detector test to be taken; may not use, accept, refer to, or ask about the results of any test. May not take adverse employment action solely on the basis of test results or a refusal to take test.

What's allowed: Nevada law allows testing in the same limited circumstances as the federal EPPA, with similar rules and restrictions on when and how the test is given.

NEW JERSEY

N.J. Stat. Ann. § 2C:40A-1

Employers covered: All

Exceptions: Employers that deal with controlled, dangerous substances

What's prohibited: Employer may not influence, request, or require applicant or employee to take a lie detector test.

What's allowed: Employers who are allowed to test must observe these rules:

- The job must require direct access to controlled substance.
- The test is limited to preceding 5 years.
- Questions must be work-related or pertain to improper handling, use, or illegal sale of legally distributed controlled dangerous substances.
- The test taker has right to legal counsel.
- The written copy of test results must be given to test taker upon request.
- Test information may not be released to any other employer or person.
- An employee or prospective employee must be informed of right to present results of a second independently administered test prior to any personnel decision being made.

Employee Polygraph Examination Laws (cont'd)

NEW YORK

N.Y. Lab. Law §§ 733 to 739

Employers covered: All

What's prohibited: Employer may not require, request, suggest, permit, or use results of a lie detector test.

OREGON

Or. Rev. Stat. Ann. §§ 659.840, 659A.300

Employers covered: All

What's prohibited: Employer may not require an employee or applicant to take a lie detector test.

PENNSYLVANIA

18 Pa. Cons. Stat. Ann. § 7321

Employers covered: All

Exceptions: Employers with positions that have access to narcotics or dangerous drugs

What's prohibited: Employer may not require an employee or applicant to take a lie detector test.

RHODE ISLAND

R.I. Gen. Laws §§ 28-6.1-1 to 28-6.1-4

Employers covered: All

What's prohibited: Employer may not request, require, subject, nor directly or indirectly cause an employee or applicant to take a lie detector test.

TENNESSEE

Tenn. Code Ann. §§ 62-27-123, 62-27-128

Employers covered: All

What's prohibited: Employer may not take any personnel action based solely upon the results of a polygraph examination. No questions may be asked about:

- religious, political, or labor-related beliefs, affiliations, or lawful activities
- beliefs or opinions about racial matters

- sexual preferences or activities
- disabilities covered by the Americans with Disabilities Act, or
- activities that occurred more than five years before the examination, except for felony convictions and violations of the state drug control act.

(Exception: Examination is part of an investigation of illegal activity in one of the above subject areas.)

What's required: Prospective examinee must be told if examiner is a law enforcement or court official and informed that any illegal activity disclosed may be used against examinee. Must receive and sign a written notice of rights including:

- right to refuse to take the test or to answer any question
- right to terminate examination at any time
- right to request an audio recording of examination and pretest interview, and
- right to request examination results within 30 days of taking it.

VERMONT

Vt. Stat. Ann. tit. 21, §§ 494 to 494e

Employers covered: All

Exceptions: Employers whose primary business is sale of precious metals, gems, or jewelry; whose business includes manufacture or sale of regulated drugs and applicant's position requires contact with drugs; employers authorized by federal law to require a test

What's prohibited: Employer may not request, require, administer, or attempt or threaten to administer a lie detector test. May not request or require that employee or applicant sign waiver of any action prohibited by state law. May not discriminate against employee who files a complaint of violation of laws.

Employee Polygraph Examination Laws (cont'd)

When testing is allowed, no questions may be asked about:

- political, religious, or labor union affiliations
- sexual practices, social habits, or marital relationship (unless clearly related to job performance), or
- any matters unrelated to job performance.

What's required: Prior to taking test examinee must receive a copy of state laws and a copy of all questions to be asked. Must be told that any information disclosed could be used against examinee or made available to employer, unless there is a signed written agreement to the contrary. Examinee must be informed of rights including:

- right to accept or refuse to take examination
- right to refuse to answer any questions or give any information
- right to stop examination at any time, and
- right to a copy of examination results and of any reports given to employer.

VIRGINIA
Va. Code Ann. § 40.1-51.4:3

Employers covered: All

What's prohibited: Employer may not require an applicant to answer questions about sexual activities in a polygraph test, unless the sexual activity resulted in a conviction for violation of state law.

What's required: Any record of examination results must be destroyed or maintained on a confidential basis, open to inspection only upon agreement of the employee.

WASHINGTON
Wash. Rev. Code Ann. § 49.44.120

Employers covered: All

Exceptions: Applicant or employee who manufactures, distributes, or dispenses controlled substances, or who works in a sensitive position directly involving national security

What's prohibited: Employer may not require, directly or indirectly, that an employee or applicant take a lie detector test.

WEST VIRGINIA
W.Va. Code §§ 21-5-5a to 21-5-5d

Employers covered: All

Exceptions: Employees or applicants with direct access to controlled substances

What's prohibited: Employer may not require or request, directly or indirectly, that an employee or applicant take a lie detector test; may not knowingly use the results of a lie detector test.

WISCONSIN
Wis. Stat. Ann. § 111.37

Employers covered: All

Exceptions: Manufacturers or distributors of controlled substances; providers or designers of security systems and other security personnel; ongoing investigation

What's prohibited: Employer may not directly or indirectly require, request, suggest, or cause an applicant or employee to take a lie detector test; may not use, accept, refer to, or inquire about the results of a test. May not take adverse employment action solely on the basis of test results or a refusal to take test. May not discriminate or retaliate against employee who files a complaint of violation of laws.

What's allowed: Wisconsin law allows testing in the same limited circumstances as the federal EPPA, with similar rules and restrictions on when and how the test is given.

State Drug and Alcohol Testing Laws

Note: The states of California, Colorado, Delaware, Kansas, Kentucky, Massachusetts, Michigan, Missouri, Nevada, New Hampshire, New Jersey, New Mexico, New York, Pennsylvania, South Dakota, Texas, Washington, West Virginia, Wisconsin, Wyoming, and the District of Columbia are not included in this chart because they do not have specific drug and alcohol testing laws governing private employers. Additional laws may apply. Check with your state department of labor for more information.

ALABAMA
Ala. Code §§ 25-5-330 to 25-5-340

Employers affected: Employers who establish a drug-free workplace program to qualify for a workers' compensation rate discount.

Testing applicants: Must test upon conditional offer of employment. Must test all new hires. Job ads must include notice that drug and alcohol testing required.

Testing employees: Random testing permitted. Must test after an accident that results in lost work time. Must also test upon reasonable suspicion; reasons for suspicion must be documented and made available to employee upon request.

Employee rights: Employees have 5 days to contest or explain a positive test result. Employer must have an employee assistance program or maintain a resource file of outside programs.

Notice and policy requirements: All employees must have written notice of drug policy. Must give 60 days' advance notice before implementing testing program. Policy must state consequences of refusing to take test or testing positive.

Drug-free workplace program: Yes.

ALASKA
Alaska Stat. §§ 23.10.600 to 23.10.699

Employers affected: Employers with one or more full-time employees.

Testing employees: Employer may test:
- for any job-related purpose
- to maintain productivity or safety
- as part of an accident investigation, or
- upon reasonable suspicion.

Employee rights: Employer must provide written test results within 5 working days. Employee has 10 working days to request opportunity to explain positive test results; employer must grant request within 72 hours or before taking any adverse employment action.

Notice and policy requirements: Before implementing a testing program employer must distribute a written drug policy to all employees and must give 30 days' advance notice. Policy must state consequences of a positive test or refusal to submit to testing.

ARIZONA
Ariz. Rev. Stat. §§ 23-493 to 23-493.11

Employers affected: Employers with one or more full-time employees.

Testing applicants: Employer must inform prospective hires that they will undergo drug testing as a condition of employment.

Testing employees: Employees are subject to random and scheduled tests:
- for any job-related purpose
- to maintain productivity or safety
- as part of an accident investigation, or
- upon reasonable suspicion.

Employee rights: Policy must inform employees of their right to explain positive results.

State Drug and Alcohol Testing Laws (cont'd)

Notice and policy requirements: Before conducting tests employer must give employees a copy of the written policy. Policy must state the consequences of a positive test or refusal to submit to testing.

Drug-free workplace program: Yes.

ARKANSAS

Ark. Code Ann. §§ 11-14-105 to 11-14-112

Employers affected: Employers who establish a drug-free workplace program to qualify for a workers' compensation rate discount.

Testing applicants: Must test for drug use upon conditional offer of employment, may test for alcohol but not required. Job ads must include notice that testing required.

Testing employees: Employer must test any employee:

- upon reasonable suspicion
- as part of a routine fitness-for-duty medical exam
- after an accident that results in injury, or
- as follow-up to a required rehabilitation program.

Employee rights: Employer may not refuse to hire applicant or take adverse personnel action against an employee on the basis of a single positive test that has not been verified by a confirmation test and a medical review officer. An applicant or employee has 5 days after receiving test results to contest or explain them.

Notice and policy requirements: Employer must give all employees a written statement of drug policy and must give 60 days' advance notice before implementing program.

Drug-free workplace program: Yes.

CONNECTICUT

Conn. Gen. Stat. Ann. §§ 31-51t to 31-51bb

Employers affected: All employers.

Testing applicants: Employer must inform job applicants in writing that drug testing is required as a condition of employment.

Testing employees: Employer may test:

- when there is reasonable suspicion that employee is under the influence of drugs or alcohol and job performance is or could be impaired
- when authorized by federal law
- when employee's position is dangerous or safety-sensitive, or
- as part of a voluntary employee assistance program.

Employee rights: Employer may not take any adverse personnel action on the basis of a single positive test that has not been verified by a confirmation test.

FLORIDA

Fla. Stat. Ann. §§ 440.101 to 440.102

Employers affected: Employers who establish a drug-free workplace program to qualify for a workers' compensation rate discount.

Testing applicants: Must inform job applicants that drug and alcohol testing is required as a condition of employment.

Testing employees: Must test any employee:

- upon reasonable suspicion
- as part of a routine fitness-for-duty medical exam, or
- as part of a required rehabilitation program.

Employee rights: Employees who voluntarily seek treatment for substance abuse cannot be fired, disciplined, or discriminated against, unless they have tested positive or have been in treatment in the past. All employees have the

State Drug and Alcohol Testing Laws (cont'd)

right to explain positive results within 5 days. Employer may not take any adverse personnel action on the basis of an initial positive result that has not been verified by a confirmation test and a medical review officer.

Notice and policy requirements: Prior to implementing testing, employer must give 60 days' advance notice and must give employees written copy of drug policy. Policy must state consequences of a positive test result or refusal to submit to testing.

Drug-free workplace program: Yes.

GEORGIA
Ga. Code Ann. §§ 34-9-410 to 34-9-421

Employers affected: Employers who establish a drug-free workplace program to qualify for a workers' compensation rate discount.

Testing applicants: Applicants are required to submit to a substance abuse test after they have been offered employment.

Testing employees: Must test any employee:
- upon reasonable suspicion
- as part of a routine fitness-for-duty medical exam after an accident that results in an injury, or
- as part of a required rehabilitation program.

Employee rights: Employees have 5 days to explain or contest a positive result. Employer must have an employee assistance program or maintain a resource file of outside programs.

Notice and policy requirements: Employer must give applicants and employees notice of testing and must give 60 days' notice before implementing program. All employees must receive a written policy statement; policy must state the consequences of refusing to submit to a drug test or of testing positive.

Drug-free workplace program: Yes.

HAWAII
Haw. Rev. Stat. §§ 329B-1 to 329B-5

Employers affected: All.

Testing applicants: Same conditions as current employees.

Testing employees: Employer may test employees only if these conditions are met:
- employer pays all costs including confirming test
- tests are performed by a licensed laboratory
- employee receives a list of the substances being tested for
- there is a form for disclosing medicines and legal drugs, and
- the results are kept confidential.

IDAHO
Idaho Code §§ 72-1701 to 72-1714

Employers affected: Employers who establish a drug-free workplace program to qualify for a workers' compensation rate discount.

Testing applicants: Employer may test as a condition of hiring.

Testing employees: May test as a condition of continued employment.

An employer who follows drug-free workplace guidelines may fire employees who refuse to submit to testing or who test positive for drugs or alcohol. Employees will be fired for misconduct and denied unemployment benefits.

Employee rights: An employee or applicant who receives notice of a positive test may request a retest within 7 working days. Employer may not take any adverse employment action on the basis of an initial positive result that has not been verified by a confirmation test. If the retest results are negative, the employer must pay for the cost; if they are positive, the employee must pay.

State Drug and Alcohol Testing Laws (cont'd)

Notice and policy requirements: Employer must have a written policy that includes a statement that violation of the policy may result in termination due to misconduct, as well as what types of testing employees may be subject to.

Drug-free workplace program: Yes (compliance is optional).

ILLINOIS

775 Ill. Comp. Stat. § 5/2-104(C)(3)

Employers affected: Employers with 15 or more employees.

Testing employees: Statute does not "encourage, prohibit, or authorize" drug testing, but employers may test employees who have been in rehabilitation.

Drug-free workplace: Yes (compliance is optional).

INDIANA

Ind. Code Ann. §§ 22-9-5-6(b), 22-9-5-24

Employers affected: Employers with 15 or more employees.

Testing employees: Statute does not "encourage, prohibit, or authorize" drug testing, but employers may test employees who have been in rehabilitation.

Drug-free workplace: Yes (compliance is optional).

IOWA

Iowa Code § 730.5

Employers affected: Employers with one or more full-time employees.

Testing applicants: Employer may test as a condition of hiring.

Testing employees: Statute does not encourage, discourage, restrict, limit, prohibit, or require

testing. Employer may test employees: during unannounced testing of employees selected from those at an entire worksite; upon reasonable suspicion; during and after rehabilitation; or following an accident that caused a reportable injury or more than $1,000 property damage.

Employee rights: Employee has 7 days to request a retest. Employers with 50 or more employees must provide rehabilitation for any employee testing positive for alcohol use who has worked for at least one year and has not previously violated the substance abuse policy. Employer must have an employee assistance program or maintain a resource file of outside programs.

Drug-free workplace program: Yes (compliance is optional).

LOUISIANA

La. Rev. Stat. Ann. §§ 49:1001 to 49:1012

Employers affected: Employers with one or more full-time employees. (Does not apply to oil drilling, exploration, or production.)

Testing applicants: Employer may require all applicants to submit to drug and alcohol test. Employer does not have to confirm a positive result of a preemployment drug screen but must offer the applicant the opportunity to pay for a confirmation test and a review by a medical review officer.

Employee rights: Employees with confirmed positive results have 7 working days to request access to all records relating to the drug test. Employer may allow employee to undergo rehabilitation without termination of employment.

State Drug and Alcohol Testing Laws (cont'd)

MAINE

Me. Rev. Stat. Ann. tit. 26, §§ 681 to 690

Employers affected: Employers with one or more full-time employees. (Law does not require or encourage employers to conduct substance abuse testing.)

Testing applicants: Employer may require applicant to take a drug test only if offered employment or placed on an eligibility list.

Testing employees: Employer may test based upon probable cause but may not base belief on a single accident; must document the facts and give employee a copy. May test when:

- there could be an unreasonable threat to the health and safety of coworkers or the public, or
- an employee returns to work following a positive test.

Employee rights: Employee who tests positive has 3 days to explain or contest results. Employee must be given an opportunity to participate in a rehabilitation program for up to 6 months; an employer with more than 20 full-time employees must pay for half of any out-of-pocket costs. After successfully completing the program, employee is entitled to return to previous job with full pay and benefits.

Notice and policy requirements: All employers must have a written policy approved by the state department of labor. Policy must be distributed to each employee at least 30 days before it takes effect. Any changes to policy require 60 days' advance notice. An employer with more than 20 full-time employees must have an employee assistance program certified by the state office of substance abuse before implementing a testing program.

MARYLAND

Md. Code Ann., [Health-Gen.] § 17-214

Employers affected: Law applies to all employers.

Testing applicants: May use preliminary screening to test applicant. If initial result is positive, may make job offer conditional on confirmation of test results.

Testing employees: Employer may require substance abuse testing for legitimate business purposes only.

Employee rights: The sample must be tested by a certified laboratory; at the time of testing employee may request laboratory's name and address. An employee who tests positive must be given:

- a copy of the test results
- a copy of the employer's written drug and alcohol policy
- a written notice of any adverse action employer intends to take, and
- a statement of employee's right to an independent confirmation test at own expense.

MINNESOTA

Minn. Stat. Ann. §§ 181.950 to 181.957

Employers affected: Employers with one or more full-time employees. (Employers are not required to test.)

Testing applicants: Employers may require applicants to submit to a drug or alcohol test only after they have been given a job offer and have seen a written notice of testing policy. May only test if required of all applicants for same position.

Testing employees: Employers are not required to test. Employers may require drug or alcohol

State Drug and Alcohol Testing Laws (cont'd)

testing only according to a written testing policy. Testing may be done if there is a reasonable suspicion that employee:

- is under the influence of drugs or alcohol
- has violated drug and alcohol policy
- has been involved in an accident, or
- has sustained or caused another employee to sustain a personal injury.

Random tests permitted only for employees in safety-sensitive positions. With 2 weeks' notice, employers may also test as part of an annual routine physical exam. Employer may test, without notice, an employee referred by the employer for chemical dependency treatment or evaluation or participating in a chemical dependency treatment program under an employee benefit plan. Testing is allowed during and for 2 years following treatment.

Employee rights: If test is positive, employee has 3 days to explain the results; employee must notify employer within 5 days of intention to obtain a retest. Employer may not discharge employee for a first-time positive test without offering counseling or rehabilitation; employee who refuses or does not complete program successfully may be discharged.

Notice and policy requirements: Employees must be given a written notice of testing policy which includes consequences of refusing to take test or having a positive test result. Two weeks' notice required before testing as part of an annual routine physical exam.

MISSISSIPPI

Miss. Code Ann. §§ 71-7-1 to 71-7-33, 71-3-205 to 71-3-225

Employers affected: Employers with one or more full-time employees. Employers who establish a drug-free workplace program to qualify for a workers' compensation rate discount must implement testing procedures.

Testing applicants: May test all applicants as part of employment application process. Employer may request a signed statement that applicant has read and understands the drug and alcohol testing policy or notice. (Must test applicants if drug-free workplace.)

Testing employees: May require drug and alcohol testing of all employees:

- upon reasonable suspicion
- as part of a routinely scheduled fitness-for-duty medical examination
- as a follow-up to a rehabilitation program, or
- if they have tested positive within the previous 12 months.

Employee rights: Employer must inform an employee in writing within 5 working days of receipt of a positive confirmed test result; employee may request and receive a copy of the test result report. Employee has 10 working days after receiving notice to explain the positive test results. Employer may not discharge or take any adverse personnel action on the basis of an initial positive test result that has not been verified by a confirmation test. Private employer who elects to establish a drug-free workplace program must have an employee assistance program or maintain a resource file of outside programs.

Notice and policy requirements: 30 days before implementing testing program employer must give employees written notice of drug and alcohol policy which includes consequences:

- of a positive confirmed result
- of refusing to take test, and
- of other violations of the policy.

Drug-free workplace program: Yes.

State Drug and Alcohol Testing Laws (cont'd)

MONTANA

Mont. Code Ann. §§ 39-2-205 to 39-2-211

Employers affected: Employers with one or more employees.

Testing applicants: May test as a condition of hire.

Testing employees: Employees may be tested:
- upon reasonable suspicion
- after involvement in an accident that causes personal injury or more than $1,500 property damage
- as a follow-up to a previous positive test, or
- as a follow-up to treatment or a rehabilitation program.

Employer may conduct random tests as long as there is an established date, all personnel are subject to testing, the employer has signed statements from each employee confirming receipt of a written description of the random selection process, and the random selection process is conducted by a scientifically valid method.

Employer may require an employee who tests positive to undergo treatment as a condition of continued employment.

Employee rights: After a positive result, employee may request additional confirmation by an independent laboratory; if the results are negative, employer must pay the test costs.

Notice and policy requirements: Written policy must be available for review 60 days before testing. Policy must state consequences of a positive test result.

NEBRASKA

Neb. Rev. Stat. §§ 48-1901 to 48-1910

Employers affected: Employers with 6 or more full-time and part-time employees.

Testing employees: Employer may require employees to submit to drug or alcohol testing and may discipline or discharge any employee who refuses.

Employee rights: Employer may not take adverse action on the basis of an initial positive result unless it is confirmed according to state and federal guidelines.

NORTH CAROLINA

N.C. Gen. Stat. §§ 95-230 to 95-235

Employers affected: Law applies to all employers.

Testing applicants: May test as a condition of hire. Applicant has right to retest a confirmed positive sample at own expense. If first screening test produces a positive result, applicant may waive a second examination that is intended to confirm the results.

Testing employees: Employers are not required to test. Employer must preserve samples for at least 90 days after confirmed test results are released.

Employee rights: Employee has right to retest a confirmed positive sample at own expense.

NORTH DAKOTA

N.D. Cent. Code §§ 34-01-15, 65-01-11

Employers affected: Any employer who requires a medical exam as a condition of hire or continued employment may include a drug or alcohol test.

Testing employees: May test following an accident or injury that will result in a workers' compensation claim, if employer has a mandatory policy of testing under these circumstances, or if employer or physician has reasonable grounds to suspect injury was caused by impairment due to alcohol or drug use.

State Drug and Alcohol Testing Laws (cont'd)

OHIO

Ohio Admin. Code §§ 4123-17-58, 4123-17-58.1

Employers affected: Employers who establish a drug-free workplace program to qualify for a workers' compensation rate discount.

Testing applicants: Must test all applicants and new hires within 90 days of employment.

Testing employees: Must test employees:
- upon reasonable suspicion
- following a return to work after a positive test
- after an accident which results in an injury requiring off-site medical attention or property damage over limit specified in drug and alcohol policy, and
- at random to meet requirements for greater discounts.

Employee rights: Employer must have an employee assistance plan. Employer must offer health care coverage which includes chemical dependency counseling and treatment. Not required for employers with fewer than 25 employees.

Notice and policy requirements: Policy must state consequences for refusing to submit to testing or for violating guidelines. Policy must include a commitment to rehabilitation.

Drug-free workplace program: Yes.

OKLAHOMA

Okla. Stat. Ann. tit. 40, §§ 551 to 565

Employers affected: Employers with one or more employees. (Drug or alcohol testing not required or encouraged.)

Testing employees: Before requiring testing, employer must provide an employee assistance program. Random testing is allowed. May test employees:
- upon reasonable suspicion

- after an accident resulting in injury or property damage over $500
- on a random selection basis
- as part of a routine fitness-for-duty examination, or
- as follow-up to a rehabilitation program.

Employee rights: Employee has right to retest a positive result at own expense; if the confirmation test is negative, employer must reimburse costs.

Notice and policy requirements: Before requiring testing employer must:
- adopt a written policy
- give a copy to each employee and to any applicant offered a job, and
- allow 30 days' notice.

  Policy must state consequences of a positive test result or refusing to submit to testing.

OREGON

Or. Rev. Stat. §§ 659.840, 659A.300, 438.435

Employers affected: Law applies to all employers.

Testing applicants: Unless there is reasonable suspicion that an applicant is under the influence of alcohol, no employer may require a breathalyzer test as a condition of employment. Employer is not prohibited from conducting a test if applicant consents.

Testing employees: Unless there is reasonable suspicion that an employee is under the influence of alcohol, no employer may require a breathalyzer or blood alcohol test as a condition of continuing employment. Employer is not prohibited from conducting a test if employee consents.

Employee rights: No action may be taken based on the results of an on-site drug test without a

State Drug and Alcohol Testing Laws (cont'd)

confirming test performed according to state health division regulations. Upon written request, test results will be reported to the employee.

RHODE ISLAND

R.I. Gen. Laws §§ 28-6.5-1 to 28-6.5-2

Employers affected: Law applies to all employers.

Testing applicants: May test as a condition of hire.

Testing employees: May require employee to submit to a drug test only if there are reasonable grounds, based on specific observations, to believe employee is using controlled substances that are impairing job performance.

Employee rights: Employee who tests positive may have the sample retested at employer's expense and must be given opportunity to explain or refute results. Employee may not be terminated on the basis of a positive result but must be referred to a licensed substance abuse professional. After referral, employer may require additional testing and may terminate employee if test results are positive.

SOUTH CAROLINA

S.C. Code Ann. §§ 41-1-15, 38-73-500

Employers affected: Employers who establish a drug-free workplace program to qualify for a workers' compensation rate discount.

Testing employees: Must conduct random testing among all employees. Must conduct a follow-up test within 30 minutes of the first test.

Employee rights: Employee must receive positive test results in writing within 24 hours.

Notice and policy requirements: Employer must notify all employees of the drug-free workplace program at the time it is established or at the time of hiring, whichever is earlier. Program must include a policy statement that balances

respect for individuals with the need to maintain a safe, drug-free environment.

Drug-free workplace program: Yes.

TENNESSEE

Tenn. Code Ann. §§ 50-9-101 to 50-9-114

Employers affected: Employers who establish a drug-free workplace program to qualify for a workers' compensation rate discount.

Testing applicants: Must test applicants upon conditional offer of employment. Job ads must include notice that drug and alcohol testing is required.

Testing employees: Employer must test upon reasonable suspicion; must document behavior on which the suspicion is based within 24 hours or before test results are released, whichever is earlier; and must give a copy to the employee upon request. Employer must test employees:

- who are in safety-sensitive positions
- as part of a routine fitness-for-duty medical exam
- after an accident that results in injury, or
- as a follow-up to a required rehabilitation program.

Employee rights: Employee has the right to explain or contest a positive result within 5 days. Employee may not be fired, disciplined, or discriminated against for voluntarily seeking treatment unless employee has previously tested positive or been in a rehabilitation program.

Notice and policy requirements: Before implementing testing program, employer must provide 60 days' notice and must give all employees a written drug and alcohol policy statement. Policy must state consequences of a positive test or refusing to submit to testing.

Drug-free workplace program: Yes.

State Drug and Alcohol Testing Laws (cont'd)

UTAH

Utah Code Ann. §§ 34-38-1 to 34-38-15

Employers affected: Employers with one or more employees.

Testing applicants: Employer may test any applicant for drugs or alcohol as long as management also submits to periodic testing.

Testing employees: Employer may test employee for drugs or alcohol as long as management also submits to periodic testing. Employer may require testing to:

- investigate possible individual employee impairment
- investigate an accident or theft
- maintain employee or public safety, or
- ensure productivity, quality, or security.

Employee rights: Employer may suspend, discipline, discharge, or require treatment on the basis of a confirmed positive test result.

Notice and policy requirements: Testing must be conducted according to a written policy that has been distributed to employees and is available for review by prospective employees.

VERMONT

Vt. Stat. Ann. tit. 21, §§ 511 to 520

Employers affected: Employers with one or more employees.

Testing applicants: Employer may not test applicants for drugs or alcohol unless there is a job offer conditional on a negative test result and applicant is given written notice of the testing procedure and a list of the drugs to be tested for.

Testing employees: Random testing not permitted unless required by federal law. Employer may not require testing unless:

- there is probable cause to believe an employee is using or is under the influence
- employer has an employee assistance program which provides rehabilitation, and
- employee who tests positive and agrees to enter employee assistance program is not terminated.

Employee rights: Employer must contract with a medical review officer who will review all test results and keep them confidential. Medical review officer is to contact employee or applicant to explain a positive test result. Employee or applicant has right to an independent retest at own expense. Employee who successfully completes employee assistance program may not be terminated, although employee may be suspended for up to 3 months to complete program. Employee who tests positive after completing treatment may be fired.

Notice and policy requirements: Must provide written policy that states consequences of a positive test.

VIRGINIA

Va. Code Ann. § 65.2-813.2

Employers affected: Employers who establish drug-free workplace programs to qualify for workers' compensation insurance discount.

Drug-free workplace program: State law gives insurers the authority to establish guidelines and criteria for testing.

State Laws on Employee Arrest and Conviction Records

The following chart summarizes state laws and regulations on whether an employer can get access to an employee's or prospective employee's past arrests or convictions. It includes citations to statutes and agency websites, as available.

Many states allow or require private sector employers to run background checks on workers, particularly in fields like child care, elder care, home health care, private schools, private security, and the investment industry. Criminal background checks usually consist of sending the applicant's name (and sometimes fingerprints) to the state police or to the FBI. State law may forbid hiring people with certain kinds of prior convictions, depending on the kind of job or license involved.

Federal law allows the states to establish procedures for requesting a nationwide background check to find out if a person has been "convicted of a crime that bears upon the [person's] fitness to have responsibility for the safety and well-being of children, the elderly, or individuals with disabilities." (42 U.S.C.A. § 5119a(a)(1).)

If your state isn't listed in this chart, then it doesn't have a *general statute* on whether private sector employers can find out about arrests or convictions. There might be a law about your particular industry, though.

It's always a good idea to consult your state's nondiscrimination enforcement agency or labor department to see what kinds of questions you can ask. The agency guidelines are designed to help employers comply with state and federal law. For further information, contact your state's agency.

ALASKA
Alaska Stat. §§ 12.62.160, 12.62.180

Agency guidelines for preemployment inquiries: Alaska Department of Labor and Workforce Development, Alaska Employer Handbook, "Preemployment Questioning," at www.labor.state.ak.us/employer/aeh.pdf.

ARIZONA
Ariz. Rev. Stat. § 13-904(E)

Rights of employees and applicants: Unless the offense has a reasonable relationship to the occupation, an occupational license may not be denied solely on the basis of a felony or misdemeanor conviction.

CALIFORNIA
Cal. Lab. Code § 432.7

Rules for employers:
- **Arrest records.** May not ask about an arrest that did not lead to conviction; may not ask about pretrial or posttrial diversion program. May ask about arrest if prospective employee is awaiting trial.
- **Convictions.** May ask about conviction even if no sentence is imposed.

Agency guidelines for preemployment inquiries: Department of Fair Employment and Housing, "Preemployment Inquiry Guidelines," DFEH-161 at www.dfeh.ca.gov/DFEH/Publications/PublicationDocs/DFEH-161.pdf.

COLORADO
Colo. Rev. Stat. §§ 24-72-308(b)(II)(f)(I), 8-3-108(m)

Rules for employers: May not inquire about arrest for civil or military disobedience unless it resulted in conviction.

Rights of employees and applicants: May not be required to disclose any information in a sealed record; may answer questions about

State Laws on Employee Arrest and Conviction Records (cont'd)

arrests or convictions as though they had not occurred.

Agency guidelines for preemployment inquiries: Colorado Civil Rights Division, "Employment Discrimination," at www.dora.state. co.us/civil-rights/publications_and_services.htm.

CONNECTICUT

Conn. Gen. Stat. Ann. §§ 46a-79, 46a-80, 31-51i

Rules for employers: State policy encourages hiring qualified applicants with criminal records. If an employment application form contains any question concerning criminal history, it must include a notice in clear and conspicuous language that (1) the applicant is not required to disclose the existence of any arrest, criminal charge, or conviction, the records of which have been erased; (2) define what criminal records are subject to erasure; and (3) any person whose criminal records have been erased will be treated as if never arrested and may swear so under oath. Employer may not disclose information about a job applicant's criminal history except to members of the personnel department or, if there is no personnel department, person(s) in charge of hiring or conducting the interview.

Rights of employees and applicants: May not be asked to disclose information about a criminal record that has been erased; may answer any question as though arrest or conviction never took place. May not be discriminated against in hiring or continued employment on the basis of an erased criminal record. If conviction of a crime has been used as a basis to reject an applicant, the rejection must be in writing and specifically state the evidence presented and the reason for rejection.

Special situations: Each consumer reporting agency that issues a consumer report that is used or is expected to be used for employment purposes and that includes in such report criminal matters of public record concerning the consumer shall provide the consumer who is the subject of the consumer report (1) notice that the consumer reporting agency is reporting criminal matters of public record, and (2) the name and address of the person to whom such consumer report is being issued.

DELAWARE

Del. Code Ann. tit. 11, § 4376

Rights of employees and applicants: Do not have to disclose an arrest or conviction record that has been expunged.

FLORIDA

Fla. Stat. Ann. § 112.011

Rights of employees and applicants: May not be disqualified to practice or pursue any occupation or profession that requires a license, permit, or certificate because of a prior conviction, unless it was for a felony or first-degree misdemeanor and is directly related to the specific line of work.

GEORGIA

Ga. Code Ann. §§ 35-3-34, 42-8-62, 42-8-63

Rules for employers: In order to obtain a criminal record from the state Crime Information Center, employer must supply the individual's fingerprints or signed consent. If an adverse employment decision is made on the basis of the record, must disclose all information in the record to the employee or applicant and tell how it affected the decision.

Rights of employees and applicants: Probation for a first offense is not a conviction; may not be disqualified for employment once probation is completed.

State Laws on Employee Arrest and Conviction Records (cont'd)

HAWAII

Haw. Rev. Stat. §§ 378-2, 378-2.5, 831-3.2

Rules for employers:

- **Arrest records.** It is a violation of law for any employer to refuse to hire, to discharge, or to discriminate in terms of compensation, conditions, or privileges of employment because of a person's arrest or court record.

- **Convictions.** May inquire into a conviction only after making a conditional offer of employment, provided it has a rational relation to job. May not examine any convictions over 10 years old.

Rights of employees and applicants: If an arrest or conviction has been expunged, may state that no record exists and may respond to questions as a person with no record would respond.

Agency guidelines for preemployment inquiries: Hawaii Civil Rights Commission, "What is Employment Discrimination?" at www.hawaii. gov/labor/hcrc/pdf/HCRCemploymdiscrim.pdf.

IDAHO

Agency guidelines for preemployment inquiries: Idaho Human Rights Commission, "Pre-Employment Inquiries Guide," in "Conducting a Lawful Employment Interview," at http://labor.idaho.gov/lawintvw3.htm.

ILLINOIS

775 Ill. Comp. Stat. § 5/2-103

Rules for employers: It is a civil rights violation to ask about an arrest or criminal history record that has been expunged or sealed, or to use the fact of an arrest or criminal history record as a basis for refusing to hire or to renew employment. Law does not prohibit employer from using other means to find out if person actually engaged in conduct for which they were arrested.

KANSAS

Kan. Stat. Ann. §§ 22-4710

Rules for employers: Cannot require an employee to inspect or challenge a criminal record in order to obtain a copy of the record, but may require an applicant to sign a release to allow employer to obtain record to determine fitness for employment. Employers can require access to criminal records for specific businesses.

Agency guidelines for preemployment inquiries: Kansas Human Rights Commission, "Guidelines on Equal Employment Practices: Preventing Discrimination in Hiring," at www. khrc.net/hiring.html.

LOUISIANA

La. Rev. Stat. Ann. § 37:2950

Rights of employees and applicants: Prior conviction cannot be used as a sole basis to deny employment or an occupational or professional license, unless conviction is for a felony and directly relates to the job or license being sought.

Special situations: Protection does not apply to medical, engineering and architecture, or funeral and embalming licenses, among others listed in the statute.

MAINE

Me. Rev. Stat. Ann. tit. 5, § 5301

Rights of employees and applicants: A conviction is not an automatic bar to obtaining an occupational or professional license. Only convictions that directly relate to the profession or occupation, that include dishonesty or false statements, that are subject to imprisonment for more than 1 year, or that involve sexual misconduct on the part of a licensee may be considered.

State Laws on Employee Arrest and Conviction Records (cont'd)

Agency guidelines for preemployment inquiries: The Maine Human Rights Commission, "Pre-Employment Inquiry Guide," at www.maine. gov/mhrc/guidance/pre-employment_inquiry_ guide.html, suggests that asking about arrests is an improper race-based question, but that it is okay to ask about a conviction if related to the job.

MARYLAND
Md. Code Ann. [Crim. Proc.], § 10-109; Md. Regs. Code §§ 09.01.10.02

Rules for employers: May not inquire about any criminal charges that have been expunged. May not use a refusal to disclose information as sole basis for not hiring an applicant.

Rights of employees and applicants: Need not refer to or give any information about an expunged charge. A professional or occupational license may not be refused or revoked simply because of a conviction; agency must consider the nature of the crime and its relation to the occupation or profession; the conviction's relevance to the applicant's fitness and qualifications; when conviction occurred and other convictions, if any; and the applicant's behavior before and after conviction.

Agency guidelines for preemployment inquiries: DLLR's Office of Fair Practices, "Guidelines for Pre-Employment Inquiries Technical Assistance Guide," at www.dllr. maryland.gov/oeope/preemp.shtml.

MASSACHUSETTS
Mass. Gen. Laws ch. 151B, § 4; ch. 276, § 100A; Mass. Regs. Code tit. 804, § 3.02

Rules for employers: If job application has a question about prior arrests or convictions, it must include a formulated statement (that appears in the statute) that states that an applicant with a sealed record is entitled to answer, "No record."
- **Arrest records.** May not ask about arrests that did not result in conviction.
- **Convictions.** May not ask about first-time convictions for drunkenness, simple assault, speeding, minor traffic violations, or disturbing the peace; may not ask about misdemeanor convictions 5 or more years old.

Rights of employees and applicants: If criminal record is sealed, may answer "No record" to any inquiry about past arrests or convictions.

Agency guidelines for preemployment inquiries: Massachusetts Commission Against Discrimination, "Discrimination on the Basis of Criminal Record," at www.mass.gov/mcad/ crimrec.html.

MICHIGAN
Mich. Comp. Laws § 37.2205a

Rules for employers: May not request information on any arrests or misdemeanor charges that did not result in conviction.

Rights of employees and applicants: Employees or applicants are not making a false statement if they fail to disclose information they have a civil right to withhold.

Agency guidelines for preemployment inquiries: Michigan Civil Rights Commission, "Preemployment Inquiry Guide," at www. michigan.gov/documents/pre-employment_ inquery_guide_13019_7.pdf.

MINNESOTA
Minn. Stat. Ann. §§ 364.01 to 364.03

Rules for employers: State policy encourages the rehabilitation of criminal offenders; employment opportunity is considered essential to rehabilitation.

State Laws on Employee Arrest and Conviction Records (cont'd)

Rights of employees and applicants: No one can be disqualified from pursuing or practicing an occupation that requires a license, unless the crime directly relates to the occupation. Agency may consider the nature and seriousness of the crime and its relation to the applicant's fitness for the occupation. Even if the crime does relate to the occupation, a person who provides evidence of rehabilitation and present fitness cannot be disqualified.

Agency guidelines for preemployment inquiries: Minnesota Department of Human Rights, "Hiring, Job Interviews, and the Minnesota Human Rights Act," at www.humanrights.state. mn.us/employers/hiring.html.

NEBRASKA
Neb. Rev. Stat. § 29-3523

Rules for employers: After one year from date of arrest, may not obtain access to information regarding arrests if no charges are completed or pending.

NEVADA
Nev. Rev. Stat. Ann. §§ 179.301, 179A.100(3)

Rules for employers: May obtain a prospective employee's criminal history record only if it includes convictions or a pending charge, including parole or probation.

Special situations: State Gaming Board may inquire into sealed records to see if conviction relates to gaming.

Agency guidelines for preemployment inquiries: Nevada Equal Rights Commission, "Guide to Pre-Employment," at http://detr.state. nv.us/Nerc_pages/premployment_guide.htm.

NEW HAMPSHIRE
N.H. Rev. Stat. Ann. § 651:5(X)(c)

Rules for employers: May ask about a previous criminal record only if question substantially follows this wording, "Have you ever been arrested for or convicted of a crime that has not been annulled by a court?"

NEW JERSEY
N.J. Stat. Ann. §§ 5:5-34.1, 5:12-89 to 5:12-91, 32:23-86; N.J. Admin. Code tit. 13, §§ 59-1.2, 59-1.6

Rules for employers: May obtain information about convictions and pending arrests or charges to determine the subject's qualifications for employment. Employers must certify that they will provide sufficient time for applicant to challenge, correct, or complete record, and will not presume guilt for any pending charges or court actions.

Rights of employees and applicants: Applicant who is disqualified for employment based on criminal record must be given adequate notice and reasonable time to confirm or deny accuracy of information.

Special situations: There are specific rules for casino employees, longshoremen and related occupations, horse racing, and other gaming industry jobs.

NEW MEXICO
Criminal Offender Employment Act, N.M. Stat. Ann. § 28-2-3

Special situations: For a license, permit, or other authority to engage in any regulated trade, business, or profession, a regulating agency may consider convictions for felonies and for misdemeanors involving moral turpitude. Such convictions cannot be an automatic bar to authority to practice in the regulated field, though.

State Laws on Employee Arrest and Conviction Records (cont'd)

NEW YORK

N.Y. Correct. Law §§ 750 to 754; N.Y. Exec. Law § 296(16)

Rules for employers:
- **Arrest records.** It is unlawful discrimination to ask about any arrests or charges that did not result in conviction, unless they are currently pending.
- **Convictions.** Employers with 10 or more employees may not deny employment based on a conviction unless it relates directly to the job or would be an "unreasonable" risk to property or to public or individual safety.

Rights of employees and applicants: Upon request, applicant must be given, within 30 days, a written statement of the reasons why employment was denied.

NORTH DAKOTA

N.D. Cent. Code § 12-60-16.6

Rules for employers: May obtain records of convictions or of criminal charges (adults only) occurring in the past three years, provided the information has not been purged or sealed.

Agency guidelines for preemployment inquiries: North Dakota Department of Labor, "Employment Applications and Interviews," www.nd.gov/labor/publications/docs/employment.pdf.

OHIO

Ohio Rev. Code Ann. §§ 2151.357, 2953.33, 2953.55

Rules for employers: May not inquire into any sealed convictions or sealed bail forfeitures, unless question has a direct and substantial relation to job.

Rights of employees and applicants: May not be asked about arrest records that are sealed; may respond to inquiry as though arrest did not occur.

OKLAHOMA

Okla. Stat. Ann. tit. 22, § 19(F)

Rules for employers: May not inquire into any criminal record that has been expunged.

Rights of employees and applicants: If record is expunged, may state that no criminal action ever occurred. May not be denied employment for refusing to disclose sealed criminal record information.

OREGON

Or. Rev. Stat. §§ 181.555–181.557 181.560, 659A.030

Rules for employers: Before requesting information, employer must notify employee or applicant; when submitting request, must tell State Police Department when and how person was notified. May not discriminate against an applicant or current employee on the basis of an expunged juvenile record unless there is a "bona fide occupational qualification."
- **Arrest records.** May request information about arrest records less than 1 year old that have not resulted in acquittal or have not been dismissed.
- **Convictions.** May request information about conviction records.

Rights of employees and applicants: Before State Police Department releases any criminal record information, it must notify employee or applicant and provide a copy of all information that will be sent to employer. Notice must include protections under federal civil rights law and the procedure for challenging information in the record. Record may not be released until 14 days after notice is sent.

State Laws on Employee Arrest and Conviction Records (cont'd)

PENNSYLVANIA

18 Pa. Cons. Stat. Ann. § 9125

Rules for employers: May consider felony and misdemeanor convictions only if they directly relate to person's suitability for the job.

Rights of employees and applicants: Must be informed in writing if refusal to hire is based on criminal record information.

Agency guidelines for preemployment inquiries: Pennsylvania Human Relations Commission at http://sites.state.pa.us/PA_Exec/PHRC/publications/literature/Pre-Employ%20QandA%208x11%20READ.pdf.

RHODE ISLAND

R.I. Gen. Laws §§ 12-1.3-4, 28-5-7(7)

Rules for employers:
- **Arrest records.** It is unlawful to include on an application form or to ask as part of an interview if the applicant has ever been arrested or charged with any crime.
- **Convictions.** May ask if applicant has been convicted of a crime.

Rights of employees and applicants: Do not have to disclose any conviction that has been expunged.

SOUTH DAKOTA

Agency guidelines for preemployment inquiries: South Dakota Division of Human Rights, "Preemployment Inquiry Guide," at www.state.sd.us/dol/boards/hr/preemplo.htm suggests that an employer shouldn't ask or check into arrests or convictions if they are not substantially related to the job.

UTAH

Utah Admin. R. 606-2(v).

Rules for employers:
- **Arrest records.** It is not permissible to ask about arrests.
- **Convictions.** Asking about felony convictions is permitted but is not advisable unless related to job.

Agency guidelines for preemployment inquiries: Utah Labor Division Anti-Discrimination Rules, Rule R606-2 "Preemployment Inquiry Guide," at www.rules.utah.gov/publicat/code/r606/r606-002.htm.

VERMONT

Vt. Stat. Ann. tit. 20, § 2056c

Rules for employers: Only employers who provide care for children, the elderly, and the disabled or who run postsecondary schools with residential facilities may obtain criminal record information from the state Criminal Information Center. May obtain record only after a conditional offer of employment is made and applicant has given written authorization on a signed, notarized release form.

Rights of employees and applicants: Release form must advise applicant of right to appeal any of the findings in the record.

VIRGINIA

Va. Code Ann. § 19.2-392.4

Rules for employers: May not require an applicant to disclose information about any criminal charge that has been expunged.

Rights of employees and applicants: Need not refer to any expunged charges if asked about criminal record.

State Laws on Employee Arrest and Conviction Records (cont'd)

WASHINGTON

Wash. Rev. Code Ann. §§ 43.43.815, 9.94A.640(3), 9.96.060(3), 9.96A.020; Wash. Admin. Code § 162-12-140

Rules for employers:

- **Arrest records.** Employer who asks about arrests must ask whether the charges are still pending, have been dismissed, or led to conviction that would adversely affect job performance, and whether the arrest occurred within the last ten years.

- **Convictions.** Employer who obtains a conviction record must notify employee within 30 days of receiving it and must allow the employee to examine it. May make an employment decision based on a conviction only if it is less than 10 years old and the crime involves behavior that would adversely affect job performance.

Rights of employees and applicants: If a conviction record is cleared or vacated, may answer questions as though the conviction never occurred. A person convicted of a felony cannot be refused an occupational license unless the conviction is less than 10 years old and the felony relates specifically to the occupation or business.

Special situations: Employers are entitled to obtain complete criminal record information for positions that require bonding, or that have access to trade secrets, confidential or proprietary business information, money, or items of value.

Agency guidelines for preemployment inquiries: Washington Human Rights Commission, "Preemployment inquiry guide," at http://apps.leg.wa.gov/WAC/default. aspx?cite=162-12.

WEST VIRGINIA

Agency guidelines for preemployment inquiries: West Virginia Bureau of Employment Programs, "Pre-employment Inquiries Technical Assistance Guide," at www.wvbep.org/Shared/ empinqu.asp. The state's website says that employers can only make inquiries about convictions directly related to the job.

WISCONSIN

Wis. Stat. Ann. §§ 111.31 and 111.335

Rules for employers: It is a violation of state civil rights law to discriminate against an employee on the basis of a prior arrest or conviction record.

- **Arrest records.** May not ask about arrests unless there are pending charges.

- **Convictions.** May not ask about convictions unless charges substantially relate to job.

Special situations: Employers are entitled to obtain complete criminal record information for positions that require bonding and for burglar alarm installers.

Agency guidelines for preemployment inquiries: Wisconsin Department of Workforce Development, Equal Rights Division, Civil Rights Bureau, "Fair Hiring & Avoiding Discriminatory Interview Questions," dwd.wisconsin.gov/dwd/ publications/erd/pdf/erd_4825_pweb.pdf.

Compensation and Hours

No matter how much you encourage creativity, camaraderie, and good cheer in your team or department, you know that employees don't show up every day for the sheer fun of it: They want to get paid (as, probably, do you). Pay is, perhaps, the most basic part of the employment relationship: Employees are paid in return for their labor. Despite the simplicity of this exchange, however, the legal rules governing pay and work can get pretty complicated. And managers—who often have to participate in setting pay levels, deciding whether employees should receive overtime, and figuring out how to pay employees who travel for business, among other things—can easily get caught in the middle.

This chapter covers some compensation basics, including:

- setting pay levels
- the minimum wage
- overtime
- paying for on-call and travel time
- flexible work schedules
- deductions and wage garnishments
- equal pay for men and women, and
- record-keeping requirements.

While not every manager will need to know the information in this chapter, it provides valuable information if you work in human resources or payroll or otherwise have to deal with compensation issues; you have some input into the pay levels of those who report to you; or you assign or approve employee schedules (including such issues as

Frequently Asked Questions About Compensation and Hours

How should I decide what to pay people?

Here are five steps to help you set pay for any given position: (1) clearly define the job and the level of talent necessary to do it well; (2) examine your company's budget to determine what you can afford to pay; (3) look internally at what others in your company are being paid for similar jobs; (4) gather external information on what other companies pay for similar jobs; and (5) find out the job candidate's pay requirements. (For an explanation of these five steps, see "Deciding What to Pay People," below.)

Do we have to pay the minimum wage to employees who receive tips?

It depends. Under federal law, as long as an employee regularly earns at least $30 per month in tips, the employee can be paid as little as $2.13 an hour. However, that amount plus the tips the employee actually earns must add up to at least the federal minimum wage. If the employee's total earnings fall short of the minimum wage, the employer must make up the difference. And some states don't allow employers to pay tipped employees less than the state minimum wage. (For more information on minimum wage laws, see "The Minimum Wage," below.)

Frequently Asked Questions About Compensation and Hours (cont'd)

Are managers entitled to overtime pay?

As long as they earn at least $455 a week and actually manage people, probably not. Under federal law, executive, professional, and administrative employees are not entitled to overtime pay. (For more, see "Overtime," below.)

If an employee goes on an overnight business trip, do we have to pay for every hour the employee spends away from home, even hours spent sleeping or eating?

No. You must pay for the hours the employee actually spends working, of course. You also have to pay for travel time, but only if the employee travels during his or her regular working hours. (These are the rules for overnight trips; the rules for one-day trips are different. For the full story, see "Travel Time," below.)

Are employees entitled to be paid for on-call time, even if they don't have to stay at work?

Employees are entitled to be paid for every on-call hour spent at the worksite. If employees aren't required to remain at the workplace, they are entitled to be paid for on-call time only if they are significantly restricted during those hours. (For more on paying for on-call time, see "On-Call Time," below.)

If I allow one or a few workers to work on a flexible schedule, do I have to allow everyone to do so?

No. Certain positions are better suited for flexible schedules than others. As long as your decision about who can work a flexible schedule isn't based on an illegal reason, such as race, gender, or age (and you stay within the bounds of overtime laws), you can allow only some workers to work flextime. (For more information, see "Flexible Work Schedules," below.)

Can I put an exempt employee on unpaid suspension while I investigate a claim that he sexually harassed a coworker?

It depends on your company's written policy. If you dock an exempt employee's pay, you risk making that employee nonexempt—and, therefore, entitled to earn overtime—unless an exception applies. Employers are allowed to put exempt employees on unpaid suspension for

Frequently Asked Questions About Compensation and Hours (cont'd)

violating workplace conduct rules, but only if the employer has a written policy regarding such suspensions that applies to all employees. (For more information, see "Pay Docking and Unpaid Suspensions," below.)

Can we deduct money from a worker's paycheck to repay a cash advance?

The answer is yes under the federal law, as long as you don't withhold so much money that the employee is effectively earning less than the minimum wage. But some states don't allow employers to make these kinds of deductions. (For more on withholding pay, see "Garnishments," below.)

Are female employees entitled to be paid as much as male employees—even if their jobs are different?

No. Under the Equal Pay Act, men and women are entitled to equal pay for doing the same work. But if men and women's job duties differ, equal pay is not required. (For more on the Equal Pay Act, see "Equal Pay," below.)

Can I get rid of employees' payroll records once they quit or are fired?

No. Federal law requires employers to keep certain records—including records on wages, hours, deductions, overtime, and pay dates—for each of its workers. You have to keep these records for three years, even if the worker leaves your company. (For more information on these rules, see "Record-Keeping Requirements," below.)

overtime, business trips, flextime, and so on) for which you'd like to know the legal rules. (This chapter may also answer some of your questions about your own paycheck.)

The Fair Labor Standards Act

The Fair Labor Standards Act (FLSA), 29 U.S.C. §§ 201 and following, is the primary federal law governing wages and hours. The FLSA sets the federal minimum wage; establishes rules for overtime pay, child labor, and paycheck deductions; and requires businesses to keep certain records showing the pay and hours of their workers.

Not every company is subject to the FLSA, although most are. Generally, a business is covered if it has $500,000 or more in annual sales. Smaller companies will still be covered if their employees work in what Congress calls "interstate commerce." Most employees are covered; engaging in interstate commerce includes making phone calls to or from another state, sending mail out of state, or handling goods that have come from or will go to another state. And the wage and hour rules also apply to employees who work out of their homes.

Certain types of workers are not entitled to the minimum wage or overtime pay. These include:

- independent contractors (only employees are covered by the FLSA—for more information about independent contractors, see Chapter 9)
- outside salespeople (a salesperson who works a route, for example)
- employees of seasonal amusement or recreational businesses (such as ski resorts or county fairs)
- employees of certain small newspapers and newspaper deliverers
- workers engaged in fishing operations
- employees who work on small farms, and
- certain switchboard operators.

Many states also have their own wage and hour laws, including some that provide workers with more protections than the FLSA (and place more obligations on companies). To make things a bit trickier, a business must follow whichever rule (state or federal) gives its workers more protection. It may have to abide by a patchwork of laws, applying a minimum federal standard in some areas and a more protective state standard in others. For example, if your company does business in a state that requires a higher minimum wage but sets lower standards for child labor, it will have to follow the state minimum wage law while applying the stricter federal child labor rules.

To find out more about your state's law—and about how it compares to federal law—contact your state labor department. (Contact information is available in the appendix.)

Deciding What to Pay People

While the bulk of this chapter covers the rules of wage and hour law, we begin with the most basic compensation question first: How do you figure out what to pay for which jobs? And what if the jobs are similar but require different levels of experience or skill? The following sections provide you with a method and the tools you need to craft compensation packages that pay fairly for the work done and, hopefully, attract employees who will do the job well.

Steps to Determine What to Pay

While there are many shifting variables to consider when determining pay, the process by which you consider these variables can be summed up in five steps:

Step 1: Clearly define the job you are paying for and the level of talent necessary to do it well.

Step 2: Examine your own budget to determine what you can afford to pay.

Step 3: Look internally at what others in your company are being paid for similar jobs (to achieve "internal equity").

Step 4: Gather external information on what other companies pay for similar jobs (called "external market data"). To do this, you may wish to gather both quantitative data—for example, surveys—and qualitative or anecdotal data—for example, asking those in your professional network what they pay or finding out what your job applicants have been earning.

Step 5: Find out the job candidate's pay requirements.

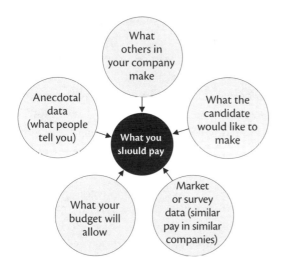

While doing this work may take a little time, it will be time well spent: You will be able to attract better candidates and justify your pay requests to your employees and management. And, the pay you determine will be fair and appropriate.

Define the Job

Until you understand precisely what you are paying for, you cannot begin to know how much you should pay. Each type of job could conceivably have many different levels or requirements that you compensate differently. Your best bet is to capture the job exactly as you know it to be currently and then begin your pay determination there.

Start with a good job description. (For help writing one, see *The Job Description Handbook*, by Margaret M. Mader-Clark (Nolo).) If you do not have a job description, spend a few minutes answering the following questions:

- What are the primary functions of this job? What must a person in this position absolutely do to get this job done successfully?
- What other responsibilities does the job have? Might you add any responsibilities in the near future?
- What skills and abilities are necessary to do this job? Are there any special requirements needed, such as licenses, certificates, or certain educational requirements?
- Are there any special characteristics of this job to consider—for example, unusual work hours, significant travel, being on call, dangerous or undesirable job duties?

Examine Your Budget

Of course, one of the biggest determinants of what you will pay an employee is how much your business can afford. After clarifying the job description, this is the first thing to consider when hiring or promoting someone into a position. How much you can afford to pay will differ depending on the type of company you work for:

- **Small businesses.** Small business owners typically know exactly what their constraints are when setting pay. Often, while they would like to hire more senior or managerial-level candidates, their budgets only allow for hiring entry-level employees.
- **Private companies.** Privately held companies vary in their level of sophistication about compensation structures. Get familiar with your company's approach and make sure that you are on the same page as your company's finance and human resources departments when getting ready to set a pay package.
- **Public companies.** Publicly owned companies are more likely to have formal compensation structures and even people to help you determine pay. Nevertheless, be prepared with a clear definition of the job, an understanding of whether your position has been budgeted for, and what that budget includes (for example, whether it covers just the salary or fringe benefits or bonuses as well).

With your budget number in hand, you now have the "top line" of what you can pay someone: an amount of compensation that you cannot exceed (although your company may have a process to do so if it's absolutely necessary). You can now move on to figure out where, from the top line down, you should set your pay.

Consider What Others in Your Company Make

Paying fairly across like positions within a company—known as "internal equity"—can be a loaded issue for many workplaces. How many times have you heard complaints about a new hire making more than someone who has been with the company for years? It's a good idea to generate a report that shows the title, level, and compensation of similarly situated employees (you don't need their names for this exercise). Then, consider the following:

- **Current pay levels.** What are people in similar positions within your company making? Keep in mind that positions need not be exactly the same or even in the same job family to be considered in an internal equity study. For instance, if you are hiring a Director of Marketing, it's helpful to understand compensation of not only other marketing directors at your company, but directors in other corporate functions as well. It is also a good idea to consider the pay of those directly below or above the position. Compression (pay that is too close to the level above or below) can lead to problems when it comes time to give someone a raise.

- **Starting pay levels.** What did people in these similar positions make when they first started (and how long ago was that)?
- **Education or experience levels.** The newcomer may have much more experience than your other employees, which may warrant more pay. If so, be prepared to justify the higher pay, because employees may very well learn what their coworkers are making.
- **Requirements of the job.** You may have added responsibilities to the position, making it different from an existing position. For example, if you are hiring an International Sales Manager to open a new sales branch for India, his or her position may be very different from the other six Sales Managers on your staff. While their titles may be the same, the other six all came to work for existing businesses and were not responsible for opening their own sales branches. This is a significant difference in the requirements of the job (as well as the experience necessary to do that job successfully) that could warrant higher pay.

Studying internal equity can be complex; don't let it become anything more than a guideline to help you set pay for a particular job. You may ultimately decide to hire at a compensation level well above or below what others are currently making. As long as you can clearly explain the differences in the job requirements or tasks, you should be able to justify the difference.

Gather External Market Data

Next, find out what other companies pay employees in the same or similar positions. There are two main sources for this data: surveys and anecdotal information. Both have advantages and disadvantages. Surveys provide concrete quantitative data across a broad spectrum, but unfortunately tend to become stale so quickly that, by the time they are published, they are already outdated (although the Internet is helping to alleviate this problem). Qualitative anecdotal data suffers from not being very scientific and tapping into a smaller pool of information, but can be even more relevant because of its freshness—it can tell you what people earn right now.

Surveys. A quick Web search can often provide fairly decent external market data on a whole variety of positions. Try visiting www.salaryexpert.com or other job websites like Monster (www.monster.com) and Jobs. com (www.jobs.com). When looking at survey information on these websites, you will see that most of the information is broken up into a few different pieces:

- **Geographical information.** Pay will always vary based on supply and demand and that, of course, varies by geography. Auto mechanics are more prevalent in Detroit than in New York City, for example, and their pay may vary accordingly.
- **Level of the job.** This is where your job definition will come in handy. Typically there are about three levels listed for any job: entry, mid, and high. Titles

used to define these three levels vary. For example, you may be hiring for an "Associate," "Junior," or "Senior" position (as in "Associate Clerk") or hiring for the position plus a "1," "2," or "3" (as in "Clerk 2"), and so on. Be sure to look for data that matches the level of the job for which you are setting pay.

- **Industry.** The industry or type of industry also helps to determine pay for any given position. Fast-growing industries, such as high-tech or biotech, typically pay more than well-established industries, such as shipping and manufacturing. Pay is often a function of supply and demand: In newer industries, you may be required to pay more for new skill sets (such as computer programming), whereas in more established industries, there are usually more people with the proper training to choose from.

Take any survey information you find with a grain of salt. As mentioned above, it may be outdated and it may not be a direct match with your position. But like internal equity, it can provide another guideline to help you set pay; use it as such, not as an absolute.

Anecdotal information. While surveys may seem scientific and important, often the freshest data will come from professional organizations, colleagues in your field, and even the candidates interested in the position themselves. Anecdotal information you glean from speaking to people can also be more relevant than survey data, because it is usually more targeted and a better match to the position you are filling.

You can gather anecdotal information from a number of different sources. At meetings of professional organizations to which you belong, check in with your peers to find out what they are currently paying people. Also, read organizational newsletters and websites, especially if they list classifieds for open positions; often a "Help Wanted" ad will list a salary range for an open position.

You can also get such information from applicants who come in to interview for the position. It's a fair question to ask them not only their current salary, but also their future salary requirements.

Understand the Candidate's Requirements

By looking at your budget, you determined the top line of what you can pay for a given position. Internal equity and external market data gave you some parameters for what you should pay to be competitive and fair. The last piece of the puzzle is finding out what the job candidate will accept. This is the bottom line of what you can pay.

Once you narrow the pool of applicants down to one or two real candidates for the position, you will need to ask the candidates both what they made in their last position (which you may have done in gathering anecdotal information from all of the applicants in the previous step) and what they would accept from you for the new position (don't phrase it this way, of course!). To make such a question sound better and not seem like you are trying to lowball the candidate, ask a question such as, "What pay would seem reasonable to you if you were to join us?" With a stroke of good luck, this number will be below your top line number and within your other guidelines. Often, however, you will need to massage the numbers and use some creative techniques (as described below) to come up with a compensation package that is acceptable to both the candidate and your company.

Putting It All Together

After going through all five steps, how do you turn all of this information into a pay package? In a perfect world, your top line is higher than your bottom line and the candidate and you agree to something in between. If this is not the case, consider the following creative techniques for making the numbers work:

- Establish base pay that reasonably falls within these parameters, but allows for pay increases in the future.
- Offer bonuses or variable pay based on performance on top of the base pay. Bonuses can be short-term (at signing or after 90 days), midterm (after six months or at annual performance appraisals), or long-term (designed to retain an employee). Make sure you communicate the entire compensation package to the candidate, not just the base pay.
- If you are a public company that offers stock to your employees, negotiate how much stock the candidate will get.
- You can often make up differences in what a candidate would like to make and what you can afford by

offering noncash compensation, such as enhanced vacation benefits, paid maternity or paternity leave, or educational assistance.

All of these elements can be part of a compensation package. Most of them will require different levels of company approval, so check your policies before offering them. If you are creative with the different tools your company has to offer and can tailor the compensation package to the individual, you should be able to hire your chosen candidate.

The Minimum Wage

Many managers will never have to worry about the minimum wage. However, if you supervise low-wage or tipped employees, you participate in determining compensation, or you implement your company's pay program (for example, you work in human resources or payroll), you need to know the basic rules.

Federal law requires employers to pay employees a minimum wage (currently $7.25 an hour). States may impose a higher minimum wage requirement, and many do. The federal law is always the minimum. That is, a company must pay the higher amount, whether it's state or federal. For information on your state's minimum wage requirements, see "State Minimum Wage Laws for Tipped and Regular Employees," at the end of this chapter.

How It's Paid

Although the minimum wage is an hourly standard, employees don't have to be paid by the hour for the minimum wage requirement to kick in. Employees entitled to the minimum wage may receive a salary, commission, wages plus tips, or piece rate, as long as the total amount paid divided by the total number of hours worked by the employee equals at least the minimum wage.

Living Wage Laws

Some cities and counties have passed "living wage" ordinances, requiring certain businesses to pay their workers more than the federal or state minimum wage. The living wage rate is usually calculated by figuring out how much a full-time worker would have to make to support a family of four at or above the poverty line in that geographic area. Some living wage laws also require employers to provide certain benefits or allow employers to pay a lower wage if they already provide benefits.

City and county governments often impose these requirements in areas where the cost of living has skyrocketed beyond that of the rest of the country (such as San Francisco and New York). If your company does business in an area with a high cost of living, there is more likely to be a living wage law.

Many of these laws cover only companies that have contracts with, or receive subsidies from, the state or county, but some apply more broadly to private employers in the area. Check city or county ordinances (or consult a local attorney) for information about local living wage laws.

Minimum Wage for Younger Workers

Under federal law, younger workers—workers under the age of 20—may be paid a lower minimum wage for a few months. These workers are entitled to at least $4.25 an hour during their first 90 days of employment. (Note that these are calendar days—including weekends and holidays—not days that the employee actually works.) Workers who reach their 20th birthday are entitled to the standard minimum wage, even if they have not yet put in 90 days at your company.

Some states don't allow a youth minimum wage. In these states, younger workers are entitled to the same minimum wage as anyone else.

Employees Who Receive Other Types of Compensation

Under federal law and the laws of some states, companies may be allowed to pay less than the minimum wage to employees who receive other types of compensation. For example, if your company provides room and board to employees, the company can deduct money from their paychecks as reimbursement—even if they'll end up with less than the minimum wage for that pay period—as long as the employee agrees to this arrangement in writing. See "Garnishments," below, for more information.

Some employers may also claim a "tip credit" under federal law. A company has to pay only $2.13 an hour to employees who make at least $30 per month in tips. However, if the employee's wage plus actual earned tips does not add up to the minimum wage for each pay period, the employer must pay the difference. And some states—including California—do not allow employers to take a tip credit. In these states, employers must pay tipped employees the minimum wage, regardless of how generous their customers are. (For information on whether your state allows a tip credit—and for how much—see "State Minimum Wage Laws for Tipped and Regular Employees," at the end of this chapter.)

Overtime

Federal and state laws require most employers to pay overtime. The overtime premium is 50% of the employee's usual hourly wage. This means an employee who works overtime must be paid "time and a half"—the employee's usual hourly wage plus the 50% overtime premium—for every overtime hour worked.

These laws contain many exceptions, so not all employees are entitled to overtime. Employees who are eligible for overtime are called "nonexempt" employees, and those who are not eligible for overtime are called "exempt" employees. Misclassifying employees can be a very costly mistake if your company faces a lawsuit or a government audit. Because this is an area where a lot of managers get in trouble, it's worth taking some time to learn the rules.

Weekly Versus Daily Standard

Federal law and the laws of most states impose a weekly overtime standard, which means that nonexempt employees are entitled to overtime for every hour more than 40 that they work in a week, regardless of how many hours they work in a day. For example, Alex is a nonexempt employee who works 12 hours on Monday and six hours on Tuesday (and doesn't work any more hours in the week). He is not entitled to receive overtime under the weekly overtime standard, even though he worked more than eight hours on Monday.

California and a handful of other states have a daily overtime standard, which means that nonexempt employees are entitled to overtime for every hour more than eight that they work in a day and every hour more than 40 that they work in a week. Let's take Alex from the paragraph above. In a daily overtime state, he would be entitled to overtime pay for the four extra hours he worked on Monday, even though he didn't even come close to working 40 hours in the week.

Which Employees Are Entitled to Overtime

If a business is covered by either the FLSA or a state overtime law, then all of its employees are entitled to overtime unless they are exempt (that is, unless they fit into an exception to the overtime rules).

Probably the most common—and confusing—exceptions to the overtime laws are for so-called "white-collar" workers. Employees who the law defines as "administrative, executive, or professional" need not be paid overtime. To be considered such, employees must be paid on a salary basis and must spend most of their time performing job duties that require the use of discretion and independent judgment.

An employee who is paid on a salary basis must earn at least $455 per week and must receive the same salary every week, regardless of how many hours the employee works or the quantity or quality of the work the employee does. There are a few circumstances in which a salaried worker may be paid less than his or her full salary for a week (for example, if the employee takes unpaid time off under the Family and Medical Leave Act). Generally, however, if an employer docks an employee's pay (for not meeting a sales target, for example), then the employee is not paid on a salary basis and is entitled to overtime. (For more information, see "Pay Docking and Unpaid Suspensions," below.)

Not every employee who earns $455 or more per week is exempt from overtime. The employee must also be performing certain types of work: generally, work that requires an advanced degree, is managerial or supervisory in nature, or requires the employee to make relatively high-level business decisions. Here are the basic requirements for the administrative, executive, and professional exemptions:

- An administrative employee must perform office or other nonmanual work that is directly related to the management or business operations of the employer or its customers and must exercise discretion and independent judgment regarding significant issues.
- An executive employee's primary duty must be managing the employer's

enterprise or a recognized division or department of that enterprise; the employee must regularly supervise at least two full-time employees (or the equivalent) and must have the authority to hire and fire or have significant input into hiring and firing decisions.

- A professional employee's primary duty must either be performing work that requires advanced knowledge in the field of science or learning, of a type that is usually attained through an advanced course of study; or performing work that requires invention, imagination, originality, or talent in a recognized creative or artistic field.

Compensatory Time Might Not Be Legal

Some companies adopt a policy of giving their employees compensatory, or "comp," time—an hour off at some later date for every extra hour worked—instead of paying them overtime. But, as many managers are surprised to learn, these policies are generally illegal under federal law, at least for private employers (state and local governments can offer comp time, in certain circumstances). The reason? They preclude employees from collecting an overtime premium: the extra pay to which they are entitled for working more than a set number of hours. (The overtime premium is 50% of the employee's usual hourly wage, so an employee who works overtime must be paid "time and a half," or the employee's usual hourly wage plus the 50% overtime premium, for every overtime hour worked.)

Classification Rules for White-Collar Employees

Administrative Employee

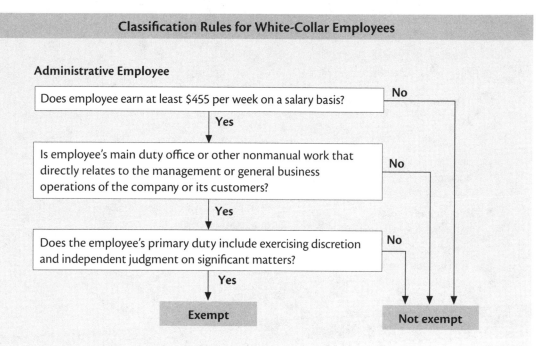

Does employee earn at least $455 per week on a salary basis?

No

Yes

Is employee's main duty office or other nonmanual work that directly relates to the management or general business operations of the company or its customers?

No

Yes

Does the employee's primary duty include exercising discretion and independent judgment on significant matters?

No

Yes

Exempt

Not exempt

Executive Employee

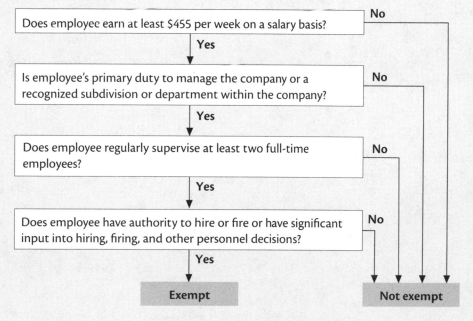

Does employee earn at least $455 per week on a salary basis?

No

Yes

Is employee's primary duty to manage the company or a recognized subdivision or department within the company?

No

Yes

Does employee regularly supervise at least two full-time employees?

No

Yes

Does employee have authority to hire or fire or have significant input into hiring, firing, and other personnel decisions?

No

Yes

Exempt

Not exempt

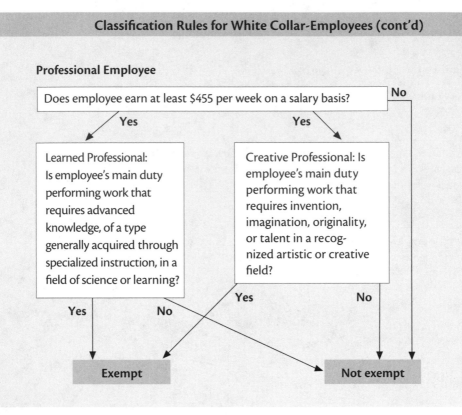

Classification Rules for White Collar-Employees (cont'd)

Professional Employee

Does employee earn at least $455 per week on a salary basis? — **No**

Yes ← → Yes

Learned Professional: Is employee's main duty performing work that requires advanced knowledge, of a type generally acquired through specialized instruction, in a field of science or learning?

Creative Professional: Is employee's main duty performing work that requires invention, imagination, originality, or talent in a recognized artistic or creative field?

Yes — No

Yes — No

Exempt

Not exempt

All of this means that if you wish to give your employees time off instead of money for extra hours worked, you cannot simply establish an hour-for-hour policy (that is, telling the employee to take an hour off for every hour of overtime worked). You may be able to handle this by adjusting an employee's hours during a pay period so that the amount of the employee's paycheck takes into account the overtime premium, yet remains constant. To make the math come out right, the employee must take an hour and a half off for every extra hour worked.

For example, if an employee who generally earns $1,600 every two weeks (or $20 an hour) works an extra ten hours during the first week of the pay period, the employee is entitled to $300 in overtime pay—ten hours multiplied by one-and-a-half times the employee's hourly rate, or $30. If the employee took 15 hours off in the second week of the pay period, however, his or her paycheck would remain the same: The employee would receive $300 in overtime pay, but would be docked $300 (15 hours multiplied by $20 an hour) for the time not worked.

Meal and Rest Breaks

The FLSA doesn't require employers to give employees time off during their work days. Federal law does, however, provide some rules on what counts as a true break, for which employees don't have to be paid, and what should be compensable work time. These rules are explained below.

Some state laws require employers to provide breaks—and some states require employers to pay for this time. In recent years, there have been a number of class action lawsuits against employers who don't provide the time off mandated by these laws. The dollar amounts in these cases add up fast: multiply what the company owes a single employee for a half-hour's work by the number of employees in the company, and multiply that by the number of days for which employees can recover (often two or even three years). Once you tack on penalties, court costs, and attorney fees (for the company and for the employee's lawyers, if they win), companies are looking at multimillion-dollar exposure. And it all could have been avoided if only they didn't make employees work through lunch.

What Counts as a Break?

Under the FLSA, employers must pay employees for brief break periods—of 20 minutes or less—during the day. Employers aren't legally required to provide this time off at all, at least under federal law. If they do, however, they must pay employees for the time.

If an employee takes more than 20 minutes off—for example, the employee takes a half-hour lunch break—the employer doesn't have to pay for any of that time. This is true only if the employee is completely relieved of all work duties during the break. If an employee has any responsibilities during the break, that time must be paid. For example, an employee who has to cover the phones or wait for a delivery while eating lunch must be paid for that time.

State Laws

As noted above, some states require employers to provide meal breaks. Typically, these statutes require employers to let employees take at least a half-hour for lunch, if they are scheduled to work more than four or five hours. And, a handful of states also require employers to provide brief paid breaks during the day. For a summary of these laws, see "State Meal and Rest Break Laws," at the end of this chapter.

Lactation Breaks

Many new mothers return to work while they are still breast-feeding, which often means that they will need one or more breaks during the day to pump breast milk. For employers, providing these breaks makes good sense. It allows women to return to work more quickly after having a baby, enhances employee loyalty, and provides mothers and babies with the proven health benefits of breast-feeding.

Now, these breaks aren't just a good idea: they are also legally required. More than a dozen states have laws requiring employers to allow employees to take unpaid breaks for this purpose. However, no federal law addressed the issue until 2010, when the Patient Protection and Affordable Care Act—better known as the health care reform law—passed. This law includes a number of provisions intended to promote preventive health care and healthy habits, including a requirement that employers allow new mothers to express breast milk at work.

What the Health Care Reform Law Requires

Under the 2010 law, employers must provide reasonable break time for nursing mothers to pump for up to one year after the child's birth. The employer must also provide private space, other than a bathroom, for this purpose. Your company doesn't have to dedicate a room solely for pumping, although it can. If an employee's office is reasonably private, she can pump there; your company may have to provide some alterations (such as a window shade) for this purpose. For employees who don't have private workspace, the company can allow them to pump in a vacant office or conference room, for example, as long as the space is adequate and private.

Although the federal law applies to all employers, it includes an exception for employers with fewer than 50 employees. These employers need not allow lactation breaks if doing so would impose an "undue hardship," defined as significant expense or difficulty, considering the employer's size, structure, and resources.

Lessons From the Real World

In December 2006, a Pennsylvania jury ordered Wal-Mart to pay more than $78 million in damages to a class of 170,000 current and former employees. The employees claimed that they were required to work through their breaks and work "off the clock"—that is, after they had punched out for the day. They argued that Wal-Mart's failure to pay them for this time violated the company's own policies and the state's laws on payment of wages and overtime.

Pennsylvania law doesn't require employers to pay for employee breaks. However, the employees claimed that they didn't really get to take breaks: Instead, they had to work through these periods, even though they weren't paid. Wal-Mart argued, among other things, that employees were encouraged to take their breaks, and that it shouldn't be held responsible if some employees chose to work instead. Apparently, the jury didn't find this argument very persuasive.

On top of the jury's award, the judge ordered Wal-Mart to pay more than $62 million in penalties and almost $50 million to the employees' attorneys, for a whopping total of more than $187 million. Wal-Mart has filed an appeal. (You can find links to decisions and articles on the case at www.walmartpaclassaction.com, a site maintained by the employees' attorneys.)

State Laws

Some state lactation break laws require only that employers allow employees to use their regular breaks to express breast milk. Other states go further and require employers to provide additional breaks, if necessary. Like the federal law, some states also require employers to provide an appropriate space for pumping.

Even if your company doesn't have to comply with the federal law (because providing breaks would pose an undue hardship, as defined above), it may still have to allow breaks under applicable state law. To find out whether your state has a law on this issue, see "State Meal and Rest Break Laws," at the end of this chapter.

Travel Time

Employees who are entitled to overtime pay also have the right to be paid for some hours they spend traveling for work. If your reports routinely travel as part of their jobs or go on business trips that take them out of the area, you'll need to be able to figure out whether (and how much) they are entitled to be paid for this time.

Although employees are not entitled to be paid for time spent commuting to and from work, they must be paid for travel time that is part of the job. If, for example, employees are required to go out on service calls, the time spent traveling to and from the customers must be paid. Also, if employees are required to take employer-provided transportation from a central location to the worksite, they may have to be paid for this time.

Even if an employee's job does not ordinarily involve travel, an employee who is required to come to the workplace at odd hours to deal with emergency situations may be entitled to pay. For example, if a mechanic works a regular 9-to-5 schedule but is sometimes called in during the night shift to repair equipment that has broken down, the mechanic is entitled to be paid for those extra hours.

Special rules apply to employees who occasionally travel to another location for business. The rules depend on whether the trip includes an overnight stay.

One-Day Trips

If you send an employee on a one-day business trip, the employee is entitled to pay for hours spent in transit. For example, if an employee has to drive two hours each way to get to an out-of-town business meeting, the company must pay for the four hours of total travel time. However, if the employee goes straight from home to the meeting, the company can deduct the time it would otherwise have taken the employee to commute to work.

Pay for Travel Time: One-Day Trip

Time spent traveling	_____
Minus usual commute time	– _____
Equals compensable travel time	= _____

EXAMPLE: It usually takes Polly about ½ hour each way to commute to the office.

You send her to a business meeting in a city that's two hours away. Polly doesn't come into the office at all that day but instead drives from her home straight to the meeting and straight home again afterwards. She is entitled to three hours of paid travel time in addition to the time she spends working:

4 hours travel time
– 1 hour usual commute time
= 3 hours compensable travel time

Overnight Trips

When an employee spends more than a day out of town, the rules are different. Of course, the employee must be paid for all of the time he or she spends actually working. However, whether the employee is entitled to pay for time spent in transit depends on when the travel takes place. Employees are entitled to pay for time spent traveling only during the hours when they regularly work (the period of the day they regularly work). However, they are entitled to be paid for weekend travel that takes place during these hours, even if they ordinarily work Monday through Friday.

Pay for Travel Time: Overnight Trip

Time spent traveling   _____

Minus travel time outside usual
work hours   – _____

Equals compensable travel time   = _____

EXAMPLE: You send Polly to attend a three-day business conference out of town. Her usual schedule is 9 a.m. to 5 p.m., Monday through Friday. She leaves her home to head for the airport at 5 a.m. Wednesday morning and arrives at the conference in time for the 9 a.m. orientation. Because the conference ends late on Friday, she returns home Saturday morning, catching an 8 a.m. flight and pulling into her driveway at home by noon. Of course, Polly is entitled to pay for all of the hours she actually spends at the conference, even if it goes beyond her regularly scheduled hours. In addition, she is entitled to three hours of travel time.

8 hours travel time
– 5 hours of travel outside usual
   work hours
= 3 hours compensable travel time

On-Call Time

Under federal law, employees are entitled to be paid for time that their employer controls and that benefits their employer. Generally, this includes time that the employee cannot spend as he or she wishes, even if that time is not spent working. For example, an employee who has to cover the phones while eating lunch is entitled to be paid for that time, even if the phones aren't ringing.

If employees are required to stay on company premises or at a customer's location while waiting for a work assignment, they are entitled to be paid even if they do not spend that time actually working. For example, a mechanic who knits a sweater while waiting for a customer to arrive, a corporate trainer who must wait for the client to gather employees and set up equipment, or a secretary who does a crossword puzzle while

Lessons From the Real World

Shelly Reimer was a nurse at Dakota Heartland Health Systems. She and her coworkers were required to spend some time "on call." They did not have to be at the workplace during this time, but they had to be reachable by cell phone, beeper, or regular phone; had to be able to report to the hospital within 20 minutes of getting called; and had to refrain from drinking alcohol or using "mind-altering" drugs or medications while on call. Dakota Heartland paid the nurses less than the minimum wage for time spent on call.

Reimer and her coworkers sued, arguing that they were entitled to regular pay for the time they spent on call. But the court disagreed. Finding that the restrictions placed on nurses were minimal, the court noted that they "could play sports, work at home, go shopping, or visit friends and neighbors" while on call. The court also found that nurses typically were not called in more than once per shift and that once a nurse was called in to work, she was paid at her regular rate. Because nurses were free to engage in a variety of activities, and because they were called in relatively rarely, the court found that their time was not spent for the benefit of Dakota Heartland and did not have to be compensated at regular rates.

Reimer v. Champion Healthcare Corp., 258 F.3d 720 (8th Cir. 2001).

waiting for an assignment is entitled to be paid for that time.

If employees must be on call elsewhere, they are entitled to be paid for those hours over which they have little or no control and which they cannot use for their own enjoyment or benefit. If you place significant restrictions on an employee who is on call, that employee should be paid. There are few hard-and-fast rules in this area—but, generally, the more constraints on an employee, the more likely he or she should be paid.

Here are some factors a court or agency might consider when deciding this issue:

- **How many calls an employee gets while on call.** The more calls an employee has to respond to, the more likely he or she is entitled to pay, particularly if any of the calls require the employee to report to work or give immediate advice or guidance over the phone.
- **How long an employee has to respond after a call.** If employees are required to report in immediately after being paged, for example, they have a better argument that they should be paid for their time.
- **Where an employee can go while on call.** Employees who must stay within a limited distance of work are more likely to be entitled to compensation.
- **What employees can do while on call.** The more rules imposed on on-call workers, such as a ban on alcohol or a requirement that they respond quickly and in person to calls (which can be difficult if the employee is out running or taking the kids to school), the more likely it is that they are entitled to pay for this time.

Flexible Work Schedules

As we all know, it can sometimes seem impossible to work full time during business hours and simultaneously meet our family and other personal obligations—whether they be caring for a child, helping an elderly parent, or taking care of our own health needs. More and more companies are starting to respond to their workers' needs for flexibility by allowing employees to work flexible schedules or what is often referred to as "flextime."

Helping employees meet their family or personal needs can pay off for the company as well. Allowing employees to work flexible schedules can reduce distractions on the job and increase worker productivity, loyalty, and job satisfaction, which in turn reduces turnover and related costs. This section describes flextime and its legality; for more on other types of personnel policies that can help employees balance work and family, see "Family-Friendly Workplace Policies" in Chapter 4.

Flextime Defined

Generally speaking, an employee who works on a flexible schedule still works full time but simply does his or her work during what may not be considered normal business hours. This means that instead of working 9:00 a.m. to 5:00 p.m., an employee may, for example, work 7:00 a.m. to 3:00 p.m. to be home to provide care for his or her children after school, work 11:00 a.m. to 7:00 p.m. in order to take an elderly parent to morning physical therapy, or work 8:00 a.m. to 6:00 p.m. four

days a week to have a full day off to care for his or her infant. (Other types of work arrangements such as working part time or job sharing are discussed in "Family-Friendly Workplace Policies" in Chapter 4.)

Flextime is not the same thing as compensatory or "comp" time: In comp time, an employee works overtime—beyond his or her regular work hours—in order to earn additional time off—a practice which may raise legal questions. (See "Compensatory Time Might Not Be Legal," above.) Flextime, on the other hand, is a policy whereby your company allows its workers to work a regular eight-hour day or 40-hour week, but doesn't require the work to be done during normal business hours.

Is Flextime Legal?

On the whole, flextime is perfectly legal, with two caveats. First, if any employee wants to work more than eight hours in one day, your company must be careful to follow any state overtime laws that apply. Under federal law, an employee who works no more than 40 hours in a week, regardless of how many hours he or she works per day, has not worked overtime and is not entitled to overtime pay. So, for example, an employee who works four ten-hour days and then has three days off need not be paid overtime. However, some states have laws that provide a daily overtime standard. In these states, workers are entitled to overtime if they work more than a set number of hours in a day, even if they ultimately work fewer than 40 hours in a week.

So, if you allow a worker to work more than the set number of hours per day, you might have to pay overtime unless the law explicitly allows you and your employees to agree on an alternative workweek. California, Colorado, and Connecticut are among the states that have a daily overtime standard. To find out the rules in your state, including whether you and your employees can arrange an alternative workweek schedule, contact your state labor department. (See the appendix for contact information.)

Second, as with any employment benefit your company may establish, you cannot discriminate unlawfully based on race, gender, religion, age, disability, or any other protected characteristic in providing the benefit. This does not mean that you have to let everyone work a flexible schedule; it just means that you cannot decide who has access to the benefit based on some impermissible characteristic. Obviously, certain jobs are more suited to a flexible schedule. For example, jobs that do not need to be done during business hours or do not require the worker to be present when other employees are present—such as editing books or accounting—may allow a flexible schedule, whereas jobs that must be done while the business is open— such as reception or computer support for employees—may not. If appropriate, flextime may also be used as a reasonable accommodation for an employee with a disability. (See "Disability," in Chapter 3, for more on reasonable accommodations.)

If your company chooses to institute flexible work schedules, however, you could hear some grumbling from those not allowed to work flexible hours. To reduce the chances of this happening, you will want to establish clear, consistent policies that can be administered fairly. For more on establishing personnel policies in general, see Chapter 4. For more information on instituting flexible work schedules, contact any of the number of organizations that work on such issues, including research organizations like the Families and Work Institute (www.familiesandwork.org), and consulting groups such as Catalyst (www. catalyst.org) and Winning Workplaces (www. winningworkplaces.com).

Pay Docking and Unpaid Suspensions

Some managers discipline employees by docking their pay or putting them on unpaid suspension for violating workplace rules. However, this type of policy can create big problems if the employee whose pay is reduced is exempt from overtime—that is, the employee is not entitled to overtime pay because he or she is paid on a salary basis and generally has to exercise a certain degree of responsibility and discretion in doing the job.

What's Wrong With Docking Pay?

To qualify as exempt, employees have to be paid a set amount each pay period, without any reductions based on the quantity or quality of work they do. If you dock their pay, you may inadvertently make them nonexempt employees and thereby entitle them to overtime. As you might guess, the money saved by docking the employee's salary could be far exceeded by the money the company could have to pay out in overtime.

Under federal law, exempt employees —those who are not entitled to overtime— must earn at least $455 per week (or $23,660 per year). To be exempt, employees must be paid on a salary basis. (For more information see "Overtime," above.) This means that all or some of the employee's salary is a fixed amount that doesn't depend on how many hours they work, how much work they accomplish, or the quality of their work. As long as employees do some work during the week, they are entitled to their full weekly pay, unless the time they take off falls into one of the exceptions described below.

Permissible Salary Deductions

Employers may make salary deductions (without jeopardizing the employee's exempt status) for one or more full days an employee takes off for the following reasons:

- to handle personal affairs
- to go on unpaid family or medical leave under the Family and Medical Leave Act (see Chapter 5 for information on the FMLA)
- for disability or illness, if the employer has a plan (such as disability insurance or sick leave) that compensates employees for this time off
- to serve on a jury, as a witness, or on temporary military leave, but the employer may deduct only the amount that the employee receives as jury or witness fees or as military pay
- during the employee's first or last week of work, if the employee does not work a full week
- as a penalty imposed in good faith for infractions of safety rules of major significance (rules that prevent serious danger in the workplace or to other employees), or
- to serve an unpaid disciplinary suspension imposed in good faith for infractions of workplace conduct rules, but only if the employer has a written policy regarding such suspensions that applies to all employees.

Penalties for Improper Deductions

A company that makes improper deductions from a salaried employee's pay can get in trouble. However, the law contains a "safe harbor" provision, which offers some protection for inadvertent deductions.

Actual Practice of Improper Deductions

A company will be penalized if it has an "actual practice" of making improper deductions. Among the factors a court or government agency will consider when making this determination are:

- the number of improper deductions
- the time period during which the deductions were made
- how many employees were subjected to improper salary deductions and where those employees worked

Lessons From the Real World

Life Time Fitness paid its senior managers a set amount of base salary twice a month, along with a monthly bonus payment based on the manager's year-to-date performance. In 2004, the compensation program reserved the company's right to take back previous bonus payments, through reducing a manager's base salary payments, if his or her performance dropped below a certain level. After 2004, the program was tweaked, but still allowed the company to reduce a manager's base pay for performance that didn't meet certain standards. In 2005, a number of managers had their base pay reduced under the program in three separate pay periods.

The managers sued, claiming that Life Time's program amounted to illegal pay docking, and that all of them were entitled to overtime pay as a result. The court had a complicated job in this case, because the Department of Labor changed the rules relating to pay docking in August of 2004. Under the old rules, an employer could be held liable for improper pay docking if it actually reduced an exempt employee's pay based on the quality or quantity of the employee's performance or if it had an employment policy creating a "significant likelihood" of such reductions. Although no managers actually received reduced pay before the rules changed, the court found that Life Time's written policies clearly communicated that deductions were likely, and so found in favor of the managers for this time period.

However, Life Time fared better for the time period after the rules changed to make employers liable only if they had an "actual practice" of making deductions. The court found that the managers were entitled to overtime compensation only during the three pay periods when illegal deductions were made, and only managers in the same job classification were covered.

Baden-Winterwood et al. v. Life Time Fitness, Inc., 566 F.3d 618 (6th Cir., 2009).

- how many managers were responsible for taking improper deductions and where those managers worked, and
- whether the company has a clearly communicated policy that either permits or prohibits improper deductions.

A company that has an actual practice of making improper deductions will lose the overtime exemption for all employees who work in the job classification(s) for which the deductions were made and who work for the same managers responsible for making the deductions. In other words, if you make improper deductions, your company will have to pay overtime (if earned by the employees) to everyone who reports to you and holds the same position as the employee whose pay you docked.

Safe Harbor Protections

A company will not be subject to the penalties noted above if:

- any improper deductions were either isolated or inadvertent, and the company reimburses the employees for the money improperly withheld, or
- the company has a clearly communicated policy prohibiting improper deductions (including a complaint procedure), reimburses employees for the money improperly withheld, and makes a good faith effort to comply with the law in the future.

Garnishments

A company may be legally obligated to deduct money from a worker's paycheck to satisfy certain debts, such as child support or tax debts. In addition, you might be allowed to deduct money to satisfy the worker's debt to the company (for a cash advance, for example). However, except in very limited circumstances, an employer is not allowed to withhold so much money that a worker's pay falls below the required minimum wage.

Wage Garnishment, Child Support Orders, and Tax Debts

If you receive a court order or notice from a government agency requiring you to withhold money from a worker's paycheck, simply follow the instructions in the documents. Generally, an employer may be required to deduct money from a worker's paycheck in three situations:

- **Wage garnishments.** A court might order your company to withhold money to satisfy certain debts, including student loan debts, alimony or spousal support, or money owed to someone who won a lawsuit against the worker. This type of order is called a wage "attachment" or "garnishment." The paperwork you receive from the court will generally tell you how much to deduct and where to send the money, although you might first have to tell the court how much the worker earns.
- **Child support orders.** When a judge orders a parent to pay child support, the judge will automatically issue a wage withholding order. This order requires the employer to deduct the amount owed each month from the worker's paycheck, then send that money to the parent who has custody of the child.
- **Wage levy notices.** The Internal Revenue Service (IRS) has the right to take some portion of a worker's wages to satisfy his or her unpaid tax debt. In these situations, the employer will receive a wage levy notice from the IRS indicating the amount to be deducted (and sent to the government). Generally, state tax agencies have the same right.

Federal law prohibits employers from firing workers because their wages have been garnished to pay any one debt, no matter how many separate orders or lawsuits have been filed to collect that debt. However, a worker whose wages are garnished to pay off more than one debt can be terminated, under federal law. Some states don't allow termination of workers because their wages have been garnished for more than one debt, however. For information on state rules, see "State Laws on Administering Wage Garnishments," at the end of this chapter.

Federal law limits how much can be deducted from a worker's paycheck for wage garnishments and child support orders. Generally, for wage garnishments an employer may deduct either 25% of the worker's actual earnings per pay period (after tax and required state and federal deductions) or the amount by which the worker's actual earnings exceed 30 times the minimum hourly wage, whichever is less. For child support or alimony orders, up to one-half of the worker's actual earnings may be taken if the worker is supporting a spouse or dependent child (other than the person for whom the money is being taken) and up to 60% if the worker is not. More may be taken from workers who are well behind in their support payments.

Wage garnishments can be tricky. If you have any questions about a wage garnishment or other withholding order, contact the authority that sent the order (for example, the IRS or a particular court). You might also consider asking a lawyer for advice.

Deductions to Pay a Debt to the Employer

If an employee owes the company money—for a salary advance, for example—the company is entitled (under federal law) to withhold money from the employee's paycheck to pay

itself back. However, you cannot deduct so much that the employee's earnings for that pay period drop below the minimum wage. If an employee owes a substantial debt, the employer can avoid running afoul of this rule by deducting money in installments.

Some states prohibit employers from deducting money from their workers' paychecks or limit the circumstances under which they can do so. For more information on your state's law, contact your state labor department (see the appendix for contact information).

Deductions for Food and Lodging

Employers are allowed to deduct the reasonable cost of meals and housing provided to workers, even if the worker's pay, after these costs are deducted, falls below the minimum wage. However, these deductions are allowed only if *all* of the following are true:

- the company regularly provides room and board for workers
- the items were provided for the benefit of the employee
- the employee was told, before the arrangement began, that the company planned to take the deductions, and
- the employee voluntarily agreed, in writing, to accept less than the minimum wage in exchange for the food and lodging provided.

Some states place additional limits on deductions for food and lodging. For example, some allow employers to deduct only a specified amount for each meal provided. To learn more about your state's law, contact your state labor department.

Other Deductions

Generally, an employer may not deduct money from its workers' paychecks to reimburse itself for other business expenses if doing so would cause the workers' pay to fall below the minimum wage. Examples of expenses subject to this rule include:

- uniforms
- tools used in the employee's work
- financial losses incurred in the ordinary course of business (for example, a short-fall in a cash register or a customer's failure to pay a bill)
- services the employee is required to purchase (such as a mandatory medical examination or a cleaning service), and
- damage to or theft of company property.

Some states prohibit employers from charging their workers for these types of business expenses, whether by wage with-holding or any other method. Check with your state department of labor to find out what expenses (if any) can be charged back to workers.

Equal Pay

The Equal Pay Act (EPA), 29 U.S.C. § 206(d), prohibits employers from paying employees of one sex at a lower rate than employees of the opposite sex for doing equal work. The law was intended to combat what the Supreme Court called the "ancient but outmoded belief that a man, because of his role in society, should be paid more than a woman." *Corning Glass Works v. Brennan*, 417 U.S. 188, 195 (1974). Despite this gender-specific intent,

however, the EPA protects both men and women from wage discrimination based on sex. (This section covers equal pay only. For more on gender discrimination, see "Gender, Pregnancy, and Sexual Harassment" in Chapter 3.)

What Is Equal Work?

Male and female employees are entitled to equal pay even if their jobs are not absolutely identical. The law requires only that their jobs be "substantially" equal for the equal pay requirement to kick in. That is, the jobs must require equal skill, effort, and responsibility, and they must be performed under similar working conditions.

Job titles do not determine whether two jobs are substantially equal. For example, you may not pay a male "administrative assistant" more than a female "secretary" if both do essentially the same tasks. Similarly, jobs that have the same official name may require different degrees of responsibility or effort, allowing men and women holding those jobs to be paid at different rates. For example, one court allowed a college to pay the male coach of its men's basketball team more than the female coach of its women's basketball team. The court decided that coaching the men's team carried with it more responsibility because the men's team had to bring in higher revenues.

What Is Equal Pay?

The EPA doesn't just apply to wages. It also applies to benefits, such as insurance coverage, pensions, and use of a company car, and other forms of compensation, like vacation time, profit sharing, and bonuses. In other words, you must also provide equal fringe benefits to workers of both sexes.

Managers can get into trouble here: If you make certain benefits or perks available to only some of your reports, you must make sure that those benefits are not being doled out along gender lines. If men and women doing the same work don't receive the same benefits, that could be an EPA violation; even if they aren't doing equal work, providing benefits based on an employee's gender could constitute sex discrimination.

However, this doesn't mean that men and women must receive identical paychecks. The EPA requires workers to be paid at the same rate, not the same amount. If workers are paid on commission or by the piece, for example, they must be paid according to the same formula (for example, 10% of the company's gross profit on each sale or $1 per piece). But it's okay if one worker earns more than another because he or she was more productive (for instance, because the worker made more sales or turned out more work in a given pay period than other workers doing the same job).

Financial incentives for good performance work the same way. You can't offer only salesmen the opportunity to earn a bonus for high sales volume while denying the same opportunity to saleswomen. But if you offer the bonus to your entire sales team and only men make enough sales to qualify, it's legal to pay the bonus only to those men.

Exceptions to the EPA

There are four exceptions to the EPA. Workers of one sex may be paid more for doing equal work if the difference is based on one of the four following factors:

- **Seniority.** Workers who have been with the company for a long time may be paid more than workers with shorter tenure, even if this results in workers of one sex making more than workers of the other.

- **Merit.** For example, if you give performance-based raises, you may give a higher raise to workers whose performance is better, regardless of gender.

- **Quantity or quality of production.** An employer may pay by the piece, for example, or pay higher rates for better quality work, as long as both men and women have the opportunity to earn this higher rate.

- **Any factor other than sex.** This "catchall" exception is intended to encompass the myriad reasons why one worker might be paid more than another—as long as they are unrelated to the worker's gender. For example, if you must pay a shift premium to entice workers to cover the night shift, that would not violate the EPA. Nor would offering a worker a higher starting rate based on his or her salary at a previous job.

For a discussion of gender discrimination, see "Gender, Pregnancy, and Sexual Harassment" in Chapter 3.

Record-Keeping Requirements

Under the Fair Labor Standards Act, employers must keep records on wages, hours, deductions, and pay dates for all of their employees. These records must be kept for three years, even after a worker leaves the company.

Although employers must create administrative systems that properly preserve these records, the good news is that you are not required to keep them in any particular form, use a time clock, or require workers to fill in time cards.

What Records Must Be Kept?

Generally, an employer must keep records showing all of the following for each employee:

- name, address, occupation, sex, and birth date (only if the worker is under the age of 19)
- hour and day when the workweek begins
- total hours worked in each workday and workweek
- total daily or weekly regular earnings
- the worker's regular hourly pay rate in any week when the worker works overtime
- total overtime pay for each workweek
- any deductions from or additions to pay for each pay period
- total wages paid each pay period, and
- date of the payment and the pay period covered for each payment.

Employers may be required to keep additional information for certain workers, including employees who work at home, employees who receive tips, employees who

live at the worksite, or employees who earn the youth minimum wage.

State law may require employers to keep additional records. To find out, contact your state labor department. (Contact information is available in the appendix.)

Penalties for Failure to Keep Records

If an employer doesn't keep records as required, an individual employee or the U.S. Department of Labor could sue the company just for inadequate record keeping. However, these claims usually come up only in the context of a larger lawsuit (for failing to pay overtime or taking improper deductions from workers' paychecks, for example).

The real danger of failing to keep adequate records is that your company will be unable to prove that it complied with wage and hour laws if the government or an employee challenges its practices. For example, if the Department of Labor decides to audit your company, you won't have any proof that you are complying with the law. This might encourage the government to dig deeper into your company's employment practices, something you probably want to avoid.

In addition, if an employer is unlucky enough to wind up on the wrong end of an employee lawsuit, it won't have records to prove the employee was paid properly. And once workers offer some evidence that they worked any hours for which they were not paid, the burden shifts to the company to prove its workers wrong, or at least to show that they are overstating their unpaid hours. A company that hasn't kept records won't be able to meet this burden.

Legal Dos and Don'ts: Compensation

Do:

- **Require approval for overtime.** If your reports work overtime—even without your knowledge or permission—the company will have to pay them for it. Cut down on surprises by requiring employees to get your approval in advance. And discipline employees who continue to work unauthorized overtime.
- **Conduct an annual job classification audit.** Once a year, review the job titles, classifications, and actual responsibilities of the employees reporting to you. Make sure employees who are classified as exempt from wage and hour laws meet the legal requirements.
- **Keep proper records.** Companies must keep certain payroll records for three years. Failing to keep required records is not only against the law; it will also hinder your company's ability to defend itself if employees sue for unpaid wages.

Don't:

- **Give comp time.** It's illegal for private employers to use comp time, but some managers have an informal practice of allowing it anyway. Even if your employees would rather take comp time than be paid overtime, don't fall into this habit.
- **Pay more attention to job titles than job duties.** When it comes to eligibility for overtime and compliance with equal pay and other wage discrimination laws, job titles don't matter. It's what employees actually do on the job that determines your company's obligations.
- **Dock an exempt employee's pay.** Find another way to discipline exempt employees for poor performance or minor misconduct. If you reduce an exempt employee's salary for these reasons, you risk making that employee—and all other employees who work for you in the same job classification—eligible for overtime.

Test Your Knowledge

Questions

1. When setting pay for a position, you should build a spreadsheet to calculate the value of the job based on the average pay internally (at your company) and at similar jobs externally (at other companies).   ☐ True   ☐ False

2. You don't have to pay tipped employees a regular wage as long as they earn at least the minimum wage in tips.   ☐ True   ☐ False

3. Only employees who are paid by the hour are entitled to earn overtime.   ☐ True   ☐ False

4. An employee who is entitled to earn overtime must be paid for every hour spent traveling for business.   ☐ True   ☐ False

5. Employees who must stay at the worksite while waiting to be called for work are entitled to be paid for that time.   ☐ True   ☐ False

6. If my company allows one employee to work a flexible schedule, it must allow all employees to do so.   ☐ True   ☐ False

7. You can never pay an exempt employee less than his or her full salary.   ☐ True   ☐ False

8. You do not have to honor a wage garnishment order unless the employee gives you permission to withhold the money from his or her paycheck.   ☐ True   ☐ False

9. All men and women who hold the same position must receive the same pay.   ☐ True   ☐ False

10. Once an employee quits or is fired, you can recycle or destroy that employee's pay records.   ☐ True   ☐ False

Answers

1. False. To set pay, you should go through a multistep process to determine your company's top line; the skills the job requires; internal equity; external market data; and the job candidate's bottom line. Setting pay is as much art as science: While averages will give you guidelines for setting pay, do not use them as absolutes.

2. False. Tipped employees must be paid at least $2.13 an hour under federal law, or more, if their tips combined with this wage don't add up to at least the minimum hourly wage. State laws often require employers to pay more, and some don't allow a tip credit at all.

3. False. The right to earn overtime is not determined by how the employee is paid, but by the employee's job duties. Some exempt employees are paid by the hour; some nonexempt employees earn a salary.

4. It depends on the length of the trip and when the travel takes place. An employee who takes a one-day trip is entitled to be paid for all hours spent traveling, less the employee's usual commute. An employee on a longer trip is entitled to be paid only for travel that falls during the employee's regular work hours.

5. True. Employees who must be on-call at the worksite are entitled to be paid for that time.

6. False. You can allow only certain employees to work flexible schedules as long as you do not make your decision for an illegal reason, such as discrimination. Seniority, whether the job is suited to a flexible schedule, and accommodating a worker with a disability, for example, are all legally valid reasons why you might allow one employee to work a flexible schedule but not another.

7. False. There are some circumstances when you can dock an exempt employee's salary (if the employee takes family and medical leave or violates an important safety rule, for example).

8. False. You must honor valid wage garnishment orders, no matter how the employee feels about it.

9. False. Men and women who hold the same position can receive different compensation if the differential is based on seniority, quantity or quality of work, merit, or any factor other than sex.

10. False. You must keep payroll records for three years after an employee leaves.

State Minimum Wage Laws for Tipped and Regular Employees

The chart below gives the basic state minimum wage laws. Depending on the occupation, the size of the employer's business, or the conditions of employment, the minimum wage may vary from the one listed here. Minimum wage rates in a number of states change from year to year; to be sure of your state's current minimum, contact your state department of labor or check its website, where most states have posted the minimum wage requirements. (See appendix for contact information.) Also, some local governments have enacted ordinances that set a higher minimum wage—contact your city or county government for more information. "Maximum Tip Credit" is the highest amount of tips that an employer can subtract from the employee's hourly wage. The employee's total wages minus the tip credit cannot be less than the state minimum wage. If an employee's tips exceed the maximum tip credit, the employee gets to keep the extra amount.

"Minimum Cash Wage" is the lowest hourly wage that an employer can pay a tipped employee

State and Statute	Notes	Basic Minimum Hourly Rate (*=tied to federal rate)	Maximum Tip Credit	Minimum Cash Wage for Tipped Employee	Minimum Tips to Qualify as a Tipped Employee (monthly unless noted otherwise)
UNITED STATES 29 U.S.C. § 206 29 U.S.C. § 203	This is the current federal minimum wage	$7.25	$5.12	$2.13	More than $30
ALABAMA	No minimum wage law				
ALASKA Alaska Stat. § 23.10.065		$7.25	No tip credit	$7.25	N/A
ARIZONA Ariz. Rev. Stat. § 23-363	Adjusts annually for inflation, posted at www.ica.state. az.us/Labor/Labor_ MinWag_main.aspx; does not apply to small businesses (those with gross revenue of less than $500,000 that are exempt from federal minimum wage laws)	$7.35	$3.00	$4.35	Averaged total of actual tips and cash minimum must equal minimum wage for each pay period
ARKANSAS Ark. Code Ann. §§ 11-4-210 and 11-4-212	Applies to employers with 4 or more employees	$6.25	$3.63	$2.63	Not specified

State Minimum Wage Laws for Tipped and Regular Employees (cont'd)

State and Statute	Notes	Basic Minimum Hourly Rate (*=tied to federal rate)	Maximum Tip Credit	Minimum Cash Wage for Tipped Employee	Minimum Tips to Qualify as a Tipped Employee (monthly unless noted otherwise)
CALIFORNIA Cal. Lab. Code § 1182.12		$8.00	No tip credit	$8.00	N/A
COLORADO Colo. Const. Art. 18, § 15; 7 Colo. Code Regs. § 1103-1	Adjusted annually for inflation, posted at www.coworkforce.com	$7.24	$3.02	$4.22	More than $30
CONNECTICUT Conn. Gen. Stat. Ann. §§ 31-58(j), 31-60, Conn. Admin. Code § 31-61-E2		$8.00 or FLSA + ½%	31% in hotel and restaurant industries; 11% bartenders; 35¢ others	$5.52 in hotel and restaurant industries; $7.12 bartenders; $7.65 others	$10 per week (full-time employees); $2 per day (part-time employees)
DELAWARE Del. Code Ann. tit. 19, § 902(a)		$7.15 or FLSA rate if higher	$4.92	$2.23	More than $30
DISTRICT OF COLUMBIA D.C. Code Ann. § 32-1003		$7 or FLSA + $1.00 ($8.25) if DC rate is below the federal rate	$5.48	$2.77	Not specified
FLORIDA Fla. Const., Art. X § 24 Fla. Stat. Ann. § 448.110	Adjusted annually, posted at www.floridajobs.org	$7.25	$3.02	$4.23	More than $30
GEORGIA Ga. Code Ann. § 34-4-3	Applies to employers with 6 or more employees and more than $40,000 per year in sales	$5.15	Minimum wage does not apply to tipped employees	N/A	N/A
HAWAII Haw. Rev. Stat. §§ 387-1 to 387-2		$7.25	25¢	$7.00	More than $20; employee's cash wage plus tips must be at least 50¢ higher than the minimum wage

State and Statute	Notes	Basic Minimum Hourly Rate (*=tied to federal rate)	Maximum Tip Credit	Minimum Cash Wage for Tipped Employee	Minimum Tips to Qualify as a Tipped Employee (monthly unless noted otherwise)
State Minimum Wage Laws for Tipped and Regular Employees (cont'd)					
IDAHO Idaho Code § 44-1502		$7.25	$3.90	$3.35	More than $30
ILLINOIS 820 Ill. Comp. Stat. § 105/4; Ill. Admin. Code tit. 56, § 210.110	Applies to employers with 4 or more employees	$8.25	40%	$4.95	At least $20
INDIANA Ind. Code Ann. § 22-2-2-4	Applies to employers with 2 or more employees	$7.25*	$5.12	$2.13	Not specified
IOWA Iowa Code § 91D.1	In first 90 calendar days of employment, minimum wage is $6.35	$7.25	40%	$4.35	At least $30
KANSAS Kan. Stat. Ann. § 44-1203	Applies to employers not covered by the FLSA	$7.25	40%	$2.13	More than $20
KENTUCKY Ky. Rev. Stat. Ann. § 337.275		$7.25*	$5.12	$2.13	More than $30
LOUISIANA	No minimum wage law				
MAINE Me. Rev. Stat. Ann. tit. 26, §§ 663(8), 664		$7.50*	50%	$3.75	More than $30
MARYLAND Md. Code Ann., [Lab. & Empl.] §§ 3-413, 3-419		$7.25*	50%	$3.63	More than $30
MASSACHUSETTS Mass. Gen. Laws ch. 151, § 1; Mass. Regs. Code tit. 455, § 2.02		$8.00 or 10¢ above FLSA rate if it is higher	$5.37	$2.63	More than $20

State and Statute	Notes	Basic Minimum Hourly Rate (*=tied to federal rate)	Maximum Tip Credit	Minimum Cash Wage for Tipped Employee	Minimum Tips to Qualify as a Tipped Employee (monthly unless noted otherwise)
State Minimum Wage Laws for Tipped and Regular Employees (cont'd)					
MICHIGAN Mich. Comp. Laws §§ 408.382 to 408.387a	Applies to employers with 2 or more employees; excludes all employers subject to the FLSA, unless state minimum wage is higher than federal	$7.40	$4.75	$2.65	Not specified
MINNESOTA Minn. Stat. Ann. § 177.24	$5.25 for small employer (business with annual receipts of less than $625,000)	$6.15	No tip credit	$6.15	N/A
MISSISSIPPI	No minimum wage law				
MISSOURI Mo. Rev. Stat. §§ 290.502, 290.512	Doesn't apply to retail or service business with gross annual sales of less than $500,000	$7.25	Up to 50%	$3.62	Not specified
MONTANA Mont. Code Ann. §§ 39-3-404, 39-3-409; Mont. Admin. R. 24.16.1508 & following	$4.00 for businesses with gross annual sales of $110,000 or less; adjusted annually. http://erd. dli.mt.gov/labor-standards/wage-and-hourwage-payment-act/state-minimum-wage.html	$7.35	No tip credit	$7.35	N/A
NEBRASKA Neb. Rev. Stat. § 48-1203	Applies to employers with 4 or more employees	$7.25	$5.12	$2.13	Not specified
NEVADA Nev. Rev. Stat. Ann. § 608.160; Nev. Admin. Code ch. 608 § 110; Nev. Const. Art. 15 § 16	Adjusted annually, posted at www. laborcommissioner .com	$6.55 if employer provides health benefits $7.55 if no health benefits provided	No tip credit	$5.85	N/A

State Minimum Wage Laws for Tipped and Regular Employees (cont'd)

State and Statute	Notes	Basic Minimum Hourly Rate (*=tied to federal rate)	Maximum Tip Credit	Minimum Cash Wage for Tipped Employee	Minimum Tips to Qualify as a Tipped Employee (monthly unless noted otherwise)
NEW HAMPSHIRE N.H. Rev. Stat. Ann. § 279:21		$7.25	55%	45%	More than $30
NEW JERSEY N.J. Stat. Ann. § 34:11-56a4		$7.25*	$5.12*	$2.13	Not specified
NEW MEXICO N.M. Stat. Ann. § 50-4-22		$7.50	$5.37	$2.13	More than $30
NEW YORK N.Y. Lab. Law § 652; N.Y. Comp. Codes R. & Regs. tit. 12, §§ 137-1.4, 138-2.1		$7.25*	Depends on occupation	Depends on occupation	Depends on occupation
NORTH CAROLINA N.C. Gen. Stat. §§ 95-25.2(14), 95-25.3		$7.25	$5.12	$2.13	More than $20
NORTH DAKOTA N.D. Cent. Code § 34-06-22; N.D. Admin. Code R. 46-02-07-01 to -03		$7.25	33% of minimum wage	67% of minimum wage	More than $30
OHIO Ohio Rev. Code Ann. § 4111.02; Ohio Const. art. II § 34a	Same as federal minimum wage for employers with gross income under $271,000; adjusted annually, posted at www.com.ohio.gov/laws	$7.40	50%	50% of minimum wage	More than $30

State Minimum Wage Laws for Tipped and Regular Employees (cont'd)					
State and Statute	Notes	Basic Minimum Hourly Rate (*=tied to federal rate)	Maximum Tip Credit	Minimum Cash Wage for Tipped Employee	Minimum Tips to Qualify as a Tipped Employee (monthly unless noted otherwise)
OKLAHOMA Okla. Stat. Ann. tit. 40, §§ 197.2, 197.4, 197.16	Applies to employers with 10 or more full-time employees OR gross annual sales over $100,000 not otherwise subject to FLSA	$7.25	50% of minimum wage for tips, food, and lodging combined	50% of minimum wage	Not specified
OREGON Or. Rev. Stat. §§ 653.025, 653.035(3)	Adjusted annually; posted at www.boli. state.or.us	$8.50	No tip credit	$8.50	N/A
PENNSYLVANIA 43 Pa. Cons. Stat. Ann. §§ 333.103 and 333.104; 34 Pa. Code §§ 231.1 and 231.103		$7.25*	$4.42	$2.83	More than $30
RHODE ISLAND R.I. Gen. Laws §§ 28-12-3 & 28-12-5		$7.40	$4.31	$2.89	Not specified
SOUTH CAROLINA	No minimum wage law				
SOUTH DAKOTA S.D. Codified Laws Ann. §§ 60-11-3 to -3.1		$7.25	$5.12	$2.13	More than $35
TENNESSEE	No minimum wage law				
TEXAS Tex. Lab. Code Ann. §§ 62.051 & 62.052		$7.25	$5.12	$2.13	More than $20
UTAH Utah Code Ann. § 34-40-102; Utah Admin. R. 610-1		$7.25	$5.12	$2.13	More than $30

State Minimum Wage Laws for Tipped and Regular Employees (cont'd)

State and Statute	Notes	Basic Minimum Hourly Rate (*=tied to federal rate)	Maximum Tip Credit	Minimum Cash Wage for Tipped Employee	Minimum Tips to Qualify as a Tipped Employee (monthly unless noted otherwise)
VERMONT Vt. Stat. Ann. tit. 21, § 384(a); Vt. Code R. 24 090 003	Applies to employers with 2 or more employees; adjusted annually; posted at www.vtlmi.info	$8.15	$4.25	$3.95 for employees of hotels, motels, restaurants, and tourist places; no tip credit otherwise	More than $120
VIRGINIA Va. Code Ann. §§ 40.1-28.9 and 28.10	Applies to employees not covered by FLSA	$7.25	Tips actually received	Minimum wage less tips actually received	Not specified
WASHINGTON Wash. Rev. Code Ann. § 49.46.020; Wash. Admin. Code § 296-126-022	Adjusted annually; posted at www.lni.wa.gov	$8.67	No tip credit	$8.55	N/A
WEST VIRGINIA W.Va. Code §§ 21-5C-1, 21-5C-2, 21-5C-4	Applies to employers with 6 or more employees at one location who are not covered by the FLSA	$7.25	20% of minimum wage	80% of minimum wage	Not specified
WISCONSIN Wis. Admin. Code DWD § 272.03		$7.25	$4.92	$2.33	Not specified
WYOMING Wyo. Stat. § 27-4-202		$5.15	$3.02	$2.13	More than $30

State Overtime Laws

This chart covers private-sector employment only. The overtime rules summarized are not applicable to all employers or all employees. Occupations that generally are not subject to overtime laws include health care and attendant care, emergency medical personnel, seasonal workers, agricultural labor, camp counselors, nonprofits exempt under FLSA, salespeople working on a commission, transit drivers, babysitters, and other household workers, and many others. For more information, contact your state's department of labor and be sure to check its website, where most states have posted their overtime rules. (See appendix for contact details.)

ALABAMA

No state overtime rules that differ from FLSA

ALASKA

Alaska Stat. § 23.10.060 and following

Time and a half after x hours per DAY: Eight

Time and a half after x hours per WEEK: 40

Employment overtime laws apply to: Employers of 4 or more employees; commerce or manufacturing businesses

Notes: Voluntary flexible work hour plan of 10-hour day, 40-hour week, with premium pay after 10 hours is permitted.

ARIZONA

No overtime limits for private sector employers

ARKANSAS

Ark. Code Ann. §§ 11-4-211, 11-4-203

Time and a half after x hours per WEEK: 40

Employment overtime laws apply to: Employers of 4 or more employees

Employment excluded from overtime laws: Employment that is subject to the FLSA

Notes: Employees in retail and service establishments who spend up to 40% of their time on nonexempt work must be paid at least twice the state's minimum wage ($572 per week).

CALIFORNIA

Cal. Lab. Code §§ 500–511; Cal. Code Regs. tit. 8, §§ 11010 and following

Time and a half after x hours per DAY: Eight; after 12 hours, double time.

Time and a half after x hours per WEEK: 40; on 7th day, time and a half for the first 8 hours; after 8 hours, double time

Employment excluded from overtime laws: Computer software employees who design, develop, create, analyze, test, or modify programs using independent judgment, or who are paid at least $36 per hour

Notes: Alternative four-day, 10-hour-day workweek is permitted, if established prior to 7/1/99.

COLORADO

7 Colo. Code Regs. § 1103-1(4)

Time and a half after x hours per DAY: 12

Time and a half after x hours per WEEK: 40

Employment overtime laws apply to: Employees in retail and service, commercial support service, food and beverage, health and medical industries

CONNECTICUT

Conn. Gen. Stat. Ann. §§ 31-76b and 31-76c; Conn. Admin. Code § 31-62-E1

Time and a half after x hours per WEEK: 40; premium pay on weekends, holidays, or 6th or 7th consecutive day

Notes: In restaurants and hotels, time-and-a-half pay required for the 7th consecutive day of work or for hours that exceed 40 per week.

State Overtime Laws (cont'd)

DELAWARE

No state overtime rules that differ from FLSA

DISTRICT OF COLUMBIA

D.C. Code Ann. § 32-1003(c); D.C. Mun. Regs. tit. 7, § 906

Time and a half after x hours per WEEK: 40

Notes: Employees must be paid one hour minimum wage for each day a split shift is worked.

FLORIDA

No state overtime rules that differ from FLSA

GEORGIA

No state overtime rules that differ from FLSA

HAWAII

Haw. Rev. Stat. §§ 387-1; 387-3

Time and a half after x hours per WEEK: 40. Dairy, sugarcane, and seasonal agricultural work: 48 hours per week

Employment excluded from overtime laws: Employees earning guaranteed compensation of $2,000 or more per month

IDAHO

No state overtime rules that differ from FLSA

ILLINOIS

820 Ill. Comp. Stat. §§ 105/3(d), 105/4a

Time and a half after x hours per WEEK: 40

Employment overtime laws apply to: Employers of 4 or more employees

INDIANA

Ind. Code Ann. § 22-2-2-4(j)

Time and a half after x hours per WEEK: 40

Employment excluded from overtime laws: Employment that is subject to the FLSA, movie theaters, seasonal camps or amusement parks, FLSA-exempt nonprofits

Notes: Collective bargaining agreements ratified by the NLRB may have different overtime provisions. Domestic service work is not excluded from overtime laws.

IOWA

No state overtime rules that differ from FLSA

KANSAS

Kan. Stat. Ann. § 44-1204

Time and a half after x hours per WEEK: 46

Employment excluded from overtime laws: Employment that is subject to the FLSA

KENTUCKY

Ky. Rev. Stat. Ann. §§ 337.050, 337.285; 803 Ky. Admin. Regs. § 1:060

Time and a half after x hours per WEEK: 40

Employment excluded from overtime laws: Retail, hotel, and restaurant businesses

Notes: 7th day, time and a half

LOUISIANA

No state overtime rules that differ from FLSA

MAINE

Me. Rev. Stat. Ann. tit. 26, § 664(3)

Time and a half after x hours per WEEK: 40

Employment excluded from overtime laws: Auto mechanics, parts clerks, service writers, and salespersons; hotels, motels, and restaurants; canning, freezing, packing, and shipping produce and perishable foods

MARYLAND

Md. Code Ann., [Lab. & Empl.] § 3-420

Time and a half after x hours per WEEK: 40; 48 hours for bowling alleys and residential employees caring for the sick, aged, or mentally ill in institutions other than hospitals; 60 hours for agricultural work

State Overtime Laws (cont'd)

MASSACHUSETTS

Mass. Gen. Laws ch. 151, § 1A

Time and a half after x hours per WEEK: 40

Employment excluded from overtime laws: Agriculture, farming, fishing; hotel, motel, or restaurant; seasonal workers less than 5 months; hospital, nursing home, or rest home; public transit

Notes: Sunday or holiday: time and a half as overtime unless already paid that rate as part of regular compensation

MICHIGAN

Mich. Comp. Laws §§ 408.382 and 408.384a

Time and a half after x hours per WEEK: 40

Employment overtime laws apply to: Employers of 2 or more employees

Employment excluded from overtime laws: Employees not subject to state minimum wage laws

MINNESOTA

Minn. Stat. Ann. § 177.25

Time and a half after x hours per WEEK: 48

MISSISSIPPI

No state overtime rules that differ from FLSA

MISSOURI

Mo. Rev. Stat. §§ 290.500 and 290.505

Time and a half after x hours per WEEK: 40; 52 hours for seasonal amusement or recreation businesses

Employment excluded from overtime laws: Employment that is subject to the minimum wage or overtime requirements of the FLSA

MONTANA

Mont. Code Ann. §§ 39-3-405 and 39-3-406

Time and a half after x hours per WEEK: 40; 48 hours for students working seasonal jobs at amusement or recreational areas.

Notes: Various employees are excluded from overtime laws. For a complete list, see *Mont. Code Ann. § 39-3-406.*

NEBRASKA

No state overtime rules that differ from FLSA

NEVADA

Nev. Rev. Stat. Ann. § 608.018

Time and a half after x hours per DAY: Eight, if employee's regular rate of pay is less than 1½ times the minimum wage

Time and a half after x hours per WEEK: 40

Notes: Employer and employee may agree to flextime schedule of four 10-hour days.

NEW HAMPSHIRE

N.H. Rev. Stat. Ann. § 279.21(VIII)

Time and a half after x hours per WEEK: 40

Employment excluded from overtime laws: Employees covered by the FLSA; employees in amusement, seasonal, or recreational business open 7 months or less a year.

NEW JERSEY

N.J. Stat. Ann. §§ 34.11-56a4 and 34.11-56a4.1

Time and a half after x hours per WEEK: 40

Employment excluded from overtime laws: June to September: summer camps, conferences, and retreats operated by nonprofit or religious groups

State Overtime Laws (cont'd)

NEW MEXICO
N.M. Stat. Ann. § 50-4-22(C)
Time and a half after x hours per WEEK: 40

NEW YORK
N.Y. Lab. Law §§ 160(3), 161; N.Y. Comp. Codes R. & Regs. tit. 12, § 142-2.2
Time and a half after x hours per WEEK: 40 for nonresidential workers; 44 for residential workers
Employment excluded from overtime laws: Same exemptions as FLSA
Notes: In some industries, employees must be given 24 consecutive hours off per week. See N.Y. Lab. Law § 161.

NORTH CAROLINA
N.C. Gen. Stat. §§ 95-25.14, 95-25.4
Time and a half after x hours per WEEK: 40; 45 hours a week in seasonal amusement or recreational establishments
Employment excluded from overtime laws: Employment that is subject to the FLSA

NORTH DAKOTA
N.D. Admin. Code § 46-02-07-02(4)
Time and a half after x hours per WEEK: 40; 50 hours per week, cabdrivers
Employment excluded from overtime laws: Various employees excluded, including computer professionals who design, develop, create, analyze, test, or modify programs using independent judgment or who are paid at least $27.63 per hour

OHIO
Ohio Rev. Code Ann. § 4111.03
Time and a half after x hours per WEEK: 40
Employment overtime laws apply to: Employers who gross more than $150,000 a year

OKLAHOMA
No state overtime rules that differ from FLSA

OREGON
Or. Rev. Stat. §§ 653.261, 653.265
Time and a half after x hours per WEEK: 40
Notes: Time and a half required after 10 hours a day in canneries, driers, packing plants, mills, factories, and manufacturing facilities

PENNSYLVANIA
43 Pa. Cons. Stat. Ann. § 333.104(c); 34 Pa. Code § 231.41
Time and a half after x hours per WEEK: 40

RHODE ISLAND
R.I. Gen. Laws §§ 28-12-4.1 and following, 5-23-2(h)
Time and a half after x hours per WEEK: 40
Notes: Time and a half for Sunday and holiday work is required for most retail businesses (these hours are not included in calculating weekly overtime).

SOUTH CAROLINA
No state overtime rules

SOUTH DAKOTA
No state overtime rules that differ from FLSA

TENNESSEE
No state overtime rules

TEXAS
No state overtime rules

UTAH
No state overtime rules

State Overtime Laws (cont'd)

VERMONT

Vt. Stat. Ann. tit. 21, §§ 382, 384(b); Vt. Code R. § 24 090 003

Time and a half after x hours per WEEK: 40

Employment overtime laws apply to: Employers of 2 or more employees

Employment excluded from overtime laws: Retail and service businesses; hotels, motels, restaurants; some amusement or recreational establishments; transportation workers exempt under FLSA

VIRGINIA

No state overtime rules

WASHINGTON

Wash. Rev. Code Ann. § 49.46.130

Time and a half after x hours per WEEK: 40

WEST VIRGINIA

W.Va. Code §§ 21-5c-1(e), 21-5c-3

Time and a half after x hours per WEEK: 40

Employment overtime laws apply to: Employers of 6 or more employees at one location

Employment excluded from overtime laws: Employees that are subject to the FLSA

WISCONSIN

Wis. Stat. Ann. § 103.01, 103.03; Wis. Admin. Code DWD §§ 274.01, 274.03, 274.04

Time and a half after x hours per WEEK: 40

Employment overtime laws apply to: Manufacturing, mechanical, or retail businesses; beauty parlors, laundries, restaurants, hotels; telephone, express, shipping, and transportation companies

Employment excluded from overtime laws: A wide variety of exclusions may apply; see Wis. Admin. Code § 274.04.

WYOMING

No state overtime rules that differ from FLSA

State Meal and Rest Break Laws

Note: The states of Alabama, Alaska, Arizona, Arkansas, District of Columbia, Florida, Idaho, Iowa, Louisiana, Maryland, Michigan, Mississippi, Missouri, Montana, New Jersey, New Mexico, North Carolina, Ohio, Oklahoma, South Carolina, South Dakota, Texas, Utah, Virginia, and Wyoming are not listed in this chart because they do not have laws or regulations on rest and meal breaks for adults employed in the private sector. Many states also exclude professional, administrative, and executive employees from these rules.

Other exceptions may apply. For example, many states have special break rules for specific occupations or industries, which are beyond the scope of this chart. Check the statute or check with your state department of labor if you need more information. (See appendix for contact list.)

CALIFORNIA
Cal. Lab. Code §§ 512, 1030; Cal. Code Regs. tit. 8, §§ 11010-11170

Applies to: Employers in most industries

Exceptions: *Motion picture and other occupations. See wage orders, Cal. Code Regs. tit. 8, §§ 11010 to 11160, for additional exceptions.*

Meal Break: 30 minutes, unpaid, after 5 hours, except when workday will be completed in 6 hours or less and employer and employee consent to waive meal break. Employee cannot work more than 10 hours a day without a second 30-minute break, except if workday is no more than 12 hours; second meal break may be waived if first meal break was not waived. On-duty paid meal period permitted when nature of work prevents relief from all duties and parties agree in writing.

Rest Break: Paid 10-minute rest period for each 4 hours worked or major fraction thereof; as practicable, in the middle of the work period; not required for employees whose total daily work time is less than 3½ hours

Breastfeeding: Reasonable time to breastfeed infant or to express breast milk; paid if taken concurrent with other break time; otherwise, unpaid

COLORADO
Colo. Code Regs. tit. 7 § 1103-1(7)-(8)

Applies to: Retail and service, food and beverage, commercial support service, and health and medical industries

Exceptions: Numerous exceptions are listed in the regulation.

Meal Break: 30 minutes, unpaid, after 5 hours of work; on-duty paid meal period permitted when nature of work prevents break from all duties.

Rest Break: Paid 10-minute rest period for each 4 hours or major fraction worked; if practical, in the middle of the work period

CONNECTICUT
Conn. Gen. Stat. Ann. §§ 31-51ii, 31-40w

Applies to: All employers, except as noted

Exceptions: Employers who pay for rest breaks as described below, those with a written agreement providing other break rules, and those granted an exemption for reasons listed in statute

Meal Break: 30 minutes, unpaid, after first 2 hours of work and before last 2 hours for employees who work 7½ or more consecutive hours

Rest Break: As alternative to meal break, a total of 30 minutes paid in each 7½-hour work period

Breastfeeding: Employee may use meal or rest break for breastfeeding or expressing breast milk.

State Meal and Rest Break Laws (cont'd)

DELAWARE
Del. Code Ann. tit. 19, § 707

Applies to: All employers, except as noted

Exceptions: Employers with alternative written agreement and those granted exemptions specified in statute. Law does not apply to teachers.

Meal Break: 30 minutes, unpaid, after first 2 hours and before the last 2 hours, for employees who work 7½ consecutive hours or more

GEORGIA
Ga. Code Ann. § 34-1-6

Applies to: All employers

Breastfeeding: Reasonable unpaid break time to breastfeed infant or to express breast milk

HAWAII
Haw. Rev. Stat. § 378-2

Applies to: All employers

Breastfeeding: Allowed during any break required by law or collective bargaining agreement

ILLINOIS
820 Ill. Comp. Stat. §§ 140/3, 260/10

Applies to: All employers

Exceptions: Employees whose meal periods are established by collective bargaining agreement

Employees who monitor individuals with developmental disabilities or mental illness, or both, and who are required to be on call during an entire 8-hour work period; these employees must be allowed to eat a meal while working.

Meal Break: 20 minutes, no later than 5 hours after the beginning of the shift, for employees who work 7½ or more continuous hours

Breastfeeding: Reasonable unpaid break time to breastfeed infant or express breast milk

INDIANA
Ind. Code §§ 22-2-14, 5-10-6-2

Applies to: All employers

Breastfeeding: Reasonable unpaid break time to express breast milk

KANSAS
Kan. Admin. Reg. 49-30-3

Applies to: Employees not covered under FLSA

Meal Break: Not required, but if less than 30 minutes is given, break must be paid.

KENTUCKY
Ky. Rev. Stat. Ann. §§ 337.355, 337.365;
Ky. Admin. Regs. tit. 803, 1:065 § 4

Applies to: All employers, except as noted

Exceptions: Written agreement providing different meal period; employers subject to Federal Railway Labor Act

Meal Break: Reasonable off-duty period close to the middle of the shift; can't be required to take it before the third or after the fifth hour of work

Rest Break: Paid 10-minute rest period for each 4-hour work period; rest period must be in addition to regularly scheduled meal period.

MAINE
Me. Rev. Stat. Ann. tit. 26, § 601

Applies to: Most employers

Exceptions: Small businesses with fewer than 3 employees on duty who are able to take frequent breaks during the workday; collective bargaining or other written agreement between employer and employee may provide for different breaks.

Meal and Rest Break: 30 minutes, unpaid, after 6 consecutive hours of work, except in cases of emergency

State Meal and Rest Break Laws (cont'd)

Breastfeeding: Adequate unpaid time to express breast milk, or employee may use rest or meal time.

MASSACHUSETTS

Mass. Gen. Laws ch. 149, §§ 100, 101

Applies to: All employers, except as noted

Exceptions: Excludes iron works, glass works, paper mills, letterpresses, print works, and bleaching or dyeing works. Attorney general may exempt businesses that require continuous operation if it won't affect worker safety. Collective bargaining agreement may also provide for different breaks.

Meal Break: 30 minutes, if work is for more than 6 hours

MINNESOTA

Minn. Stat. Ann. §§ 177.253, 177.254, 181.939

Applies to: All employers

Exceptions: Excludes certain agricultural and seasonal employees

A collective bargaining agreement may provide for different rest and meal breaks.

Meal Break: Sufficient unpaid time for employees who work 8 consecutive hours or more

Rest Break: Paid adequate rest period within each 4 consecutive hours of work to utilize nearest convenient rest room

Breastfeeding: Reasonable unpaid break time to breastfeed infant or express milk

NEBRASKA

Neb. Rev. Stat. § 48-212

Applies to: Assembly plant, workshop, or mechanical establishment

Exceptions: Other written agreement between employer and employees

Meal Break: 30 minutes off premises for each 8-hour shift

NEVADA

Nev. Rev. Stat. Ann. § 608.019

Applies to: Employers of two or more employees

Exceptions: Employees covered by collective bargaining agreement; exemptions for business necessity

Meal Break: 30 minutes for 8 continuous hours of work

Rest Break: Paid 10-minute rest period for each 4 hours or major fraction worked; as practicable, in middle of the work period; not required for employees whose total daily work time is less than 3½ hours.

NEW HAMPSHIRE

N.H. Rev. Stat. Ann. § 275:30-a

Applies to: All employers

Meal Break: 30 minutes after 5 consecutive hours, unless the employer allows the employee to eat while working and it is feasible for the employee to do so

NEW YORK

N.Y. Lab. Law §§ 162, 206-c

Applies to: Factories, workshops, manufacturing facilities, mercantile (retail and wholesale) establishments

Meal Break: Factory employees, 60 minutes between 11 a.m. and 2 p.m.; mercantile employees, 30 minutes between 11 a.m. and 2 p.m. If a shift starts before 11 a.m. and ends after 7 p.m., every employee gets an additional 20 minutes between 5 p.m. and 7 p.m. If a shift starts between 1 p.m. and 6 a.m., a factory employee gets 60 minutes, and a mercantile employee gets 45 minutes, in the middle of the

State Meal and Rest Break Laws (cont'd)

shift. Labor commissioner may permit a shorter meal break; the permit must be in writing and posted conspicuously in the main entrance of the workplace.

Breastfeeding: Reasonable unpaid break time to express breast milk for up to three years after child's birth

NORTH DAKOTA
N.D. Admin. Code § 46-02-07-02

Applies to: Applicable when two or more employees are on duty

Exceptions: Waiver by employee or other provision in collective bargaining agreement

Meal Break: 30 minutes for each shift over 5 hours; unpaid if employee is completely relieved of duties

OREGON
Or. Admin. R. §§ 839-020-0050, 839-020-0051

Applies to: All employers except as noted

Exceptions: Agricultural workers and employees covered by a collective bargaining agreement

Meal Break: 30 minutes, unpaid if relieved of all duties; paid time to eat if employee cannot be relieved of duty; a 20-minute paid break, if employer can show that it is industry practice or custom. If shift of 7 hours or less, meal break must occur between hours 2 and 5; if shift longer than 7 hours, meal break must be between hours 3 and 6.

Rest Break: Paid 10-minute rest period for each 4 hours or major fraction worked; if practical, in the middle of the work period

Rest period must be in addition to usual meal break and taken separately; can't be added to meal period or deducted from beginning or end of shift to reduce length of total work period.

Rest period is not required for certain solo adult employees serving the public, although they must be allowed to use rest room.

Breastfeeding: Reasonable unpaid rest period, no greater than 30 minutes for each 4 hours worked, to express milk for child 18 months or younger

PENNSYLVANIA
43 Pa. Cons. Stat. Ann. § 1301.207

Applies to: Employers of seasonal farmworkers

Meal Break: 30 minutes after 5 hours

RHODE ISLAND
R.I. Gen. Laws §§ 28-3-8, 28-3-14, 23-13-2.1

Applies to: Employers with 5 or more employees

Exceptions: Employers of health care facility or employers with fewer than 3 employees on any shift

Meal Break: 20 minutes, unpaid, within a 6-hour shift or 30 minutes, unpaid, within an 8-hour shift

Breastfeeding: Reasonable unpaid break time to breastfeed infant or express breast milk

TENNESSEE
Tenn. Code Ann. §§ 50-2-103(h), 50-1-305

Applies to: Employers with 5 or more employees

Meal and Rest Break: 30 minutes unpaid for employees scheduled to work 6 consecutive hours or more unless work is such that there is ample time for breaks throughout the day

Breastfeeding: Reasonable unpaid break time to breastfeed infant or express breast milk, and employer shall make reasonable efforts to provide a space (other than a toilet stall) for employee to express breast milk in privacy.

State Meal and Rest Break Laws (cont'd)

VERMONT

Vt. Stat. Ann. tit. 21, § 304

Applies to: All employers

Meal Break: Employees must be given reasonable opportunities to eat and use toilet facilities during work periods.

WASHINGTON

Wash. Admin. Code §§ 296-126-092, 286-131-020

Applies to: All employers except as noted

Exceptions: Newspaper vendor or carrier, domestic or casual labor around private residence, sheltered workshop; separate provisions for agricultural labor.

Meal Break: 30-minute break, if work period is more than 5 consecutive hours, not less than 2 hours nor more than 5 hours from beginning of shift. This time is paid if employee is on duty or is required to be at a site for employer's benefit. Employees who work 3 or more hours longer than regular workday are entitled to an additional half hour, before or during overtime.

Agricultural employees: 30 minutes if working more than 5 hours; additional 30 minutes if working 11 or more hours in a day

Rest Break: Paid 10-minute rest break for each 4-hour work period, scheduled as near as possible to midpoint of each work period. Employee cannot be required to work more than 3 hours without a rest break.

Scheduled rest breaks are not required where nature of work allows employee to take intermittent rest breaks equivalent to required standard.

WEST VIRGINIA

W.Va. Code § 21-3-10a; W.Va. Code St. R. § 42-5-2(2.6)

Applies to: All employers

Meal Break: At least 20-minute break for each 6 consecutive hours worked, unless employees are allowed to take breaks as needed or to eat lunch while working

Rest Break: Rest breaks of 20 minutes or less must be counted as paid work time.

WISCONSIN

Wis. Admin. Code § DWD 274.02

Applies to: All employers

Meal Break: Recommended but not required: 30 minutes close to usual meal time or near middle of shift. Shifts of more than 6 hours without a meal break should be avoided. If employee is not free to leave the workplace, meal period is considered paid time.

State Laws on Administering Wage Garnishments

This chart describes state laws for administering wage garnishments, including permissible fees employers may charge to administer garnishments, as well as laws prohibiting employer discrimination or retaliation because of wage garnishments. Other state statutes may apply.

ALABAMA

Ala. Code §§ 15-18-142, 15-18-143, 30-3-70, 30-3-71

Applies to: Child support garnishments and restitution to victims of crime.

Employee protections that exceed federal law: No employer shall discharge an employee or refuse to hire a person because of an order of child support withholding or order for restitution to crime victim.

Employer's fee: $2 per month (child support only).

Employer penalties, general wage garnishment: Contempt of court. For garnishments for restitution for crime victims, employer may not discharge employee solely because of garnishment and, in addition to contempt of court, may be required to reinstate the employee.

ALASKA

Alaska Stat. § 25.27.062

Applies to: Child support garnishments only.

Employee protections that exceed federal law: An employer may not discharge, discipline, or refuse to employ an obligor on the basis of a child support withholding order.

Employer's fee: $5 per payment.

Employer penalties, child support withholding: If employer discharges, disciplines, or refuses to hire someone because of having child support withholding orders, may be fined up to $1,000 and be required to reinstate and/or provide restitution to the employee.

ARIZONA

Ariz. Rev. Stat. §§ 23-722.02, 25-505.01

Applies to: Child support or spousal maintenance garnishment.

Employee protections that exceed federal law: Newly hired, rehired, or returning employees may be asked to disclose any child support wage assignment orders but may not be discriminated against, fired, or disciplined because of having them.

Employer's fee: $1 per pay period or $4 per month.

Employer penalties, child support withholding: Employer who refuses to hire, discharges, or disciplines employee because of having child support withholding orders is subject to contempt of court and fines. Employer who fails without good cause to comply with income withholding order may be liable for amounts not paid, reasonable attorneys' fees and costs, and may be subject to contempt of court. Employee wrongfully refused employment, wrongfully discharged, or otherwise disciplined may recover damages and may be reinstated, if appropriate, and be entitled to recovery of attorneys' fees and costs.

ARKANSAS

Ark. Code Ann. §§ 9-14-226, 9-14-227, 9-14-515

Applies to: Child support garnishments and child's health care coverage orders.

Employee protections that exceed federal law: Employer is prohibited from discharging, refusing to employ, or taking other disciplinary action against a noncustodial parent under an income withholding order.

Employer's fee: $2.50 per pay period.

State Laws on Administering Wage Garnishments (cont'd)

Employer penalties, child support withholding: If discharge, refuse to employ, or take other disciplinary action against a noncustodial parent under an income withholding order, subject to contempt of court and fine of up to $50 per day.

CALIFORNIA
Cal. Fam. Code §§ 5235, 5241; Lab. Code § 2929

Employee protections that exceed federal law: Employee may not be discharged for being threatened with a wage garnishment.

Employer's fee: $1.50 per payment.

Employer penalties, child support withholding: In child support cases, if employer willfully fails to withhold, can be held in contempt of court. If employer does not withhold or does not forward payments, liable to obligee for amount of payments plus interest.

COLORADO
Colo. Rev. Stat. §§ 5-5-107, 13-54.5-110, 14-14-111.5, 14-14-112, 26-13-121.5

Employee protections that exceed federal law: Employee may not be discharged because a consumer creditor garnishes or attempts to garnish wages (no limit on number of garnishments).

Employer's fee: Up to $5 per month for child support garnishments.

Employer penalties, general wage garnishment: Liable to discharged employee for up to six weeks' wages, reinstatement, court costs, and attorneys' fees (applies to general wage garnishments, child support, and child national medical support and child health insurance withholding orders).

Employer penalties, child support withholding: If the employer fails to withhold income, the employer may be held in contempt of court; for wrongful failure to withhold, liable for both the amount that should have been withheld and any other penalties set by state law.

CONNECTICUT
Conn. Gen. Stat. Ann. §§ 46b-88, 52-361, 52-362

Employee protections that exceed federal law: Employee may not be disciplined, suspended, or discharged for having wages garnished unless there are more than seven within a calendar year.

Employer penalties, general wage garnishment: Liable to employee for all wages and benefits from time of discipline or discharge to reinstatement.

Employer penalties, child support withholding: Fine of up to $1,000 for discharging, refusing to employ, disciplining, or discriminating against an employee because of a withholding order. Also applies to child health care coverage.

DELAWARE
Del. Code Ann. tit. 10, § 3509; tit. 13, § 513

Employee protections that exceed federal law: Employer may not dismiss employee because employer was summoned to appear in court in a garnishment proceeding.

Employer penalties, child support withholding: For failing to comply with law or terminating employee, fine of up to $1,000 or up to 90 days' imprisonment, or both, for first offense; for each subsequent offense, fine of up to $5,000 or up to one year's imprisonment, or both. For refusing to employ because of a support withholding order, fine of up to $200 for each offense. Corporations are subject to criminal charges. Also applies to child health care coverage and spousal support.

State Laws on Administering Wage Garnishments (cont'd)

DISTRICT OF COLUMBIA

D.C. Code Ann. §§ 16-573, 46-212(d), 46-219

Employee protections that exceed federal law: In any month, employer cannot withhold more than 10% of gross wages until at least $200 of the employee's wages have been withheld that month; cannot collect more than 20% until at least $500 has been withheld. Employee may not be discharged because a creditor garnishes or attempts to garnish wages (no limit on number of garnishments).

Employer's fee: $2 for each child support payment.

Employer penalties, child support withholding: Employer who discharges, refuses to employ, takes disciplinary action against, or otherwise discriminates against employee is subject to a penalty of up to $10,000, which employee may use to offset support obligations. Any adverse action employer takes within 90 days of receiving notice to withhold wages is presumed to be in violation of law.

FLORIDA

Fla. Stat. Ann. §§ 61.12(2), 61.1301

Applies to: Child or spousal support garnishments.

Employee protections that exceed federal law: Employer may not fire, refuse to hire, or discipline employee who has wages garnished for child or spousal support.

Employer's fee: $5 for first deduction, $2 for each subsequent deduction.

Employer penalties, general wage garnishment: Employer who refuses to hire, discharges, or disciplines employee because of having spousal support order is subject to fine of up to $250 for first violation and up to $500 for each subsequent

violation; employer may also be held in contempt of court. Employee entitled to reinstatement and wages/benefits lost.

Employer penalties, child support withholding: Employer who refuses to hire, discharges, or disciplines employee because of having child support order is subject to fine of up to $250 for first violation and up to $500 for each subsequent violation; employer may also be held in contempt of court. Employee entitled to reinstatement and wages/benefits lost.

GEORGIA

Ga. Code Ann. § 19-11-20

Applies to: Child support garnishments.

Employee protections that exceed federal law: Employers may not terminate the services of an employed parent who executes a wage assignment for child support purposes.

Employer's fee: $25 for first child support deduction, $3 for each subsequent deduction.

HAWAII

Haw. Rev. Stat. §§ 378-2, 378-32, 571-52, 576E-16, 710-1077

Employee protections that exceed federal law: Employer may not fire, suspend, or discriminate against employee for having wages garnished or because employer was summoned as a garnishee in an action or proceeding where the employee is the debtor. Employer who refuses to hire or discharges an employee who has wages garnished for child support is guilty of unlawful discrimination.

Employer's fee: $2 for each deduction.

Employer penalties, child support withholding: Employer who discriminates against employee is guilty of criminal contempt of court.

State Laws on Administering Wage Garnishments (cont'd)

IDAHO

Idaho Code §§ 28-45-105, 32-1210, 32-1211

Employee protections that exceed federal law: Employee may not be discharged because a consumer creditor garnishes or attempts to garnish wages (no limit on number of garnishments). In child support cases, garnishment plus the employer's processing fee cannot exceed 50% of the employee's disposable income.

Employer's fee: $5 for each deduction (child support).

Employer penalties, child support withholding: For discharging, disciplining, or refusing to hire an employee: liable for double lost wages and other damages, costs, and attorneys' fees; and may be fined up to $300 for each violation and ordered to hire or reinstate employee.

ILLINOIS

735 Ill. Comp. Stat. §§ 5/12-818, 5/12-814; 740 Ill. Comp. Stat. § 170/10; 750 Ill. Comp. Stat. §§ 28/35, 28/50

Employee protections that exceed federal law: May not discharge or suspend employee for any indebtedness or for one wage garnishment.

Employer's fee: 2% of entire amount withheld for general wage garnishment; $5 per month for child support.

Employer penalties, general wage garnishment: Discharging or suspending employee because wage garnishment for one indebtedness or one wage garnishment is a Class A misdemeanor, which carries a fine of up to $2,500 and imprisonment for up to one year.

Employer penalties, child support withholding: Liable for amount of wages not withheld or paid; if employer discriminated against employee, may be fined up to $200 and

ordered to hire or reinstate employee. Any officer or employee of any payor who has the control, supervision, or responsibility for withholding and paying and who wilfully fails to withhold or pay shall be personally liable for a penalty equal to the total amount that was not withheld or paid.

INDIANA

Ind. Code Ann. §§ 24-4.5-5-105 to 24-4.5-5-106

Employee protections that exceed federal law: Employer may not discharge employee because creditor has garnished or attempted to garnish wages (no limit on number of garnishments).

Employer's fee: $12 or 3% of entire amount withheld, whichever is greater, for general wage garnishment, 50% paid by employee and 50% by creditor; $2 per deduction for child support.

IOWA

Iowa Code § 252D.17

Employee protections that exceed federal law: Employer may not discharge, refuse to employ, or take disciplinary action against an obligor based upon income withholding for child support.

Employer's fee: $2 for each child support payment.

Employer penalties, child support withholding: Employer who fails to withhold or remit payment for the first offense is guilty of a misdemeanor, and a serious misdemeanor for each subsequent offense, and in either case may have to pay costs, interest, and attorneys' fees for collection. An employer who discharges, refuses to employ, or takes disciplinary action against an employee because of a wage garnishment is guilty of a simple misdemeanor and may be subject to contempt of court proceedings.

State Laws on Administering Wage Garnishments (cont'd)

KANSAS

Kan. Stat. Ann. §§ 23-4,108, 60-2311

Employee protections that exceed federal law: Illegal to discharge employee because of wage garnishment of any type.

Employer's fee: $5 per pay period or $10 per month for income withheld for child or spousal support, whichever is less.

Employer penalties, general wage garnishment: Illegal to discharge employee because of wage garnishment of any type.

Employer penalties, child support withholding: For not withholding and remitting payments, or discharging, refusing to employ, or taking disciplinary action against an employee because of garnishment, subject to a fine of up to $500 and other equitable relief. Liable to obligee for three times amount owed and reasonable attorneys' fees if fails to pay without just cause.

KENTUCKY

Ky. Rev. Stat. Ann. §§ 405.465, 405.467, 405.991

Applies to: Child or medical support orders only.

Employee protections that exceed federal law: No child or medical support withholding shall be grounds for discharging from employment, refusing to employ, or taking disciplinary action against any obligor.

Employer's fee: $1 per payment for child or medical support withholding.

Employer penalties, child support withholding: If discharge, refuse to employ, or take disciplinary action against employee, subject to fine of up to $500 or up to one year in the county jail, or both.

LOUISIANA

La. Rev. Stat. Ann. §§ 13:3921, 23:731

Employee protections that exceed federal law: Employee cannot be discharged or denied employment because of a single wage garnishment. Employee may be fired for a wage garnishment if there are three or more garnishments for unrelated debts in a two-year period. However, employee may not be fired if garnishment resulted from an accident or illness that caused employee to miss ten or more consecutive workdays.

Employer's fee: $3 per pay period for as long as garnishment is in effect

Employer penalties, general wage garnishment: Discharged employee is entitled to reinstatement and back pay, but not damages. A person denied employment solely because of garnishment is entitled to reasonable damages.

MAINE

Me. Rev. Stat. Ann. tit. 9-A, § 5-106; tit. 14, § 3127-B; tit. 19-A, §§ 2306, 2662, 2663

Employee protections that exceed federal law: Employee cannot be fired because creditor garnishes or attempts to garnish wages (number of garnishments not specified).

Employer's fee: $1 per check issued to creditor for general wage garnishment; child support fee allowed, set by administrative rule.

Employer penalties, child support withholding: For knowingly failing to withhold or remit payments, fine of up to $100 for each failure to withhold. For discharging, refusing to employ, or disciplining employee, fine of up to $5,000; liable for actual and punitive damages plus attorneys' fees and court costs.

State Laws on Administering Wage Garnishments (cont'd)

MARYLAND

Md. Code Ann. [Com. Law] § 15-606; [Fam. Law] § 10-129

Employee protections that exceed federal law: Employer cannot discharge employee for having one garnishment in a single year.

Employer's fee: $2 for each child support deduction.

Employer penalties, general wage garnishment: Employer who discharges employee who is subject to only one wage garnishment in a calendar year is subject to fine up to $10,000 and imprisonment of up to one year, or both.

Employer penalties, child support withholding: Employer who fails to withhold or remit payments is liable for amount of wages not withheld or paid. Employer may not use garnishment as reason for reprisal, dismissal, refusal to hire, or refusal to promote employee.

MASSACHUSETTS

Mass. Gen. Laws ch. 119A, § 12

Applies to: Child support garnishments only.

Employee protections that exceed federal law: Employer may not discipline, suspend, discharge, or refuse to hire an employee because of having child support withholding orders.

Employer's fee: $1 per pay period.

Employer penalties, child support withholding: For violating employee rights, liable for lost wages and benefits plus a fine of up to $1,000; for failing to comply with a withholding order, liable for amount not withheld, plus fine of that amount or up to $500, whichever is greater.

MICHIGAN

Mich. Comp. Laws §§ 552.623, 600.4012, 600.4015

Employee protections that exceed federal law: Employer may not refuse to hire, discharge, take disciplinary action against, or impose a penalty against an employee because of a wage garnishment, including using the fact that the employee had an occupational, recreational, or driver's license suspended under child support laws, unless license is legally required for employee's job.

Employer's fee: $6 per writ of garnishment.

Employer penalties, general wage garnishment: Must reinstate employee and pay back all lost wages and benefits.

Employer penalties, child support withholding: Guilty of a misdemeanor punishable by a fine of up to $500; must reinstate employee with back pay.

MINNESOTA

Minn. Stat. Ann. §§ 518A.53, 571.927

Employee protections that exceed federal law: Employer shall not discharge or otherwise discipline an employee as a result of an earnings garnishment (no number specified).

Employer's fee: $1 for each child support payment.

Employer penalties, general wage garnishment: Employee entitled to reinstatement and employer liable to employee for double wages lost.

Employer penalties, child support withholding: To obligee: for intentional failure to withhold or remit funds, liable for amount not paid, plus interest from the time payments were due, and attorneys' fees, and may be subject to sanctions for contempt. To employee: for

State Laws on Administering Wage Garnishments (cont'd)

discharging, refusing to hire, or disciplining employee because of child support withholding orders, liable for double lost wages and subject to a fine of no less than $500.

MISSISSIPPI

Miss. Code Ann. § 93-11-111

Applies to: Child support garnishments.

Employee protections that exceed federal law: Employer may not discharge, discipline, refuse to hire or otherwise penalize the employee because of the duty to withhold income.

Employer's fee: $2 per payment inside Mississippi. If interstate withholding, determined by rules/laws of state where obligor works.

MISSOURI

Mo. Rev. Stat. §§ 452.350, 454.505, 525.230

Employee protections that exceed federal law: An employer shall not discharge or otherwise discipline, or refuse to hire, an employee as a result of a child support withholding notice.

Employer's fee: 2% or $8, whichever is greater, for general wage garnishment; up to $6 per month per payment for child support withholding.

Employer penalties, child support withholding: For failing to withhold or remit payments, employer is liable to obligee for support not withheld and may be held in contempt of court. If discharges, disciplines, or refuses to hire employee as a result of withholding notice, may be fined up to $500, payable to county general fund. For discharging, refusing to hire, or disciplining an employee because of garnishment, liable for fine of up to $150, order to reinstate employee, and payment of back wages, costs, and

attorneys' fees, plus support which should have been withheld during time employee was wrongfully discharged. (Discharge within 30 days of receipt of support order is presumed wrongful.)

MONTANA

Mont. Code Ann. §§ 39-2-302, 40-5-416, 40-5-422

Employee protections that exceed federal law: Employee may not be discharged or laid off because of wage garnishment (number not specified).

Employer's fee: $5 per month for child support payments.

Employer penalties, child support withholding: If employer discharges, disciplines, or refuses to hire employee because of garnishment, subject to a fine of $150 to $500; must reinstate employee with full restitution, including back pay.

NEBRASKA

Neb. Rev. Stat. §§ 42-364.01, 42-364.12, 43-1725

Employee protections that exceed federal law: Employer may not fire, demote, discipline, or penalize employee because of any proceeding to collect child support.

Employer's fee: $2.50 per month for child support payments.

Employer penalties, child support withholding: For failing to remit payments, liable for entire amount owed plus interest, costs, and attorneys' fees; for violating employee rights, liable for damages plus interest, costs, and attorneys' fees. May also be liable for a civil fine of up to $500 per violation, and may be required to make full restitution to employee, including reinstatement and back pay.

State Laws on Administering Wage Garnishments (cont'd)

NEVADA

Nev. Rev. Stat. Ann. §§ 31.296, 31.297, 31.298, 31A.090, 31A.120

Employee protections that exceed federal law: It is unlawful to discharge or discipline an employee because employer required to withhold earnings because of a garnishment (no number specified).

Employer's fee: $3 per pay period up to $12 per month for general wage garnishments; $3 per child support payment withheld.

Employer penalties, general wage garnishment: For willfully refusing to withhold payments, deliver payments to the enforcing authority, or misrepresenting employee's income, employer must pay entire amount not withheld; may be liable for punitive damages of up to $1,000 per pay period.

Employer penalties, child support withholding: For refusing to hire, discharging, or taking disciplinary action against an employee, employer must reinstate employee and is liable for any payments not withheld plus a $1,000 fine; if employee wins in court, employer liable for not less than $2,500, plus costs and attorneys' fees. For willfully refusing to withhold payments or misrepresenting employee's income, must pay entire amount not withheld; may be liable to obligee for punitive damages of up to $1,000 per pay period.

NEW HAMPSHIRE

N.H. Rev. Stat. Ann. §§ 161-H:5, 458-B:6

Applies to: Child support and child's medical support garnishments.

Employee protections that exceed federal law: Employer may not discharge, refuse to employ, or take any disciplinary action against an employee because of child support or child medical support garnishments.

Employer's fee: $1 per support payment.

Employer penalties, child support withholding: For discharging, refusing to employ, or taking any disciplinary action against an employee, guilty of a misdemeanor with a fine of up to $1,000; for failing to withhold payments, a fine up to $100 per pay period.

NEW JERSEY

N.J. Stat. Ann. §§ 2A:17-56.11, 2A:17-56.12, 2C:40A-3

Employee protections that exceed federal law: Employer may take no disciplinary action against employee because of wage garnishment (no number specified).

Employer's fee: $1 per garnishment (child support).

Employer penalties, general wage garnishment: For discharging or disciplining an employee because of a wage garnishment, guilty of a disorderly person offense; must rehire and compensate employee for damages.

Employer penalties, child support withholding: For discharging, failing to employ, or disciplining an employee because of a wage garnishment, employer liable for a fine and civil damages and must reinstate employee; if employee wins in court, liable for attorneys' fees, twofold compensatory damages, including court costs, and lost income. For failing to withhold child support payments, liable for a fine up to amount not withheld as well as interest and attorneys' fees. For failing to withhold payments under a medical support order, liable for children's medical expenses and any other amount that should have been withheld.

State Laws on Administering Wage Garnishments (cont'd)

NEW MEXICO

N.M. Stat. Ann. §§ 40-4A-8, 40-4A-11

Applies to: Child or spousal support garnishments.

Employer's fee: $1 per payment.

Employee protections that exceed federal law: Employer may not discharge, discipline, refuse to hire, or otherwise penalize the employee because of the duty to withhold income under a child or spousal support order.

Employer penalties, child support withholding: Employer who willfully fails to pay liable to a fine for total amount not withheld. For discharging, disciplining, refusing to hire, or otherwise penalizing an employee because of a wage garnishment, liable for reinstatement and damages; subject to action for contempt of court.

NEW YORK

N.Y. C.P.L.R. Law §§ 5241, 5252

Employee protections that exceed federal law: Current employee may not be fired, laid off, refused promotion, or disciplined, and prospective employee may not be refused employment because of one or more current, past, or pending garnishments.

Employer penalties, general wage garnishment: Liable to employee for reinstatement or hiring and up to six weeks' lost wages, plus fine of up to $500 for first offense and up to $1,000 for each additional offense. May also be liable for civil contempt of court.

Employer penalties, child support withholding: For failure to deduct or remit child or spousal support deductions: liable to creditor for fine of up to $500 for first offense and up to $1,000 for each additional offense.

NORTH CAROLINA

N.C. Gen. Stat. §§ 110-136, 110-136.8, 110-136.13, 131E-49, 131E-50

Applies to: Child and medical support garnishments, wage garnishments for public hospital debts.

Employee protections that exceed federal law: Employee may not be discharged or disciplined for having wages garnished to pay a public hospital debt. Employer shall not discharge from employment, refuse to employ, or otherwise take disciplinary action against employee because of child support withholding (including medical support orders).

Employer's fee: $1 per child support payment; $1 per payment to public hospital.

Employer penalties, general wage garnishment: An employer who discharges or disciplines employees for having wages garnished to pay public hospital debt may be liable for damages, including back pay, reinstatement, costs, and attorneys' fees.

Employer penalties, child support withholding: If employer fails to employ, discharges, or takes disciplinary action against employee because of garnishment, liable to employee for reinstatement and reasonable damages. May also be liable for a fine of $100 for first offense; $500 for second; and $1,000 for third (also applies to child medical support orders). For violating the terms of an order, may be liable for contempt.

NORTH DAKOTA

N.D. Cent. Code §§ 14-09-08.11, 14-09-09.3, 14-09-09.6, 32-09.1-18

Employee protections that exceed federal law: Employee may not be discharged because of wage garnishment (no number specified).

State Laws on Administering Wage Garnishments (cont'd)

Employer's fee: $3 per month for child support (voluntary garnishment).

Employer penalties, general wage garnishment: For discharging employee because of a garnishment, liable for twice lost wages and reinstatement.

Employer penalties, child support withholding: For failing or refusing to withhold or deliver income, may be punished for contempt of court. May be liable for amount of income that should have been withheld or delivered as well as costs, interest, and attorneys' fees. May owe late fees as well. Employer who refuses to employ, dismisses, demotes, disciplines, or in any way penalizes the employee because of a proceeding to collect child support is liable for damages, costs, interest, and attorneys' fees, and may be required to make restitution, including reinstatement and back pay.

OHIO
Ohio Rev. Code Ann. §§ 2716.041, 2716.05, 3121.18, 3123.20, 3123.99

Employee protections that exceed federal law: Employee may not be discharged because of wage garnishments by a single creditor in a 12-month period or because of child support order garnishment.

Employer's fee: $3 per pay period that earnings withheld for general wage garnishment; $2 per support order or 1% of amount withheld, whichever is greater, for child support.

Employer penalties, child support withholding: For discharging employee because of child support order, subject to fine of $50 to $200 and ten to 30 days in jail.

OKLAHOMA
Okla. Stat. Ann. tit. 12, §§ 1171.3, 1190; tit. 14A, § 5-106; tit. 56, § 240.2

Employee protections that exceed federal law: Employee may not be discharged because of a garnishment to collect on a consumer credit transaction, unless the employee has more than two such garnishments in one year.

Employer's fee: $5 per payment (up to $10/ month) for child support; $10 for each general wage garnishment.

Employer penalties, child support withholding: For discharging, disciplining, suspending or refusing to promote employee, liable for wages and benefits lost from time of discharge, discipline, suspension or refusal to promote to time of reinstatement or promotion. For failing to withhold or remit payments, liable for amount not withheld, plus fine of up to $200 for each payment not made.

OREGON
Or. Rev. Stat. §§ 18.385, 25.414, 25.424, 659A.885

Employee protections that exceed federal law: Employer may not discharge employee because of a wage garnishment (no number specified).

Employer's fee: $5 per month for child support withholding.

Employer penalties, child support withholding: For failure to withhold, liable for all amounts and damages not paid as well as a fine of $250 for each willful or grossly negligent failure to pay. For discharging, refusing to hire, or discriminating, disciplining, or retaliating against employee, may be liable for reinstatement, back pay, compensatory damages or $200 (whichever is greater), punitive damages, costs, and attorneys' fees.

State Laws on Administering Wage Garnishments (cont'd)

PENNSYLVANIA

23 Pa. Cons. Stat. Ann. § 4348

Applies to: Child support garnishments only.

Employee protections that exceed federal law: Employer may not refuse to employ, discharge, discipline, or demote employee because of a child support garnishment.

Employer's fee: 2% of amount withheld per support payment.

Employer penalties, child support withholding: For violating employee rights, liable for damages and subject to a fine of up to $1,000. For failing to withhold payment, may be jailed and fined for contempt of court.

RHODE ISLAND

R.I. Gen. Laws §§ 10-5-8, 15-5-24, 15-5-26, 15-29-5

Employee protections that exceed federal law: Employer may not dismiss, demote, discipline, or penalize employee due to child support garnishments; may not discharge, refuse to employ, or discipline employee due to child health garnishments.

Employer's fee: $5 per general garnishment order; $2 per child support payment.

Employer penalties, child support withholding: For failure to withhold income, personally liable for amount failed to withhold, together with costs, interest, attorney's fees. For dismissing, demoting, disciplining, or penalizing employee, liable for damages, interest, court costs, and attorneys' fees, and may be required to reinstate employee with back pay; subject to a fine of up to $100. For discharging, refusing to employ, or disciplining an employee because of a wage garnishment for child medical support, or failing to withhold for the same, liable for a $100 fine.

SOUTH CAROLINA

S.C. Code Ann. §§ 63-17-1420, 37-5-106, 63-17-1550, 63-17-1460

Employee protections that exceed federal law: Employee may not be discharged because of wage garnishment (no number specified).

Employer's fee: $3 per child support payment.

Employer penalties, child support withholding: For discharging, refusing to hire, or penalizing employee because of child or spousal support withholding, liable for a fine of up to $500.

SOUTH DAKOTA

S.D. Codified Laws Ann. §§ 21-18-9, 25-7A-46, 25-7A-59

Applies to: Child support and children's health garnishments only.

Employee protections that exceed federal law: Employer may not discharge, refuse to employ, discipline, or penalize an employee because of a child support wage garnishment.

Employer's fee: $15 for preparing a garnishment disclosure.

Employer penalties, child support withholding: Child support orders: for violating employee rights or failing to withhold or pay garnishment, guilty of petty offense. Child health support garnishments: for failure to withhold or pay garnishment, guilty of petty offense.

TENNESSEE

Tenn. Code Ann. §§ 36-5-501, 40-35-111

Applies to: Child and spousal support garnishments only.

Employee protections that exceed federal law: Employee whose wages are ordered withheld for either child or spousal support may not be fired or disciplined.

State Laws on Administering Wage Garnishments (cont'd)

Employer's fee: Up to 5% of amount withheld (no more than $5/month) for child support and spousal orders.

Employer penalties, child support withholding: For child and spousal support orders: refusing to employ, discharging, or taking disciplinary action against an employee, or refusing to withhold is a Class C misdemeanor, which carries a fine of up to $50 or up to 30 days' imprisonment, or both.

TEXAS

Tex. Civ. Prac. & Rem. Code Ann. § 63.006; Fam. Code §§ 8.204, 8.206 to 8.209, 158.204, 158.209, 158.210

Applies to: Child and spousal support garnishments only.

Employee protections that exceed federal law: Employee may not be fired, disciplined, or refused employment because of wage withholding orders for child or spousal support.

Employer's fee: Actual cost or up to $10 per month, whichever is less, for general wage garnishments under state or federal law; $10 per month for child support payments; $5 per month for spousal support payments.

Employer penalties, child support withholding: For violating employee rights, employer must reinstate employee with full benefits and seniority and is liable for wages plus court costs and attorneys' fees. For knowingly failing to withhold or remit child or spousal support payments, liable for the amount withheld but not paid as well as attorneys' fees and costs, $200 for each instance.

UTAH

Utah Code Ann. §§ 62A-11-316, 62A-11-406, 62A-11-410, 78A-2-216; Utah R. Civ. Proc. Rule 64D

Applies to: Child support garnishments.

Employee protections that exceed federal law: Employer may not discharge or prejudice an employee because of any child support garnishments.

Employer's fee: $10 for a single garnishment and $25 for a continuing garnishment.

Employer penalties, child support withholding: For discharging, refusing to hire, or disciplining because of a child support garnishment, liable to employee for damages; liable to state child support enforcement agency for amount of garnishment or $1,000, whichever is greater, plus interest, costs, and attorneys' fees.

VERMONT

Vt. Stat. Ann. tit. 12, §§ 3171, 3172; tit. 15, §§ 787, 790

Employee protections that exceed federal law: Employee may not be discharged because of garnishment (Vermont uses term "trustee process"). If employee is discharged within 60 days of a garnishment order, presumed to be in violation of law. Employee may not be discharged or subject to disciplinary action due to child support garnishment.

Employer's fee: $5 per month for child support withholding.

Employer penalties, general wage garnishment: Liable to discharged employee for reinstatement, back wages, and damages; if employee wins in court, also liable for costs and reasonable attorneys' fees. For failure to withhold, liable for amount of garnishment plus interest, costs, and attorneys' fees.

State Laws on Administering Wage Garnishments (cont'd)

Employer penalties, child support withholding: Liable to discharged or disciplined employee for reinstatement, back wages, and damages; if employee wins in court, also liable for costs, attorneys' fees, and $100 fine. Employers failing to forward payments may be subject to penalties of up to $100 for first violation and up to $1,000 for second or subsequent violations.

VIRGINIA

Va. Code Ann. §§ 8.01-512.2, 20-79.3, 63.2-1944

Employee protections that exceed federal law: Employee who voluntarily assigns earnings to settle a child support debt or who is subject to child support garnishment may not be discharged because of assignment.

Employer's fee: $10 for each general wage garnishment summons; $5 per child support withholding payment.

Employer penalties, child support withholding: For discharging, taking disciplinary action against, or refusing to employ an employee, fine of up to $1,000 for violating employee rights.

WASHINGTON

Wash. Rev. Code Ann. §§ 6.27.170, 26.18.110, 26.23.090, 74.20A.080, 74.20A.230, 74.20A.240

Employee protections that exceed federal law: Employee may not be discharged unless there are garnishments for three or more separate debts within a 12-month period. Employee may not be fired, disciplined, or refused employment because of wage withholding orders for child or spousal support.

Employer's fee: $10 for first payment, $1 for each successive payment for child or spousal support withholding; $15 for first payment, $1 for each successive payment for processing earnings

assignment issued by Department of Social and Health Services.

Employer penalties, child support withholding: Child or spousal support orders: for discharging, disciplining, or refusing to hire, liable to employee for double lost wages, other damages, costs, and attorneys' fees; may also be required to reinstate or hire employee. Liable for a civil fine up to $2,500 per violation. For failing to withhold, liable for full payment plus costs, interest, and attorneys' fees (includes child health care support).

WEST VIRGINIA

W.Va. Code §§ 46A-2-131, 46B-6-5, 48-14-406, 48-14-407, 48-14-418

Employee protections that exceed federal law: Employer may not take any form of reprisal against employee because of wage garnishment to pay judgment for consumer credit, consumer lease/loan, or rent-to-own transaction.

Employer's fee: $1 per child support withholding order.

Employer penalties, child support withholding: Employer who discharges, refuses to employ, or takes disciplinary action against an employee because of a child support garnishment is guilty of a misdemeanor, punishable by a fine of $500 to $1,000.

WISCONSIN

Wis. Stat. Ann. §§ 425.110, 767.75; 812.43

Employee protections that exceed federal law: Employer may not charge a fee or take any adverse action because of a general wage garnishment (no number specified); may not discharge an employee because of consumer credit garnishment.

State Laws on Administering Wage Garnishments (cont'd)

Employer's fee: Up to $3 per child or spousal support payment.

Employer penalties, general wage garnishment: For general wage garnishments: employee subject to fee or adverse action may sue for reinstatement, back wages and benefits, restoration of seniority, and attorneys' fees. For consumer credit garnishments: employee shall recover back wages and be reinstated, if files an action for relief within 90 days of discharge.

Employer penalties, child support withholding: Child and spousal support, and child health support: for discharging, disciplining, or denying employment, fine of up to $500, and full restitution (including reinstatement and back pay).

WYOMING

Wyo. Stat. §§ 1-15-509, 20-6-212, 20-6-218, 40-14-506

Employee protections that exceed federal law: Employee may not be discharged for having wages subject to continuing garnishment for any judgment or for a judgment from a consumer credit transaction (no number specified).

Employer's fee: $5 per child support payment.

Employer penalties, general wage garnishment: Employee may sue for reinstatement, 30 days' lost wages, costs, and attorneys' fees.

Employer penalties, child support withholding: For discharging, disciplining, or otherwise penalizing employee, subject to fine of up to $200. For failing to withhold, liable for amount that should have been withheld and fine of up to $200.

Discrimination

Discrimination is a negative force in American culture, but it's particularly destructive when it occurs in the workplace, where an individual's livelihood is at stake. Discrimination undermines employee loyalty, destroys employee morale, and reduces productivity and work quality. It can also lead to costly and painful lawsuits and do irreparable harm to a company's reputation.

In addition to the obvious moral and ethical reasons to prevent discrimination, it makes good business sense for employers to keep discrimination out of the workplace. And the burdens of preventing and remedying discrimination fall heavily on managers; after all, you are the ones who represent the company to its employees, have an opportunity to see what's really going on in the workplace, and are responsible for important personnel decisions that could form the basis for a discrimination lawsuit.

This chapter provides an overview of the kinds of employment discrimination that federal and state laws prohibit, tips on how you can prevent discrimination and harassment in your workplace, and what to do if an employee complains of discrimination.

Frequently Asked Questions About Discrimination

What types of discrimination are illegal in the workplace?

If a characteristic is specifically listed in a federal or state antidiscrimination law, or even in a local ordinance, then it is illegal to discriminate against someone on the basis of that characteristic. Under federal law, employers may not discriminate on the basis of race, color, national origin, religion, sex, disability, age, genetic information, or citizenship status. State and local laws may prohibit discrimination on the basis of additional characteristics, such as marital status or sexual orientation. (See "Antidiscrimination Laws," below, for more information.)

Can we require employees to speak only English when customers are present?

It depends on the reasons for the policy. If your company can show that the rule is necessary for business reasons and that the rule is not too restrictive, an English-only rule will probably pass legal muster. However, you must tell employees when they have to speak English and inform them of the consequences of breaking the rule. (See "Race and National Origin," below, for more information.)

Frequently Asked Questions About Discrimination (cont'd)

Is it age discrimination to hire a younger applicant who knows a broad range of cutting-edge computer programs over an older applicant who barely understands word processing?

No. You are not discriminating when you choose the most qualified candidate for a position. As long as the job requires the type of computer skills the younger applicant has, you're on safe ground. Age discrimination problems arise when you make assumptions based on age—for example, if you simply assumed that the older applicant didn't have up-to-date computer skills but he or she was actually a technology whiz, you could get into trouble. (For more information, see "Age," below.)

Can I choose to reassign a pregnant employee to a job that requires less physical work or travel?

Generally not. Unless the employee requests an accommodation or reassignment, you cannot force one upon her. As long as a pregnant employee can perform her job duties, treating her differently based solely upon her pregnancy is a form of sex discrimination. If the pregnant worker is having difficulty performing her job based on physical conditions due to her pregnancy, you should treat her the same way you treat other temporarily disabled employees, such as workers who have had a heart attack or broken a leg. (For more information, see "Gender, Pregnancy, and Sexual Harassment," below.)

Is it illegal to receive genetic information about an employee if we didn't request it?

Generally, no. Although the Genetic Information Nondiscrimination Act (GINA) makes it illegal for employers to acquire genetic information about employees and their family members, there's an exception for information you receive inadvertently. For example, if an employee tells you that he has a genetic condition or you overhear a conversation about it, that doesn't violate the law. This exception also applies if you receive genetic information from a health-care provider in response to a lawful request for medical information (for example, as part of an FMLA certification), as long as you tell the provider not to give genetic information. GINA includes suggested language you can use to tell providers not to give genetic information. (For more on these rules, see "Genetic Information," below.)

Frequently Asked Questions About Discrimination (cont'd)

Our company has a largely gay clientele; can we give an edge in hiring to gay and lesbian applicants?

As a legal matter, it depends on the laws of your city and state. More than 20 states, the District of Columbia, and many cities and counties prohibit discrimination in private workplaces on the basis of sexual orientation, and this applies equally to heterosexuals and homosexuals. Even if this type of discrimination isn't prohibited where you do business, however, discrimination is never a good idea. It can lead to other types of lawsuits, bad publicity, and more. And really, what should be important to your company is that employees understand the needs of its primarily gay customers, not whether the employees are gay themselves. (See "Sexual Orientation," below, for more information.)

Do we have to let a religious employee take his or her Sabbath day off?

It depends on how that would affect your company. Employers are required to accommodate their employees' religious practices, but only if accommodation doesn't cause hardship. If it's relatively easy to switch employee schedules around, you may be legally obligated to give this employee the day off. On the other hand, if no other employees are willing to work that day and employee schedules depend on seniority, this employee may not have the right to an accommodation. (See "Religion," below, for more information.)

If an employee with a disability asks for a particular reasonable accommodation, do we have to provide it?

Not necessarily. Once an employee asks for an accommodation, the employer must brainstorm with the employee to figure out what kinds of accommodations might work. However, you don't have to provide exactly the accommodation the worker requests, nor do you have to provide an accommodation if it would cause your company undue hardship. (For information on accommodating disabilities, see "Disability," below.)

Antidiscrimination Laws

Discrimination becomes a legal issue only when a state or federal law or local ordinance declares that a characteristic is "protected." Once that happens, an employer subject to the law cannot base employment decisions on that characteristic.

To know what forms of discrimination are prohibited, you must know a little about your federal, state, and local laws. Some of these laws apply only to businesses of a particular size. For example, five or more employees. In addition, each state's law is slightly different. For example, some states prohibit discrimination on the basis of sexual orientation, while others do not. To learn which characteristics are protected by your state antidiscrimination laws, see "State Laws Prohibiting Discrimination in Employment," at the end of this chapter.

Employer Duties Under Antidiscrimination Laws

In addition to not discriminating against its own employees, an employer must take steps to prevent discrimination. And when discrimination does occur, the company must stop it—and fast.

This means employers must:
- have policies that prohibit discrimination and tell employees what to do if they experience discrimination
- make sure its managers and supervisors don't discriminate
- make sure its policies and procedures don't have an unfair impact on a protected group of people (discussed in more detail below)
- investigate complaints of discrimination (see "Investigating Complaints" in Chapter 11), and
- take effective action against those who discriminate.

All of this may sound complicated, but it really isn't. If you and the company's other managers base all of your employment decisions on criteria related to the job, that's half the battle. And if someone does complain about discrimination, or if prejudicial behavior otherwise comes to your attention, follow your company's reporting policies. Don't retaliate or allow retaliation against the victim.

Federal Antidiscrimination Laws

The main federal laws that managers should be aware of are:
- Title VII of the Civil Rights Act ("Title VII")
- the Age Discrimination in Employment Act (ADEA)
- the Equal Pay Act (EPA)
- the Immigration Reform and Control Act (IRCA)
- the Americans with Disabilities Act (ADA), and
- the Genetic Information Nondiscrimination Act (GINA).

We describe each of these laws below. Even if your company is so small that some of these federal laws don't apply, that's not a license to discriminate. Not only is it bad business, but it also might violate a state law that covers smaller employers.

Although they each protect separate characteristics, federal antidiscrimination laws have a lot in common:

- **They prohibit retaliation.** All of the federal laws (and most state laws) prohibit employers from retaliating against applicants or employees who assert their rights under the law. For example, an employer cannot fire someone for complaining about race discrimination. This is an area in which managers can really get into trouble, because they are often the ones who have to decide whether to separate, move, discipline, or otherwise take action that affects the employees involved. To learn more about this issue, see "Retaliation" in Chapter 11.

- **They cover the entire employment relationship.** The federal laws prohibit discrimination in all terms, conditions, and privileges of employment, including hiring, firing, compensation, benefits, job assignments, shift assignments, promotions, and discipline.

- **They prevent neutral practices that harm a protected group.** Each law prohibits employer practices that seem neutral but have a disproportionate or unfair impact on a protected group of people. A neutral practice that has an unfair impact on a certain group is legal only if the employer has a valid business reason for using it. For example, a strength requirement for a job might be legal—even though it could exclude a disproportionately high number of women from that job—if an employer

is filling a position for which lifting a certain amount is a requirement, such as a job in the logging industry. A strength requirement would not, however, be valid for a desk job.

- **Harassment is always a no-no.** In addition to prohibiting discrimination on the basis of the listed characteristics, all of the laws prohibit harassment based on those characteristics as well.

Title VII of the Civil Rights Act of 1964

Title VII of the Civil Rights Act of 1964 ("Title VII"), 42 U.S.C. §§ 2000e and following, prohibits employers from discriminating on the basis of:

- race or color
- religion
- sex (including pregnancy and childbirth), or
- national origin (including membership in a Native American tribe).

A very narrow exception to Title VII allows an employer to discriminate on the basis of religion, sex, or national origin (but not race) if a characteristic is intrinsic to the job—called a "bona fide occupational qualification" or "BFOQ" in legal lingo. For example, if you need to hire an actor to play the role of Hamlet's mother or you need to hire attendants for a women's restroom, you can discriminate against men in filling these positions. To rely on this exception, an employer must be able to show that no member of the group it discriminated against could perform the job, which is a very tough standard to meet.

Title VII applies to:

- private employers with 15 or more employees
- state governments and their political subdivisions and agencies
- the federal government
- employment agencies
- labor organizations, and
- joint labor-management committees and other training programs.

The Age Discrimination in Employment Act

The Age Discrimination in Employment Act (ADEA), 29 U.S.C. §§ 621–634, prohibits discrimination against employees who are age 40 or older. It does not protect people who are younger than 40 from being discriminated against on the basis of age. (Some state laws do, however.)

The ADEA applies to:

- private employers with 20 or more employees
- the federal government and its agencies
- interstate agencies
- employment agencies, and
- labor unions.

Although state government workers are protected by the ADEA, they do not have the right to sue their employers (the state for which they work) in court to enforce their rights. Only the Equal Employment Opportunity Commission (EEOC), the federal agency that interprets and enforces the ADEA, may sue a state to protect state employees from age discrimination.

To learn more about age discrimination, see "Age," below.

The Equal Pay Act

The Equal Pay Act (EPA), 29 U.S.C. § 206(d), requires that employers provide men and women with equal pay for equal work. It applies to all employers, regardless of size. For more about this law, see "Equal Pay" in Chapter 2.

The Immigration Reform and Control Act of 1986

The Immigration Reform and Control Act of 1986 (IRCA), 8 U.S.C. § 1324, prohibits employers from discriminating against applicants or employees on the basis of their citizenship or national origin. On the flip side, however, the IRCA also makes it illegal for employers to knowingly hire or employ people who are not legally authorized to work in the United States. Employers must keep records verifying that their employees are authorized to work in the United States.

The IRCA applies to employers with four or more employees. For more information, see "Race and National Origin," below.

The Americans with Disabilities Act

The Americans with Disabilities Act (ADA), 42 U.S.C. §§ 12101–12213, prohibits employers from discriminating against a person with a disability in any aspect of employment.

The ADA applies only to:

- private employers with 15 or more employees

- local governments and their agencies
- employment agencies, and
- labor unions.

Employees of the federal government are protected from disability discrimination by the Rehabilitation Act. Like the ADEA, the ADA protects state employees, but those employees do not have the right to sue their state employer in court. Only the EEOC may sue a state to protect its employees from disability discrimination.

Genetic Information Nondiscrimination Act

The most recent addition to the civil rights laws is named GINA: the Genetic Information Nondiscrimination Act, 42 U.S.C. §§ 200 and following, effective November 2009. GINA prohibits health insurers from using genetic information to deny insurance coverage or determine premiums. It also prohibits covered employers from making employment decisions based on an applicant's or employee's genetic

Which Federal Antidiscrimination Laws Apply to Your Company?

Not every antidiscrimination law applies to every employer. Federal antidiscrimination laws apply to only private employers with more than a minimum number of employees, and the minimum number is different for each law.

Name of Law:	Discrimination Prohibited on the Basis of:	Applies to:
Title VII	Race, color, religion, sex, or national origin	Employers with 15 or more employees
Age Discrimination in Employment Act	Age (age 40 or older)	Employers with 20 or more employees
Americans with Disabilities Act	Physical or mental disability	Employers with 15 or more employees
Equal Pay Act	Sex (wage discrimination only)	All employers
Immigration Reform and Control Act	Citizenship status, national origin	Employers with 4 or more employees
Civil Rights Act of 1866	Race, ethnicity	All employers
Genetic Information Nondiscrimination Act	Genetic information	Employers with at least 15 employees

information, and requires employers to keep employee genetic information confidential.

GINA applies to:

- private employers with 15 or more employees
- the federal government
- state governments
- private and public employment agencies
- labor organizations, and
- joint labor-management committees.

Race and National Origin

Employment discrimination on the basis of race or national origin still happens more often than anyone wants to believe. It exacts a very high price, both from its victims and from the companies where it occurs. Recent lawsuits prove the point: Large companies have paid millions of dollars to compensate victims of race and national origin discrimination and to pay for their own complicity in encouraging or allowing a discriminatory atmosphere to flourish in the workplace.

Race Discrimination

An employer commits race discrimination when it makes job decisions on the basis of race or when it adopts seemingly neutral job policies that disproportionately affect members of a particular race.

Federal and state laws forbid race discrimination in every aspect of the employment relationship, including hiring, firing, promotions, compensation, job training, or any other term or condition of employment. For example, an employer discriminates when it refuses to hire Latinos, promotes only white employees to supervisory positions, requires only African American job applicants to take a drug test, or refuses to allow Asian American employees to deal with customers.

An employer that discriminates on the basis of physical characteristics associated with a particular race—such as hair texture or color, skin color, or facial features—also commits race discrimination.

Even employment policies or criteria that seem to be neutral may be discriminatory if they have a disproportionate impact on members of a particular race. For example, a height requirement may screen out disproportionate numbers of Asian American and Latino job applicants. Or an employment policy requiring men to be clean-shaven may discriminate against African American men, who are more likely to suffer from Pseudofolliculitis barbae (a painful skin condition caused and exacerbated by shaving).

Rules or policies that have a disproportionate impact on people of a certain race will pass legal muster only if the employer can show that there is a legitimate and important work reason for the policy. For example, a height requirement might be legitimate if the company can show that an employee must be at least a certain height to operate a particular type of machinery.

National Origin Discrimination

An employer discriminates on the basis of national origin when it makes employment decisions based on a person's ancestry, birthplace, or culture, or on linguistic characteristics or surnames associated with a particular ethnic group. For example, an employer who refuses to hire anyone with a Hispanic-sounding last name discriminates, as does an employer who won't allow anyone with an accent to work with the public.

Language Rules

An employer may be able to prohibit on-duty employees from speaking any language other than English if it can show that the rule is necessary for business reasons. If your company has an English-only rule, you must tell employees when they have to speak English (for example, whenever customers are present) and the consequences of breaking the rule. And, if an employee challenges the English-only rule, the company will have to defend the rule's scope: A rule that forbids workers from ever speaking another language, even during breaks or when a customer who speaks that language is present, is probably too broad.

Accent Rules

Because an employee's accent is often associated with his or her national origin, employers must tread carefully when making employment decisions based on accent. An employer may decide not to hire or promote an employee to a position that requires

 Lessons From the Real World

A federal judge in Dallas ordered a Texas company to pay its Spanish-speaking workers $700,000 in damages for requiring them to speak only English on company premises. The judge said that the policy discriminated against the workers because language is part of one's national origin. Although the judge might have allowed the policy if the company could have come forward with a business justification, the company could not.

The company's policy was so broad that it prohibited workers from speaking Spanish during lunch, on breaks, when making personal telephone calls, and before and after work if they were in the building.

The rule even prevented a Spanish-speaking husband and wife from speaking Spanish to each other when they ate lunch together.

The company disciplined and terminated employees who violated the policy. Even employees who tried to follow the policy but occasionally slipped up and allowed a Spanish word or phrase to enter into the conversation were disciplined.

The only time employees were allowed to speak Spanish was when serving the company's Spanish-speaking customers.

Equal Employment Opportunity Commission v. Premier Operator Services, Inc., 113 F.Supp.2d 1066 (N.D. Texas 2000).

clear oral communication in English if the employee's accent substantially affects his or her ability to communicate clearly. However, if the employee's accent does not impair his or her ability to be understood, you may not make job decisions on that basis. For example, a company cannot simply adopt a blanket rule that employees who speak accented English may not work in customer service positions.

Harassment Based on Race or National Origin Is Illegal

Harassment on the basis of race and national origin is also prohibited. Harassment is any conduct based on a person's race or national origin that creates an intimidating, hostile, or offensive work environment or interferes with the person's work performance. Harassing conduct might include racial slurs, jokes about a particular ethnic group, comments or questions about a person's cultural habits, or physical acts of particular significance to a certain racial or ethnic group, such as hanging or posting an offensive picture or object near an employee's workspace, like a swastika or noose.

Companies Pay the Price for Discrimination

Companies have been hit with huge verdicts—or have agreed to pay massive settlements—to employees who have been discriminated against or harassed on the basis of race or national origin. For example:

- Consolidated Freightways Corporation of Delaware agreed to pay $2.75 million to settle a racial harassment lawsuit filed by the EEOC. Twelve African American employees alleged that they were subjected to racial intimidation, threats, assault, racist graffiti, and property damage, among other things.
- The Equal Employment Opportunity Commission (EEOC) announced a $50 million settlement of a race and sex

discrimination lawsuit against the clothing retail company Abercrombie & Fitch. Among the allegations was a claim that the clothier refused to hire female and nonwhite applicants because they did not fit the image or "look" the company was trying to project in the marketplace.

- Coca-Cola settled a class action race discrimination lawsuit for $192.5 million. African American employees said that Coke imposed a racial "glass ceiling" by discriminating against them in pay and promotions. Of the total settlement, $36 million was earmarked for monitoring the company's employment practices to make sure that the discrimination stopped.

Lessons From the Real World

In 2006, a California jury awarded two Federal Express drivers more than $61 million in damages, one of the largest verdicts in the nation that year. The drivers, who were Lebanese-American, claimed that they were harassed and discriminated against based on their national origin. They said they were called names, such as "terrorists," "camel jockeys," and "Hezbollah," and that management did nothing to stop the harassment, despite repeated complaints.

In this case, the drivers were not employees, but instead independent contractors, who are also protected from discrimination under California law. The jury awarded the drivers even more than they requested, ordering FedEx to pay them $5 million each in compensatory damages and $25 million each in punitive damages. The jury also ordered the manager who harassed them to pay more than $500,000 to each driver.

"Top Ten Jury Verdicts of 2006: Lebanese-American FedEx Drivers Win Workplace Harassment Suit," by Dick Dahl (*Lawyers USA*).

Age

There is an adage: "Hire a young doctor and an old lawyer." A young doctor, the theory holds, will have cutting-edge skills and knowledge of all the latest research and techniques; the old lawyer will have the experience and gravitas needed to convince a jury. If the adage resonates with you, you are not alone—stereotypes based on age fill our culture, from the irresponsible, beer-loving college student to the stale and slow, 60-something middle manager.

While the stereotypes may abound, it is illegal for your company to act on such age-based preconceptions when making employment decisions. A number of state and federal laws prohibit you from discriminating against employees and applicants because of their age.

The Age Discrimination in Employment Act

The Age Discrimination in Employment Act (ADEA), 29 U.S.C. §§ 621–634, is the major federal law that addresses age discrimination. This law prohibits employers from discriminating against employees and applicants who are 40 years of age or older on the basis of their age. It does not, however, prohibit discrimination against people who are younger than 40. (Some state laws do; see the discussion below.) If you are a private employer with 20 or more employees, you must follow the ADEA.

The ADEA prohibits discrimination in all phases of the employment relationship, except benefits and early retirement, which are addressed by a different law. (See "Discrimination in Benefits," below.) Not only does the ADEA prohibit you from discriminating against older workers in favor of those who are younger than 40, it also prohibits you from discriminating among older workers. For example, you can't hire a 43-year-old over a 53-year-old simply because of age.

The ADEA also prohibits seemingly neutral employment practices that have a disparate impact on older workers, but the rules for these cases are slightly different than for other types of discrimination claims. In a disparate impact age discrimination case, the employee must point to a specific employment practice (such as a policy, screening test, or job requirement) that led to the disparate impact. And, the employer can escape liability if it can prove that its practice was based on a reasonable factor other than age, even if that factor often correlates largely with age, such as seniority. Because of these different standards, it is generally thought to be more difficult for employees to win disparate impact claims based on age.

State Laws

Many state laws also prohibit discrimination on the basis of age. Although some of these laws essentially mirror the federal law and only protect people older than 40, other laws are broader and protect workers of all ages.

State laws tend to cover employers with fewer than 20 employees, so you might have to comply with your state law even if your company isn't covered by the federal law. To find out more about the age discrimination law in your state, contact your state fair employment office. (See the appendix for contact information.)

Discrimination in Benefits

The federal Older Workers Benefit Protection Act (OWBPA), 29 U.S.C. §§ 623 and following, makes it illegal to use an employee's age as a basis for discrimination in benefits. Like the ADEA, this Act only protects people who are at least 40 years old. Also like the ADEA, this Act applies to private employers with 20 or more employees, government employers, and unions.

The OWBPA prohibits age discrimination in the provision of fringe benefits, such as life insurance, health insurance, disability benefits, pensions, and retirement benefits. Typically, this means that employers must provide equal benefits to older and younger workers. For some types of benefits, however, employers can meet this nondiscrimination requirement by spending the same amount on the benefit provided to each group, even if older workers receive lesser benefits. In some circumstances, employers are also allowed to provide lesser benefits to older workers if those workers receive additional benefits— from the government or the employer—to make up the difference. Because these rules can get complicated, you'll need to talk to a lawyer to make sure you're in compliance.

Gender, Pregnancy, and Sexual Harassment

As with race or national origin discrimination, employment discrimination on the basis of sex continues to persist with surprising regularity today. Despite federal and state laws prohibiting discrimination on the basis of sex—which the law defines to include pregnancy and related conditions—employers still make the mistake of making decisions along gender lines or treating pregnant employees differently just because they are pregnant. Such mistakes can cost a company dearly in lawsuit judgments and settlements.

Gender and Pregnancy Discrimination

An employer commits sex discrimination when it makes job decisions on the basis of sex or pregnancy or when it adopts seemingly neutral job policies that disproportionately affect members of one gender.

Federal and state laws forbid sex discrimination in every aspect of the employment relationship, including hiring, firing, promotions, compensation, job training, or any other term or condition of employment. For example, an employer discriminates based on gender when it promotes only men to supervisory positions, hires only women to work in tipped service positions, denies only women the chance to participate in training opportunities, or reassigns pregnant employees to "dead-end" positions based on the assumption that they won't return to work after giving birth.

As with race discrimination, even employment policies or criteria that seem to be neutral may be discriminatory if they have a disproportionate impact on members of a particular gender. For example, a height or strength requirement may screen out disproportionate numbers of female job applicants. Again, such rules or policies will pass legal muster only if the employer can show that there is a legitimate and important work reason for the policy. For example, a strength requirement might be legitimate if the company can show that an employee must be able to lift a certain amount of weight in order to load and transport heavy goods.

When it comes to pregnancy, you can avoid sex discrimination by following two basic rules: (1) Do not make any decisions about the employee based solely on the fact that she is pregnant, and (2) Treat pregnant employees the same way you would treat any other temporarily disabled employees, such as a worker who suffered a heart attack or broke a leg. If your pregnant employee is able to perform her job duties, you may not reassign her or change any of her job duties or any other term or condition of her job simply because she is pregnant. If she is having trouble performing her job duties due to pregnancy-related conditions (for example, extreme nausea or medically required bed rest), under basic federal antidiscrimination law, you must treat her as you would any nonpregnant, temporarily disabled worker. For instance, if you offer light duty at full pay or paid time off for a worker who cannot perform his or her job duties because the worker injured his or her back, you must offer your pregnant employee the same type of accommodation on the same terms.

Beyond Title VII, however, your pregnant employee may have additional rights under the federal and/or state family and medical leave laws or under additional state laws that protect pregnant workers or require transfer or reasonable accommodation if the worker requests it. For more information, see "Family and Medical Leave" and "Pregnancy and Parental Leave" in Chapter 5, and contact your state labor and fair employment agencies. (Contact information is included in the appendix.)

Sexual Harassment

Sexual harassment is a form of sex discrimination. As with sex discrimination, Title VII is the main federal law that prohibits sexual harassment. (See "Antidiscrimination Laws," above.) In addition, each state has its own law prohibiting sexual harassment.

Sexual harassment is any unwelcome sexual advance or conduct on the job that creates an intimidating, hostile, or offensive working environment. Any conduct of a sexual nature that makes an employee uncomfortable has the potential to be sexual harassment. Sexual harassment can also include harassment that is not sexual in nature, but is based on one's gender, just as racial harassment is based on one's race. This type of harassment often takes place when women enter workplaces that have been traditionally male-dominated and are belittled and treated poorly because they are women.

Given such a broad definition, it is not surprising that sexual harassment comes in many forms. The following are all examples of sexual harassment:

- A supervisor implies to an employee that the employee must go on a date with him or her to receive a promotion. (In legal lingo, this is sometimes called "quid pro quo" harassment.)

- Employees regularly tell sexually explicit jokes within earshot of the office manager, who finds the jokes offensive.
- A cashier at a store pinches and fondles a coworker against the coworker's will.
- Several employees post sexually explicit jokes on an office intranet bulletin board.
- An employee sends emails to coworkers that contain sexually explicit language and jokes.
- A male sales clerk makes demeaning comments about female customers to his coworkers.
- A secretary's coworkers belittle her and refer to her by sexist or demeaning terms.
- The only woman on an otherwise all-male construction crew routinely has her work tools taken or damaged by her male coworkers.

The harasser can be the victim's supervisor, manager, or coworker. The harasser can even be a nonemployee, if the person is on the premises with permission (for example, a customer or a vendor).

Anyone Can Be Sexually Harassed

Although it may sound counterintuitive, sexual harassment knows no gender: Men can sexually harass women, and women can sexually harass men.

Harassment based on a person's sexual orientation is not illegal under federal law (although some states prohibit it; see "Sexual Orientation," below). A worker who is harassed for being gay or straight is not protected, but a worker who is harassed—even by a member of the same gender—because of his or her sex is. Sound confusing? That's because the courts are still trying to figure out how to handle same-sex harassment.

The bottom line is that you should try to prevent harassment in any form, regardless of where it falls on the legal spectrum. For information on how you can—and should— prevent sexual harassment in the workplace, see "Preventing Sexual Harassment" in Chapter 4.

Genetic Information

Although more than half of the states ban genetic discrimination, federal law didn't prohibit genetic discrimination by private employers until quite recently. The Genetic Information Nondiscrimination Act (GINA) makes it illegal for employers to gather or use genetic information, and requires employers to maintain the confidentiality of any genetic information they obtain through legal means.

The nondiscrimination provision is fairly straightforward: Employers may not make employment decisions based on an employee's or applicant's genetic information, or the genetic information of an employee's or applicant's family member. Genetic information includes the results of genetic tests or the manifestation of a particular disease or disorder in the employee's family. For example, an employer may not refuse to hire an applicant because she carries BRCA1 or BRCA2 (the genes thought responsible for most inherited breast cancers), or fire an employee because he carries the trait for sickle cell anemia. Whether the employer is motivated by stereotypes or stigma associated with the disease or by a desire to reduce health care costs, decisions like these are illegal.

Acquiring Genetic Information

With a few exceptions, GINA prohibits employers from requiring or asking employees to provide genetic information (for example, by requiring genetic testing as a condition of employment). Employers also may not purchase genetic information about employees or their family members.

As explained below, there are a handful of exceptions to the general prohibition on acquiring genetic information from employees. Even if one of these exceptions applies, however, employers may not use the genetic information as a basis for employment decisions. Employers must also keep the information confidential as explained in "Confidentiality of Genetic Information," below.

It isn't illegal for an employer to obtain genetic information on an employee or employee's family member if one of these six exceptions applies:

1. The employer requests or requires such information "inadvertently." This exception is intended to cover casual conversations among coworkers, overheard comments, information volunteered by employees, or unsolicited email messages (for example, a request that coworkers sponsor an employee on a walkathon to support research into a particular genetic disease).

Navigating GINA's Safe Harbor for Discrimination

If your company requests medical information about employees (for example, to support an employee's request for a reasonable accommodation under the ADA or request for medical leave under the FMLA), it might receive genetic information in response. This will be considered inadvertent—and fall within the first exception to GINA—as long as your company tells the information provider, up front, not to give you genetic information. The final regulations interpreting GINA suggest using this language to make sure you gain the protection of this safe harbor:

"The Genetic Information Nondiscrimination Act of 2008 (GINA) prohibits employers and other entities covered by GINA Title II from requesting or requiring genetic information of an individual or family member of the individual, except as specifically allowed by this law. To comply with this law, we are asking that you not provide any genetic information when responding to this request for medical information. 'Genetic information' as defined by GINA, includes an individual's family medical history, the results of an individual's or family member's genetic tests, the fact that an individual or an individual's family member sought or received genetic services, and genetic information of a fetus carried by an individual or an individual's family member or an embryo lawfully held by an individual or family member receiving assistive reproductive services."

2. The employer acquires the information through health or genetic services it offers (as part of a wellness program, for example), if all of the following are true:
   - Providing information is voluntary, meaning that employees are not required to provide it or penalized for choosing not to provide it. If financial inducements are offered for participation, the employer must make clear that the inducement will be paid whether or not the employee provides genetic information. The employee gives prior, knowing, voluntary, and written authorization for the services.
   - Only the employee or family member receiving services, along with the genetic counselor or health care professional involved in providing the services, receive individually identifiable information about the results.
   - Any individually identifiable information resulting from the services is available only for the purpose of those services and is not disclosed to the employer except in aggregate terms that don't reveal individual identities.

3. The employer requires family medical history from the employee to comply with the certification requirements of the Family and Medical Leave Act (see Chapter 5) or a similar requirement under a state family and medical leave law, or an employer policy.

4. The employer gets the information from documents that are commercially and publicly available. This exception applies to newspapers, magazines, and books, for

example, but not to medical databases or court records. This exception doesn't apply if the employer accesses these sources with the intent to gather employee genetic information or was likely to acquire genetic information from viewing them.

5. The employer conducts DNA analysis for law enforcement purposes as a forensic laboratory or to identify human remains, and requests or requires genetic information from its employees only for analysis of DNA identification markers as a means of detecting sample contamination— that is, to separate employee DNA from the DNA the lab is examining.

6. The information acquired is to be used for genetic monitoring of the biological effects of toxic substances in the workplace, but only if all of the following are true:

   • The employer provides written notice of the monitoring to employees.

   • Employees give prior, knowing, voluntary, and written authorization to the monitoring, or the monitoring is required by law.

   • The employee is informed of his or her own results.

   • The monitoring complies with federal or state genetic monitoring regulations (depending on whether the state has its own genetic monitoring program under the authority of OSHA).

   • Other than a licensed health care professional or genetic counselor involved in the program, the employer receives results from the program only in aggregate form, which does not disclose the identity of individual employees.

Confidentiality of Genetic Information

Employers that have genetic information about an employee must keep it on separate forms and in separate files, and treat it as a confidential medical record. This means the employer must treat this information as it treats medical information under the ADA: The information must be kept separately from regular personnel files and revealed only in limited circumstances to certain people (for example, to government officials investigating the company's compliance with the law).

Genetic information may be disclosed only in the following circumstances:

   • To the employee or family member, on written request.

   • To an occupational or health researcher for research conducted in compliance with part 46 of Title 45 of the Code of Federal Regulations (these are the Department of Health and Human Services' rules for the protection of human research subjects).

   • In response to a court order, but the employer may disclose only the genetic information expressly authorized by that order. If the court order was obtained without the employee's or family member's knowledge, the employer must notify the employee or family member of the order and of any genetic information that was disclosed as a result.

   • To government officials investigating compliance with GINA, if the information is relevant to the investigation.

- In connection with the employee's compliance with the certification requirements of the Family and Medical Leave act or a similar state law.
- To a government health agency, an employer may disclose only information about the manifestation of a disease or disorder in an employee's family member if that information concerns a contagious disease that presents an imminent hazard of death or life-threatening illness. The employer must inform the employee of the disclosure.

Sexual Orientation

Traditionally, gay and lesbian employees have had little protection from discrimination and harassment in the workplace. Times are changing, however, and a growing number of employers must now provide these workers the same thing they must provide to members of other traditionally oppressed groups: a workplace free of discrimination and harassment.

Although federal law doesn't currently prohibit private employers from discriminating on the basis of sexual orientation, a number of state and local laws do. Almost half the states prohibit sexual orientation discrimination in private employment, along with the District of Columbia, and numerous cities and counties also prohibit sexual orientation discrimination in the workplace.

To find out whether your state, county, or city has a law prohibiting discrimination on the basis of sexual orientation, contact your state labor department or your state fair employment office. (See the appendix for contact information.) You can also visit the Lambda Legal Defense and Education Fund website at www.lambdalegal.org. There, you will find a state-by-state list of antidiscrimination laws.

Even if there is no law in your state, city, or county prohibiting sexual orientation discrimination, that's not a license to discriminate. If a gay or lesbian employee feels unfairly treated and/or injured based on sexual orientation, that employee can still sue your company under a number of other legal theories. These include:

- intentional or negligent infliction of emotional distress
- assault
- battery
- invasion of privacy
- defamation
- interference with employment contract, and
- wrongful termination in violation of public policy.

Religion

The laws against religious discrimination present employers with a seeming contradiction: They prohibit employers from making decisions based on a person's religion, but they sometimes also require employers to make decisions based on a person's religion.

This apparent contradiction comes from the fact that religion is a set of practices and beliefs. The law prohibits employers from discriminating based on the fact of someone's religion (for example, that an employee is Jewish, Catholic, Muslim, or Baptist), and it requires employers to make allowances for a person's religious practices and beliefs (for example, that an employee needs time after lunch to pray or that an employee needs Saturdays off to observe a Sabbath).

The first part is fairly simple. You can't refuse to hire someone, decide to promote someone, or make any other employment decisions because of the person's religion.

The second part is more complicated. You must work with employees to make it possible for them to practice their religious beliefs, within reason. This might mean not scheduling an employee to work on a Sabbath day, or relaxing a company dress code so that an employee can wear religious garments. The only time an employer does not have to accommodate an employee is when it would pose a hardship for the business. For instance, if changing an employee's schedule to accommodate a religious belief would wreak havoc on your company's seniority-based scheduling system and cause severe morale problems among other employees, you might not have to accommodate the worker.

As with many legal terms, it can be tough to figure out exactly what "accommodation" and "hardship" mean in the practical context of your workplace. The following sections look at the meaning of these terms.

Accommodation

If an employee has a sincere religious belief that conflicts with an employment rule or requirement, the law requires you to accommodate the employee's beliefs, working with the employee to find a way around the conflict. This does not mean that you have to accept any accommodation that the employee suggests. If you don't like the employee's idea, you can suggest one of your own. In this way, the two of you should engage in a negotiation process that balances the employee's religious rights with your need for the job to get done.

Examples of reasonable accommodations include:

- flexible scheduling
- changes to a grooming or dress code
- splitting shifts, and
- transferring the employee to a different position.

Undue Hardship

You do not have to make an accommodation for an employee's religious beliefs that will cause your company an undue hardship. This means that you can deny an accommodation that would:

- cost too much money (anything more than a minor cost is too much in the eyes of the law)
- substantially harm the morale of other employees (in other words, more than mere grumbling), or
- substantially disrupt work routines.

Expression of Religious Beliefs

Some employees wish to—or believe that their religion requires them to—express their religious beliefs in the workplace by, for

Lessons From the Real World

As part of a workplace diversity program, Hewlett Packard hung posters of employees, including one featuring an employee who was labeled as gay. In response, Richard Peterson posted passages from the Bible condemning homosexuality. Peterson claimed that he had a duty to expose evil, and that he intended the messages to be hurtful to his gay and lesbian coworkers whom he hoped would read the messages, repent, and be saved.

After Peterson was fired for refusing to take down the passages, he sued for discrimination on the basis of religion. A federal Court of Appeals rejected his claim. The Court found that Peterson's desire to express his religious beliefs could not be accommodated without requiring his employer to allow other employees to be demeaned.

Peterson v. Hewlett-Packard, 359 F.3d 599 (9th Cir. 2004).

example, posting religious messages in their workspace, using religious language (such as "God bless you" or "Praise the Lord") when communicating with others, or attempting to proselytize coworkers. In these situations, it can be difficult to balance the rights of the religious employee with the rights of others who do not share that employee's beliefs.

According to the EEOC, employers must allow employees to engage in religious expression as long as it doesn't create an undue hardship. And, employers may not restrict religious expression more heavily than other forms of expression that have a similar impact on workplace efficiency.

What do these rules mean in practice? Unfortunately, it's not entirely clear. Some courts have held that an employer has no duty to accommodate an employee's religious expression when it could constitute harassment against other employees or it contravenes the employer's diversity or nondiscrimination policies. On the other hand, some courts have found in the employee's favor if his or her behavior was merely "annoying" or created discomfort for others. In light of this confusion, the best practice is to consult with a lawyer if an employee's religious expression is causing others to feel uncomfortable.

Disability

Federal and state laws also prohibit discrimination at work on the basis of a worker's disability. The federal Americans with Disabilities Act (ADA), 42 U.S.C. §§ 12101–12213, and similar state laws prohibit discrimination against people with disabilities and require employers to accommodate employees'—and applicants'—disabilities when possible.

Who Is Covered

The ADA and most state laws protect "qualified workers with disabilities." A qualified worker is someone who can perform the essential duties of the job, with or without some form of accommodation from the employer.

A worker who falls into one of these three categories is considered disabled under the ADA:

- The worker has a physical or mental impairment that substantially limits a major life activity (such as the ability to walk, talk, see, hear, breathe, reason, work, or take care of oneself) or a major bodily function (such as the proper functioning of the immune system, cell growth, brain, or respiratory system). Impairments that are episodic or in remission qualify as disabilities if they substantially limit a major life activity when active.
- The worker has a record or history of impairment. In other words, you may not make employment decisions based on an employee's past disability.
- The employer regards the worker—even incorrectly—as having a disability. In other words, you can't treat workers less favorably because you believe that they have disabilities, even if you are wrong.

In addition, for an impairment to be a disability under the ADA, it must be long-term. Temporary impairments, such as pregnancy or broken bones, are not covered by the ADA (but they may be covered by other laws; for example, see "Gender and Pregnancy Discrimination," above).

Measures an employee takes or uses to mitigate the effects of a disability may not be considered in determining whether the employee's impairment limits major life activities or major bodily functions. For example, an employee may have a serious condition that is largely controlled by medication. When considering whether that employee has a disability, the employer must look at the employee's condition as it would be if the employee were not using medication to control it. The only exception to this rule is for the corrective power of ordinary prescription glasses and contact lenses, which may be considered when determining whether an employee has a disability.

Reasonable Accommodation

Accommodating a worker means providing assistance or making changes in the job or workplace that will enable the worker to do the job. For example, an employer might change the height of a desktop to accommodate a worker in a wheelchair, provide TDD telephone equipment for a worker whose hearing is impaired, or provide a quiet, distraction-free workspace for a worker with attention deficit disorder.

It is the employee's responsibility to inform you of the disability and request a reasonable accommodation; managers are not legally required to guess at what might help the employee do the job. However, once an employee reveals a disability, you must engage in what the law calls a "flexible interactive process," which is essentially a brainstorming dialogue with the worker to figure out what kinds of accommodations might be effective and practical. Your company does not have to provide the precise accommodation the worker requests, but you must work together to come up with a reasonable solution.

However, you don't have to provide an accommodation if it would cause your company "undue hardship." For instance, if the cost of an accommodation would eat up an entire year's profits (building a new wing on an office building, for example), it isn't required. Whether implementing an accommodation qualifies as undue hardship depends on a number of factors, including:

- the cost of the accommodation
- the size and financial resources of the business
- the structure of the business, and
- the effect the accommodation would have on the business.

Your company and the employee may have different opinions about what constitutes a reasonable accommodation and what would be an undue hardship. If you're unsure whether a disabled employee is entitled to a specific accommodation, you might want to get some legal help.

Alcohol and Drugs

Alcohol and drug use pose special problems under the ADA. Employees who use (or have used) alcohol or drugs may have disabilities under the law. However, an employer can require these employees to meet the same work standards—including not drinking or using drugs on the job—as everyone else. Here are some guidelines to follow when dealing with these tricky issues:

- **Alcoholism.** Alcoholism is a disability covered by the ADA. This means that an employer cannot fire or discipline a worker simply because he or she is an alcoholic. However, an employer can fire or discipline an alcoholic worker for failing to meet work-related performance and behavior standards imposed on all employees, even if the worker fails to meet these standards because of drinking.
- **Illegal drug use.** The ADA does not protect employees who currently use or are addicted to illegal drugs. These workers do not have disabilities within the meaning of the law and therefore don't have the right to be free from discrimination or to receive a reasonable accommodation. However, the ADA does cover workers who are no longer using drugs and have successfully completed (or are currently participating in) a supervised drug rehabilitation program.
- **Use of legal drugs.** If an employee is taking prescription medication or over-the-counter drugs to treat a disability, you may have to accommodate that employee's use of drugs and the side effects that the drugs have on the employee.

Legal Dos and Don'ts: Discrimination

Do:

- **Use only job-related criteria when making decisions.** If you always have sound business reasons for your actions, employees are less likely to complain of discrimination, and much less likely to win any discrimination claims they might make.
- **Keep an open door.** The more comfortable employees are talking to you about problems and concerns, the more likely they are to come to you for help rather than running to a lawyer. Communication is the best way to nip problems in the bud.
- **Act out of enlightened self-interest.** Most managers want to keep their companies out of trouble. But if you need a little more incentive to refrain from harassing or discriminatory behavior, remember this: In some states, managers can be personally liable for harassment or discrimination they commit themselves.

Don't:

- **Hurt by helping.** Although it may seem like a good idea to move a victim out of a discriminatory or harassing environment, even well-intentioned actions taken against a victim might constitute retaliation. Solve these types of problems by moving the accused, not the accuser.
- **Drag your feet.** When you don't take immediate action to stop discrimination or harassment, you cost the company money. Allowing misconduct to continue causes morale and productivity to drop, and could set your company up to lose a million-dollar lawsuit.
- **Jump to conclusions.** Always report claims of discrimination and harassment. Managers get in trouble when they make assumptions that they know what happened, that their employees wouldn't lie to them, or that "it could never happen here," for instance.

Test Your Knowledge

Questions

1. Only large companies need to worry about complying with antidiscrimination laws.   ☐ True   ☐ False

2. Once a manager learns about discrimination, he or she should report it immediately, even if the employee is reluctant to come forward.   ☐ True   ☐ False

3. It is illegal to consider an employee's accent when filling a position, even if the job requires extensive customer communication.   ☐ True   ☐ False

4. It is discriminatory to hire or promote an employee based on age, even if all of the applicants are over the age of 40.   ☐ True   ☐ False

5. If an employee voluntarily reveals that he or she has a particular genetic disease, you may take that information into account when making decisions about promotions and other employment matters.   ☐ True   ☐ False

6. You may require an employee to accept a light-duty position if she is pregnant.   ☐ True   ☐ False

7. Because no federal law prohibits discrimination based on sexual orientation, employers are free to discriminate against gay and lesbian applicants or employees.   ☐ True   ☐ False

8. You are never allowed to take an employee's religion into account when making employment decisions.   ☐ True   ☐ False

9. As a manager, you are responsible for asking your reports whether they have a disability and whether they need an accommodation to do their jobs.   ☐ True   ☐ False

10. An employee can sue your company for disability discrimination even if he or she does not have a disability.   ☐ True   ☐ False

Answers

1. False. Some federal antidiscrimination laws apply to very small companies. And every state has an antidiscrimination law; some of these laws apply to every employer in the state, regardless of size.

2. True. Once you know about discrimination, the company is legally responsible to take steps to stop it, even if the employee who tells you about it doesn't want to come forward.

3. False. If an employee's accent is so pronounced that it seriously impairs the employee's ability to be understood, you may refuse to place that employee in a position that requires strong communication skills.

4. True. If you hire a 45-year-old applicant rather than a 65-year-old applicant because of age, that's discriminatory.

5. False. Even if the employee provides the information voluntarily, you may not make employment decisions based on genetic information.

6. False. As long as the employee is able to work her usual job, you may not move her simply because she is pregnant.

7. False. Some 20 states, the District of Columbia, and many cities and counties prohibit discrimination on the basis of sexual orientation. And, even if it's not prohibited in your region, making decisions based on an employee's sexual orientation can lead to other kinds of legal trouble.

8. False. If a worker needs a reasonable accommodation to practice his or her religious beliefs, you are legally required to take the worker's needs into account in deciding whether you can offer an accommodation.

9. False. Employees are responsible for telling you that they have a disability and need an accommodation. Once an employee does so, you are legally obligated to work with the employee to try to come up with an accommodation that will work for the employee and the company.

10. True. If you make decisions based on your erroneous belief that an employee has a disability, or based on an employee's history of disability, that's disability discrimination.

State Laws Prohibiting Discrimination in Employment

ALABAMA
Ala. Code §§ 25-1-20, 25-1-21

Law applies to employers with: 20 or more employees

Private employers may not make employment decisions based on:

Age: 40 and older

ALASKA
Alaska Stat. §§ 18.80.220, 47.30.865

Law applies to employers with: One or more employees

Private employers may not make employment decisions based on:

Age: 40 and older

Ancestry or national origin:

Disability: physical or mental

AIDS/HIV

Gender

Marital status: includes changes in status

Pregnancy, childbirth, and related medical conditions: includes parenthood

Race or color

Religion or creed

Additional protected categories: Mental illness

ARIZONA
Ariz. Rev. Stat. §§ 41-1461, 41-1463, 41-1465

Law applies to employers with: 15 or more employees

Private employers may not make employment decisions based on:

Age: 40 and older

Ancestry or national origin

Disability: physical or mental

AIDS/HIV

Gender

Race or color

Religion or creed

Genetic testing information

ARKANSAS
Ark. Code Ann. §§ 16-123-102, 16-123-107, 11-4-601, 11-5-403

Law applies to employers with: Nine or more employees

Private employers may not make employment decisions based on:

Ancestry or national origin

Disability: physical, mental, or sensory

Gender

Pregnancy, childbirth, and related medical conditions

Race or color

Religion or creed

Genetic testing information

CALIFORNIA
Cal. Gov't. Code §§ 12920, 12926.1, 12940, 12941, 12945; Cal. Lab. Code § 1101

Law applies to employers with: Five or more employees

Private employers may not make employment decisions based on:

Age: 40 and older

Ancestry or national origin

Disability: physical or mental

AIDS/HIV

Gender

Marital status

Pregnancy, childbirth, and related medical conditions

Race or color

Religion or creed

State Laws Prohibiting Discrimination in Employment (cont'd)

Sexual orientation

Genetic testing information

Additional protected categories:

- gender identity
- medical condition
- political activities or affiliations

COLORADO

Colo. Rev. Stat. §§ 24-34-301, 24-34-401, 24-34-402, 24-34-402.5, 27-65-115

Law applies to employers with: One or more employees

Private employers may not make employment decisions based on:

Age: 40 to 70

Ancestry or national origin

Disability: physical, mental, or learning

AIDS/HIV

Gender

Pregnancy, childbirth, and related medical conditions

Race or color

Religion or creed

Sexual orientation: includes perceived sexual orientation

Additional protected categories:

- lawful conduct outside of work
- mental illness

CONNECTICUT

Conn. Gen. Stat. Ann. §§ 46a-51, 46a-60, 46a-81a, 46a-81c

Law applies to employers with: Three or more employees

Private employers may not make employment decisions based on:

Age: 40 and older

Ancestry or national origin

Disability: present or past physical, mental, learning, or mental retardation

AIDS/HIV

Gender

Marital status: includes civil unions

Pregnancy, childbirth, and related medical conditions

Race or color

Religion or creed

Sexual orientation: includes having a history of being identified with a preference

Genetic testing information

DELAWARE

Del. Code Ann. tit. 19, §§ 710, 711, 724

Law applies to employers with: Four or more employees

Private employers may not make employment decisions based on:

Age: 40 and older

Ancestry or national origin

Disability: physical or mental

AIDS/HIV

Gender

Marital status

Pregnancy, childbirth, and related medical conditions

Race or color

Religion or creed

Sexual orientation

Genetic testing information

State Laws Prohibiting Discrimination in Employment (cont'd)

DISTRICT OF COLUMBIA

D.C. Code Ann. §§ 2-1401.01, 2-1401.02, 2-1402.82, 7-1703.03, 32-131.08

Law applies to employers with: One or more employees

Private employers may not make employment decisions based on:

Age: 18 and older

Ancestry or national origin

Disability: physical or mental

AIDS/HIV

Gender

Marital status: includes domestic partnership

Pregnancy, childbirth, and related medical conditions: includes parenthood and breast-feeding

Race or color

Religion or creed

Sexual orientation

Genetic testing information

Additional protected categories:

- enrollment in vocational, professional, or college education
- family duties
- source of income
- place of residence or business
- personal appearance
- political affiliation
- victim of intrafamily offense
- gender identity or expression
- any reason other than individual merit
- tobacco use

FLORIDA

Fla. Stat. Ann. §§ 760.01, 760.02, 760.10, 760.50, 448.075

Law applies to employers with: 15 or more employees

Private employers may not make employment decisions based on:

Age

Ancestry or national origin

Disability: "handicap"

AIDS/HIV

Gender

Marital status

Race or color

Religion or creed

Additional protected categories: sickle cell trait

GEORGIA

Ga. Code Ann. §§ 34-1-2, 34-5-1, 34-5-2, 34-6A-1 and following, 45-19-20 and following

Law applies to employers with: 15 or more employees (disability)

10 or more employees (gender)

Private employers may not make employment decisions based on:

Age: 40 to 70

Disability: physical, mental, or learning or mental retardation

Gender: wage discrimination only

Additional protected categories: domestic and agricultural employees are not protected

HAWAII

Haw. Rev. Stat. §§ 378-1, 378-2, 378-2.5

Law applies to employers with: One or more employees

State Laws Prohibiting Discrimination in Employment (cont'd)

Private employers may not make employment decisions based on:

Age

Ancestry or national origin

Disability: physical or mental

AIDS/HIV

Gender

Marital status

Pregnancy, childbirth, and related medical conditions: includes breast-feeding

Race or color

Religion or creed

Sexual orientation

Genetic testing information

Additional protected categories:

- arrest and court record (unless there is a conviction directly related to job)
- credit history or credit report, unless the information in the individual's credit history or credit report directly relates to a bona fide occupational qualification

IDAHO

Idaho Code §§ 39-8303, 67-5902, 67-5909, 67-5910

Law applies to employers with: five or more employees

Private employers may not make employment decisions based on:

Age: 40 and older

Ancestry or national origin

Disability: physical or mental

Gender

Pregnancy, childbirth, and related medical conditions

Race or color

Religion or creed

Genetic testing information

ILLINOIS

410 Ill. Comp. Stat. § 513/25; 775 Ill. Comp. Stat. §§ 5/1-102, 5/1-103, 5/1-105, 5/2-101, 5/2-102, 5/2-103; 820 Ill. Comp. Stat. §§ 105/4, 180/30; Ill. Admin. Code tit. 56, § 5210.110

Law applies to employers with: 15 or more employees; one or more employees (disability)

Private employers may not make employment decisions based on:

Age: 40 and older

Ancestry or national origin

Disability: physical or mental

AIDS/HIV

Gender

Marital status

Pregnancy, childbirth, and related medical conditions

Race or color

Religion or creed

Sexual orientation

Genetic testing information

Additional protected categories:

- citizenship status
- military status
- unfavorable military discharge
- gender Identity
- arrest record
- victims of domestic violence
- order of protection status

INDIANA

Ind. Code Ann. §§ 22-9-1-2, 22-9-2-1, 22-9-2-2, 22-9-5-1 and following

Law applies to employers with: six or more employees

Private employers may not make employment decisions based on:

State Laws Prohibiting Discrimination in Employment (cont'd)

Age: 40 to 75 (applies to employers with one or more employees)

Ancestry or national origin

Disability: physical or mental (15 or more employees)

Gender

Race or color

Religion or creed

Additional protected categories: off-duty tobacco use

IOWA

Iowa Code §§ 216.2, 216.6, 729.6, 216.6A

Law applies to employers with: four or more employees

Private employers may not make employment decisions based on:

Age: 18 or older

Ancestry or national origin

Disability: physical or mental

AIDS/HIV

Gender

Pregnancy, childbirth, and related medical conditions

Race or color

Religion or creed

Sexual orientation

Genetic testing information

Additional protected categories:

- gender identity
- wage discrimination

KANSAS

Kan. Stat. Ann. §§ 44-1002, 44-1009, 44-1112, 44-1113, 44-1125, 44-1126, 65-6002(e)

Law applies to employers with: four or more employees

Private employers may not make employment decisions based on:

Age: 40 or older

Ancestry or national origin

Disability: physical or mental

AIDS/HIV

Gender

Race or color

Religion or creed

Genetic testing information

Additional protected categories: military service or status

KENTUCKY

Ky. Rev. Stat. Ann. §§ 207.130, 207.135, 207.150, 342.197, 344.010, 344.030, 344.040

Law applies to employers with: eight or more employees

Private employers may not make employment decisions based on:

Age: 40 or older

Ancestry or national origin

Disability: physical or mental

AIDS/HIV

Gender

Pregnancy, childbirth, and related medical conditions

Race or color

Religion or creed

Additional protected categories:

- occupational pneumoconiosis with no respiratory impairment resulting from exposure to coal dust
- off-duty tobacco use

State Laws Prohibiting Discrimination in Employment (cont'd)

LOUISIANA

La. Rev. Stat. Ann. §§ 23:301 to 23:368

Law applies to employers with: 20 or more employees

Private employers may not make employment decisions based on:

Age: 40 or older

Ancestry or national origin

Disability: physical or mental

Gender

Pregnancy, childbirth, and related medical conditions: applies to employers with 25 or more employees

Race or color

Religion or creed

Genetic testing information

Additional protected categories: sickle cell trait

MAINE

Me. Rev. Stat. Ann. tit. 5, §§ 19302, 4552, 4553, 4571 to 4576, 23; tit. 26, § 833; tit. 39-A, § 353

Law applies to employers with: One or more employees

Private employers may not make employment decisions based on:

Age

Ancestry or national origin:

Disability: physical or mental

Gender

Pregnancy, childbirth, and related medical conditions

Race or color

Religion or creed

Sexual orientation: includes perceived sexual orientation

Genetic testing information

Additional protected categories:

• gender identity or expression

• past workers' compensation claim

• past whistle-blowing

• medical support notice for child

MARYLAND

Md. Code, State Government, §§ 20-101, 20-601 to 20-608

Law applies to employers with: 15 or more employees

Private employers may not make employment decisions based on:

Age

Ancestry or national origin

Disability: physical or mental

Gender

Marital status

Pregnancy, childbirth, and related medical conditions

Race or color

Religion or creed

Sexual orientation

Genetic testing information

Additional protected categories: Civil Air Patrol membership

MASSACHUSETTS

Mass. Gen. Laws ch. 149, § 24A; ch. 151B, §§ 1, 4

Law applies to employers with: six or more employees

Private employers may not make employment decisions based on:

Age: 40 or older

Ancestry or national origin

Disability: physical or mental

AIDS/HIV

State Laws Prohibiting Discrimination in Employment (cont'd)

Gender

Marital status

Race or color

Religion or creed

Sexual orientation

Genetic testing information

Additional protected categories:

- military service
- arrest record

MICHIGAN

Mich. Comp. Laws §§ 37.1103, 37.1201, 37.1202, 37.2201, 37.2202, 37.2205a, 750.556

Law applies to employers with: One or more employees

Private employers may not make employment decisions based on:

Age

Ancestry or national origin

Disability: physical or mental

AIDS/HIV

Gender

Marital status

Pregnancy, childbirth, and related medical conditions

Race or color

Religion or creed

Genetic testing information

Additional protected categories:

- height or weight
- misdemeanor arrest record

MINNESOTA

Minn. Stat. Ann. §§ 144.417, 181.81, 181.974, 363A.03, 363A.08

Law applies to employers with: One or more employees

Private employers may not make employment decisions based on:

Age: 18 to 70

Ancestry or national origin

Disability: physical or mental

AIDS/HIV

Gender

Marital status

Pregnancy, childbirth, and related medical conditions

Race or color

Religion or creed

Sexual orientation: includes perceived sexual orientation

Genetic testing information

Additional protected categories:

- gender identity
- member of local commission
- receiving public assistance

MISSISSIPPI

Miss. Code Ann. § 33-1-15

Law applies to employers with: One or more employees

Protected categories:

- military status
- no other protected categories unless employer receives public funding

MISSOURI

Mo. Rev. Stat. §§ 191.665, 213.010, 213.055, 375.1306

Law applies to employers with: six or more employees

Private employers may not make employment decisions based on:

Age: 40 to 70

State Laws Prohibiting Discrimination in Employment (cont'd)

Ancestry or national origin

Disability: physical or mental

AIDS/HIV

Gender

Race or color

Religion or creed

Genetic testing information

MONTANA

Mont. Code Ann. §§ 49-2-101, 49-2-303, 49-2-310

Law applies to employers with: One or more employees

Private employers may not make employment decisions based on:

Age

Ancestry or national origin

Disability: physical or mental

Gender

Marital status

Pregnancy, childbirth, and related medical conditions

Race or color

Religion or creed

NEBRASKA

Neb. Rev. Stat. §§ 20-168, 48-236, 48-1001 to 48-1010, 48-1102, 48-1104

Law applies to employers with: 15 or more employees

Private employers may not make employment decisions based on:

Age: 40 or older (applies to employers with 20 or more employees)

Ancestry or national origin

Disability: physical or mental

AIDS/HIV

Gender

Marital status

Pregnancy, childbirth, and related medical conditions

Race or color

Religion or creed

Genetic testing information: applies to all employers

NEVADA

Nev. Rev. Stat. Ann. §§ 613.310 and following

Law applies to employers with: 15 or more employees

Private employers may not make employment decisions based on:

Age: 40 or older

Ancestry or national origin

Disability: physical or mental

Gender

Pregnancy, childbirth, and related medical conditions

Race or color

Religion or creed

Sexual orientation: includes perceived sexual orientation

Genetic testing information

Additional protected categories:

- opposing unlawful employment practices
- use of service animal

NEW HAMPSHIRE

N.H. Rev. Stat. Ann. §§ 141-H:3, 354-A:2, 354-A:6, 354-A:7

Law applies to employers with: six or more employees

Private employers may not make employment decisions based on:

Age

State Laws Prohibiting Discrimination in Employment (cont'd)

Ancestry or national origin

Disability: physical or mental

Gender

Marital status

Pregnancy, childbirth, and related medical conditions

Race or color

Religion or creed

Sexual orientation

Genetic testing information

NEW JERSEY

N.J. Stat. Ann. §§ 10:5-1, 10:5-4.1, 10:5-5, 10:5-12, 10:5-29.1, 34:6B-1, 43:21-49

Law applies to employers with: One or more employees

Private employers may not make employment decisions based on:

Age: 18 to 70

Ancestry or national origin

Disability: past or present physical or mental

AIDS/HIV

Gender

Marital status

Pregnancy, childbirth, and related medical conditions

Race or color

Religion or creed

Sexual orientation: includes affectional orientation and perceived sexual orientation

Genetic testing information

Additional protected categories:

- gender identity
- atypical heredity cellular or blood trait
- accompanied by service or guide dog
- military service

NEW MEXICO

N.M. Stat. Ann. §§ 24-21-4, 28-1-2, 28-1-7, 50-4A-4

Law applies to employers with: four or more employees

Private employers may not make employment decisions based on:

Age: 40 or older

Ancestry or national origin

Disability: physical or mental

Gender

Marital status: applies to employers with 50 or more employees

Pregnancy, childbirth, and related medical conditions

Race or color

Religion or creed

Sexual orientation: includes perceived sexual orientation; applies to employers with 15 or more employees

Genetic testing information

Additional protected categories:

- gender identity (employers with 15 or more employees)
- serious medical condition
- domestic abuse leave

NEW YORK

N.Y. Exec. Law §§ 292, 296; N.Y. Lab. Law § 201-d

Law applies to employers with: four or more employees

Private employers may not make employment decisions based on:

Age: 18 and over

Ancestry or national origin

Disability: physical or mental

AIDS/HIV

Gender

State Laws Prohibiting Discrimination in Employment (cont'd)

Marital status

Pregnancy, childbirth, and related medical conditions

Race or color

Religion or creed

Sexual orientation: includes perceived sexual orientation

Genetic testing information

Additional protected categories:

- lawful recreational activities when not at work
- military status or service
- observance of Sabbath
- political activities
- use of service dog
- arrest or criminal accusation
- domestic violence victim status

NORTH CAROLINA

N.C. Gen. Stat. §§ 95-28.1, 127B-11, 130A-148, 143-422.2, 168A-5

Law applies to employers with: 15 or more employees

Private employers may not make employment decisions based on:

Age

Ancestry or national origin

Disability: physical or mental

AIDS/HIV

Gender

Race or color

Religion or creed

Genetic testing information

Additional protected categories:

- military status or service
- sickle cell or hemoglobin C trait

NORTH DAKOTA

N.D. Cent. Code §§ 14-02.4-02, 14-02.4-03, 34-01-17

Law applies to employers with: One or more employees

Private employers may not make employment decisions based on:

Age: 40 or older

Ancestry or national origin

Disability: physical or mental

Gender

Marital status

Pregnancy, childbirth, and related medical conditions

Race or color

Religion or creed

Additional protected categories:

- lawful conduct outside of work
- receiving public assistance

OHIO

Ohio Rev. Code Ann. §§ 4111.17, 4112.01, 4112.02

Law applies to employers with: four or more employees

Private employers may not make employment decisions based on:

Age: 40 or older

Ancestry or national origin

Disability: physical or mental

Gender

Pregnancy, childbirth, and related medical conditions

Race or color

Religion or creed

Additional protected categories:

- armed services

State Laws Prohibiting Discrimination in Employment (cont'd)

- caring for a sibling, child, parent, or spouse injured while in the armed services

OKLAHOMA

Okla. Stat. Ann. tit. 25, §§ 1301, 1302; tit. 36, § 3614.2; tit. 40, § 500; tit. 44, § 208

Law applies to employers with: 15 or more employees

Private employers may not make employment decisions based on:

Age: 40 or older

Ancestry or national origin

Disability: physical or mental

Gender:

Pregnancy, childbirth, and related medical conditions: except abortions where the woman is not in "imminent danger of death"

Race or color

Religion or creed

Genetic testing information

Additional protected category: military service

OREGON

Or. Rev. Stat. §§ 25-337, 659A.030, 659A.122 and following, 659A.303

Law applies to employers with: One or more employees

Private employers may not make employment decisions based on:

Age: 18 or older

Ancestry or national origin

Disability: physical or mental (applies to employers with 6 or more employees)

Gender

Marital status

Pregnancy, childbirth, and related medical conditions

Race or color

Religion or creed

Sexual orientation

Genetic testing information

Additional protected categories:

- parent who has medical support order imposed by court
- domestic violence victim status
- refusal to attend an employer-sponsored meeting with the primary purpose of communicating the employer's opinion on religious or political matters
- credit history

PENNSYLVANIA

43 Pa. Cons. Stat. Ann. §§ 954–955

Law applies to employers with: four or more employees

Private employers may not make employment decisions based on:

Age: 40 to 70

Ancestry or national origin

Disability: physical or mental

Gender

Pregnancy, childbirth, and related medical conditions

Race or color

Religion or creed

Additional protected categories:

- relationship or association with disabled person
- GED rather than high school diploma
- use of service animal

State Laws Prohibiting Discrimination in Employment (cont'd)

RHODE ISLAND

R.I. Gen. Laws §§ 12-28-10, 23-6.3-11, 28-5-6, 28-5-7, 28-6-18, 28-6.7-1

Law applies to employers with: four or more employees; one or more employees (gender-based wage discrimination)

Private employers may not make employment decisions based on:

  Age: 40 or older

  Ancestry or national origin

  Disability: physical or mental

  AIDS/HIV

  Gender

  Pregnancy, childbirth, and related medical conditions

  Race or color

  Religion or creed

  Sexual orientation: includes perceived sexual orientation

  Genetic testing information

  Additional protected categories:

  • domestic abuse victim

  • gender identity or expression

SOUTH CAROLINA

S.C. Code §§ 1-13-30, 1-13-80

Law applies to employers with: 15 or more employees

Private employers may not make employment decisions based on:

  Age: 40 or older

  Ancestry or national origin

  Disability: physical or mental

  Gender

  Pregnancy, childbirth, and related medical conditions

  Race or color

  Religion or creed

SOUTH DAKOTA

S.D. Codified Laws Ann. §§ 20-13-1, 20-13-10, 60-2-20, 60-12-15, 62-1-17

Law applies to employers with: One or more employees

Private employers may not make employment decisions based on:

  Ancestry or national origin

  Disability: physical or mental

  Gender

  Race or color

  Religion or creed

  Genetic testing information

  Additional protected category: Preexisting injury

TENNESSEE

Tenn. Code Ann. §§ 4-21-102, 4-21-401 and following, 8-50-103, 50-2-201, 50-2-202

Law applies to employers with: eight or more employees; one or more employees (gender-based wage discrimination)

Private employers may not make employment decisions based on:

  Age: 40 or older

  Ancestry or national origin

  Disability: physical, mental, or visual

  Gender

  Pregnancy, childbirth, and related medical conditions: Refer to chart on State Family and Medical Leave Laws in Chapter 5

  Race or color

  Religion or creed

  Additional protected categories:

  • use of guide dog

State Laws Prohibiting Discrimination in Employment (cont'd)

- volunteer rescue squad worker responding to an emergency

TEXAS

Tex. Lab. Code Ann. §§ 21.002, 21.051, 21.082, 21.101, 21.106, 21.402

Law applies to employers with: 15 or more employees

Private employers may not make employment decisions based on:

Age: 40 or older

Ancestry or national origin

Disability: physical or mental

Gender

Pregnancy, childbirth, and related medical conditions

Race or color

Religion or creed

Genetic testing information

UTAH

Utah Code Ann. §§ 26-45-103, 34A-5-102, 34A-5-106

Law applies to employers with: 15 or more employees

Private employers may not make employment decisions based on:

Age: 40 or older

Ancestry or national origin

Disability: physical or mental

AIDS/HIV

Gender

Pregnancy, childbirth, and related medical conditions

Race or color

Religion or creed

Genetic testing information

VERMONT

Vt. Stat. Ann. tit. 21, § 495, 495d; tit. 18, § 9333

Law applies to employers with: One or more employees

Private employers may not make employment decisions based on:

Age: 18 or older

Ancestry or national origin

Disability: physical, mental, or emotional

AIDS/HIV

Gender

Race or color

Religion or creed

Sexual orientation

Genetic testing information

Additional protected category: Place of birth

VIRGINIA

Va. Code Ann. §§ 2.2-3900, 2.2-3901, 40.1-28.6, 40.1-28.7:1, 51.5-41

Law applies to employers with: One or more employees

Private employers may not make employment decisions based on:

Age

Ancestry or national origin

Disability: physical or mental

Gender

Marital status

Pregnancy, childbirth, and related medical conditions

Race or color

Religion or creed

Genetic testing information

State Laws Prohibiting Discrimination in Employment (cont'd)

WASHINGTON

Wash. Rev. Code Ann. §§ 38.40.110, 49.60.040, 49.60.172, 49.60.180, 49.12.175, 49.44.090, 49.76.120, 49.60.030; Wash. Admin. Code § 162-30-020

Law applies to employers with: eight or more employees; one or more employees (gender-based wage discrimination)

Private employers may not make employment decisions based on:

Age: 40 or older

Ancestry or national origin

Disability: physical, mental, or sensory

AIDS/HIV

Gender

Marital status

Pregnancy, childbirth, and related medical conditions: including breast-feeding

Race or color

Religion or creed

Sexual orientation

Genetic testing information

Additional protected categories:

- hepatitis C infection
- member of state militia
- use of service animal
- gender identity
- domestic violence victim

WEST VIRGINIA

W.Va. Code §§ 5-11-3, 5-11-9, 16-3C-3, 21-5B-1, 21-5B-3

Law applies to employers with: 12 or more employees; one or more employees (gender-based wage discrimination)

Private employers may not make employment decisions based on:

Age: 40 or older

Ancestry or national origin

Disability: physical, mental, or blindness

AIDS/HIV

Gender

Race or color

Religion or creed

WISCONSIN

Wis. Stat. Ann. §§ 111.32 and following

Law applies to employers with: One or more employees

Private employers may not make employment decisions based on:

Age: 40 or older

Ancestry or national origin

Disability: physical or mental

AIDS/HIV

Gender

Marital status

Pregnancy, childbirth, and related medical conditions

Race or color

Religion or creed

Sexual orientation: includes having a history of or being identified with a preference

Genetic testing information

Additional protected categories:

- arrest or conviction record
- member of National Guard/state defense force/military reserve
- declining to attend a meeting or to participate in any communication about religious matters or political matters

State Laws Prohibiting Discrimination in Employment (cont'd)

WYOMING

Wyo. Stat. §§ 27-9-102, 27-9-105, 19-11-104

Law applies to employers with: two or more employees

Private employers may not make employment decisions based on:

  Age: 40 or older

  Ancestry or national origin

  Disability

  Gender

  Pregnancy, childbirth, and related medical conditions

  Race or color

  Religion or creed

  Additional protected category: military service or status

Personnel Basics

Effective management starts with good personnel policies. Fair and sensible policies can help improve performance and productivity while discouraging misconduct. They can also help prevent lawsuits by employees or government agencies, or at least lay the groundwork for a solid defense. Here, you'll find information on:

- at-will employment
- employee handbooks
- antiharassment policies
- communication skills
- performance evaluations
- personnel files, and
- policies to help employees balance work and family obligations.

Even if your job duties don't include creating policies, you'll want to be familiar with the information in this chapter. It will help you understand the legal framework within which you carry out your day-to-day supervisory responsibilities. And it will help you with basic management tasks, such as evaluating performance, communicating with employees, keeping personnel records, and more.

Frequently Asked Questions About Personnel Policies

What is at-will employment?

If employees work at will, the company has the right to fire them at any time, for any reason that is not illegal, and they have the right to quit at any time. In every state but Montana, employees are presumed to work at will unless they have an employment contract limiting the employers' right to fire. (For more on at-will employment, including steps you can take to avoid changing an at-will employee's status inadvertently, see "At-Will Employment," below.)

Does every company need an employee handbook?

No law requires employers to have an employee handbook, but it's a good idea. A handbook tells employees about workplace rules in an efficient, uniform way. Employees will know what is expected of them and what they can expect of the company. And your company will be able to prove that all employees were aware of the rules if a worker later decides to sue. (For suggestions on what to include in an employee handbook, see "Employee Handbooks," below.)

Do we need a sexual harassment policy?

Absolutely. The Supreme Court has held that an effective antiharassment policy, which includes a procedure for making complaints, can provide a defense to certain types of sexual harassment lawsuits. And a good policy can prevent sexual harassment from happening in the first place, by letting workers know what kinds of behavior cross the line, and what action the company will take against a harasser. (To learn more, see "Preventing Sexual Harassment," below.)

Frequently Asked Questions About Personnel Policies (cont'd)

How can I improve my communication with my coworkers and employees?

Here are a few principles you can follow to improve your communication at work: listen first; understand your audience; tailor your message appropriately (for your goals and your audience); deliver your message using the right medium (email is appropriate only for certain things); and speak and write clearly and concisely. (For an explanation of these principles, see "Communicating With Employees Effectively," below.)

How do I avoid legal problems when giving employee performance evaluations?

First, decide on the job requirements and performance goals you want each employee to meet. Create specific criteria that are directly related to the employee's success on the job. Write down the criteria you choose and let your employees know the basis for their evaluations—or, better yet, ask your employees to help you come up with appropriate performance goals. (For more on evaluating your workers, see "Performance Appraisal," below.)

What documents should I keep in an employee's personnel file?

Your company should have a personnel file for each employee. Keep every important job-related document in the file, including job applications, offer letters, employment contracts, benefits and salary information, government forms, performance evaluations, and memos about disciplinary actions. (For more on personnel files, including who has access to them, see "Creating and Maintaining Personnel Files," below.)

What are some of the things I can do to make our workplace more family-friendly without costing the company a lot of money?

There are many policies you can institute in the workplace that can help your employees balance the competing demands of work and family without significant cost to your company, including: flexible work schedules; telecommuting; job sharing or part-time work schedules; flexible spending accounts; and employee assistance programs that provide help finding child care, after-school care, or elder care. (For more on such policies, see "Family-Friendly Workplace Policies," below.)

Personnel Policies and the Law

There are surprisingly few legal requirements when it comes to personnel policies. For example, no law dictates what a company must put in its employee handbook—or even requires companies to have one in the first place. (Although there are a few types of policies you may have to put in writing—such as a notice about family and medical leave or, in some states, a smoking policy—you don't have to put them in an employee handbook.) You aren't legally obligated to evaluate your employees, let alone use a particular form or follow a specified timetable. And although federal and state laws prohibit harassment, employers don't have to adopt a certain type of antiharassment policy.

So why take the time and trouble to develop sound personnel policies? Because they keep the workplace running smoothly and keep your company out of legal trouble. Written policies tell workers what the company expects of them and what they can expect in return. A fair evaluation process helps managers keep track of workers' performance, notice and reward those workers who are doing well, and warn and assist those workers who are getting off track. A good sexual harassment policy will help prevent misconduct in the first place, as well as encourage workers to bring problems to the company's attention so they can be resolved before they get out of control. And policies that help employees balance work and family obligations will decrease distractions and absenteeism, while increasing worker productivity and loyalty.

We can't emphasize the legal benefits of solid personnel policies enough. If your company is unfortunate enough to be sued by a former worker, good personnel policies will be crucial to its defense. Performance evaluations can be used to show that a worker fired for poor performance was given notice and an opportunity to improve before being shown the door. Written policies can help show that a worker fired for misconduct knew the rules and the consequences of violating them. And if your company maintains complete personnel files, it will have all the documents necessary to prove that, for example, a worker generated customer complaints, signed a noncompete agreement, or received written performance warnings.

State Law

Some states have laws that apply to various personnel issues. For example, many states give workers the right to see their personnel files (or, at least, certain documents in those files). (See "State Laws on Access to Personnel Records," at the end of this chapter, for information on your state's law.) In addition, many states have codified the principle of employment at will. This age-old legal doctrine is not written down in any federal statute, but virtually every state (except Montana) recognizes it, and many have incorporated it into their own statutes. Again, your state labor department should be able to tell you whether your state has such a law or any other laws that relate to your personnel policies.

At-Will Employment

Private employers in the United States start off with the law on their side when dealing with employees. Although workers have specified rights in some situations, employers generally have plenty of latitude to make the employment decisions they feel are right for their businesses. This latitude is protected by the legal doctrine of "employment at will," which means just about what it sounds like: At-will employees are free to quit at any time, for any reason, and employers are free to fire them at any time, for any reason, unless that reason is illegal. An illegal reason is one that is discriminatory (see Chapter 3) or retaliatory (see "Retaliation" in Chapter 11), violates a statute or public policy, or is in bad faith (see "Illegal Reasons for Firing Employees" in Chapter 12).

Companies that avoid these no-nos may fire an at-will employee for even the most whimsical or idiosyncratic reasons—for having annoying mannerisms, poor fashion sense, or lousy eating habits, for example. Employers are also free to change the terms of employment—job duties, compensation, or hours, for example—for any reason that isn't illegal. Workers can agree to these changes and continue working or reject the changes and quit. In other words, the employment relationship is voluntary. An employer cannot force its employees to stay forever, and employees cannot require their employers to keep them on indefinitely.

Montana is the only state that does not recognize the doctrine of employment at will. Employers in the Big Sky state must have "good cause" to fire an employee who has completed the company's probationary period or worked for the company for at least six months (if there is no probationary period). (For more on what constitutes good cause, see Chapter 12.)

Legal Limitations on At-Will Employment

The doctrine of employment at will gives employers protection from wrongful termination claims. But this protection is limited in two ways:

- **Employment contract.** The doctrine doesn't apply to employees who have an employment contract, whether written, oral, or implied, that puts some limits on the company's right to fire them. For these employees, the language or nature of the contract usually spells out the terms of employment, including when and for what reasons the employees can be fired. (See "Firing Employees With Employment Contracts" in Chapter 12 for more information.)

- **State or federal laws.** Congress, state legislatures, and judges have carved out several exceptions to the doctrine of employment at will. Generally, as stated above, these exceptions prevent employers from taking any negative action against an employee (including disciplining, demoting, or firing) that is illegal—in bad faith, in violation of public policy, or for a discriminatory or retaliatory reason. (See "Illegal Reasons for Firing Employees" in Chapter 12 for more information.)

Practical Limitations on At-Will Employment

Although the law gives employers the right to fire or change the job of an at-will employee for any reason, no matter how frivolous, employers who lack a sensible basis for employment decisions take legal and practical risks. These risks include:

- **Productivity and morale problems.** If you fire or discipline a worker without a good reason, the rest of the workforce will be confused and uneasy. Employees who believe they might be fired or demoted even if they are doing a good job have less incentive to follow performance standards and other rules of the workplace.
- **Recruiting and hiring difficulties.** Once word gets out that an employer fires or disciplines employees without good reason, new employees will be harder to find. After all, why should an employee take a job where he or she could get fired at any time if another employer offers a little job security or at least a fair shake?
- **Lawsuits.** An employee who has been treated unfairly is more motivated to sue. And despite the doctrine of employment at will, most jurors have been or are employees and will empathize with the fired worker. Juries find ways to punish an employer they perceive to be unfair, arbitrary, or callous. And even if the employee ultimately loses the lawsuit, the employer will spend precious time and money fighting it in court.

Because of this, many employers fire or demote workers only for legitimate business reasons, which other workers (and a judge or jury, if it comes to that) will understand. However, smart employers also hang on to their at-will rights, just in case. Even if your company generally fires only for cause, maintaining the right to fire at will can provide a valuable legal theory to fall back on if your company ever has to defend its actions in court.

Preserving Your At-Will Rights

If you want to keep your company's right to fire and discipline employees on its own terms, don't make promises or adopt policies that restrict that right. For example, don't state that employees will only be fired for certain reasons or that employees will have a job as long as they do good work. Despite your good intentions, a disgruntled former employee can use these statements as evidence of an employment contract that eliminates employment at will.

Here are some steps you can take to protect your company's right to fire and discipline employees at will:

- **State that employment is at will.** In written employment policies, including the employee handbook or personnel manual, state clearly that employment at your company is at will and explain what this means.
- **Ask employees to sign an at-will agreement.** Consider asking employees to sign a simple form or offer letter acknowledging that their employment is at will. A

worker who has signed such a form will have a difficult time refuting it later.

• **Don't promise continued employment.** If you tell employees that their jobs are secure, that they will not be fired without good cause, or even that the company has never had to fire a worker, you risk creating an expectation that they will not be fired. Avoid these types of comments; they are particularly common when interviewing potential employees and giving performance reviews.

• **Train managers.** With few exceptions, the actions and statements of company managers will be legally attributable to your company. If your job includes training other managers, make sure they understand company policies and procedures, especially regarding discipline, performance reviews, and employment at will. If managers make any statements or take any actions contrary to these policies—like promising that workers won't be fired—

Lessons From the Real World

Annunzio Ferraro worked as a security guard at the Hyatt hotel in Milwaukee. His job application form, which he signed, said that his employment could be terminated at any time. However, Hyatt's employment manual stated that employees would only be fired for just cause and outlined a progressive discipline policy under which employees would generally receive at least two prior warnings for similar offenses before getting fired. The manual allowed the company to fire an employee immediately for a "severe rule violation."

Ferraro was fired for physically assaulting a hotel guest. Amazingly, he then sued for wrongful termination, claiming that the hotel breached an implied employment contract by firing him without the two prior warnings promised in its disciplinary policy.

The Wisconsin Supreme Court agreed with Ferraro on one important issue: The court found that Hyatt's disciplinary policy created an implied contract promising that Ferraro would be fired only for just cause.

However, the court found that Ferraro's assault on a hotel guest constituted a "severe rule violation" and gave the hotel ample cause for termination, particularly since it was not Ferraro's first offense. Ferraro had previously hit an intoxicated guest, raised his voice in argument with a guest, and been accused of harassing the hotel's female employees, all in the space of less than a year. Faced with this less-than-stellar record, the court threw out a jury's verdict in Ferraro's favor, finding that no jury could reasonably believe Hyatt had breached Ferraro's implied employment contract.

Ferraro v. Koelsch et al., 368 N.W.2d 666 (Wis. 1985).

the company just may lose its at-will rights.

- **Keep disciplinary options open.** If your company has a progressive discipline policy, make sure it includes clear language preserving the right to fire employees at will. If the policy lists offenses for which firing is appropriate, it should state that the list is not exhaustive and that the company reserves the right to fire for any reason.

- **Don't refer to employees as "permanent."** Many employers have an initial probationary or temporary period for new employees, during which the company is free to fire the worker. Workers who survive this period are called permanent employees, entitled to benefits and so forth. To some courts, this language implies that an employee who becomes permanent can be fired only for good cause. If your company uses a probation period and you are responsible for writing company policies, make clear that the company retains the right to fire at will once the probationary period is over.

Employee Handbooks

Many companies—especially smaller businesses—get along fine without any written employment policies. But at some point, particularly as your company grows, it makes good business sense to create an employee handbook. Although compiling the policies will take some effort, your company will save time, headaches, and possibly legal fees in the long run.

The benefits of having an employee handbook are many. Every employee will receive the same, consistent information about workplace rules, benefit policies, company procedures, and other important issues. Employees will know what is expected of them and what they can expect from your company, particularly in the areas of performance, attendance, and discipline. The handbook can tell workers a bit about the history of the business and the company's structure and values. And the handbook will provide a measure of legal protection if an employee or former employee decides to sue.

What to Include in an Employee Handbook

Effective employee handbooks vary widely in size, style, and content. Some large corporations produce handbooks that come in multiple volumes and cover every possible aspect of the business. Smaller companies might have a more limited handbook that covers only the basics and could probably fit into a pamphlet.

No matter which approach your company chooses, its handbook should incorporate the company's style and values. A handbook doesn't have to be written in legalese to be effective. In fact, the best policies are written in plain English. A handbook should communicate policies to workers in language they will understand.

Here are some topics to consider covering in a handbook. If you are assigned the responsibility for creating, updating, or troubleshooting your company's handbook, you can use this list as a starting point. For more detailed information and sample policies that you can modify, cut, and paste for use in your company, see *Create Your Own Employee Handbook,* by Lisa Guerin and Amy DelPo (Nolo).

- **Information about the company.** If your company has an organizational chart, mission statement, or written history, you can include it here.
- **At-will statement.** If your company is an "at-will" employer, you should include a statement to that effect in the handbook. (See "At-Will Employment," above, for more information.)
- **Hiring rules.** Explain any rules or policies the company follows when hiring workers, including job posting, affirmative action or antidiscrimination policies, referral bonuses, and any testing required of new workers or applicants.
- **Pay.** Set out the rules on overtime, show up or on-call time, wage garnishments, and so on. If the company has policies on expense reimbursements and pay advances, include them as well. And let workers know when they will be paid and according to what formula (for example, by commission or piece rate).
- **Hours.** Set the rules on rest breaks and meal breaks, attendance policies, schedules, flextime or other flexible scheduling arrangements, and time cards, if applicable. (For more information on compensation and hours, see Chapter 2.)

- **Leave.** If your company offers sick leave, vacation time, parental leave, pregnancy or disability leave, leave for civic duties, sabbaticals, bereavement leave, or other time off, explain those policies here. (You can find information on leave policies in Chapter 5.)
- **Performance.** If your company gives performance evaluations, explain the process here. (See "Performance Appraisal," below, for more information.)
- **Benefits.** Explain the benefits available to employees, including health insurance, dental and vision coverage, life insurance, disability insurance, pensions or other retirement plans, profit sharing, and the like.
- **Discrimination and harassment.** Include a statement that discrimination and harassment violate company policies and will not be tolerated. State that immediate action will be taken against wrongdoers. (For more on discrimination and sexual harassment, see "Preventing Sexual Harassment," below, and Chapter 3.)
- **Complaints and investigations.** Describe how employees can report harassment or other misconduct. Tell employees how to make complaints, describe what steps the company will take to investigate, and state that retaliation will not be allowed against a worker who complains in good faith. Encourage them to report any concerns immediately. (For more on investigations, see "Investigating Complaints" in Chapter 11.)
- **Health and safety.** Detail any safety-related workplace rules (for example,

that hard hats must be worn in certain areas) and any special health and safety issues that apply to your company. And encourage workers to bring health and safety concerns to management for resolution. (For more on health and safety issues, see Chapter 7.)

- **Violence.** State clearly that violence and threats of violence will be taken seriously. Explain how employees can report threats and violent incidents, and lay out your company's safety plan in case of violence. (For more on violence, see "Workplace Violence" in Chapter 11.)

- **Privacy.** If your company monitors workers' phone calls, voice mail, email messages, or Internet use, or if it conducts any workplace search or surveillance, let workers know. (For more about privacy issues in the workplace, see Chapter 6.)

- **Use of company property.** Be clear about employee use of computer equipment, email, and the Internet. You should also cover use of company cars, communications equipment (phones and cell phones, for example), copiers, and so on.

- **Workplace conduct.** Include not only company standards of conduct (for example, no fighting or no conflicts of interest) but also policies on grooming, uniforms, and bringing children (or pets) to work.

- **Discipline.** If your company has a progressive discipline policy, describe it here. You can also describe what infractions constitute grounds for termination, but be sure to keep management's

options open. (Disciplinary policies are covered in "Disciplining Workers" in Chapter 11.)

- **Firing.** Detail any layoff and termination policies, including provisions regarding severance, recall rights, and references. (Firing and layoffs are covered in Chapters 12 and 13.)

Don't Create Obligations That Will Haunt Your Company Later

Some courts—and employees—interpret the language in employee handbooks as contracts that create binding obligations on employers. If you include any unconditional promises in the employee handbook, there's a very real possibility that employees or former employees might try to enforce those promises in court. Here are some of the most common trouble spots:

- **Promises of continued employment.** Don't put language in the handbook that promises employees a job as long as they follow company rules. A court might interpret this as a contract of employment, guaranteeing that employees will not be fired without good cause. State in the handbook that your company reserves the right to terminate employees for reasons not stated in the handbook or for no reason at all. Even though the company may never have to rely on this language to provide a legal defense to a wrongful termination claim, at least employees will know where they stand. (See "At-Will Employment," above, for more details.)

- **Conduct not covered by the handbook.** Of course, no handbook can cover every possible workplace situation. It's best to make this clear to employees by saying so in the handbook. Otherwise, employees may argue that any action the company takes that goes beyond what's explicitly set forth in the handbook is unfair.

- **Progressive discipline.** Many employers follow some form of "progressive discipline" for performance problems or less serious forms of misconduct (attendance problems, difficulties getting along with coworkers, or missing deadlines, for example). Often, discipline starts with informal coaching, then a verbal warning, followed by a written warning, then termination. Whatever system your company uses, don't obligate managers to follow a particular disciplinary pattern for every employee in every circumstance. It's better to leave the company's options open, to make sure it can fire workers, if necessary, without facing a legal challenge. (See "Disciplining Workers" in Chapter 11 for more information.)

- **Right to change the handbook.** You cannot be sure that the employment policies you come up with today will stand the test of time. Your company might later decide to change or get rid of a policy or to branch out into other endeavors that make additional policies necessary. Either way, the handbook should state that the company reserves the right to change the policies at any time, for any reason. This will give your

company the necessary leeway to keep its policies in tune with its business.

Once you've created a comprehensive employee handbook, set aside time to review and update it regularly as company policies and procedures change. An outdated handbook doesn't do the company or its employees any good; it might even create confusion or unwanted legal obligations. And a periodic handbook review will help you identify changes you want—or need—to make to company policies.

Preventing Sexual Harassment

Private employers have a responsibility to provide a workplace that is free of sexual harassment. This is a legal obligation, but it also makes good business sense. Companies that allow sexual harassment to flourish will pay a high price in terms of poor employee morale, low productivity, and lawsuits.

As a manager, you are on the front lines when it comes to avoiding, preventing, and reporting harassment. You also have the legal authority to act on behalf of your company, which means that your failure to act appropriately can get the company in a lot of trouble. If you harass employees yourself, your company will be legally responsible for your actions. And if employees report harassment to you or you otherwise become aware that harassment is taking place, your company will be on the hook, even if you choose to look the other way. That's why it's so important to learn what harassment is and what you should do if it takes place.

Sexual Harassment Defined

Sexual harassment is any unwelcome sexual advance or conduct on the job that creates an intimidating, hostile, or offensive working environment. Any conduct of a sexual nature that makes an employee uncomfortable has the potential to be sexual harassment. Sexual harassment can also include harassment that is not sexual in nature but is based on one's gender. This type of harassment typically occurs when women enter workplaces that have been traditionally male-dominated. For example, a woman who joins an all-male construction crew might find sexist graffiti on her locker, her car defaced, or that her male coworkers won't back her up on dangerous work tasks. For examples of behavior that might qualify as sexual harassment, see "Gender, Pregnancy, and Sexual Harassment" in Chapter 3.

Strategies for Prevention

There are a number of steps that a company can take to reduce the risk of sexual harassment:

- **Adopt a clear sexual harassment policy.** In its employee handbook, your company should include a clear policy prohibiting sexual harassment. The policy should define sexual harassment; state in no uncertain terms that sexual harassment will not be tolerated; warn that the company will discipline or fire any wrongdoers; set out a clear procedure for filing sexual harassment complaints; state that complaints will be investigated fully; and assert that the company will not tolerate retaliation against anyone who complains about harassment.

- **Train employees.** Once a year, your company should require employees to attend sexual harassment training. These sessions should teach employees what sexual harassment is, explain that employees have a right to a workplace free of sexual harassment, review the company's complaint procedure, and encourage employees to come forward with concerns.

- **Train supervisors and managers.** At least once a year, your company should train supervisors and managers in a separate session. (A few states, including California, now require such trainings, at least for certain employers.) The sessions should educate managers and supervisors about sexual harassment and explain how to deal with complaints they receive or problems they observe.

- **Monitor your workplace.** You and other managers should walk the floor periodically. Talk to employees about the work environment. Ask for their input. Look around the workplace itself. Do you see any offensive posters or notes? Keep the lines of communication open.

- **Take all complaints seriously.** If someone complains about sexual harassment, immediately follow your company's reporting procedure. Prompt and thorough investigation can help your company defend against harassment lawsuits. If the complaint turns out to be valid, the company's response should be swift and effective. (For more information, see "Investigating Complaints" in Chapter 11.)

Lessons From the Real World

A male employee successfully sued his employer for sexual harassment because his coworkers made fun of him for not being "manly" enough.

Antonio Sanchez endured a lot of abuse for his less-than-macho ways. Coworkers referred to him as "she" and "her," told him that he walked and carried his tray "like a woman," made derisive comments because he did not have sex with a female friend, and taunted him for behaving like a woman.

Understandably, this barrage of verbal abuse upset and angered Sanchez. He complained to the general manager, an assistant manager, and the human resources director, but got no relief.

Eventually he sued, arguing that the abuse amounted to illegal sexual harassment. The court agreed. It said that Sanchez's coworkers abused him because he did not conform to their gender-based stereotypes. This was sexual harassment, plain and simple, and the employer had a legal obligation to stop the harassment once it knew about it.

Nichols v. Azteca Restaurant Enterprises, Inc., 264 F.3d 864 (9th Cir. 2001).

Communicating With Employees Effectively

More than any other aspect of successful management and leadership, good communication skills can have an enormously positive impact on your workforce. On the flip side, few things are as damaging to a workplace as poor communication. There are countless advantages to mastering good communication skills. Effective communication enhances your ability to:

- solve problems (and perhaps even anticipate them)
- supervise others successfully
- develop solid work relationships
- create a clear and compelling vision for your team (and your company)
- manage workflow between individuals and groups
- make well-informed decisions
- manage good performance, and
- eliminate poor performance.

Most of us believe that we know what we mean before we say something. Why, then, do so many people consistently misunderstand us and get what we say wrong? Good communication is multifaceted. To communicate effectively, you need to get your point across in a way that whomever you're talking to can truly understand. Here are a few guiding principles to help you make yourself heard:

- listen first
- understand your audience
- tailor your message appropriately (for your goals and your audience)

- deliver your message using the right medium, and
- speak and write well.

Listen

Listening to others is probably the most overlooked aspect of good communication in the workplace. In their haste to make their own points, direct others, provide input, or just get things done, many managers issue declarative statements and pay little attention to the effect they have on those who hear them. Your ability to really listen, to understand what someone else is saying, and to incorporate that information into whatever you are doing, directly improves your skills and abilities as a manager.

The easiest way to build your listening skills is in a one-on-one environment. As you go about communicating something to an employee or coworker, stop and ask if he or she is clear on what you are saying. As he or she answers, listen closely and then repeat the answer back to the speaker, paraphrasing. Then ask, "Am I understanding you correctly?" Too often, managers ask questions and, as those questions are being answered, are already preparing their responses. By knowing that you will have to paraphrase the answer you hear back to the speaker, you can train yourself to really listen to what is being said.

Depending on your responsibilities as a manager, you may have to communicate with small and large groups in addition to individuals. Yet the importance of listening to your audience remains. How many times have you been sitting in a meeting, listening to a presentation, and noticed that your mind has wandered—perhaps sinking you into such boredom that you might even shut your eyes? If the speaker was paying close attention and listening to the cues of the audience, he or she would have known to either shorten the presentation or punch it up somehow to recapture the audience. When you are the speaker in such a situation, always stay alert to how your information is being received. Check in with your audience frequently for questions (you're really testing to see if they are still listening!) and shorten or modify your material if you see that you are losing people.

Understand Your Audience

Another common mistake in workplace communication is failing to consider whom you are speaking to and how that listener best receives information. Do not assume that everyone absorbs information like you do: Although it may be more comfortable for you to fall back on what works best for you, chances are that what works for you won't work for everyone.

In one-on-one communication, especially with employees you manage, simply ask the listener how he or she would prefer to hear things. Some employees may wish to receive a written email rather than a phone call or voicemail if you are providing directives or instructions. Others may wish to have a back-and-forth conversation. Some employees may require time to process or think about issues before they discuss them. For such folks, you'll want to set up meetings thoughtfully and provide an agenda in advance so that they know what you are expecting of them.

When it comes to providing criticism or negative feedback, you should be particularly sensitive to the needs of individual employees. For instance, it is never appropriate to criticize someone's work in a group setting. Some people need to be taken aside, have the issue pointed out to them, and then participate in deciding how to correct the issue. Others may want to be told what is wrong and how they could do it better, directly and forthrightly. By spending time with your team and learning how each of them hears things best, you will be much more effective in the long run.

In larger audiences, know whom you are talking to and how well they understand the material being presented. We have all heard the old adage that newspaper articles are written at the sixth-grade level, so that they are understood by all. While this guideline may work for the public as a whole, if you present a sixth-grade level presentation to the Board of Directors of your company, you'll probably be searching for a new job soon. Your audience will greatly appreciate being engaged at the appropriate level of their knowledge and interests.

Tailor Your Message Appropriately

Once you know your audience, put that information to work. There are many ways to tailor a message; knowing what you want to accomplish is key to getting the message across effectively. You should consider not only your audience, but also the goal of your communication: what you want to accomplish.

If you need to deliver the same information to a variety of different people, you may need to tailor your message differently depending on your goal for communicating with each group. For example, imagine that you are a manager in a small company that is about to be sold to a larger company. You manage a very diverse group of employees, from warehouse personnel to freelance writers. You know that the information will affect your reports differently, so you should prepare the appropriate communication for each group you will face. When delivering the news to the freelance writers, you might, for example, focus more on the future plans of the new company and how the work they are currently doing will be folded into those plans. For the warehouse staff, however, you might focus on their employment status in particular, letting them know what will likely happen to their positions.

Deliver Your Message Using the Right Medium

Another key to effective communications at work is to deliver your message using the right medium of communication, whether in a conversation, an email, a meeting, or a written memo.

While the advent of email has been a huge boon to efficiency and consistency, email can be very dangerous when used to avoid difficult conversations or to vent frustrations. Email is appropriate for getting your simple questions answered quickly, making large group announcements, or documenting a conversation after the fact. But, unfortunately, email is often misused, allowing people who are uncomfortable with direct confrontation to raise difficult subjects while avoiding the reactions they provoke. This can be terribly destructive to effective communication at work because it can feel inappropriate or even cruel to the recipient. Also, when you send an email, you have no way of knowing how the recipient is interpreting your communication, which can cause needless and sometimes harmful misunderstandings.

Given the obvious limitations of email, even if it is your preferred method of communicating with employees, you must consider all of the possible ways you can deliver information at work and choose the most appropriate and effective medium. Consider the following:

- **Email.** As mentioned above, email is a great tool to update people, pass along materials, make brief announcements, provide status reports, ask and answer simple questions, and the like. It is not appropriate for many kinds of communication.

- **Voicemail.** A bit more personal than email, voicemail allows you to convey meaning with your tone of voice. It is appropriate for leaving a short instruction or requesting an in-person conversation or meeting. Larger companies often use voicemail to send out a "blast message," or company announcement, to employees. This allows everyone to hear the same message but does not allow two-way communication.

- **One-on-one conversations.** These are in-person meetings (or telephone conversations if the person you are speaking to is at another location). Conversation is a terrific medium for reviewing any performance issues, getting updated on work in progress, setting goals, and discussing how your employee is doing overall. It also provides direct and immediate feedback, the key to strong two-way communication.

- **Small group meetings.** This medium is best for making group decisions, gathering input from multiple sources, educating or training people, brainstorming ideas, and so on. A small group meeting should still involve two-way communication, allowing discussions, questions, and feedback.

- **Large group meetings.** This medium is best for bringing a larger number of people up to speed on specific issues in the same way at the same time. The larger the group, the more difficult it will be to engage in two-way communication, collect feedback, or make decisions.

- **Informal gatherings or hallway conversations.** Take advantage of these opportunities to get to know your team (and their communication preferences) better outside the work environment. Be careful not to hand out or take on any action items during such communication, as assignments can be quickly forgotten.

The key point here is to match your medium or vehicle for communication with the message. Don't use a large group meeting to be critical of an employee, but do use it to celebrate someone's accomplishments. Don't use email to blow off steam if you're angry, but do use it to appropriately share information on a specific issue. And, most importantly, don't hide behind passive communication vehicles like email or voice-mail when you really need to have a direct, courageous conversation with someone.

Speak and Write Well

Finally, put some time and care into your written and spoken communication. Be clear and concise. Use words correctly. Check for typos and misspellings, even in internal emails, and especially in external presentations, memos, or correspondence. Such carelessness in a business setting is distracting and looks unprofessional.

Beyond these negatives, there are many more positive reasons why you should put care and thought into all your communications in the workplace:

- You appear more professional and knowledgeable.
- You garner credibility and respect.
- You will convey your point without distraction.
- You can be much more compelling when making an argument.
- You can effectively model good communication practices for employees and coworkers.

Improving your communication skills will not only help you in your current workplace, but is also an investment in your own professional development. There are countless books and training courses available on how to write more clearly, improve your presentation skills, and the like. A few places for more information include the American Management Association, online at www.amanet.org, which provides training and seminars on communication skills; and the book *Harvard Business Review on Effective Communications,* by Ralph G. Nichols, et al.

Performance Appraisal

Managers who routinely review employee performance and conduct regular employee evaluations reap tremendous benefits. The evaluation process nips a lot of employment problems in the bud. Your reports will know what you expect of them; will receive feedback, praise, and criticism of their work; and will have notice of any shortfalls in their performance or conduct. You can recognize and reward good employees and identify and coach workers who are having trouble. And the communication involved in any good evaluation process ensures that you will stay in tune with the needs and concerns of the workers you supervise

Performance evaluations can also keep your company out of legal trouble. They help you track and document employee problems. If you ever need to fire or discipline a worker, you will have written proof that you gave the employee notice and a chance to correct the problem, which will go a long way toward convincing a jury or judge that you acted fairly. This section provides an overview of the performance appraisal process; for more detailed information and forms you can use in your workplace, see *The Performance Appraisal Handbook,* by Amy DelPo (Nolo).

Create Job Requirements and Performance Goals

Before you can accurately evaluate an employee's performance, you need some way to measure that performance. For each employee in a particular position, you will need to come up with performance objectives: job requirements and performance goals.

Job requirements describe what you want a worker in a particular job to accomplish and how you want the job done. These requirements apply across the board, to every worker who holds the same position. For example, a job requirement for a salesperson might be to make $40,000 in sales per quarter; for a customer service representative, to answer each call cheerfully; for a delivery driver, to have a missed delivery rate of 5% or less. Make sure requirements are achievable and directly related to the employee's job. If other managers supervise some employees who hold the same position, work together to come up with requirements all of you will use.

Performance goals should be tailored to each employee; they will depend on the individual worker's strengths and weaknesses. For example, a goal for a graphic artist might be learning a new software design program;

for an accounting professional, a goal might be to take the exam to become a Certified Public Accountant. Your workers can help you figure out what reasonable goals should be.

Once you have defined the requirements and goals for each position and worker, write them down and hand them out to your reports. This will let employees know what you expect and what they will have to achieve during the year to receive a positive evaluation.

Keep Track of Employee Performance

Throughout the year, track the performance of each employee. Keep a performance log for each worker, either on your computer or on paper. Note memorable incidents or projects involving that worker, whether good or bad. For example, you might note that a worker was absent without calling in, worked over-time to complete an important project, or participated in a community outreach program on behalf of the company.

If an employee does an especially wonderful job on a project or really fouls something up, consider giving immediate feedback. Orally or in writing, let the employee know that you noticed and appreciate the extra effort (or that you are concerned about the employee's performance). If you choose to give this kind of feedback orally, make a written note of the conversation for the employee's personnel file.

Conduct Performance Evaluations

At least once a year, formally evaluate the worker both by writing a performance evaluation and by meeting with the worker to discuss the evaluation. First, gather and review all of the documents and records relating to the employee's performance, productivity, and behavior. Review your performance log for the employee and the employee's personnel file. You might also want to take a look at other company records relating to the worker, including sales records, call reports, productivity records, time cards, budget reports, and the like.

Once you have reviewed these records and gathered your thoughts about the employee's work, write the evaluation (or, if you will solicit input from other managers, ask each of them to complete an evaluation and compile them). Although a performance evaluation can take many forms, it should include:

- each requirement or goal you set for that worker and that job
- your conclusion as to whether the employee met the requirement or goal, and
- the reasons that support your conclusion.

Many companies use some kind of numerical scale or grading system to indicate how well the employee did on each goal or requirement. If yours is one of them, you should include these ratings in your evaluation. You should also leave space on the form for the employee's comments and your notes on your meeting with the employee.

When you have finished writing the evaluation, set up a meeting to discuss it with the employee. Remember, this is likely to be one of the most important meetings you have with that worker all year so be sure to schedule enough time to discuss each issue thoroughly.

At the meeting, let the worker know what you think he or she did well and what he or she needs to improve. Using your evaluation as a guide, explain your conclusions about each requirement and goal. Listen carefully to the worker's comments, and ask the worker to write them down on the evaluation form. Take notes on the meeting and include those notes on the form.

Tips for Performance Appraisal

Giving evaluations can be difficult. A worker who is criticized might react defensively. And, sometimes, no one understands what merits a positive evaluation. If workers feel that you take it easy on some of them while coming down hard on others, resentment will build. Avoid problems by following these rules:

- **Be specific.** When you set requirements and goals for your workers, spell out exactly what they will have to do to achieve them. For example, don't say "work harder" or "improve quality." Instead, say "increase sales by 20 percent over last year" or "make three or fewer errors per day in data input." Similarly, when you evaluate a worker, give specific examples of what the employee did to achieve—or fall short of—the requirement or goal.
- **Give deadlines.** If you want to see improvement, give the worker a timeline for turning things around. If you expect something to be done by a certain date, say so.
- **Be realistic.** If you set unrealistic or impossible requirements and goals,

everyone will be disheartened. They will have little incentive to do their best if they know they will still fall short. Don't make your requirements too easy to achieve, but do take into account the realities of your workplace.

- **Be honest.** If you avoid telling a worker of performance problems, the worker won't know which areas need improvement. Be sure to give the bad news, even if it is uncomfortable.

- **Be complete.** Write your evaluation so that an outsider reading it would be able to understand exactly what happened and why. Remember, the evaluation could potentially become evidence in a lawsuit, should the employee ever sue. If it does become evidence, you will want the judge and jury to see why you rated the employee as you did.

- **Evaluate performance, not personality.** Focus on how well (or poorly) the worker did the job, not on the worker's personal characteristics or traits. Don't say, "You are angry and emotional." Instead, focus on the workplace conduct that is the problem. For example, you might write "You have been insubordinate to your supervisor twice in the past six months. This behavior is unacceptable and must stop."

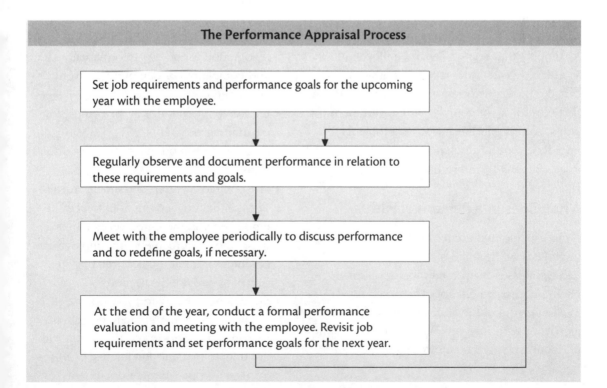

The Performance Appraisal Process

Set job requirements and performance goals for the upcoming year with the employee.

Regularly observe and document performance in relation to these requirements and goals.

Meet with the employee periodically to discuss performance and to redefine goals, if necessary.

At the end of the year, conduct a formal performance evaluation and meeting with the employee. Revisit job requirements and set performance goals for the next year.

- **Listen to your employees.** The evaluation process will seem fairer to workers if they have an opportunity to express their concerns, too. Ask employees what they enjoy about their jobs and working at the company. Also ask about any concerns or problems each employee has. You'll gain valuable information, and the employee will feel like a real participant in the process. In rare cases, you might even learn something that could change your evaluation.

Creating and Maintaining Personnel Files

Paperwork can be a bore, but setting up and maintaining personnel files will pay off in the long run. You will have all the important documents that relate to each employee in one place, easily accessible when it's time to make decisions on promotions or layoffs, file tax returns, or comply with government audits. And if you have to fire a problem employee, careful documentation can protect your company from legal trouble.

What Goes in a Personnel File

Begin a personnel file for each of your employees on the date of hire. (If you are a manager or supervisor, talk to your human resources department about who should set up the personnel file and whether you should keep your own files on your reports or submit all documents to the employee's main file.)

All important job-related documents should go in the file, including:

- the employee's job application and/or résumé
- letters of reference provided by or for the employee or notes from your conversations with references
- the offer letter
- IRS Form W-4: *Employee's Withholding Allowance Certificate*
- forms relating to the employee's benefits
- forms providing next of kin and emergency contacts for the employee
- a signed acknowledgment that the employee received and read the employee handbook
- performance evaluations
- other documents relating to the employee's performance (such as written warnings, memos on disciplinary actions, recognition for good performance, and complaints or compliments from customers)
- records of attendance at, or completion of, training programs
- records of promotions, pay raises, and transfers
- any contract, written agreement, receipt, or other acknowledgment between the employee and the employer (such as a noncompete agreement, an employment contract, or an agreement relating to a company-provided car), and
- documents relating to the worker's departure from the company (such as reasons why the worker was fired or let go, unemployment documents, COBRA forms, and other benefit documents).

Although an employee's personnel file should contain every important job-related document, don't go overboard. In many states, employees have the right to view their personnel files (or at least certain items, such as contracts or other documents they have signed). In the worst-case scenario, that file may turn into evidence in a lawsuit brought by a disgruntled former employee. Indiscreet entries that do not directly relate to an employee's job performance and qualifications—like references to an employee's private life or political beliefs; unsubstantiated criticisms; or comments about an employee's race, sex, or religion—will come back to haunt your company. A good rule of thumb: Don't put anything in a personnel file that you would not want a jury to see.

What Does Not Go in a Personnel File

Although most employment-related documents should be kept in a worker's personnel file, there are a couple of exceptions to this rule. First, medical records should not go in a worker's personnel file. If a worker has a disability, the employer is legally required to keep all of the worker's medical records in a separate file—and limit access only to a very few people. A similar rule applies to records of genetic information (under the Genetic Information Nondiscrimination Act, as explained in Chapter 3) and family and medical leave records (under the Family and Medical Leave Act, covered in Chapter 5). The best practice is to segregate all medical information into a separate file for each

worker, whether or not it fits squarely within the definition provided by one of these laws.

Second, Form I-9, the form you must complete for each employee verifying eligibility to work in this country, should be kept in a separate file. The U.S. Citizenship and Immigration Service (USCIS), the agency that replaced the INS, is entitled to inspect these forms. If you keep these forms in a worker's personnel file, the USCIS will be looking at all those other documents as well. Not only does this compromise workers' privacy, but it also might open your company up to additional questions and investigation.

How to Maintain a Personnel File

Establish a time to periodically review each employee's personnel file, perhaps when you conduct the employee's evaluation. During this review, consider whether the documents in the file are accurate, up to date, and complete. Some questions to consider:

- Does the file reflect all of the employee's raises, promotions, and commendations?
- Does the file contain every written evaluation of the employee?
- Does the file show every warning or other disciplinary action taken against the employee?
- If company policy provides that written warnings or other records of discipline will be removed from an employee's file after a certain period, have they been removed?
- If the employee was on a performance improvement plan, a probationary or training period, or other temporary

status, has it ended? Has the file been updated to reflect the employee's current status?

- If the employee handbook has been updated since the employee started work, does the file contain a receipt or acknowledgment for the most recent version?
- Does the file contain current versions of every contract or other agreement between the company and the employee?

Once you get a regular filing system in place (for example, to make sure every new document a worker signs goes in the personnel file), these annual reviews should only take a few minutes.

Who May See Personnel Files

Generally, personnel files should be treated as private records belonging to the company and its employees. Obviously, not everyone in the company should be allowed to rummage through the performance evaluations, salaries, and job applications of employees. But, some employees may have a legitimate need to view the information in a personnel file. For example, you or another manager may need to review performance evaluations to decide whether to promote an employee, or the human resources manager may need to review an employee's salary information to decide what to pay a new hire in the same position.

Treat personnel files like any other private company records: Keep them confidential and store them in a locked cabinet. Allow only those with legitimate business reasons to have access to the files. For example, a reasonable policy might give only the human resources manager, the individual employee's manager, and the employee the right to see the employee's file. This will protect employees' privacy and limit opportunities for inappropriate documents to find their way into the files.

Employees' Rights to See Their Own Personnel Files

Most states give employees some right to view the contents of their own personnel files. This right may be limited, however. In some states, employers have to provide workers with copies of certain documents in their files. In others, the employee may only review the file in person, sometimes in the presence of a company representative. And in some states, the company can withhold certain documents that might compromise another person's privacy, such as letters of reference or investigation reports that include witness statements. To find out your state's rules, see "State Laws on Access to Personnel Records," at the end of this chapter.

Even if your state does not expressly allow employees to inspect their personnel files, however, it's a sensible policy to allow them to do so, or at least to inform them about documents that are in their files. If you are planning to take action against an employee based on material in the personnel file—a complaint or documented performance problems, for example—let the employee know. That way, the employee will have a chance to explain or discuss the problem and an opportunity to improve. An employee who finds negative information in a file only after being fired is likely to believe, rightly or wrongly, that those documents were created after the fact.

Family-Friendly Workplace Policies

In addition to the personnel policies that you must adopt, an increasing number of companies today are choosing to adopt policies that help their employees to meet the competing demands of work and family.

Family-Friendly Policies Defined

For a variety of reasons, a growing number of companies today are adopting personnel policies that help their employees balance work and family obligations. Such policies are often referred to as "family-friendly policies," yet they do not benefit only employees with young children. In fact, employees with elderly parents or other relatives for whom they must care or employees who have their own health or personal needs that can interfere with work can benefit from such policies as well.

Adopting family-friendly policies can be an inexpensive yet effective way to attract workers to your company these days, when the costs of employee benefits can be astronomical. You may not think of allowing workers more flexibility with their schedules or providing workers help to identify child or elder care services, for example, as traditional

employment benefits. Yet such policies can be valuable and inexpensive tools to attract the best workers, especially if your company may not be able to afford to pay for the most comprehensive health insurance plan for workers or to make large matching contributions to their 401(k)s.

In addition, your company can reap cost savings by adopting policies that let employees deal with the family or other matters that often distract or interrupt their work. Family-friendly policies can increase loyalty, job satisfaction, and productivity, while reducing absenteeism, turnover, and the associated costs of finding and training new workers. Global consulting company Deloitte & Touche estimated that offering flexible work arrangements to 30,000 employees in the U.S. helped save $41.5 million in turnover and affiliated costs in 2003, while pharmaceutical company Merck & Co. estimated that it cost $38,000 to give an average employee a six-month parental leave with partial pay and benefits, as compared to $50,000 to replace the employee. (Elyane Robertson Demby, "Do Your Family-Friendly Programs Make Cents?" *HR Magazine*, January 2004.)

Below are some of the types of family-friendly policies that companies around the nation are implementing. (Note that these are just a handful of potential policies: The possibilities are limited only by the imaginations of your company's policymakers.)

- **Flexible work schedules.** This means allowing employees to work full time, yet outside of normal business hours, whether it be 7:00 a.m. to 3:00 p.m., ten hours for four days a week, or a varying schedule each day. It can also mean the flexibility to leave work when necessary to take an elderly parent to a doctor's appointment or pick up a sick child early from school. For more on flextime, see "Flexible Work Schedules" in Chapter 2.

- **Telecommuting.** This refers to allowing employees to work off-site—for example, from home—for some or all of their workweek.
- **Job sharing.** This means allowing two employees to share one full-time job, alternating days or shifts (one working mornings and the other afternoons, for example).
- **Flexible spending accounts.** These are tax-saving vehicles that allow employees to set aside pretax money from their income (like a 401(k)) which they can then use to reimburse their dependent care costs and medical expenses.
- **Employee assistance programs (EAPs) or work/life programs.** These are general terms for a host of supportive services that companies provide to their employees, such as resource lists or other help finding child care, after-school care, or elder care providers
- **Caregiving services.** Some companies go as far as providing financial assistance for child care nearby, providing on-site child care, or providing emergency caregiver services to be used when planned child or elder care falls through.
- **Allowing employees to donate sick or vacation time to each other.** Should one employee have an emergency situation, this allows others to help that employee

out (while not requiring the company to provide any additional sick or vacation leave). For more on sick and vacation time, see "Vacation and Sick Leave" in Chapter 5.

- **Providing additional family and medical leave.** This means either providing more unpaid leave than is legally required or providing partial or total pay during an employee's otherwise unpaid leave. For more on family and medical leave, see Chapter 5.

Are Family-Friendly Policies Legal?

As with all employment benefits your company provides, any family-friendly policies your company decides to offer will be legally sound as long as the company offers and administers such policies fairly and consistently and free from illegal discrimination. Again, this does not mean that you have to provide every worker with the same family-friendly benefits; it just means that you cannot decide who gets such benefits based on an impermissible reason, such as race, gender, national origin, religion, age, or disability. Your company may, for example, decide to provide paid family and medical leave only for top executives as part of an executive compensation package. Or you may decide who gets to work a flexible schedule based on seniority with the company.

In addition, where appropriate, some of these policies may be used as reasonable accommodations for employees with disabilities (for example, allowing a worker to work flextime, share a job, or telecommute).

(See "Disability" in Chapter 3 for more on reasonable accommodations.)

Once you make such a policy, however, you cannot discriminate in offering it by, for example, allowing only mothers access to such benefits, but not fathers. One note of caution here: Some state and local laws may prohibit discrimination based on sexual orientation and/or marital status in addition to the characteristics protected by federal law, so be sure to follow any such laws that apply to your company when administering family-friendly policies. For more information on impermissible discrimination, see Chapter 3 and contact your state fair employment practices agency. (Contact information is in the appendix.)

While some may complain that family-friendly policies favor workers who have children over those who don't or favor women over men, this is not necessarily true, as long as you make such policies available equally to all workers who may need them. For example, if you offer paid maternity leave, offer paid paternity leave, too. If you offer flexible work schedules to care for children after school, offer this benefit equally to mothers and fathers. If you allow job-sharing or part-time work for parents of young children, allow the same for workers who may need to care for an elderly parent or sick spouse. In short, be sure to make all of your family-friendly policies clear and consistent and to administer them fairly, without regard to race, gender, national origin, religion, age, disability, or any other characteristics protected by your state and local laws.

For more information on family-friendly workplace policies, consult any of the many organizations that focus on helping employees balance work and family, including the following:

- The Families and Work Institute (www.familiesandwork.org)
- The National Partnership for Women and Families (www.nationalpartnership.org)
- Workplace Flexibility 2010 (www.workplaceflexibility2010.org)
- Catalyst (www.catalyst.org)
- Winning Workplaces (www.winningworkplaces.com), and
- *Working Mother Magazine* (www.workingmother.com), which publishes an annual list of the best 100 companies to work for based on their family-friendly policies.

Legal Dos and Don'ts: Personnel Basics

Do:

- **Keep your door open.** All good management practices and policies are based on communication between workers and managers. Keep your ear to the ground by having an open door policy that encourages your reports to come to you with concerns or ideas, and by listening to what they have to say. You may be surprised at what you hear.

- **Blaze a paper trail.** Any time you evaluate, discipline, take a complaint from, or investigate an employee, write it down. Keeping a written record of an employee's performance and conduct is the best way to keep your company out of court. If you later have to fire that employee, your documents will make it much harder for him or her to find a lawyer willing to take the case.

- **Get help from your reports.** Your policies and practices will be most effective if workers believe they are reasonable and fair, especially if they had a hand in their development. Encourage employees to help you develop performance requirements and goals, come up with training programs, or suggest ways you can help them do their jobs more effectively.

Don't:

- **Sugarcoat the truth.** Most of us dislike giving bad news or disappointing others. But when you are giving evaluations or administering discipline, you have to be honest. Employees will improve only if you tell them exactly what you expect and where they have fallen short.

- **Treat some workers better than others.** Discrimination claims start with inconsistency: treating some workers better (or worse) than others. By knowing your company's policies and applying them evenhandedly, you will avoid playing favorites or picking on scapegoats, practices sure to land your company in legal trouble.

- **Procrastinate.** Putting off important tasks is a bad habit for a variety of reasons, but managers who procrastinate can create lots of unnecessary problems. If you are always timely with your performance evaluations and personnel documents, you will be able to avoid claims that you created evidence after the fact to justify termination or other discipline.

Test Your Knowledge

Questions

1. All employees work at will unless they have a written employment contract stating otherwise. ☐ True ☐ False

2. Managers should always have a good reason for firing an employee, even if the employee works at will. ☐ True ☐ False

3. As long as company policies are written down in an employee handbook, managers are free to supervise employees and make decisions as they see fit. ☐ True ☐ False

4. You have no obligation to report or take action to stop sexual harassment unless the victim is willing to make a complaint in writing. ☐ True ☐ False

5. Sexual harassment training is not just a good idea; it may also be legally required. ☐ True ☐ False

6. Because it is so efficient, you should always communicate with employees you supervise via email. ☐ True ☐ False

7. You should give employees feedback throughout the year, not just at formal, year-end reviews. ☐ True ☐ False

8. I-9 forms should not be kept in employees' regular personnel files. ☐ True ☐ False

9. Employees are not entitled to see what's in their personnel files. ☐ True ☐ False

10. Family-friendly policies are discriminatory because they only benefit workers who have children. ☐ True ☐ False

Answers

1. False. If you make promises about continued employment to an employee, orally or in writing (for example, in an employee handbook), you risk creating an oral or implied contract that the employee will be fired only for good cause or other specified reasons.

2. True. Even if you have the legal right to fire at will, you don't gain anything by using it. Firing employees without a good reason leads to morale problems and employee lawsuits.

3. False. Written policies in an employee handbook are meaningless if managers don't follow those policies consistently.

4. False. Once a manager learns of harassment—whether through a complaint, personal observation, or any other means—the company is legally responsible to take action to stop it. Employees need not make a written complaint to put the company on notice.

5. True. Some states require companies to provide sexual harassment training to managers.

6. False. Email is a great tool for certain types of communication, such as to document a conversation after it occurs or make brief announcements. It is not, however, appropriate for many kinds of communication, such as providing feedback on an employee's performance or delivering bad news. Never use email as a way to avoid conversations that make you uncomfortable.

7. True. Ongoing feedback, both positive and negative, is an important part of a successful performance evaluation system.

8. True. I-9 forms should be kept in a separate file, so government auditors will be able to review them without rummaging through other employee personnel documents.

9. False. Most states give employees and former employees a right to see at least some of the documents in their personnel files.

10. False. Instituting policies that help workers balance the demands of work and family can benefit all workers, regardless of whether they have children or not. Flexible work schedules, job sharing, and flexible spending accounts can all help workers to care for elderly parents or sick spouses or partners or to meet their own health or other needs. As long as such policies are written and applied consistently, fairly, and without regard to such protected characteristics as gender, race, national origin, age, and the like, they are legally sound.

State Laws on Access to Personnel Records

This chart deals with only those states that authorize access to personnel files. Generally, an employee is allowed to see evaluations, performance reviews, and other documents that determine a promotion, bonus, or raise; access usually does not include letters of reference, test results, or records of a criminal or workplace-violation investigation. Under other state laws, employees may have access to their medical records and records of exposure to hazardous substances; these laws are not included in this chart.

ALASKA

Alaska Stat. § 23.10.430

Employers affected: All.

Employee access to records: Employee or former employee may view and copy personnel files.

Conditions for viewing records: Employee may view records during regular business hours under reasonable rules.

Copying records: Employee pays (if employer so requests).

CALIFORNIA

Cal. Lab. Code §§ 1198.5; 432

Employers affected: All employers subject to wage and hour laws.

Employee access to records: Employee has right to inspect at reasonable intervals any personnel records relating to performance or to a grievance proceeding.

Conditions for viewing records: Employee may view records at reasonable times, during break or nonwork hours. If records are kept off-site or employer does not make them available at the workplace, then employee must be allowed to view them at the storage location without loss of pay.

Copying records: Employee also has a right to a copy of any personnel document employee has signed.

CONNECTICUT

Conn. Gen. Stat. Ann. §§ 31-128a to 31-128h

Employers affected: All.

Employee access to records: Employee has right to inspect personnel files within a reasonable time after making a request, but not more than twice a year. Employer must keep files on former employees for at least one year after termination.

Written request required: Yes.

Conditions for viewing records: Employee may view records during regular business hours in a location at or near worksite. Employer may require that files be viewed on the premises and in the presence of employer's designated official.

Copying records: Employer must provide copies within a reasonable time after receiving employee's written request; request must identify the materials employee wants copied. Employer may charge a fee that is based on the cost of supplying documents.

Employee's right to insert rebuttal: If employee disagrees with information in personnel file and cannot reach an agreement with employer to remove or correct it, employee may submit an explanatory written statement. Rebuttal must be maintained as part of the file.

DELAWARE

Del. Code Ann. tit. 19, §§ 730 to 735

Employers affected: All.

Employee access to records: Current employee, employee who is laid off with reemployment rights, or employee on leave of absence may inspect personnel record; employee's agent is not entitled to have access to records. Unless there is

State Laws on Access to Personnel Records (cont'd)

reasonable cause, employer may limit access to once a year.

Written request required: At employer's discretion. Employer may require employee to file a form and indicate either the purpose of the review or what parts of the record employee wants to inspect.

Conditions for viewing records: Records may be viewed during employer's regular business hours. Employer may require that employees view files on their own time and may also require that files be viewed on the premises and in the presence of a designated official.

Copying records: Employer is not required to permit employee to copy records. Employee may take notes.

Employee's right to insert rebuttal: If employee disagrees with information in personnel file and cannot reach an agreement with employer to remove or correct it, employee may submit an explanatory written statement. Rebuttal must be maintained as part of the personnel file.

ILLINOIS
820 Ill. Comp. Stat. §§ 40/1 to 40/12

Employers affected: Employers with 5 or more employees.

Employee access to records: Current employee, or former employee terminated within the past year, is permitted to inspect records twice a year at reasonable intervals, unless a collective bargaining agreement provides otherwise. An employee involved in a current grievance may designate a representative of the union or collective bargaining unit, or other agent, to inspect personnel records that may be relevant to resolving the grievance. Employer must make records available within 7 working days after

employee makes request (if employer cannot meet deadline, may be allowed an additional 7 days).

Written request required: At employer's discretion. Employer may require use of a form.

Conditions for viewing records: Records may be viewed during normal business hours at or near worksite or, at employer's discretion, during nonworking hours at a different location if more convenient for employee.

Copying records: After reviewing records, employee may get a copy. Employer may charge only actual cost of duplication. If employee is unable to view files at worksite, employer, upon receipt of a written request, must mail employee a copy.

Employee's right to insert rebuttal: If employee disagrees with any information in the personnel file and cannot reach an agreement with employer to remove or correct it, employee may submit an explanatory written statement. Rebuttal must remain in file with no additional comment by employer.

IOWA
Iowa Code §§ 91B.1, 91A.2

Employers affected: All employers with salaried employees or commissioned salespeople.

Employee access to records: Employee may have access to personnel file at time agreed upon by employer and employee.

Conditions for viewing records: Employer's representative may be present.

Copying records: Employer may charge copying fee for each page that is equivalent to a commercial copying service fee.

State Laws on Access to Personnel Records (cont'd)

MAINE

Me. Rev. Stat. Ann. tit. 26, § 631

Employers affected: All.

Employee access to records: Within 10 days of submitting request, employee, former employee, or authorized representative may view and copy personnel files.

Written request required: Yes.

Conditions for viewing records: Employee may view records during normal business hours at the location where the files are kept, unless employer, at own discretion, arranges a time and place more convenient for employee. If files are in electronic or any other nonprint format, employer must provide equipment for viewing and copying.

Copying records: Employee entitled to one free copy of personnel file during each calendar year, including any material added to file during that year. Employee must pay for any additional copies.

MASSACHUSETTS

Mass. Gen. Laws ch. 149, § 52C

Employers affected: All. (Employers with 20 or more employees must maintain personnel records for 3 years after termination.)

Employee access to records: Employee or former employee must have opportunity to review personnel files within 5 business days of submitting request, but not more than twice a calendar year. (Law does not apply to tenured or tenure-track employees in private colleges and universities.) Employer must notify an employee within 10 days of placing in the employee's personnel record any information to the extent that the information is, has been used, or may be used, to negatively affect the employee's qualification for employment,

promotion, transfer, additional compensation, or the possibility that the employee will be subject to disciplinary action. (This notification does not count toward employee's two allotted opportunities to view personnel file.)

Written request required: Yes.

Conditions for viewing records: Employee may view records at workplace during normal business hours.

Copying records: Employee must be given a copy of record within 5 business days of submitting a written request.

Employee's right to insert rebuttal: If employee disagrees with any information in personnel record and cannot reach an agreement with employer to remove or correct it, employee may submit an explanatory written statement. Rebuttal becomes a part of the personnel file.

MICHIGAN

Mich. Comp. Laws §§ 423.501 to 423.505

Employers affected: Employers with 4 or more employees.

Employee access to records: Current or former employee is entitled to review personnel records at reasonable intervals, generally not more than twice a year, unless a collective bargaining agreement provides otherwise.

Written request required: Yes. Request must describe the record employee wants to review.

Conditions for viewing records: Employee may view records during normal office hours either at or reasonably near the worksite. If these hours would require employee to take time off work, employer must provide another time and place that is more convenient for the employee.

Copying records: After reviewing files, employee may get a copy; employer may charge only actual

State Laws on Access to Personnel Records (cont'd)

cost of duplication. If employee is unable to view files at the worksite, employer, upon receipt of a written request, must mail employee a copy.

Employee's right to insert rebuttal: If employee disagrees with any information in personnel record and cannot reach an agreement with employer to remove or correct it, employee may submit a written statement explaining his or her position. Statement may be no longer than five 8½" by 11" pages.

MINNESOTA
Minn. Stat. Ann. §§ 181.960 to 181.966

Employers affected: 20 or more employees.

Employee access to records: Current employee may review files once per 6-month period; former employee may have access to records once only during the first year after termination. Employer must comply with written request within 7 working days (14 working days if personnel records kept out of state). Employer may not retaliate against an employee who asserts rights under these laws.

Written request required: Yes.

Conditions for viewing records: Current employee may view records during employer's normal business hours at worksite or a nearby location; does not have to take place during employee's working hours. Employer or employer's representative may be present.

Copying records: Employer must provide copy free of charge. Current employee must first review record and then submit written request for copies. Former employee must submit written request; providing former employee with a copy fulfills employer's obligation to allow access to records.

Employee's right to insert rebuttal: If employee disputes specific information in the personnel record, and cannot reach an agreement with employer to remove or revise it, employee may submit a written statement identifying the disputed information and explaining his or her position. Statement may be no longer than 5 pages and must be kept with personnel record as long as it is maintained.

NEVADA
Nev. Rev. Stat. Ann. § 613.075

Employers affected: All.

Employee access to records: An employee who has worked at least 60 days and a former employee, within 60 days of termination, must be given a reasonable opportunity to inspect personnel records.

Conditions for viewing records: Employee may view records during employer's normal business hours.

Copying records: Employer may charge only actual cost of providing access and copies.

Employee's right to insert rebuttal: Employee may submit a reasonable written explanation in direct response to any entry in personnel record. Statement must be of reasonable length; employer may specify the format; employer must maintain statement in personnel records.

NEW HAMPSHIRE
N.H. Rev. Stat. Ann. § 275:56

Employers affected: All.

Employee access to records: Employer must provide employees a reasonable opportunity to inspect records.

Copying records: Employer may charge a fee reasonably related to cost of supplying copies.

State Laws on Access to Personnel Records (cont'd)

Employee's right to insert rebuttal: If employee disagrees with any of the information in personnel record and cannot reach an agreement with the employer to remove or correct it, employee may submit an explanatory written statement along with supporting evidence. Statement must be maintained as part of personnel file.

OREGON
Or. Rev. Stat. § 652.750

Employers affected: All.

Employee access to records: Within 45 days after receipt of request, employer must provide employee a reasonable opportunity to inspect personnel records used to determine qualifications for employment, promotion, or additional compensation, termination, or other disciplinary action. Employer must keep records for 60 days after termination of employee.

Conditions for viewing records: Employee may view records at worksite or place of work assignment.

Copying records: Within 45 days after receipt of request, employer must provide a certified copy of requested record to current or former employee (if request made within 60 days of termination). If employee makes request after 60 days from termination, employer shall provide a certified copy of requested records if employer has records at time of the request. May charge amount reasonably calculated to recover actual cost of providing copy.

PENNSYLVANIA
43 Pa. Cons. Stat. Ann. §§ 1321 to 1324

Employers affected: All.

Employee access to records: Employer must allow employee to inspect personnel record at reasonable times. (Employee's agent, or employee who is laid off with reemployment rights or on leave of absence, must also be given access.) Unless there is reasonable cause, employer may limit review to once a year by employee and once a year by employee's agent.

Written request required: At employer's discretion. Employer may require the use of a form as well as a written indication of the parts of the record employee wants to inspect or the purpose of the inspection. For employee's agent: Employee must provide signed authorization designating agent; must be for a specific date and indicate the reason for the inspection or the parts of the record the agent is authorized to inspect.

Conditions for viewing records: Employee may view records during normal business hours at the office where records are maintained, when there is enough time for employee to complete the review. Employer may require that employee or agent view records on their own time and may also require that inspection take place on the premises and in the presence of employer's designated official.

Copying records: Employer not obligated to permit copying. Employee may take notes.

Employee's right to insert rebuttal: The Bureau of Labor Standards, after a petition and hearing, may allow employee to place a counterstatement in the personnel file, if employee claims that the file contains an error.

RHODE ISLAND
R.I. Gen. Laws § 28-6.4-1

Employers affected: All.

Employee access to records: Employer must permit employee to inspect personnel files when given at least 7 days' advance notice (excluding

State Laws on Access to Personnel Records (cont'd)

weekends and holidays). Employer may limit access to no more than 3 times a year.

Written request required: Yes.

Conditions for viewing records: Employee may view records at any reasonable time other than employee's work hours. Inspection must take place in presence of employer or employer's representative.

Copying records: Employee may not make copies or remove files from place of inspection. Employer may charge a fee reasonably related to cost of supplying copies.

WASHINGTON

Wash. Rev. Code Ann. §§ 49.12.240 to 49.12.260

Employers affected: All.

Employee access to records: Employee may have access to personnel records at least once a year within a reasonable time after making a request.

Employee's right to insert rebuttal: Employee may petition annually that employer review all information in employee's personnel file. If there is any irrelevant or incorrect information in the file, employer must remove it. If employee does not agree with employer's review, employee may request to have a statement of rebuttal or correction placed in file. Former employee has right of rebuttal for two years after termination.

WISCONSIN

Wis. Stat. Ann. § 103.13

Employers affected: All employers who maintain personnel records.

Employee access to records: Employee and former employee must be allowed to inspect personnel records within 7 working days of making request. Access is permitted twice per calendar year unless a collective bargaining agreement provides otherwise. Employee involved in a current grievance may designate a representative of the union or collective bargaining unit, or other agent, to inspect records that may be relevant to resolving the grievance.

Written request required: At employer's discretion.

Conditions for viewing records: Employee may view records during normal working hours at a location reasonably near worksite. If this would require employee to take time off work, employer may provide another reasonable time and place for review.

Copying records: Employee's right of inspection includes the right to make or receive copies. If employer provides copies, may charge only actual cost of reproduction.

Employee's right to insert rebuttal: If employee disagrees with any information in the personnel record and cannot come to an agreement with the employer to remove or correct it, employee may submit an explanatory written statement. Employer must attach the statement to the disputed portion of the personnel record.

Time Off

We all know that a little time off is a good thing. Workers get a chance to have fun and recharge their batteries, and deal with personal and family obligations as they arise. And your company benefits, too: A company is more productive if its employees (and managers!) are healthy, rested, and focused on their jobs.

Whether your company offers a generous leave program or only the minimum required by law, this chapter will give you an overview of the rules on:

- vacation time
- sick leave
- family and medical leave
- pregnancy and parental leave
- time off for jury duty
- voting leave
- leave for military service
- domestic violence leave, and
- other types of legally required leave.

If you are responsible for setting company policy, this chapter will help you create sensible leave policies that stay well within the bounds of the law. If your job is to supervise employees, this information will help you figure out how to handle requests for leave, how to enforce your company's policies, and what kinds of requests should alert you to a potential legal problem for your company.

Frequently Asked Questions About Leave

Is my company legally required to offer paid vacation and sick leave?
Probably not. In most places, no law requires employers to offer paid time off (Washington, DC, and San Francisco are exceptions, as is the State of Connecticut; all require employers to offer a certain amount of paid sick leave). Although a few states require paid family or medical leave, employees typically are paid through a state fund, not directly by your company. Even if they aren't required to do so, however, most employers do offer some form of paid leave. A well-designed leave program can help a company attract high-quality employees—and improve office productivity and morale. (For more information, see "Vacation and Sick Leave," below.)

Does my company have to provide family and medical leave?
It depends on how many employees work for your company. Under the federal Family and Medical Leave Act (FMLA), employers must allow employees to take leave only if they employ more than 50 people within a 75-mile radius. Even if a business is covered by the FMLA, only employees who have worked there for at least a year are eligible for leave. Some states have their own leave laws in addition to the FMLA, so be sure to find out about these, too. (For more on the requirements of the FMLA, see "Family and Medical Leave," below.)

Frequently Asked Questions About Leave (cont'd)

Can I fire a pregnant employee for poor attendance, even if the absences are pregnancy-related?

It's illegal to fire an employee because she is pregnant. However, if you would fire any employee with poor attendance, you may legally fire your pregnant employee for that reason, as long as the absences for which you are firing her are not protected by the FMLA or a similar state law. (For more on pregnancy leave, see "Pregnancy and Parental Leave," below.)

One of the employees I supervise just got called for jury duty. If she gets seated on a jury, can I replace her?

No. Almost every state prohibits employers from firing or disciplining an employee for being called to jury duty and serving on a jury. However, most states do not require companies to pay employees for time spent on jury duty unless their own employment policies provide for such pay. (For more on employees and jury duty, see "Jury Duty and Voting," below.)

Does my company have to pay employees for time spent voting?

It depends on where your workplace is. Almost half of the states require employers to provide at least a few hours of paid leave so employees can vote, if the employee would not have enough time to vote without taking time off from work. Even if your company does business in a state that does not require paid leave for voting, you must not discipline any employee for taking time off to cast a ballot. (For more on leave to vote, see "Jury Duty and Voting," below.)

Does my company have to give employees time off for National Guard training or other military service?

Most likely. Federal law requires employers to reinstate workers who take up to five years of leave to serve in the armed forces. And in almost every state, employers must allow their employees to take leave for certain types of military service. In some states, only employees called for active duty are entitled to leave; other states require leave for training as well. (For more on leave for military duties, see "Military Leave," below.)

Are employees entitled to take time off to handle domestic violence issues?

It depends on the situation and the laws of your state. If the employee has a serious health condition or needs to care for a family member with a serious health condition due to domestic violence, the Family and Medical Leave Act (or a similar state law) may give the employee the right to take time off. About a dozen states have laws that give victims of domestic violence a right to time off work to deal with medical issues, relocate, or take legal action against their abusers. (For more information, see "Domestic Violence Leave," below.)

Vacation and Sick Leave

Most employers do not currently have to provide paid sick or vacation leave, although this issue is a hot topic of debate in federal, state, and local legislatures. In recent years, California and New Jersey have passed laws that allow employees to receive some pay while they're off work for certain family or medical reasons. However, employees in these states are paid through a state insurance fund, not directly by their employers.

In 2011, Connecticut became the first state to require employers to offer traditional paid sick leave (paid by the employer rather than the state, that is). This law applies only to employers with at least 50 employees, and covers only service employees. Employees protected by the law will be entitled to accrue an hour of paid sick leave for every 40 hours worked, up to a maximum of 40 hours in a year. Other states are considering paid sick leave legislation, as is Congress. And some localities, including San Francisco and Washington, DC, already require employers to provide paid sick leave. Because this area is in flux, you should check in regularly with your state and local government—and check www.nolo.com for updates on federal legislation—to find out whether any new laws apply to your company.

If your company isn't required to offer paid leave, it might decide not to (although such a policy would make it tough to attract and retain high-quality employees). If your company decides to adopt a paid leave policy, keep these guidelines in mind:

- **Apply the policy consistently to all employees.** Don't make individual decisions on who can take leave and for how long. Adopt a policy that applies to all workers in a particular position or all workers at your company. If your company already has a policy, apply it evenhandedly. If some employees are offered a more attractive leave package than others in the same position, you are opening your company up to claims of unfair treatment and possible discrimination lawsuits.

- **Require employees to schedule leave in advance, if possible.** Sometimes, an employee cannot know ahead of time that he or she will need time off (for a sudden illness or family emergency, for example). In all other circumstances, however, you should ask your reports to schedule leave—particularly vacations—at least a month in advance. This will help you meet your staffing needs, particularly during summers and holidays.

- **Adopt a sensible vacation accrual policy.** Many employees enjoy taking a longer vacation from time to time, and a policy that allows employees to save up a long stretch of vacation time—four weeks, say—for this purpose is reasonable. Your company may want to cap how much vacation time an employee can accrue or specify how much vacation an employee can take at one time, however. Otherwise, you may suddenly have several employees asking for months off at a time. And until those employees take their long vacation, they may suffer from job burn-out from years of work without time off.

- **Don't allow abuse of sick leave time.** Some employees treat sick leave as an extra allotment of vacation days. Crack down by requiring employees to call in each day they are ill, requiring a doctor's note for serious illnesses, and monitoring patterns of sick leave use. Do you have employees who only seem to call in sick on Mondays and Fridays? Do some employees claim illness at the end of every year, in an effort to take advantage of unused sick time? Counsel these employees about the proper use of sick leave, and discipline those who abuse the system.

- **Consider what you will pay when an employee quits or is fired.** If your company allows employees to accrue vacation days, it must decide whether to pay departing employees for unused leave. Some states, including California, require employers to pay for this accrued vacation time when employment ends. (See "State Laws That Control Final Paychecks," at the end of Chapter 12, for information on your state's rules.) Although employers are generally not required to pay out unused sick days, some do anyway, perhaps believing that this encourages employees not to misuse sick leave.

Family and Medical Leave

Working people often have a tough time balancing the demands of a job with personal and family needs. In response to this much-discussed problem, Congress passed the Family and Medical Leave Act (FMLA), 29 U.S.C. §§ 2601 and following, then amended it in 2008 to cover military family leave. The FMLA requires certain employers to allow their employees up to 12 weeks of unpaid leave a year to care for a seriously ill family member, to deal with their own serious illness, to take care of a newborn or newly adopted child, or to handle a qualifying exigency arising out of a family member's call to active duty in the military. As amended in 2008, the FMLA also requires employers to allow employees to take up to 26 weeks of leave in a single leave year to care for a family member who suffers a serious injury or illness while serving on active duty.

In most cases, the employer must reinstate an employee returning from leave to either the same position or to a position that is comparable in every important respect—including pay, benefits, and status. (For detailed information on the FMLA, see *The Essential Guide to Family and Medical Leave,* by Lisa Guerin and Deborah C. England (Nolo).)

When the FMLA Applies

An employer must comply with the FMLA if these three requirements are met:

- The company has 50 or more employees who work within a 75-mile radius. All employees on the payroll—including those who work part time and those on leave—count toward this total.
- The employee seeking leave has worked for the company for at least 12 months.
- The employee has worked at least 1,250 hours (about 25 hours a week) during the 12 months immediately preceding the leave.

When all three of these requirements are met, an employee is entitled to take FMLA leave only for specified reasons. Not every personal or family emergency qualifies for FMLA leave. The employee must be seeking leave for:

- **Birth, adoption, or foster care.** A new parent or foster parent may take FMLA leave within one year after the child is born or placed in the parent's home. A parent may go out on leave before the child arrives, if necessary for prenatal care or preparations for the child. If both parents work for the same employer, they may be entitled to less leave.

- **An employee's serious health condition.** The FMLA provides a specific definition of a "serious health condition." Generally, an employee who requires inpatient treatment, has a chronic health problem, or is unable to perform normal activities for three days while under the treatment of a doctor has a serious health condition.

- **A family member's serious health condition.** An employee who needs to care for an ill family member is also entitled to leave. Under this provision of the FMLA, only parents, spouses, and children count as family members. Grandparents, same-sex partners, in-laws, and siblings are not included.

- **Qualifying exigencies.** Employees may take leave to handle certain matters when a parent, spouse, or child who is a member of the reserve, National Guard, or regular armed forces is called to active duty. Qualifying exigencies include making legal and financial arrangements, changing child care, or attending military events or ceremonies, among other things.

- **Seriously injured or ill family member.** An employee whose family member suffers or aggravates a serious injury or illness while on active military duty is eligible for FMLA leave. The law also allows time off to care for veterans who were in the military in the last five years and are undergoing treatment, therapy, or recuperation for a qualifying injury or illness (this provision is intended to cover conditions that might not manifest fully until military service has ended, such as posttraumatic stress disorder). For this provision, family members include the service member's "next of kin," which could be a sibling, grandparent, or aunt or uncle, for example.

Amount of Leave Available

An employee who takes leave for a serious health condition, a family member's serious health condition, a new child, or a qualifying exigency, may take 12 weeks of leave per 12-month period. The 12-week entitlement is for all of these types of leave combined. For example, an employee who takes ten weeks off to spend with a new child has only two weeks of leave to use for any other purpose in the 12-month leave year.

Different rules apply to FMLA leave taken to care for a family member who suffers a serious illness or injury while on active military duty. Employees may take up to 26 weeks of leave for this purpose in a single

12-month leave year, beginning on the first day of leave. However, this leave entitlement doesn't renew every 12 months: Instead, it is a per-injury, per-service-member entitlement. Once an employee takes this leave, he or she cannot take it again unless the same family member suffers a different injury on active duty, or a different family member suffers an injury on active duty.

Reinstatement and Benefits

When the employee's leave is over, the company must reinstate the employee to the same position the employee held prior to taking leave, or to a position that is comparable in every important respect, subject to these conditions:

- Employees have no greater right to reinstatement than they would have had if they had not taken leave. In other words, if an employee works in the accounting department and your company decides, while the employee is on leave, to cut the entire department and outsource its bookkeeping needs, the employee does not have a right to be reinstated just because he or she was on FMLA leave.
- Your company doesn't have to reinstate certain highly paid or high-level employees. The FMLA recognizes how difficult it would be for many businesses to function without their top executives. The law allows an employer to refuse reinstatement if (1) the employee is among the highest-paid 10% of the salaried workers employed within 75 miles of the employee's workplace, and (2) taking back the employee would cause "sub-stantial and grievous economic injury" to the company's business.

If your company has a group health plan for employees, it must also maintain insurance coverage for employees on FMLA leave. However, the company can choose to require the employee to reimburse it for the insurance premiums it paid for the employee if the employee chooses voluntarily not to return to work when the leave ends (but not if a serious health condition for which the employee took the leave continues or other circumstances beyond the employee's control prevent the employee's return to work). Employers aren't required to continue any other employee benefits while an employee is on leave, nor must they allow a worker to accrue seniority, vacation leave, sick time, or other benefits while on leave. However, an employee who returns to work is entitled to benefits reinstatement as well—that is, the company must provide the same benefits that were available to the worker previously.

You cannot discipline a worker for taking FMLA leave. This means not only that you can't fire or demote a worker for going on leave, but also that you cannot count a worker's FMLA leave as an absence under a no-fault attendance policy. For example, if you give workers a disciplinary warning after ten absences in any year and fire workers after 15 absences, you may not count any days that a worker takes as FMLA leave as an "absence" under the policy.

Paid Leave

FMLA leave is unpaid. In some situations, however, employers must allow—or may require—employees to use their accrued paid leave while on FMLA leave. Paid leave may be used for FMLA leave only if the employee's reason for leave is covered by your company's paid leave policy. For example, if your company's paid sick leave policy covers employees who take time off to care for sick family members, then an employee may use paid sick leave for FMLA leave to care for a family member with a serious health condition. If your policy covers only the employee's own illness, however, the employee may not use paid sick leave while caring for a family member.

Your company may require employees to follow its usual procedures for paid leave. For example, if your company requires employees to give two weeks of notice to use vacation time, you don't have to allow an employee to use paid vacation time while out on FMLA leave for a medical emergency until two weeks have passed since the employee first notified you of the need for leave. However, you may not deny the employee's FMLA leave for those two weeks: Your company's policies dictate only when an employee can take paid leave, not whether the employee is eligible for FMLA leave.

Scheduling and Notice Requirements

An employee's absence can disrupt the workplace. Recognizing this, the FMLA requires employees to give 30 days' notice if the need for leave is foreseeable (except for qualifying exigency leave). The most common "foreseeable" leave is leave the employee will take for the birth or adoption of a child or to care for a family member recovering from

scheduled surgery or other planned medical treatment.

If the employee's need for leave is not foreseeable or the employee is taking qualifying exigency leave, the employee has to give whatever notice is possible and practical under the circumstances. For example, it would be impossible for an employee to give advance notice of a medical emergency such as a car accident or appendectomy.

In some circumstances, an employee may want to take the leave intermittently rather than all at once. If an employee requires physical therapy for a serious injury, for example, or needs to care for a spouse receiving periodic medical treatment, it might make more sense for the employee to take several hours off per week. This arrangement might also make more sense for your company, because you get to keep your employee's part-time services instead of planning for a protracted absence.

If it is medically necessary for an employee to take intermittent leave to care for a family member or for his or her own serious health condition, the employee has a right to do so. Employees may also take intermittent leave for a qualifying exigency. However, if an employee wants to take time off to care for a new child, you may, but are not required to, allow the employee to take leave on an intermittent schedule.

Certifications

Your company can ask employees to provide proof that they really need leave for an FMLA purpose. If an employee is taking leave for a serious health condition, for example, you can require the employee to provide a medical certification from a health care provider, giving certain information about the condition and need for leave. You may also require an employee to submit a certification regarding qualifying exigency leave or leave to care for a military service member. The Department of Labor has developed optional forms you can use for this purpose (available online at www.dol.gov).

There are detailed rules covering when and how you may request clarification of a certification, second and third opinions, and requests for recertification of a serious health condition. You can find all of the details in *The Essential Guide to Family and Medical Leave*, by Lisa Guerin and Deborah C. England (Nolo).

State Leave Laws

Some states have their own family and medical leave laws in addition to the federal FMLA. If your company does business in one of these states, it will have to follow whichever law—federal or state—gives workers the most protection. For example, if your state has a family and medical leave law that gives workers the right to take more than 12 weeks off to bond with a new child, your company will have to follow state law, even though the federal law doesn't require as much. And if state and federal law offer workers different benefits, your company has to follow both of them. For example, if your state law requires employers to offer family leave to allow parents to attend a child's school conference (a right that the federal law doesn't include), your company must

let parents take that time in addition to their 12 weeks of federal FMLA leave.

To find out more about your state's laws on leave, see "State Family and Medical Leave Laws," at the end of this chapter.

Lessons From the Real World

On September 26, 1995, Chem-Tronics fired Javier Mora for violating its attendance policy. Mr. Mora had taken a number of absences to care for his teenage son, Javier Jr., who suffered from AIDS and related infections. On these occasions, Mr. Mora cared for his son at home and took his son to necessary medical appointments.

The company claimed that Mr. Mora was not entitled to FMLA leave because his wife, Javier Jr.'s stepmother, should have handled Javier Jr.'s medical needs. Mr. Mora explained to company representatives that his wife was not his son's biological mother, that he was closer to his son, and that his son wanted him to provide care—all to no avail.

The company also argued that it didn't know that Javier Jr. suffered from a serious health condition covered by the FMLA. However, this argument was dramatically undercut by the company's own newsletter—in which an article appeared detailing Mr. Mora and his son's trip to the Superbowl, courtesy of the Make a Wish Foundation (a group that provides special experiences for terminally ill children).

Mora v. Chem-Tronics, Inc., 16 F.Supp.2d 1192 (S.D. Cal. 1998).

Pregnancy and Parental Leave

Some employers assume that they must provide paid maternity leave to new mothers. Generally, however, this is not the case. You might be surprised to learn that in the United States (unlike most European countries), no law requires employers to provide paid maternity leave. A couple of states (California and New Jersey) have insurance programs that pay employees a portion of their usual salary for time spent on parental leave, but these programs are paid by a state fund, not directly by employers.

Your company may be required to offer unpaid parental leave or leave to pregnant employees who are temporarily unable to work. It will have to offer paid leave to pregnant employees who are temporarily unable to work only if it provides paid leave to workers who are temporarily disabled for other reasons. And it must provide benefits evenhandedly to avoid discrimination claims.

Unpaid Leave

As explained above, the Family and Medical Leave Act (FMLA) requires employers who meet certain criteria to provide up to 12 weeks of unpaid leave.

FMLA leave can be used as pregnancy or parental leave in certain situations. Here are some of the rules that apply:

- Pregnant employees are entitled to use FMLA leave if complications from pregnancy constitute a serious health condition. As a practical matter, if a woman's doctor determines that it is medically necessary for her to take time off from work, she will be able to use FMLA leave for that purpose. FMLA leave is also available for routine prenatal care, such as monthly checkups.

- New parents may use FMLA leave as parental leave following the birth or adoption of a child or the placement of a foster child. This leave may be taken any time during the first year after the new child arrives. However, a worker is entitled to only 12 weeks of FMLA leave, total, in a single year (unless caring for a family service member). So, if a worker has to take two weeks off for medical reasons during her pregnancy, she will have only ten weeks of FMLA leave remaining to use as parental leave (unless state law provides additional leave).

- If both parents work for your company (and are married to each other), they are entitled to a combined total of 12 weeks of parental leave. This rule does not apply to an employee who must take time off for her own serious health condition, however. So if an employee had a difficult birth and is unable to work for 12 weeks, her husband will still be entitled to a full 12 weeks of parental leave.

- Parental leave may be taken intermittently, but only with an employer's permission. For example, new parents may wish to work part time for a period or take some leave immediately following the birth and some leave later. As long as your company agrees, you and the employee can work out a flexible leave arrangement under the FMLA.

Some states require employers to provide more than 12 weeks of leave, particularly if the leave is for "maternity disability": the legal term for the period of time when women are actually unable to work because of pregnancy and childbirth. In a few of these states (including California), the maternity disability leave provided under state law is in addition to the leave provided by the FMLA or similar state statutes—in other words, the worker may take her full leave under the FMLA and then take her full leave under state law, as long as she qualifies for leave under the relevant statutes. To find out what your state requires, see "State Family and Medical Leave Laws," at the end of this chapter.

Paid Leave

Your company may be required to provide paid leave to pregnant employees and new parents, depending on its employment policies. Generally, if your company makes paid leave available to other workers in similar situations, it must make it available to pregnant employees and new parents. For example, if employees who are temporarily disabled (unable to work) for other medical reasons (such as a heart attack or stroke) typically receive paid time off, employees who are unable to work because of pregnancy must be given the same benefit.

A handful of states (including California and New York) offer temporary disability insurance (TDI)—or require employers to provide it as a job benefit—to employees who are temporarily unable to work due to a disability, including pregnancy disability. An employee who can't work due to pregnancy or childbirth is typically entitled to some wage replacement for that time. However, these programs are not intended as parental leave: They are available only for the period of time when the employee is actually unable to work.

Similarly, if your company provides personal or vacation leave to employees, new parents must be allowed to use this time off as parental leave as long as they meet the other requirements of the policy (for example, providing adequate notice or scheduling the leave with a supervisor). Employers also have the right to require employees to use their accrued paid leave as FMLA leave—and most employers do. This allows companies to put an outer limit on employee absences. If your company doesn't require substitution, employees can take their total FMLA allotment —and then use their paid vacation or sick days to extend their time off.

In California and New Jersey, employees may be eligible to receive partial wage replacement from a state insurance fund for parental leave (time taken off to bond with and care for a new child). For more information on New Jersey's program, go to http://lwd.dol.state.nj.us/labor/fli/fliindex. html; you can find information on California's program at www.edd.ca.gov/Disability/Paid_ Family_Leave.htm.

Discrimination Claims

Federal and state laws prohibit discrimination on the basis of gender, including pregnancy. This means, of course, that you may not fire, demote, or take any other negative employment action against a worker because she is pregnant. Here are a few tips that will help you stay within the law when dealing with these issues:

- Employers cannot require a worker to take pregnancy or maternity leave. In the not-so-distant past, an employer could force a pregnant worker to stop working when she reached a certain stage of her pregnancy or was "showing." This is no longer legal. As long as she can get the job done, you must allow her to work, even up to the date she gives birth.

- Treat a pregnant employee who needs time off like any other temporarily disabled worker (an employee who suffers a back injury or has a mild heart attack, for example). Employers don't have to offer special benefits to pregnant workers, but these workers should get the same treatment as other workers who are temporarily unable to do their jobs because of disability or illness. Similarly, you may fire a pregnant employee who has excessive absences for pregnancy-related health problems (morning sickness, for example) if you would fire a nonpregnant employee for the same conduct. But make sure you are not penalizing a pregnant worker for absences taken under the FMLA or other state law. And make sure your state's law does not require you to provide a reasonable accommodation for your worker's pregnancy-related condition. (Check with your state's fair employment agency; the appendix contains contact information.)

- Offer parental leave, not maternity leave. And don't discourage new fathers from taking parental leave or penalize them for doing so. If your company offers any time off for a parent to spend with a newborn child, make it available to both fathers and mothers. If an employer offers a benefit that can only be used by women—like maternity leave—it might be accused of gender discrimination.

Jury Duty and Voting

Almost every state prohibits employers from firing or disciplining employees for jury service. A few states go further and make it illegal for employers to discourage or intimidate an employee from serving on a jury.

For most employers, the most important issue is whether they must pay an employee for time spent on jury duty. Generally, unless your company has promised otherwise in your employment policies or handbook, it does not have to pay employees for leave taken to serve on a jury. However, some states require at least some payment for this time off. See "State Laws on Jury Duty," at the end of this chapter, for information on your state's rules.

Similarly, workers are entitled to time off work to cast their ballots. Almost every state prohibits employers from disciplining or firing an employee who takes time off work to vote. In many states, an employer must grant a certain number of hours of leave for employees to get to the voting booth, but only if the employee is unable, because of his or her work schedule or the distance the employee must travel to cast a ballot, to vote outside of work hours. In most of these states, an employer must pay the worker for this time off. To find out what your state requires, see "State Laws on Taking Time Off to Vote," at the end of this chapter.

Military Leave

A federal law, the Uniformed Services Employment and Reemployment Rights Act of 1994 (USERRA), 38 U.S.C. §§ 4301 and following, prohibits discrimination against members of the United States military or those who serve in the military reserves. This law also requires employers to reinstate an employee who has taken time off to serve in the armed forces, if the employee meets these conditions:

- The employee must have given notice, before taking leave, that the leave was for military service.
- The employee must have spent no more than five years on leave for military service.
- The employee must have been released from military service under honorable conditions.
- The employee must report back or apply for reinstatement within specified time limits; these limits vary depending on the length of the employee's leave.

USERRA requires employers to reinstate workers to the "escalator position": the same position they would have held had they been continuously employed throughout their leave, provided they are otherwise qualified for that job. This means that your company cannot simply return the worker to his old position; the worker is entitled to any promotions, increased pay, or additional job responsibilities that he or she would have gotten if not for taking leave, if the worker is qualified to do that job. If the worker is not qualified, your company must try to get him or her qualified. The worker is also entitled to the benefits and seniority that he or she would have earned if continuously employed. For purposes of benefits plans and leave policies, the time the worker spent on leave must be counted as time worked.

Returning members of the military receive one additional benefit: They cannot be fired without cause for up to one year after they are reinstated (the exact length of this protection depends on the length of the worker's military service). Thus, no matter what your company's employment policies say, these workers are no longer at-will employees for a limited period after they return. (For more on at-will policies and cause for firing, see "At-Will Employment" in Chapter 4.)

State Laws

Almost every state has a law prohibiting discrimination against those in the state's militia or National Guard. Most state laws also require employers to grant leave to employees for certain types of military service. Some states require leave only for those employees called to active duty; other states require leave for those called for training as well. Employers don't generally have to pay employees who take military leave, although some states provide paid leave for public employees.

Lessons From the Real World

Charley Hill started working for Michelin North America in the early 1980s. In 1995, he became a member of the Naval Reserves of the United States, a position that required Hill to be absent from work for two weeks per year.

In 1998, Hill began working in the "Q-Laboratory" at Michelin. Although Hill wanted to keep working in the Q-Lab, his supervisor didn't think the lab could accommodate Hill's Navy Reserve schedule. Hill was required to transfer to another assignment, even though he wanted to stay in the Q-Lab.

Hill filed a lawsuit against Michelin, arguing that the company discriminated against him by making him transfer out of the Q-Lab. The court agreed, finding that the Q-Lab had better working conditions and a more regular work schedule, which made it superior to the job to which he was transferred. The court held that if Michelin transferred Hill because of his military service requirements, that effectively denied Hill the benefits of the Q-Lab job, in violation of the Uniformed Services Employment and Reemployment Rights Act.

Hill v. Michelin North America, Inc., 252 F.3d 307 (4th Cir. 2001).

When an employee takes military leave, your company must usually reemploy him or her without any loss of benefits or status or reduction in pay. These reemployment guarantees vary from state to state and sometimes contain additional conditions. To find out your state's rules, see "State Laws on Military Leave," at the end of this chapter.

Domestic Violence Leave

Employees who are victims of domestic violence may have the right to take time off from work. The federal Family and Medical Leave Act (FMLA) may require employers to give domestic abuse victims time off in certain circumstances, and some states have passed laws that specifically require employers to provide domestic violence leave: time off to handle the medical, legal, psychological, and practical ramifications of domestic violence.

Domestic violence—mental or physical abuse at the hands of an intimate partner—often affects the victim's ability to work. According to Legal Momentum, an advocacy group, victims of domestic violence lose an average of 137 hours of work a year. Some need time off to seek medical attention, get a restraining order, or relocate to a safe place. Others are prevented from getting to work when an abuser disables or takes the car, sabotages child care arrangements, or leaves the victim without cash to use public transportation.

These problems have led a number of states to pass domestic violence leave laws, which give victims of domestic violence the right to take time off for certain reasons. Some states allow those who are victims of (or witnesses to) any crime to take time off to attend court proceedings; these laws protect victims of domestic violence, although they also apply more generally. And the FMLA may also provide a right to leave for some domestic violence victims.

State Domestic Violence Leave Laws

Almost a dozen states—including California, Florida, Illinois, and Washington—and the District of Columbia have passed laws requiring employers to provide domestic violence leave. These laws vary significantly in the details, including:

- **How much time off.** Some states allow employees to take up to a set amount of days or weeks off; others allow employees to take a "reasonable" amount of leave or simply prohibit employers from disciplining or firing employees who take time off for reasons related to domestic violence.
- **Reasons for leave.** The list of covered activities varies by state, but most allow time off for medical care and psychological counseling, relocation or other safety planning, and seeking a restraining order or participating in legal proceedings relating to domestic violence.
- **Notice and paperwork requirements.** Most states require employees to give reasonable advance notice that they will need leave, although these laws also recognize that the employee may be facing an emergency and be unable to give notice. State law may also require

employees to provide some written proof that they took leave for reasons related to domestic violence.
- **Use of paid leave.** Currently, no state requires employers to pay employees for this time off; only the District of Columbia does. Some states allow employees to use their paid leave (such as sick or vacation days) while taking time off for domestic violence; others require employees to use up all of their paid leave before taking domestic violence leave.

You can find information on each state's domestic violence leave laws at www. legalmomentum.org.

State Crime Victim Laws

In addition to laws that require employers to provide domestic violence leave, most states have laws that protect employees who must take time off for legal matters relating to a criminal case in which they are a victim or witness. These laws differ in the legal matters they cover: Some states protect only employees who have been subpoenaed to appear in court and testify; others cover more activities, such as seeking a restraining order, attending court hearings, or preparing to testify.

Family and Medical Leave Act (FMLA)

The FMLA allows certain employees to take up to 12 weeks off every 12 months for their own serious health condition, to care for a family member with a serious health condition, or to care for a new child (among other things). An employee who is physically injured or develops psychological trauma as a result of domestic violence might be entitled to FMLA leave. An employee might also be able to take time off to care for a parent or child who has been a victim of domestic violence.

Restraining Orders for Employers

A restraining order (often called a "stay away" order) requires a perpetrator of domestic violence to stay a certain distance away from the victim. A restraining order often also requires the abuser to stay away from certain places, such as the victim's home and the school attended by the victim's children, if applicable. The purpose of a restraining order is to allow law enforcement to step in before anyone gets hurt. A batterer who gets too close to the victim has violated the order and can be detained by the police.

Some states allow businesses to get their own restraining orders if they are threatened with violence, and employers can use these laws to get restraining orders against an employee's batterer. Such a restraining order requires the batterer to stay a certain distance away from the employer's property or face arrest. You can find detailed information about workplace restraining orders at the website of Legal Momentum, www.legalmomentum.org.

Other Types of Leave

In addition to the kinds of leave covered above, many states require employers to provide leave for specified activities. Some of these entitlements are part of the state's family and medical leave law; others are stand-alone benefits. If your company does

business in a state that has any such laws and meets the other coverage requirements (most often, that it have a certain minimum number of employees), it will have to provide the mandated leave.

Details on every state law requiring employers to grant time off is beyond the scope of this book. For information on requirements imposed by your state, contact your state department of labor. (Contact information is in the appendix.) Here are some common state leave requirements:

- **Time off to be an organ or bone marrow donor.** A handful of states require private employers to give employees time off to donate bone marrow or be an organ donor. Sometimes, this leave counts toward the employee's entitlement to state family and medical leave.

- **Use of sick leave to care for an ill family member.** Some states give employees the right to use accrued sick leave to care for a sick family member, even if the employer's own policies don't provide for it.

- **Time off for court proceedings.** Many states give employees the right to take time off to appear as a witness in a court case.

- **Time off to serve as a volunteer firefighter or other emergency worker.** Some states require private employers to give workers time off to serve as a disaster relief worker, volunteer firefighter, emergency rescue worker, or Red Cross volunteer.

- **Time off for school activities.** In some states, parents are entitled to take a certain amount of leave each year to attend school functions, parent-teacher conferences, special education meetings, and the like.

Legal Dos and Don'ts: Leave

Do:

- **Help employees balance work and family.** Smart managers know that workers who can take time off occasionally to attend school conferences, care for a sick child, or take an elderly parent to the doctor will be more productive on the job. And companies that have a family-friendly reputation are better able to recruit—and retain—a high-quality workforce.
- **Be consistent.** Make sure you follow your company's policies faithfully when considering leave requests. If you play favorites, you could be setting your company up for a lawsuit.
- **Encourage employees to take accrued leave.** You don't want sick workers showing up, unable to work efficiently and infecting the rest of your team. Similarly, you don't want good employees to burn out because they never take a vacation.

Don't:

- **Allow abuse of leave.** Require sick employees to call in. Have your reports schedule vacation well in advance. And crack down on any employee who misuses leave. As long as you are evenhanded in applying these policies, they will go a long way toward keeping your workers in line.
- **Forget about fathers.** Although we've come a long way, many companies still offer only maternity leave, or discourage fathers from taking leave under seemingly neutral parental leave policies. These kinds of policies and practices can lead straight to the courthouse steps in a gender discrimination lawsuit.
- **Deny a leave request without checking the law.** If an employee asks to take time off for a particular reason, check with your human resources department—or your state labor department—to find out whether your state protects that type of leave. If you leap without looking, you may be violating the law.

Test Your Knowledge

Questions

1. All companies must give their employees some paid sick leave. ☐ True ☐ False

2. Employers are not allowed to cap the amount of vacation leave employees may accrue. ☐ True ☐ False

3. Only employees who work full time are entitled to take FMLA leave. ☐ True ☐ False

4. Employers may ask employees who take FMLA leave for their own serious health condition to provide a medical certification. ☐ True ☐ False

5. If both parents work for one company, each is entitled to a full 12 weeks of FMLA leave to care for their new baby. ☐ True ☐ False

6. Employees can take up to 26 weeks of FMLA leave each year to care for a family member who suffers a serious injury while serving in the military. ☐ True ☐ False

7. Employers must pay employees for time spent on jury duty. ☐ True ☐ False

8. Employees who are reinstated after serving in the military cannot be fired without good cause for up to one year, even if they work for an at-will employer. ☐ True ☐ False

9. Employers must pay employees for time spent on military leave. ☐ True ☐ False

10. Your company may have a legal obligation to allow employees to take time off to serve as a witness in court. ☐ True ☐ False

Answers

1. False. Employers in most places are generally not required to provide paid sick leave to their employees, although they may have to provide unpaid leave under the FMLA.

2. False. Some states prohibit employers from taking away accrued vacation time (by zeroing out an employee's balance at the end of the year, for example). But it is legal to put a limit on how much vacation time an employee may accrue in the first place.

3. False. An employee who has worked 1,250 hours for your company in the last 12 months and meets the other eligibility requirements is entitled to take FMLA leave. This works out to about 25 hours a week.

4. True. An employer may require an employee to provide a certification: proof that the employee (or the employee's family member) actually has a serious health condition.

5. False. If both parents work for one company and are married to each other, they are entitled to a combined 12 weeks of parental leave. (Unmarried parents get 12 weeks each.) However, you may have to give more time off if one parent needs leave for a serious health condition, such as complications from a difficult childbirth.

6. False. Employees may take military caregiver leave only once, unless the same family member suffers a different injury on active duty, or a different family member is injured. This right doesn't renew every 12 months, like other types of FMLA leave.

7. It depends on the laws of your state. Most do not require employers to pay for this time, but some do.

8. True. Employees who are reinstated after taking military leave enjoy this special job protection for up to one year (the exact length of the protection depends on the length of the employee's military service).

9. False. Although many private employers choose to pay employees for at least some portion of their military service, this is not a legal requirement.

10. True. Some states give employees the right to take time off work to serve as a witness.

State Family and Medical Leave Laws

CALIFORNIA

Cal. Gov't. Code §§ 12945 and 12945.2; Cal. Lab. Code §§ 230 and following; Cal. Unemp. Ins. Code §§ 3300 and following

Employers Covered: For pregnancy leave: employers with 5 or more employees; for domestic violence leave and school activity leave: employers with 25 or more employees; for family medical leave: employers with 50 or more employees; for paid family leave: employers whose employees contribute to state temporary disability insurance (SDI) fund

Eligible Employees: For pregnancy, domestic violence, or school activity leave: all employees; for family medical leave: employee with more than 12 months of service with the employer, and who has at least 1,250 hours of service with the employer during the previous 12-month period; for paid family leave benefits program: employees who contribute to SDI fund

Family Medical Leave: Up to 4 months for disability related to pregnancy (in addition to 12 weeks under family leave law); up to 12 weeks of leave per year to care for seriously ill family member. Employees who contribute to SDI fund may receive paid family leave benefits for up to 6 weeks of leave per year to care for a seriously ill family member (including a registered domestic partner) or bond with a new child.

School Activities: 40 hours per year, not more than 8 hours per calendar month

Domestic Violence: Reasonable time for issues dealing with domestic violence or sexual assault, including health, counseling, and safety measures. Family member or domestic partner of a victim of a felony may take leave to attend judicial proceedings related to the crime.

COLORADO

Colo. Rev. Stat. §§ 19-5-211; 24-34-402.7

Employers Covered: For adoption leave: all employers who offer leave for birth of a child; for domestic violence leave: employers with 50 or more employees

Eligible Employees: For adoption leave: all employees; for domestic violence leave: employees with one year of service

Family Medical Leave: Employee must be given same leave for adoption as allowed for childbirth (doesn't apply to stepparent adoption).

Domestic Violence: Up to 3 days' leave in any 12-month period to seek restraining order, obtain medical care or counseling, relocate, or seek legal assistance for victim of domestic violence, sexual assault, or stalking

CONNECTICUT

Conn. Gen. Stat. Ann. §§ 31-51kk to 31-51qq; 46a-60

Employers Covered: For pregnancy leave: employers with 3 or more employees; for family medical or serious health leave: employers with 75 or more employees

Eligible Employees: For pregnancy leave: all employees; for family medical or serious health condition leave: any employee with one year and at least 1,000 hours of service in last 12 months

Family Medical Leave: Reasonable amount of pregnancy leave required; 16 weeks per any 24-month period for childbirth, adoption, employee's serious health condition, care for family member with serious health condition, or bone marrow or organ donation; 26 weeks per 12-month period for each family member who is also a current member of the armed forces and is undergoing medical treatment

State Family and Medical Leave Laws (cont'd)

DISTRICT OF COLUMBIA

D.C. Code Ann. §§ 32-501 and following; 32-1202, 32-131.01 and following

Employers Covered: Employers with 20 or more employees

Eligible Employees: Employees who have worked at company for at least one year and at least 1,000 hours during the previous 12 months

Family Medical Leave: 16 weeks per any 24-month period for childbirth, adoption, pregnancy/maternity, domestic violence, or care for family member with serious health condition; additional 16 weeks per any 24-month period for employee's serious health condition; paid leave for the employee's or family member's physical or mental illness, injury, or medical condition; for the employee's or family member's medical care, diagnosis, or preventive medical care. Amount of paid leave depends on employer size: Employers with 100 or more employees must provide at least one hour of paid leave for every 37 hours worked, up to seven days of leave per year; employers with 25 to 99 employees must provide at least one hour of paid leave for every 43 hours worked, up to five days of leave per year; employers with fewer than 25 employees must provide at least one hour of paid leave for every 87 hours worked, up to three days of leave per year.

School Activities: Up to 24 hours of unpaid leave per year (all employees, all employers)

Domestic Violence: Paid leave, described under "Family Medical Leave," may also be used for employee or family member who is a victim of stalking, domestic violence, or abuse to get medical attention, get services, seek counseling, relocate, take legal action, or take steps to enhance health and safety.

FLORIDA

Fla. Stat. § 741.313

Employers Covered: All employers

Eligible Employees: All employees

Domestic Violence: Up to 3 working days in any 12-month period if employee or family/household member is victim of domestic violence, with or without pay at discretion of employer; applies to employers with 50 or more employees, and employee must be employed for at least 3 months

HAWAII

Haw. Rev. Stat. §§ 398-1 to 398-11; 378-1, 378-71 to 378-74

Employers Covered: For childbirth, adoption, and serious health condition leave: employers with 100 or more employees; for pregnancy leave and domestic violence leave: all employers

Eligible Employees: For childbirth, adoption, and serious health condition leave: employees with 6 months of service; for pregnancy and maternity leave: all employees

Family Medical Leave: 4 weeks per calendar year for childbirth, adoption, or care for family member with serious health condition; "reasonable period" of pregnancy/maternity leave required by discrimination statute and case law; may include up to 10 days' accrued leave or sick leave

Domestic Violence: Employer with 50 or more employees must allow up to 30 days' unpaid leave per year for employee who is a victim of domestic or sexual violence or if employee's minor child is a victim. Employer with 49 or fewer employees must allow up to 5 days' leave.

State Family and Medical Leave Laws (cont'd)

ILLINOIS

820 Ill. Comp. Stat. §§ 147/1 and following; 180/1 and following

Employers Covered: Employers with 15 or more employees

Eligible Employees: For school activities leave: employees who have worked at least half-time for 6 months; for domestic violence leave: all employees

School Activities: Eight hours per year (no more than 4 hours per day); required only if employee has no paid leave available

Domestic Violence: If employer has at least 50 employees, up to 12 weeks' unpaid leave per 12-month period for employee who is a victim of domestic violence or sexual assault or for employee with a family or household member who is a victim; if employer has at least 15 but not more than 49 employees, up to 8 weeks' unpaid leave during any 12-month period

IOWA

Iowa Code § 216.6

Employers Covered: Employers with 4 or more employees

Eligible Employees: All employees

Family Medical Leave: Up to 8 weeks for disability due to pregnancy, childbirth, or legal abortion

KENTUCKY

Ky. Rev. Stat. Ann. § 337.015

Employers Covered: All employers

Eligible Employees: All employees

Family Medical Leave: Up to 6 weeks for adoption of a child under 7 years old

LOUISIANA

La. Rev. Stat. Ann. §§ 23:341 to 23:342; 23:1015 and following; 40:1299.124

Employers Covered: For pregnancy/maternity leave: employers with 25 or more employees; for leave to donate bone marrow: employers with 20 or more employees; for school activities leave: all employers

Eligible Employees: For pregnancy/maternity or school activities leave: all employees; for leave to donate bone marrow: employees who work 20 or more hours per week

Family Medical Leave: "Reasonable period of time" not to exceed four months for pregnancy/maternity leave, if necessary for pregnancy or related medical condition; up to 40 hours' paid leave per year to donate bone marrow

School Activities: 16 hours per year

MAINE

Me. Rev. Stat. Ann. tit. 26, §§ 843 and following

Employers Covered: For domestic violence leave: all employers; for family medical leave: employers with 15 or more employees at one location

Eligible Employees: All employees for domestic violence leave; employees with at least one year of service for family medical leave

Family Medical Leave: 10 weeks in any two-year period for childbirth, adoption (for child 16 or younger), employee's serious health condition, or care for family member with serious health condition

Domestic Violence: "Reasonable and necessary" leave for employee who is victim of domestic violence, sexual assault, or stalking, or whose parent, spouse, or child is a victim, to prepare for and attend court, for medical treatment, and for other necessary services

State Family and Medical Leave Laws (cont'd)

MARYLAND

Md. Code Ann., Lab. & Empl. § 3-801, 3-802

Employers Covered: Employers with 15 or more employees

Eligible Employees: All employees

Family Medical Leave: Employee must be given same leave for adoption as allowed for childbirth.

MASSACHUSETTS

Mass. Gen. Laws ch. 149, §§ 52D, 105D; ch. 151B, § 1(5)

Employers Covered: For maternity and adoption leave: employers with 6 or more employees; for school activities leave: employers with 50 or more employees

Eligible Employees: For maternity and adoption leave: full-time female employees who have completed probationary period, or 3 months of service if no set probationary period; for all other leave: employees who are eligible under FMLA

Family Medical Leave: Eight weeks total for childbirth/maternity or adoption of child younger than 18 (younger than 23 if disabled); additional 24 hours total per year (combined with school activities leave) to accompany minor child or relative age 60 or older to medical and dental appointments

School Activities: 24 hours per year total (combined with medical care under "other")

MINNESOTA

Minn. Stat. Ann. §§ 181.940 and following

Employers Covered: For childbirth/maternity and adoption leave: employers with 21 or more employees at one site; for bone marrow donation: employers with 20 or more employees; for school activities: all employers

Eligible Employees: For maternity leave: employees who have worked at least half-time for one year; for bone marrow donation: employees who work at least 20 hours per week; for school activities: employees who have worked at least one year

Family Medical Leave: Six weeks for childbirth/maternity or adoption; up to 40 hours paid leave per year to donate bone marrow; parent can use accrued sick leave to care for sick or injured child.

School Activities: 16 hours in 12-month period; includes activities related to child care, preschool, or special education

MONTANA

Mont. Code Ann. §§ 49-2-310, 49-2-311

Employers Covered: All employers

Eligible Employees: All employees

Family Medical Leave: Reasonable leave of absence for pregnancy/maternity and childbirth

NEBRASKA

Neb. Rev. Stat. § 48-234

Employers Covered: Employers that allow workers to take leave for the birth of a child

Eligible Employees: All employees

Family Medical Leave: Employee must be given same leave as allowed for childbirth to adopt a child, unless child is over 8 (or over 18 for special needs child); does not apply to stepparent or foster parent adoptions

NEVADA

Nev. Rev. Stat. Ann. §§ 392.920, 613.335, 392.4577

Employers Covered: All employers

Eligible Employees: All employees

Family Medical Leave: Same sick or disability leave policies that apply to other medical conditions must be extended to pregnancy, miscarriage, and childbirth.

State Family and Medical Leave Laws (cont'd)

School Activities: Employers may not fire or threaten to fire a parent, guardian, or custodian for attending a school conference or responding to a child's emergency. Employers with 50 or more employees must provide parent with a child in private school a leave of 4 hours per school year, which must be taken in increments of at least 1 hour, to attend parent-teacher conferences, attend school-related activities during regular school hours, attend school-sponsored events, or volunteer or be involved at the school.

NEW HAMPSHIRE

N.H. Rev. Stat. Ann. § 354-A:7(VI)

Employers Covered: Employers with 6 or more employees

Eligible Employees: All employees

Family Medical Leave: Temporary disability leave for pregnancy/childbirth or related medical condition

NEW JERSEY

N.J. Stat. Ann. §§ 34:11B-1 and following; 43-21-1 and following

Employers Covered: Employers with 50 or more employees; for paid family leave, employers subject to the New Jersey Unemployment Compensation Law

Eligible Employees: Employees who have worked for at least one year and at least 1,000 hours in previous 12 months; for paid family leave benefits program: employees who worked 20 calendar weeks in covered New Jersey employment; or earned at least 1,000 times New Jersey minimum wage during 52 weeks preceding leave

Family Medical Leave: 12 weeks (or 24 weeks reduced-leave schedule) in any 24-month period for pregnancy/maternity, childbirth, adoption, or care for family member with serious health condition. Employees may receive paid family leave benefits for up to 6 weeks of leave per year to care for a seriously ill family member (including a registered domestic partner) or bond with a new child.

NEW MEXICO

N.M. Stat. Ann. § 50-4A-1 and following

Employers Covered: All employers

Eligible Employees: All employees

Domestic Violence: Employer must provide intermittent paid or unpaid leave time for up to fourteen days in any calendar year, taken by an employee for up to eight hours in one day, to obtain or attempt to obtain an order of protection or other judicial relief from domestic abuse or to meet with law enforcement officials, to consult with attorneys or district attorneys' victim advocates or to attend court proceedings related to the domestic abuse of an employee or an employee's family member.

NEW YORK

N.Y. Lab. Law §§ 201-c; 202-a

Employers Covered: Employers that allow workers to take leave for the birth of a child must allow adoption leave; employers with 20 or more employees at one site must allow leave to donate bone marrow.

Eligible Employees: All employees are eligible for adoption leave; employees who work at least 20 hours per week are eligible for leave to donate bone marrow.

Family Medical Leave: Employees must be given same leave as allowed for childbirth to adopt a child of preschool age or younger, or no older than 18 if disabled; up to 24 hours' leave to donate bone marrow.

State Family and Medical Leave Laws (cont'd)

NORTH CAROLINA

N.C. Gen. Stat. §§ 95-28.3, 50B-5.5

Employers Covered: All employers

Eligible Employees: All employees

School Activities: Parents and guardians of school-aged children must be given up to 4 hours of leave per year.

Domestic Violence: Reasonable time off from work to obtain or attempt to obtain relief from domestic violence and sexual assault

OREGON

Or. Rev. Stat. §§ 659A.029, 659A.150 and following, 659A.312, 659A.270 and following

Employers Covered: For childbirth, adoption, and serious health condition leave: employers with 25 or more employees; for domestic violence leave: employers with 6 or more employees; for leave to donate bone marrow: all employers

Eligible Employees: For childbirth, adoption, serious health condition or domestic violence leave: employees who have worked 25 or more hours per week for at least 180 days; for leave to donate bone marrow: employees who work an average of 20 or more hours per week

Family Medical Leave: 12 weeks per year for pregnancy/maternity, adoption, or childbirth; additional 12 weeks per year for serious health condition, care for family member with serious health condition, or care for child who has an illness, injury, or condition that requires home care; up to 40 hours or amount of accrued paid leave (whichever is less) to donate bone marrow

Domestic Violence: Reasonable leave for employee who is victim of domestic violence, sexual assault, or stalking, or whose minor child is a victim, to seek legal treatment, medical services, counseling, or to relocate/secure existing home

RHODE ISLAND

R.I. Gen. Laws §§ 28-48-1 and following

Employers Covered: Employers with 50 or more employees

Eligible Employees: Employees who have worked an average of 30 or more hours a week for at least 12 consecutive months

Family Medical Leave: 13 weeks in any two calendar years for childbirth, adoption of child up to 16 years old, employee's serious health condition, or care for family member with serious health condition

School Activities: Up to 10 hours a year

SOUTH CAROLINA

S.C. Code Ann. § 44-43-80

Employers Covered: Employers with 20 or more workers at one site in South Carolina

Eligible Employees: Employees who work an average of at least 20 hours per week

Family Medical Leave: Up to 40 hours paid leave per year to donate bone marrow—employers are not required to grant such leave.

TENNESSEE

Tenn. Code Ann. § 4-21-408

Employers Covered: Employers with 100 or more employees

Eligible Employees: Employees who have worked 12 consecutive months as full-time employees

Family Medical Leave: Up to 4 months of unpaid leave for pregnancy/maternity and childbirth (includes nursing); employee must give 3 months' notice unless a medical emergency requires the leave to begin sooner; these laws must be included in employee handbook.

State Family and Medical Leave Laws (cont'd)

VERMONT

Vt. Stat. Ann. tit. 21, §§ 471 and following

Employers Covered: For childbirth and adoption leave: employers with 10 or more employees; for family medical leave: employers with 15 or more employees

Eligible Employees: Employees who have worked an average of 30 or more hours per week for at least one year

Family Medical Leave: 12 weeks per year for childbirth, adoption of child age 16 or younger, employee's serious health condition, or care for family member with a serious health condition; combined with school activities leave, additional 4 hours of unpaid leave in a 30-day period (up to 24 hours per year) to take a family member to a medical, dental, or professional well-care appointment or respond to a family member's medical emergency

School Activities: Combined with leave described above, 4 hours' total unpaid leave in a 30-day period (but not more than 24 hours per year) to participate in child's school activities

WASHINGTON

Wash. Rev. Code Ann. §§ 49.78.010 and following, 49.12.265 and following, 49.12.350 and following, 49.76.010 and following, 49.86.005 and following

Employers Covered: All employers must allow employees to use available paid time off to care for sick family members (including state registered domestic partners); employers with 50 or more employees must provide leave to care for newborn, adopted, or foster child, or family member with serious health condition.

Eligible Employees: All employees who accrue paid sick leave may use it to care for sick family members (including state registered domestic partners); employees who have worked at least 1,250 hours in the previous year are eligible for parental leave to care for newborn, adopted, or foster child, or leave to care for a family member with serious health condition.

Family Medical Leave: In addition to any leave available under federal FMLA, employee may take leave for the period of time when she is sick or temporarily disabled due to pregnancy or childbirth; employers with 50 or more employees must allow up to 12 weeks during any 12-month period for the birth or placement of a child, employee's serious health condition, or care for a family member with a serious health condition; all employees can use paid sick leave to care for a sick family member.

Domestic Violence: Reasonable leave from work, with or without pay, for employee who is victim of domestic violence, sexual assault, or stalking, or whose family member is a victim, to prepare for and attend court, for medical treatment, and for other necessary services.

WISCONSIN

Wis. Stat. Ann. § 103.10

Employers Covered: Employers with 50 or more employees

Eligible Employees: Employees who have worked at least one year and 1,000 hours in the preceding 12 months

Family Medical Leave: 6 weeks per 12-month period for pregnancy/maternity, childbirth, or adoption; additional 2 weeks per 12-month period to care for family member (including domestic partner) with a serious health condition; additional 2 weeks per 12-month period to care for the employee's own serious health condition

State Laws on Jury Duty

ALABAMA

Ala. Code §§ 12-16-8 to 12-16-8.1

Paid leave: Full-time employees are entitled to usual pay minus any fees received from the court.

Notice employee must give: Must show supervisor jury summons the next working day; must return to work the next scheduled hour after discharge from jury duty.

Employer penalty for firing or penalizing employee: Liable for actual and punitive damages.

ALASKA

Alaska Stat. § 09.20.037

Unpaid leave: Yes.

Employer penalty for firing or penalizing employee: Liable for lost wages and damages; may be required to reinstate the fired employee.

ARIZONA

Ariz. Rev. Stat. § 21-236

Unpaid leave: Yes.

Additional employee protections: Employee may not lose vacation rights, seniority, or precedence. Employer may not require employee to use annual, sick, or vacation hours.

Employer penalty for firing or penalizing employee: Class 3 misdemeanor, punishable by a fine of up to $500 or up to 30 days' imprisonment.

Note: Employers with 5 or fewer full-time employees: Court must postpone an employee's jury service if another employee is already serving as a juror.

ARKANSAS

Ark. Code Ann. § 16-31-106

Unpaid leave: Yes.

Additional employee protections: Absence may not affect sick leave and vacation rights.

Employer penalty for firing or penalizing employee: Class A misdemeanor, punishable by a fine of up to $2,500.

CALIFORNIA

Cal. Lab. Code §§ 230, 230.1

Unpaid leave: Employee may use vacation, personal leave, or comp time.

Additional employee protections: Victims of crime, domestic violence, or sexual assault are protected against discharge, discrimination, or retaliation for attending a court proceeding or seeking judicial relief.

Notice employee must give: Reasonable notice.

Employer penalty for firing or penalizing employee: Employer must reinstate employee with back pay and lost wages and benefits. Willful violation is a misdemeanor.

COLORADO

Colo. Rev. Stat. §§ 13-71-126, 13-71-133 to 13-71-134

Paid leave: All employees (including part-time and temporary who were scheduled to work for the 3 months preceding jury service): regular wages up to $50 per day for first 3 days of jury duty. Must pay within 30 days of jury service.

Additional employee protections: Employer may not make any demands on employee which will interfere with effective performance of jury duty.

Employer penalty for firing or penalizing employee: Class 2 misdemeanor, punishable by a fine of $250 to $1,000 or 3 to 12 months' imprisonment, or both. May be liable to employee for triple damages and attorney's fees.

State Laws on Jury Duty (cont'd)

CONNECTICUT
Conn. Gen. Stat. Ann. §§ 51-247 and 51-247a

Paid leave: Full-time employees: regular wages for the first 5 days of jury duty; after 5 days, state pays up to $50 per day.

Employer penalty for firing or penalizing employee: Criminal contempt: punishable by a fine of up to $500 or up to 30 days' imprisonment, or both. Liable for up to 10 weeks' lost wages for discharging employee. If employer fails to pay the employee as required, may be liable for treble damages and attorney's fees.

DELAWARE
Del. Code Ann. tit. 10, § 4515

Unpaid leave: Yes.

Employer penalty for firing or penalizing employee: Criminal contempt: punishable by a fine of up to $500 or up to 6 months' imprisonment, or both. Liable to discharged employee for lost wages and attorney's fees and may be required to reinstate the fired employee.

DISTRICT OF COLUMBIA
D.C. Code Ann. §§ 11-1913, 15-718

Paid leave: Full-time employees: regular wages for the first 5 days of jury duty.

Employer penalty for firing or penalizing employee: Criminal contempt: punishable by a fine of up to $300 or up to 30 days' imprisonment, or both, for a first offense; up to $5,000 or up to 180 days' imprisonment, or both, for any subsequent offense. Liable to discharged employee for lost wages and attorney's fees and may be required to reinstate the fired employee.

FLORIDA
Fla. Stat. Ann. § 40.271

Unpaid leave: Yes.

Additional employee protections: Employee may not be threatened with dismissal.

Employer penalty for firing or penalizing employee: Threatening employee is contempt of court. May be liable to discharged employee for compensatory and punitive damages and attorney's fees.

GEORGIA
Ga. Code Ann. § 34-1-3

Unpaid leave: Yes.

Additional employee protections: Employee may not be discharged, penalized, or threatened with discharge or penalty for responding to a subpoena or making a required court appearance.

Notice employee must give: Reasonable notice.

Employer penalty for firing or penalizing employee: Liable for actual damages and reasonable attorney's fees.

HAWAII
Haw. Rev. Stat. § 612-25

Unpaid leave: Yes.

Employer penalty for firing or penalizing employee: Petty misdemeanor: punishable by a fine of up to $1,000 or up to 30 days' imprisonment. May be liable to discharged employee for up to 6 weeks' lost wages and may be required to reinstate the fired employee.

IDAHO
Idaho Code § 2-218

Unpaid leave: Yes.

Employer penalty for firing or penalizing employee: Criminal contempt: punishable by a fine of up to $300. Liable to discharged employee for triple lost wages.

State Laws on Jury Duty (cont'd)

ILLINOIS

705 Ill. Comp. Stat. § 310/10.1

Unpaid leave: Yes.

Additional employee protections: A regular night-shift employee may not be required to work if serving on a jury during the day. May not lose any seniority or benefits.

Notice employee must give: Must give employer a copy of the summons within 10 days of issuance.

Employer penalty for firing or penalizing employee: Employer will be charged with civil or criminal contempt, or both; liable to employee for lost wages and benefits.

INDIANA

Ind. Code Ann. §§ 34-28-4-1, 35-44-3-10

Unpaid leave: Yes.

Additional employee protections: Employee may not be deprived of benefits or threatened with the loss of them.

Employer penalty for firing or penalizing employee: Class B misdemeanor: punishable by up to 180 days' imprisonment; may also be fined up to $1,000. Liable to discharged employee for lost wages and attorney's fees and may be required to reinstate the fired employee.

IOWA

Iowa Code § 607A.45

Unpaid leave: Yes.

Employer penalty for firing or penalizing employee: Contempt of court. Liable to discharged employee for up to 6 weeks' lost wages and attorney's fees and may be required to reinstate the fired employee.

KANSAS

Kan. Stat. Ann. § 43-173

Unpaid leave: Yes.

Additional employee protections: Employee may not lose seniority or benefits. (Basic and additional protections apply to permanent employees only.)

Employer penalty for firing or penalizing employee: Liable for lost wages and benefits, damages, and attorney's fees and may be required to reinstate the fired employee.

KENTUCKY

Ky. Rev. Stat. Ann. §§ 29A.160, 29A.990

Unpaid leave: Yes.

Employer penalty for firing or penalizing employee: Class B misdemeanor: punishable by up to 89 days' imprisonment or fine of up to $250, or both. Liable to discharged employee for lost wages and attorney's fees. Must reinstate employee with full seniority and benefits.

LOUISIANA

La. Rev. Stat. Ann. § 23:965

Paid leave: Regular employee entitled to one day full compensation for jury service. May not lose any sick, vacation, or personal leave or other benefit.

Additional employee protections: Employer may not create any policy or rule that would discharge employee for jury service.

Notice employee must give: Reasonable notice.

Employer penalty for firing or penalizing employee: For each discharged employee: fine of $100 to $1,000; must reinstate employee with full benefits. For not granting paid leave: fine of $100 to $500; must pay full day's lost wages.

State Laws on Jury Duty (cont'd)

MAINE

Me. Rev. Stat. Ann. tit. 14, § 1218

Unpaid leave: Yes.

Additional employee protections: Employee may not lose or be threatened with loss of health insurance coverage.

Employer penalty for firing or penalizing employee: Class E crime: punishable by up to 6 months in the county jail or a fine of up to $1,000. Liable for up to 6 weeks' lost wages, benefits, and attorney's fees.

MARYLAND

Md. Code Ann., [Cts. & Jud. Proc.] § 8-502

Unpaid leave: Yes.

Additional employee protections: An employee may not be required to use annual, sick, or vacation leave. Employer penalty for violating this provision is a fine up to $1,000.

MASSACHUSETTS

Mass. Gen. Laws ch. 234A, §§ 48 and following

Paid leave: All employees (including part-time and temporary who were scheduled to work for the 3 months preceding jury service): regular wages for first 3 days of jury duty. If paid leave is an "extreme financial hardship" for employer, state will pay. After first 3 days state will pay $50 per day.

MICHIGAN

Mich. Comp. Laws § 600.1348

Unpaid leave: Yes.

Additional employee protections: Employee may not be threatened or disciplined; may not be required to work in addition to jury service, if extra hours would mean working overtime or beyond normal quitting time.

Employer penalty for firing or penalizing employee: Misdemeanor, punishable by a fine of up to $500 or up to 90 days' imprisonment, or both. Employer may also be punished for contempt of court, with a fine of up to $7,500 or up to 93 days' imprisonment, or both.

MINNESOTA

Minn. Stat. Ann. § 593.50

Unpaid leave: Yes.

Employer penalty for firing or penalizing employee: Criminal contempt: punishable by a fine of up to $700 or up to 6 months' imprisonment, or both. Also liable to employee for up to 6 weeks' lost wages and attorney's fees and may be required to reinstate the fired employee.

MISSISSIPPI

Miss. Code Ann. §§ 13-5-23, 13-5-35

Unpaid leave: Yes.

Additional employee protections: Employee may not be required to use annual, sick, or vacation leave for jury service.

Notice employee must give: Reasonable notice is required.

Employer penalty for firing or penalizing employee: If found guilty of interference with the administration of justice: at least one month in the county jail or up to 2 years in the state penitentiary, or a fine of up to $500, or both. May also be found guilty of contempt of court, punishable by a fine of up to $1,000 or up to 6 months' imprisonment, or both.

Note: Employers with 5 or fewer full-time employees: Court must postpone an employee's jury service if another employee is already serving as a juror.

State Laws on Jury Duty (cont'd)

MISSOURI

Mo. Rev. Stat. § 494.460

Unpaid leave: Yes.

Additional employee protections: Employer may not take or threaten to take any adverse action. Employee may not be required to use annual, sick, vacation, or personal leave.

Employer penalty for firing or penalizing employee: Employer may be liable for lost wages, damages, and attorney's fees and may be required to reinstate the fired employee.

MONTANA

Mont. Admin. R. 24.16.2520

Paid leave: No paid leave laws regarding private employers.

NEBRASKA

Neb. Rev. Stat. § 25-1640

Paid leave: Normal wages minus any compensation (other than expenses) from the court.

Additional employee protections: Employee may not lose pay, sick leave, or vacation or be penalized in any way; may not be required to work evening or night shift.

Notice employee must give: Reasonable notice.

Employer penalty for firing or penalizing employee: Class IV misdemeanor, punishable by a fine of $100 to $500.

NEVADA

Nev. Rev. Stat. Ann. § 6.190

Unpaid leave: Yes.

Additional employee protections: Employer may not recommend or threaten termination; may not dissuade or attempt to dissuade employee from serving as a juror, and cannot require the employee to work within 8 hours before jury duty or if employee's duty lasts four hours or more (including travel time to and from the court), between 5 p.m. that day and 3 a.m. the next day. Cannot be required to take paid leave.

Notice employee must give: At least one day's notice.

Employer penalty for firing or penalizing employee: Terminating or threatening to terminate is a gross misdemeanor, punishable by a fine of up to $2,000 or up to one year's imprisonment, or both; in addition, employer may be liable for lost wages, damages equal to lost wages, and punitive damages to $50,000 and must reinstate employee. Dissuading or attempting to dissuade is a misdemeanor, punishable by a fine of up to $1,000 or up to 6 months in the county jail, or both.

NEW HAMPSHIRE

N.H. Rev. Stat. Ann. § 500-A:14

Unpaid leave: Yes.

Employer penalty for firing or penalizing employee: Employer may be found guilty of contempt of court; also liable to employee for lost wages and attorney's fees and may be required to reinstate the fired employee.

NEW JERSEY

N.J. Stat. Ann. § 2B:20-17

Unpaid leave: Yes.

Employer penalty for firing or penalizing employee: Employer may be found guilty of a disorderly persons offense, punishable by a fine of up to $1,000 or up to 6 months' imprisonment, or both. May also be liable to employee for economic damages and attorney's fees and may be ordered to reinstate the fired employee.

State Laws on Jury Duty (cont'd)

NEW MEXICO

N.M. Stat. Ann. §§ 38-5-18 to 38-5-19

Unpaid leave: Yes.

Additional employee protections: An employee may not be required to use annual, sick, or vacation leave.

Employer penalty for firing or penalizing employee: Petty misdemeanor, punishable by a fine of up to $500 or up to 6 months in the county jail, or both.

NEW YORK

N.Y. Jud. Ct. Acts Law § 519

Unpaid leave: Yes.

Paid leave: Employers with more than 10 employees must pay first $40 of wages for the first 3 days of jury duty.

Notice employee must give: Must notify employer prior to beginning jury duty.

Employer penalty for firing or penalizing employee: May be found guilty of criminal contempt of court, punishable by a fine of up to $1,000 or up to 30 days in the county jail, or both.

NORTH CAROLINA

N.C. Gen. Stat. § 9-32

Unpaid leave: Yes.

Additional employee protections: Employee may not be demoted.

Employer penalty for firing or penalizing employee: Liable to discharged employee for reasonable damages; must reinstate employee to former position.

NORTH DAKOTA

N.D. Cent. Code § 27-09.1-17

Unpaid leave: Yes.

Additional employee protections: Employee may not be laid off, penalized, or coerced

because of jury duty, responding to a summons or subpoena, serving as a witness, or testifying in court.

Employer penalty for firing or penalizing employee: Class B misdemeanor, punishable by a fine of up to $1,000 or up to 30 days' imprisonment, or both. Liable to employee for up to 6 weeks' lost wages and attorney's fees and may be required to reinstate the fired employee.

OHIO

Ohio Rev. Code Ann. § 2313.18

Unpaid leave: Yes.

Additional employee protections: An employee may not be required to use annual, sick, or vacation leave.

Notice employee must give: Reasonable notice. Absence must be for actual jury service.

Employer penalty for firing or penalizing employee: May be found guilty of contempt of court, punishable by a fine of up to $250 or 30 days' imprisonment, or both, for first offense; a fine of up to $500 or 60 days' imprisonment, or both, for second offense; a fine of up to $1,000 or 90 days' imprisonment, or both, for third offense.

Note: Employers with 25 or fewer employees: Court must postpone an employee's jury service if another employee is already serving as a juror.

OKLAHOMA

Okla. Stat. Ann. tit. 38, §§ 34, 35

Unpaid leave: Yes.

Additional employee protections: Employee can't be required to use annual sick or vacation leave.

Notice employee must give: Reasonable notice.

Employer penalty for firing or penalizing employee: Misdemeanor, punishable by a fine

State Laws on Jury Duty (cont'd)

of up to $5,000. Liable to discharged employee for actual and exemplary damages; actual damages include past and future lost wages, mental anguish, and costs of finding suitable employment.

OREGON
Or. Rev. Stat. § 10.090

Unpaid leave: Yes (or according to employer's policy).

Additional employee protections: Employee may not be threatened, intimidated, or coerced.

Employer penalty for firing or penalizing employee: Employer must reinstate discharged employee with back pay.

PENNSYLVANIA
42 Pa. Cons. Stat. Ann. § 4563; 18 Pa. Cons. Stat. Ann. § 4957

Unpaid leave: Yes (applies to retail or service industry employers with 15 or more employees and to manufacturers with 40 or more employees).

Additional employee protections: Employee may not lose seniority or benefits. (Any employee who would not be eligible for unpaid leave will be automatically excused from jury duty.) Employee who must appear in court as a victim or witness, or as a family member of a victim or witness, must also be given unpaid leave.

Employer penalty for firing or penalizing employee: Liable to employee for lost benefits, wages, and attorney's fees; may be required to reinstate the fired employee.

RHODE ISLAND
R.I. Gen. Laws § 9-9-28

Unpaid leave: Yes.

Additional employee protections: Employee may not lose wage increases, promotions, length of service, or other benefit.

Employer penalty for firing or penalizing employee: Misdemeanor punishable by a fine of up to $1,000 or up to one year's imprisonment, or both.

SOUTH CAROLINA
S.C. Code Ann. § 41-1-70

Unpaid leave: Yes.

Additional employee protections: Employee may not be demoted or dismissed for responding to a subpoena to testify.

Employer penalty for firing or penalizing employee: For discharging employee, liable for one year's salary; for demoting employee, liable for one year's difference between former and lower salary.

SOUTH DAKOTA
S.D. Codified Laws Ann. §§ 16-13-41.1, 16-13-41.2

Unpaid leave: Yes.

Additional employee protections: Employee may not lose job status, pay, or seniority.

Employer penalty for firing or penalizing employee: Class 2 misdemeanor, punishable by a fine of up to $500 or up to 30 days in the county jail, or both.

TENNESSEE
Tenn. Code Ann. § 22-4-106

Paid leave: Regular wages minus jury fees, as long as the employer has at least 5 employees and the employee has been employed for at least 6 months.

Additional employee protections: Night-shift employees are excused from shift work during and for the night before the first day of jury service.

ork.

me art over roprly.

State Laws on Jury Duty (cont'd)

Notice employee must give: Employee must show summons to supervisor the day after receiving it.

Employer penalty for firing or penalizing employee: Violating employee rights or any provisions of this law is a Class A misdemeanor, punishable by up to 11 months, 29 days imprisonment or a fine up to $2,500, or both. Liable to employee for lost wages and benefits and must reinstate employee.

TEXAS
Tex. Civ. Prac. & Rem. Code Ann. §§ 122.001, 122.002

Unpaid leave: Yes.

Notice employee must give: Employee must notify employer of intent to return after completion of jury service.

Employer penalty for firing or penalizing employee: Liable to employee for not less than one year's nor more than 5 years' compensation and attorney fees. Must reinstate employee.

Note: Only applies to permanent employees.

UTAH
Utah Code Ann. § 78B-1-116

Unpaid leave: Yes.

Additional employee protections: Employee may not be requested or required to use annual or sick leave or vacation.

Employer penalty for firing or penalizing employee: May be found guilty of criminal contempt, punishable by a fine of up to $500 or up to 6 months' imprisonment, or both. Liable to employee for up to 6 weeks' lost wages and attorney's fees and may be required to reinstate the fired employee.

VERMONT
Vt. Stat. Ann. tit. 21, § 499

Unpaid leave: Yes.

Additional employee protections: Employee may not be penalized or lose any benefit available to other employees; may not lose seniority, vacation credit, or any fringe benefits. Protections also apply to an employee appearing as a witness in court or testifying before a board, commission, or tribunal.

Employer penalty for firing or penalizing employee: Fine of up to $200.

VIRGINIA
Va. Code Ann. § 18.2-465.1

Unpaid leave: Yes.

Additional employee protections: Employee may not be subject to any adverse personnel action and may not be forced to use sick leave or vacation. Employee who has appeared for 4 or more hours cannot be required to start a shift after 5 p.m. that day or before 3 a.m. the next morning. Protections also apply to an employee summoned or subpoenaed to appear, except criminal defendants.

Notice employee must give: Reasonable notice.

Employer penalty for firing or penalizing employee: Class 3 misdemeanor, punishable by a fine of up to $500.

WASHINGTON
Wash. Rev. Code Ann. § 2.36.165

Unpaid leave: Yes.

Additional employee protections: Employee may not be threatened, coerced, harassed, or denied promotion.

Employer penalty for firing or penalizing employee: Intentional violation is a misdemeanor,

State Laws on Jury Duty (cont'd)

punishable by a fine of up to $1,000 or up to 90 days' imprisonment, or both; also liable to employee for damages and attorney's fees and may be required to reinstate the fired employee.

WEST VIRGINIA

W.Va. Code § 52-3-1

Unpaid leave: Yes.

Additional employee protections: Employee may not be threatened or discriminated against; regular pay cannot be cut.

Employer penalty for firing or penalizing employee: May be found guilty of civil contempt, punishable by a fine of $100 to $500. May be required to reinstate the fired employee. May be liable for back pay and for attorney's fees.

WISCONSIN

Wis. Stat. Ann. § 756.255

Unpaid leave: Yes.

Additional employee protections: Employee may not lose seniority or pay raises; may not be disciplined.

Employer penalty for firing or penalizing employee: Fine of up to $200. May be required to reinstate the fired employee with back pay.

WYOMING

Wyo. Stat. § 1-11-401

Unpaid leave: Yes.

Additional employee protections: Employee may not be threatened, intimidated, or coerced.

Employer penalty for firing or penalizing employee: Liable to employee for up to $1,000 damages, costs, and attorney's fees. May be required to reinstate the fired employee with no loss of seniority.

State Laws on Taking Time Off to Vote

Note: The states of Connecticut, Delaware, District of Columbia, Florida, Idaho, Indiana, Louisiana, Maine, Michigan, Mississippi, Montana, New Hampshire, New Jersey, North Carolina, Oregon, Pennsylvania, Rhode Island, South Carolina, Vermont, and Virginia are not listed in this chart because they do not have laws or regulations on time off to vote that govern private employers. Check with your state department of labor if you need more information. (See appendix for contact list.)

ALABAMA
Ala. Code § 17-1-5

Time off work for voting: Necessary time up to one hour. The employer may decide when hours may be taken.

Time off not required if: Employee has 2 nonwork hours before polls open or one nonwork hour after polls are open.

Time off is paid: No.

Employee must request leave in advance: "Reasonable notice."

ALASKA
Alaska Stat. § 15.56.100

Time off work for voting: Not specified.

Time off not required if: Employee has 2 consecutive nonwork hours at beginning or end of shift when polls are open.

Time off is paid: Yes.

ARIZONA
Ariz. Rev. Stat. § 16-402

Time off work for voting: As much time as will add up to 3 hours when combined with nonwork time. Employer may decide when hours are taken.

Time off not required if: Employee has 3 consecutive nonwork hours at beginning or end of shift when polls are open.

Time off is paid: Yes.

Employee must request leave in advance: Prior to the day of the election.

ARKANSAS
Ark. Code Ann. § 7-1-102

Time off work for voting: Employer must schedule employees' work schedules on election days to enable employees to vote.

Time off is paid: No.

CALIFORNIA
Cal. Elec. Code § 14000

Time off work for voting: Up to 2 hours at beginning or end of shift, whichever gives employee most time to vote and takes least time off work.

Time off not required if: Employee has sufficient time to vote during nonwork time.

Time off is paid: Yes (up to 2 hours).

Employee must request leave in advance: 2 working days before election.

COLORADO
Colo. Rev. Stat. § 1-7-102

Time off work for voting: Up to 2 hours. Employer may decide when hours are taken, but employer must permit employee to take time at beginning or end of shift, if employee requests it.

Time off not required if: Employee has 3 nonwork hours when polls are open.

Time off is paid: Yes (up to 2 hours).

Employee must request leave in advance: Prior to election day.

State Laws on Taking Time Off to Vote (cont'd)

GEORGIA
Ga. Code Ann. § 21-2-404

Time off work for voting: Up to 2 hours. Employer may decide when hours are taken.

Time off not required if: Employee has 2 nonwork hours at beginning or end of shift when polls are open.

Time off is paid: No.

Employee must request leave in advance: "Reasonable notice."

HAWAII
Haw. Rev. Stat. § 11-95

Time off work for voting: 2 consecutive hours excluding meal or rest breaks. Employer may not change employee's regular work schedule.

Time off not required if: Employee has 2 consecutive nonwork hours when polls are open.

Time off is paid: Yes.

Employee required to show proof of voting: Only if employer is verifying whether employee voted when they took time off to vote. A voter's receipt is proof of voting by the employee. If employer verifies that employee did not vote, hours off may be deducted from pay.

ILLINOIS
10 Ill. Comp. Stat. §§ 5/7-42, 5/17-15

Time off work for voting: 2 hours. Employer may decide when hours are taken except that employer must permit a 2-hour absence during working hours if employee's working hours begin less than 2 hours after opening of polls and end less than 2 hours before closing of polls.

Time off is paid: Yes.

Employee must request leave in advance: Prior to the day of election. One day in advance (for general or state election). Employer must give consent (for primary).

IOWA
Iowa Code § 49.109

Time off work for voting: As much time as will add up to 3 hours when combined with nonwork time. Employer may decide when hours are taken.

Time off not required if: Employee has 3 consecutive nonwork hours when polls are open.

Time off is paid: Yes.

Employee must request leave in advance: In writing "prior to the date of the election."

KANSAS
Kan. Stat. Ann. § 25-418

Time off work for voting: Up to 2 hours or as much time as will add up to 2 hours when combined with nonwork time. Employer may decide when hours are taken, but it may not be during a regular meal break.

Time off not required if: Employee has 2 consecutive nonwork hours when polls are open.

Time off is paid: Yes.

KENTUCKY
Ky. Const. § 148; Ky. Rev. Stat. Ann. § 118.035

Time off work for voting: "Reasonable time," but not less than 4 hours. Employer may decide when hours are taken.

Time off is paid: No.

Employee must request leave in advance: One day before election.

Employee required to show proof of voting: No proof specified, but employee who takes time off and does not vote may be subject to disciplinary action.

State Laws on Taking Time Off to Vote (cont'd)

MARYLAND

Md. Code Ann. [Elec. Law] § 10-315

Time off work for voting: 2 hours.

Time off not required if: Employee has 2 consecutive nonwork hours when polls are open.

Time off is paid: Yes.

Employee required to show proof of voting: Yes; also includes attempting to vote. Must use state board of elections form.

MASSACHUSETTS

Mass. Gen. Laws ch. 149, § 178

Time off work for voting: First 2 hours that polls are open. (Applies to workers in manufacturing, mechanical, or retail industries.)

Time off is paid: No.

Employee must request leave in advance: Must apply for leave of absence (no time specified).

MINNESOTA

Minn. Stat. Ann. § 204C.04

Time off work for voting: May be absent for the time necessary to appear at the employee's polling place, cast a ballot, and return to work.

Time off is paid: Yes.

MISSOURI

Mo. Rev. Stat. § 115.639

Time off work for voting: 3 hours. Employer may decide when hours are taken.

Time off not required if: Employee has 3 consecutive nonwork hours when polls are open.

Time off is paid: Yes (if employee votes).

Employee must request leave in advance: "Prior to the day of election."

Employee required to show proof of voting: None specified, but pay contingent on employee actually voting.

NEBRASKA

Neb. Rev. Stat. § 32-922

Time off work for voting: As much time as will add up to 2 consecutive hours when combined with nonwork time. Employer may decide when hours are taken.

Time off not required if: Employee has 2 consecutive nonwork hours when polls are open.

Time off is paid: Yes.

Employee must request leave in advance: Prior to or on election day.

NEVADA

Nev. Rev. Stat. Ann. § 293.463

Time off work for voting: If it is impracticable to vote before or after work: Employee who works 2 miles or less from polling place may take 1 hour; 2 to 10 miles, 2 hours; more than 10 miles, 3 hours. Employer will decide when hours are taken.

Time off not required if: Employee has sufficient nonwork time when polls are open.

Time off is paid: Yes.

Employee must request leave in advance: Prior to election day.

NEW MEXICO

N.M. Stat. Ann. § 1-12-42

Time off work for voting: 2 hours. (Includes Indian nation, tribal, and pueblo elections.) Employer may decide when hours are taken.

Time off not required if: Employee's workday begins more than 2 hours after polls open or ends more than 3 hours before polls close.

Time off is paid: Yes.

State Laws on Taking Time Off to Vote (cont'd)

NEW YORK

N.Y. Elec. Law § 3-110

Time off work for voting: As many hours at beginning or end of shift as will give employee enough time to vote when combined with nonwork time. Employer may decide when hours are taken.

Time off not required if: Employee has 4 consecutive nonwork hours at beginning or end of shift when polls are open.

Time off is paid: Yes (up to 2 hours).

Employee must request leave in advance: Not more than 10 or less than 2 working days before election.

NORTH DAKOTA

N.D. Cent. Code § 16.1-01-02.1

Time off work for voting: Employers are encouraged to give employees time off to vote when regular work schedule conflicts with times polls are open.

Time off is paid: No.

OHIO

Ohio Rev. Code Ann. § 3599.06

Time off work for voting: "Reasonable time."

Time off is paid: Yes.

OKLAHOMA

Okla. Stat. Ann. tit. 26, § 7-101

Time off work for voting: 2 hours, unless employee lives so far from polling place that more time is needed. Employer may decide when hours are taken or may change employee's schedule to give employee nonwork time to vote.

Time off not required if: Employee's workday begins at least 3 hours after polls open or ends at least 3 hours before polls close.

Time off is paid: Yes.

Employee must request leave in advance: One day before election.

Employee required to show proof of voting: Yes.

SOUTH DAKOTA

S.D. Codified Laws Ann. § 12-3-5

Time off work for voting: 2 consecutive hours. Employer may decide when hours are taken.

Time off not required if: Employee has 2 consecutive nonwork hours when polls are open.

Time off is paid: Yes.

TENNESSEE

Tenn. Code Ann. § 2-1-106

Time off work for voting: "Reasonable time" up to 3 hours during the time polls are open. Employer may decide when hours are taken.

Time off not required if: Employee's workday begins at least 3 hours after polls open or ends at least 3 hours before polls close.

Time off is paid: Yes.

Employee must request leave in advance: Before noon on the day before the election.

TEXAS

Tex. Elec. Code Ann. § 276.004

Time off work for voting: Employer may not refuse to allow employee to take time off to vote, but no time limit specified.

Time off not required if: Employee has 2 consecutive nonwork hours when polls are open.

Time off is paid: Yes.

UTAH

Utah Code Ann. § 20A-3-103

Time off work for voting: 2 hours at beginning or end of shift. Employer may decide when hours are taken.

State Laws on Taking Time Off to Vote (cont'd)

Time off not required if: Employee has at least 3 nonwork hours when polls are open.

Time off is paid: Yes.

Employee must request leave in advance: "Before election day."

WASHINGTON
Wash. Rev. Code Ann. § 49.28.120

Time off work for voting: Employer must either arrange work schedule so employee has enough nonwork time (not including meal or rest breaks) to vote, or allow employee to take off work for a "reasonable time," up to 2 hours.

Time off not required if: Employee has 2 nonwork hours when polls are open or enough time to get an absentee ballot.

Time off is paid: Yes, if employee's work schedule does not give the employee 2 free hours (not including meal or rest breaks) when polls are open.

WEST VIRGINIA
W.Va. Code § 3-1-42

Time off work for voting: Up to 3 hours. (Employers in health, transportation, communication, production, and processing facilities may change employee's schedule so that time off doesn't impair essential operations but must allow employee sufficient and convenient time to vote.)

Time off not required if: Employee has at least 3 nonwork hours when polls are open.

Time off is paid: Yes (if employee votes).

Employee must request leave in advance: Written request at least 3 days before election.

Employee required to show proof of voting: None specified, but time off will be deducted from pay if employee does not vote.

WISCONSIN
Wis. Stat. Ann. § 6.76

Time off work for voting: Up to 3 consecutive hours. Employer may decide when hours are taken.

Time off is paid: No.

Employee must request leave in advance: "Before election day."

WYOMING
Wyo. Stat. § 22-2-111

Time off work for voting: One hour, other than a meal break. Employer may decide when the hour is taken.

Time off not required if: Employee has at least 3 consecutive nonwork hours when polls are open.

Time off is paid: Yes (if employee votes).

Employee required to show proof of voting: None specified, but pay contingent on employee voting.

State Laws on Military Leave

ALABAMA

Alabama Stat. §§ 31-12-1 to 31-12-4

Alabama National Guard members called to active duty for at least 30 consecutive days or for federally funded duty for service other than training have the same leave and reinstatement rights and benefits guaranteed under USERRA.

ALASKA

Alaska Stat. § 26.05.075

Employees called to active service in the state militia are entitled to unlimited unpaid leave and reinstatement to their former or a comparable position, with the pay, seniority, and benefits the employee would have had if not absent for service. Employee must return to work on next workday, after time required for travel. Disabled employee must request reemployment within 30 days of release; if disability leaves the employee unable to do the job, employee must be offered a position with similar pay and benefits.

ARIZONA

Ariz. Rev. Stat. §§ 26-167, 26-168

Members of the National Guard, Arizona National Guard, and U.S. armed forces reserves called to active duty have the same leave and reinstatement rights and benefits guaranteed under USERRA. Members of the National Guard called to participate in maneuvers or drills are entitled to unlimited unpaid leave and reinstatement to their former or a higher position with the same seniority and vacation benefits. Employer may not dissuade employees from enlisting in state or national military forces by threatening economic reprisal.

ARKANSAS

Ark. Code Ann. § 12-62-413

Employees called by the governor to active duty in the Arkansas National Guard or the state militia have the same leave and reinstatement rights and benefits guaranteed under USERRA.

CALIFORNIA

Cal. Mil. & Vet. Code §§ 394, 394.5, 395.06

Members of the California National Guard called to active duty are entitled to unlimited unpaid leave and reinstatement to their former position or to a position of similar seniority, status, and pay without loss of retirement or other benefits, unless the employer's circumstances have so changed as to make reinstatement impossible or unreasonable. Employee must apply for reinstatement within 40 days of discharge, and cannot be terminated without cause for one year. Employees in the U.S. armed forces reserves, National Guard, or Naval Militia are entitled to 17 days' unpaid leave per year for training or special exercises. Employer may not terminate employee or limit any benefits or seniority because of a temporary disability resulting from duty in the National Guard or Naval Militia (up to 52 weeks). Employer cannot discriminate against employee because of membership in the military services.

COLORADO

Colo. Rev. Stat. §§ 28-3-609, 28-3-610.5

Employees who are members of Colorado National Guard or U.S. armed forces reserves are entitled to 15 days' unpaid leave per year for training and reinstatement to their former or a similar position with the same status, pay, and seniority. Employees called to active service in the Colorado National Guard are entitled to unlimited unpaid leave and reinstatement to

State Laws on Military Leave (cont'd)

their former or comparable position, with the pay, seniority, and benefits the employee would have had if not absent for service.

CONNECTICUT

Conn. Gen. Stat. Ann. §§ 27-33a, 27-34a

Members of the Connecticut National Guard ordered into active duty are entitled to the same rights and benefits guaranteed under USERRA, except those pertaining to life insurance. Employees who are members of the military are entitled to take leave to attend military reserve or National Guard meetings or drills that take place during regular work hours, without loss or reduction of vacation or holiday benefits. Employer may not discriminate in terms of promotion or continued employment.

DELAWARE

Del. Code Ann. tit. 20 § 905

National Guard members who are called to state active duty shall be entitled to the same rights, privileges, and protections as they would have had if called for military training under federal law protecting reservists and National Guard members.

FLORIDA

Fla. Stat. Ann. §§ 250.482, 627.6692(5)

Employees who are members of the Florida National Guard and are called into active duty may not be penalized for absence from work. Employees not covered by COBRA whose employment is terminated while on active duty are entitled to a new 18-month benefit period beginning when active duty or job ends, whichever is later. Upon return from service, employee is entitled to reinstatement with full benefits unless employer's circumstances have

changed to make reinstatement impossible or unreasonable or impose an undue hardship. Employee cannot be terminated without cause for one year after reinstatement.

GEORGIA

Ga. Code Ann. § 38-2-280

Members of U.S. uniformed services or Georgia National Guard called into active federal or state service are entitled to unlimited unpaid leave for active service and up to 6 months' leave in any 4-year period for service school or annual training. Employee is entitled to reinstatement with full benefits unless employer's circumstances have changed to make reinstatement impossible or unreasonable. Employee must apply for reinstatement within 90 days of discharge or within 10 days of completing school or training.

HAWAII

Haw. Rev. Stat. § 121-43

Members of the National Guard are entitled to unlimited unpaid leave and reinstatement to the same or a position comparable in seniority, status, and pay. If an employee is not qualified for his or her former position because of a disability sustained during service but is qualified for any other position, the employee is entitled to the position that is most similar to his or her former position, unless employer's circumstances have changed to make reinstatement impossible or unreasonable. Employee cannot be terminated without cause for one year after reinstatement. Employer cannot discriminate against employee because of any obligation as a member of the National Guard.

State Laws on Military Leave (cont'd)

IDAHO

Idaho Code §§ 46-224, 46-225, 46-407

Members of Idaho National Guard or National Guard of another state ordered to active duty may take up to one year of unpaid leave and are entitled to reinstatement to former position or a comparable position with like seniority, status, and pay. If an employee is not qualified for former position because of a disability sustained during service but is qualified for another position, the employee is entitled to the position that is most similar to the former position in seniority, status, and pay. Employee must apply for reinstatement within 30 days of release. Returning employees may not be fired without cause for one year. Members of the National Guard and U.S. armed forces reserves may take up to 15 days' leave per year for training without affecting the employee's right to receive normal vacation, sick leave, bonus, advancement, and other advantages of employment. Employee must give 90 days' notice of training dates.

ILLINOIS

20 Ill. Comp. Stat. §§ 1805/30.15, 1805/30.20; 330 Ill. Comp. State. § 60/4

Members of the National Guard are entitled to unlimited leave and reinstatement with the same increases in status, seniority, and wages that were earned during the employee's military duty by employees in like positions, or to a position of like seniority, status, and pay, unless employer's circumstances have changed so that reinstatement would be unreasonable or impossible or impose an undue hardship. If employee is no longer qualified for the position because of a disability acquired during service but is qualified for any other position, then the employee is entitled to the position that will provide like seniority, status, and pay. If reasonably possible, employee must give advance notice of military service. Members of the National Guard must submit request for reemployment the day after finishing duty if duty lasted less than 31 days, within 14 days if duty lasted longer than 30 days, or within 90 days if duty lasted longer than 180 days. Members of the U.S. uniformed services must submit request for reemployment within 90 days. Employee can't be discharged without cause for one year.

INDIANA

Ind. Code Ann. §§ 10-17-4-1 to 10-17-4-5

Members of U.S. armed forces reserves may take up to 15 days' unpaid (or paid at employer's discretion) leave per year for training. Employee must provide evidence of dates of departure and return, and proof of completion of the training upon return. Leave does not affect vacation, sick leave, bonus, or promotion rights. Employee must be reinstated to former or a similar position with no loss of seniority or benefits.

IOWA

Iowa Code § 29A.43

Members of the U.S. armed forces reserves, National Guard, or the civil air patrol called into temporary duty are entitled to reinstatement to former or a similar position. Leave does not affect vacation, sick leave, bonuses, or other benefits. Employee must provide proof of satisfactory completion of duty and of qualifications to perform the job's duties.

State Laws on Military Leave (cont'd)

KANSAS
Kan. Stat. Ann. §§ 48-517, 48-222

Members of state military forces called into active duty are entitled to reinstatement to the same position or a comparable position with like seniority, status, and pay. If an employee is not qualified for former position because of a disability sustained during service but is qualified for another position, the employee is entitled to the position that is most similar to the former position in seniority, status, and pay. Employee must report to work within 72 hours of release from duty or recovery from service-related injury or illness. Reemployment not required if employer's circumstances have changed so as to make reemployment impossible/unreasonable or if reemployment would impose undue hardship on employer. In addition to unlimited leave for active duty, employees are entitled to 5 to 10 days' leave each year to attend Kansas National Guard training camp.

KENTUCKY
Ky. Rev. Stat. Ann. §§ 38.238, 38.460

Members of National Guard are entitled to unlimited unpaid leave for active duty or training and reinstatement to former position with no loss of seniority or benefits. Employer may not in any way discriminate against employee or use threats to prevent employee from enlisting in the Kentucky National Guard or active militia.

LOUISIANA
La. Rev. Stat. Ann. §§ 29:38, 29:38.1, 42:394

Employees called into active duty in National Guard, state militia, or any branch of the state military forces are entitled to reinstatement to same or comparable position with same seniority, status, benefits and pay. If employee is not

qualified for former position because of disability sustained during active duty, but is otherwise qualified to perform another position, employer or successor shall employ person in other or comparable position with like seniority, status, benefits, and pay provided the employment does not pose a direct threat or significant risk to the health and safety of the individual or others that cannot be eliminated by reasonable accommodation. Employees on leave are entitled to the benefits offered to employees who take leave for other reasons. Employee must report to work within 72 hours of release or recovery from service-related injury or illness and cannot be fired, except for cause, for one year after reinstatement. Employees in the U.S. National Guard or military reserves are entitled to 15 days of paid leave annually for training. Employer cannot discriminate against employee because of any obligation as a member of the state military forces.

MAINE
Me. Rev. Stat. Ann. tit. 37-B, § 342

Employer may not discriminate against employee for membership or service in National Guard or United States armed forces reserves.

MARYLAND
Md. Code Ann. [Public Safety] § 13-705

Members of the state National Guard and Maryland Defense Force ordered to military duty have the same leave and reinstatement rights and benefits guaranteed under USERRA.

MASSACHUSETTS
Mass. Gen. Laws ch. 149, § 52A

Employees who are members of armed forces reserves may take up to 17 days per year for training. Leave does not affect vacation, sick leave, bonus, or promotion rights. Employee who

State Laws on Military Leave (cont'd)

is qualified must be reinstated to former or a similar position. Employee must give employer notice of departure and anticipated return date.

MICHIGAN
Mich. Comp. Laws §§ 32.271 to 32.274

Members of state or U.S. uniformed services called into active state or federal duty may take unpaid leave; employee may also take unpaid leave to take a physical, enlist, be inducted, or attend training. Returning employee must generally be reinstated to former position. Employee must apply for reinstatement within 45 days of release from service, or 90 days if service was more than 180 days. Employer may not in any way discriminate against employee or use threats to prevent employee from enlisting in the state armed forces.

MINNESOTA
Minn. Stat. Ann. § 192.34

Employer may not discharge employee, interfere with military service, or dissuade employee from enlisting by threatening employee's job. Applies to employees who are members of the U.S., Minnesota, or any other state military or naval forces.

MISSISSIPPI
Miss. Code Ann. §§ 33-1-19, 33-1-21

Members of U.S. armed forces reserves or U.S. military veterans are entitled to unpaid leave for military training or duty. If still qualified to perform job duties, employee entitled to reinstatement to previous or similar position. Employee must give evidence of completion of training.

MISSOURI
Mo. Rev. Stat. § 41.730

Employer may not discharge employee, interfere with employee's military service, or use threats to dissuade employee from enlisting in the state militia or U.S. armed forces.

MONTANA
Mont. Code Ann. §§ 10-1-1005, 10-1-1006, 10-1-1007

Members of the state-organized militia called to active service during a state-declared disaster or emergency are entitled to leave for duration of service. Leave may not be deducted from sick leave, vacation, or other leave, although employee may voluntarily use that leave. Returning employee is entitled to reinstatement to same or similar position with the same seniority, status, pay, health insurance, pension, and other benefits. Employer may not in any way discriminate against employee or dissuade employee from enlisting.

NEBRASKA
Neb. Rev. Stat. § 55-161

Employees who are members of the Nebraska National Guard and are called into active state duty have the same leave and reinstatement rights and benefits guaranteed under USERRA.

NEVADA
Nev. Rev. Stat. Ann. §§ 412.139, 412.606

Employers may not discriminate against members of the Nevada National Guard and may not discharge any employee because he or she is called into active service.

State Laws on Military Leave (cont'd)

NEW HAMPSHIRE

N.H. Rev. Stat. Ann. §§ 110-B:65, 110-C:1

Members of the state National Guard or militia called to active duty have the same leave and reinstatement rights and benefits guaranteed under USERRA. Employer may not discriminate against employee because of connection or service with National Guard; may not dissuade employee from enlisting by threatening job.

NEW JERSEY

N.J. Stat. Ann. § 38:23C-20

An employee is entitled to take unpaid leave for active service in the U.S. or state military services. Upon return, employee must be reinstated to the same or a similar position, unless employer's circumstances have changed to make reinstatement impossible or unreasonable. If same or similar position is not possible, employer shall restore such person to any available position, if requested by such person, for which the person is capable and qualified to perform the duties. Employee must apply for reinstatement within 90 days of release from service. Employee may not be fired without cause for one year after returning from service. Employee is also entitled to take up to 3 months' leave in 4-year period for training or assemblies relating to military service. Employee must apply for reinstatement within 10 days.

NEW MEXICO

N.M. Stat. Ann. §§ 28-15-1, 28-15-2, 20-4-6

Members of the U.S. armed forces, National Guard, or organized reserve may take unpaid leave for service (or for up to one year of hospitalization after discharge). Employee who is still qualified must be reinstated in former or similar position with like status, seniority, pay

unless employer's circumstances have changed to make reinstatement impossible or unreasonable. Employee may not be fired without cause for one year after returning from service. Employee must request reinstatement within 90 days. Employer may not discriminate against or discharge employee because of membership in the National Guard; may not prevent employee from performing military service.

NEW YORK

N.Y. Mil. Law §§ 317, 318

Members of the U.S. armed forces or organized militia are entitled to unpaid leave for active service; reserve drills or annual training; service school; initial full-time or active duty training. Returning employee is entitled to reinstatement to previous position, or to one with the same seniority, status, and pay, unless the employer's circumstances have changed and reemployment is impossible or unreasonable. Employee must apply for reinstatement within 90 days of discharge from active service, 10 days of completing school or annual training, or 60 days of completing initial training. Employers may not discriminate against persons subject to military duty.

NORTH CAROLINA

N.C. Gen. Stat. §§ 127A-201, 127A-202, 127A-202.1, 127B-14

Members of the North Carolina National Guard called to active duty by the governor are entitled to take unpaid leave. Unless the employer's circumstances now make it unreasonable: returning employee must be restored to previous position or one of comparable seniority, status, and salary; if no longer qualified, employee must be placed in another position with appropriate

State Laws on Military Leave (cont'd)

seniority, status, and salary. Employee must apply for reinstatement, in writing, within 5 days of release or recovery from service-related injury or illness. Employer may not discriminate against or discharge an employee because of membership in the National Guard or discharge an employee called up for emergency military service.

OHIO
Ohio Rev. Code Ann. § 5903.02

Employees who are members of the Ohio organized militia or National Guard called for active duty or training; members of the commissioned public health service corps; or any other uniformed service called up in time of war or emergency have the same leave and reinstatement rights and benefits guaranteed under USERRA.

OKLAHOMA
Okla. Stat. Ann. tit. 44, §§ 71, 208.1

Employees called to duty in the Oklahoma National Guard have the same leave and reinstatement rights and benefits guaranteed under USERRA. Members of the National Guard may take leave to attend state National Guard drills, ceremonies, exercises, or other duties.

OREGON
Or. Rev. Stat. § 659A.086

Members of Oregon or other states' organized militias called into active duty may take unpaid leave for term of service. Returning employee is entitled to reinstatement with no loss of seniority or benefits including sick leave, vacation, or service credits under a pension plan. Employee must return to work within 7 calendar days of release from service.

PENNSYLVANIA
51 Pa. Cons. Stat. Ann. §§ 7302 to 7309

Employees who enlist or are drafted during a time of war or emergency called by the president or governor, along with reservists or members of Pennsylvania National Guard called into active duty, are entitled to unpaid military leave. Leave expires 90 days after enlistment/draft period, 90 days after military duty for reservists, 30 days after state duty for Pennsylvania National Guard members. Returning employee must be reinstated to same or similar position with same status, seniority, and pay. If no longer qualified due to disability sustained during military duty, employer must restore to position with like seniority, status, and pay unless employer or successor's circumstances have changed so as to make it impossible or unreasonable to do so. Employers may not discharge or discriminate against any employee because of membership or service in the military. Employees called to active duty are entitled to 30 days' health insurance continuation benefits at no cost.

RHODE ISLAND
R.I. Gen. Laws §§ 30-11-2 to 30-11-9; 30-21-1

Members of state military forces and Rhode Island National Guard members on state active duty have the same leave and reinstatement rights and benefits guaranteed under USERRA. Members of the National Guard or U.S. armed forces reserves are entitled to unpaid leave for training and are entitled to reinstatement with the same status, pay, and seniority. Employees in the U.S. armed forces are entitled to reinstatement to the same position or a position with similar seniority, status, and pay unless the employer's circumstances make reinstatement impossible or unreasonable. Employee must

State Laws on Military Leave (cont'd)

request reinstatement within 40 days. Employer may not discriminate against or discharge employee because of membership in the military reserves, interfere with employee's military service, or dissuade employee from enlisting by threatening employee's job.

SOUTH CAROLINA
S.C. Code Ann. §§ 25-1-2310 to 25-1-2340

Members of the South Carolina National Guard and State Guard called to state duty by the governor are entitled to unpaid leave for service. Unless employer's circumstances make reinstatement unreasonable: returning employee must be reinstated to previous position or one with same seniority, status, and salary; if no longer qualified, must be given another position. Employee must apply for reinstatement in writing, within 5 days of release from service or related hospitalization.

SOUTH DAKOTA
S.D. Codified Laws Ann. § 33-17-15.1

Members of the South Dakota National Guard ordered to active duty by governor or president have the same leave and reinstatement rights and benefits guaranteed under USERRA.

TENNESSEE
Tenn. Code Ann. § 58-1-604

Employer may not terminate or refuse to hire an employee because of Tennessee National Guard membership or because employee is absent for a required drill or annual training.

TEXAS
Tex. Gov't. Code Ann. § 431.006

Members of the Texas or other military forces called to active duty or training are entitled to reinstatement to the same position with

no loss of time, efficiency rating, vacation, or benefits unless employer's circumstances have changed so that reemployment is impossible or unreasonable.

UTAH
Utah Code Ann. § 39-1-36

Members of U.S. armed forces reserves who are called to active duty, active duty for training, inactive duty training, or state active duty may take up to 5 years of unpaid leave. Upon return, employee is entitled to reinstatement to previous employment with same seniority, status, pay, and vacation rights. Employer may not discriminate against an employee based on membership in armed forces reserves.

VERMONT
Vt. Stat. Ann. tit. 21, § 491

Employees who are members of U.S. armed forces reserves, an organized unit of the National Guard, or the ready reserves and are called to active duty or training are entitled to 15 days per year of unpaid leave. Returning employee must be reinstated to former position with the same status, pay, and seniority, including any seniority that accrued during the leave of absence. Employer may not discriminate against an employee who is a member or an applicant for membership in the state or federal National Guard.

VIRGINIA
Va. Code Ann. §§ 44-93.2 to 44-93.4

Members of the Virginia National Guard, Virginia State Defense Force, or naval militia called to active duty are entitled to take unpaid leave and may not be required to use vacation or any other accrued leave (unless employee wishes). Returning employee whose absence does not exceed five years must be reinstated to previous position

State Laws on Military Leave (cont'd)

or one with same seniority, status, and pay; if position no longer exists, then to a comparable position unless employer's circumstances would make reemployment unreasonable. Employee must apply for reinstatement, in writing, within (a) 14 days of release from service or related hospitalization if service length did not exceed 180 days, or (b) 90 days of release from service or related hospitalization if service length exceeded 180 days. Employer cannot discriminate against employees because of membership in state military service.

WASHINGTON
Wash. Rev. Code Ann. §§ 73.16.032 to 73.16.035

Unless the employer's circumstances have changed so that reinstatement is impossible or unreasonable or would be an undue hardship: members of the uniformed services are entitled to reinstatement to the same position or a position of like seniority, status, and pay; if the employee is no longer qualified for the position because of a disability sustained during service, but is qualified for another position, the employee is entitled to a position with the same seniority, status, and pay. Time limits set forth governing written application for reinstatement based on length of uniformed service. Employer cannot discriminate against employees because of membership in uniformed services.

WEST VIRGINIA
W.Va. Code § 15-1F-8

Employees who are members of the organized militia in active state service have the same leave and reinstatement rights and benefits guaranteed under USERRA.

WISCONSIN
Wis. Stat. Ann. § 321.64

Employees who enlist, are inducted, or are ordered to serve in the U.S. armed forces for 90 days or more, or civilians requested to perform national defense work during an officially proclaimed emergency, may take up to 5 years' leave for military service and/or training unless period of service is extended by law. Returning employee is entitled to reinstatement to previous position, or to one with the same seniority, benefits, and pay, unless the employee is no longer qualified or the employer's circumstances have changed and reemployment is impossible or unreasonable. Employee must apply for reinstatement within 90 days of release or 6 months of release from service-related hospitalization and must present evidence of completion of training or service. Employee may not be fired without cause for one year after returning from service.

WYOMING
Wyo. Stat. §§ 19-11-103, 19-11-104, 19-11-107, 19-11-111

Employees who are members of, or who apply for membership in, the uniformed services; employees who report for active duty, training, or a qualifying physical exam; or who are called to state duty by the governor, may take up to 5 years' leave of absence. Employee must give advance notice of service. Employee may use vacation or any other accrued leave but is not required to do so. Returning employee is entitled to reemployment with the same seniority, rights, and benefits, plus any additional seniority and benefits that employee would have earned if there had been no absence, unless employer's circumstances have changed so that

State Laws on Military Leave (cont'd)

reemployment is impossible or unreasonable or would impose an undue hardship. Time limits set forth governing written application for reinstatement based on length of uniformed service. Employee is entitled to complete any training program that would have been available to employee's former position during period of absence. Employee may not be terminated without cause for one year after returning to work. Employer cannot discriminate against applicant or member of the uniformed services.

Privacy

As a manager, you may occasionally need (or want) to gather information about the employees you supervise. For example, you might want to monitor employee productivity by keeping track of Internet use, search the workspace of an employee suspected of theft, or ask applicants for promotion to take a personality test.

However, you must balance your or your company's need (or desire) for this information with your employees' privacy rights. You certainly don't want to go so far overboard that your workers start thinking of your company as "Big Brother." And, of course, you should follow the basic legal rules that relate to employee privacy in order to steer clear of potential lawsuits.

This chapter covers some employment practices that might lead your company to run afoul of privacy protections—including testing, monitoring employee communications, and looking into an employee's off-duty conduct. We explain what you can and cannot do when it comes to gathering information about your employees.

Frequently Asked Questions About Workplace Privacy

Can I require a worker to take a drug test?

Generally, it isn't a good idea to require every worker to submit to a drug test. However, you can require drug testing for a particular employee if you reasonably suspect drug use (if the employee has glassy or red eyes, concentration problems, or other signs of impairment at work, for example). (For more on drug testing of job applicants, see "Testing Applicants" in Chapter 1. For more on drug testing of current employees, see "Testing Current Employees," below.)

Can we prohibit all personal use of the Internet by employees?

Yes, but it isn't necessarily the best policy. Consider how much most of us use the Internet, and for how many purposes. Because the Internet is such a common fact of modern life, you would have to assume that your "no personal use" policy would be violated fairly often. This means that enforcement of the policy will necessarily be inconsistent and lead to claims of favoritism. Most companies don't mind an employee's occasional check of the stock market or sports scores; what they mind is an employee who watches streaming movies, downloads gaming apps (and then plays them), or spends all day sending email from a personal account. The better approach is to adopt a policy that prohibits abuses like these. (For more information, see "Internet Monitoring," below.)

Frequently Asked Questions About Workplace Privacy (cont'd)

Can my company read employees' email messages?

Probably, although it might depend on your company's policies. If you have a policy of email privacy (if you tell your employees that their email will be confidential or will not be read by the company, for example), then you should abide by it. Otherwise, you have the right to monitor employee email, as long as you have a legitimate business purpose for doing so. (For more information, see "Why Your Company Needs an Email Policy," below.)

Can we prohibit employees from saying anything about our company on social networking sites, like Facebook?

The National Labor Relations Board has determined that online posts and comments about the terms and conditions of employment—which includes, for example, complaining about the company's dealings with a union, taking issue with company policies, and even criticizing supervisors—qualify as protected activities, for which employees may not be disciplined or fired. This is a rapidly evolving area of law, but so far employers who prohibit employees from any online discussion of their employer or work lives have found themselves on the losing end. (For more information, see "Employee Posts and Social Networking," below.)

Can we refuse to hire smokers?

It depends on the laws of your state. Some states forbid employers from making job decisions based on an employee or applicant's activities outside of work, including smoking. In fact, some of these laws were passed explicitly to prohibit discrimination against smokers, and that's the only off-duty conduct they protect. (For more information, see "Off-Duty Conduct," below.)

Can my company randomly search employees to discourage theft?

Generally, you can perform a workplace search in order to serve important, work-related interests—as long as you don't unduly intrude on your workers' privacy rights. Random searches are less likely to pass legal muster than a search of a particular employee whom you reasonably suspect of theft. And, even if you have a reasonable suspicion, you must not search too invasively. (For more information, see "Workplace Searches," below.)

The Right to Privacy

Worker privacy is one of the more complex areas of law that employers have to navigate. The basic rule is fairly simple: An employer should stay out of its workers' personal lives, opinions, communications, and belongings. However, there are numerous exceptions to this basic rule—circumstances in which an employer can intrude even into these private areas, if there is a business-related reason to do so. We explain these guidelines in the discussions of specific topics that follow.

Privacy law is tricky, in part, because it comes from so many different legal sources. There is no one federal statute that lays out the content and limits of the right to privacy. Instead, privacy principles derive mainly from the "common law," a group of legal theories inherited from England when our nation was founded. There are additional privacy protections in the U.S. Constitution, some state constitutions, various state and federal statutes, and court decisions by state and federal judges. Here's a brief roadmap through this complicated terrain of workplace privacy law.

Common Law

The term "common law" is used by lawyers to refer to legal rules that are not codified in a statute or constitution. Many of these rules originated in England and came to this country along with the colonists. As time passes and legal issues evolve, judges apply these ancient principles to more modern situations. In the sphere of privacy,

for example, judges have had to stretch the time-honored right to be left alone to cover everything from people's homes to Internet chat rooms to celebrity weddings.

Most of the privacy rules that employers must follow come from the common law. Because the common law isn't codified, however, you have to read cases—written records of judicial decisions—to find out precisely how judges in your state have interpreted these rules.

Generally speaking, courts recognize that employees have a right to be free from overly intrusive actions by their employers. If an employee claims that his or her right to privacy has been violated, courts generally sort it out by weighing two competing concerns. On the one hand, the court will consider the employee's legitimate expectations of privacy: whether the employee reasonably believed that the area searched or monitored (such as a locker, desk, email messages, or off-duty conduct) was private, and on what basis. On the other hand, the court will look at the reason for the intrusion: whether the employer had a legitimate, job-related reason for searching or monitoring, and whether the employer could have gathered the same information in a less intrusive way.

Constitutional Protections

The U.S. Constitution does not explicitly grant a right to privacy. Nonetheless, the U.S. Supreme Court has decided, in a series of decisions dealing primarily with sex and reproductive choice, that the Bill of Rights implies a right to privacy. However, private employers don't need to worry too much about exactly what this right entails: It applies mostly to the government. Private employers generally cannot be sued for violating the federal constitution.

However, some state constitutions also contain an explicit right to privacy—and some apply this right to private employers as well as state governments. Provisions like these can put more weight on the employee's side of the scale when a court balances the employee's right to privacy against the employer's reasons for intruding.

Federal Statutes

No single federal law lays out comprehensive rules on privacy. However, a few federal laws set down some privacy guidelines for employers. For example, the Fair Credit Reporting Act (discussed in more detail in "Background Checks" in Chapter 1) requires employers to get written consent from an employee or applicant before reviewing that person's credit report. The Employee Polygraph Protection Act generally prohibits employers from subjecting their workers to lie detector tests. (See "Testing Current Employees," below, for more information.) And the National Labor Relations Act prohibits employers from monitoring a worker's union activity, including off-the-job meetings. (See "Off-Duty Conduct," below, for more on this topic.)

State Statutes

Many states have laws banning particular privacy violations. For example, some states prohibit employers from considering an appli-cant's arrest records, require employers to notify workers when they listen in to a worker's telephone conversation, or prohibit employers from using particular surveillance techniques (such as a one-way mirror or video camera) in areas like restrooms and locker rooms. To find out more about your state's privacy laws, contact your state labor department.

Testing Current Employees

Workplace testing has become increasingly popular as employers screen their workers in an effort to figure out who would be the best candidate for promotion or who is responsible for a workplace problem. As long as a test is designed to predict a worker's actual ability to do the job and is relatively noninvasive—for example, it doesn't require a worker to reveal personal information—it is probably legal. For example, an employer can generally require typing tests for clerical jobs or agility/strength tests for positions that require certain physical skills (but make sure that the test doesn't unfairly screen out disabled workers who could do the job with a reasonable accommodation; see "Applicants With Disabilities" in Chapter 1 for more information).

Generally, an employer should have a sound, work-related reason to require a current employee to submit to a test. But that might not be enough: If the test is too intrusive or delves too deeply into personal issues, it might invade the employee's right to privacy (and result in a lawsuit).

Unfortunately for employers, there are no hard-and-fast rules about whether a particular test is legal; courts generally decide these issues on a case-by-case basis, looking at all the facts and circumstances. For the most part, employers can stay out of trouble by using simple common sense. An employer who inquires into an employee's sex life, religious beliefs, or political affiliations probably crosses the line, while an employer who tests only for necessary job skills is probably on safe ground.

In addition to these general considerations, specific rules apply to the following types of tests.

Medical Examinations

Once an employee is on the job, an employer's right to conduct a medical examination is usually limited to so-called "fitness for duty" situations. If an employee has shown objective signs that he or she is physically or mentally unfit to perform the essential functions of the job—for example, by claiming that an injury prevents him or her from working—an employer may request that the employee's fitness for the job be evaluated by a medical examiner. Although the examiner can take a full history of the employee and conduct any tests necessary to evaluate the employee's fitness, the employer may not be entitled to all of this information. Many states also impose strict limits on the information a doctor may disclose to an employer or an insurance company without the worker's consent.

The federal Americans with Disabilities Act (ADA) also requires certain privacy protections for the results of a medical examination.

Data gathered in medical examinations must be kept in a separate file available only to those with a demonstrable need to know, such as supervisors who need information about the employee's work restrictions or reasonable accommodations, and first aid and safety personnel (if the employee's disability might require emergency treatment or special evacuation procedures). (Similar rules apply to records of genetic information—pursuant to the Genetic Information Nondisclosure Act, covered in Chapter 3—and medical certifications and other records gathered in connection with the Family and Medical Leave Act, covered in Chapter 5.)

Drug Tests

Although an employer can generally require those applying for a job to submit to drug testing, an employer's right to test current employees is less clear. (For more on drug testing applicants, see "Testing Applicants" in Chapter 1 and "Drugs and Alcohol" in Chapter 7.) No federal law clearly authorizes drug testing of employees, except for certain workers in the defense and transportation industries. And many state laws limit the circumstances under which an employer may test and the types of tests an employer may conduct.

Because the law of drug testing is changing rapidly, and because state law varies widely in terms of what is allowed and prohibited, employers have to tread very carefully in this area. Before undertaking any drug testing, an employer should consult with a knowledgeable lawyer.

Lessons From the Real World

Marya Norman-Bloodsaw worked as an accounting administrator at the Lawrence Berkeley Laboratory (a research facility jointly operated by the State of California and the federal government). When she started work, Bloodsaw and other clerical and administrative employees were given a "general physical," including a blood test.

Employees were also offered the option of further "periodic health examinations" during their employment. But the Lab didn't just give workers a physical. It also tested them for syphilis, sickle cell trait, and pregnancy—without their consent or knowledge. When Bloodsaw found out, she and some of her co-workers filed a class-action complaint against the Lab, arguing that the Lab had violated their right to privacy.

The U.S. Court of Appeals for the Ninth Circuit agreed, saying, "[O]ne can think of few subject areas more personal and more likely to implicate privacy interests than that of one's health or genetic make-up."

The Lab agreed to settle the case, in December 1999, for $2.2 million.

Bloodsaw v. Lawrence Berkeley Laboratory, 35 F.3d 1260 (9th Cir. 1998); Dorothy Wertz, "Genetic Testing in the Workplace: The Lawrence Berkeley Labs Case," *The Gene Letter* (April 3, 2000); Matt Fleischer, "Protecting Genome Privacy Proves Hard," *The National Law Journal* (July 20, 2000).

Employers are on safest ground if they have a strong, legitimate reason for testing workers. Your company is most likely to withstand a legal challenge if it limits testing to:

- workers whose jobs carry a high risk of injury to themselves or others (such as a pilot or a security guard who carries a gun)
- workers who have been involved in an accident that suggests the possibility of drug use (for example, a delivery person who causes a collision by driving erratically)
- workers who are currently in or have completed a rehabilitation program, and
- workers whom a manager or supervisor reasonably suspects are using drugs (based on obvious signs of impairment—for example, slurred speech or glassy eyes).

For information on your state's current rules, see the chart entitled "State Drug and Alcohol Testing Laws," at the end of Chapter 1.

Psychological Screening

Some employers use pencil and paper (or keyboard and screen) psychological tests to attempt to predict whether an employee will steal, fight, or engage in other workplace misconduct. There are two problems with using such tests. First, mental health experts disagree about whether these tests can actually predict an employee's future conduct. Second, some of these tests include questions that are highly personal and invade the employee's privacy. For the most part, employers would be well-advised to steer clear of psychological tests absent some compelling justification, and some reason to believe that the test you use will yield relevant, accurate information about the employee.

Lie Detector Tests

A federal law, the Employee Polygraph Protection Act, 29 U.S.C. § 2001, prohibits all private employers from requiring workers to submit to lie detector tests, with a few exceptions. Employers who manufacture or distribute pharmaceuticals or provide certain security services may be allowed to require polygraphs. And an employer may require a worker accused of theft or embezzlement to take a polygraph, under certain circumstances.

Aside from these limited exceptions, however, a private employer may not require a current employee to take a lie detector test, use the results of any such test in making employment decisions, or discipline or fire any employee who refuses to take one. And, even if an exception applies, the employer must meet very strict technical requirements regarding the way the test is administered and interpreted, the employee's privacy rights, how the test results may be used, and more.

Internet Monitoring

Remember when we had to track shipments by phone, book travel at a travel agent's office, locate information in the library, plan trips using a paper map, or go shopping in stores? The Internet sure has changed all of that! As most businesses are aware, however, the Internet's convenience comes with a dark side. As a virtual gateway in and out of the company, the Internet tempts employees to spend work time on personal pursuits like bargain hunting, watching live sports, conversing in chat rooms, posting to the Facebook pages, or even looking for a new job. In addition, employees can use the Internet to access inappropriate material—such as pornography, gambling, and hate speech—which offends coworkers.

Employee access to the Web can also inadvertently damage the company's computer system and software. And, the Internet provides a backdoor by which employees can send information out of the company, whether by transmitting company data through personal email or posting personal comments (which can be traced back to your company) to outside sites. For all these reasons and more, it's a good idea to have a company policy on use of the Internet.

Prohibited Uses of the Internet

To protect your company against abuses, your policy should explain what types of Internet activities are allowed and forbidden. In addition to banning sites with offensive material, many companies ban downloads that violate the law or could infect the company's computer system. Also, consider your company's bandwidth: Streaming audio or video can quickly overload the system, particularly during popular events like the NCAA tournament or the finale of a daytime soap opera. Your company may want to consider limits like these:

- Employees may not view websites that offer pornography, gambling, violent images, or other inappropriate content.
- Employees may not use the company's computer system to operate an outside business, online auction, or other sales site.
- Employees may not download or copy software, games, text, photos, or any other works in violation of copyright laws.
- Employees may not stream, run, or download music, video, games, widgets, or any form of multimedia.

Personal Use of the Internet

Some companies ban any personal use of the Internet. This type of rule can lead to problems, however. Because most employees will probably violate the policy at some point, disciplining employees will inevitably lead to accusations of unfairness and inconsistent application of the rules. Especially if your company's employees work at computers all day long, they are likely to feel some resentment that they aren't allowed to even check the weather or take a quick look at the news headlines. A more sensible approach is to allow limited personal use of the Internet during lunch, breaks, and so on, as long as that use is not excessive and doesn't violate the company's other rules about Internet use.

Privacy Concerns

If it doesn't already monitor employee Internet use, there may come a day when your company needs to do so. To guard against potential legal problems, you should tell employees—in a written policy—that their use of the Internet on company equipment is not private and may be monitored. That way, if you have to investigate employee complaints that a manager is viewing pornography, look into online rumors about your company's products that appear to come from within the building, or find out whether declining productivity can fairly be blamed on streaming video of the World Cup, you can check up on employee Internet use without running afoul of privacy rights.

Warning employees that they may be monitored has another benefit, too: It will prevent employees from using the Internet inappropriately in the first place. All of us are less likely to break the rules if we know we can get caught. By telling employees, up front, that their Internet use is not private, you not only reserve your right to look into wrongdoing after it's taken place, but also increase the chances that employees won't commit online misconduct at all.

Why Your Company Needs an Email Policy

Does your company make computers and email available to your employees? If so, you should seriously consider adopting a policy explaining the rules for using email and reserving the company's right to monitor the messages sent and received on its equipment.

Lessons From the Real World

When Nissan hired Bonita Bourke to help car dealership personnel with its computer system, the company probably had no idea just how much Ms. Bourke planned to use that computer.

The first sign of trouble was during a training session. While demonstrating how dealership management could use email effectively, one of Ms. Bourke's coworkers pulled up a message at random to use as a teaching tool. Unfortunately for Ms. Bourke, it was a personal, sexual message she had sent to a dealership employee.

After the plaintiff's coworker reported the incident to management, the company reviewed the entire workgroup's email messages. It found a number of personal messages, including messages with sexual overtones, sent by Ms. Bourke.

After she was fired for poor performance, Ms. Bourke sued Nissan for violating her privacy rights, among other things. However, the court found that Ms. Bourke's privacy was not violated. Ms. Bourke had signed a form indicating her understanding that company policy restricted use of company computers to business purposes only. She also knew that email messages were, on occasion, read by someone other than the intended recipient. Therefore, the court found that, even though Ms. Bourke had a confidential password to use the computer, she could not have reasonably expected that her email messages were private.

Bourke v. Nissan Motor Corp., No. B068705 (California Court of Appeal, 2nd District, 1993) (unpublished decision). You can find this case at www.loundy.com/CASES/Bourke_v_Nissan.html.

Benefits of Having an Email Policy

There are several very good reasons to adopt an email policy. First and foremost, you need to let employees know that your company may monitor their messages. Even if you have never read employee email and don't plan to make a regular practice of it, you should protect the company's right to do so. If you don't, your company might be unable to fully investigate claims of harassment, discrimination, theft, and other misconduct. An employee might even threaten a lawsuit, claiming that your investigation violated his or her privacy.

Consider these statistics: In a survey commissioned by Elron Software, more than 60% of workers admitted to sending or receiving adult-oriented personal email at work; more than 55% admitted to sending or receiving personal email messages that are racist, sexist, or otherwise offensive; one in ten employees admitted receiving confidential information about another company in personal email; and a significant number admitted sending messages that included confidential information about their own companies.

If your company is ever faced with an employee who uses email to transmit pornographic images, reveal trade secrets, or send racist or sexist messages—and these statistics demonstrate that you may very well find yourself in this position—you will have to read the messages to figure out what to do. If your company doesn't have a policy warning employees that their messages can be read at any time, an employee might sue for violation of privacy. Although these lawsuits are generally unsuccessful—that is, employees have lost most of them—your company will still have to spend time and money to defend its actions in court.

In addition, some states—including Connecticut and Delaware—require employers who monitor email messages to let their employees know. Every year, more states consider imposing similar requirements. Putting this information in a workplace policy helps you meet these legal obligations.

Finally, you can use an email policy to tell your employees how you expect them to use the email system and what uses are prohibited. Laying down the rules clearly, in writing, will go a long way toward preventing abuses in the first place.

What to Include in an Email Policy

Your company's email policy should address these issues:

- **Personal use of the email system.** Explain whether employees can use email for personal messages. If your company places any restrictions on personal messages (for example, that employees can send them only during nonwork hours, must exercise discretion as to the number and type of messages sent, or

may not send personal messages with large attachments), describe those rules.
- **Monitoring.** Reserve the company's right to monitor employee email messages at any time. Explain that any messages employees send using company equipment are not private, even if the employee considers them to be personal. If your company will monitor regularly using a particular system—for example, a system that flags key words or copies every draft of a message—explain it briefly. This will help deter employees from sending offensive messages in the first place.
- **Rules.** Make clear that all of your workplace policies and rules—such as rules against harassment, discrimination, violence, solicitation, and theft of trade secrets—apply to employee use of the email system. Remind employees that all email messages sent on company equipment should be professional and appropriate. Some employers also include so-called netiquette rules: style guidelines for email writing.
- **Deleting email.** Establish a regular schedule for purging email messages. Otherwise, your company will eventually run into a storage problem. Let employees know how they can save important messages from the purge.

Sample Email Policy

An example of a company email policy is provided on the next three pages. This example is for illustrative purposes only; be sure any policy you adopt is appropriate for your workplace and consistent with your state's and federal law.

Email Policy

Use of the Email System

The email system is intended for official Company business. Although you may use the email system occasionally for personal messages, you may do so during nonworking hours only. If you send personal messages through the Company's email system, you must exercise discretion as to the number and type of messages you send. You must also ensure that your personal use of the email system does not interfere in any way with your job duties or performance. Any employee who abuses this privilege may be subject to discipline.

Email Is Not Private

Email messages, including attachments, sent and received on Company equipment are the property of the Company. We reserve the right to access, monitor, read, and/or copy email messages at any time, for any reason. You should not expect privacy for any email you send using Company equipment, including messages that you consider to be personal, or label with a designation such as "Personal" or "Private."

In addition, the Company's software automatically searches the messages you send for questionable content, including sexual or racial comments, threats, trade secrets, competitive information, and inappropriate language. Any message deemed questionable will be forwarded to, and read by, Company management.

All Conduct Rules Apply to Email

All of our policies and rules of conduct apply to employee use of the email system. This means, for example, that you may not use the email system to send harassing or discriminatory messages, including messages with explicit sexual content or pornographic images; to send threatening messages; or to reveal Company trade secrets or confidential information.

No Solicitation by Email

You may not use the email system to solicit others to patronize an outside business or to support an outside organization, a political candidate or cause, or a religious cause.

Professional Tone and Content

We expect you to exercise discretion in using electronic communications equipment. When you send email using the Company's equipment, you are representing the Company. Make sure that your messages are professional and appropriate, in tone and content. Remember, although email may seem like a private conversation, email can be printed, saved, and forwarded to unintended recipients. You should not send any email that you wouldn't want your boss, your mother, or our Company's competitors to read.

Guidelines for Email Writing

1. Always spell-check or proofread your email messages. Email is official Company correspondence. Spelling errors in email are all too common, and they look sloppy and unprofessional.

2. Use lowercase and capital letters in the same way that you would in a letter. Using all capital letters is the email equivalent of shouting at someone—and it can be hard on the eyes. Failing to use capital letters at all (to begin a sentence or formal noun) can confuse readers and seem overly cute. Unless you are writing poetry, use standard capitalization.

3. Remember your audience. Although email encourages informal communication, that might not be the most appropriate style to use if you are addressing the CEO of an important customer. And, remember that your email can be forwarded to unintended recipients, some of whom may not appreciate joking comments or informalities.

4. Don't use email for confidential matters. Again, remember the unintended recipient. Your email might be forwarded to someone you didn't anticipate or might be sitting at a printer for all to see. If you need to have a confidential discussion, do it in person or over the phone.

5. Send messages sparingly. There is rarely a need to copy everyone in the Company on an email. Carefully consider who really needs to see the message, and address it accordingly.

6. Always think before you send. Resist the urge to respond in anger, to "flame" your recipient, or to get emotional. Although email gives you the opportunity to respond immediately, you don't have to take it.

7. Don't leave the subject line blank. Always include a brief description, so readers will know what your email is about at a glance. This makes it easier for all of us to manage our email—and makes it more likely that you will receive a response to your message.

8. Don't overuse the "urgent" tag. Mark a message as urgent only if it is truly important and must be answered right away.

Email Security

To avoid email viruses and other threats, employees should not open email attachments from people and businesses they don't recognize, particularly if the email appears to have been forwarded multiple times or has a nonexistent or peculiar subject heading. Even if you know the sender, do not open an email attachment that has a strange name or is not referenced in the body of the email—it may have been transmitted automatically, without the sender's knowledge.

If you believe your computer has been infected by a virus, worm, or other security threat to the Company's system, you must inform the IT department immediately.

Employees also may not share their email passwords with anyone, including coworkers or family members. Revealing passwords to the Company's email system could allow an outsider to access the Company's network.

Retaining and Deleting Email Messages

Because email messages are electronic records, certain messages must be retained for compliance purposes. Please refer to our record-keeping policy for guidance on which records must be kept, and for how long. If you have any questions about whether and how to retain a particular email message, please ask your manager.

Because of the large volume of emails our Company sends and receives each day, we discourage employees from storing large numbers of email messages that are not subject to the retention rules explained above. Please make a regular practice of deleting email messages once you have read and/or responded to them. If you need to save a particular message, you may print out a paper copy, archive the email, or save it on your hard drive or disk. The Company will purge email messages that have not been archived after 90 days.

The Company may have occasion to suspend our usual rules about deleting email messages (for example, if the Company is involved in a lawsuit requiring it to preserve evidence). If this happens, employees will be notified of the procedures to follow to save email messages. Failing to comply with such a notice could subject the Company to serious legal consequences, and will result in discipline, up to and including termination.

Employee Posts and Social Networking

Chances are good that many of your company's employees post personal content on the Internet. Perhaps they have their own Facebook or MySpace page, tweet their observations throughout the day, keep a blog, post comments on other websites, upload photos, or chat with others online.

Many employers are understandably wary about trying to crack down on personal posts. Blogs and social media provide a creative outlet, a way for friends to keep in touch, a place to share opinions and be part of a larger community of pug owners, single parents, or recycling enthusiasts. They are, in a word, personal, and few employers really want to read employees' personal writings or be known as a company that stifles personal expression.

Unfortunately, however, not all employees like their jobs; even those who do may not successfully navigate the line between appropriate and inappropriate content. An employee blog or post that reveals company trade secrets, slams a company product, or threatens or harasses other employees can present an unmitigated disaster for a company. Even posts that have nothing to do with work can create major trouble if they express extreme or unpopular views, racist comments, or violent fantasies, for example.

A quick look through news reports shows that employees have used social networking sites and blogs to post:

- a YouTube video showing an employee of a restaurant chain stuffing cheese up his nose—before putting it on a pizza
- Facebook posts by an employee chronicling his dates with coworkers
- MySpace posts by employees of an auto club, commenting on their coworkers' weight and sexual orientation—and on their plans to slow down the company's roadside assistance to motorists
- a Facebook post by an employee threatening to punch a coworker in the face "before the end of my shift," and
- a MySpace page a teacher created to communicate with his students, which included nude photos, inappropriate conversation, and curse words.

Employers have the right to control what employees do with the time and equipment it pays for, generally speaking. However, when employees use their own computers to express their own opinions on their own time, an employer's legal rights are more limited.

Legal Protections for Employees Who Post Online

A host of laws protect an employee's right to speak—at least about certain topics—online. These laws include:

- **Off-duty conduct laws.** As explained in "Off-Duty Conduct," below, a number of states have laws that prohibit employers from disciplining or firing employees for activities they pursue on their own time. Although some of these laws were originally intended to protect smokers from discrimination, others protect any employee conduct that doesn't break the law, which might include employee blogging or posting.

- **Protections for political views.** A handful of states protect employees from discrimination based on their political views or affiliation. In these states, disciplining an employee for a political post (for example, one that endorses a candidate or cause) could be illegal.

- **Protections for "whistle-bloggers."** An employee who raises concerns about safety hazards or illegal activity at work may be protected as a whistle-blower (called a "whistle-blogger" if the concerns are raised in a blog).

- **Prohibitions on retaliation.** Many employment laws protect employees from retaliation for claiming that their rights have been violated. If an employee complains online about workplace discrimination, harassment, violation of the Family and Medical Leave Act, wage and hour violations, or other legal transgressions, that employee may be protected from disciplinary action.

- **Concerted activity protections.** The National Labor Relations Act and similar state laws protect employees' rights to communicate with each other about the terms and conditions of employment, and to join together—in a union or otherwise—to bring concerns about these issues to their employer. Under these laws, an employee who is fired for posting about low wages, poor

benefits, or long work hours could have a plausible legal claim.

Adopting a Commonsense Policy

Online posts are easy to dash off and virtually impossible to retract once published. When employees aren't at work, they probably aren't thinking of the potential consequences of making fun of a coworker's accent or revealing little-known facts about a client. Most likely, they're simply trying to be funny and attract readers.

So what can your company do to curb inappropriate employee posts without running afoul of the law or becoming known as Corporate Big Brother? Adopt a policy letting employees know that their personal pages, blogs, and posts could get them in trouble at work, and explain the types of content that could create problems.

A good online posting policy should explain that, while the company appreciates that employees want to express themselves in the virtual world, problems might arise if their personal posts appear to be associated with the company or violate the rights of the company or other employees. Here are some topics you should cover:

- **Use of company resources.** Your policy should prohibit employees from using the company's equipment or network to write or publish personal content, or from doing so on company time.

- **Company policies apply online.** It's a good idea to remind employees that company policies prohibiting harassment, protecting trade secrets, and so on apply whether an employee makes these statements online or in the bricks and mortar world.

- **Company name and marks.** Your policy should prohibit employees from using the company's trademarks, logos, or other images, and should also prohibit employees from making false statements about the company. If employees choose to identify themselves as employees of the company in an online post, require them to clearly state that the views they express online are their own and that they do not speak for the company.

- **Inappropriate disclosures.** Remind employees that the company may have a legal duty to keep certain facts confidential, such as information on stock offerings. If employees have concerns about whether something they plan to post falls into this category, they should raise the issue with a manager.

- **Inappropriate comments.** It should go without saying, but news reports tell us it doesn't: Inform employees that it is inappropriate to make embarrassing or unkind comments about employees, customers, clients, or competitors. Remind them that personal posts can be read by virtually anyone and that they should use common sense when deciding what types of content are appropriate.

For sample policy language on blogs and online posts—as well as policies on use of the Internet, email, cell phones, and much more—pick up a copy of *Smart Policies for Workplace Technologies*, by Lisa Guerin (copublished by SHRM and Nolo).

Rules for Online Product Endorsements

If your company sells products on sites that allow users to comment or post reviews, or products that are discussed in blogs or on social networking sites or user boards, you need to make sure that employees always identify themselves—and their relationship to your company—when discussing company products online. This is required by regulations released in 2009 by the Federal Trade Commission (FTC), the federal government agency that regulates deceptive advertising.

The FTC already had rules about product endorsements, but the 2009 changes made clear that these rules also apply to statements and reviews made online. The purpose of these rules is to make sure consumers fully understand the relationship between the product and the person endorsing or discussing it, so they can make informed decisions about how much weight to give the endorser's statement. After all, a paid actor or spokesperson isn't as credible as an actual user of the product.

The upshot of these new rules is that employees must identify themselves as employees of your company when posting anything about its products online. The FTC has said that an employment relationship is the type of connection that a consumer would want to know about in evaluating product endorsements. So, your online posting policy should tell employees that they must be up front about their relationship to the company when making any statements about it or its products online.

Off-Duty Conduct

Today, employers have the technological means, and occasionally the inclination, to find out what workers are doing on their own time. However, there are legal limits to a company's right to monitor its employees' conduct off the job and to make decisions based on that conduct.

Privacy Law

Employees of government and public entities have a constitutional right to privacy that protects them from most employer monitoring of, or even questions about, their off-the-job conduct. For public employers, then, monitoring of off-duty activities is largely off limits.

In the private sector, a number of laws prohibit employers from intruding into their employees' private lives. As noted, some state constitutions specifically contain a right to privacy, which prevents private employers from looking into their employees' off-duty activity. Some states also have laws prohibiting employers from taking any job-related action against a worker based on that worker's lawful conduct off the job, including smoking or other use of tobacco products.

Even in states that don't provide private workers with a constitutional or statutory right to privacy, it is generally illegal for an employer to intrude unreasonably into the "seclusion" of an employee. This means that physical areas in which an employee has a reasonable expectation of privacy (personal belongings, for instance) are off-limits to employers, unless there is a very good reason to intrude. And an employer is never allowed to physically enter an employee's home without consent (even when searching for allegedly stolen company property).

The same balancing approach applies to private information. Generally speaking, employers should not inquire about or otherwise obtain facts about employees' private lives. For example, an employer may not ask employees about their sexual practices.

Courts and legislatures have created some specific rules for certain types of private, off-duty activities, as described in the sections that follow.

Union Activity

Under the National Labor Relations Act (NLRA), 29 U.S.C. §§ 151 and following, it is illegal for an employer to monitor or conduct any surveillance of employee union activities, including off-the-job meetings or gatherings. This rule applies to any concerted activity (that is, activity undertaken by workers acting together, rather than individually), even if no union is involved, as long as employees are discussing their work conditions or terms of employment. An employer who sends a supervisor to eavesdrop on such meetings or plants a spy among employees engaged in this conduct violates the NLRA. (For more on this rule, see "Representation Elections and Organizing Campaigns" in Chapter 8.)

Drug Testing

Because drug testing has the potential to reveal an employee's use of drugs outside of work hours, it has been the subject of much privacy litigation. In general, drug testing is usually allowed of job applicants, employees who perform safety or security-sensitive work, or employees who have given an employer some reason to believe that they are impaired by drugs at work. (See "Testing Current Employees," above, for more information about drug testing.)

Moonlighting

Generally speaking, working more than one job is lawful. However, an employer has the right to limit after-hours work that is in conflict with the employer's own business. For instance, going to work for the competition could provide grounds for discipline or discharge. As a general rule, the more senior the employee, the more likely a court will take a dim view of the employee moonlighting for a competitor.

Marital Status

Many states make it illegal for employers to discriminate on the basis of marital status. Employers in these states may not keep track of whether their employees are single, married, or divorced, except as may be necessary for providing certain benefits such as health insurance.

However, tricky issues can arise when, for example, one spouse applies for a position in which he or she would supervise the other, or an applicant's spouse works for your company's major competitor. To find out whether your state prohibits marital status discrimination, and how its law might apply to situations like these, contact your state fair employment practices agency. (You can find contact information in the appendix.)

Lawful Activities

A number of states prohibit employers from taking action against employees based on their off-the-job activities, as long as those activities are not illegal. The form of these protections varies: Some states protect an employee's right to engage in any lawful activities, some protect an employee's right to use lawful products off the job, and some protect only an employee's right to smoke or use other tobacco products off the job.

Although these laws are often invoked to prohibit employers from firing or refusing to hire those who smoke, the broader version—those that protect employees who engage in lawful activities—applies to a wide range of conduct. For example, such a law would protect an employee who works for a particular political candidate or collects signatures for a controversial ballot measure.

Workplace Searches

It happens to even the best employers: a sudden rash of thefts, a worker threatening violence, or some other possible misconduct or illegal activity in the workplace. Your company's first step must be to investigate the situation. (See "Investigating Complaints" in

Chapter 11.) As part of the investigation, you might even want to search a worker's desk or locker, install some kind of monitoring device (a video camera, for example), or ask to look inside an employee's purse or backpack. The following sections explain how you can get the information you need without violating workers' right to privacy.

Reasonable Expectations of Privacy

When judges evaluate whether a particular workplace search is legal, they usually try to balance two competing concerns. First, the law considers the employer's justification for performing the search: An employer with a strong work-related reason for searching has the best chance of prevailing. For example, an employer who receives a complaint that an employee brought a gun to work and has threatened to use it has a strong justification for a locker search.

On the other hand, workers have reasonable expectations of privacy. A worker who legitimately expects, based on the employer's policies, past practice, and common sense, that the employer will not search certain areas has the strongest argument here. For example, a worker has a high expectation of privacy in an employee rest room or changing area, particularly if the employer has not warned workers that these areas might be monitored.

To decide if a workplace search is legal, a court considers the relative strengths of these two competing interests. The more steps employers take to diminish their workers' expectations of privacy and the stronger the employer's reason to search, the more likely

a court is to find the search legal. Courts also have to consider whether a particular state or federal law prohibits the search.

Search Considerations

Privacy is a highly volatile area of law. Every year, workers bring lawsuits claiming that an employer invaded their privacy by conducting an improper search. The outcome of these cases depends on the judge's view of the worker's misconduct and the employer's methods for getting to the bottom of things. Because there are no legal guarantees in this area of law, most employers should talk to a lawyer before conducting any but the most routine searches. Here are a few considerations to keep in mind:

- **Search only if necessary.** In many companies, there will rarely be a need to search. Unless your employees routinely handle large amounts of money or valuable, easily hidden items (such as prescription drugs or jewelry), you may not need to search at all. If you do want to conduct a search, make sure you have a legitimate business reason (theft, for example).

- **If you plan to search, have a policy.** If you warn your employees in advance that certain areas (like desks or lockers) might be subject to search, employees will have lower expectations of privacy in those areas, and less reason to complain about a particular search.

- **Don't conduct random searches.** Courts tend to frown on employers who conduct random searches, even if the employer's policy puts employees on notice of this possibility. These searches, particularly if conducted when the employer has no reason to suspect any wrongdoing, can get employers into trouble.

- **Never search an employee's body.** Some employers become so zealous that they want to physically search their workers for contraband or stolen items. This is always a bad idea. Workers have a very strong privacy interest in their own bodies. If your search reaches this level, consider calling the police in for help.

- **Rest rooms and changing rooms are off limits.** Most workers legitimately expect that they will not be monitored while using the bathroom or changing their clothes. This expectation is highly reasonable. If you must monitor these areas, warn employees and monitor only to the extent necessary. For example, if you have received reports that some employees are selling illegal drugs in the rest room, you might install a camera or post a guard in the main part of the room, after notifying your workers. However, you would probably be going too far if you posted cameras in each stall. And some states prohibit any surveillance of these private areas.

- **Consider the worker's privacy expectations.** Before you search, think about whether an average worker would consider a particular space private in your workplace. Do employees routinely lock their desk drawers? If so, they might have higher expectations of privacy. On the other hand, if no one has an assigned desk or if workers routinely use each other's desks, they shouldn't expect their desk drawers to be private.

- **Don't hold employees against their will.** Some employers detain workers in connection with a search, either to keep the worker out of the area being searched or to exert a little pressure on the worker to consent to a search ("No one is leaving this room until you show me what's in your backpack!") This is a bad idea. Under a legal theory called "false imprisonment," an employee can sue an employer who leads the employee to believe that he or she is not free to leave. Although these claims often come up in the context of questioning (when employers refuse to let their employees leave the workplace until they have answered certain questions, for example), they also surface when searches are conducted.

Legal Dos and Don'ts: Workplace Privacy

Do:

- **Search, test, and monitor only if you really need to.** Let's face it: Most smaller businesses will never have a strong need to dig into their employees' purses, psyches, or private lives. Absent a compelling reason to pry—such as a theft problem—your best course of action is to stay out of the spy business (and, hopefully, out of the courtroom).
- **Adopt clear written policies.** The more steps your company takes to diminish employee expectations of privacy, the better its legal position will be. And, telling employees that you reserve the right to monitor and search will help deter them from engaging in misconduct in the first place.
- **Get some legal advice if you need it.** The law of workplace privacy changes all the time, and your state may have some special requirements you should know about. Before installing surveillance cameras, adopting a search policy, or tailing employees off-site, talk to a lawyer.

Don't:

- **Detain employees physically.** If you prevent workers from leaving a room or building, or you lead them to believe they are not free to go, you are buying legal trouble for your company.
- **Use lie detector tests.** In most situations, it is illegal to require a worker to take a polygraph "test" or make any decisions based on the results of such a test. And even in the rare circumstances when polygraphs are allowed, employers must follow a number of technical rules to protect the worker's rights. The best rule of thumb for most employers: Just don't do it.
- **Become "Big Brother."** Too much monitoring will quickly lead to employee resentment. When you dig too deeply into workers' private lives, you risk alienating them. This type of resentment leads not only to lawsuits, but also to poor performance, plummeting morale, and retention problems.

Test Your Knowledge

Questions

1. Employers can require current employees to take lie detector tests as a condition of promotion. ☐ True ☐ False

2. Employers may never require employees to take a medical examination. ☐ True ☐ False

3. Employees may not post online reviews or endorsements of their own company's products. ☐ True ☐ False

4. Employers are not allowed to read employee email messages if those messages are marked "private" or "confidential." ☐ True ☐ False

5. Even though it's sneaky, it isn't illegal for an employer to send a manager to eavesdrop on an off-site employee meeting to discuss forming a union. ☐ True ☐ False

6. A company can fire employees for off-duty conduct, as long as the employees work at will. ☐ True ☐ False

7. The First Amendment of the U.S. Constitution protects employees from being fired for what they write in a personal blog. ☐ True ☐ False

8. Employers are legally entitled to search anyone who enters or leaves company property. ☐ True ☐ False

9. If an employee won't answer legitimate questions about employee theft or other misconduct, the employer is legally entitled to detain the employee until he or she starts talking. ☐ True ☐ False

10. A company's email policy should always reserve the employer's right to read email messages, even if the company has no current plans to do so. ☐ True ☐ False

Answers

1. False. With a few very limited exceptions, employers may not require employees to take polygraph tests.

2. False. There are circumstances in which an employer may require an employee to take a "fitness for duty" exam, to prove that the employee is able to work following an illness or injury.

3. False. Employees may post reviews, comments, and endorsements, as long as they identify themselves as company employees.

4. False, as long as the employer has warned employees that email messages are not private.

5. False. Employers may not send spies or otherwise monitor employee discussions on union issues.

6. Not necessarily. It depends on the conduct and the laws of your state. Some states protect employees from being fired for lawful activity off the job, for example. And the employee's actions might be protected under other laws, such as the National Labor Relations Act (see Chapter 8).

7. False. The First Amendment protects only against limits the government sets on speech, not against the actions of private employers.

8. False. Even if an employer adopts a strict search policy, its employees may have a legitimate claim for invasion of privacy if they are routinely subjected to a physical search every time they leave the worksite.

9. False. Detaining an employee against his or her will is called "false imprisonment," and it is illegal.

10. True. A company should always reserve the right to monitor, just in case it faces a situation in which it must read employee email. ●

Health and Safety

Most employers want to maintain a healthy and safe work environment for their employees. Not only is it the humane thing to do, but it is also good for business. Employees are happier and more productive in a safe, secure work environment. And the company will save money—with fewer workers' compensation claims and lower rates of absenteeism—by keeping employees and their work environment as healthy and safe as possible.

In addition to these practical concerns, your company also has a legal obligation to provide a safe workplace. Federal and state governments have passed laws designed to ensure healthy and safe work environments. These laws impose safety standards and posting, reporting, and record-keeping requirements on all employers. Your company will face investigations, fines, and—in serious cases—closure if it ignores these important laws.

In this chapter, we provide an overview of health and safety laws. We also look at workers' compensation statutes, drug and alcohol issues, smoking, and use of cell phones while driving.

Frequently Asked Questions About Health and Safety

What kinds of penalties are imposed on companies that violate health and safety laws?

Penalties range from minimal to major fines. The exact penalty depends on a number of factors, including the employer's record of violations, the severity of the violation, and whether the employer acted in good faith. (See "Health and Safety Laws," below, for more information about penalties.)

Can an employee who is injured at work sue for damages?

Usually, an employee who suffers a work-related injury is limited to the benefits provided by workers' compensation; that is, the employee may not sue the employer for the injuries. If the employer willfully or recklessly caused the injury, however (for example, if the company knew about the hazardous condition that caused the worker's accident but didn't do anything about it), then the employee may be able to bypass the workers' compensation system and sue the company for damages. (See "Workers' Compensation," below, for more information.)

Do we need any special rules for employee use of cell phones while driving?

Yes. Studies have shown that using a cell phone while driving increases the risk of accidents. Employees who dial, talk, or text while driving not only create a safety hazard, they also create a legal risk for your company, which might be liable for any harm they cause if they are having a work-related conversation or driving for work. To minimize the dangers, every company should have cell phone rules for employees. (See "Cell Phones and Driving," below, for more information.)

Frequently Asked Questions About Health and Safety (cont'd)

Can we fire—or refuse to hire—employees who smoke?

It depends on the laws of your state. Many states prohibit employers from discriminating against workers or applicants just because they smoke; in other states, however, companies are free to make hiring and firing decisions on this basis. (See "Smoking," below, for more information.)

Can we fire an employee for being an alcoholic?

No. You cannot fire or discipline an employee merely for being an alcoholic. You can, however, fire an employee for drinking at work or appearing at work under the influence of alcohol. You can also fire or discipline an employee for not meeting the conduct and performance standards that apply to all workers. (For more information about this issue, see "Drugs and Alcohol," below, as well as "Disability" in Chapter 3.)

Health and Safety Laws

All companies, regardless of size or industry, must comply with federal and state health and safety laws.

The Occupational Safety and Health Act

The major federal health and safety law is the Occupational Safety and Health Act (OSH Act), 29 U.S.C. §§ 651 to 678. The OSH Act requires employers to provide a workplace that is free of "recognized hazards" that are likely to cause serious harm or death to employees. As you can imagine, the term "recognized hazards" encompasses a wide range of things, from sharp objects to dangerous chemicals to radiation.

Employers must also conduct safety training sessions to educate employees about the materials and equipment they will be using, any workplace hazards (especially toxic chemicals), and the steps the company is taking to control those hazards.

In addition, employers must comply with some administrative requirements. For instance, companies must post a notice informing employees of health and safety regulations, report employee deaths and hospitalizations, and maintain records of:

- employee injuries and illnesses
- employee exposure to hazardous chemicals and substances, and
- employee safety training.

There are thousands of pages of federal regulations interpreting this law and defining employer duties and obligations. That's the bad news. The good news is that you do not have to wade through all this paper to learn about the law. The U.S. Occupational Safety and Health Administration (OSHA), the federal agency that enforces the law, publishes lots of information designed especially for small businesses and employers. You can find this information on the agency's website, www.osha.gov.

Also, each state has an OSHA-funded agency that offers free on-site consultations. If you ask for a consultation, an expert will walk through your worksite with you, pointing out risks and hazards and providing practical advice on how to correct problems and comply with the law. You can ask for this consultation without fear that your company will be fined for any violations or hazards that the expert sees. You'll find a list of OSHA consultation agencies organized by state on the OSHA website, at www.osha.gov; select "Cooperative Programs," then "Find a Cooperative Program" for more information.

Companies that disregard their health and safety obligations run the risk of being investigated and perhaps fined by OSHA inspectors. Fines depend on a variety of factors. Generally, employers that knowingly and intentionally violate the law, fail to correct a problem that OSHA warned them about, and put their employees at risk of serious injury or death are going to face the largest penalties. Depending on these factors, fines range from minimal all the way up to $70,000. If OSHA identifies a hazard that your company fails to eliminate, it can impose a fine of for each day that the hazard goes uncorrected.

If your company has ten or fewer employees and does business in an industry with a low injury rate, it is exempt from random inspections by OSHA. If not, OSHA can inspect the workplace at any time without advance notice. And it can issue citations and impose penalties based on what it finds.

In addition to fines and citations, your company could face lawsuits from an injured employee—or from the family of a deceased employee—if the employee was hurt or killed because the company intentionally violated a workplace safety law.

State Laws

In addition to the federal health and safety law, you must comply with the laws of your state. State laws regulating workplace health and safety can include occupational health and safety laws (usually similar to the federal law described above), workers' compensation laws, drug testing laws, substance abuse laws, and smoking laws, among others.

To find out about your state health and safety laws, contact your state labor department and state OSHA agency. You'll find contact information for both in the appendix.

(For more information about workers' compensation laws, see "Workers' Compensation," below. For more information about smoking laws, see "Smoking," below.)

Employee Rights

Federal and state laws give employees the right to complain about hazards in the workplace and legal violations. They also give employees the right to refuse to do something that endangers their safety or the safety of others.

This means that you can't discipline or take any other negative action against an employee who exercises a right under these laws. If you do, you might face additional fines or even a lawsuit.

Lessons From the Real World

The U.S. Occupational Health and Safety Administration (OSHA) sent investigators to Party City Corporation after employees complained of unsafe conditions. When investigators looked around the workplace, they found a whole host of problems, including:

- locked fire exits
- obstructed fire exits
- no training in the use of fire extinguishers
- no handrails on stairs
- no exit signs, and
- dangerously stacked boxes.

Even though no employees had been injured or harmed by the violations, OSHA imposed a hefty $111,150 fine because the potential for harm was so high. The possibility that employees might be unable to escape a fire or other emergency was unacceptable to the agency.

Workers' Compensation

Through the workers' compensation system, employers purchase insurance that provides benefits to employees who suffer work-related injuries and illnesses. The system strikes a compromise between employers and employees. Employees get benefits regardless of who was at fault: themselves, their employer, a customer, or a coworker. In return, the employer gets protection from lawsuits by injured employees seeking damages for pain and suffering or mental anguish.

Workers' compensation systems are governed by state, not federal, law. Although each state's system differs slightly in the details, the structure and operation of the overall system is the same from state to state. (The main differences are the rates paid to injured employees and the procedures to be followed for making a claim, seeing a doctor, filing an appeal, and so on.) To find out the details of your state's law, contact your state department of industrial relations or workers' compensation. You can also find a state-by-state description of these laws at the U.S. Department of Labor's website, at www.dol. gov. From the home page, click "Audiences: Employers," then "Workers' Compensation," then "State Workers' Compensation Laws."

Coverage

An employee's injury or illness must be work-related to be covered by workers' compensation law. It does not have to occur in the workplace, however. As long as it's job-related, it's covered. For example, employees are covered if they are injured while traveling on business, doing a work-related errand, or even attending a required business-related social function.

Workers' compensation covers injuries ranging from sudden accidents, such as falling off a scaffolding, to illnesses, such as those that result from exposure to workplace chemicals or radiation. Many workers receive compensation for repetitive stress injuries, including carpal tunnel syndrome and back problems. Workers may also receive compensation for illnesses and diseases that are the gradual result of work conditions, such as heart conditions, lung disease, and stress-related digestive problems.

Of course, not all problems that occur in the workplace are covered. Generally, workers' compensation will not cover injuries that are caused by an employee who is intoxicated or using illegal drugs. Coverage may also be denied in situations involving:

- self-inflicted injuries (including those caused by a person who starts a fight)
- injuries a worker suffers while committing a serious crime
- injuries an employee suffers off the job, and
- injuries an employee suffers when engaged in conduct that violates company policy.

Similarly, employers aren't protected from all employee lawsuits related to injuries. If the employee is injured because of some intentional or reckless action by the company, that employee can bypass the workers' compensation system to sue the employer for a full range of damages, including punitive damages, pain and suffering, and mental anguish.

Benefits

The workers' compensation system provides replacement income, pays for medical expenses, and sometimes pays for vocational rehabilitation benefits: on-the-job training, education, or job placement assistance.

An employee who is temporarily unable to work will usually receive two-thirds of his or her average wage up to a fixed ceiling. An employee who becomes permanently unable to do the work he or she was doing prior to the injury, or unable to work at all, may be eligible for long-term or lump-sum benefits. The system also pays death benefits to surviving dependents of workers who are fatally injured in a work-related incident.

Health Care Reform

The president signed the health care reform law—officially called the Patient Protection and Affordable Care Act—in March 2010. The law makes substantial changes to the health insurance system in this country. Because many people currently receive their health insurance through their jobs, the law will have a significant impact on employers. However, most changes don't take effect right away. And, because several aspects of the law are facing legal challenges across the country, the future of the law—particularly the individual and employer mandates, described below—is somewhat unclear. Here, we provide some basic information on major provisions of the law as written; to stay up to date and get detailed information on your

Lessons From the Real World

The Exxon Corporation got a lesson in the limits of workers' compensation laws. Usually, these laws protect companies from lawsuits filed by employees who are injured on the job. As this case illustrates, however, the law only goes so far.

For several weeks, four workers welded sheets of steel to the inside of a huge tower at an Exxon plant in Louisiana. Exxon did not give the welders safety equipment such as masks or air-supplied respirators; it did not give the welders safety instructions on the equipment they were using; and it did not ventilate the tower with clean air. As a result, the welders inhaled carcinogenic smoke and fibers while they worked.

After just a few days of work, the welders complained of physical problems, such as nosebleeds, blurry vision, night sweats, and vomiting blood. Still, day after day, the company sent them back to work in the tower without any safety equipment or training. This went on for a period of several weeks until the welders quit.

As it turned out, the manufacturer of the equipment the welders were using had given the company a safety manual that warned of severe physical problems and that suggested safety precautions. Not only did Exxon not pass the warnings on to the welders, it also failed to take a single one of the safety precautions suggested by the manufacturer.

The welders sued for punitive damages. The company argued that the welders had no right to go to court, because they were limited to the benefits that they could get from the workers' compensation system.

The court disagreed, concluding that the company's actions—or inactions—amounted to intentional conduct: "When an employer repeatedly sends employees back to work without safety equipment or without remedial measures being taken, and the employees are inevitably injured each time they are sent back to work, then the employer can be considered to have committed an intentional act." And when an employer intentionally harms an employee, the employer cannot hide behind the workers' compensation laws.

Abney v. Exxon Corporation, 755 So.2d 283 (La. App. 1st Cir. 1999).

obligations, check out the resources at the end of this section.

Lactation Breaks

The health care reform law requires employers to allow new mothers to express breast milk. Employers must provide reasonable break time for nursing mothers to pump for up to one year after birth. The employer need not pay for this time unless state law requires it; many states already require employers to offer lactation breaks.

(For more information, see "Lactation Breaks," in Chapter 2.)

Tax Credit for Small Businesses That Offer Health Insurance

Small businesses—defined as those with fewer than 25 full-time employees (or equivalent) and an average annual salary of less than $50,000 per employee—are eligible for a tax credit if they provide health insurance to their employees. To qualify, the business must pay at least half of the premium for covering a single person (not a family). Businesses can get a credit of up to 35% of the premiums they paid; nonprofit employers can get a credit of up to 25% of the premiums they paid (these percentages are set to increase in 2014). The maximum credit is available to the smallest employers: those with ten or fewer employees with average annual wages of less than $25,000.

Temporary Reimbursement to Employers That Provide Retiree Health Coverage

The Early Retiree Reinsurance Program gives a subsidy to employers that provide health care coverage to retirees who do not yet qualify for Medicare (those between the ages of 55 and 64). Coverage for spouses, surviving spouses, and dependents of the retiree is also covered. The subsidy covers up to 80% of claims incurred after June 1, 2010, but only after the retiree has made at least $15,000 in annual claims. (And the subsidy cuts off once the retiree has made $90,000 in annual claims.)

Plan sponsors must apply for this subsidy. This is a temporary program, scheduled to end on January 1, 2014, when retirees will be able to get insurance through state insurance exchanges. However, the program has a limited budget, to be paid out on a first-come, first-served basis.

Requirements and Restrictions on Health Care Plans

For plan years that began on October 1, 2010 or later, new restrictions and requirements apply to health care plans. There are more requirements for new plans; existing (grandfathered) plans won't have to comply with all of these requirements right away.

Rules for Existing Plans

Here are some of the requirements that will apply to existing plans:

- There can be no lifetime dollar limits on the care provided for essential health benefits. Which benefits go on this list will be decided by the Health and Human Services (HHS) Department, but the list must include certain items, such as emergency care, hospitalization, maternity and newborn care, prescription drugs, laboratory services, mental health, and preventive care.
- Insurers can apply annual benefit limits, subject to certain restrictions in order to ensure access to necessary services.

- Children up to the age of 26 who are not covered at their own jobs must be allowed to enroll in a parent's plan.
- Children up to the age of 18 may not be denied coverage for preexisting conditions.
- Plans may rescind (cancel) coverage only if the insured commits fraud or intentionally misrepresents a material fact.
- Additional requirements for grandfathered plans will start in 2014.

Rules for New Plans

New plans will have to comply with the rules for existing plans, along with some additional requirements, including:

- Plans must fully cover preventive care, with no deductible or co pay.
- Employers that choose to offer wellness programs must pay the full cost, with no deductible or co-pay.
- Employees must be able to go to the emergency room and ob-gyn visits without prior authorization; participation in clinical trials must be covered.
- Group health plans may not discriminate in favor of highly compensated employees.

Again, additional requirements will apply in 2014.

Long-Term Care Insurance: CLASS Act

The health care reform law includes the Community Living Assistance Service and Supports Act (the CLASS Act), a new program that provides limited payments for long-term care. The CLASS Act is a federal insurance program, like Social Security or Medicare. Unlike those programs, however, participation is voluntary for both employers and employees.

Beginning in 2011, employers who choose to participate in the program may allow employees to opt in or may automatically enroll employees and allow them to opt out of the program. Employees pay the full price of the premiums, which are withheld as a regular payroll deduction. Once employees have paid into the program for at least five years, they are eligible for cash benefits (estimated at about $50 per day) if they are limited in at least two daily living activities, such as bathing, dressing, or caring for themselves.

Changes to HSAs and FSAs

Over-the-counter drugs are no longer reimbursable through flexible savings accounts (FSAs) or health savings accounts (HSAs) unless a doctor prescribes them. The health care reform law also caps annual contributions to an FSA to $2,500 beginning in 2013. And employees under the age of 65 who make nonqualified withdrawals from their HSA (in other words, don't use the money for health care purposes) will have to pay a 20% penalty.

Reporting and Notice Requirements

The health care reform law imposes several new informational requirements on employers. They include:

- Employers must report the value of the health benefits they provide to employees on each employee's W-2 Form. This requirement kicks in at the beginning of 2012 for benefits provided in 2011.
- Employers must give employees information about the state insurance exchange program, including how to get premium assistance if necessary. This requirement starts in 2013.
- Beginning in 2014, larger employers must report certain information about the health coverage they provide to employees.

Play or Pay: The Employer Mandate

Beginning in 2014, the individual mandate will kick in. Everyone will have to be covered by health insurance or pay a fine; those who can't afford insurance will be eligible for assistance.

The employer mandate kicks in at the same time. Employers with at least 50 employees must provide health care benefits or pay a penalty. Employers who provide benefits may still have to pay a penalty, depending on the cost of benefits to employees and employee ability to pay. Here are the basics:

- Employers that have more than 50 employees and don't offer coverage must pay an annual fine of $2,000 per full-time employee (those working at least 30 hours a week). The first 30 employees are "free"; the fine begins with employee number 31.
- Even employers that offer coverage may face a penalty if the employer doesn't pay for at least 60% of the actuarial value of the benefits the plan provides or the employee's cost for coverage is more than 9.5% of the employee's household income. In this situation, a full-time employee would be eligible to receive government-subsidized coverage. If this happens, the employer would have to pay a penalty of $3,000 per full-time employee who receives the subsidy, up to a limit.
- Employers must offer a voucher to employees who (1) have an income that is less than four times the federal poverty level, (2) would have to pay more than 8% of their income for employer-provided coverage, and (3) choose to enroll in a plan from a state insurance exchange. The voucher requires the employer to pay what it would have paid to enroll the employee in its own plan.

Larger employers will also have to automatically enroll employees in their health insurance plan.

For More Information

To learn more about the health care reform law, check out:

- www.healthreform.gov, the federal government's website on the law
- http://healthreform.kff.org, a comprehensive site maintained by the Kaiser Family Foundation, and

- www.shrm.org, the Society for Human Resource Management's site, which includes detailed articles and a timeline for health care reforms affecting employers (some of the articles are available only to members).

Cell Phones and Driving

Studies show that drivers who are distracted cause more accidents, and that cell phones and other forms of wireless technology are increasingly to blame for our lack of attention to the road. If your company's employees drive for work or use cell phones for work, chances are good that they occasionally do both at the same time; 81% of drivers do, according to a 2008 survey by Nationwide Insurance Company. To make sure employees are safe and don't cause harm to others (or expose the company to liability), you should have rules dictating whether and how employees may use their cell phones while driving.

State Law Restrictions

A growing number of states have passed laws that limit the use of cell phones while driving. These laws take several forms: Some prevent only texting; some require drivers to use a hands-free device if they want to talk on the phone; some prohibit younger or less experienced drivers from using any type of cell phone; and some allow officers to cite drivers for using a hand-held cell phone if the driver is pulled over for another offense. (To learn the laws of your state, go to the website

of the Governors Highway Safety Association, www.statehighwaysafety.org, and select "State Laws and Funding.")

If your company does business in a state that limits the use of cell phones while driving, of course you'll want to require employees to follow the law. However, even companies in states that haven't legislated in this area need cell phone rules. Simply put, using a cell phone while driving is dangerous. And, if an employee causes an accident while doing business on a cell phone, your company could be held liable for the damages.

Employer Liability Concerns

There have been plenty of big settlements in lawsuits against companies whose employees injured or killed someone while talking on a cell phone. Why are the companies sued? Because they typically have much deeper pockets than the employee who actually caused the accident. Consider these real-life examples:

- A stockbroker from Smith Barney was making a cold call to a potential client while driving when he struck and killed a motorcyclist. Although the broker was using his own cell phone and driving to a nonbusiness event, the plaintiff argued that Smith Barney should be liable because it encouraged employees to use their cell phones for cold calling without training them on safety issues. Smith Barney eventually settled the case for $500,000.
- A lawyer was making a business call on her cell phone while driving home

from work. She hit something, which she though was a deer, and kept driving; sadly, she actually hit—and killed—a teenager. The attorney served a year in jail for hit-and-run driving and was ordered to pay the victim's family more than $2 million. Her law firm settled its part of the case for an undisclosed amount.

- An employer of International Paper was using her company cell phone when she rear-ended another driver on the freeway, causing injuries that eventually required the other driver to have her arm amputated. The company paid $5.2 million to settle the case.

As explained in "Liability for an Employee's Actions" in Chapter 11, your company can be held liable for actions an employee takes within the scope of employment. So, if the call, the driving, or both are work-related, your company may be on the hook for damages.

Sensible Cell Phone Rules

To promote employee safety (and avoid liability), your company should adopt a policy on use of cell phones while driving. Your policy should:

- Prohibit employees from using cell phones for work-related matters while driving.
- Tell employees what to do if they receive or must place a call while driving: Pull over safely and stop the car before taking or making the call.
- Explain the rules on hands-free devices. If your company wants to allow employees to use hands-free equipment

while driving, your policy should say so. However, it should also state that employees must concentrate fully on the road while driving. If bad weather, traffic, or other conditions make it difficult to talk on the phone and drive safely at the same time, employees should pull over and park before having their hands-free conversation. (If you know employees use cell phones for work, it's a good idea to issue them hands-free equipment, to make sure they can comply with the policy.)

Smoking

Smoking used to be as accepted a workplace activity as drinking coffee, but not any more. Concerns about the impact of secondhand smoke and the comfort of nonsmokers have prompted most states to enact laws—commonly called clean air laws—that severely restrict smoking in the workplace.

Some states prohibit smoking in all enclosed private workplaces. Other state laws prohibit smoking except in designated areas, prohibit smoking in private workplaces if the employer has more than a minimum number of employees, or prohibit smoking in certain kinds of workplaces, such as hospitals and restaurants.

In addition to these state laws, many cities and counties have also enacted ordinances against smoking in the workplace.

Many employers choose to ban smoking in their workplaces, even if no state law requires them to do so. Smokers generally have higher-than-average health care costs and higher absenteeism rates than nonsmokers. In addition, nonsmokers complain about the quality of the air and about the smoking breaks that their smoking colleagues take.

However, many states prohibit employers from discriminating against smokers. This means that employers can limit an employee's on-site smoking but may not make job decisions based on an employee's or applicant's decision to smoke outside of work. (For more about this issue, see "Off-Duty Conduct" in Chapter 6.)

To check your state's rules on smoking, see "State Laws on Smoking in the Workplace," at the end of this chapter.

To learn whether your city or county has an ordinance that prohibits or restricts smoking in the workplace, contact your local government offices.

Drugs and Alcohol

Employees who abuse alcohol and drugs (including illegal drugs, prescription drugs, and over-the-counter drugs)—either on their own time or at work—can pose significant and wide-ranging problems for their employers, managers, and coworkers. These problems can include diminished job performance, lowered productivity, absenteeism, tardiness, high turnover, and increased medical and workers' compensation bills. Employees who abuse drugs and alcohol can also make a workplace more volatile and more dangerous, and they can expose employers to legal liability.

Alcohol Use at Work

Your company's employee handbook (or its verbally announced workplace policies) should make clear to employees that drinking on the job is not allowed. If you catch an employee actually drinking alcohol at work, you can deal with it through your company's standard disciplinary procedures. Depending on the circumstances and on your company's policies, the punishment can range from an oral reminder to immediate termination.

The consequences should depend in part on whether the employee has endangered the health and safety of others. For example, an employee who drinks a beer while operating a forklift might deserve more severe discipline than a secretary who has a beer while sitting at a desk.

Off-Hours, Off-Site Use of Alcohol

Many people use alcohol when not at work. Most employers aren't concerned about an employee's occasional drink—or even the occasional overindulgence—as long as it doesn't affect the employee's work performance. But when off-site, off-hours drinking begins to take its toll on the worker's ability to do the job, employers may have reason to take action.

Handling a worker with a drinking problem is tricky business. As discussed in Chapter 3, the federal Americans with Disabilities Act (ADA) and many state disability rights laws protect alcoholics from workplace discrimination. (See "Disability" in Chapter 3 for more about the ADA.) The ADA doesn't allow employers to make an employment decision based solely on the fact that an employee is an alcoholic. An employer can, however, make a decision—including a decision to discipline or terminate—based on the employee's inability to meet the same performance and productivity standards that it imposes on all employees.

Legal Drug Use

Many employees properly use prescribed or over-the-counter drugs, such as sleeping aids, cold medicine, or painkillers. Most employers sensibly believe that this is none of their business, as long as the drugs don't impair the employee's job performance.

Things get trickier, however, if legitimate drug use affects an employee's ability to do the job safely and well. For example, medications that cause drowsiness might make it downright dangerous for a worker to do a job that requires driving or operating machinery. Medication may also impair judgment and abilities, which could impair a worker's ability to meet job requirements.

If an employee's performance is affected by the proper use of prescription or over-the-counter drugs, state and federal disability laws may limit an employer's options. Depending on how the drug use affects the employee, and whether the employee suffers from a disability within the meaning of these laws, your company may have to accommodate the employee's use of the drugs. (See "Disability" in Chapter 3 for more information about disability rights laws and your duty to accommodate an employee's legal drug use.)

Illegal Drug Use and Possession

If an employee is under the influence of illegal drugs at work, disability rights laws do not limit your company's options. You may deal with that employee through your company's standard disciplinary procedures. If the employee has not created a safety threat and does not hold a highly sensitive position, a written reprimand might be appropriate for a first offense.

However, if the employee endangers the physical safety of others—for example, by driving the company van after smoking marijuana at home—something more drastic is called for. If the employee has a drug problem, one option is to suspend the worker until he or she successfully completes a treatment program. Some employers, however, opt for a zero-tolerance policy under these circumstances and immediately suspend and then terminate the employee.

Because using, selling, or possessing illegal drugs is a crime, most employers immediately terminate employees who engage in this type of behavior at work.

Drug Testing Current Employees

Drug testing is a dicey legal issue for employers—and one that should be approached with extreme caution. Drug tests are highly intrusive, yet they can also be invaluable tools for preventing drug-related accidents and safety problems.

The law of drug testing is changing rapidly as more courts rule on employee lawsuits claiming that a particular drug test violated their right to privacy. Because drug testing is so intrusive, a worker who convinces a jury that a test was illegal (in violation of either your state's drug testing laws or your state's privacy laws) could cost your company a lot of money, and ruin its reputation as a fair employer. Before performing any drug test or adopting a drug test policy, you must get some legal advice. If you decide to proceed with legal assistance, here are some guidelines to consider.

Whom to test. Avoid testing every employee for drugs, and avoid random drug testing. Unless all of your company's workers perform dangerous jobs, these sorts of tests cast too wide a net. A drug test is most likely to withstand legal scrutiny if you have a particular reason to suspect an employee of illegal drug use or the employee's job carries a high risk of injury.

When to test. Your company will be on the safest legal ground if your primary motive is to ensure the safety of workers, customers, and members of the general public. Employers are most likely to withstand a legal challenge if they limit testing to:

- employees whose jobs carry a high risk of injury to themselves or others (such as a forklift operator or pilot) or involve security (a security guard who carries a gun, for example)
- workers who have been involved in accidents (for instance, a delivery driver who inexplicably ran a red light and hit a pedestrian)
- employees who are currently in or have completed a drug rehabilitation program, and
- workers whom a manager or supervisor reasonably suspects are illegally using drugs.

How to test. Even if you have strong reasons for testing, your company can still get into legal trouble over the way the test is administered and interpreted. To be safe, employers should:

- use a test lab that is certified by the U.S. Department of Health and Human Services or an equivalent state agency
- consult with a lawyer in developing testing policy and procedures
- use a testing format that respects the privacy and dignity of each employee
- have a written policy in place about drug use in the workplace (including a discussion of the disciplinary steps the company will take and under what circumstances) and testing procedures (including when the test will be given, how the test will be administered, and what substances—at what levels—the test will detect)
- require employees to read the drug and alcohol policy and testing policy and sign an acknowledgment that they have done so
- for every drug test administered, document why it was necessary and how the test was performed
- keep the test results confidential, and
- be consistent in how the company deals with workers who test positive.

Employers cannot force workers to take a drug test against their will. However, an employee who refuses to take a drug test can be fired for that reason, as long as the employer had a solid basis for asking the employee to submit to the drug test in the first place.

Legal Dos and Don'ts: Health and Safety

Do:

- **Help employees stop smoking.** While many states prohibit employers from discriminating against smokers, nothing prevents your company from sponsoring programs to help employees kick the habit. It's generally easier for smokers to quit within the context of a supportive program than on their own, and your company will reap rewards like lower absenteeism and health care costs.

- **Consider rehab leave.** Workers with substance abuse problems cost a company plenty in lost productivity, higher health care costs, and missed work. Encourage these employees to clean up their acts by offering some paid leave to enter a rehabilitation program. You will more than earn that money back if the worker successfully rehabilitates and returns to work more productive and more dedicated to the company.

- **Seek professional help for health and safety concerns.** Many experts offer free workplace consultations, so it makes sense to get an expert to come to your workplace and point out health and safety concerns, free of charge. This could save you a bundle in workers' compensation claims, fines, and health care costs.

Don't:

- **Disregard employee complaints.** If an employee expresses concern about a workplace hazard or other safety issue, take it seriously. If you don't, the employee might take his or her complaint to a federal or state agency. More seriously, workers might be injured or worse if the employee's fears were valid.

- **Ignore OSHA's advice.** If a federal or state inspector tells your company to make changes, do it. These agencies do not like to be ignored and won't hesitate to impose fines on employers that buck the system. Disregarding these recommendations also leaves a company more vulnerable to lawsuits from employees, customers, and vendors.

- **Go without workers' compensation coverage.** If you think your company is so safe that it doesn't need workers' compensation coverage, think again. Most states require all but the smallest employers to purchase coverage. Even smaller employers would be wise to get a policy. Otherwise, one workplace accident could wipe the company out.

Test Your Knowledge

Questions

1. Small companies don't have to worry about complying with OSHA. ☐ True ☐ False

2. Employees can be fired for complaining about a health or safety issue. ☐ True ☐ False

3. If an injury is covered by workers' compensation, the injured employee cannot sue the employer for damages. ☐ True ☐ False

4. An injury must occur at the workplace to be covered by workers' compensation. ☐ True ☐ False

5. As long as a company requires employees to use hands-free devices to use a cell phone when driving, it won't be responsible for any resulting accidents. ☐ True ☐ False

6. All employers must create a designated smoking area for employees who wish to smoke. ☐ True ☐ False

7. Employees who take breaks to smoke outside must stand at least a certain distance away from the workplace. ☐ True ☐ False

8. It is illegal to fire an employee for using alcohol at work, because that might be a sign of alcoholism, which is a disability. ☐ True ☐ False

9. Employers can fire an employee whose use of prescription or over-the-counter drugs interferes with his or her ability to do the job. ☐ True ☐ False

10. Drug testing current employees is illegal. ☐ True ☐ False

Answers

1. False. Although small employers (those with fewer than ten employees) and employers in industries with a low injury rate are exempt from some OSHA requirements, other OSHA obligations—including the obligation to maintain a safe workplace and report serious injuries and deaths to the government—apply to all employers, regardless of size.

2. False. Retaliating against employees who complain of workplace safety or health violations is illegal.

3. True. An employee whose injury is covered by workers' compensation is entitled to the benefits that system provides but may not sue the employer for damages relating to the injury.

4. False. An injury need not take place at the worksite; it must only be work-related. If an employee is injured at an off-site work event or while driving a delivery route, for example, that injury is covered by workers' compensation.

5. Not necessarily. Your policy should tell employees that they must concentrate fully on the road, no matter what technology they are using. If they can't drive safely while using a hands-free device—for example, because the conversation is heated and distracting, or the weather makes driving difficult—they should hang up.

6. False. Employers are generally free to prohibit smoking, if they wish to do so. Many states impose requirements on employers who choose to allow smoking (for example, that smoking areas be designated and separately ventilated).

7. It depends on local laws. Some cities prohibit smoking within a certain distance of the entrance, exit, and/or ventilation openings of certain buildings (for example, those that are open to the public).

8. False. Although the Americans with Disabilities Act prevents employers from firing an employee simply because he or she is an alcoholic, employers are free to discipline employees who use alcohol at work.

9. It depends on whether the employee has a disability. Employers must make reasonable accommodations for employees with disabilities. One such change might involve making minor alterations to an employee's job responsibilities to accommodate the effects of drugs necessitated by the employee's disability.

10. It depends on state law and on how the test is administered. Most states allow some drug testing of current employees, depending on the situation.

State Laws on Smoking in the Workplace

Note: These rules typically don't apply to some types of businesses, such as those that primarily sell or research tobacco products, theatrical productions, hotel rooms, private clubs, private conventions, and workplaces that are private residences (except to provide medical care or to care for children). For a complete list of exceptions in your state, refer to the listed statutes or contact your state department of labor or state or local health department.

ALABAMA
Ala. Code §§ 22-15A-3 and 22-15A-5

Workplaces where laws apply: Enclosed places of employment with five or more employees.

Exceptions: Common work areas if a majority of the workers who work in that area agree that a smoking area will be designated.

Where smoking prohibited: Employer may prohibit smoking in all or part of workplace. Individual employee may designate his or her own work area as a nonsmoking area. No smoking in common work areas unless majority of workers in that area agree to designate it as a smoking area.

Where smoking permitted: Majority of workers in an area may decide to designate common work area as smoking area, unless employer prohibits.

Smoking area requirements: Ventilated or separated to minimize toxic effects of smoke.

Accommodations for nonsmokers: Employers must provide signs to post if an employee designates his or her own work area as nonsmoking.

Employer smoking policy: Written policy must meet minimum requirements and be communicated to all employees.

ALASKA
Alaska Stat. §§ 18.35.300, 18.35.310, and 18.35.320

Workplaces where laws apply: Any private place of business that posts signs regulating smoking; restaurants serving more than 50; grocery stores.

Exceptions: (1) A portion of a place or vehicle that is designated as a smoking section under § 18.35.320; (2) a limousine for hire or taxicab, if the driver consents and the driver ascertains that all passengers consent to smoking in the vehicle.

Where smoking prohibited: Throughout workplace except in designated smoking area. Employer may designate entire site nonsmoking. A smoking section may not be designated under § 18.35.320 for students on the grounds of or in an elementary or secondary school, indoors or outdoors.

Where smoking permitted: Designated smoking area.

Smoking area requirements: Ventilated or separated to protect nonsmokers from active byproducts of smoke.

Accommodations for nonsmokers: Reasonable accommodations to protect the health of nonsmokers.

ARIZONA
Ariz. Rev. Stat. § 36-601. 01

Workplace where laws apply: Any enclosed workplace.

Where smoking prohibited: Entire enclosed workplace. Employer may permit smoking

State Laws on Smoking in the Workplace (cont'd)

outside so long as people entering or leaving the building will not be subject to breathing tobacco smoke and the smoke does not enter the building.

Protection from discrimination: No employer may discharge or retaliate against an employee for exercising rights under this law.

ARKANSAS
Ark. Code Ann. §§ 20-27-1804 and 20-27-1805, Ark. Admin. Code §§ 016 24 002

Workplace where laws apply: Any enclosed workplace.

Exceptions: Nonpublic workplaces with fewer than 3 employees.

Where smoking prohibited: Entire enclosed workplace.

Smoking area requirements: When smoking is permitted, employer must post signs that meet certain size and placement criteria and say: "HEALTH WARNING. THIS IS A SMOKING AREA. OCCUPANTS WILL BE EXPOSED TO SECONDHAND SMOKE. IT IS UNLAWFUL FOR ANYONE UNDER 21 YEARS OF AGE TO ENTER OR WORK IN ANY PART OF THE ESTABLISHMENT AT ALL TIMES."

Protection from discrimination: No employer may discharge or retaliate against an employee for making a complaint under this law or furnishing information about a violation to an enforcement authority.

Employer smoking policy: The prohibitions on smoking shall be communicated to each prospective employee upon application for employment.

CALIFORNIA
Cal. Lab. Code §§ 96,98.6, 6404.5

Workplaces where laws apply: Workplaces with more than 5 employees.

Exceptions: Designated lobby areas; meeting and banquet rooms when food is not being served; warehouses over 100,000 sq. ft. with fewer than 20 employees; truck cabs if no nonsmoking employees are present.

Where smoking prohibited: Employer may not knowingly or intentionally permit smoking in any enclosed workplace; must take reasonable steps to prevent nonemployees from smoking. May designate entire site nonsmoking.

Where smoking permitted: Break rooms designated for smokers.

Smoking area requirements: Break room must be in a nonwork area. No employee may be required to enter room as part of job (does not apply to custodial work when room is unoccupied). Air must be exhausted directly to the outside with a fan and may not recirculate to other areas of the building.

Accommodations for nonsmokers: If there is a break room for smokers, must be enough break rooms for all nonsmokers.

Accommodations for smokers: None required. However, employers with 5 or fewer employees may permit smoking if:
- all the employees agree
- no minors are allowed in the smoking area, and
- no employee is required to enter smoking area.

State Laws on Smoking in the Workplace (cont'd)

COLORADO

Colo. Rev. Stat. §§ 25-14-204 to 25-14-205; 24-34-402.5

Workplaces where laws apply: Any indoor workplace.

Exceptions: Places of employment not open to the public, under the control of the employer, and with 3 or fewer employees.

Where smoking is prohibited: The common areas of retirement facilities, publicly owned housing facilities, and, except as specified in section 25-14-205(1)(k), nursing homes, but not including any resident's private residential quarters or areas of assisted living facilities specified in section 25-14-205 (1)(k).

Accommodations for nonsmokers: Exempted employers must designate a smoke-free area if requested by an employee.

Protection from discrimination: Employee may not be fired for lawful conduct off-site during nonwork hours.

CONNECTICUT

Conn. Gen. Stat. Ann. §§ 31-40q, 31-40s

Workplaces where laws apply: Employers with 5 or more employees must prohibit smoking, except in designated smoking rooms. Enclosed facilities.

Where smoking prohibited: Employer may prohibit smoking throughout the workplace.

Smoking area requirements: Employers with fewer than 5 employees: Existing physical barriers and ventilation systems. Employers with 5 or more employees: Air must be exhausted directly outside with a fan and cannot recirculate to other areas of the building; room must be in a nonwork area where no employee is required to enter.

Accommodations for nonsmokers: Each smoking room designated by an employer shall be in a nonwork area for the use of employees only; air from the smoking room shall be exhausted directly to the outside by an exhaust fan, and no air from such room shall be recirculated to other parts of the building.

Protection from discrimination: Employer may not require employee to refrain from smoking as a condition of employment.

DELAWARE

Del. Code Ann. tit. 16, §§ 2902 to 2907

Workplaces where laws apply: Indoor areas.

Exceptions: Restaurants serving 50 or fewer.

Where smoking prohibited: Any indoor enclosed area where the general public is permitted or may be invited.

Protection from discrimination: Employer may not discriminate against or retaliate against employee who files a complaint or testifies in a proceeding about violation of workplace smoking laws.

DISTRICT OF COLUMBIA

D.C. Code Ann. §§ 7-1701 to 7-1703.03

Workplaces where laws apply: Any private employer.

Where smoking prohibited: Throughout the workplace except for designated smoking area.

Where smoking permitted: Designated smoking area.

Smoking area requirements: Physical barrier or separate room.

Accommodations for smokers: Employer required to provide smoking area.

State Laws on Smoking in the Workplace (cont'd)

Smoking area requirements: Physical barrier or separate room.

Protection from discrimination: Employee may not be fired or discriminated against in hiring, wages, benefits, or terms of employment because of being a smoker.

Employer smoking policy: Must have written policy that designates a smoking area; must notify each employee orally and post policy within 3 weeks after adopting it.

FLORIDA
Fla. Stat. Ann. §§ 386.201 to 386.209

Workplaces where laws apply: All enclosed indoor workplaces. (More than 50% covered and surrounded by physical barriers.)

Exceptions: Stand-alone bars.

Where smoking prohibited: Smoking is prohibited throughout the workplace.

Smoking area requirements: A customs smoking room in an airport in-transit lounge may not be designated in any common area; must be enclosed by physical barriers that are impenetrable by secondhand tobacco smoke, and exhaust tobacco smoke directly to the outside, and comply with the signage requirements.

Employer smoking policy: Employer must develop and enforce a policy prohibiting smoking in the workplace. May post "No Smoking" signs to increase awareness.

GEORGIA
Ga. Code Ann. §§ 31-12A-1 to 31-12A-13, Ga. Comp. R. & Regs. § 290-5-61.03

Workplace where laws apply: Any enclosed workplace.

Where smoking prohibited: Entire indoor workplace except for designated smoking area.

Employer may designate the entire workplace nonsmoking.

Where smoking permitted: Any designated smoking area.

Smoking area requirements: Smoking area must be in a nonwork area where no employee is required to enter (except to perform custodial and maintenance work when the smoking area is unoccupied). Must have ventilation systems that exhaust air outdoors; have no air recirculating to nonsmoking areas; and be only for employee use.

Employer smoking policy: Smoking prohibition must be communicated to all applicants when they apply.

HAWAII
Haw. Rev. Stat. §§ 328J-1 to 328J-7

Workplaces where laws apply: Any enclosed area.

Where smoking prohibited: Entire enclosed workplace and within a "presumptively reasonable" distance of 20 feet from any entrance, exit, or ventilation intake.

Protection from discrimination: Employer may not discharge, refuse to hire, or retaliate against employee or applicant for attempting to prosecute a violation of this law.

IDAHO
Idaho Code §§ 39-5501 and following

Workplaces where laws apply: Enclosed indoor area used by the general public, including restaurants that seat 30 or more, retail stores, and grocery stores.

Exceptions: Bowling alleys, bars.

Where smoking prohibited: Everywhere except designated smoking area; not required to provide smoking area.

State Laws on Smoking in the Workplace (cont'd)

Where smoking permitted: Employer or proprietor designates.

Smoking area requirements: Must not be accessible to minors, must be separated from the rest of the building by a floor-to-ceiling partition; must not be the sole entrance to the workplace or restroom, and must be located in an area where no employee is required to enter as part of the employee's work responsibilities. Must post "Warning: Smoking Permitted" signs.

Protection from discrimination: Employer may not discharge or discriminate against employee because employee has made a complaint or has given information to the department of health and welfare or the department of labor for violation of this law.

ILLINOIS
410 Ill. Comp. Stat. §§ 82/1 and following; 820 Ill. Comp. Stat. § 55/5

Workplaces where laws apply: Any enclosed indoor workplace.

Where smoking prohibited: Entire workplace and within 15 feet of entrance, exit, or ventilation intake of workplace.

Protection from discrimination: Employee may not be discriminated against for asserting rights under the clean indoor air laws. May not be refused a job, fired, or discriminated against in terms of compensation or benefits because of using lawful products outside of work. Different insurance rates or coverage for smokers are not discriminatory if:
- difference is based on cost to employer, and
- employees are given a notice of carriers' rates.

INDIANA
Ind. Code Ann. § 22-5-4-1

Protection from discrimination: Employer may not: require prospective employee to refrain from using tobacco products outside of work in order to be hired; discriminate against employee who uses them in terms of wages, benefits, or conditions of employment.

IOWA
Iowa Code §§ 142D.1 to 142D.9.

Workplaces where laws apply: All enclosed indoor areas.

Exceptions: State fairgrounds; designated smoking areas of National Guard and correctional facilities.

Where smoking prohibited: All enclosed indoor areas.

Where smoking permitted: Outdoor areas not otherwise prohibited by law, unless employer chooses to prohibit smoking there. Such areas must be marked with signs.

Protection from discrimination: An employer shall not discharge, refuse to employ, or in any manner retaliate against an employee, applicant for employment, or customer because that employee, applicant, or customer exercises any rights under this law, registers a complaint, or attempts to prosecute a violation of the law.

KANSAS
Kan. Stat. Ann. §§ 21-4009 to 21-4011

Workplaces where laws apply: Any enclosed workplace.

Where smoking prohibited: Anywhere other than designated smoking areas.

Where smoking permitted: Designated smoking areas.

State Laws on Smoking in the Workplace (cont'd)

Smoking area requirements: Existing barriers and ventilation systems are to be used to minimize the toxic effect of smoke in nonsmoking areas.

Employer smoking policy: Written policy must prohibit smoking without exception in all areas of the place of employment. Policy shall be communicated to all current employees within one week of its adoption and to all new employees upon hiring. Written policy available upon request.

KENTUCKY
Ky. Rev. Stat. Ann. § 344.040(3)

Protection from discrimination: As long as employee complies with workplace smoking policy, employer may not: discharge employee or discriminate in terms of wages, benefits, or conditions of employment because of being a smoker or nonsmoker; require employee to refrain from using tobacco products outside of work as a condition of employment. A difference in employee contribution rates for smokers and nonsmokers in relation to an employer-sponsored health plan is a lawful practice, as well as the offering of incentives or benefits offered to employees who participate in a smoking cessation program.

LOUISIANA
La. Rev. Stat. Ann. §§ 40:1300.251 to 40:1300.263, 23:966

Workplaces where laws apply: Any enclosed workplace.

Exceptions: Bars, outdoor patios.

Where smoking prohibited: Any enclosed workplace.

Where smoking permitted: Outdoors, unless employer posts signs prohibiting smoking in the outdoor area.

Protection from discrimination: Employer may not:
- require prospective employee to refrain from using tobacco products outside of work as a condition of employment;
- discriminate against smokers or nonsmokers regarding termination, layoffs, wages, benefits, or other terms of employment.

MAINE
Me. Rev. Stat. Ann. tit. 22, §§ 1580-A; tit. 26, § 597

Workplaces where laws apply: Structurally enclosed business facilities.

Where smoking prohibited: Employer may prohibit throughout entire workplace.

Where smoking permitted: Designated smoking area, meaning in an outdoor area where smoking is permitted, which must be at least 20 feet from entryways, vents, and doorways.

Protection from discrimination: Employer may not discriminate or retaliate against employee for assisting with enforcement of workplace smoking laws. As long as employee follows workplace smoking policy employer may not:
- discriminate in wages, benefits, or terms of employment because of use of tobacco products outside of work;
- require employee to refrain from tobacco use as a condition of employment.

Employer smoking policy: Written policy concerning smoking and nonsmoking rules. State bureau of health will assist employees and employers with creating policy.

State Laws on Smoking in the Workplace (cont'd)

MARYLAND

Md. Code Ann. [Health-Gen.] §§ 24-501 and following; Md. Regs. Code §§ 09.12.23.01 to 09.12.23.04

Workplaces where laws apply: Any indoor work area.

Where smoking prohibited: Entire indoor workplace.

Protection from discrimination: Employer may not discharge or discriminate against an employee because that employee has made a complaint or charge against the employer under this law or or has testified or is about to testify in a proceeding regarding this law.

MASSACHUSETTS

Mass. Gen. Laws ch. 270, § 22

Workplaces where laws apply: Any enclosed workspace.

Where smoking prohibited: Where employees work in an enclosed workspace.

MINNESOTA

Minn. Stat. Ann. §§ 144.411 to 144.417, 181.938

Workplaces where laws apply: Enclosed indoor workplace.

Where smoking prohibited: Entire indoor workplace.

Protection from discrimination: Employer cannot discharge, refuse to hire, penalize, discriminate against, or in any manner retaliate against an employee or applicant because the individual exercises any right to a smoke-free environment.

MISSISSIPPI

Miss. Code Ann. § 71-7-33

Workplaces where laws apply: Employer may not make it a condition of employment for prospective or current employee to abstain from smoking during nonwork hours, as long as employee complies with laws or policies that regulate workplace smoking.

MISSOURI

Mo. Rev. Stat. §§ 191.765 to 191.771, 290.145

Workplaces where laws apply: Enclosed indoor workplaces.

Exceptions: Bars or restaurants seating fewer than 50 people, bowling alleys and billiard parlors, and stadiums seating more than 15,000 people.

Where smoking prohibited: Entire workplace except for designated smoking area.

Where smoking permitted: Designated smoking area (may not be more than 30% of workplace).

Smoking area requirements: Existing physical barriers and ventilation systems that isolate area.

Protection from discrimination: Employer may not refuse to hire, discharge, or in any way discriminate against employee for lawful use of tobacco off-site during nonwork hours, unless use interferes with employee's or coworkers' performance or employer's business operations.

MONTANA

Mont. Code Ann. §§ 50-40-104; 39-2-313

Workplaces where laws apply: Any enclosed indoor workplace.

Where smoking prohibited: Entire workplace.

Protection from discrimination: Employer may not discharge, refuse to hire, or discriminate

State Laws on Smoking in the Workplace (cont'd)

against employee in regard to compensation, promotion, benefits, or terms of employment because of lawful tobacco use off-site during nonwork hours. Use that affects job performance, other workers' safety, or conflicts with a genuine job requirement is not protected. It is not discrimination to have different insurance rates or coverage for smokers if:

• difference is based on cost to employer, and
• employees are given a written statement of carriers' rates.

NEBRASKA

Neb. Rev. Stat. §§ 71-5716 to 71-5734

Workplaces where laws apply: Any enclosed indoor workplace.

Where smoking prohibited: Entire workplace.

NEVADA

Nev. Rev. Stat. Ann. § 613.333

Protection from discrimination: Employer may not: fail or refuse to hire, discharge, or discriminate in terms of compensation, benefits, or conditions of employment, because of employee's lawful use of any product off-site during nonwork hours, unless use adversely affects job performance or the safety of other employees.

NEW HAMPSHIRE

N.H. Rev. Stat. Ann. §§ 155:64 to 155.77; 275:37-a

Workplaces where laws apply: Enclosed workplaces where 4 or more people work.

Where smoking prohibited: Throughout the workplace except for designated smoking area. If smoking area cannot be effectively segregated, smoking will be totally prohibited. Employer may declare entire workplace nonsmoking.

Where smoking permitted: Designated smoking area, but no smoking area is permitted in certain workplaces, including restaurants, cocktail lounges, or grocery stores.

Smoking area requirements: Must be effectively segregated, which means procedures for accurately and fairly determining preference have been followed; the size and location of no-smoking and smoking-permitted areas are designed, designated, or juxtaposed so that smoke does not cause harm or unreasonably intrude into the area occupied by persons who are not smoking; and in buildings with existing ventilation systems, smoking areas are near exhaust vents.

Accommodations for nonsmokers: Special consideration for employees with medically proven conditions adversely affected by smoke, as documented by an occupational physician.

Employer penalties and liabilities: Employment discrimination: misdemeanor with a fine of up to $1,000 and up to one year in prison.

Employer smoking policy: Written policy outlining either smoking prohibition or areas where smoking permitted. Policy must be handed out or posted; employees must receive policy orientation. If there is a designated smoking area, must be written training procedures for:

• enforcing smoking policy
• handling complaints and violations, and
• accommodating employees with medical conditions.

Protection from discrimination: Employer may not require employee or applicant to refrain from using tobacco products outside of work as a condition of employment, as long as employee complies with workplace smoking

State Laws on Smoking in the Workplace (cont'd)

policy. Employer may not retaliate or discriminate against any employee who exercises rights under smoking laws; however, laws do not give employee right to refuse to perform normal duties, even if duties require entering a smoking area.

NEW JERSEY

N.J. Stat. Ann. §§ 26:3D-56 to 26:3D-61; 34:6B-1

Workplaces where laws apply: Any indoor workplace.

Where smoking prohibited: Entire workplace.

Protection from discrimination: Employer may not discharge or discriminate in terms of hiring, compensation, benefits, or conditions of employment because employee does or does not smoke, unless smoking or not smoking relates to work and job responsibilities.

NEW MEXICO

N.M. Stat. Ann. § 50-11-3

Protection from discrimination: Employer may not:

- refuse to hire, discharge, or disadvantage an employee with respect to compensation, terms, conditions, or privileges of employment because the individual is a smoker or nonsmoker, or
- require that an employee abstain from tobacco products during nonwork hours.
- Employer may restrict smoking if it relates to a genuine occupational requirement or if it materially threatens a legitimate conflict of interest policy.

NEW YORK

N.Y. Pub. Health Law §§ 1399-n to 1399-x; N.Y. Lab. Law § 201-d(2b),(6)

Workplaces where laws apply: Indoor workspaces.

Where smoking prohibited: Smoking is prohibited throughout the workplace, in copy machine and common equipment areas, and in company vehicles.

Protection from discrimination: Employee may not be discharged, refused employment, or discriminated against in terms of compensation or benefits because of lawful use of products off-site during nonwork hours when not using employer's equipment or property. It is not discrimination to offer insurance with different rates or coverage for smokers if:

- difference is based on cost to employer, and
- employees are given a written statement of carriers' rates.

Employer smoking policy: Must post "No Smoking" signs; must make good-faith effort to ensure that employees do not smoke.

NORTH CAROLINA

N.C. Gen. Stat. § 95-28.2

Workplaces where laws apply: Discrimination laws apply to employers with 3 or more employees.

Protection from discrimination: Employer may not discharge, refuse to hire, or discriminate in regard to compensation, benefits, or terms of employment because of employee's use of lawful products off-site during nonwork hours. Use that affects employee's job performance, other workers' safety, or conflicts with a genuine job requirement is not protected. It is not

State Laws on Smoking in the Workplace (cont'd)

discrimination to offer insurance with different rates or coverage for smokers if:
- difference is based on cost to employer
- employees are given written notice of carriers' rates, and
- employer makes equal contribution for all employees.

NORTH DAKOTA
N.D. Cent. Code §§ 14-02.4-03, 23-12-09 and 23-12-10

Workplace where laws apply: Any enclosed workplace.

Exceptions: Outdoors, bars, adults-only areas of truckstops.

Where smoking prohibited: Entire indoor workplace.

Protection from discrimination: Employer cannot discharge, refuse to hire, or retaliate against employee or applicant for exercising rights related to this law. Employer may not refuse to hire, discharge, or discriminate with regard to training, apprenticeship, tenure, promotion, compensation, benefits, or conditions of employment because of employee's lawful activity off-site during nonwork hours, unless it is in direct conflict with employer's essential business-related interests.

OHIO
Ohio Rev. Code Ann. §§ 3794.01 to 3794.09, Ohio Admin. Code §§3701-52-01 to 3710-52-09

Workplace where laws apply: Any enclosed workplace.

Exceptions: Family owned and operated business in which all employees are related to the employer and the area is not open to the public, as long as the smoke will not migrate to nonsmoking areas.

Where smoking prohibited: Entire indoor workplace and outside immediately adjacent to entrances or exits to the building. Employer may designate the entire workplace nonsmoking.

Where smoking permitted: Outdoors, including outdoor patios that are physically separate from enclosed areas, as long as windows and doors prevent migration of the smoke into enclosed areas.

Smoking area requirements: Employer must ensure that tobacco smoke does not enter enclosed areas through entrances, windows, ventilation systems, or other means.

Protection from discrimination: Employer may not discharge, refuse to hire, or in any manner retaliate against any individual for exercising any right, including reporting a violation of the law.

OKLAHOMA
Okla. Stat. Ann. tit. 40, §§ 500 to 503; Okla. Admin. Code §§ 310:355-5-1 and following

Workplace where laws apply: Any indoor workplace.

Exceptions: Family owned and operated business in which all employees are related to the employer or where all the employees are nonsmokers, and there is only occasional public access.

Where smoking prohibited: Throughout workplace except in designated smoking area. Employer may designate entire site nonsmoking. All buildings owned by an educational facility.

Where smoking permitted: Designated smoking area.

State Laws on Smoking in the Workplace (cont'd)

Smoking area requirements: Smoking area must be in a nonwork area where no employee is required to enter (except to perform custodial and maintenance work when the smoking area is unoccupied). Must: have ventilation systems that exhaust air outdoors at least 15 feet from entrances, exits, or air intake; be fully enclosed; no air recirculating to nonsmoking areas; and under negative air pressure so that no smoke can drift or circulate into a nonsmoking area.

Protection from discrimination: Employer may not:

- discharge or disadvantage employee in terms of compensation, benefits, or conditions of employment because of being a nonsmoker or smoking during nonwork hours, or
- require that employee abstain from using tobacco products during nonwork hours as a condition of employment.

Employer may restrict nonwork smoking if it relates to a genuine occupational requirement.

OREGON
Or. Rev. Stat. §§ 433.835 to 433.875, 659A.315

Workplaces where laws apply: All enclosed areas used by employees.

Where smoking prohibited: Entire workplace unless there are employee lounges designated for smoking. Beginning 1/1/09, within 10 feet of a building exit, entrance, open window, or vent intake serving an enclosed area.

Where smoking permitted: Employee lounges designated for smoking.

Smoking area requirements: Lounge must be inaccessible to minors. Lounge must be in a nonwork area. Air must be exhausted directly to the outside with a fan. Air may not recirculate to other areas of building. No employee may

be required to enter lounge as part of job (does not apply to custodial work when lounge is unoccupied).

Accommodations for nonsmokers: If there is a lounge for smokers, must be enough lounges for nonsmokers.

Protection from discrimination: Employer may not require that employee refrain from lawful use of tobacco products during nonwork hours as a condition of employment, unless there is a genuine occupational requirement.

PENNSYLVANIA
35 Pa. Cons. Stat. Ann. §§ 637.2 to 637.11

Workplaces where laws apply: All indoor workplaces.

Exceptions: Some annual charitable events; bars; outdoor areas at entertainment venues.

Where smoking prohibited: All indoor workplaces.

Where smoking permitted: Outdoor area, if employer permits.

Smoking area requirements: Must have a "Smoking Permitted" sign.

Protection from discrimination: An employer may not discharge an employee, refuse to hire an applicant for employment, or retaliate against an employee because the individual exercises a right to a smoke-free environment.

RHODE ISLAND
R.I. Gen. Laws §§ 23-20.7-1 to 23-20.10-14

Workplaces where laws apply: Smoking shall be prohibited in all enclosed facilities within places of employment. Required signs must be posted.

State Laws on Smoking in the Workplace (cont'd)

Where smoking permitted: Employer may designate outdoor area.

Smoking area requirements: Must be physically separate from enclosed workspace, to prevent smoke from getting into the workplace.

Protection from discrimination: Employers cannot prohibit the use of tobacco outside of work, and cannot discriminate in compensation, terms, or benefits for tobacco use outside of work, or retaliate against an employee for reporting or attempting to prosecute a violation of the law.

SOUTH CAROLINA
S.C. Code Ann. § 41-1-85

Protection from discrimination: Employer may not take personnel actions, including hiring, discharge, demotion, or promotion, based on use of tobacco outside the workplace.

SOUTH DAKOTA
S.D. Codified Laws Ann. §§ 22-36-2 to 22-36-4

Workplaces where laws apply: Any enclosed space under control of a private or public employer.

Where smoking prohibited: The entire workplace.

Protection from discrimination: Employer may not discharge employee because of using tobacco products offsite during nonwork hours, unless not smoking is a genuine occupational requirement. It is not discrimination to have insurance policies with different rates or coverage for smokers.

TENNESSEE
Tenn. Code Ann. §§ 39-17-1801 to 39-17-1812, 50-1-304(e); Tenn. Comp. R. & Regs. §§ 0800-6-1-.01 to 0800-6-1-.08

Workplaces where laws apply: All enclosed workplaces.

Exceptions: Age-restricted venues; businesses with 3 or fewer employees (smoking permitted in area not accessible to the public).

Where smoking is prohibited: All enclosed workplaces.

Where smoking is permitted: Nonenclosed spaces, including outdoor patios.

Employer smoking policy: Prohibition must be communicated to all current employees and all prospective employees upon application for employment.

UTAH
Utah Code Ann. §§ 26-38-2 and 26-38-3; Utah Admin. Code §§ R392-510-1 to R392-510-14

Workplaces where laws apply: All enclosed indoor workplaces unless owner-operated with no employees and not open to the public.

Exceptions: Vehicles that are workplaces when not occupied by nonsmokers.

Where smoking prohibited: Entire workplace; within 25 feet of any entranceway, exit, open window, or air intake of a building where smoking is prohibited. Employer can choose to prohibit smoking outdoors.

Smoking area requirements: Any enclosed area where smoking is permitted must be designed and operated to prevent exposure of persons outside the area to tobacco smoke generated in the area.

State Laws on Smoking in the Workplace (cont'd)

Employer smoking policy: An employer shall establish a policy to prohibit employee smoking within 25 feet of any entranceway, exit, open window, or air intake of a building where smoking is prohibited.

Protection from discrimination: An employer may not discriminate or take any adverse action against an employee or applicant because that person has sought enforcement of the provisions of this law or the smoking policy of the work-place or otherwise protests the smoking of others.

VERMONT
Vt. Stat. Ann. tit. 18, §§ 1421 to 1428

Workplaces where laws apply: All enclosed structures where employees perform services.

Where smoking prohibited: Entire enclosed structure.

Protection from discrimination: Employer may not discharge, discipline, or otherwise discriminate against employee who assists in enforcement of workplace smoking laws.

VIRGINIA
Va. Code Ann. § 15.2-2828

Workplaces where laws apply: Restaurants; educational and recreational facilities; retail establishments of at least 15,000 square feet serving the public. For all other private workplaces, state law prohibits local ordinances that regulate smoking except that employer may, if allowed by local ordinance: regulate smoking if smoking and nonsmoking areas are designated by written agreement between employer and employees; or totally ban smoking if a majority of the affected employees vote for it.

Where smoking prohibited: Educational, health care, recreational facilities, and retail establishments must designate reasonable no-smoking areas. Restaurants: entire establishment.

Where smoking permitted: Restaurants: outdoor areas; areas that are structurally separate from no-smoking areas. Educational, health care, recreational facilities, and retail establishments: everywhere except designated no-smoking areas.

Smoking area requirements: Restaurants must be structurally separate and separately vented from no-smoking area. At least one public entrance to restaurant must be into no-smoking area.

WASHINGTON
Wash. Admin. Code §§ 70.160.011 to 70.160.900

Workplaces where laws apply: Any enclosed workplace.

Exceptions: Outdoor structures, gazebos, and lean-tos provided for smokers that are at least 25 feet from entrances and exits.

Where smoking prohibited: Any area which employees are required to pass through or within 25 feet of an entrance or exit.

WEST VIRGINIA
W.Va. Code § 21-3-19

Protection from discrimination: Employer may not refuse to hire, discharge, or penalize an employee with respect to compensation, conditions of employment, or other benefits for using tobacco products off-site during nonwork hours. It is not discrimination to have insurance policies with different rates or coverage for smokers if:
- difference is based on cost to employer, and
- employees are given a notice of carriers' rates.

State Laws on Smoking in the Workplace (cont'd)

WISCONSIN

Wis. Stat. Ann. §§ 101.123; 111.35

Workplaces where laws apply: All places of employment, which covers any enclosed place employees normally frequent in the course of employment, including offices, work areas, elevators, employee lounges, restrooms, conference and meeting rooms, classrooms, hallways, stairways, lobbies, common areas, vehicles, and employee cafeterias.

Where smoking prohibited: All places of employment.

Protection from discrimination: Employer may not discriminate against employee who uses or does not use lawful products off-site during nonwork hours. Use that impairs employee's ability to perform job or conflicts with a genuine occupational requirement is not protected. It is not discrimination to have insurance policies with different coverage and rates for smokers and nonsmokers if:

- difference is based on cost to employer, and
- each employee is given a written statement of carriers' rates.

WYOMING

Wyo. Stat. § 27-9-105(a)(iv)

Protection from discrimination: Employer may not make use or nonuse of tobacco products outside of work a condition of employment unless nonuse is a genuine occupational qualification. May not discriminate regarding compensation, benefits, or terms of employment because of use or nonuse of tobacco products outside of work. It is not discrimination to offer insurance policies with different rates and coverage for smokers and nonsmokers if:

- difference reflects actual cost to employer, and
- employees are given written notice of carriers' rates.

Unions

Many companies—particularly small businesses—will never have to deal with a union. In fact, union membership has steadily decreased in recent years, from 20.1% of the workforce in 1983 (the first year the government compiled statistics) to 11.9% of workers in the year 2010 (and only 6.9% of private sector employees). The type of work your company does will also dictate how much contact you have with unions, which are more common in certain industries than others. For instance, there are more union workers in government than in private industry, where union membership is concentrated heavily in the fields of transportation, utilities, manufacturing, and construction.

If there is a union (or more than one) in your workplace—or even if workers at your company are just interested in forming one—a special set of rules comes into play. Federal and state labor laws dictate how management (including you) must deal with unions, as well as what rules can be imposed on workers. In this chapter, we explain the laws relating to:

- elections and organizing campaigns
- union discussions and literature in the workplace
- union dues
- union shops
- collective bargaining
- company unions, and
- strikes.

Frequently Asked Questions About Unions

Can managers join a union?

No. Some workers are excluded from the National Labor Relations Act (NLRA, the set of federal laws that governs union issues. These workers include agricultural workers, domestic servants, those employed by a parent or spouse, and independent contractors, as well as managers and supervisors. (For more on these laws, including how they are enforced, see "The National Labor Relations Act," below.)

If a union says it represents workers at our company, do we have to recognize it?

An employer can recognize a union as the bargaining representative of its employees only if the union has the support of a majority of workers in the "bargaining unit": a group of employees who do similar types of work and have common concerns about wages, hours, and working conditions. Even if the union can show that a majority of workers signed union authorization cards (statements indicating that the workers want a union to represent them), the employer can refuse to recognize the union, at least under current law. Then, the union will have to ask for a secret election to prove its support. (For more on bargaining units, authorization cards, and elections, see "Representation Elections and Organizing Campaigns," below.)

Frequently Asked Questions About Unions (cont'd)

Are there limits on what managers and other company officials can say about the union?

During an election campaign—the period of time between when the union asks for an election and when the election is actually held—management representatives have to watch their mouths. Employers and managers may voice their opinions about the union but cannot punish union supporters, threaten employees who support the union, make promises to workers if they vote against the union, spy on union activities, or ask workers about the union in a coercive manner. (For more on what you can and can't do, see "Election Statements," below.)

Can the company ban workers from talking about the union on the job?

An employer may prohibit workers from talking about union matters on work time, but only if it prohibits them from talking about other nonwork issues as well. The company can also prohibit workers from holding union discussions in work areas, even during nonwork hours, but only if this rule applies across the board to all nonwork topics. But the company cannot prohibit workers from talking about the union while off the clock in nonwork areas—like a lunch room or locker area. (For more on union discussions and literature, see "Shop Talk," below.)

Can union workers strike whenever they want?

They can, but the strike might not be legal. There are two kinds of legal strikes: strikes to gain economic concessions from the employer and strikes to protest an employer's unfair labor practice. And even one of these two types of strikes might be illegal if it violates a no-strike provision in the collective bargaining agreement, or if the striking workers engage in serious misconduct. (For more on strikes—including when a company can replace striking workers—see "Strikes," below.)

The National Labor Relations Act

Several federal laws cover labor-management relations. Together, these laws make up the National Labor Relations Act (NLRA), 29 U.S.C. §§ 151 and following, which establishes the rights and obligations of employers, unions, and individual workers in the workplace.

Many states also have labor laws that apply to public employees: those who work for state or local governments and are not covered by the NLRA.

The Act Itself

The cornerstone of the NLRA is the Wagner Act, passed in 1935. The Wagner Act guarantees covered employees the right to join a union, to bargain collectively with their employer, and to be free from discrimination or retaliation for belonging to a union. It also prohibits certain employer "union-busting" tactics and establishes the procedures for union elections. And it created the National Labor Relations Board (NLRB), the federal government agency that interprets and enforces the law. (See "The Role of the NLRB," below.)

In 1947, Congress passed the second piece of the puzzle, the Labor-Management Relations Act (LMRA), better known as the Taft-Hartley Act. The primary purpose of the LMRA was to rein in the unions' power. The Act outlawed certain kinds of strikes, including the secondary boycott (a strike against a company that is not a party to a labor dispute, like a customer or client of the employer), sympathy strike (a strike by one union to show support for another), and jurisdictional strike (a strike by one of two or more unions competing to represent the same group of workers). The act also declares an individual's right not to join a union and protects this right by prohibiting unions from using violence, threats, or fraud to coerce workers to become members.

Finally, Congress passed the Labor-Management Reporting and Disclosure Act (LMRDA), also known as the Landrum-Griffin Act, in 1959. The LMRDA regulates internal union affairs: how officers are elected, what information the union must provide to its members and the government, and the rights of union members vis-à-vis the union. The LMRDA also imposes additional restrictions on union workers' rights to strike and picket.

Which Employees Are Covered

Not all workers are covered by the NLRA. The NLRA specifically excludes certain types of workers, including:

- agricultural workers
- domestic servants
- persons employed by a parent or spouse
- independent contractors
- government workers, and
- managers and supervisors.

A 2006 NLRB decision clarifies which employees qualify as supervisors or managers, who aren't protected by the NLRA and cannot join a union. The NLRA says that a supervisor or manager is an employee who has the authority, in the interest of the employer, to take any of the following actions toward an employee:

- hire
- transfer
- suspend
- lay off
- recall
- promote
- discharge
- assign
- reward
- discipline
- responsibly direct
- adjust grievances, or
- effectively recommend any of the above actions.

It isn't enough for the supervisor to take any one of these actions: The supervisor's actions must not be merely routine or clerical in nature, but instead must require the use of independent judgment.

This is where the 2006 decision created controversy. Previous NLRB decisions held that employees who use ordinary technical skill or judgment in directing other employees don't qualify as supervisors, because they aren't using independent judgment. These decisions meant that employees of the "assistant manager" variety, who do largely the same work as other employees but also set schedules and determine assignments, were not classified as supervisors. In the case of *Oakwood Healthcare Inc.*, 348 N.L.R.B. 37 (2006), however, the Board found that employees who have the authority to make work assignments or direct the work of other employees may be supervisors if those tasks require some independent judgment and discretion, even if they spend only 10% to 15% of their time on these supervisory duties.

Which Employers Are Covered

The NLRA applies only to businesses that are engaged in "interstate commerce." The National Labor Relations Board and the courts interpret the term "interstate commerce" very broadly. Most employees are covered: Engaging in interstate commerce includes making phone calls to or from another state, sending mail out of state, or handling goods that have come from or will go to another state. However, the NLRB will generally step in to resolve labor disputes only if the company involved has reached a certain size, as measured by its volume of business or revenue. Thresholds vary depending on the industry. For example, the NLRB will get involved in a dispute involving a retail establishment that does $500,000 or more in annual business volume, while it will step in to a dispute at a private university only if the school has at least $1 million in gross annual revenue.

Legal Rights and Wrongs Under the NLRA

The NLRA protects the rights of individual employees to form or join a union and to bargain collectively with their employer. An employer who interferes with these rights commits an illegal "unfair labor practice." Unfair labor practices include:

- firing, demoting, or taking other negative action (or threatening any of these actions) against employees who join or vote for a union
- threatening to close down a company if the workers unionize

- giving or promising to give benefits to workers for refusing to support a union
- asking employees about their union activities in a coercive or intimidating way
- spying on union meetings
- creating a "company union" or favoring one union over another, and
- firing, refusing to rehire, or otherwise penalizing employees for participating in legally protected union activities, such as legal strikes or proceedings before the National Labor Relations Board.

A union can also commit unfair labor practices. For example, a union may not coerce workers to join or require workers to pay excessive union fees or dues. Unions are also prohibited from taking certain actions against or making certain demands on employers, including:

- "featherbedding" (receiving payment for work that is not performed)
- striking to force the employer to bargain with a union other than the union elected by the employer's workers, and
- striking or picketing against an employer who is not a party to a labor dispute (for example, a "secondary strike" against a customer of the employer intended to convince that customer to take its business elsewhere).

The Role of the NLRB

As noted above, the National Labor Relations Board (NLRB) administers and enforces the NLRA. The NLRB is run by five appointed board members who decide cases that come before the agency. The NLRB also has a general counsel (who investigates charges and issues complaints) as well as regional and field offices throughout the country.

The NLRB conducts representation elections—in which workers decide whether they want a particular union to represent them—and stops unfair labor practices. In either scenario, the NLRB gets involved only when a party to the dispute requests its help. For instance, if an employer refuses to acknowledge a union after a representation election, the NLRB will conduct a secret representation election if either party (usually, the union) requests it.

The Board itself functions as a sort of court to decide cases alleging unfair labor practices. Administrative law judges (decision makers hired by the federal government) decide these cases, which the losing party can appeal up to the five-member Board. The Board has the power to order unions and/or employers to do certain things—or stop doing certain things. At that point, the losing party must obey the Board's order or ask a federal Court of Appeals to overrule the Board.

From the end of 2007 through 2010, the NLRB was down to two members, one Republican and one Democrat. These two members decided about 600 cases in which they could agree on the outcome; if the panel split, no decision was issued. In *New Process Steel v. National Labor Relations Board*, 130 S.Ct. 1117 (2010), the Supreme Court found that the NLRB wasn't authorized to issue decisions while it had only two members, which left the parties in these cases up in the air about their rights and obligations.

Any decision that either party appealed to federal court was returned to the Board for reconsideration—and a new decision—by at least three board members.

Representation Elections and Organizing Campaigns

Efforts to unionize a workplace often begin with employee dissatisfaction. Workers might start talking about unionizing in response to an unpopular workplace rule, low wages, or a perception that the company doesn't care about their concerns.

An actual union—as opposed to a group of unhappy workers—might enter a workplace in a number of ways. A worker might contact an existing union and ask for information and help. A union might send an organizer out to the company to look into whether a union campaign is likely to succeed. Or the workers might decide to form their own union—not a typical scenario, but certainly possible. Regardless of how a union starts, its goal will be the same: to earn the right to represent workers in their dealings with the company.

Bargaining Units

A union may only represent workers who form an appropriate "bargaining unit." A bargaining unit is a group of employees who do similar types of work and have common concerns about wages, hours, and working conditions. A bargaining unit generally won't combine professional with nonprofessional employees, nor will it contain workers with significantly different job duties, skills, or working conditions. If the employer claims that a particular bargaining unit is inappropriate (a strategy employers often use to challenge a successful representation election), the NLRB will also consider what the workers themselves want.

A bargaining unit can include employees from several different facilities. For example, all the cashiers in a chain of retail stores might be included in a single bargaining unit. And a single workplace might contain more than one bargaining unit. In a grocery store, for example, the butchers might be represented by one union, the checkers by another, and the janitors by yet another.

Authorization and Election

In order to represent a bargaining unit in negotiations with the company, a union must have the support of a majority of the workers in the unit. The union usually demonstrates this support by asking workers to sign authorization cards—forms that workers fill in and sign to indicate that they want the union to represent them in bargaining with the employer.

If the union gets support from the majority of workers in the unit, it will probably ask the company to recognize the union voluntarily. If the company decides to do this (and it has good reason to believe that the union's majority support is genuine), the company and the union can immediately begin hammering out a collective bargaining agreement. (See "Collective Bargaining," below.)

But many companies choose not to recognize a union voluntarily. Perhaps the company doubts the signatures on the authorization cards are authentic or suspects that the union coerced workers into signing. Or maybe the company just wants to do whatever it can to keep a union out of its workplace for as long as possible. For whatever reason, the company may refuse to recognize the union. In that case, the union will probably file a petition with the NLRB, asking it to hold an election.

The NLRB will then conduct a secret election in the workplace to figure out whether workers really support the union. Before the election, the union and the employer can engage in a pro- or antiunion campaign (subject to the rules discussed in "Election Statements," below). If the union receives a majority of the votes cast, the NLRB will certify it as the bargaining representative of the unit. Note that the union only has to get a majority of those workers who vote, not a majority of all the workers in a unit. This means turnout in secret elections can play a major role in the outcome.

As we go to press, the NLRB has just released proposed regulations that would streamline and speed up the election process. Some of these regulations merely bring the election process into the modern age by, for example, allowing documents to be filed with the NLRB electronically rather than in hard copy. Others are more controversial, particularly changes that would shorten the time between when an election petition is filed and the election is actually held (a period employers often use to challenge

the union's claims and try to defeat the campaign). The NLRB will have to take comments on the rules, consider those comments and make changes as needed, and then issue final rules before anything goes into effect, a process that can take a year or more. For information on this developing issue, check the NLRB's website at www.nlrb.gov or look for updates at www.nolo.com.

Challenging an Election

Usually, everyone accepts the outcome of a representation election and moves on to the negotiating table. However, either the company or the union may object to the election results. Usually, one side will claim that the other side unfairly influenced the outcome of the election. For example, if the union incites workers to violence or offers special privileges to workers who vote for the union, the NLRB might set aside a union victory. Similarly, if the company threatens to fire workers who vote for the union or promises to give benefits to workers who oppose the union, the NLRB might void the election results and could even declare the union to have won by default.

The union or the employer can also challenge the conduct of the election itself. Just as in a government election, certain NLRA rules restrict what can be posted near the voting booth. And the NLRB generally prohibits both unions and employers from making campaign speeches to groups of employees on company time within 24 hours of the election.

Decertifying a Union

Even a union once championed by employees might lose support as time goes on. This can happen for many reasons. Perhaps the union hasn't been able to negotiate successfully for the workers, has corrupt leadership, or imposes dues and fees the workers find oppressive. Employees who wish to challenge the union can file a petition for a decertification election with the NLRB. In such an election, workers will vote on whether they still want the union to represent them in negotiations with their employer. If a majority of workers voting oppose the union, the union no longer has the right to represent the workers.

Election Statements

Many employers are not eager to deal with unionized workers and want to defeat a union organizing campaign. However, there are limits to how far employers can go in fighting the union. Employers hold the power of the purse and the pink slip, not to mention the opportunity to make their workers a captive audience for any opinions they might want to express. Recognizing this, the NLRA prohibits employers from using this advantage to unfairly influence the outcome of an election.

The NLRB will set aside the results of an election if the employer engages in conduct that tends to interfere with the employees' right to freely choose—or reject—a union, without fear of reprisal. If the employer's actions confuse or incite fear in its workers, the election won't count. However,

employers—like everyone else—have free speech rights. The trick is to differentiate between free speech and coercion.

What You Cannot Do

Any of the following activities constitute unfair labor practices and might cause the NLRB to overturn a decision against union representation:

- **Punishing union supporters.** You may not retaliate or discriminate against workers who support the union.
- **Making threats.** You cannot threaten to fire, demote, impose pay cuts on, or otherwise take any negative job action against workers for supporting a union. And employers can't threaten to shut down or move the business if the union is successful.
- **Inducements.** You are not allowed to promise or give benefits to workers who oppose the union. And, once an organizing campaign has begun, the company may not increase workers' benefits—by giving a pay raise or health insurance coverage, for example—to discourage them from forming or joining the union.
- **Infiltration.** Conducting surveillance of union meetings or of employees who support the union is coercive, as is planting a spy in union gatherings to report back to management.
- **Interrogation.** You may not question workers about their union membership, union meetings, or their support for the union. Similarly, you should not ask

employees to report workplace union activities to you or tell you how their coworkers feel about the union.

- **Gag rules.** You may not prohibit workers from discussing the union in work areas unless you prohibit all conversations that aren't related to work. (See "Shop Talk," below.)

What You Can Do

Once you rule out the spying, threats, and strong-arming, what's left? Quite a bit, obviously. Employers are free to express their opinions, present reasons why a union might not be in the workers' best interests, and give employees information about the union, as long as these actions aren't coercive and the information is accurate.

Here are some examples of employer statements and actions that courts and the NLRB have said are okay:

- **Voicing an opinion.** Employers can tell employees that they don't want a union in the workplace, and explain why.
- **Providing information.** Employers can publicize true information about the union, such as how much it charges members for dues, the rules it imposes on members, and how often it has gone on strike at other companies.
- **Explaining workplace changes.** Employers can inform workers of changes a union might bring to the workplace (for example, that workers might have to bring problems to a shop steward instead of to a supervisor).
- **Giving wage and benefit comparisons.** Employers can compare the benefits and wages they offer workers to the benefits and wages the union has been able to negotiate from other companies.

Shop Talk

The one location where all of a company's workers are certain to gather is the workplace. Recognizing this, workers who are in favor of a union often spread their views or pass out union material in the workplace, whether in the lunchroom or on the assembly line.

For various reasons, some employers try to keep union organizing out of the workplace, arguing that their facility is private company property and that management dictates what goes on within its walls. And certainly, employers want to minimize the amount of work time employees spend on nonwork activities.

The NLRB and the courts try to balance these competing concerns by creating some rules about what union-related activities are allowed in the workplace. Here are the basic rules that apply to employees (but note that these rules do not apply to nonemployees who work for the union):

- Companies may prohibit workers from talking about nonwork issues in work areas during work hours.
- Companies must allow workers to talk about union matters during nonwork hours in nonwork areas (like the company lunchroom). Union discussions may be prohibited in work areas during nonwork hours only if such a rule is necessary to maintain productivity or discipline and the rule applies to all nonwork topics.

- Companies may prohibit distribution of union literature (such as pamphlets and fact sheets) in work areas at all times— as long as the prohibition applies to all nonwork literature, not just union literature.
- Companies cannot single out union communications for special rules. For example, an employer cannot forbid employees to distribute union materials in work areas but allow them to distribute other nonwork documents.
- Companies cannot prevent workers from wearing clothing bearing pro-union logos or symbols, such as a button or cap, unless that type of apparel creates a safety hazard.

Using Company Email

Email has added a modern twist to these rules. As is true of other types of communications, an employer may not single out union-related messages for harsher treatment. For example, if an employer allows employees to send personal messages using company email, it must allow them to send union-related email messages. Similarly, an employer that allows employees to solicit coworkers on behalf of various organizations may not prohibit messages soliciting on behalf of a union.

Until recently, it wasn't clear whether employers could ban employees from sending any personal messages without running afoul of the NLRA. As indicated above, employers must allow employees to talk about union issues on nonwork time. And the NLRB had previously indicated that a broad prohibition

against all personal email could prevent employees from exercising these rights.

More recently, however, the NLRB issued a decision that allows employers to adopt broad rules prohibiting certain types of email communications—for example, personal messages or solicitations—without violating the NLRA. *(In re The Guard Publishing Co., 351 NLRB No. 70 (2007).)* As long as the policy doesn't explicitly prohibit only union-related messages, and the company enforces it evenhandedly, such a rule doesn't violate the NLRA.

Another issue might arise for employers that monitor employee email messages: What if the employer reads a message about union activity? Would the NLRB view this as an example of illegal employer eavesdropping, or of a legitimate, consistently applied business practice that should be allowed? As the Board continues to consider how evolving technology and workplace norms affect traditional union rights, more guidance on these issues should be forthcoming.

Union Shops and Union Dues

Workers have the right, under the NLRA, to refuse to join a union. However, some collective bargaining agreements require a company to employ only union workers to do certain jobs. One major reason unions want these contracts is to share the burden of the union's work. The union is required to represent everyone in the bargaining unit, regardless of their union membership. Requiring everyone who gets the benefit of the contract to be a union member solves the problem of so-called "free riders," workers who reap the windfall of the union's work but don't pay the price.

Generally, a company can't require a worker to become a full union member as a condition of employment, but the worker may have to pay at least some portion of union dues, depending on the basis of his or her objection to the union and the laws of the state where the employer is located.

Union Security Agreements and "Right to Work" Laws

The NLRA allows a union and an employer to enter into a contract called a "union security agreement." Although these contracts cannot require a worker to join a union, they can require workers to make certain "agency fee" payments to the union as a condition of getting or keeping a job. An employer that enters into one of these agreements will be required to fire a worker who doesn't make the payments called for in the contract.

However, the NLRA also allows states to prohibit these agreements, and many states have done so. In these states, workers who decide not to join the union cannot be required to pay any fees to the union, and cannot be fired or otherwise penalized for failing to do so. These statutes, called "right to work" laws, basically require that every unionized workplace be an "open shop," in which workers are free to choose whether or not to join or support the union. To find out whether your state has such a law, see "State Right to Work Laws," at the end of this chapter.

Dues Objectors

Workers who object to paying union dues either on religious grounds or because they don't support the union's political or other activities (usually those that are unrelated to representing the workers in the bargaining unit) are also entitled to alternative arrangements, even in states that allow union security agreements.

A worker who refuses to join a union or pay union dues for religious reasons may be exempt from paying dues or fees. However, these workers can be required to make a similar contribution to a nonlabor, nonreligious charity organization. And the union can require them to pay the reasonable cost of any grievances the union handles on their behalf.

In states that allow union security agreements, nonmember workers who object to the union's use of fees for political or other nonrepresentational activities are entitled to get that money back. However, they still have to pay their fair share of union money spent on representing the bargaining unit's workers—including the costs of collective bargaining, contract administration, and grievance processing. Some states require the union to get the permission of workers, whether they are members of the union or dues-paying nonmembers—before collecting any fees for activities not related to representing the workers.

Lessons From the Real World

The Washington Education Association (WEA), the state's largest teachers' union, was sued by the state of Washington and several nonunion members, claiming that it had improperly used agency fees—fees collected from teachers who did not want to join the union—to fund political causes.

Under Washington law, the union was required to get explicit authorization from nonmembers before using their fees for this purpose. Instead, the union adopted a procedure by which nonmembers had to "opt out" by objecting to this use of their fees within 30 days. When challenged, the WEA claimed that the state law requiring it to get authorization from nonmembers imposed an unconstitutional burden on the union.

The Supreme Court disagreed, however. The Court found that the voters of Washington were within their rights in passing a law that required the union to get permission before spending money it collected from state employees on political issues.

Davenport v. Washington Education Association, 127 S.Ct. 2372 (2007).

Collective Bargaining

"Collective bargaining" refers to the negotiation process between the union (on behalf of the bargaining unit it represents) and the company to work out an agreement that will govern the terms and conditions of the workers' employment. The agreement reached through this negotiating process is called a collective bargaining agreement (CBA).

The NLRA requires a duly elected union and an employer to meet and negotiate over wages, hours, and other employment terms, as well as to negotiate over issues that may arise under an existing CBA. The two sides don't have to reach an agreement, but they always have to bargain in good faith. Although neither side is required to make a particular concession, a party that refuses to bend on a single issue or to put any offer on the table might be acting in bad faith.

Employers Have to Supply Information

Employers have a clear bargaining advantage over the union in one important respect: Employers have access to more information. Although the union can poll its members to find out what they know, the employer is almost always better informed about a variety of issues, especially the company's financial picture.

To level the playing field a bit, the NLRB and the courts require employers to make certain types of information available to the union during the collective bargaining process. For example, if an employer claims that financial problems prohibit it from granting a requested wage increase, the union has the right to request and review documents that support the company's claims. Similarly, employers may have to supply the union with current employee salary and benefit data so the union can base its demands on accurate information.

Mandatory Bargaining Issues

An employer doesn't have to bargain over every conceivable employment issue. However, employers must bargain with the union over issues that are central to the employment relationship, such as wages, hours, and layoff procedures. Employers must give the union advance notice of any proposed workplace changes that involve these issues, but only if the union requests it. An employer who refuses to bargain or takes unilateral action in one of these mandatory bargaining areas commits an unfair labor practice. At that point, the NLRB can step in to remedy the situation, but the union may also take certain actions against the employer, including a strike.

Given these dire consequences, you might think that there would be a clear list of mandatory bargaining topics included in labor laws. Unfortunately, that's not the case. Although there is general agreement that mandatory bargaining is required on some issues—including wages, hours, layoff procedures, production quotas, and other substantial work rules—many other issues fall into a gray area. And this is where employers often find themselves in trouble.

Part of the problem is that some subjects may or may not qualify as mandatory bargaining topics, depending on the reasons for the employer's action. For instance, if the employer decides to close a plant in order to avoid paying union wages, that might be a mandatory bargaining topic. But if the employer bases its decision on concerns unrelated to the union—for example, if the employer's customer base in the area has dried up or the employer can reap significant tax advantages by moving to another location—the employer might not have to bargain on the issue.

What constitutes a mandatory bargaining topic is an evolving area of law. Consult an experienced labor lawyer if your company is trying to figure out whether it has to bargain a particular issue.

Acting Unilaterally Can Get Employers in Trouble

Before changing a workplace rule or policy that clearly requires bargaining (such as adjusting pay scales or revamping a seniority system), a company must ask the union to negotiate. Mandatory bargaining applies whether the changes will benefit or harm workers. In other words, a company cannot give an across-the-board pay raise or offer more generous paid leave on its own initiative without consulting with the union.

Sounds silly? Consider that some employers make positive changes on their own to convince workers that they don't need a union. And some employers might try to disguise a controversial change as a "benefit"

Lessons From the Real World

Workers at the Frontier Hotel & Casino in Las Vegas belonged to a union. When the collective bargaining agreement between the union and Frontier expired, the two sides were unable to negotiate a new agreement.

And then things got ugly. A member of Frontier's management started eavesdropping on conversations between workers and their union representative. When it didn't like what it heard, Frontier kicked the union representative out of the workplace. Then Frontier instituted 63 new work rules and stopped making contributions to the employees' pension fund.

The union filed a charge against Frontier with the NLRB. Both the NLRB and the Ninth Circuit Court of Appeals decided that Frontier's actions were illegal under the NLRA. The eavesdropping was an obvious no-no, but the court also decided that ejecting the union representative from the premises interfered with the workers' right to discuss union issues.

Further, the court decided that Frontier's decision to issue major changes in work rules—including a requirement that workers suspected of being drunk or high on illegal drugs had to agree to undergo a medical exam or risk immediate termination—violated its duty to bargain with the union before implementing a major change. Even though the first collective bargaining agreement had expired, Frontier was legally required to negotiate these issues, as well as its decision to stop paying into the pension fund, with the union before taking action. Its failure to do so—and its insistence on filing legal appeals on issues that were such clear losers—convinced the court to slap the company and its attorney with a hefty fine for wasting everyone's time.

NLRB v. Unbelievable, Inc., 71 F.3d 1434 (9th Cir. 1995).

(for example, by tying a wage increase to higher production rates).

Yet the process of bargaining on mandatory topics isn't as onerous as it sounds. In the real world, if the proposed change is beneficial, the union is likely to agree to it without a lengthy negotiating session. And by seeking the union's approval, the employer avoids a claim that it committed an unfair labor practice.

Company Unions and Employee Committees

Under the NLRA, employers may not establish, dominate, or interfere with any labor organization. This rule exists to outlaw sham unions: company groups that appear to represent employees but are really employer-controlled. The reason for this rule is simple: Fair collective bargaining requires genuine employee participation. If an employer negotiates with a union of its own creation, the employees' chair at the bargaining table is empty.

To figure out whether an employer unfairly controls a particular union, the courts and the NLRB look at all the circumstances, including whether the employer started the group, whether the employer played a role in the group's organization and function, whether management actually attends the group's meetings or otherwise tries to set its agenda, and what the group's purpose is.

Employee Committees May Cross the Line

Many companies have established "committees": informal groups of workers and management that meet to resolve workplace problems. Common examples include committees on safety, policy review, or productivity. But even if these groups are not unions, they may still constitute employer-dominated labor organizations, which are illegal under the NLRA.

Whether these groups qualify as sham unions depends on their purpose and on the role both employees and management play in their activities. To constitute an illegal sham union, the group must deal with the employer on traditional union bargaining topics, such as wages, hours, or working conditions. The group doesn't have to bargain formally with the employer; even a group that simply comes up with proposals for management to consider might be considered illegal, if those proposals involve bargaining issues.

Lessons From the Real World

Crown Cork & Seal, a company that manufactures aluminum cans, adopted an unusual decision-making structure at its Texas plant. Under the "Socio-Tech System," employees serve on one of four production teams. These teams have substantial authority to make and carry out workplace decisions, including decisions on safety, discipline, training, production, and more.

One level above the production teams are three more committees, which recommend changes in policies, terms and conditions of employment, safety procedures, and pay. These committees make their recommendations to the plant manager, who has always adopted them without question.

The NLRB found that these teams and committees were not illegal company unions because they did not "deal with" management; in effect, they *were* management. They had the power to make important decisions—to discipline employees, shut down the production line, or stop delivery of products—that are traditionally made by managers. Even though the plant manager had the right to disapprove some of these decisions, he never did so, instead letting the committees and teams effectively run the plant.

Crown Cork & Seal Company, Inc., 334 NLRB No. 92 (2001).

To be illegal, management must also dominate or support the group. For example, if a group is established by the company, management chooses the employee representatives to the group, management employees sit in on the meetings, or management sets the committee's agenda, this group is probably dominated by the company.

Strikes

Strikes are, perhaps, the most common image that comes to mind when people think of the history of unions over the last century. But strikes are much less common than they were in the past. For a number of reasons—including "no-strike" clauses in contracts, employers' right to replace some striking workers, and a decline in union membership generally—many employers will never have to face a strike.

However, if your company's workforce does take to the streets, you need to know whether their actions are protected by law and what steps the company can legally take to stay open for business.

Legal Strikes

The right to strike is protected by the NLRA, but not all strikes are legal. Whether a strike is lawful depends on the purpose of the strike, when the strike takes place, and the conduct of the strikers.

To qualify for protection under the NLRA, a strike must have a legal motive. Generally, a strike has a protected purpose if the workers are striking (1) for economic reasons or (2) to protest an unfair labor practice by the employer. In the first scenario, workers strike to try to get some economic concession from the employer, like higher wages, increased benefits, or better working conditions. In the second, workers strike because the employer has engaged in some practice that violates the NLRA, like refusing to bargain with the union or discriminating against union members.

However, even a strike that has a lawful purpose might be illegal if the workers strike in violation of a "no-strike" provision in the collective bargaining agreement. With a few limited exceptions, these strikes are not protected by the Act. And a strike to end or change a collective bargaining agreement might be illegal if the workers haven't complied with whatever conditions the agreement sets for such changes.

Finally, even a lawful strike may cross the line if the strikers engage in serious misconduct. Workers who are violent or threaten violence, who physically prevent others from entering or leaving the workplace, or who engage in a sit-down strike—a strike in which employees refuse to leave the workplace and refuse to work—are not legally protected.

Strike Replacements

Although the NLRA protects the right to strike, employers do not have to shut down their business for the duration of the walkout. Instead, employers are legally allowed to hire replacement workers (sometimes called "scabs" in union lingo) to take the place of strikers during the strike. Once the strike ends, the

Tips for Nonunion Employers

If your workplace is not unionized, you might think that the rules in this chapter don't apply to you. In fact, some of these rules apply to all employers who are covered by the NLRA, regardless of whether their workers are represented by a union or not. The NLRA applies generally to any collective action workers take in an effort to change their working conditions or wages, whether or not a union is involved and whether or not workers are explicitly trying to form a union.

Here are some tips for nonunion companies:

- All of the rules described above about union discussions—that employers cannot prohibit such discussions in nonwork areas when employees are off duty, for example—apply to employee discussions of wages, benefits, hours, and other working conditions as well. And employers may not adopt a policy prohibiting workers from discussing their salaries with each other.

- All of the NLRA's prohibitions on retaliation, threats, coercion, and so on apply equally to nonunion employers. An employer may not, for example, fire employees for joining together to ask the company for a raise or a better benefit plan, plant a spy in an employee meeting where employees are discussing working conditions, or threaten to demote employees who are trying to convince other workers to protest a work rule.

- A nonunion employer may not create a company or "sham" union: an employee group that is dominated or supported by management and deals with the company on traditional bargaining issues (wages, working conditions, and so on). Even though such a group doesn't compete with an existing union, it is illegal under the NLRA.

employer's obligation to rehire the striking workers depends on the reasons for the strike.

Workers who strike to protest an unfair labor practice cannot be fired or permanently replaced. When the strike is over, these strikers must be reinstated to their jobs, even if it means replacement workers have to be let go.

However, workers who strike for economic reasons don't enjoy the same right. Although they cannot be fired, they can be replaced. And if they are replaced permanently, they aren't entitled to their jobs back. Instead, if they are unable to find similar employment, employers are required only to call them back for job openings as they occur.

Legal Dos and Don'ts: Unions

Do:

- **Make employees happy.** If your company is intent on keeping a union out of the workplace, it should give workers what a union would get for them. This might include competitive pay, good benefits, safe working conditions, some form of job protection, and a meaningful complaint process.
- **Review your company's employee handbook.** Work rules must allow employees to exercise their rights under the NLRA. Make sure, for example, that your company's dress code doesn't prohibit workers from wearing pro-union messages and that your email policy doesn't single out union talk.
- **Get some help if you plan to fight the union.** The rules about what employers can and can't do to defeat a union in a representation election are very nuanced. Sometimes, a single word or act can make the difference between a sustainable victory and an unfair labor practices charge. If your company is planning to get into it, get some help from an experienced labor lawyer.

Don't:

- **Prevent employees from discussing union issues.** Although your company can prohibit workers from discussing any nonwork issue in work areas, it cannot selectively enforce this policy to prohibit only union matters, and it cannot prohibit union discussions in nonwork areas when employees are off duty. If you, as a representative of management, try to discourage workers from exercising this right, you could get the company in big trouble.
- **Bypass the union.** If your company has a union, it must bargain with the union before changing the terms and conditions of employment. This means no new policies on wages, hours, or working conditions without consulting the union.
- **Coerce workers during a union election.** As a manager, what you say and do will be attributed to the company. If you threaten to fire workers who vote for the union, promise benefits to workers who vote against the union, or otherwise put pressure on workers, the NLRB might find that you've unduly influenced the outcome of the election and declare the union to have won by default.

Test Your Knowledge

Questions

1. Managers can join a union, as long as the union is made up of managers and employees who work in the same field. ☐ True ☐ False

2. Independent contractors may not join a union. ☐ True ☐ False

3. Employers should not make any statements about the union during a union election. ☐ True ☐ False

4. If employees try to organize a union and they are unsuccessful, the employer may discipline or fire them. ☐ True ☐ False

5. Employers can prohibit employees from talking about union issues anywhere on the employer's premises. ☐ True ☐ False

6. Closed shops—in which employers may hire only union members—are illegal. ☐ True ☐ False

7. Although employees can be required to join a union, they cannot be forced to pay union dues. ☐ True ☐ False

8. An employer may not decide, on its own, to offer more generous benefits; it must bargain on this issue with the union. ☐ True ☐ False

9. Companies may establish safety committees, made up of employees and managers, as long as those committees don't have the power to make decisions. ☐ True ☐ False

10. Once workers go out on strike, their jobs are not protected. ☐ True ☐ False

Answers

1. False. Managers may not join a union, period.

2. True. Independent contractors may not join a union, even if the union is composed of employees who do similar types of work for the same company.

3. False. Although employers should not make threats, coerce, or interrogate workers during an election, they can give accurate information about the union and express their opinions about whether workers should unionize.

4. False. Employees who engage in "concerted activity" are protected from retaliation, even if they ultimately fail in their efforts.

5. False. Companies must allow workers to talk about union issues in nonwork areas—such as a lunch area, locker room, or break room—on nonwork time.

6. True. Employees cannot be required to join a union.

7. False. This is exactly backwards: Employees cannot be required to join a union. However, they can be required to pay at least some portion of union dues in states that have not enacted a "right to work" law.

8. True. Even if the employer is trying to do something good for its workers, it must include the union in the decision. (If it's really a win for workers, chances are good that the union will agree to it.)

9. False. Even if the committee simply makes recommendations, it might be considered a company union if it deals with the company on traditional topics of union bargaining and is dominated by management. A committee that has the right to make important decisions might be legal if it is acting in the place of management.

10. It depends on the reasons for the strike. Workers who strike over an unfair labor practice are entitled to get their jobs back when the strike is over.

State Right to Work Laws

Alabama	Ala. Code §§ 25-7-30 to 25-7-35
Alaska	No right to work law.
Arizona	Ariz. Const. art. 25; Ariz. Rev. Stat. §§ 23-1301 to 23-1307
Arkansas	Ark. Const. amend. 34; Ark. Code Ann. §§ 11-3-301 to 11-3-304
California	No right to work law.
Colorado	No right to work law.
Connecticut	No right to work law.
Delaware	No right to work law.
District of Columbia	No right to work law.
Florida	Fla. Const. art. 1, § 6; Fla. Stat. Ann. § 447.17
Georgia	Ga. Code Ann. §§ 34-6-20 to 34-6-28
Hawaii	No right to work law.
Idaho	Idaho Code §§ 44-2001 to 44-2009
Illinois	No right to work law.
Indiana	No right to work law.
Iowa	Iowa Code § 731.1
Kansas	Kan. Const. art. 15, § 12; Kan. Stat. Ann. §§ 44-808(5), 44-831
Kentucky	No right to work law.
Louisiana	La. Rev. Stat. Ann. §§ 23:981 to 23:987 (all workers) and 23:881 to 23:889 (agricultural workers)
Maine	No right to work law.
Maryland	No right to work law.
Massachusetts	No right to work law.
Michigan	No right to work law.
Minnesota	No right to work law.
Mississippi	Miss. Const. Art. 7, § 198-A; Miss. Code Ann. § 71-1-47
Missouri	No right to work law
Montana	No right to work law.
Nebraska	Neb. Const. art XV, §§ 13 to 18; Neb. Rev. Stat. § 48-217
Nevada	Nev. Rev. Stat. Ann. §§ 613.230 to 613.300
New Hampshire	N.H. Rev. Stat. Ann §§ 275:1 to 275:2
New Jersey	No right to work law.
New Mexico	N.M. Stat. Ann. §§ 50-2-1- to 50-2-4
New York	No right to work law.
North Carolina	N.C. Gen. Stat. §§ 95-78 to 95-84
North Dakota	N.D. Cent. Code § 34-01-14
Ohio	Ohio Rev. Code Ann. § 4113.02
Oklahoma	Okla. Const. Art. 23, § 1A
Oregon	No right to work law.
Pennsylvania	No right to work law.
Rhode Island	No right to work law.
South Carolina	S.C. Code Ann. §§ 41-7-10 to 41-7-100
South Dakota	S.D. Const. art. VI, § 2; S.D. Codified Laws Ann. §§ 60-8-3 to 60-8-8
Tennessee	Tenn. Code Ann. §§ 50-1-201 to 50-1-204
Texas	Tex. Lab. Code Ann. §§ 101.051 to 101.053
Utah	Utah Code Ann. §§ 34-34-1 to 34-34-17
Vermont	No right to work law.
Virginia	Va. Code Ann. §§ 40.1-59 to 40.1-69
Washington	No right to work law.
West Virginia	No right to work law.
Wisconsin	No right to work law.
Wyoming	Wyo. Stat. §§ 27-7-108 to 27-7-115

Independent Contractors

ndependent contractors exist in virtually every type of workplace, large and small, blue collar and professional. The federal Bureau of Labor Statistics estimates that more than ten million people work as independent contractors in occupations ranging from farming to computer technology to upper-level management. Contractors go by any one of a number of names—consultants, freelancers, the self-employed, entrepreneurs, and business owners—but they all have two common traits: They are in business for themselves, and they don't rely on a single employer for their livelihood.

Hiring independent contractors can be a smart, cost-effective alternative to taking on employees. They can add a lot of flexibility and expertise to a company's workforce without the financial and legal burdens of hiring employees.

Using independent contractors does have some drawbacks, however. The biggest potential problem is that numerous federal and state government agencies keep a close watch on any employer who uses independent contractors. These agencies want to make sure employers aren't taking advantage of workers (and skipping out on their tax obligations) by calling them independent contractors when they should really be classified as employees. Companies that try to get the benefits of the arrangement without following the rules can end up in legal trouble.

In this chapter, you'll find:

- an overview of the issues that arise when companies hire independent contractors

- an examination of the various government definitions of independent contractor and employee, as well as advice on how to steer clear of legal trouble

- the benefits and drawbacks of this type of arrangement, and

- advice on creating a written independent contractor agreement.

Frequently Asked Questions About Independent Contractors

What is an independent contractor?

Independent contractors, also sometimes referred to as freelancers or consultants, are independent businesspeople who perform services for other people or businesses. In other words, they are people who do work for a company but are not its employees. Figuring out the difference between employees and independent contractors is not always easy, and the answer often depends on who is asking the question. (For more about this, see "Classifying Workers," below.)

Frequently Asked Questions About Independent Contractors (cont'd)

What are the benefits of using independent contractors?

Because companies don't have to pay taxes or provide benefits (such as health insurance) for independent contractors, it can be less expensive to use them. Using independent contractors also gives a company flexibility and reduces its exposure to certain kinds of lawsuits. (For more, see "Benefits and Drawbacks of Using Independent Contractors," below.)

What are the drawbacks of using independent contractors?

A company does not have the same right to control independent contractors as it does employees, nor can a company demand or expect the same type of loyalty from independent contractors. In addition, independent contractors can sue your company if they are injured while working for you, while employees cannot. (See "Benefits and Drawbacks of Using Independent Contractors," below.)

Do we need to use any special paperwork to hire independent contractors?

Your company can greatly reduce the chances of a worker being reclassified as an employee by requiring the worker to fill out an independent contractor questionnaire, provide copies of business licenses, and sign a written independent contractor agreement. (For more information, see "Important Documents When Hiring Independent Contractors," below.)

Do we have to use a written agreement with independent contractors?

With a few exceptions, the law does not require companies to use a written agreement with independent contractors. Still, it's a good idea to write things down, for a number of reasons. (To learn more about this, see "Written Agreements With Independent Contractors," below.)

Who owns the rights to the intellectual property we hire an independent contractor to create for us?

Unless the work falls into one of nine categories defined by law, the intellectual property rights to any works an independent contractor creates will belong to the independent contractor, not to your company. This is true even if you hired and paid the independent contractor specifically to create the product for your company. But you can use a written contract to ensure that the copyright belongs to your company. (For more information, see "Copyright Ownership," below.)

Classifying Workers

You may think that a worker's status as an independent contractor or an employee depends on what your company and the worker decide. As long as both parties agree on the terms of the relationship, that's all that matters, right?

Wrong. The federal and state governments care a lot about how workers are classified. Not surprisingly, the root of their concern is money. Your company doesn't have to withhold or pay taxes (including expensive payroll taxes such as Social Security and Medicare) for an independent contractor, and it will have fewer legal obligations to an independent contractor than to an employee. Thus, it's often in a company's interest to call a worker an independent contractor. (For more on this, see "Benefits and Drawbacks of Using Independent Contractors," below.) By contrast, it's in the government's interest to label the worker as an employee. The more employees there are in this world, the more money flows straight into government coffers through payroll withholding (and the fewer opportunities workers have to hide or underreport their income).

Unfortunately, there are as many tests to determine whether a worker qualifies as an independent contractor as there are government agencies that deal with workers, from your state unemployment office to the federal Internal Revenue Service. Figuring out how to treat a worker so that agencies classify the worker as an independent contractor can be a complicated undertaking.

Employers who don't learn the rules before they hire an independent contractor can get into trouble with one agency or another. To avoid problems such as audits, fines, and taxes, you should learn the rules of all of the following agencies before you hire a worker. (For more about fines and taxes, see "Benefits and Drawbacks of Using Independent Contractors," below.)

The Internal Revenue Service

The Internal Revenue Service (IRS) is probably the most important agency to satisfy when it comes to classifying a worker as an independent contractor. Under the IRS's test, workers are considered employees if the company they work for has the right to direct and control the way they work, including the details of when, where, and how the job is accomplished. In contrast, the IRS will consider workers independent contractors if the company they work for does not manage how they work, except to accept or reject their final results.

The IRS looks at a number of factors when determining whether a worker is an employee or an independent contractor. The agency is more likely to classify as an independent contractor a worker who:

- can earn a profit or suffer a loss from the activity
- furnishes the tools and materials needed to do the work
- is paid by the job
- works for more than one company at a time
- invests in equipment and facilities

- pays his or her own business and traveling expenses
- hires and pays assistants, and
- sets his or her own working hours.

On the other hand, the IRS is more likely to classify as an employee a worker who:

- can be fired at any time
- is paid by the hour
- receives instructions from the company
- receives training from the company
- works full time for the company
- receives employee benefits
- has the right to quit without incurring liability, and
- provides services that are an integral part of the company's day-to-day operations.

If the IRS would consider the worker an independent contractor, your company does not have to withhold federal payroll taxes as you would for an employee, including Social Security taxes, federal disability taxes, and federal income taxes. If you're not sure how to classify a worker, you can ask the IRS to determine the worker's status, but we don't recommend it. Not surprisingly, the IRS will usually decide that the worker is an employee (and your company will be stuck with that decision). If you're really confused, you're better off consulting with an experienced employment lawyer.

To find out more about the IRS independent contractor test, you can refer to the agency's website at www.irs.gov.

The U.S. Department of Labor

The U.S. Department of Labor also cares about how your company classifies workers:

If a worker is an independent contractor, then the worker is not covered by the Fair Labor Standards Act (FLSA), the major federal law regarding wages and hours. This means, among other things, that the worker is not entitled to minimum wage or overtime.

Like the IRS, the Department of Labor has no single rule or test for determining whether someone is an independent contractor under the FLSA. However, the U.S. Supreme Court has said that the following factors are significant when determining whether a worker is an independent contractor under the FLSA:

- whether the worker's services are an integral part of your company's business (this points to employee status)
- the permanency of the relationship (the more permanent the relationship, the more likely it is that the worker is an employee)
- whether the worker has invested in facilities and equipment (if so, this points to independent contractor status)
- how much control your company has over the worker (the more control, the more likely it is that the worker is an employee)
- whether the worker has opportunities to make a profit or suffer a loss (as opposed to always earning a set amount of money no matter what happens, like an employee)
- whether the worker competes in the open market (if so, this points to independent contractor status), and
- the extent to which the worker operates a truly independent business (the more

independence, the more likely the worker is an independent contractor).

The U.S. Supreme Court has also said that the following things have no bearing on whether a worker is an independent contractor or an employee:

- where the worker performs the work
- the absence of a formal employment contract, and
- whether the worker is licensed by a state or local government.

For more information about the Department of Labor's test, refer to the Wage and Hour portion of the agency's website at www.dol.gov. For more about wages and hours, see Chapter 2.

Your State Unemployment Compensation Board

If the worker meets your state unemployment compensation board's definition of independent contractor, your company doesn't need to pay unemployment insurance for the worker. If the worker does not meet this test, your company should provide unemployment coverage for the worker, even if the worker qualifies as an independent contractor under other tests (such as the IRS test).

To learn more about your state unemployment department's test, contact your state unemployment compensation board or your state department of labor. You can also try your local office of the Small Business Administration (SBA). For a list of local SBA offices, refer to the SBA's website, at www.sba.gov.

As a manager, it's a good idea to learn about your state's unemployment department test for independent contractor status *before* you hire an independent contractor. That way, you can create an independent contractor relationship from the beginning that satisfies the test and averts possible problems later.

Your company could get into trouble if a worker who you thought was an independent contractor decides to apply for unemployment compensation, a benefit that is reserved for employees. Should this happen, it will be your company's word against the worker's: You say the worker was an independent contractor, but the worker—eager for that unemployment check—claims to have been an employee. In such a situation, you'll have to be prepared to back up your assertion.

Your State Workers' Compensation Insurance Agency

As with unemployment insurance, only employees are entitled to receive workers' compensation. If a worker meets your state workers' compensation agency definition of independent contractor, your company does not have to pay for workers' compensation coverage for that worker. Otherwise, your company should pay for workers' compensation coverage, even if the worker qualifies as an independent contractor under other tests.

To find out more about the workers' compensation test in your state, contact your state department of industrial relations or workers' compensation or your state labor department. Your local office of the Small

Lessons From the Real World

Bennett Harrington, who worked as a hunting guide for Gueydan Duck Club in Louisiana, was injured one day when his dog stepped on a client's loaded gun, causing it to go off. The shell ripped into Mr. Harrington's leg, seriously injuring him.

When Mr. Harrington applied for workers' compensation benefits, he was surprised to learn that the club owner had classified him as an independent contractor. This meant that Mr. Harrington could not get the benefits, which were for employees only.

The Louisiana Court of Appeal looked at the relationship between Mr. Harrington and the club and decided that Mr. Harrington was entitled to benefits because he should have been classified as an employee. The court based its opinion on the amount of control the club had over Mr. Harrington. The court decided that the following facts, taken together, made Mr. Harrington an employee:

- The club had recruited Mr. Harrington to work as a guide.
- The club, not Mr. Harrington, set the price that the clients paid for the guided hunt.

- The clients paid the club, not Mr. Harrington.
- There was no formalized agreement between Mr. Harrington and the club, which meant that the club could choose not to use Mr. Harrington at any time, for any reason.
- The club assigned clients to Mr. Harrington.
- The club told Mr. Harrington which hunting blind to use.
- The club told Mr. Harrington how to act around the clients—to entertain them, to make them happy, and to ensure their safety.
- The club maintained facilities and land for its guides, including Mr. Harrington, to use.
- The club provided blinds and decoys for the hunts.
- The club provided cell phones and transportation to the guides.
- Mr. Harrington thought he was an employee.

Harrington v. Herbert, 2001 WL 541772 (La. App. 3d Cir. 2001).

Business Association (SBA) might also have information on the subject. (For a list of SBA offices, refer to the SBA's website, at www. sba.gov.)

Again, you should find out what test your state's workers' compensation board uses before you hire an independent contractor. If

an independent contractor is injured on the job and applies for workers' compensation—a benefit reserved for employees—your company might face an audit.

Your State Tax Department

If your state collects income tax, then you need to know your state tax department's rules regarding independent contractors. If the worker will qualify as an independent contractor under your state tax department's test, your company does not need to withhold state income taxes from the worker's compensation. Otherwise, you must withhold state income taxes (if your state imposes them), even if the worker qualifies as an independent contractor under other tests. Contact your state tax board for details. This is an especially important test to learn, because many independent contractor audits begin with a state tax agency: state tax agencies are often more aggressive about independent contractor audits than the IRS.

Your State Department of Labor

If your state department of labor would consider the worker an independent contractor, then your company does not have to pay the worker minimum wage or overtime according to your state wage and hour laws. (But federal wage and hour laws might apply—see above for more information.) Contact your state labor department for details. (See the appendix for contact information.)

Benefits and Drawbacks of Using Independent Contractors

Using independent contractors is a double-edged sword. For every benefit, there is an equally important drawback. In the end, your company will have to weigh all of the factors and decide what is best for the business when deciding what sort of worker to hire.

Benefits

Independent contractors require a much smaller cash outlay than do new employees. As a result, cash-strapped companies are often tempted to classify workers as independent contractors. Companies that hire independent contractors instead of employees reap these financial benefits:

- They do not have to pay a whole host of federal taxes for independent contractors, including Social Security and Medicare taxes.
- They do not have to withhold any state or federal income taxes from an independent contractor's paycheck.
- They do not have to pay workers' compensation insurance for independent contractors.
- They do not have to pay unemployment insurance for independent contractors
- They do not have to provide employee benefits (such as health insurance, paid sick leave, paid holidays, and retirement benefits) to independent contractors.
- Unless the project requires otherwise, they do not have to provide facilities, equipment, or training to independent contractors.

These and other expenses associated with employees add about 20% to 30% to a company's payroll costs. Although independent contractors generally earn more per hour than employees for doing the same work, the company will still pay less overall because it won't have to pay these extra employee expenses and administrative costs.

In addition to the monetary benefits, independent contractors give companies the flexibility to add expertise to their workforce as needed. A company can hire independent contractors for specific tasks and take advantage of their specialized knowledge and experience without the cost and obligations of hiring full-time employees. This allows a company to run a lean operation, using employees for integral parts of the business and independent contractors for other projects as they arise.

Companies also have less exposure to lawsuits from independent contractors than from employees. Antidiscrimination laws and wrongful termination laws are all designed to protect employees, not independent contractors. In addition, employees have the right to unionize; independent contractors do not.

Companies that hire independent contractors also have less exposure to lawsuits from third parties. Although a company is liable to third parties for anything an employee does on the job, it is not liable for what an independent contractor does unless the company had some part in causing the injury or accident (for example, it gave the independent contractor poor directions or hired an independent contractor who wasn't qualified for the job).

Drawbacks

After reading about the financial and other benefits of hiring independent contractors, it might be tempting to convert your company's entire workforce to independent contractors. Not so fast: There are some definite drawbacks to using independent contractors instead of employees.

The primary drawback of classifying any worker an independent contractor is the risk that one government agency or another will audit your company and reclassify the worker as an employee. According to *Business Wire* magazine, the government loses about $20 billion a year in taxes because more than half of the independent contractors in the country are really misclassified employees. The government—particularly the IRS— does not take these losses lightly, and it is happy to audit any company it suspects is misclassifying workers.

State agency audits are even more common, spurred by independent contractors who apply for unemployment benefits and workers' compensation, benefits exclusively reserved for employees. If a government agency decides that your company has misclassified a worker, your company will owe all of the back taxes associated with that worker, plus interest on those taxes and penalties. This could add up to quite a hefty sum. In addition, the worker might be entitled to overtime and back pay, as well as any unpaid unemployment or workers' compensation benefits.

Another drawback to classifying a worker as an independent contractor is that your

Lessons From the Real World

When Julianne Eisenberg sued the warehouse at which she worked for sexual harassment, the warehouse claimed that she was an independent contractor, not an employee, so she was not protected by workplace anti-discrimination laws. As proof of her status, the warehouse pointed out that it called her an independent contractor in tax documents and didn't provide her with any employee benefits.

The warehouse's arguments did not convince the federal court that reviewed the case, however. Looking at the way the warehouse treated Ms. Eisenberg, the court said she was an employee, not an independent contractor. That meant the warehouse was on the hook for the sexual harassment that Ms. Eisenberg suffered.

What tipped the balance in Ms. Eisenberg's favor? The court noted the following facts:

- The warehouse gave Ms. Eisenberg, whose job was to load and unload trucks, orders on a daily basis.
- At the job site, someone from the warehouse would instruct the crew, of which Ms. Eisenberg was a member, on what objects to move and where.

- Ms. Eisenberg's job did not require any specialized skill. (Examples of jobs that require a specialized skill include computer programmers, architects, graphic artists, and photographers. A worker with specialized skills is more likely to be classified as an independent contractor than an unskilled laborer.)
- The warehouse supplied all of the necessary supplies and equipment for Ms. Eisenberg to do her job.
- Ms. Eisenberg performed her job almost exclusively in the warehouse or on its trucks.
- Ms. Eisenberg was not hired for a specific move or project. Instead, she worked on whatever move or project the warehouse had at the time.
- Ms. Eisenberg was paid on an hourly basis, not by project.
- Ms. Eisenberg's job was an integral part of the warehouse's business.

Eisenberg v. Advance Relocation & Storage, Inc., 237 F.3d 111 (2d Cir. 2000).

company will not be able to control that worker as it could an employee (for instance, setting work hours or requiring a project to be done in a certain manner). Under all of the agency tests, control is a big factor. The more the hiring company controls (or has the right to control) the way the worker does the job, the more likely it is that one agency or another will classify that worker as an employee instead of an independent contractor. When your company hires an independent contractor, it must allow the worker to do the job as he or she wishes, or suffer the consequences.

Control isn't the only thing your company loses by using an independent contractor. It also loses continuity when independent contractors come and go for short-term projects. Each new independent contractor will have to become familiar with your business and the project, and you'll have to establish a working relationship with each new person you bring on. In contrast, employees know your company's inner workings and needs. They know your company's people and practices, which can improve the efficiency and consistency of your operations.

Your company also can't simply get rid of an independent contractor who isn't working out. Unlike an employee, who can usually be fired for any reason at any time (see "At-Will Employment" in Chapter 4 for more information), an independent contractor will be protected by the terms of the contract, and your company will have to honor that contract or risk a lawsuit. (For more about contracts, see "Written Agreements With Independent Contractors," below.)

If your company hires an independent contractor to create works that can be copyrighted, the company might not own the rights to the work unless the contractor signs a written agreement transferring copyright ownership in advance. This is not the case with employees; for the most part, your company owns copyrightable works created by its employees. (For more about this, see "Copyright Ownership," below.)

Although independent contractors usually cannot sue your company for violating federal antidiscrimination laws, they can sue for on-the-job injuries, if your company was at fault. Employees, on the other hand, cannot: They are limited to the benefits provided by the workers' compensation system. (See "Workers' Compensation" in Chapter 7 for more information.)

Important Documents When Hiring Independent Contractors

If your company hires an independent contractor, there are certain key steps you can—and should—take to reduce the chances of a government agency reclassifying the contractor as an employee. You can take these steps even before the independent contractor starts work. If you gather the documents described here, you will have already gone a long way toward establishing the worker's independent contractor status.

Independent Contractor Questionnaire

Ask prospective independent contractors to complete an independent contractor questionnaire. Design the questionnaire to elicit information that will help prove that the independent contractor is a separate business entity and not merely an employee in independent contractor's clothing. The questionnaire should ask the prospective hire about the following:

- whether the independent contractor has a fictitious business name
- how the independent contractor's business is structured (for example, sole proprietorship, partnership, corporation, or limited liability company)
- the independent contractor's business address and phone number
- the number of people, if any, the independent contractor employs
- any professional licenses the independent contractor holds
- any business licenses the independent contractor holds
- contact information for other companies for whom the person has worked as an independent contractor
- how the independent contractor markets his or her business (for example, in the yellow pages or other advertising)
- whether the independent contractor has an office separate from home
- a description of the business equipment and facilities the independent contractor owns

- whether the independent contractor has business cards, professional stationery, and invoice forms, and
- a list of all types of business insurance the independent contractor carries.

The answers to these questions will help you accurately assess whether the worker is an independent contractor. However, none of them is conclusive evidence of independent contractor status. Each answer is just one factor among many you should consider when deciding how to classify the worker.

Make sure that anyone you may hire as an independent contractor fills out this questionnaire instead of your company's standard employment application. A government agency can—and probably will—try to use the fact that the independent contractor filled out an "employment" application as evidence that the worker is actually an employee.

Business Documents

Once you've received a completed questionnaire and conducted the interview, the next step is to make sure you have enough documentation to establish that the worker is a separate business entity if the government decides to audit your company. Make copies of all these documents and file them along with the questionnaire described above:

- copies of any business or professional licenses
- certificates showing that the independent contractor has insurance, including

general liability insurance and workers' compensation insurance (if the independent contractor has employees)

- copies of the independent contractor's business card and stationery
- copies of any advertising that the independent contractor has done, including advertising in the yellow pages or printouts of online ads
- a copy of the independent contractor's white pages business listing, if there is one
- if the independent contractor is operating under a fictitious or assumed business name, a copy of the fictitious or assumed business name statement or application
- a copy of the invoice form that the independent contractor uses to bill for services
- if the independent contractor rents business space, a copy of the office lease
- if the independent contractor has employees, a document containing the independent contractor's unemployment insurance number
- copies of IRS Form 1099-MISC other firms have issued to the independent contractor, and
- if the independent contractor is a sole proprietor and will agree to do so (this is a big if), copies of the independent contractor's tax returns for the previous two years showing that the independent contractor has filed a Schedule C, *Profit or Loss From a Business* (which will show that the independent contractor has been operating as an independent business).

Although the contractor may balk at showing you a few of these items—especially those that contain sensitive financial information—stress that you will keep everything confidential and that you only want these items to verify the contractor's status.

Written Agreements With Independent Contractors

For most types of projects, the law does not require companies to enter into a written contract with independent contractors. You can talk to the independent contractor, agree on the terms of the arrangement, and have an oral contract that any court will enforce.

As your mother no doubt told you, however, just because you can do something doesn't mean you should. Oral agreements invite costly misunderstandings because there's no clear written statement of what the independent contractor is to do, how much your company will pay, or what will happen if a dispute arises. These misunderstandings might be innocent—you and the independent contractor genuinely may have different memories about what was agreed to—or they may not. Either way, it'll be your word against the worker's, and there is no telling whom a judge or jury will believe. It's much safer to rely on a written document that clearly sets out the details of your relationship.

Even better, a written independent contractor agreement can also help establish a worker's independent contractor status by showing the IRS and other agencies that both your company and the worker intended to create a hiring firm/independent contractor relationship, not an employer/employee relationship. But don't expect the written agreement to be a magic bullet: A written agreement won't make much difference if your company treats the worker like an employee. (For more about classification rules, see "Classifying Workers," above.)

When writing the independent contractor agreement, remember the tests for classifying workers. Don't put anything in the agreement that would tend to show the worker is an employee rather than an independent contractor For example, don't describe in the agreement the details of how the independent contractor is to accomplish the work; remember, if the hiring company controls the details of the work, that's a sign that the worker is really an employee.

A written independent contractor agreement should contain at least the following terms:

- a description of the services the independent contractor will perform
- a description of how much your company will pay the worker (usually either a fixed fee for a finished product or a sum based on unit of time—for example, by the hour or by the week)
- a description of how and when the worker will be paid
- an explanation of who will be responsible for expenses (independent contractors are usually responsible for their own expenses, although this isn't true in every field)

- an explanation of who will provide materials, equipment, and office space (independent contractors usually provide these things, but not always)
- a statement that your company and the worker agree to an independent contractor relationship
- a statement that the independent contractor has all of the permits and licenses that the state requires for the work
- a statement that the independent contractor will pay all state and federal income taxes
- an acknowledgment that the independent contractor is not entitled to any of the benefits your company provides employees
- a statement that the independent contractor carries liability insurance
- a description of the term of the agreement (for example, one week, one season, or until the project is completed)
- a description of the circumstances under which your company or the independent contractor can terminate the agreement, and
- an explanation of how any disputes will be resolved.

Other terms you could include range from copyright ownership (see below) to naming who will be responsible for the independent contractor's employees.

Sometimes, You Have to Write It Down

While agreements between your company and the independent contractor can generally be oral (even though we don't recommend relying on oral understandings), many states' laws require certain kinds of contracts to be in writing to be enforceable. These laws, usually called a state's "Statute of Frauds," typically require that the following types of agreements be in writing:

- any contract that will last longer than a year
- contracts for the sale of goods (tangible property, such as a work of art or a car) worth $500 or more
- a promise to pay someone else's debt
- contracts involving the sale of real estate
- real estate leases that last for more than one year, or
- any transfer of copyright ownership.

If your company's agreement with the independent contractor meets any of these definitions (for instance, your relationship will last longer than a year, or the contractor is assigning or transferring copyright ownership to the company), then the agreement will probably need to be in writing to be enforceable.

Sample Independent Contractor Agreement

Below is an example of an agreement one company used to hire an independent contractor (referred to as the "Consultant"). This example is for illustrative purposes only; be sure any agreement you create is appropriate for your situation and consistent with your state's and federal law. For sample contract language you can use to create your own agreements, see *Consultant & Independent Contractor Agreements*, by Stephen Fishman (Nolo).

Independent Contractor Agreement

This Agreement is made between FunWorks, Inc., ("Client"), with a principal place of business at Berkeley, California, and John Cunningham ("Consultant"), with a principal place of business at Berkeley, California.

1. Services to Be Performed

Consultant agrees to perform the following consultant services on Client's behalf:

Create new design for Client's packaging and promotional materials.

2. Payment

In consideration for the services to be performed by Consultant, Client agrees to pay Consultant $10,000 according to the terms of payment set forth below.

3. Terms of Payment

Client shall pay according to the schedule of payments set forth in Exhibit A, attached to this Agreement.

4. Expenses

Consultant shall be responsible for all expenses incurred while performing services under this Agreement.

5. Materials

Consultant will furnish all materials, equipment, and supplies used to provide the services required by this Agreement.

6. Independent Contractor Status

Consultant is an independent contractor, and neither Consultant nor Consultant's employees or contract personnel are, or shall be deemed, Client's employees. In its capacity as an independent contractor, Consultant agrees and represents, and Client agrees, as follows:

- Consultant has the right to perform services for others during the term of this Agreement.

- Consultant has the sole right to control and direct the means, manner, and method by which the services required by this Agreement shall be performed.

- Consultant has the right to perform the services required by this Agreement at any place or location and at such times as Consultant may determine.

- Consultant has the right to hire assistants as subcontractors or to use employees to provide the services required by this Agreement.

- The services required by this Agreement shall be performed by Consultant, consultant's employees, or contract personnel, and Client shall not hire, supervise, or pay any assistants to help Consultant.

- Neither consultant nor Consultant's employees or contract personnel shall receive any training from Client in the professional skills necessary to perform the services required by this Agreement.

7. Business Permits, Certificates, and Licenses

Consultant has complied with all federal, state, and local laws requiring business permits, certificates, and licenses required to carry out the services to be performed under this Agreement.

8. State and Federal Taxes

Client will not:

- withhold FICA (Social Security and Medicare taxes) from Consultant's payments or make FICA payments on Consultant's behalf

- make state or federal unemployment compensation contributions on Consultant's behalf, or

- withhold state or federal income tax from Consultant's payments.

9. Fringe Benefits

Consultant understands that neither Consultant nor Consultant's employees or contract personnel are eligible to participate in any employee pension, health, vacation pay, sick pay, or other fringe benefit plan of Client.

10. Workers' Compensation

Client shall not obtain workers' compensation insurance on behalf of Consultant or Consultant's employees. If Consultant hires employees to perform any work under this

Agreement, Consultant will cover them with workers' compensation insurance and provide Client with a certificate of workers' compensation insurance before the employees begin work.

11. Term of Agreement

This agreement will become effective when signed by both parties and will terminate on the earlier of:

- the date Consultant completes the services required by this Agreement
- November 30, 20xx, or
- the date a party terminates the Agreement as provided below.

12. Terminating the Agreement

Either party may terminate this agreement at any time by giving 30 days' written notice to the other party of the intent to terminate.

13. Exclusive Agreement

This is the entire agreement between Consultant and Client.

14. Intellectual Property Ownership

Consultant assigns to Client all patent, copyright, trademark, and trade secret rights in anything created or developed by Consultant for Client under this Agreement. Consultant shall help prepare any papers that Client considers necessary to secure any patents, copyrights, trademarks, or other proprietary rights at no charge to Client. However, Client shall reimburse Consultant for reasonable out-of-pocket expenses incurred.

Consultant must obtain written assurances from Consultant's employees and contract personnel that they agree with this assignment. Consultant agrees not to use any of the intellectual property mentioned above for the benefit of any other party without Client's prior written permission.

15. Resolving Disputes

If a dispute arises under this Agreement, the parties agree to first try to resolve the dispute with the help of a mutually agreed-upon mediator in Berkeley, California. Any costs and fees other than attorney fees associated with the mediation shall be shared equally by the parties.

If the dispute is not resolved within 30 days after it is referred to the mediator, any party may take the matter to court.

16. Applicable Law

This Agreement will be governed by the laws of the state of California.

Signatures

Client: FunWorks, Inc.

By: _____

   Dylan Irons, President

Date: _____

Consultant: _____

   John Cunningham

Taxpayer ID#: _____   _____

Date: _____

Copyright Ownership

When your company hires an independent contractor to create a work for the company—such as a computer program, written work, artwork, musical work, photograph, or multimedia work—you might wonder who will own the copyright. Generally, whoever owns the copyright to a work owns significant rights, including the right to use, license, or sell the work to someone else.

Although you might think that your company owns any work it pays a contractor to create, that isn't automatically the case. Copyright law contains a major trap for the unwary: Unless the work an independent contractor creates falls into one of nine "work for hire" categories described below, your company will *not* automatically own the copyright to the work. The independent contractor must "assign" the copyright to the company in writing. It's critical to obtain this assignment (transfer of copyright ownership) before an independent contractor starts work so that there is no disagreement later over who owns the copyright. You can include the copyright assignment in the written independent contractor agreement described above.

If the work was specially commissioned or ordered by the hiring company and falls into one of the nine categories described, it is considered a "work for hire" in legal parlance. The hiring company automatically owns the copyright to such works for hire; however, your company and the independent contractor must sign a written agreement stating that the work is made for hire. Again, you can include this statement in the independent contractor agreement described above.

Works for hire include:

1. a contribution to a collective work, such as a work created by more than one author like a newspaper, magazine, anthology, or encyclopedia
2. a part of an audiovisual work (for example, a motion picture screenplay)
3. a translation
4. supplementary works, such as forewords, afterwords, supplemental pictorial illustrations, maps, charts, editorial notes, bibliographies, appendixes, and indexes
5. a compilation (for example, an electronic database)
6. an instructional text
7. a test
8. answer material for a test, and
9. an atlas.

Legal Dos and Don'ts: Independent Contractors

Do:

- **Say what you mean.** Never use the words "employment" or "employee" when referring to the independent contractor. Have the worker complete an independent contractor questionnaire (*not* an employment application) and be careful when naming or referring to any written agreement you create (do *not* call it an "employment contract").

- **Spread the work around.** The more consistently a worker works for your company, the more likely an agency is to view the worker as an employee who depends on your company for a living. If you can, don't use the same independent contractor every time.

- **Hire corporations.** If you have the choice, hire independent contractors who have incorporated or formed a limited liability company. This will go a long way toward establishing that the worker has a separate business.

Don't:

- **Buck the trend.** When deciding whether a worker is an independent contractor, auditors will sometimes look at how others in the same industry categorize those workers. If workers who do particular types of jobs are always characterized as employees, your company is more likely to attract an audit if it tries to call them contractors.

- **Rely on labels.** When it comes to classifying workers, it's what you do that matters, not what you say. If you treat an independent contractor like an employee (especially by trying to control every aspect of how the worker does the job), you'll find yourself paying fines and taxes, no matter what you call the worker.

- **Take the worker's word for it.** Don't just accept a worker's claim that he or she operates an independent business: Get proof. You never know when the worker might decide to argue that he or she was really an employee (for instance, to receive workers' compensation or unemployment benefits).

Test Your Knowledge

Questions

1. As long as your company calls a worker an independent contractor and doesn't withhold employment taxes, it won't have to worry about government audits. ☐ True ☐ False

2. A company has essentially the same obligations to independent contractors as it does to its employees, except that it doesn't have to withhold and pay taxes for contractors. ☐ True ☐ False

3. Independent contractors are not entitled to workers' compensation benefits if they are injured on the job. ☐ True ☐ False

4. It is generally more expensive to hire employees than it is to hire independent contractors. ☐ True ☐ False

5. Someone who works for more than one company at a time cannot be classified as your company's employee. ☐ True ☐ False

6. You can use your company's regular employment application with independent contractors. ☐ True ☐ False

7. Even very basic arrangements with independent contractors should be put in writing. ☐ True ☐ False

8. Your company shouldn't hire independent contractors unless they have incorporated their own businesses. ☐ True ☐ False

9. If your company hires someone to create a work of art, the company will automatically own the copyright to the work, regardless of whether the worker is an employee or an independent contractor. ☐ True ☐ False

10. Even if your company pays an independent contractor to create a work, the contractor might own the copyright. ☐ True ☐ False

Answers

1. False. What matters is how your company treats the worker. Not paying taxes and calling the worker an employee are a good start, but the real issues are whether the worker is truly operating an independent business and whether your company has the right to exercise a great degree of control over how the work gets done.

2. False. Employees are protected by laws that require overtime pay, prohibit discrimination, and provide benefits for on-the-job injuries. These protections generally don't extend to independent contractors.

3. True. Independent contractors are not covered by the workers' compensation system.

4. True. Although independent contractors typically command higher pay than employees, your company won't have to pay taxes; provide benefits, workspace, and training; or otherwise lay out so much overhead for independent contractors.

5. False. An employee might work two part-time jobs, for example. What matters is whether the worker has an independent business and whether your company controls how the worker does the job.

6. False. You shouldn't use an employment application with independent contractors, because a court or agency might see that as proof that you thought the worker was really an employee.

7. True. The best course of action is to always use a written agreement, spelling out the terms of the job.

8. False. Although it's safest to hire contractors who have formed corporations or LLCs, it's fine to hire an unincorporated contractor—as long as he or she is really running an independent business.

9. False. Although a company generally owns the copyright to works created by its employees, this is not the case with independent contractors.

10. True. Your company must have a written agreement with the contractor either stating that the work is a work for hire (if it falls into one of the nine listed categories) or assigning the copyright to your company.

Trade Secrets

Often, workers never seem more precious to their employer than they do the moment they walk out the door—taking a vast amount of knowledge and a keen understanding of the employer's business with them, perhaps to the doorstep of a competitor.

Companies do not have to sit back and just watch this happen, however. You can help protect your company's confidential business information, while also protecting valuable employees and independent contractors. In this chapter, we look at how the law protects company trade secrets and what steps companies can take to stop them from leaking out.

Frequently Asked Questions About Trade Secrets

What is a trade secret?

The answer varies slightly depending on the state where your company does business. Generally speaking, a trade secret is a novel piece of information that gives the business a competitive advantage. A trade secret can be anything from a formula to a marketing plan to a customer list to the recipe for Coca Cola (one of the most famous trade secrets in history). (For more information, see "The Law of Trade Secrets," below.)

Can we prevent employees from revealing the company's trade secrets?

Yes. You can take many steps to prevent current and former employees from revealing your company's trade secrets, including the most basic step of letting employees know about them on a need-to-know basis only. (To learn how, see "Protecting Trade Secrets," below.)

What is a nondisclosure agreement?

A nondisclosure agreement is a contract an employee or independent contractor signs promising to protect the confidentiality of secret information learned while working for your company. The company must give something of value in exchange, such as money, a promotion, or a raise. (For more information, see "Nondisclosure Agreements," below.)

What is a noncompete agreement?

A noncompete agreement is a contract an employee or independent contractor signs promising not to work for a direct competitor for a specified period of time after leaving your company. As it would for a nondisclosure agreement, the company must give something of value in exchange for the worker's promise. (For more information, see "Noncompete Agreements," below.)

Frequently Asked Questions About Trade Secrets (cont'd)

What is a nonsolicitation agreement?

A nonsolicitation agreement is a contract an employee or independent contractor signs promising not to solicit your company's clients and customers after leaving your company. This type of agreement can also contain a promise not to solicit other employees to leave. Again, in exchange for signing the agreement, your company must provide the worker with something of value. (For more about this, see "Nonsolicitation Agreements," below.)

Does it violate trade secret law to hire an employee from a competitor?

You can hire employees who worked for a competitor, but you should always be careful when you do so, especially if the new hire signed a nondisclosure or noncompete agreement with the previous employer. (For more information, see "Hiring From Competitors," below.)

The Law of Trade Secrets

More often than not, what gives a business a competitive advantage over others is the specialized knowledge it has gained through ingenuity, innovation, or just plain old hard work. This specialized knowledge could be something as mundane as a list of customers who use or need your company's services or as glamorous as the top secret formula for its best-selling product, from a cookie recipe to an industrial chemical.

Each state has a trade secret law designed to protect these confidential bits of specialized knowledge. Although each law differs in the details, the basic structure tends to be the same. In fact, the vast majority of states have adopted a law called the Uniform Trade Secrets Act, which means that there's a lot of consistency from one state to the next.

There are many complicated definitions of trade secrets under the law, but generally, a trade secret is information that has the following characteristics:

- **Value.** The information has economic value to your company's business because you know it and competitors don't. (In other words, it's valuable because it is a secret.) Information that doesn't give your company a competitive edge is not a trade secret.

- **Secrecy.** The information is not generally known, nor is it easy to find out. If a competitor could learn the same information easily without much work or ingenuity, it's probably not a trade secret. Similarly, if some competitors already know the information, then it is not a trade secret.

- **Effort.** Your company must take reasonable steps to keep the information as secret as possible. For example, if a company posts the information in a place where anyone, including employees, customers, and vendors, can see it, then it's probably not a trade secret. Similarly, it's not a trade secret if it's posted on the company's public website.

Examples of trade secrets include a formula for a sports drink, survey methods used by professional pollsters, a recipe, a new invention for which a patent application has not yet been filed, marketing strategies, manufacturing techniques, and computer algorithms.

Unlike other forms of intellectual property such as patents, copyrights, or trademarks, trade secrecy is basically a do-it-yourself form of protection. Companies don't register with the government to secure their trade secrets; it's the company's responsibility to keep the information confidential and make sure it fits the definition laid out above. Trade secret protection lasts for as long as the secret is kept confidential. Once a trade secret is made available to the public, trade secret protection ends, sometimes even if the secret was taken or disclosed without permission.

Rights of the Trade Secret Owner

A trade secret owner has the right to prevent the following groups of people from copying, using, and benefiting from its trade secrets, or disclosing them to others without permission:

- people who are automatically bound by a duty of confidentiality not to disclose or use trade secret information (for example, your company's employees)
- people who acquire a trade secret through improper means such as theft, industrial espionage, or bribery

- people who knowingly obtain trade secrets from people who have no right to disclose them (for example, a competitor who hires one of your company's employees and then intentionally tries to exploit that employee's knowledge of your company's trade secrets)
- people who learn about a trade secret by accident or mistake but have reason to know that the information is a protected trade secret (for example, a competitor who hires one of your company's employee's away and accidentally learns information from the employee that turns out to be a trade secret), and
- people who sign nondisclosure agreements (also known as "confidentiality agreements") promising not to disclose trade secrets without authorization from the owner. (For more about these, see "Nondisclosure Agreements," below.)

Each state imposes a duty of loyalty on current and former employees not to disclose a company's trade secrets, so they automatically come under the umbrella of trade secret laws. Your company does not have to ask its employees to sign a nondisclosure agreement to require them to keep its secrets, but it's still a good idea to do so. (See "Nondisclosure Agreements," below, for some reasons why a company might want to take this extra step.)

Unlike current and former employees, however, the only way to impose liability on independent contractors, customers, or vendors for disclosing trade secrets is to have them sign a nondisclosure agreement. (For more about this, see "Nondisclosure

Lessons From the Real World

Christopher Warman devised the perfect recipe for fudge and turned it into a successful business called Christopher M's Hand Poured Fudge, Inc.

Warman hired Clyde Hennon to work as his assistant in daily operations. In the course of his employment, Hennon learned all about Warman's fudge-making operations, from the details of Warman's secret fudge recipe to Warman's unique manufacturing process.

After a year of working at Christopher M's, Hennon struck out on his own, opening his own fudge-making operation called The Fudge Works, Inc. Warman sued, arguing that Hennon was illegally using trade secret information he had learned from Warman including, among other things, Warman's secret fudge recipe.

The court agreed with Warman and ordered Hennon to stop making fudge. The court decided that the fudge recipe was a trade secret based on the following facts:

- Warman developed the recipe after several years of trial and error from a recipe that he had purchased for $140,000.
- Certain aspects of the recipe were unique and were not commonly used in the industry.
- Warman took great care to protect the secrecy of the recipe. He kept only one written copy of the recipe that he stored off the premises; he compartmentalized the manufacturing process so that employees only knew the portion of the recipe relating to their specific tasks; and he revealed the entire recipe to only a handful of people.
- The recipe had a multimillion-dollar value.

Christopher M's Hand Poured Fudge, Inc., v. Hennon and The Fudge Works, Inc., 699 A.2d 1272 (1997).

Agreements," below.) Unless such people sign a nondisclosure agreement, they are free to disclose any trade secrets they learn while working for or with your company to others, because trade secret law does not impose a duty on them to keep quiet.

Finally, there is one group of people whom your company cannot prevent from using its trade secret information: people who discover the secret independently, without using illegal means or violating agreements or state laws. For example, it is not a violation of trade secret law to analyze (or "reverse engineer") any lawfully obtained product to determine its trade secret. Although it's highly unlikely, if someone managed to exactly reproduce Kentucky Fried Chicken's 11-herb-and-spice recipe by experimenting in the kitchen, Kentucky Fried Chicken could not sue that person for violating trade secret laws.

Protecting Trade Secrets

Employees and independent contractors pose a thorny dilemma for businesses with valuable trade secrets. After all, your company has to let some of these people in on its trade secrets. Perhaps they need the information to do their jobs, or they helped develop the information in the first place. Yet these same people may leave your company and take that special knowledge with them, into business for themselves or to work for a competitor.

Simple preventive measures can reduce the risk that departing employees or independent contractors will take your company's trade secrets with them on their way out the door. We suggest a six-step approach:

- First, identify your company's trade secrets.
- Second, grant access to these trade secrets only on a need-to-know basis.
- Third, tell employees and independent contractors which information the company considers confidential.
- Fourth, use nondisclosure agreements.
- Fifth, make sure the company keeps its own secrets.
- Sixth, conduct exit interviews with departing employees and independent contractors.

The following sections look at each of these steps in more detail.

Identify Trade Secrets

You can't protect something if you don't know it exists. The first step in protecting your company's trade secrets is to figure out what valuable information needs to be protected.

Periodically, take an "information inventory" and ask yourself and other managers and supervisors the following questions:

- What information does my company know that gives us an advantage?
- Do our competitors know this information?
- Is it information that they would want to know or find valuable?
- How did we gain the information? Was the process difficult? Time-consuming? Expensive? Unique?
- What kind of damage would our business suffer if competitors discovered this information?
- What do we know that we really don't want our competitors to know?

Because businesses are in an almost constant process of developing this information, you should probably conduct this sort of review once a year.

Limit Access

The fewer people who know your company's trade secrets, the better. Limiting access to trade secrets limits the number of potential loose lips. And departing employees or independent contractors can't reveal secrets that they don't know.

Of course, no companies can keep all of its employees and independent contractors in the dark about everything. But always carefully consider whether an individual actually needs to know a secret you or other managers are about to reveal. Once you give it some thought, you might realize that an individual needs to know only one piece of the puzzle; other times, you might realize that the individual needs only a summary of the information, not the details.

If employees or independent contractors really need to know a trade secret to work effectively, go ahead and reveal it. But before you do, make sure they know it's a trade secret, which they are obligated to keep under wraps (see below).

Tell Workers That the Information Is Secret

Once you've identified your company's trade secrets and the employees or contractors who need to know them, the next step is to inform them that they must keep the secrets confidential. After all, you can't expect them to keep information a secret if they don't know that they are supposed to.

Often, your company's internal security procedures will be enough to put people on notice about trade secrets. (See "Keep the Secret," below.) But you should review these security procedures periodically to make sure that they're still appropriate. For example, once a formula that's been in research and development hits the production line, your company will need to change its security procedures to include the production floor and any workers involved in the manufacturing process.

Use Nondisclosure Agreements

Because employees have an automatic duty to keep trade secrets confidential, telling them that something is confidential is technically sufficient: You do not have to ask them to sign a nondisclosure agreement to impose this legal duty on them. Still, nondisclosure agreements underscore the importance of confidentiality and clear up any ambiguity about what information your company considers a trade secret. They can also be helpful if your company ever has to haul that employee into court for revealing the trade secret, whether the employee is still working for your company or not.

Independent contractors do not have an automatic duty to protect your company's confidential information, so you should make a practice of presenting a nondisclosure agreement to every independent contractor who will learn any trade secrets before you share those secrets. When you disclose confidential information to independent contractors, tell them that the information is confidential and remind them of their obligations under any nondisclosure agreement. (For more about this type of contract, see "Nondisclosure Agreements," below.)

Keep the Secret

As explained above, information can't qualify as a trade secret if your company doesn't take steps to protect it and keep it confidential. And once information loses its trade secret status, your company loses the right to prevent employees and others from disclosing it to competitors. The security measures you take to protect a trade secret can make or break your company's rights to the exclusive use of the information.

Security measures include the following:

- labeling all documents that contain trade secret information "Confidential" (which you can do using a "Confidential" ink stamp, available for a few dollars at most stationery stores)
- keeping a log of all confidential documents and the people who have access to them
- keeping a list of all trade secrets and the people who know them
- keeping all documents and evidence of trade secrets in a locked cabinet, locked room, or secure online location
- requiring employees to sign out confidential documents and materials and return them when they're done
- using a paper shredder to destroy any discarded documents that contain trade secret information
- password-protecting any computer files that contain proprietary information
- requiring all visitors to sign in, wear badges, and be accompanied by an employee at all times
- locking all exterior doors
- using nondisclosure agreements with employees, independent contractors, vendors, and customers
- using noncompete and nonsolicitation agreements with key employees and independent contractors, and
- periodically providing employees who have access to confidential information with a list identifying which pieces of information your company views as confidential.

Although it's rare that a business will want to use all of these security measures, using at least some of them will go a long way toward maintaining the confidentiality of its trade secrets. Moreover, if someone does pilfer your company's trade secrets, implementing these procedures will show a judge that the company has taken reasonable steps to keep the information a secret.

Conduct Exit Interviews

When an employee or independent contractor stops working for your company—for whatever reason—you must take extra care to ensure that the individual does not turn around and disclose the company's trade secrets to competitors.

An effective way to do this is to conduct an exit interview. Identify all of the trade secret information that the employee has learned and remind him or her of the obligation to keep the information confidential. If possible, present the worker with a topical list of all trade secrets so that there is no doubt about what the company expects. If the person leaving has any documents that are confidential, retrieve them at the interview.

If the individual signed a nondisclosure or noncompete agreement, review that at the interview and reiterate that your company will enforce it, if necessary.

Finally, once employees or independent contractors are gone, make sure they no longer have access to the company's computer files and physical premises, by retrieving keys and changing passwords.

Checklist: Trade Secret Protection Program

Once you identify your company's trade secrets, how can you keep them confidential? Here are some tips:

☐ Require anyone who will have access to your company's trade secrets to sign a nondisclosure agreement ahead of time.

☐ Maintain the physical security of your company's trade secrets by, for example, keeping them in a locked room, file cabinet, or desk drawer.

☐ Increase computer security to prevent unauthorized access to the system. For example, you should use secret passwords, firewalls, and access procedures; keep trade secrets in coded or encrypted form; and/or consider using a separate computer system, without Internet or network access, for your company's most sensitive information.

☐ Stamp or label your company's trade secrets "confidential."

☐ Don't write down trade secrets; tell others what they need to know orally.

☐ Limit employee access to trade secrets by, for example, having them sign confidential materials in and out and creating project logs to keep track of which employees have access to which confidential information.

☐ Restrict photocopying. Many trade secrets are lost through unauthorized photocopying. A good way to limit this is by requiring employees to use key cards and passwords every time they use a company copy machine.

☐ Shred documents. Whenever anyone at your company disposes of a document that includes confidential information, it should be shredded, not left in a dumpster or garbage can for the world to see.

☐ Screen employee presentations. Companies can inadvertently lose trade secret protection if an employee reveals or refers to them in a speech or presentation at a trade show, convention, or professional conference.

☐ Restrict camera phones. Cell phones with a camera feature make it all too easy for employes to photograph confidential documents, products, or processes.

Nondisclosure Agreements

A nondisclosure agreement—also called an NDA or a confidentiality agreement—is a contract in which the parties promise to protect the confidentiality of secret information that they learn during employment or another type of business transaction. A company can use a non-disclosure agreement to protect any type of trade secret or confidential information. For example, a nondisclosure agreement can prohibit someone from disclosing a secret invention design, an idea for a new website, or confidential financial information about your company.

If your company has entered into a nondisclosure agreement with someone who then uses or discloses its trade secrets without permission, your company can ask a court to stop the violator from making any further disclosures and sue for damages.

There are five important elements in a nondisclosure agreement:

- definition of confidential information
- exclusions from confidential information
- obligations of receiving party
- time periods, and
- miscellaneous provisions.

This section looks at each of these elements in more detail.

Definition of confidential information. Every nondisclosure agreement provides a general description of the types or categories of confidential information or trade secrets that the agreement covers. The purpose is to establish the boundaries or subject matter of

the disclosure, without actually disclosing the secrets.

Exclusions from confidential information. Every nondisclosure agreement excludes some information from protection. The party that receives the trade secret has no obligation to protect the excluded information. Typical areas of excluded information include:

- information that is already generally known outside of the business at the time the nondisclosure agreement is signed
- information that becomes known outside of the business through no fault of the employee or independent contractor
- information the employee or independent contractor knew prior to working for your company, and
- information the employee or indepen-dent contractor learns independently.

Obligations of the receiving party. The employee or independent contractor generally must keep the information in confidence and limit its use. Under most state laws, he or she can neither reveal the information nor assist others in acquiring it improperly or revealing it.

Time periods. Most nondisclosure agreements provide that the employee or independent contractor cannot disclose confidential information either during or after employment with your company.

Miscellaneous provisions. Miscellaneous standard terms are usually included at the end of the agreement. They include such matters as which state's law will apply if the agreement is breached, whether the parties will use arbitration to settle disagreements over the contract, and whether attorneys' fees will be awarded to the party who wins.

As noted above, even if an employee already has a legal duty to keep your company's secrets confidential under your state's trade secrets law, it's still a good idea to ask an employee to sign a nondisclosure agreement. A nondisclosure agreement:

- shows a judge that your company takes its responsibility to protect its trade secrets seriously
- defines exactly what information the employee must keep secret, and
- can specify the jurisdiction in which disputes will be resolved, the state's law that will apply, and any dispute resolution method the parties agree on.

Nondisclosure agreements are even more important for independent contractors, customers, and vendors, because none of these people have a duty to keep your company's secrets confidential without an agreement.

Noncompete Agreements

Sometimes, an employee or independent contractor is so integral to your company's business or so thoroughly immersed in its trade secrets that his or her departure— particularly to work for a competitor—would cause your company a great deal of harm. In such a situation, a nondisclosure agreement probably will not be sufficient to protect your company. Instead, you should ask, or require, the worker to sign a noncompete agreement. A noncompete agreement takes nondisclosure

one step further by prohibiting the worker from performing services for a direct competitor—or by prohibiting the worker from competing against you in his or her own business—for a specified period of time after leaving the company.

You do not need to ask every worker to sign a noncompete agreement. Indeed, you should reserve this type of contract for the most valuable and key members of the workforce. So how do you determine which workers fall into this category? Consider the following questions:

- Is the worker so valuable and, if he or she is an employee, has the company spent so much money training the employee, that losing him or her to a competitor would damage your company's business?
- Does the worker have access to a great deal of important information that you don't want revealed to a competitor?
- If that individual were to work for a competitor, is it practically inevitable that he or she would use your company's trade secrets in the new job?

Noncompete agreements are not enforce-able against employees in some states, including California. If your company does business in one of these states, it will have a difficult time using noncompete agreements to protect its business. However, you can use nonsolicitation agreements and nondisclosure agreements to protect trade secrets, client lists, and employees when a worker leaves. (For more about these types of contracts, see "Nondisclosure Agreements," above, and "Nonsolicitation Agreements," below.)

Make the Agreement Legal

While noncompete agreements may be an effective way to protect your company's trade secrets, the legal system also puts a high value on a person's right to earn a living. This means that a court will balance your company's interest in protecting itself against an individual's interest in being able to work where he or she wants to work. If the agreement isn't reasonable and necessary, your company will have a hard time convincing a court to enforce it.

If your company follows the guidelines set out in this section, its agreements should pass legal muster (in states that allow noncompetes).

Have a good business reason. First and foremost, your company must have a good business reason for asking an employee to sign a noncompete agreement. In other words, you can't simply use the agreement to punish someone for leaving the company. The typical business reason is to protect trade secrets or a customer base that a company has worked long and hard to develop. By being selective about which workers are asked to sign noncompete agreements, your company can increase its chances of success, because judges are much more likely to

---

Lessons From the Real World

Anita Walia worked as an Account Manager in the San Francisco office of Aetna U.S. Healthcare. Aetna decided, in 1997, to start requiring its employees to sign noncompete agreements. When Walia was asked to sign the agreement, which would have prohibited her from working for any health care organization in the state of California for six months after leaving Aetna, she did some research on the Internet and learned that noncompete agreements are generally illegal in California.

Walia spoke to four Aetna managers, starting with her supervisor, about her concerns. She offered to sign the nondisclosure and confidentiality provisions of the agreement if the noncompete were removed. She had a lawyer write to Aetna's president, explaining that the noncompete portion was illegal in California. Her efforts were unsuccessful, however, and Aetna eventually fired her for refusing to sign the agreement.

Walia sued, claiming that she was illegally terminated. A jury agreed, and awarded her more than $1.2 million, most of it for punitive damages. Aetna's failure to take a closer look at California law, even after Walia and her attorney told the company that its agreement was illegal, led the jury to believe that the company needed a wake-up call.

Walia v. Aetna, Inc., 93 Cal.App.4th 1213 (2001).

enforce noncompete agreements against workers who truly possess inside information.

Provide a benefit. Next, your company must provide a benefit to the worker in exchange for the promise not to compete. Making a job offer contingent on signing a noncompete agreement probably satisfies this requirement, because the worker is receiving a benefit (a job) in exchange for the promise. It's more difficult to provide an existing worker with a benefit, but usually coupling the agreement with a promotion or a raise will do the trick.

Be reasonable. A noncompete agreement must also be "reasonable." This means that the agreement can't:

- last too long
- cover too wide a geographic area, or
- prohibit a former worker from engaging in too many types of businesses.

Generally, the biggest issue with noncompete agreements is how long the noncompete agreement lasts. In most states, there's no set rule, and noncompete agreements ranging from six months to two years are generally considered "reasonable," while anything longer than that will receive closer scrutiny. Some states place statutory limits on how long a noncompete agreement can last. Check your state's law to make sure any agreement you create complies with your state's legal restrictions.

Nonsolicitation Agreements

It's inevitable: If your company is a service or sales business, workers will develop relationships with the company's best clients and customers. Similarly, employees often develop close working relationships with each other. But when an employee or independent contractor leaves, your company will probably want to stop him or her from using those relationships to solicit its clients' business and steal away other valuable workers. With a little advance planning, you can accomplish this by using a nonsolicitation agreement.

A nonsolicitation agreement is exactly what it sounds like: an agreement in which the worker promises not to solicit your company's clients and customers, for his or her own benefit or for the benefit of a competitor, after leaving your company. A nonsolicitation agreement can also contain a promise by the worker not to solicit other employees to leave when he or she quits or moves on.

Often, a nonsolicitation agreement is part of a larger employment agreement, noncompete agreement, or nondisclosure agreement. But it doesn't need to be. For example, if your company isn't concerned about a former employee competing against it but just wants to prevent him or her from stealing its customers and clients, a nonsolicitation agreement alone will do the trick.

Nonsolicitation agreements are effective tools for protecting your company's clients and customers. And if your company is located in a state such as California, which doesn't enforce noncompete agreements against employees, nonsolicitation agreements may be one of the only ways to discourage employees from going to work for a competitor or opening a competing business.

Of course, there are some limits on nonsolicitation agreements. Courts sometimes won't enforce a nonsolicitation agreement that makes it too difficult for an employee to earn a living or unfairly limits a competitor's ability to hire workers or solicit customers through legitimate means. Generally, courts will balance your company's and the employee's circumstances to judge whether a nonsolicitation agreement is fair.

As with most things in law, the key to drafting an effective nonsolicitation agreement is to be reasonable. A judge who thinks the agreement is overreaching may refuse to enforce it at all. For instance, if your company is worried about an employee stealing only a specific client or clients, it's best to limit the nonsolicitation agreement to those clients instead of creating a blanket prohibition on soliciting any customers. Similarly, if there are a few specific employees you're afraid the departing employee will try to take, list them, too. Remember, the more reasonable the agreement, the easier it will be to enforce (if it comes to that).

Just like noncompete agreements, nonsolicitation agreements must comply with some basic legal requirements before a judge will agree to enforce them.

Your company must have a valid business reason. A judge who reviews a nonsolicitation agreement will want to see a valid business reason for putting restraints on a former employee. (As tempting as it might be, a company can't keep a former employee from soliciting its customers and employees just because it wants to.) This valid business reason can include:

- protecting a valuable customer list
- protecting trade secrets and other confidential information, or
- protecting the business from the mass departure of valuable employees with specialized skills, knowledge, and access to trade secrets.

Your company's customer list has to be worth protecting. If the average person could figure out who your company's customers or clients are just by looking in the yellow pages, a judge probably won't enforce a nonsolicitation agreement against a former employee who tries to get the company's business. Unless your company has spent a lot of time, energy, and money establishing its client database (and it contains information that isn't readily available to the general public), the list may not merit protection.

Employees and customers can leave voluntarily. Nonsolicitation agreements generally don't (and can't) prevent a client, customer, or employee from moving to a competitor voluntarily. There isn't much a company can do to stop its other employees from leaving to join the former employee at a new company, as long as the departing employee hasn't improperly solicited them (and as long as the departing employees aren't subject to noncompete agreements). And if customers want to take their business to a competitor, a nonsolicitation agreement probably isn't going to be much help, unless the departing employee has improperly pressured them or used your company's information (for example, the prices the company has charged the customer in the past) to get their business.

Hiring From Competitors

Although your company may be most concerned about protecting its own business, trade secret laws are a two-way street: Competitors are just as intent on preventing your company from taking what belongs to them. If your company oversteps the bounds of trade secret laws—even unwittingly—it might end up in a heap of trouble.

Sometimes, what makes a prospective employee most desirable is also what makes him or her a risky hire. Although no law could require a person to erase his or her memory, a new employee who uses a former employer's trade secrets while working for your company poses a serious lawsuit risk.

Some potential trade secret violations are obvious, such as explicitly asking a new employee to reveal trade secrets, violate a confidentiality agreement, or violate a nonsolicitation agreement. Always tread very carefully if you want to hire someone who is bound by a noncompete agreement; you might want some help from a good employment law attorney. Even if your company wins, fights between competitors over employees bound by noncompete agreements can be expensive and downright nasty.

Although it's less obvious, it's just as important not to create a situation in which the employee will be likely to, or even tempted to, reveal trade secrets. Even if no one at your company specifically asks for the information, the company could be liable for a trade secret law violation if an employee reveals a former employer's trade secrets and your company created a fertile environment for the deed. For example, if you hire someone who you know has knowledge of a competitor's trade secrets, and put that employee in a job where it's likely he or she will use that trade secret information to your advantage, your company could be held liable in a trade secret misappropriation or unfair trade practices lawsuit, even if no one directly asked the employee to use the competitor's trade secrets.

To avoid winding up on the losing end of a trade secret lawsuit, consider the following:

- **Honor noncompete agreements.** If you really want to hire someone who's bound by a noncompete agreement, be honest about it. Talk to the former employer and negotiate some sort of arrangement. Sometimes, companies will allow a new employer to buy out an employee's noncompete, or they will agree to release an employee from a noncompete if your company promises to impose certain security measures.
- **Get promises from the new hire.** Before hiring employees, verify that they will not be bringing trade secrets and will not need to use a former employer's trade secrets in order to do their jobs well.

- **Do your own research.** Don't trust the employee's opinion about who owns what. Many employees don't understand intellectual property laws and think that anything they create belongs to them. This isn't always so. Many people also don't take agreements they signed seriously, but your company should. Ask to review any agreement the new hire signed with a former employer, even if the employee assures you it's "nothing serious" or it doesn't apply to the new job.

- **Manage the situation.** Don't put an employee in a job where use of a former employer's trade secrets is inevitable.

Legal Dos and Don'ts: Trade Secrets

Do:

- **Keep your own secrets.** Treat your company's trade secrets like the valuable commodities they are by keeping them in a secure location (such as a locked file cabinet) and revealing them only if and when necessary. If your company doesn't treat its trade secrets in a confidential way, it will be tough to convince a court to help you stop others from revealing them.
- **Keep track of who knows what.** Carefully label everything your company considers a trade secret, and implement procedures to track which employees have access to them. For example, you might require employees to use a sign-in sheet to access confidential information or keep a roster of all employees who have access to customer lists.
- **Use nondisclosure agreements.** From employees to independent contractors to customers to vendors, using confidentiality agreements gives your company a triple dose of protection. The agreements let these people know what information you consider secret, bind people to keep those secrets, and provide proof that your company actively safeguarded its trade secrets.

Don't:

- **Dip into your competitor's pool.** No matter how tempting it is, your company shouldn't hire a competitor's employee in order to get at the competitor's trade secrets. Company executives who engage in this type of sneaky behavior risk a lawsuit, fines, and possible jail time.
- **Cry "wolf."** If you classify every company document as a trade secret, employees won't know what's really worthy of protection. Courts won't know, either, and your company might actually get less protection for its real trade secrets as a result.
- **Overreach in trying to restrict your employees.** Do some research (and perhaps talk to a lawyer) before implementing a noncompete, nondisclosure, or nonsolicitation agreement. Companies that go too far in their efforts to prohibit employees from taking away business, other employees, or information can find themselves in court.

Test Your Knowledge

Questions

1. Your company must get a patent to make sure its trade secrets are protected from unauthorized use by others. ☐ True ☐ False

2. Independent contractors have a duty not to reveal their clients' trade secrets, even if they never sign a nondisclosure agreement. ☐ True ☐ False

3. All of a company's internal documents should be marked "Confidential," just to be safe. ☐ True ☐ False

4. A company can lose its trade secret protection if it reveals the secret information on its website or in publicly available documents. ☐ True ☐ False

5. Companies can use nondisclosure agreements to prohibit nonemployees with whom it works—such as vendors or customers—from revealing trade secrets. ☐ True ☐ False

6. All companies should ask every employee to sign a noncompete agreement. ☐ True ☐ False

7. Companies should give employees something in exchange for signing a noncompete or nonsolicitation agreement. ☐ True ☐ False

8. A company can use a nonsolicitation agreement to prevent customers from taking their business to a competitor. ☐ True ☐ False

9. As long as no one at your company asks a new hire to reveal a former employer's trade secrets, your company cannot be sued for trade secret theft. ☐ True ☐ False

10. It's best not to ask an applicant whether he or she is subject to a noncompete agreement, because that protects your company from legal problems. ☐ True ☐ False

Answers

1. False. Trade secret protection is do-it-yourself; you don't have to file anything with the government.

2. False. Although employees have an automatic duty not to reveal their employer's trade secrets, independent contractors do not—which is why they should be required to sign a nondisclosure agreement if they will work with the company's trade secrets.

3. False. You should designate only truly secret information as "Confidential," so employees know what they are obligated to protect and courts will know that your company didn't unreasonably restrict employees.

4. True. If your company reveals its own trade secrets, it cannot expect a court to prevent others from revealing them.

5. True. Your company can enter into nondisclosure agreements with customers, vendors, other businesses with which it's considering joint ventures, and others who are not employees.

6. False. Noncompete agreements are illegal in some states, and others prohibit employers from using them unless they are necessary. If you ask every employee to sign a noncompete agreement, your company will have a tough time convincing a court that it really had to go to such lengths to protect its business.

7. True. Your company should give something of value to employees whom it asks to sign a noncompete or nonsolicitation agreement, to make sure that a court treats it as a legally binding contract.

8. False. Your customers are free to take their business wherever they wish. A nonsolicitation agreement prohibits a former employee from actively going after their business but doesn't limit your customers in any way.

9. False. Your company can also get in trouble if it puts an employee in a work situation where disclosure of the former employer's trade secrets is virtually inevitable.

10. False. If your company hires an employee who is bound by a noncompete agreement with a previous employer, the previous employer might ask you to fire the employee or otherwise honor the agreement. If your company fails to comply, it could be facing a lawsuit.

Handling Workplace Problems

No manager likes dealing with workplace problems. Misconduct, harassment, interpersonal problems, and violent outbursts are all issues most of us would rather avoid if at all possible. But, as a manager, you must get involved. If you ignore such issues, you risk even more serious problems for you and your company, ranging from poor performance and bad morale to workplace injuries, violence, and lawsuits.

In this chapter, we provide some information about, and techniques for handling, common workplace problems. We cover:

- creating and enforcing discipline policies
- tips on handling a workplace investigation
- retaliation
- violence in the workplace, and
- a company's responsibility for employees' actions.

Frequently Asked Questions About Handling Workplace Problems

How can I safely discipline employees?

Make sure your company has a clear written disciplinary policy that sets out the consequences of failing to meet its performance standards. Apply the policy fairly and consistently to all employees. And avoid claims of discrimination or favoritism by imposing similar discipline for similar offenses. (To learn more, see "Disciplining Workers," below.)

What should I do if an employee complains of harassment or other misconduct?

The most important thing to do is to take the complaint seriously. Make sure not to take any negative action against an employee who complains; this could be considered illegal retaliation. Report the complaint immediately, in accordance with company policy. If you are responsible for handling the complaint, investigate thoroughly. Once you get to the bottom of things, take action to remedy the situation, if necessary. (For more on handling workplace complaints, see "Investigating Complaints," below.)

How can my company prevent violence in the workplace?

There's no way to guarantee that violence will never occur in your company, but there are steps you can take to minimize the risk. For example, screen applicants to make sure that they have no criminal convictions for violent conduct. Make sure your company has both a zero-tolerance policy for threats or violence and a strict no-weapons policy. You can also learn and train other managers about the warning signs of violence. Most importantly, treat workers—even those you must discipline or fire—with dignity and respect. (For more, see "Workplace Violence," below.)

Frequently Asked Questions About Handling Workplace Problems (cont'd)

Can I fire or discipline an employee for complaining about discrimination or another workplace problem?

No. Most antidiscrimination laws forbid retaliation against employees who assert certain rights, such as complaining about discrimination, reporting unsafe working conditions, or making a workers' compensation claim. Both firing and discipline constitute retaliation. (To learn more about what retaliation is and how to avoid it, see "Retaliation," below.)

Is the company responsible if one of our workers injures a customer?

Yes and no. If the worker is doing his or her job when the injury happens, your company is probably legally responsible. The company might also be liable for criminal acts a worker commits against a customer, client, or coworker if the company knew, or should have known, that the worker was dangerous and failed to prevent it. (For more, see "Liability for an Employee's Actions," below.)

Disciplining Workers

Most managers don't like to discipline employees. It's unpleasant to give criticism, even when an employee desperately needs it. But an effective, carefully administered disciplinary policy is an invaluable workplace tool.

Advantages of a Good Disciplinary Policy

A clear and effective disciplinary policy offers many benefits, including:

- **Clear guidelines for employee behavior.** A straightforward, easy-to-understand disciplinary policy will tell employees what the company expects of them and what conduct will not be tolerated. Enforcing the policy uniformly will show

employees that you take these rules seriously and administer them fairly.

- **Improved performance.** Employees who don't know what you expect—or don't know that they aren't measuring up—are not going to improve. A disciplinary meeting allows you to let the employee know what's going on, listen to the employee's explanation, and collaborate together to come up with a solution.

- **Employee morale.** The employee you discipline is not likely to enjoy a morale boost, but the rest of your employees will. Just like siblings, other employees do not like to see a coworker "getting away with it." And if a problem employee is allowed to misbehave without suffering any consequences, others in the workforce will assume that they can get away with slacking off or misbehaving, creating an even larger problem.

- **Protection against employee lawsuits.** If your company informs employees of the consequences of poor behavior and enforces its policy fairly, it can buy itself some insurance in future disputes. It will be more difficult for an employee to argue wrongful termination if the company can show that employees knew what types of conduct would result in discipline and that this particular employee violated a clearly defined workplace rule.

Writing a Disciplinary Policy

The trick to writing an effective disciplinary policy is to give employees clear notice of the consequences of poor behavior without locking the company into following one course of action in every situation. For example, even though your company may generally follow a policy of progressive discipline (for instance, a first offense is met with a verbal warning, a second offense with a written warning, and so on), you want to reserve the right to immediately fire an employee who crosses the line.

More importantly, you should avoid even a hint of a promise that employees will not be fired unless they engage in specified misconduct. You may find that employees dream up bad acts you never considered or that your company has to fire employees for reasons entirely unrelated to their performance or behavior (an economic downturn or a plant closing, for example).

Breaking the Bad News

If an employee violates a company rule or fails to live up to performance standards, you will have to dispense the discipline promised in your company's disciplinary policy. Here are some guidelines for doing so:

- **Don't procrastinate.** Set up a meeting with the employee right away. The sooner you let the employee know there's a problem, the sooner he or she will have an opportunity to improve.
- **Keep it private.** Meet one on one with the employee to discuss the problem. Make sure to meet in a private place, out of the earshot of coworkers or others to avoid embarrassing the employee.
- **Be honest.** The purpose of this meeting is to notify the employee of his or her poor behavior or performance so that the employee can improve. You must tell the employee precisely what the problem is, so you can figure out, together, how to correct it.
- **Collaborate.** Employees are most likely to improve when they participate in coming up with an action plan for improvement. When you meet with the employee, explain why the employee's performance or conduct is creating problems for the company and ask for the employee's help in coming up with a solution. You're much more likely to get positive results if you work with the employee to resolve the problem.
- **Be respectful.** Even bad news should be delivered with respect. Let the employee know that you want to see

improvement and that you will help if you can. Set aside enough time for the meeting so that the employee will have an opportunity to respond. Make sure to listen to the employee's concerns; it may be that a performance problem is the result of a misunderstanding or could be easily corrected if you work together.

- **Write it down.** Document every disciplinary meeting, action, or discussion you have with an employee and place that record in the employee's personnel file. In the case of a written warning, give the employee a copy of the warning and ask him or her to sign it to acknowledge receipt. These records help the company show that you informed the employee of the problem if the employee decides to file a lawsuit later.

- **Follow up.** If you tell an employee that you must see improvement by a certain date, make sure to follow up. Check with the employee periodically to make sure that things are going smoothly and improving. If the problem persists, get ready to take the next step in your disciplinary policy.

Investigating Complaints

Most managers are anxious when faced with complaints of workplace misconduct, such as violence or harassment. And with good reason: Such complaints can lead to workplace tension, government investigations, and even costly legal battles. If the company mishandles the complaint, even

unintentionally, it may unwittingly put itself out of business.

However, a company that takes complaints seriously and follows a careful strategy for dealing with them can reduce the likelihood of a lawsuit and even improve employee relations in the process.

This section provides some basic rules to follow if you receive a complaint of workplace misconduct. (For an in-depth discussion of how to conduct an investigation of harassment or other misconduct at work, see *The Essential Guide to Workplace Investigations*, by Lisa Guerin (Nolo).)

- **Promptly report any complaints you receive.** If your company has established procedures for making or reporting complaints, follow them to the letter. As a manager, you are considered a representative of the company. Once you know about a complaint, the company is considered to be on notice—and it will be responsible for taking action to resolve the issue. This means that you must report complaints to the appropriate person or department right away.

- **Keep an open mind.** Many managers have a hard time believing that harassment, violent behavior, or other misconduct could be happening right under their noses. As a result, they often fail to take complaints seriously, assuming that the complaint could not possibly be true. Unfortunately, ignoring a complaint is a surefire way to land your company in court.

- **Treat the employee with respect.** Employees often find it extremely difficult to come forward, particularly if the complaint involves harassment. They feel vulnerable and afraid, which can have an impact on the quality of their work. It can also lead them to seek outside assistance from a lawyer. When an employee comes to you with concerns, be understanding. An employee who feels that you are taking the complaint seriously is less likely to take the complaint to a government agency or to court.

- **Don't retaliate against the complainer.** It is against the law to punish someone for complaining about discrimination, harassment, illegal conduct, or unsafe working conditions. The most obvious forms of retaliation are termination, discipline, demotion, pay cuts, or threats to do any of these things. More subtle forms of retaliation may include changing the shift hours or work area of the accuser, changing the accuser's job responsibilities, or isolating the accuser by leaving him or her out of meetings and other office functions. (To learn more, see "Retaliation," below.)

- **Follow established procedures.** If your company has an employee handbook or other documented policies relating to discrimination, harassment, or other workplace misconduct, follow those policies. Don't open the company up to claims of unfair treatment by bending the rules for a favorite employee.

- **Interview the people involved.** If you are responsible for investigating the complaint, start by talking to the person who complained. Find out exactly what the employee's concerns are. Get the details: who said or did what, when, where, and who else was there. Take notes of your interviews. Then talk to any employees who are being accused of misconduct. Get details from them as well. Be sure to interview any witnesses who may have seen or heard problematic conduct.

- **Look for corroboration or contradiction.** Many workplace complaints, especially those of harassment, come down to one person's word against another's. Often, the accuser and the accused offer different versions of incidents, leaving you with no way of knowing who's telling the truth. If you conduct the investigation, you may have to turn to other sources for clues. For example, schedules, time cards, and other attendance records (for trainings, meetings, and so on) may help you determine whether everyone was where they claimed to be. Witnesses— including coworkers, vendors, customers, or friends—may have seen all or part of an incident. And in some cases, documents will prove one side right. After all, it's hard to argue with a sexually provocative email or a written threat to harm a coworker.

- **Keep it confidential.** Complaints can polarize a workplace. Workers will likely side with either the complaining employee or the accused employee, and the rumor mill will start working overtime. Worse, if too many details about the complaint are leaked, you may be accused of damaging the reputation of the alleged victim or alleged wrongdoer, and get yourself (and the company) slapped with a defamation lawsuit. Avoid these problems by insisting on confidentiality and practicing it in your investigation.

- **Write it all down.** Take notes during your interviews, if you conduct the investigation. Before the interview is over, go back through your notes with the interviewee to make sure you got it right. Keep a log of your investigation. Write down the steps you take to get at the truth, including the dates and places of interviews you conduct. Keep track of any documents you review. Document any action taken against the accused or the reasons for deciding not to take action. This written record will protect the company later if the employee claims that you ignored the complaint or conducted a one-sided investigation.

- **Cooperate with government agencies.** If the employee makes a complaint with a government agency—such as the federal Equal Employment Opportunity Commission (EEOC) or Occupational Safety and Health Administration (OSHA)—the agency may investigate. It will probably ask your company to provide certain documents, give its side of the story, and explain any efforts it made to deal with the complaint. Be cautious but cooperative. Try to provide the agency with the materials it requests, but remember that the agency

is gathering evidence that could be used against the company later. This is a good time to consider hiring a lawyer.

- **Consider hiring an experienced investigator.** Many law firms and private consulting agencies will investigate workplace complaints for a fee. You might consider bringing in outside help if more than one employee complains; the accused is a high-ranking official in your business (like the president or CEO); the accuser has publicized the complaint, either in the workplace or in the media; the accusations are extreme (allegations of rape or assault, for example); or you feel too personally involved to make a fair, objective decision.

- **Take appropriate action against the wrongdoer(s).** If you are responsible for disciplinary decisions, you'll have to decide how to handle the complaint. Once you have gathered all the information available, sit down and decide what you think really happened. If you conclude that some form of misconduct occurred, figure out how to discipline the wrongdoer(s) appropriately. Termination may be warranted for violence, extreme misconduct, or egregious harassment, such as threats, stalking, or repeated and unwanted physical contact. Lesser discipline, such as a warning or counseling, might be in order if the misconduct arises out of a misunderstanding (a blundered attempt to ask a coworker on a date, for example). Once you have decided on an appropriate action, take it quickly, document it, and notify the accuser.

Checklist: Ten Steps to an Effective Workplace Investigation

If you are tapped to conduct a workplace investigation, follow these steps to get the job done right. (For more information on investigating workplace issues, including detailed instructions on looking into harassment, discrimination, violence, and theft, see *The Essential Guide to Workplace Investigations*, by Lisa Guerin (Nolo).)

1. **Decide whether to investigate.** Before you put on your detective's hat, take some time to decide whether you really need to investigate. In a few situations—for example, if all employees agree on what happened or the problem appears to be minor—you may reasonably decide that a full-blown investigation is unnecessary. Usually, however, it's best to err on the side of conducting an investigation. If the problem is more serious than it seemed, failing to investigate can lead to legal trouble and continuing problems. And sometimes, you just can't tell how widespread or substantial a problem is until you do a little poking around.

2. **Take immediate action, if necessary.** You might have to act right away—even before you begin your investigation—if a situation is volatile or could otherwise cause immediate harm to your company. If an employee is accused of sexually assaulting a coworker, stealing valuable trade secrets, or bringing a weapon to work, you'll probably want to suspend the accused employee temporarily, with pay, while you look into the matter. But be careful not to prejudge the situation or lead the accused employee to believe that you've already made up your mind.

3. **Choose an investigator.** You'll want an investigator who is experienced in investigation techniques, is impartial and perceived as impartial by the employees involved, and is capable of acting—and, if necessary, testifying in court—professionally about the situation. If your company has someone who meets this job description on the payroll (perhaps you!) you're in luck. If not, you can look into hiring an outside investigator.

4. **Plan the investigation.** Take some time up front to organize your thoughts. Gather any information you already have about the problem, including an employee complaint, a supervisor's report, written warnings, or materials that are part of the problem (such as X-rated emails or threatening letters). Using this information as your guide, think about what you'll need to find out to decide what happened. Whom will you interview and what will you ask? Are there additional documents that employees or supervisors might have? Is there anyone who witnessed important events (or should have)?

5. **Conduct interviews.** The goal of every investigation is to gather information, and the most basic way to do that is by asking people questions. Most investigations involve at least two interviews: one of the employee accused of wrongdoing and another of the employee who complained or was the victim. Sometimes, you will also want to interview witnesses who

Checklist: Ten Steps to an Effective Workplace Investigation (cont'd)

may have seen or heard something important. When you interview people, try to elicit as much information as possible by asking open-ended questions.

6. **Gather documents and other evidence.** Almost every investigation will rely to some extent on documents: personnel files, email messages, company policies, correspondence, and so on. And some investigations will require you to gather other types of evidence, such as drugs, a weapon, photographs, or stolen items.

7. **Evaluate the evidence.** The most challenging part of many investigations—especially if witnesses disagree or contradict each other—is figuring out what actually happened. There are some proven methods of deciding where the truth lies, which all of us use in our everyday lives. You'll want to consider, for example, whose story makes the most sense, whose demeanor was more convincing, and who (if anyone) has a motive to deceive you. And in some situations, you may just have to acknowledge that you don't have enough information to decide what happened.

8. **Take action.** If you conclude that serious wrongdoing occurred, you will have to take disciplinary action quickly to make sure your company isn't held liable for that employee's behavior and to protect your company and other workers from harm. In deciding how to handle these situations, you should consider a number of factors, including how serious the actions were and how your company has handled similar problems.

9. **Document the investigation.** Once your investigation is complete, you should write an investigation report that explains what you did and why. This will not only give the company some protection from lawsuits relating to the investigation, but will also provide a written record in case of future misconduct by the same employee(s). Among other things, your report should explain how and when the problem came to the company's attention, what interviews you conducted, what evidence you considered, what conclusions you reached, and what you did about the problem.

10. **Follow up.** The last step is to follow up with the employees to make sure that you've solved the problem that led to the investigation. Has the misconduct stopped? Has the wrongdoer met any requirements imposed as a result of the investigation, such as a training course on sexual harassment? If the investigation revealed any systemic workplace problems (such as widespread confusion about company policy or lack of training on issues like workplace diversity or proper techniques for dealing with customers), some training might be in order.

Retaliation

When an employee exercises a legal right—such as complaining about discrimination, harassment, or unsafe working conditions—you must treat that employee with care. Don't take any action that the employee might see as punishment or retaliation for complaining. It is illegal to retaliate against an employee for complaining about these issues, and retaliation is often in the eye of the beholder.

All employers, managers, supervisors, and human resources professionals should become familiar with the law of retaliation, because retaliation claims are becoming more and more common, especially with respect to complaints about discrimination and harassment. And they are also becoming more costly: Juries seem especially offended by retaliation and tend to slam retaliating employers with high damage awards. Even if the original complaint turns out to be unfounded, the employee can still win a retaliation claim by showing that something negative happened because of the complaint.

Retaliation Defined

An employer retaliates when it punishes a worker for reporting or complaining of discrimination, harassment, or even unsafe working conditions. Any negative job action, such as demotion, discipline, firing, salary reduction, negative evaluation, change in job assignment, or change in shift assignment, can constitute retaliation.

The Supreme Court has held that any materially adverse action against an employee may constitute retaliation under Title VII, if the action taken might deter a reasonable employee from making a complaint. (*Burlington Northern & Santa Fe Railway v. White*, 548 U.S. 53 (2006).) The Court found that enforcement of Title VII depends on employees' willingness to come forward with complaints, so the statute must be interpreted to provide broad protection from retaliation.

Employees are also protected from retaliation for participating in an investigation of discrimination or harassment. In other words, the employee need not be the source of the complaint: If the employee acts as a witness or answers an investigator's questions about another employee's complaint, the employee is protected. (*Crawford v. Metropolitan Government of Nashville and Davidson County, Tennessee*, 129 S.Ct. 846 (2009).)

Good Intentions Can Still Be Retaliatory

Retaliation obviously includes any action intended to punish the employee for complaining. However, it can also include actions that managers take with the best of intentions, if those actions have a negative impact on the employee.

For example:

- A female employee complains that her supervisor is sexually harassing her. In response, you change the employee from the day shift to the night shift so that she doesn't have to work with the supervisor anymore. Even though you didn't intend to hurt the employee, this action could

Lessons From the Real World

Jayson Lewis and Michael Gonzales, two employees at Video Only, went to an attorney after they felt they were subjected to harassment on the basis of their race, national origin, and religion. The attorney sent a letter to the store's owner, detailing a number of incidents by managers and coworkers. The owner called in the company's area manager and the manager of the store where the employees worked, and asked them to look into the matter and report back to him. He also asked the company's general manager to hire an investigator to be ready to investigate the complaint.

The general manager hired Lynn McKinney, a private investigator who had done some theft investigations for the company before, to "check out" Lewis and Gonzales. He didn't tell McKinney about the harassment complaints. McKinney ran criminal background checks on Lewis and Gonzales, asked the mother of Lewis's fiancée whether Lewis had ever beaten her, and asked Lewis's former coworkers if Lewis had ever sued anybody for race

discrimination. Gonzales was told by his former manager and family members that a private investigator was also asking disturbing questions about him. Gonzales and Lewis filed charges of harassment and retaliation at the EEOC.

The court found that Video Only had retaliated against Lewis and Gonzales by investigating them. The court found that the investigation was an adverse employment action that most employees would find aggravating, and that might dissuade employees from complaining about discrimination. The court also found that the investigation was conducted precisely because the employees complained of harassment. Although the company argued that it had intended to investigate the harassment claims rather than the employees, and its investigator had simply misunderstood what the company wanted, the court rejected that argument.

Equal Employment Opportunity Commission v. Gonzales et al., Civil Case No. 06-1362 (D. Oregon 2008).

be retaliatory if the employee preferred the day shift.

• An African American employee complains that the store in which he works is racially hostile toward him because his coworkers tell racial jokes and refer to him with racially derogatory names. In response, you transfer the employee to another store. This action

could be retaliatory if the new store is farther from the employee's home or is less desirable in some other way.

In both of the above examples, the manager made the mistake of focusing on the complaining employee rather than focusing on the problem. When someone complains or exercises a legal right, the employer's job is to fix the problem, not to avoid it by removing the complaining employee from the situation. By focusing on the complaining employee, the manager took actions that could be viewed as retaliatory.

With discrimination and harassment, you won't need to separate workers every time someone makes a complaint. Unless the complaining worker and the accused worker share an office, work closely together, or have a reporting relationship, you can simply tell each to stay away from the other until you (or someone else assigned to investigate) get to the bottom of things. However, if the complaint is serious and the employees work together, your best bet is to separate them by moving the accused worker. Even if the investigation later shows that the complaint was unfounded, the accused worker will have a hard time showing that your action was unreasonable, given the circumstances.

Strategies to Prevent Retaliation

As soon as an employee complains about discrimination, harassment, or unsafe working conditions, retaliation becomes a possibility. You can reduce your chances of facing retaliation claim by taking the following precautionary steps:

- **Establish a policy against retaliation.** Your company should have in place a clear policy against retaliation. It should spell out exactly what retaliation is, and it should make perfectly clear that retaliation will not be tolerated. It should also tell employees what steps to take if they feel they are being retaliated against.

- **Communicate with the complaining employee.** Explain that the company is taking the complaint seriously. Tell the employee that you want to hear about anything that the employee considers hostile or negative. Refer the employee to your company's antiretaliation policy and explain what retaliation is.

- **Keep complaints confidential.** The fewer people who know about a complaint, the smaller the chances are that someone will retaliate against the complainer. Of course, if you investigate the employee's complaint, you will have to tell some people about it. Make sure that you only tell the people who absolutely need to know. And when you tell them, explain what retaliation is and tell them that it is prohibited. Take immediate disciplinary action against any employee who retaliates against a complaining employee.

- **Document, document, document.** Take notes of everything you do to prevent retaliation. Send the complaining employee a letter confirming what you have said about retaliation.

Actions That Are Not Retaliatory

An adverse action is retaliatory only if it is done *because* the employee complained. The company is free to take adverse actions against an employee for other reasons, even if that employee has complained or participated in an investigation. For example, the following actions would not qualify as retaliation:

- If the employee performs poorly, you can give the employee a negative evaluation.
- If the employee is habitually late for work, you can discipline the employee for tardiness.
- If the employee brings a gun to work, you can fire the employee.

The problem is that some employees may claim that an adverse action is retaliation even if your decision had nothing to do with the employee's complaint or participation in an investigation.

If you must take an adverse action against an employee who has complained, be prepared to show that you had valid reasons, unrelated to the complaint, for taking the action. Your reasons will be most persuasive if they are supported by documentation—like performance evaluations and disciplinary warnings—showing that the employee's performance problems predated the complaint.

(For more information on employees who report workplace health and safety issues, see Chapter 7. For more information on illegal reasons to fire employees, see Chapter 12.)

Workplace Violence

Unless you've been hiding under a rock, you've heard horror stories about violence in the workplace. A disgruntled worker, an employee's former lover, or an enraged customer or client bursts through the door, shooting first and asking questions later.

Workplace violence is a major problem in the United States: Government studies estimate that there are about two million assaults and violent threats made against workers each year. And such violence costs businesses more than $36 billion each year, according to the Workplace Violence Research Institute.

So what can you do to prevent violence in the workplace? More than you might think. You can't guarantee your company will never face a violent incident, but you can take steps to reduce its risk. And your company can adopt a policy and a safety plan to improve its chances of avoiding trouble.

Workplace Violence Defined

Workplace violence can take many forms and come from several different sources. Perhaps the most familiar source of violence is the infamous "disgruntled employee": the former or current worker who returns to the workplace to avenge a perceived injustice or settle a score. But violence might also be committed by an angry customer or client or by a stranger intent on robbing a business or assaulting its workers. And domestic violence can spill into the workplace.

You should treat any conduct that is menacing or assaulting as violence under your company's policies. This includes threats, actual assaults, unwelcome physical contact, destruction of property, stalking, and intimidation.

Lessons From the Real World

Rena Weeks walked into the lion's den in July of 1991, when she started working as a secretary to Martin Greenstein, a partner in the law firm of Baker & McKenzie. Greenstein treated Weeks boorishly right from the start, reaching into her breast pocket, grabbing her rear end, asking her about "the wildest thing she'd ever done," and pulling her shoulders back so he could see "which breast is bigger."

Weeks complained almost immediately. The firm transferred her to another position, but she still felt uncomfortable. Shortly thereafter, Weeks's performance was questioned, and she left the firm. Weeks's complaint was not investigated.

Sound like the wrong way to handle a complaint? The jury sure didn't like it, especially when they heard that Greenstein had been accused by at least seven other women of sexual harassment and the firm had never done a thing about it. There was no documentation in Greenstein's file, he was never disciplined, and no investigation was ever conducted. What's worse, many of the women who complained were transferred or fired.

Perhaps the final blow to the law firm's defense was the fact that Greenstein himself was finally fired—in the midst of the lawsuit—but not for sexual harassment. He was fired immediately when the firm learned that he had been improperly dating documents. Apparently that was an offense that merited firing, but propositioning and fondling a long line of female subordinates was not. The law firm was ordered to pay Weeks almost $4 million, not including attorney fees.

Weeks v. Baker & McKenzie, 63 Cal.App.4th 1128 (1998).

Warning Signs

There is no "profile" of a perpetrator of workplace violence; like any other crime, just about anyone can commit workplace violence. But experts agree that an employee who commits a violent act often exhibits certain signs of trouble. All managers should keep an eye out for clues that intervention might be necessary. They include:

- an unexplained rise in absences
- angry outbursts at coworkers and customers
- verbal abuse or threats toward coworkers

- strained workplace relationships
- overreaction or resistance to even minor changes in the workplace
- lack of attention to one's own appearance, including hygiene
- comments about firearms or weapons
- signs of paranoia ("everyone's out to get me") or withdrawal, and
- substance abuse problems.

Clearly, not every worker who displays some of these traits poses a threat. There are numerous reasonable explanations for absences (a sick child, for example) or a decline in personal appearance (perhaps the end of a personal relationship that has nothing to do with the workplace). But a worker who demonstrates a number of these indicators—especially if the behavior appears to be intensifying—may need some help.

Preventing and Addressing Violence

In addition to watching for danger signs, there are a few other things you can do to reduce the incidence of violence in the workplace:

- **Screen applicants before hiring.** Check for past criminal convictions (if your state allows it), restraining orders, or a history of difficulties with coworkers. (See "Background Checks" in Chapter 1 for more information.) This is important to protect other workers, but also to protect the company's bottom line. An employer who doesn't properly investigate a potentially violent employee could face a lawsuit from a coworker or customer who is injured or harmed when the employee becomes violent.

- **Conduct evaluations and use your company's progressive discipline policy.** Experts say that employees are more likely to become violent if they believe they have been treated unfairly, taken by surprise, or sandbagged. Prevent these reactions by giving employees fair warning and a chance to improve on minor problems.

- **Treat workers with respect.** Always treat workers decently, especially when you have to discipline or fire them. Depriving a worker of dignity—by disparaging the person in front of coworkers or calling

the employee names—can trigger violent behavior.

- **Adopt a zero-tolerance policy toward workplace violence.** Create a company policy that states that violence of any kind—as defined above—will not be tolerated. Violence should be grounds for immediate termination.

- **Never allow weapons in the workplace.** Unless employees have a compelling need to be armed (for example, they work as security guards), don't allow weapons in the workplace. Ban weapons on company property, including the parking lot (if your state allows it; some don't). Immediately discipline any employee who violates the rule.

- **Consider an employee assistance program.** Workplace violence often begins off-site, with a failing marriage, a substance abuse problem, or money troubles. Help employees manage these problems with an employee assistance program (EAP) before they result in workplace violence. An EAP might include counseling, rehabilitation services, or anger management classes. For information on offering an EAP to employees, contact your company's insurance carrier; many offer EAP services as part of an overall mental health benefit.

- **Take threats seriously.** Investigate every incident of violence. Don't assume a worker "didn't mean it" or was just "blowing off steam." While you may think an incident was misperceived or exaggerated, you should make that decision only after looking into all the facts. If a threat seems serious, increase security and tell the police.

- **Develop a safety plan.** Instruct employees on what to do if violence starts. Plan escape routes and know where first aid supplies are. And have the telephone numbers of local police or building security handy, preferably on speed dial.
- **Require reporting.** Your company should require all employees to report any incident of violence that they witness. Stress that employees who report incidents of violence will be assured confidentiality to encourage reporting.
- **Train managers.** If you are responsible for company training, make sure other managers know the warning signs for violence, the safety plan, and the requirements of your company's reporting policy.

Domestic Violence in the Workplace

An employee's domestic violence issues can make their way into the workplace. Because the perpetrator is usually not a company employee, this presents unique prevention concerns. Among the strategies a company can adopt to address this problem are:

- increasing security whenever you become aware that an employee is a victim of domestic violence
- encouraging employees who are victims of domestic violence to report any potential problems or developments (if the employee's violent partner made a threat or is getting out of jail, for example)

- making sure that the security staff in the office or building are aware of any outstanding restraining orders or threats against your employees and know what the abuser looks like
- getting a restraining order (or helping the employee get one) that prohibits the abuser from entering the workplace; a handful of states allow employers to apply for such orders directly, and
- moving a victim of violence so she is not easily located by her abuser (for example, to a different floor or wing), which will protect her and buy your company some time to defuse a potentially violent encounter.

Liability for an Employee's Actions

Under a handful of legal theories, courts have held employers liable (that is, have allowed them to be sued) for injuries their employees have inflicted on others—whether the injured person is a coworker, a customer, or a complete stranger. Here, we explain those theories, along with a few steps you can take to keep your company out of this kind of trouble.

Employer Liability for Actions Within the Scope of Employment

Under a legal doctrine sometimes referred to in legal jargon as "respondeat superior," an employer is legally responsible for the actions of its employees. However, there's a big exception to this rule: An employer is liable only if the employee acted within the course and scope of the employment. In other words, if the employee was doing his or her job, carrying out company business, or acting on the employer's behalf, the employer will generally be liable.

The purpose of this rule is fairly simple: to hold employers responsible for the costs of doing business, including the cost of employee carelessness and misconduct. If the injury the employee caused is simply one of the risks of the business, the employer will be liable. But if the employee acted independently or purely out of personal motives, the employer might not be liable. Here are a couple of examples to illustrate the difference:

- A restaurant promises delivery in 30 minutes "or your next order is free." If a delivery person hits a pedestrian while trying frantically to beat the deadline, the company may be liable to the pedestrian.

- A technology services company gives its sales staff company cars to make sales calls. After work hours, a sales person hits a pedestrian while using the car to do personal errands. Most likely, the company cannot be sued for the incident.

Lessons From the Real World

Charles Smith was the superintendent of Amtrak's Rail Weld and Cropping Plant in New Haven, Connecticut. On March 20, 1981, Smith reprimanded one of the employees he supervised, Joseph Leonetti, for sitting in a restaurant eating breakfast when he should have been at work.

A few hours later, Leonetti came into Smith's office and shot Smith twice with a shotgun. Smith's kneecap was shattered, he was hospitalized for months, and he suffered a heart attack and a stroke related to the shooting.

Smith sued Amtrak, arguing that the company put him in harm's way by ignoring previous incidents involving Leonetti, who was never reported or disciplined for some prior violent behavior. Smith argued that Amtrak's failure to take these earlier incidents seriously led to his injury.

Amtrak contended that Smith would have been injured regardless of what it did. Amtrak pointed out that when Smith reprimanded Leonetti, he immediately responded violently. Therefore, the company argued, if Leonetti had been disciplined for his earlier misconduct, those disciplinary measures would have resulted in violence as well.

But the jury didn't buy it. They found that Amtrak's failure to take action after the earlier incidents led to the shooting and awarded Smith $3.5 million in damages.

Smith v. National Railroad Passenger Corporation, 856 F.2d 467 (2d Cir. 1988).

If your company is sued under this legal theory, the employee's victim generally won't have to show that the company should have known the employee might cause harm, or even that the company did anything demonstrably wrong. If the employee caused the harm while acting within the scope of employment, your company will have to answer to the victim.

Employer Carelessness in Hiring and Retaining Employees

Under two different legal theories, known as "negligent hiring" and "negligent retention," someone who is injured by an employee can sue the employer for failing to take reasonable care in selecting its workers. These legal theories apply even to actions workers take that are outside the scope of employment. In fact, they often are used to hold an employer responsible for a worker's violent criminal acts on the job, such as rape, murder, or robbery. However, an employer is responsible under these theories only if it acted carelessly (in other words, if it knew or should have known that an applicant or employee was unfit for the job, yet did nothing about it).

Here are a few situations in which employers have had to pay up:

- A pizza company hired a delivery driver without looking into his criminal past, which included a sexual assault conviction and an arrest for stalking a woman he met while delivering pizza for another company. After he raped a customer, he was sent to jail for 25 years and the pizza franchise was liable to his victim for negligent hiring.
- A car rental company hired a man who later raped a coworker. Had the company verified his résumé claims, it would have discovered that he was in prison for robbery during the years he claimed to be in high school and college. The company was liable to the coworker.
- A furniture company hired a delivery man without requiring him to fill out an application or performing a background check. The employee assaulted a female customer in her home with a knife. The company was liable to the customer for negligent hiring.

Many states have allowed claims for negligent hiring and retention. Although these lawsuits have not yet appeared in every state, the clear legal trend is to allow injured third parties to sue employers for hiring or keeping on a dangerous worker. So what can you do to keep your company out of trouble? Here are a few tips:

- **Perform background checks.** Run a routine background check before you hire an applicant. Verify information on résumés, look for criminal convictions (but only to the extent legally allowed in your state; see "Background Checks" in Chapter 1 for more information), and check driving records. These simple steps will weed out many dangerous workers and help show that your company was not careless in its hiring practices.

- **Use special care in hiring workers who will have a lot of public contact.** A company is more likely to be found responsible for a worker's actions if the job involves working with the public. Workers who go to a customer's home (those who make deliveries, perform home repairs, or manage apartment buildings, for example), workers who deal with children or the elderly, and workers whose jobs give them access to weapons (like security guards) all require more careful screening.

- **Root out problem employees immediately.** Under the theory of negligent retention, your company can be responsible for keeping a worker on after it learns (or should have been aware) that the worker posed a potential danger. If an employee has made violent threats against customers, brought an unauthorized weapon to work, or racked up a few moving violations, for example, take immediate action.

Lessons From the Real World

Minimed Inc. hired a pest control company to rid its facility of fleas. The company sprayed pesticide overnight. Some employees who reported to work the next day felt nauseated and ill from the fumes. One was Irma Hernandez, who felt sick and left work at noon. Her supervisor asked whether she felt well enough to drive home, and she said she did.

Ms. Hernandez rear-ended a car stopped at a red light on her way home. She told officers that she felt dizzy and light-headed immediately before the crash. The person Ms. Hernandez hit, Barbara Bussard, sued Minimed for her injuries, claiming that Ms. Hernandez was acting within the scope of her employment when she drove home.

The court agreed and held Minimed responsible for the accident. Although an employer is ordinarily not legally liable for any actions an employee might take while commuting to and from work, the court found that Ms. Hernandez was exposed to pesticide at work, within the scope of her employment. The court decided that it was fair to attribute the injuries to Minimed's actions because they were a foreseeable result of the pesticide exposure, even though they occurred after Ms. Hernandez left work.

Bussard v. Minimed, Inc., 105 Cal.App.4th 798 (Cal.App. 2d District, 2003).

Legal Dos and Don'ts: Handling Workplace Problems

Do:

- **Consider zero-tolerance policies.** Some workplace misconduct is so serious that firing is called for. If, after an investigation, you conclude that a worker has made serious threats of violence, committed egregious harassment, or brandished a weapon, show that worker the door.

- **Make the punishment fit the crime.** Just as some types of misconduct are clearly firing offenses, others just as clearly are not. A progressive discipline policy that differentiates between serious and minor problems will help employees know what is expected of them, and help you weed out the real troublemakers while getting minor miscreants to shape up.

- **Get help on the tough issues.** If you are faced with a potentially violent employee and you don't know what to do, a workplace violence consultant can help. A professional investigator can help you get to the bottom of a workplace dispute, if you feel like you are in over your head. You can find these professionals in the phone book or on the Internet.

Don't:

- **Drag your feet.** Once you discover or learn about an employment problem—whether it's a performance issue, harassing conduct, or threats of violence—take action right away. It's only human to put off unpleasant confrontations, but procrastinating will only compound the problem.

- **Minimize threats and outbursts.** None of us wants to believe that someone we know could become violent. But if you assume that a worker who threatens or rages is only "blowing off steam," you could be putting others in danger. Take all threats and violent acts seriously.

- **Blame the messenger.** Though it might not seem like it, a worker who complains of a workplace problem is doing you a favor. You then have a chance to investigate and act quickly to nip the problem in the bud. Take action against the problem, not against the worker who brought it to your attention.

Test Your Knowledge

Questions

1. Your company's progressive discipline policy should try to anticipate every conceivable type of employee misconduct, so employees will know what discipline will be imposed. ☐ True ☐ False

2. Employees can use a poorly written progressive discipline policy as part of a lawsuit against your company. ☐ True ☐ False

3. If an employee complains that she was sexually harassed, but the alleged harasser denies it, there's nothing the company can do. ☐ True ☐ False

4. You don't have to investigate every workplace incident or complaint. ☐ True ☐ False

5. If an employee complains that another employee is harassing him or her, it's best to move the complaining employee to another work area until you figure out what really happened. ☐ True ☐ False

6. Keeping complaints confidential can help you avoid claims of retaliation. ☐ True ☐ False

7. There's very little a company can do to reduce its risk of a violent workplace incident. ☐ True ☐ False

8. Employers in some states can get a restraining order that prohibits someone who has committed domestic violence against one of their employees from coming on the worksite. ☐ True ☐ False

9. A company can be sued for damage caused by an employee only for incidents that take place on the worksite, during work hours. ☐ True ☐ False

10. A company can be legally liable for an employee's criminal behavior. ☐ True ☐ False

Answers

1. False. You couldn't possibly list every possible employee offense, and you shouldn't try to. The best progressive discipline policies reserve the company's right to decide how to handle incidents on a case-by-case basis.

2. True. If the policy appears to lock the company into a particular course of action, and the company departs from it, then the worker might have a legal claim for breach of contract.

3. False. The investigator can talk to any witnesses, examine relevant documents (such as emails between the workers), and consider each employee's demeanor, motives, and consistency.

4. True. Although it's best to err on the side of investigating, there may be situations in which the alleged wrongdoing is extremely minor or the employees involved agree about what happened. In these cases, you may be able to skip the investigation.

5. False. If you move the employee who complained, the company could be accused of retaliation. If you must separate workers temporarily, it's a better idea to move the accused employee.

6. True. A negative employment action qualifies as retaliation only if it is done because an employee complained. Only people who know about a complaint are in a position to commit illegal retaliation.

7. False. Although there are no guarantees, treating employees with respect, and giving them fair warning of misconduct and performance problems through evaluations and progressive discipline, can help avert trouble.

8. True. Traditionally, only a victim of abuse could get this type of order, but the laws of some states allow employers to get them to protect an employee, as well.

9. False. A company can be held liable for any harm an employee causes within the course and scope of the employment, whether on-site or off, during work hours or not. But if the employee acted independently or purely out of personal motives, the employer probably won't be liable.

10. True. A company can be held liable for criminal acts a worker commits against a customer, client, or coworker if the company knew, or should have known, that the worker was dangerous and failed to prevent potential crimes (for example, by conducting a background check or screening before hiring a delivery- or repairperson who will enter customers' homes).

Firing Employees

Firing an employee is one of the toughest tasks you'll face as a manager. And because of the emotional stakes involved, it's also the task most likely to land your company in legal trouble. When you fire a worker, some amount of his or her dignity, self-esteem, and livelihood is on the line; it's understandable that a poorly handled termination might lead a disgruntled employee to the courthouse door.

Because firing poses considerable risks to your company, it pays to consider the decision carefully. In this chapter, we will explain some of the legal rules that govern employment termination, discuss some factors you should consider in deciding whether to fire, and give you advice about how to break the news. We cover:

- legal and illegal reasons for firing
- special rules for employees with contracts
- deciding whether to fire workers, and
- how to conduct the termination meeting.

(Layoffs are covered in Chapter 13. For information on your company's obligations to departing workers—whether they quit, are fired, or are laid off—see Chapter 14.)

Frequently Asked Questions About Firing Employees

Can at-will workers be fired for any reason?

No. A company cannot fire an at-will worker for illegal reasons, such as to discriminate, retaliate, or get rid of a whistleblower. However, as long as your reason is not illegal, you don't need a business-related reason to let an at-will worker go. For example, you can fire an at-will worker simply because you don't get along with him or her. (See "Illegal Reasons for Firing Employees," below, for more information.)

Does a written employment contract limit our right to fire?

If an employee has a written contract, the terms of the contract will dictate the circumstances under which the worker can be fired. (See "Firing Employees With Employment Contracts," below, for more on written agreements.)

How can I protect our company from lawsuits when firing workers?

Make sure you always have a legitimate, business-related reason—known in the legal world as "good cause"—to fire. (While this is not required to fire an at-will worker, it is always a good idea.) And make sure you have documented evidence that the worker didn't meet company standards, in the form of performance reviews, disciplinary warnings, and so on. Consistency is also important. (For more tips, see "Making the Decision to Fire," below.)

Frequently Asked Questions About Firing Employees (cont'd)

Does it really matter how we fire workers?

In a word, yes. Surveys have shown that the manner in which a worker is fired plays a very important role in determining whether that worker decides to file a wrongful termination lawsuit. (For more information on how to break the bad news, see "How to Fire," below.)

Illegal Reasons for Firing Employees

If your company employs workers at will, you don't need good cause to fire them. You can let them go for any reason or for no reason at all. (See "At-Will Employment" in Chapter 4.) However, you can't fire them for an illegal reason. Here, we list some of the most common illegal reasons for firing an employee. (If you want to end your company's relationship with an independent contractor, see Chapter 9.)

Discrimination

Federal law makes it illegal for most employers to fire an employee because of the employee's race, gender, national origin, disability, religion, genetic information, or age (if the person is at least 40 years old). Federal law also prohibits most employers from firing a worker because she is pregnant, has recently given birth, or has a pregnancy-related medical condition.

Most states also have antidiscrimination laws that include all of the characteristics listed in the federal law—and then some. Many state laws impose additional limits (for example, prohibiting discrimination on the basis of sexual orientation or marital status). Some also include a wider range of employers—for example, they cover employers of fewer employees than federal law. For more information on antidiscrimination laws, see Chapter 3.

Retaliation

It is illegal for employers to fire employees for asserting their rights under the state and federal antidiscrimination laws described above. You cannot fire an employee for complaining of discrimination or harassment, filing a lawsuit or a charge with a government agency alleging discrimination or harassment, or testifying on behalf of a coworker who was discriminated against or harassed. (For more, see "Retaliation" in Chapter 11.)

Refusal to Submit to a Lie Detector Test

A federal law, the Employee Polygraph Protection Act, prohibits most employers from firing employees for refusing to take a lie detector test. Many state laws contain a similar prohibition. (See "Testing Current Employees" in Chapter 6 for more.)

Alien Status

Under the federal Immigration Reform and Control Act (IRCA), an employer cannot fire an employee based on lack of citizenship. As long as the employee is legally eligible to work in the United States, the employer cannot discriminate against the worker based on alien or legal resident status.

Whistleblowing

Generally, you may not fire an employee for complaining about illegal or unethical conduct in the workplace. A number of laws protect an employee's right to complain to a government agency or to company management about potential workplace illegalities. Some of these types of whistleblowing are covered by the laws that prohibit retaliation. For example, an employee who files an OSHA complaint or files a charge of discrimination with the EEOC cannot be fired for doing so.

However, protections for whistleblowers go quite a bit further. For example, an employee who complains about financial irregularities or improprieties relating to a government contract cannot be fired for doing so. A number of laws protect the right to blow the whistle on improper employer conduct, including the Sarbanes-Oxley Act of 2002, which protects employees who complain of accounting irregularities and potential shareholder fraud.

Because so many types of whistleblowing are protected, the safest course of action is never to fire an employee for complaining of illegal or unethical behavior. Before you take any disciplinary action against an employee

Lessons From the Real World

Kaaren Yarborough worked as a manager in the recruiting department of PeopleSoft, Inc., a software maker in California. Because PeopleSoft has significant contracts with the Department of Defense and other federal agencies, it was required to comply with federal guidelines relating to the recruiting and hiring of women and minority workers.

In 1995, Ms. Yarborough saw reports that management sent to the Office of Federal Contract Compliance, a government agency that monitors companies with government contracts. According to Ms. Yarborough's lawyer, these reports falsely claimed that the company had a significantly higher percentage of female and minority workers than it actually did. Although the company claimed that 60% of its workforce was female and 21.7% were racial minorities, the true figures were 45% and 13%, respectively.

Ms. Yarborough reported these problems but was fired two days before she was scheduled to meet with auditors from the federal agency. Although PeopleSoft claimed it fired Ms. Yarborough for poor performance, the Alameda County jury that heard the case thought otherwise. The jury awarded Ms. Yarborough $5.45 million in damages on August 16, 2001.

John Roemer, "Wrongful Termination Suit Brings $5.45M," *The Daily Journal*, August 17, 2001; "PeopleSoft Whistleblower Awarded $5.4 Million," Reuters, August 16, 2001.

who has made this type of complaint, talk to an experienced employment lawyer.

Violations of Public Policy

Most states prohibit employers from firing an employee in violation of public policy—that is, for reasons that most people would find morally or ethically wrong. Of course, morals and ethics are relative things, so the range of prohibited reasons for firing varies from state to state. Some state and federal laws explicitly prohibit employers from firing workers for taking advantage of certain rights, like taking family medical leave or supporting a union. In some states, a worker can successfully argue that he or she was fired in violation of public policy even if no statute spells out exactly what the employer can and cannot do.

Although the laws and rules vary from state to state, most states agree that firing an employee for any of the following reasons would violate public policy:

- refusing to commit an illegal act (like falsifying insurance claims or submitting false tax returns)
- complaining about illegal workplace conduct (see "Whistleblowing," above), and
- exercising a legal right (such as voting or filing a workers' compensation claim).

To find out more about the law regarding public policy in your state, contact your state labor department or your state fair employment office. (You'll find contact information in the appendix.)

Firing Employees With Employment Contracts

If an employee has an employment contract— whether written or oral, express or implied— that contract may limit your ability to fire the employee. Usually, if an employment contract exists (which is not always easy to figure out), the company must treat the employee fairly and fire him or her only for "good cause."

Is There a Contract?

Before you fire someone, you have to determine whether your company has an employment contract with that worker. This might be as simple as looking in the employee's personnel file for a document labeled "employment contract," but often it's not that easy.

Employers sometimes create employment contracts without meaning to or even knowing they are doing so. These types of contracts—called implied contracts because they are not written down, but instead are inferred from your actions and statements— are every bit as binding as signed, written contracts.

Employers create implied contracts when they promise the employee something, usually job security. You might inadvertently make these promises in all sorts of circumstances, such as during a casual conversation with an employee or as part of a discussion in an employee handbook. No matter how the promise is made, if the promise has enough weight and the employee has relied on that promise (usually by taking the job or staying there), a court might decide that the promise is a contract your company must honor.

Figuring out whether the company has unintentionally created one of these types of contracts can be a tricky business. However, past court decisions do provide some guidance. Courts have found implied contracts in the following circumstances:

- While trying to convince a prospective employee to take a job, an employer promises the employee that he or she will be fired only if he or she does not do the job well.
- An employee manual states that once new workers successfully make it through a 90-day probation period, they become "permanent" employees.
- During an evaluation, a supervisor gives an employee a glowing review and tells the employee he or she has a long future at the company unless he or she really messes up. (See "At-Will Employment" in Chapter 4 for more on creating implied contracts.)

Don't let the specter of implied contracts worry you too much, however. The vast majority of employees in this country are working without a contract, written or implied. If you are dealing with an employee who has only been with your company for a short time (say, a year or two) and you are sure no one ever promised the employee job security, chances are good that the employee does not have an implied contract. This means the employee is at will and you can fire the employee for any reason that isn't illegal. (See "Illegal Reasons for Firing Employees," above).

Remember, too, that a contract doesn't mean you can never fire a worker. It just limits the circumstances under which the worker can be terminated. For workers with implied contracts, this generally means that you must have good cause—such as poor performance or violation of important workplace rules—to fire the employee. For workers with written contracts, you must abide by whatever limits the contract places on the company's right to fire.

Firing Employees With Written Contracts

If your company has a formal written contract with an employee, it will usually list the reasons for which the employee can be fired. If you want to terminate that employee, you must follow what the contract says. Often, contracts simply state that an employee can only be terminated for good cause. Sometimes, however, the contract will be more detailed. For example, some contracts say that a worker can be fired only for gross misconduct, for committing a crime, or in connection with a sale of the company. Either way, you must follow the contract terms or risk a lawsuit.

Good Cause

As explained above, many written employment contracts—and almost all implied contracts—allow employers to terminate the employee only for good cause. What exactly constitutes good cause varies from state to state, but generally it means what it says:

You must have a legitimate reason for firing the employee. In general, the termination must be based on reasons related to business needs and goals. Firing an employee because you don't like the fact that she is a single mother, for example, isn't good cause. Firing an employee because he harasses female coworkers is.

Other examples of good cause include the following:

- poor job performance
- low productivity
- refusal to follow instructions
- habitual tardiness
- excessive absences from work
- possession of a weapon at work
- threats of violence
- violating company rules
- stealing or other criminal activity
- dishonesty
- endangering health and safety
- revealing company trade secrets
- harassing coworkers
- disrupting the work environment
- conviction of a felony or a crime involving "moral turpitude"
- preventing coworkers from doing their jobs, and
- insubordination.

Good Faith and Fair Dealing

If your company has a contract with an employee, then it has an obligation to be fair and honest in its dealings with that employee. Although this rule might seem to override your company's ability to terminate contracted employees, it really doesn't. To breach this obligation, employers have to engage in very egregious conduct, such as:

- firing employees to prevent them from collecting sales commissions
- firing employees just before their retirement benefits vest, or
- fabricating evidence of poor performance to fire workers when the real motivation is to replace them with employees who will work for lower pay.

Lessons From the Real World

If an employee has a contract, you must abide by the terms of the agreement or face a breach of contract lawsuit. That's the very expensive lesson learned by Metris Companies, a credit card issuer that fired its CEO, Ronald Zebeck.

Zebeck claimed that he was fired in anticipation of a sale in the company, which triggered the generous severance provisions of his employment contract; Zebeck also argued that he was fired because he was planning to report financial improprieties to government regulators. Metris claimed that he was fired for cause, and so forfeited the right to receive severance. Ultimately, the jury sided with Zebeck and ordered Metris to pay him more than $30 million in damages.

Making the Decision to Fire

Most employers start thinking about firing a worker in one of two situations. In the first, a worker commits a single act of serious misconduct that's dangerous or potentially harmful to the business, such as threatening or committing violence, stealing from the company, violating major safety rules, or revealing important company information to a competitor. These problems require a quick and careful response.

More commonly, a "problem" employee has persistent performance or conduct problems (despite managerial efforts to counsel and correct). An employee who is repeatedly absent or tardy, is insubordinate, or simply can't seem to meet reasonable performance and productivity goals falls into this category. Though not as urgent, these problems can also threaten your company's well-being. Left unchecked, they will eventually erode the morale of other workers and the productivity of the business.

No matter what your reasons are, consider all the angles before you take action. Remember, firing is the one decision you will make as a manager that is most likely to land your company in court. Stay out of legal trouble by making sure you give the worker a fair shake before showing him or her the door. We provide some suggestions below.

Questions to Ask Yourself Before Firing

If you're contemplating firing an employee, ask yourself these important questions:

- **Do we have a legitimate reason?** Make sure you have good cause—that is, a solid, business-related reason—to fire the worker. (While this is not required for at-will employees, it is always a good idea.) In either of the two scenarios described above, you probably will have good cause. But don't use that reason as an excuse to fire a worker for an illegal motive (for example, because the worker complained about unsafe working conditions or asked for a reasonable accommodation for a disability; see "Illegal Reasons for Firing Employees," above, for more information.)

- **Should we investigate first?** If the incident has already been investigated or if the accused worker admits committing the misconduct in question, you can skip this step. But if the situation is not so clear-cut, you have to figure out what happened. Take the time to investigate, even when the employee is caught "in the act." There is always the possibility, no matter how slim, that things are not what they appear to be. And the worker might have an explanation or reason for the misconduct that is not immediately apparent. (See "Investigating Complaints" in Chapter 11 for more information on performing an investigation.)

- **Does the worker's personnel file support the reasons for firing?** Always review the employee's personnel file before firing. If you are considering firing for persistent problems (poor performance or attendance, for example), make sure these problems are documented in evaluations and disciplinary warnings. And make sure the file does not contradict your reason for firing: An employee fired for poor performance should not be able to point to merit increases and glowing performance reviews, for example. If you are firing for a single serious offense, the worker's file might not mention any problems. That's fine as long as there haven't been any.

- **Have we followed company policy?** If your company has written work rules or disciplinary policies, make sure they have been followed to the letter. Was the worker notified that the conduct could result in termination? Did the worker receive any promised warnings and opportunities to improve? Also check to see if company policies put any limitations on your right to fire. If employees work at will, this shouldn't be a problem.

- **Does the worker have a contract?** If the worker has a written employment contract, you can fire only for the reasons stated in the contract. If the worker doesn't have a written contract, consider whether any company representative made any promises or statements that the worker would be fired only for certain reasons. Have employees been told that they would only be fired for serious misconduct? If promises like these have been made, make sure you have honored them. (See "Firing Employees With Employment Contracts," above, for more information.)

- **Would firing this worker be consistent with the way the company has handled similar problems?** Think about how your company has dealt with other employees who have committed similar offenses. Have they always been fired? Or have some of them been given a second chance? If your company isn't consistent with discipline, it may be at risk for a claim of discrimination or unfair treatment.

- **Is this worker likely to sue?** Although it's always hard to predict what another person will do, you should take some time to consider whether this worker seems likely to sue. Has he or she threatened to sue, thrown legal terms around with ease, or talked about hiring a lawyer? Does the employee have a history of butting heads with people—such as neighbors or previous employers—and running to the courthouse? Will the employee have difficulty finding another job? Does the employee consistently see him- or herself as the victim? Has your company treated the employee unfairly? If your answer to any of these questions is "yes," your company might be at higher risk for a lawsuit, so handle the termination very carefully.

- **Is there an alternative to firing?** Would less extreme discipline be effective? Do you think it's likely that the employee will be able and willing to improve? If so, you might want to give the employee some time to fix things instead of firing immediately. Just make sure you don't play favorites or bend the rules without a good reason. You especially might want to consider an alternative to termination if the worker's problems are due to difficulties outside of work, increased responsibilities that the employee can't handle, or trouble working with a particular supervisor, or if your company has made some managerial missteps with the worker.

- **Is the firing decision impartial and fair?** Make sure your decision makes sense and can be defended if necessary. Get a second opinion from a colleague. This will help ensure that your decision is legitimate, reasonable, and well supported. A secondary review should make sure that the decision is based on objective, work-related concerns and has not been influenced by favoritism, discrimination, or other subjective factors.

- **Should we talk to a lawyer?** If it's a close call, or if the company has made some management mistakes, consider talking to a lawyer before firing. For example, getting legal help is probably a good idea if firing would dramatically change workplace demographics, the worker recently complained of discrimination or harassment, the worker has an employment contract that strictly limits your company's right to fire, the worker is due to vest pension or other benefits soon, or the worker denies the acts for which you are firing.

Once you have run through these questions and are satisfied with the answers, the only thing left to do is to document your decision. Write an internal memorandum to the worker's file explaining why you have decided to fire the worker. It doesn't have to be a novel; a concise statement of your reasons for firing is enough. Describe any misconduct the worker has committed and, if the worker has had ongoing performance or other problems, the dates and details of any prior evaluations or warnings and any efforts the company has made to try to help the worker improve.

How to Fire

The 15 minutes or so you spend telling an employee that you are terminating his or her employment may be the most important in your company's relationship with that worker. And they will certainly be the most unpleasant: Surveys have shown that managers dread this aspect of their jobs more than any other.

Although you might be tempted to rush the process—a hurried review of the employee's personnel file, a quick check-in with other managers to make sure they're on board with the decision—this isn't the best approach. While you might want to get the task off your plate as soon as possible, the time you spend planning this meeting (such as deciding who will break the news, where it will be held, and what will be said) will pay off in the long run. Prior planning helps ensure that you treat the employee with respect, provide all necessary information, and avoid doing or saying anything unnecessarily cruel or provocative, all of which will make the meeting a bit easier and help you avoid future legal trouble.

Who Should Break the News

The person who actually fires the employee should be someone with whom the worker has a positive, or at least a neutral, relationship. Don't assign someone who has clashed frequently with the worker or who is emotionally involved in the decision to fire the employee. This means the employee's supervisor might be the wrong person for the job. If you have a human resources manager, that person might be a good choice.

Where and When to Hold the Meeting

There are many different theories about when an employee should be fired. Some say it's best to fire a worker early in the week, to give him or her the chance to immediately begin her job search and hook up with outplacement services while businesses are still open. Others advise waiting until Friday, reasoning that this will give the worker a chance to exit quietly and use the weekend to let the news sink in. Unless you fear violence from a fired worker (in which case, you should break the news at the end of the day on Friday, when few other workers are around), you should do whatever feels right.

Whichever day you choose, make sure to tell the worker early in the day. This will give him or her the chance to pack, tie up loose ends, and say goodbye to coworkers.

Above all, respect the worker's privacy. Hold the meeting in a private, quiet place away from prying eyes. An open cubicle is a lousy spot for a termination meeting, as is a conference room that coworkers can see into, a lunchroom, or any other common area. If possible, avoid holding the meeting in a location that will require the worker to make a long, sad march past coworkers after the meeting is over. The best place to break the news is probably the worker's own office, if it is private. This will allow you to end the meeting when you wish (by getting up and leaving) and will give the fired worker a chance to process the news privately before having to face coworkers.

What to Say

At the meeting, be firm but kind. Don't joke around or make pleasant small talk with the employee to put off the inevitable. It will ring hollow or, worse, seem cruel once the real purpose of the meeting becomes apparent.

Start the meeting by telling the employee that his or her employment is being terminated and why. Long explanations or justifications will only draw the worker into an argument or an effort to change your mind, so skip them. It can be tough to strike the right tone in giving this information: If you're too direct, you risk seeming cold. But if you sugarcoat it, the worker won't understand why he or she is being fired and might use your sympathetic words against you later to show that the termination wasn't justified. It's a difficult line to walk; the best you can do is to try for an honest, professional tone.

Once the deed is done, explain what will happen next and discuss tying up loose ends. Give the worker his or her final paycheck and any accrued vacation pay. (To find out your state's requirements for final paychecks, see "State Laws That Control Final Paychecks," at the end of this chapter.) Explain the worker's severance package, if you will offer one. Let the worker know whether you will continue to pay for benefits for any period of time, or of the right to continued health insurance coverage under COBRA. Explain your company's reference policy. (See "References" in Chapter 14.) This is also a good time to review any confidentiality or noncompete agreements the worker has signed, to make sure those obligations are clear. (See Chapter 10 for more information on these agreements.)

Finally, try to end the meeting on a positive note. Shake hands, wish the worker good luck, and give him or her the name of someone at the company to contact with any questions.

Company Property

Figuring out when and how to collect company property and block the employee's access to the building and computer system is a matter of judgment and tact. If you trust the employee and don't fear violence or sabotage, don't treat the employee like a criminal, especially at a time when he or she is apt to

be feeling pretty low. Unless you fear violence or sabotage, you shouldn't march the worker off the premises. Give the worker time to digest the termination before you swoop in for the company credit card and cell phone.

If you do fear violence, theft, or sabotage—or if the employee held a highly sensitive position in your company (such as managing your computer system)—act quickly to block the employee's access to the computer system, confidential files, trade secrets, and the building. If you can arrange it, the best time to have access blocked is while you are in the termination meeting with the employee. If you choose this route, explain the steps you have taken during the meeting. Offer to help the employee retrieve any personal information that might be located on your computer network or in his or her email account. Tell the employee what kinds of reply email messages and voice mail messages will be established to explain his or her absence, and implement them right away.

Documenting the Meeting

As soon after the meeting is over as possible, write down what happened. Note what you said and how the employee responded. Also keep a record of any issues left up in the air (for example, if the employee wants to negotiate a different severance package or continue to use the company car for a few weeks).

Checklist: Things to Do Before the Termination Meeting

☐ Cut a final paycheck for the employee that includes all unused accrued vacation time (if required by company policy or your state's law). Also include earned commissions.

☐ Issue any outstanding expense reimbursements.

☐ Tell the payroll or accounting staff to drop the employee from the payroll.

☐ Determine who else needs to know about the termination and inform them.

☐ Choose someone (if not you) to conduct the termination meeting.

☐ Choose someone to be the employee's contact after the meeting.

☐ Make sure that the person who conducts the meeting is familiar with the employee's personnel file and benefits status.

☐ Plan an exit interview, if you choose to conduct one.

☐ Decide whether the employee will be offered a severance package.

☐ If the employee had access to confidential information, take steps to make sure that the employee understands his or her obligations to keep that information secret.

☐ Create an action plan for handing off the employee's current projects.

☐ Decide how the company will handle calls from prospective employers seeking a reference for the employee.

☐ Decide what you will tell coworkers about the termination.

☐ If you think the employee might turn violent, arrange for security personnel and an escort for the employee.

☐ Make arrangements to have the employee's password and computer privileges turned off.

☐ If the employee has an assigned parking space, remove the employee's name from the list and reassign the space.

☐ Cancel the employee's company credit card and long-distance phone card.

☐ Collect company property from the employee.

☐ Identify someone to handle any mail that comes for the employee after his or her departure.

☐ Remove the employee's name from company lists, including routing slips, email lists, and telephone rosters. Also remove the employee's name from letterhead, if applicable.

Lessons From the Real World

Malcolm Bolton was a social work specialist at the Fergus Falls Regional Treatment Center, working with developmentally disabled people. He challenged the Center's decision to place a resident in a community group home. Based on this disagreement, Bolton was eventually fired.

Bolton sued the Center over his termination and lost on every count but one: that the manner in which he was fired damaged his reputation. On Bolton's last day, one of the directors of the Center walked Bolton to his office, stayed while he packed his belongings,

and then marched him to the front door, in full view of Bolton's coworkers.

The Minnesota Court of Appeals found that these actions might constitute defamation, because they conveyed a negative message about Bolton every bit as much as a statement would have. And the message was "that Bolton was dishonest and was not to be trusted to leave the building unaccompanied." The Court allowed Bolton to present this claim to a jury.

Bolton v. Department of Human Services, 527 N.W.2d 149 (Minn. Ct. App. 1995).

Legal Dos and Don'ts: Firing Employees

Do:

- **Document everything.** We can't say it enough: You should always have a written record to back up your reasons for firing an employee. If you are firing someone for ongoing problems, the employee's personnel file should reflect that the employee has had notice of those problems and an opportunity to correct them. Nothing in the file should contradict your reasons for firing.
- **Consider your decision carefully.** It's important to think through your decision to fire. Are your reasons legitimate and documented? Are you sure you know the facts? Have you followed company policy and past practice? Is there any reason why it might make sense to talk to a lawyer? Taking the time to troubleshoot your decision now will save your company a lot of time (and money) down the road.
- **Fire only for good cause.** Although your company has the right to fire an at-will worker for any reason that is not illegal, you shouldn't exercise that right very often. If you fire only for legitimate business reasons, you give workers an incentive to perform well and follow workplace rules. And your company will gain a reputation for being fair and reasonable, which will help in recruiting new workers, retaining employees, and fighting off wrongful termination lawsuits.

Don't:

- **Treat fired employees like criminals.** The way you fire someone largely determines whether your company will face a lawsuit over that termination. Unless you have legitimate concerns about violence, sabotage, or other extreme behavior, let workers gather their thoughts and belongings, say goodbye to coworkers, and exit your company for the last time under their own steam.
- **Take workers by surprise.** A firing should not come as a complete surprise to the employee who gets the bad news. A worker fired for cause should have been on notice that his or her actions or performance were unsatisfactory and might lead to termination.
- **Postpone the inevitable.** We know that it's difficult to fire an employee. But it's often the best thing for your company. Once an employee has proven that he or she can't meet the company's expectations or has committed serious misconduct, it's time to terminate. The longer you put it off, the more intractable the employee's problems will become.

Test Your Knowledge

Questions

1. An at-will employee can be fired for any reason. ☐ True ☐ False

2. If an employee has an employment contract, he or she can be fired only for good cause. ☐ True ☐ False

3. As long as an employee works at will, you don't need to bother reviewing the personnel file before you fire him or her. ☐ True ☐ False

4. It's a good idea to explain in detail the reasons why an employee is being fired. ☐ True ☐ False

5. An employee's direct supervisor should always be the one to do the firing. ☐ True ☐ False

6. You should always ask security to escort someone you've fired off the premises, just in case. ☐ True ☐ False

7. You may have to pay a fired employee on the spot, rather than issuing a final paycheck on your usual payroll schedule. ☐ True ☐ False

8. As long as you have a good reason to fire an employee, it doesn't really matter how other managers handle similar problems. ☐ True ☐ False

9. An employee may have a valid legal claim for breach of contract even without a written employment agreement. ☐ True ☐ False

10. You should always turn off an employee's access to the company's network and computer system before the termination meeting, to avoid sabotage. ☐ True ☐ False

Answers

1. False. At-will employees cannot be fired for reasons that are illegal, such as discrimination or retaliation.

2. It depends on the contract. Many contracts (and virtually all implied contracts) require good cause for termination, but some contracts may impose different requirements. For example, it might say the employee can be fired only for committing a crime or for serious financial mismanagement.

3. False. A terminated employee's personnel file should support the reasons for firing, if possible. An employee who is fired for persistent performance problems or misconduct should have been on notice that the problems could lead to termination.

4. False. Although you should tell an employee why his or her employment is being terminated, you should not get into details. This will only encourage arguments.

5. It depends on the relationship between the employee and the supervisor. If the relationship is generally good, the supervisor should handle the firing. If there is friction, however, another manager might be better suited to the task.

6. False. Unless you have a legitimate concern about violence or sabotage, don't have the worker marched off the premises. This only leads to bad feelings, for the employee you fired and the employees who see how you treated him or her.

7. True. This issue is governed by state law, and some states require you to give a fired employee a final paycheck right away. See "State Laws That Control Final Paychecks," at the end of this chapter, for information on your state's rules.

8. False. Inconsistent treatment can lead to claims of unfairness and discrimination. You should make sure that all managers at your company are handling employee problems according to the same set of rules.

9. True. The employee may have an oral or implied contract that limits the company's right to fire, even if nothing was ever put in writing.

10. False. If you turn off access before the termination meeting, the employee will already know that there's a problem before you have a chance to fire him or her. If you fear sabotage, you can arrange to have access turned off while you are meeting with the employee.

State Laws That Control Final Paychecks

Note: The states of Alabama, Florida, Georgia, and Mississippi are not included in this chart because they do not have laws specifically controlling final paychecks. Contact your state department of labor for more information. (See appendix for contact list.)

State	Paycheck due when employee is fired	Paycheck due when employee quits	Unused vacation pay due	Special employment situations
Alaska *Alaska Stat.* *§ 23.05.140(b)*	Within 3 working days.	Next regular payday at least 3 days after employee gives notice.	Only if required by company policy.	
Arizona *Ariz. Rev. Stat.* *§§ 23-350, 23-353*	Next payday or within 3 working days, whichever is sooner.	Next payday.	Yes, if company has policy or practice of making such payments.	
Arkansas *Ark. Code Ann.* *§ 11-4-405*	Within 7 days from discharge date.	No provision.	No provision.	Railroad or railroad construction: day of discharge.
California *Cal. Lab. Code* *§§ 201 to 202,* *227.3*	Immediately.	Immediately if employee has given 72 hours' notice; otherwise, within 72 hours.	Yes.	Motion picture business: next payday. Oil drilling industry: within 24 hours (excluding weekends and holidays) of termination. Seasonal agricultural workers: within 72 hours of termination.
Colorado *Colo. Rev. Stat.* *§ 8-4-109*	Immediately. (Within 6 hours of start of next workday, if payroll unit is closed; 24 hours if unit is offsite.) Employer decides check delivery.	Next payday.	Yes.	
Connecticut *Conn. Gen. Stat.* *Ann. §§ 31-71c,* *31-76k*	Next business day after discharge.	Next payday.	Only if policy or collective bargaining agreement requires payment on termination.	

State Laws That Control Final Paychecks (cont'd)				
State	Paycheck due when employee is fired	Paycheck due when employee quits	Unused vacation pay due	Special employment situations
Delaware *Del. Code Ann. tit. 19, § 1103*	Next payday.	Next payday.	No provision.	
District of Columbia *D.C. Code Ann. § 32-1303*	Next business day.	Next payday or 7 days after quitting, whichever is sooner.	Yes, unless there is an agreement to the contrary.	
Hawaii *Haw. Rev. Stat. § 388-3*	Immediately or next business day, if timing or conditions prevent immediate payment.	Next payday or immediately, if employee gives one pay period's notice.	No.	
Idaho *Idaho Code §§ 45-606, 45-617*	Next payday or within 10 days (excluding weekends and holidays), whichever is sooner. If employee makes written request for earlier payment, within 48 hours of receipt of request (excluding weekends and holidays).	Next payday or within 10 days (excluding weekends and holidays), whichever is sooner. If employee makes written request for earlier payment, within 48 hours of receipt of request (excluding weekends and holidays).	No provision.	
Illinois *820 Ill. Comp. Stat. § 115/5*	At time of separation if possible, but no later than next payday.	At time of separation if possible, but no later than next payday.	Yes.	
Indiana *Ind. Code Ann. §§ 22-2-5-1, 22-2-9-1, 22-2-9-2*	Next payday.	Next payday. (If employee has not left address, (1) 10 business days after employee demands wages or (2) when employee provides address where check may be mailed.)	Yes.	Does not apply to railroad employees.

State Laws That Control Final Paychecks (cont'd)

State	Paycheck due when employee is fired	Paycheck due when employee quits	Unused vacation pay due	Special employment situations
Iowa *Iowa Code §§ 91A.4, 91A.2(7)(b)*	Next payday.	Next payday.	Yes.	If employee is owed commission, employer has 30 days to pay.
Kansas *Kan. Stat. Ann. § 44-315*	Next payday.	Next payday.	Only if required by employer's policies or practice.	
Kentucky *Ky. Rev. Stat. Ann. §§ 337.010, 337.055*	Next payday or 14 days, whichever is later.	Next payday or 14 days, whichever is later.	Yes.	
Louisiana *La. Rev. Stat. Ann. § 23:631*	Next payday or within 15 days, whichever is earlier.	Next payday or within 15 days, whichever is earlier.	Yes.	
Maine *Me. Rev. Stat. Ann. tit. 26, § 626*	Next payday or within 2 weeks of requesting final pay, whichever is sooner.	Next payday or within 2 weeks of requesting final pay, whichever is sooner.	Yes.	
Maryland *Md. Code Ann., [Lab. & Empl.] § 3-505*	Next scheduled payday.	Next scheduled payday.	Yes, unless employer has contrary policy.	
Massachusetts *Mass. Gen. Laws ch. 149, § 148*	Day of discharge.	Next payday. If no scheduled payday, then following Saturday.	Yes.	
Michigan *Mich. Comp. Laws §§ 408.471 to 408.475; Mich. Admin. Code R. 408.9007*	Next payday.	Next payday.	Only if required by written policy or contract.	Hand-harvesters of crops: within one working day of termination.

			Unused vacation pay due	
State Laws That Control Final Paychecks (cont'd)				
State	**Paycheck due when employee is fired**	**Paycheck due when employee quits**	**Unused vacation pay due**	**Special employment situations**
Minnesota Minn. Stat. Ann. §§ 181.13, 181.14, 181.74	Immediately.	Next payday. If payday is less than 5 days from last day of work, then following payday or 20 days from last day of work, whichever is earlier.	Only if required by written policy or contract.	Migrant agricultural workers who resign: within 5 days.
Missouri Mo. Rev. Stat. § 290.110	Day of discharge.	No provision.	No.	
Montana Mont. Code Ann. § 39-3-205; Mont. Admin. Code § 24.16.7521	Immediately if fired for cause or laid off (unless there is a written policy extending time to earlier of next payday or 15 days).	Next payday or within 15 days, whichever comes first.	Yes.	
Nebraska Neb. Rev. Stat. §§ 48-1229 to 48-1230	Next payday or within 2 weeks, whichever is earlier.	Next payday or within 2 weeks, whichever is earlier.	Only if required by agreement.	Commissions due on next payday following receipt.
Nevada Nev. Rev. Stat. Ann. §§ 608.020, 608.030	Immediately.	Next payday or 7 days, whichever is earlier.	No.	
New Hampshire N.H. Rev. Stat. Ann. §§ 275:43(V), 275:44	Within 72 hours. If laid off, next payday.	Next payday, or within 72 hours if employee gives one pay period's notice.	Yes.	
New Jersey N.J. Stat. Ann. § 34:11-4.3	Next payday.	Next payday.	Only if required by policy.	
New Mexico N.M. Stat. Ann. §§ 50-4-4, 50-4-5	Within 5 days.	Next payday.	No provision.	If paid by task or commission, 10 days after discharge.

State Laws That Control Final Paychecks (cont'd)

State	Paycheck due when employee is fired	Paycheck due when employee quits	Unused vacation pay due	Special employment situations
New York N.Y. Lab. Law §§ 191(3), 198-c(2)	Next payday.	Next payday.	Yes, unless employer has a contrary policy.	
North Carolina N.C. Gen. Stat. §§ 95-25.7, 95-25.12	Next payday.	Next payday.	Yes, unless employer has a contrary policy.	If paid by commission or bonus, on next payday after amount calculated.
North Dakota N.D. Cent. Code § 34-14-03; N.D. Admin. Code R. 46-02-07-02(12)	Next payday, or 15 days, whichever is earlier.	Next payday.	Yes.	
Ohio Ohio Rev. Code Ann. § 4113.15	First of month for wages earned in first half of prior month; 15th of month for wages earned in second half of prior month.	First of month for wages earned in first half of prior month; 15th of month for wages earned in second half of prior month.	Yes, if company has policy or practice of making such payments.	
Oklahoma Okla. Stat. Ann. tit. 40, §§ 165.1(4), 165.3	Next payday.	Next payday.	Yes.	
Oregon Or. Rev. Stat. §§ 652.140, 652.145	End of first business day after termination (must be within 5 days if employee submits time records to determine wages due).	Immediately, with 48 hours' notice (excluding weekends and holidays); without notice, within 5 business days or next payday, whichever comes first (must be within 5 days if employee submits time records to determine wages due).	Only if required by policy.	Seasonal farm workers: fired or quitting with 48 hours' notice, immediately; quitting without notice, within 48 hours or next payday, whichever comes first.

State Laws That Control Final Paychecks (cont'd)

State	Paycheck due when employee is fired	Paycheck due when employee quits	Unused vacation pay due	Special employment situations
Pennsylvania *43 Pa. Cons. Stat. Ann. §§ 260.2a, 260.5*	Next payday.	Next payday.	Only if required by policy or contract.	
Rhode Island *R.I. Gen. Laws § 28-14-4*	Next payday.	Next payday.	Yes, if employee has worked for one full year and the company has verbally or in writing awarded vacation.	
South Carolina *S.C. Code Ann. §§ 41-10-10(2), 41-10-50*	Within 48 hours or next payday, but not more than 30 days.	No provision.	Only if required by policy or contract.	
South Dakota *S.D. Codified Laws Ann. §§ 60-11-10, 60-11-11, 60-11-14*	Next payday (or until employee returns employer's property).	Next payday (or until employee returns employer's property).	No.	
Tennessee *Tenn. Code Ann. § 50-2-103*	Next payday or 21 days, whichever is later.	Next payday or 21 days, whichever is later.	Only if required by policy or contract.	Applies to employers with 5 or more employees.
Texas *Tex. Lab. Code Ann. §§ 61.001, 61.014*	Within 6 days.	Next payday.	Only if required by policy or contract.	
Utah *Utah Code Ann. §§ 34-28-5; Utah Admin. Code 610-3*	Within 24 hours.	Next payday.	Only if required by policy or contract.	

State Laws That Control Final Paychecks (cont'd)

State	Paycheck due when employee is fired	Paycheck due when employee quits	Unused vacation pay due	Special employment situations
Vermont *Vt. Stat. Ann. tit. 21, § 342(c)*	Within 72 hours.	Next regular payday or next Friday, if there is no regular payday.	No provision.	
Virginia *Va. Code Ann. § 40.1-29(A.1)*	Next payday.	Next payday.	Only if agreed to in a written statement.	
Washington *Wash. Rev. Code Ann. § 49.48.010*	End of pay period.	End of pay period.	No provision.	
West Virginia *W.Va. Code §§ 21-5-1, 21-5-4*	Within 72 hours.	Immediately if employee has given one pay period's notice; otherwise, next payday.	Yes.	
Wisconsin *Wis. Stat. Ann. §§ 109.01(3), 109.03*	Next payday or 1 month, whichever is earlier. If termination is due to merger, relocation, or liquidation of business, within 24 hours.	Next payday.	Yes.	Does not apply to managers, executives, or sales agents working on commission basis.
Wyoming *Wyo. Stat. Ann. §§ 27-4-104, 27-4-507(c)*	5 working days.	5 working days.	Yes.	

Layoffs

As the economic downturn continues, many companies have had to lay off employees to stay in business. Many more have tried to be creative in coming up with others ways to cut payroll, either in addition to or instead of layoffs. Furloughs, cuts in pay and/or hours, and trimming benefits have all become common strategies to save jobs.

Even if your company absolutely must trim its staff, that doesn't make the job of deciding whom to lay off—and actually delivering the bad news—any easier. Layoffs are very delicate, for legal and practical reasons. First and foremost, layoffs are painful, most especially for the employees who lose their jobs, but also for those who remain (and for the managers who have to carry out the decision). Unless your decisions rest on sound business reasons, your company could face lawsuits arising out of layoffs, probably just what you don't need when money is tight. And, layoffs that aren't handled in a professional, reassuring manner can lead to anxiety, poor morale, and high turnover among the employees who remain.

This chapter explains some of the legal rules that govern layoffs and other cost-cutting measures, as well as some practical strategies that will help you keep employees on track if you have to resort to job or compensation cuts. We cover:

- how to figure out whether layoffs are necessary
- how to handle alternatives to layoffs, such as hours or pay cuts, without violating the law
- how to decide whom to lay off
- how to conduct a layoff, and
- how to make sure your company meets its notice requirements.

Frequently Asked Questions About Layoffs

What should we consider before laying workers off?

Think carefully about whether the company really needs to lay workers off. If other, less drastic alternatives would help, start there. Make sure your company has valid, business-related reasons for the layoff. Also consider possible constraints on your company's right to lay off workers, such as a collective bargaining agreement or employment contracts. (For more information on deciding whether to lay workers off, see "Before Conducting a Layoff," below.)

We're cutting employee hours and pay in order to save as many jobs as possible; are there any potential legal pitfalls we should be aware of?

Yes. Wage and hour laws may limit your ability to cut hours or pay, or restrict the ways you can implement these measures. Even though employees generally support cuts like these if they're necessary to avoid layoffs, you could still face legal problems if you aren't careful. (See "Alternatives to Layoffs," below, for more information.)

Frequently Asked Questions About Layoffs (cont'd)

How should we choose the workers who will be laid off?

From a legal perspective, it's safest to use objective criteria: factors that can be measured and compared, such as seniority, productivity, or sales figures. If you want to use some subjective measures—like quality of work, skills, or teamwork—you must apply them consistently in evaluating workers. And, make sure your list doesn't include a disproportionately large number of workers in a protected class. (For more on deciding whom to lay off, see "Making the Cut," below.)

How should we tell our workforce about the layoffs?

Resist the temptation to just get it over with by laying workers off in a group, in an email, or in a rush. Meet with each targeted employee, explain the decision, and take the time to answer questions about what will happen next. And, don't forget about the employees who haven't been laid off: You should also meet with them, once the layoffs have been carried out, to explain why cuts were made and how your company plans to succeed in the future. (See "Conducting a Layoff," below, for more information.)

Can we wait until the last minute to tell employees about a layoff, to avoid unnecessary gossip and wasted work time?

Legally, it depends on the size of your company, how many people are losing their jobs, and why. If the layoff is subject to the Worker Adjustment Retraining and Notification (WARN) Act, you must give employees who will be laid off at least 60 days' advance notice, with a few exceptions. Even if you aren't legally required to give this much notice, however, your plan to avoid gossip might not be furthered by laying people off suddenly. Whatever work time you save up front will probably be lost after the layoffs become public. (For more information about the WARN Act and layoff notice, see "Notice Requirements for Layoffs," below.)

Before Conducting a Layoff

When you're considering layoffs, it pays to understand the most common mistakes companies make when letting workers go and how to avoid them. Here, we cover some issues to think about before deciding to lay workers off. (If you aren't in on the layoff decisions—that is, if your job is to carry those decisions out rather than to make them in the first place—you can skip this section.)

If your company is faced with the tough decision of whether to lay off workers— many of whom you may like and wish you could keep—you have a lot to consider. Your company's first priority is probably turning the business around, by cutting costs to make the company more profitable. However, surveys have shown that downsizing doesn't always pay off in this way. According to the American Management Association, only a minority of companies that downsize report any increase in productivity or long-term gains in shareholder value.

Layoffs can be costly in other ways as well. Your company may have to pay for increased unemployment claims, severance packages, and outplacement services. And it will certainly risk declines in productivity and morale in the workers who remain. It may even face lawsuits, depending on how the layoff is conducted. Given the risks, companies should carefully consider whether they really need to conduct layoffs and whether they can do so legally. Consider the following questions:

- **Are there good business reasons for the layoffs?** Before handing out pink slips, consider why a layoff is necessary. Make sure there's a legitimate business reason for the layoff, such as a decrease in sales, overstaffing, changes in the company's direction, or technological changes that render some employees obsolete. If your company has a sound justification for the layoff, workers will have a more difficult time challenging the decision in court. However, if your company has illegal motives for laying off workers—such as a desire to get rid of older workers or retaliate against union supporters—it may find itself on the receiving end of a lawsuit.

- **Will layoffs solve your company's problem?** It's worth remembering an obvious point: When you lay employees off, there are fewer employees left to do the work. Although cutting payroll costs will save you some money, that won't help much if your company can't turn a profit with the employees it has left. A company that really is supporting too many employees to do the available work can realize significant benefits from layoffs. A company whose employees all have plenty to do might be better served by looking at ways to make more money rather than ways to cut costs, such as focusing its energy and resources on the most profitable areas of the business for now, leaving more speculative or long-term growth possibilities for better days.

- **Are alternatives to layoffs available?** Think about whether your company can achieve its cost-cutting goals with less drastic measures. Some less painful alternatives might include a freeze on hiring, promotions, or pay raises; cutting back on budgets for things like continuing education, travel, or entertainment; or a freeze on filling positions left vacant when employees leave voluntarily. You might also consider pay cuts, asking employees to take time off, or reducing authorized overtime. (For more information on all of these options, see "Alternatives to Layoffs," below.) Finally, some employers provide voluntary termination incentives to allow employees to decide whether to quit in exchange for a package of benefits. If your company considers or implements some of these alternatives before laying workers off, fewer workers will question whether the layoff was truly necessary.

- **Do the company's written personnel policies address layoffs?** Gather together your company's employee handbook, manual, or other written personnel policies. Do they discuss layoffs? If so, you will have to follow the company's guidelines or risk a lawsuit for breach of contract. Some companies lay down specific rules about when and how layoffs will be conducted, give workers bumping rights (the right to take the job of a worker with less seniority rather than be laid off), or promise severance pay to laid-off workers. You'll need to factor in these limits—and the additional costs they often entail—when determining whether layoffs make economic sense.

- **Do the company's actual policies or past practices limit its ability to lay workers off?** Even if your company's written policies don't deal with layoffs, it might have restricted its ability to lay workers off by actions or statements. For example, if the company president has announced that no one who is performing well will be fired, the company could face legal trouble if it lays off good performers. Or, if your company has previously given severance pay to every worker fired for economic reasons, it may have to provide severance to workers who are laid off this time around.

- **Are layoff decisions limited by employment contracts?** If a worker has an employment contract, that contract might limit the company's right to fire the worker. (See "Firing Employees With Employment Contracts," in Chapter 12.) For example, a worker whose contract says that he or she can be fired only for serious misconduct cannot be laid off for economic reasons. Similarly, if a contract gives the worker bumping rights or promises severance pay if the worker is laid off, you will have to abide by that agreement.

- **Is the workplace unionized?** If so, check the collective bargaining agreement for any limitations on the company's right to lay workers off. Workers may be entitled to bumping rights, to be retained according to seniority, or to be paid severance. Also consider whether the company will have to negotiate with the union over how layoffs are conducted. (See "Collective Bargaining" in Chapter 8.)

- **Will the company offer severance or other termination benefits?** Even if severance is not legally required (see "Severance" in Chapter 14), providing it can be a very good idea. By giving laid-off workers something to tide them over until they find another job, you show them that the company values their contributions and is concerned for their welfare. This will only improve the company's standing in the eyes of the laid-off workers, the remaining workforce, and the public.

Alternatives to Layoffs

Layoffs generally come from a need to cut payroll costs. After all, payroll is often the largest single line item in a company's budget, and often the first place companies look when they need to save some money. Before your company lets any workers go, it's a good idea to consider other ways to cut costs here. You might save enough money to avoid layoffs altogether. Even if you still need to cut some staff, at least employees will know that layoffs were a last resort. Here are some alternatives to consider, as well as some legal restrictions on your company's ability to cut in the areas of wages and hours.

Attrition and Freezes

Before you cut anything, it makes sense to consider a freeze on hiring (including replacing employees who leave voluntarily), promotions, and raises. A freeze is one of the least cruel means of saving payroll dollars, because it doesn't take anything away from employees. Employees continue on in their same positions, at their same salaries; it's status quo for everyone.

There are a couple of drawbacks to counting on a freeze to save money. For one, it takes a while to pay off. Because your company isn't taking anything away from anyone, it won't realize any savings right away. However, if your company's budget allowed for several new hires, raises, and so on, that money will be freed up for other things (or, if your company is doing poorly, you won't have to figure out a way to come up with that money in the first place).

Also, a freeze might not be the best way to plan for your company's future. You may really need to expand in some areas of the company and contract in others, rather than simply limiting the company's overall size. Especially if you combine a freeze with an attrition program (by which employees who leave the company aren't replaced), you may not have enough people—or enough of the right people with the right skills—to keep the company moving forward.

Despite these drawbacks, however, a freeze is often a good first cost-cutting step. It should free up at least some money, and it will also lay the groundwork for further cuts, if necessary. After all, your employees won't be pleased to learn that, while they have seen their pay cut or watched colleagues lose their jobs, the company has been bringing on new workers. By putting a freeze on new hires, your company can demonstrate that it's trying to put its existing workforce first.

Overtime

If employees at your company routinely work overtime, cutting back on authorized overtime hours is another good way to cut costs. But remember: Even though overtime may look like extra pay to you, it probably doesn't look that way to employees. An employee who routinely works overtime likely does so because he or she needs the money, and cutting that employee's paycheck is going to hurt, no matter how you classify the cut.

Furloughs and Hour Cuts

Many companies have resorted to reducing the number of hours employees work each week as a way to save money. Some (including some state and local governments) have introduced furloughs, by which employees take, for example, every other Friday off, or take off one week per month, in order to cut payroll cuts. Some companies have simply cut employee hours across the board by 10% or 20%.

If your company must actually reduce employee pay (beyond a freeze), this is the fairest way to do it. At least employees get some time off to compensate for their lost pay. But therein lies the legal rub: If you institute a cut in hours, you must make sure that you don't violate wage and hour laws. This means that, for nonexempt employees (those who are entitled to overtime pay), you must make sure they aren't actually working the hours when they're supposed to be off. And for exempt employees, you must make sure that your hours cut doesn't look like pay docking (which, as explained in Chapter 2,

can result in these employees becoming entitled to earn overtime).

Nonexempt Employees

Unlike exempt employees, who must be paid on a salary basis, nonexempt employees are entitled to pay for all of the time they spend working. So, if your company institutes a furlough or hours cut, you must make sure that nonexempt employees are not working this time anyway. If they are, you will have to pay them for those hours. And, if they are working enough extra hours to merit overtime, you must pay them the overtime premium—time and a half—for those hours.

To make sure employees spend their cut hours doing other things, your company must make very clear that it does not expect employees to work those hours. This can be tricky, especially because your company probably cut hours in the first place because times are tough. But you must make sure that you don't send the message, inadvertently or otherwise, that employees who don't work the cut hours aren't "team players." If you cut employee hours, you have to honor the cut and give employees that time off.

Some lawyers advocate that companies take steps to make it harder for employees to work remotely during cut hours, such as requiring employees to leave laptops or smartphones at work when they leave for a furlough, or disabling outside access to the company's network during the cut hours. As long as these measures won't hamper employees from getting their work done during the hours for which they're actually paid, they could be a sensible way to make sure that employees aren't putting in unauthorized time.

Exempt Employees

For exempt employees, the issues are a bit different. As explained in Chapter 2, exempt employees must be paid on a salary basis. This means they must be paid a set salary of at least $455 every week, no matter how much work they do. An employer may reduce an employee's salary only in limited circumstances. Improper deductions in a salaried employee's compensation can result in that employee—and all other employees in the same job classification—being considered nonexempt and therefore eligible to earn overtime.

A furlough or hours cut—with an accompanying cut in salary—might be considered illegal pay docking, depending on how it's handled. One sure way to avoid this problem is to furlough employees for an entire week. Exempt employees are entitled to their full salary in any week when they do any work. So, as long as you furlough them for a solid week, you may cut their pay proportionately without worrying about the pay docking rule. Of course, you'll have to make sure that exempt employees do absolutely no work during that week. And, you'll have to weigh whether you can really get along without your exempt employees (who are probably your most senior staff) for an entire week.

There's more risk involved in a shorter furlough (for example, every other Friday off) or hours cut (such as half a day off each week). However, the DOL has said that a reduced workweek and concomitant pay cut would not violate the salary basis test as long as the exempt employee still receives at least $455 per week, the cut is prospective, and the employer

has a bona fide reason for the cuts (that is, the employer isn't just trying to get around the salary basis requirement). In short, the cuts must reflect the long-term needs of the business. Under this test, employees will no longer be exempt if their hours are reduced on a day-to-day or week-to-week basis, depending on the operating requirements of the employer. An employer may cut an exempt employee's salary from $1,000 to $900 per week, if that cut is intended to continue as long as necessary, in response to the economic downturn. But it may not cut the employee's salary to $900 this week, $800 the next, and bump it back up to $1,000 the following week, based on its day-to-day levels of business. This type of strategy starts to look a lot like simply paying employees for the hours they work rather than paying them a salary. That's how exempt employees can be converted to nonexempt employees, who are entitled to overtime when they work more than 40 hours per week (which, for many salaried employees, is fairly often).

Pay Cuts

Some employers cut employee pay without reducing hours. There are a number of ways to do this. Some companies give everyone the same percentage wage reduction across the board; others reduce the wages of those who are paid more by a higher percentage. Sometimes, a company's top executives will cut their own pay publicly and drastically (for example, reducing their annual salary to one dollar), as a way both to cut costs and to demonstrate to employees that they are not suffering alone.

For exempt employees, pay cuts can raise some of the same issues discussed above. For example, your company must make sure that the exempt employee's salary remains at least $455 per week after the pay cut, the cut must be prospective, and the cut must reflect long-term business needs, not daily, weekly, or monthly "adjustments" based on cash flow or available work.

For nonexempt employees, you don't need to worry about the salary basis test. However, you must make sure that employees are still receiving at least the minimum wage after the cut. (See Chapter 2 for more on the minimum wage.)

Making the Cut

If your company decides that layoffs are necessary, you'll have to figure out who gets the axe. If the company is getting rid of an entire department or outsourcing particular work tasks, the answer will be obvious. However, if you need to make cuts across the board or simply reduce staff in some areas, there will be some tough decisions to make.

Ultimately, who you lay off should depend on your company's needs and projected future: What is your strategic plan, and what kinds of human resources will you need to get there? It's also a very good idea to have a lawyer review your layoff plan before you actually start breaking the news, to make sure the layoffs will be fair and legally defensible. Here are tips that will help you come up with your initial plan:

- **Decide what the company will need going forward.** Before deciding whom to cut, the company will have to think about its future direction. Is the company shrinking in some areas? Expanding in others? Is the corporate focus shifting? What are the essential positions that must be filled for this plan to succeed? The decision makers should meet to hash out these issues. Once you figure out the functions the company will require in the future, you'll know which jobs can safely be cut.

- **Figure out which departments or positions will be cut.** Now that you know your company's goals, you will be able to figure out which areas need to be scaled back. For example, if the company is cutting back on direct sales to focus more attention on research and development, the sales department can be safely targeted for cuts. At this point, you should focus on jobs and positions, not on individual workers. At the end of this process, you should have a sense of which departments will face cuts and how many workers will have to be laid off from each.

- **Establish the criteria for layoff decisions.** Once you have a sense of what skills the company will need going forward, you can decide how to select workers for layoff. The safest course, legally, is to use objective criteria, like seniority, productivity, sales numbers, client base, and so on. After all, it's hard to argue with numbers that can be double-checked and agreed upon. However, many companies want to include subjective considerations in deciding whom to lay off, such as quality of work, skills, ability to supervise, willingness to learn new tasks, communication, leadership skills, or team spirit. If you will consider subjective qualities, make sure everyone applies these criteria consistently.

- **Make a list.** After the criteria are set, apply them to the workers in the targeted departments to come up with an initial layoff list. Some companies choose to rank or rate their workers according to how well they meet the criteria and then weed out those with the lowest scores.

- **Check it twice.** Once the initial list is finished, look it over for potential problems. Consider the demographics of the workforce before the layoff and after. If you lay off the workers on your list, will the company be getting rid of a disproportionate number of women or minority workers? If so, the company could face a disparate impact discrimination lawsuit. (See Chapter 3 for more information about discrimination claims.)

- **Keep enough people to do the work.** Make sure the workers who are left will be able to do the work that remains, and don't get rid of anyone who is essential to the business. Even after the layoffs, the company still has to function. Workers who remain will quickly begin searching for new jobs if they are asked to do twice as much work to make up the shortfall. If the company makes drastic reductions in its workforce, you will also have to reduce the workload you expect the remaining workers to handle.

Conducting a Layoff

Layoffs are stressful for everyone. The workers whose jobs are cut will face unemployment, job searches, money worries, and possibly worse. The workers who remain will feel uncertain about their future with the company. And the managers who have to break the news will dislike having to be the bad guys.

There is nothing you can do to make layoffs pleasant for everyone; it's undeniably a bad situation for the entire company. But you can take a few steps to make sure that layoffs are handled respectfully, with full recognition of workers' concerns and contributions to the company.

Before Announcing the Layoffs

Realistically, by the time the pink slips get passed around, most of the workforce will know that layoffs are coming. Why? Because layoffs are an open secret. Workers will likely have some inkling of the reasons for the layoff, whether job cuts are required by declining profits, changes in the marketplace, or the elimination of a product line. Savvy employees may have noticed the closed-door management meetings, the human resources department working overtime, or the stress on the faces of their supervisors.

Because news of layoffs often leaks out, some experts advise employers to take the initiative by announcing that reductions might be necessary, even before layoff plans are finalized. If your company chooses to go this route, a company officer or manager should

Lessons From the Real World

Schott North America made a decision to change its business operations in the United States. Previously, the company had produced optical glass (typically used in military, medical, aerospace, and other highly technical fields) and ophthalmic glass (used in ordinary eyeglasses). It decided to move all of its ophthalmic glass production to a plant in Germany, and reorganize its U.S. plant to produce only optical glass.

The company did not lay off all of the employees who worked on the ophthalmic glass line. Instead, it decided to create a new position that consolidated the work necessary for creating optical glass, then purported to rate employees on how well they met the requirements for this position. The company chose the employees for the position by coming up with a list of required job skills, asking managers to assign those skills a relative weight in terms of their importance to the job, then grading each employee for each skill. The top 40 employees were offered a position; the rest lost their jobs either through layoff or voluntary resignation.

A group of women sued the company, claiming that the layoff was discriminatory because many more men than women were offered positions. The company tried to have the lawsuit thrown out, arguing that it made its layoff decisions based on legitimate criteria. The court found that the employees should have a chance to argue their case to a jury.

The former employees argued that the plant had been highly segregated by gender before the reorganization, and that sex discrimination against women had been rampant. They also argued that the rating system for determining who would get the new jobs unfairly gave more weight to the skills associated with positions largely held by men, and didn't accurately measure the skills necessary for the new position. They also claimed that managers ranked individual employees unfairly, based on gender. Because the former employees presented evidence supporting each of these arguments, the court refused to throw out the case before trial.

EEOC v. Schott North America, Inc., 104 F.E.P.C. 1194 (M.D. Penn. 2008).

gather employees together and let them know that the company is considering job cuts. Explain why the cuts may be necessary, when decisions will be made, and how the layoffs will be handled (for example, whether severance will be offered, whether employees will be given incentives to quit, and so on). And be sure to talk about any actions the company is taking to try to tighten its belt; workers are more likely to cooperate in cost-cutting efforts if they know that layoffs could be next.

Of course, other experts advise employers to keep their lips sealed until all of the layoff plans have been hammered out. The aim of this approach is to keep things confidential for as long as possible and prevent workers from leaving like rats fleeing a sinking ship.

If you're in on this decision, you'll have to consider what makes sense for your company. Consider how many people will be involved in the layoff planning, how likely it is that others will find out about the layoffs, and how the company has handled communications with employees in the past. Consider also your company's philosophy on worker involvement. If it places a high value on open communication and group decision making, keeping layoffs a secret might do serious damage to the company's credibility with its workers.

Breaking the News to Laid-Off Workers

We have all heard layoff horror stories: groups of employees herded into conference rooms to be canned en masse, workers fired by email,

staff marched out of the office by armed security guards, and so on. Each of these actions illustrates a callous disrespect for employees and their contributions to the company. And employers reap the negative consequences, by creating legions of hurt ex-employees whose righteous anger at the way they were treated fuels their march to a lawyer's office.

The lesson to be learned from these fiascoes is clear: Be respectful when you lay workers off. Remember that they have made valuable contributions to the company, often for many years, and are suffering a significant loss. Here are a few tips to help you keep things positive:

- **Involve the top brass.** Layoffs are a major event and should be handled by top company executives. Employees may not expect every layoff to be conducted personally by the CEO, but higher-ups should show their faces at meetings and make sure laid-off employees don't feel unimportant or ignored.

- **Give advance notice.** A federal law, the Workers Adjustment and Retraining Notification Act (WARN), requires larger employers to give workers 60 days' notice before a plant closing or mass layoff. (To learn more, see "Notice Requirements for Layoffs," below.) Many states have similar laws; see "State Layoff and Plant-Closing Laws," at the end of this chapter.

- **Don't lay off workers in a group.** Whenever possible, take the time to inform workers individually that they will be laid off. Hold the meeting confidentially, allow enough time to answer the worker's questions and give any necessary information. Don't rush through the meeting or make the worker feel like one stop on the layoff express.

- **Timing is everything.** Don't let laid off workers be the last to know that they're losing their jobs. They deserve to learn the news from their managers, before the rest of the work force. At the same time, don't wait too long to tell the rest of the company: It isn't a good idea for everyone else to learn of a layoff from a former coworker's "keep in touch" email message or from a hallway parade of departing employees carrying cardboard boxes. Experts advise breaking the news to the company while employees are being laid off, or very shortly thereafter.

- **Explain the decision.** Tell the worker why layoffs were necessary and why he or she was chosen to be laid off. Also discuss whether the worker will be eligible for recall or will have any bumping rights to take the position of less senior workers.

- **Be gracious.** A layoff hits workers who have done a good job for the company. Be sure to express your gratitude for the worker's contributions and your sympathy about the termination.

- **Discuss what will happen next.** If the company will offer severance, explain the package. Tell the worker when his or her last day will be and what will happen in the meantime. And give the worker the name of someone in the company to contact with questions.

 Lessons From the Real World

According to the *New York Times*, one company's layoff practices might have cost it millions of dollars in damage to its computer system.

The employer, a chemical company in New Jersey, laid off 50 people in February 2001. One of the unfortunate pink slip recipients was the company's manager of information management systems, who had the inside scoop on the company's computer network. After he was fired, he used another executive's password to tap into the computer system and delete important inventory and personnel files, costing the company $20 million in damages and postponing indefinitely a public stock offering.

Why did he resort to sabotage? In an anonymous letter he wrote to the company president, he gave some clues about the source of his anger: "I have been loyal to the company in good and bad times for over 30 years ... I was expecting a member of top management to come down from his ivory tower to face us with the layoff announcement, rather than sending the kitchen supervisor with guards to escort us off the premises like criminals. You will pay for your senseless behavior."

Eve Tahmincioglu, "Electronic Workplace Vulnerable to Revenge," *The New York Times*, Aug. 6, 2001.

Handling Security Concerns

One reason why some companies treat laid-off workers disrespectfully is that they fear violence or sabotage. And these are legitimate concerns: According to a survey of 186 companies by the Computer Security Institute and the FBI, disgruntled workers caused their former employers $378 million worth of damage in the year 2000 alone.

So how can you protect your company without treating workers like criminals? First, bring in security personnel only if you legitimately fear violence. If workers are resentful or have made threats, or if the situation seems particularly volatile, consider having extra security on hand for the layoffs. But don't ask them to guard the doors, escort workers out, or use any strong-arm tactics unless things really get out of hand.

Protect your company's computer system by turning off employee email and disabling passwords. The best time to do this is during the termination meeting itself. Do it too early and the employee will be left wondering what's going on; do it too late and you leave yourself open to sabotage. Also, make sure to collect company property—keys, credit cards, cell phones, laptop computers, and so on—on the worker's last day. And once the layoffs are through, most companies take the extra step of changing locks and security codes.

Dealing With the Rest of the Workforce

No one would dispute that the workers hit hardest by a layoff are those who lose their jobs. But a layoff is no picnic for the workers who avoid the axe either. They are likely to feel wary about their employment prospects, and quite possibly resentful of the company for firing their coworkers. At the same time, they will likely be expected to work harder, take on new responsibilities, and pick up the work done by their former coworkers. It's no wonder that studies have shown employee turnover rises significantly after a layoff.

To ease the burden and reassure the employees who remain, you can:

- **Provide training.** Unless your company is eliminating an entire product line or company service, the work that used to be done by the laid-off workers still has to get done. This means that remaining employees might have to take on new jobs or added responsibilities. Consider providing some job training to these employees, so they will have an opportunity to learn their new roles. Training can reduce the frustration and anxiety employees feel after a layoff. It can also keep the business running more smoothly.

- **Overcommunicate.** After a layoff, employees are going to be worried about the future of the company and the security of their jobs. Especially if your company had to lay workers off because it isn't doing well financially, make an effort to let employees know how the company plans to turn things around. Check in frequently to tell employees about progress the company is making toward its goals. The more you can keep employees in the loop, the more likely you will be able to hold on to your most valued workers.

- **Avoid burnout.** Employees burn out when they are asked to do more work than they can handle. Remember, if the company is getting rid of a significant number of employees, it is not enough simply to cut those jobs. You must also cut the workload required of the new, streamlined workforce. If you expect remaining employees to simply pick up the slack and do all the work that used to be done by a much larger group, those employees will quickly move on to greener pastures.

- **Retain the employees you keep.** One unfortunate consequence of a layoff is that your company may even lose the employees it chooses not to lay off. After all, the best of these employees are likely to be able to find work elsewhere and may not want to stick around to see how things shake out after the layoffs. To keep these employees, reward good performance. Recognize employees who do well with positive performance evaluations and promotions, even if you can't afford any raises right now.

- **Boost morale.** After a layoff, workers will likely have questions and concerns. You and other managers should be available to provide answers, including the reasons for the layoff. While you should not make promises that the company can't keep, you can tell workers about the company's future plans and expectations. Assure workers

that you value their contributions and you appreciate them staying on in this difficult time.

- **Share the pain.** If your company laid off workers to save money and increase profitability, the yearly management team retreat to Aspen isn't going to go over well with the remaining workforce. Employees want the company to turn around financially, but they also want to know that management- and executive-level employees are in the same boat and feel their pain. Now is not the time to order fancy new office furniture or throw a big expensive party.

Notice Requirements for Layoffs

The Worker Adjustment and Retraining Notification (WARN) Act requires certain larger employers to give some advance notice of an impending plant closing or mass layoff that will result in job losses for a specified percentage or number of employees. The law was passed to help ease the transition for workers who lose their jobs in these circumstances. The WARN Act requires employers to give notice not only to the employees and unions that will be affected by the job cuts, but also to state government agencies that provide assistance to dislocated workers.

Many states have similar laws. See the "State Layoff and Plant-Closing Laws" chart at the end of this chapter for more information.

WARN Act Coverage

The WARN Act doesn't apply to every employer, every employee, or even every layoff. Only large private employers must comply with the WARN Act, and then only if they engage in a plant closing or mass layoff.

Which Employers Are Covered

Federal, state, and local governments are not covered by the WARN Act. Private employers are covered if:

- they have 100 or more employees, not counting part-time employees (those who average fewer than 20 hours per week or have been employed for less than six months before the date when notice would be required under the WARN Act), or
- they have 100 or more employees (including part-time employees) who work a combined total of at least 4,000 hours per week.

Independent contractors don't count toward the total. However, employees who are on temporary layoff or leave must be counted, if they have a reasonable expectation of being recalled or otherwise returning to work. For example, an employee who is taking FMLA leave should be counted, because that employee is entitled to reinstatement after the leave is over. (See Chapter 5 for more on the FMLA).

Lessons From the Real World

After the attacks of September 11, 2001, Congress transferred responsibility for airport security to the federal government. This change meant that many passenger screeners and other security employees who worked for private employers lost their jobs (although some were rehired by the federal agency in charge of airport security).

A group of security employees who were laid off by a company that provided security at San Jose International Airport sued their employers, claiming that they should have received 60 days' notice under the WARN Act. The Ninth Circuit Court of Appeals disagreed, however. The Court found that the WARN Act applies only when an employer orders a layoff or plant closing. Because the layoffs at the airport were due to government action rather than an employer order, the WARN Act didn't apply and the employees were not entitled to notice.

Deveraturda v. Globe Aviation Security Services, 454 F.3d 1043 (9th Cir. 2006).

Which Employees Are Covered

All employees who may reasonably be expected to lose their jobs or to have their hours cut by more than 50% for six consecutive months due to a covered layoff are entitled to notice under the WARN Act. Part-time employees are entitled to notice, even though they are not counted in determining whether the WARN Act applies.

Independent contractors are not covered by WARN and are not entitled to notice.

Which Layoffs Are Covered

Not every reduction in force by a covered employer triggers the WARN Act's notice requirements. An employer must comply with the WARN Act only if it plans to conduct a:

- **Plant closing:** the permanent or temporary shutdown of a single employment site or one or more facilities or operating units within a single employment site, which results in job loss for 50 or more employees (not including part-time employees) during a 30-day period.
- **Mass layoff:** a reduction in force that results in job loss at a single employment site, during a 30-day period, for (1) 500 or more employees (excluding part-time employees), or (2) 50 to 499 employees (excluding part-time employees) if the laid off employees make up at least 1/3 of the employer's active workforce.
- **Staged plant closing or mass layoff:** a plant closing or mass layoff, as defined above, that occurs in stages over a 90-day period. This rule is intended to prevent employers from getting around the

WARN Act's requirements by conducting a series of smaller layoffs.

Required Notice

If a layoff is covered by the WARN Act, the employer must give written notice of the layoff 60 days in advance. The notice must be provided to:

- each employee who will be affected, except those in a union
- the bargaining representative(s) of all union members who will be affected
- the state's dislocated worker unit (sometimes called the rapid response coordinator), and
- the local government in the area where the layoff will occur.

The contents of the notice depend on the recipient. For example, employees who are not in a union must be told whether the planned action is expected to be temporary or permanent; whether an entire plant will be closed; the date when the layoff or closure is expected to begin; the date when the employee will be terminated; whether the employee will have bumping rights; and the name and phone number of a company official the employee can call for more information. (For detailed information on the WARN Act, including the contents of the notice required to each recipient, check out the resources at the Department of Labor's WARN Act page, www.dol.gov/compliance/laws/comp-warn.htm.)

The notice must be based on the best available information when it is given. If that information later proves to be wrong because of subsequent changes in events or inadvertent errors, the employer will not be liable.

Employers that don't provide the required notice may have to pay each employee up to 60 days of compensation and benefits; pay a fine of up to $500 for each day of violation; and pay attorney fees and court costs of workers who sue the employer successfully for violating the law.

Exceptions

In some circumstances, an employer does not have to give notice, or may give notice less than 60 days before a covered layoff.

No Notice Required

The WARN Act doesn't apply—and therefore, an employer need not give any advance notice of a layoff—in these circumstances:

- **Temporary facilities or projects.** If an employer closes a facility that was intended to be open only temporarily or lays off workers who were hired only for a specific project once that project is complete, no notice is required. However, this exception applies only if the laid-off workers understood when they were hired that their employment was limited to the duration of the facility or project.
- **Strikes and lockouts.** If a layoff results from a union strike or an employer lockout, no notice is required.

Notice of Less Than 60 Days Allowed

An employer may comply with the WARN Act by giving as much notice as possible under the circumstances—even if the employer can't give a full 60 days' notice—in some situations. If one of these exceptions applies, the employer must give as much notice as it can and must explain in the written notice why it couldn't give the 60 days' notice that would otherwise be required:

- **Natural disasters.** If an earthquake, flood, or other natural disaster forces a layoff, an employer may give less than 60 days' notice.
- **Unforeseeable business circumstances.** If the layoff is caused by business circumstances that were not reasonably foreseeable when the employer should have given 60 days' notice, a shorter notice period is allowed.
- **Faltering company.** If a company is struggling financially at the time it should have given 60 days' notice of a plant closing, it can give a shorter period of notice. However, the company must show that it was actively seeking business or money that would have allowed it to avoid or postpone the closing, and that it reasonably believed, in good faith, that providing the 60 days' notice would have precluded it from obtaining the necessary business or money. This exception does not apply to mass layoffs, only to plant closings.

Lessons From the Real World

A group of employees sued their former employer Hale-Halsell Co ("HHC"), a grocery distribution and warehouse center, for failing to give 60 days' notice before laying them off under the WARN Act. HHC argued that it couldn't give notice because the layoffs occurred unexpectedly, after it lost a key account following on top of other economic problems, and were therefore covered by the unforeseeable business circumstances exception to the WARN Act.

The employees argued that they should have received notice because there had been problems brewing with the account for more than a year, which had resulted in declining orders from the customer and numerous discussions about the problem. However, the court found in favor of HHC. Although the problems in the relationship were evident, the court found that this didn't trigger the WARN Act's requirements: "Free enterprise always involves risk ... [b]usiness downturns in a cyclical economy are not unusual, and we should not burden employers with the task of notifying employees of possible contract cancellation and concomitant layoffs every time there is a cost overrun or similar difficulty" (internal quotations omitted).

Gross, et al. v. Hale-Halsell Co., 554 F.3d 870 (10th Cir. 2009).

Legal Dos and Don'ts: Layoffs

Do:

- **Plan layoffs carefully.** Surveys have shown that layoffs often cost more than they are worth. Companies may cut too deep, lose critical performers to post-layoff attrition, or have to hire contract workers to pick up the slack. And layoffs are fraught with potential danger, including lawsuits. The lessons for the savvy manager are to think long and hard before undertaking layoffs, and to make sure the layoff plan is legally and practically sound.

- **Research notice requirements.** In the current economic climate, layoffs are increasingly common, and government authorities are increasingly interested in making sure that employers meet their notice obligations. Companies that are struggling and laying off workers piecemeal must be especially careful: A series of smaller layoffs may turn Into a "staged" layoff that's covered by the WARN Act. And don't forget to research state law, which may be stricter than the WARN Act.

- **Overcommunicate with workers who remain.** If you want to hang on to your best employees, you must give them reasons to stay. Attrition is often high after a layoff because employees are worried about the company's future. Keeping workers in the loop is a good way to quell this anxiety. Tell workers how the company plans to turn things around, deadlines by which you expect to see progress, and milestones that will indicate better prospects for the future. Even if your company already holds regular quarterly or annual meetings, it's a good idea to meet more frequently and explain how things are going.

Don't:

- **Disrespect workers on the way out the door.** The way in which you lay off workers is hugely important for many reasons. Remaining workers will judge you and the company by these actions. And your actions will play a major role in determining whether the worker decides to sue over the termination.

- **Start with layoffs.** Before anyone loses a job, your company should already have tried some lesser measures, such as a hiring or promotion freeze, cutting back on overtime, or even pay or hours cuts. Workers should see that the company is tightening its belt. If layoffs become necessary, employees will know that the company resorted to letting people go only as a last resort.

- **Go it alone.** Pay and hour cuts can lead to potential wage and hour problems, and layoffs can lead straight to the courthouse. If you have any concerns or questions about your plans to cut costs, consult with an employment attorney.

Test Your Knowledge

Questions

1. A company is free to cut hours, cut pay, or furlough employees, as long as employees agree to it as a way to save jobs. ☐ True ☐ False

2. You should keep your layoff plans secret for as long as possible, to make sure you don't lose employees you wanted to keep. ☐ True ☐ False

3. Layoffs provide a good cover for getting rid of employees with performance, attendance, or conduct problems. ☐ True ☐ False

4. As long as you tell employees that their hours have been cut, it's okay if some employees keep putting in a full week; after all, the company needs the help. ☐ True ☐ False

5. Employees should be laid off in a group, to make sure everyone gets the same information. ☐ True ☐ False

6. Layoffs are a great way to save money. ☐ True ☐ False

7. Companies should decide which departments or positions will be cut before deciding which particular employees will be laid off. ☐ True ☐ False

8. Companies should try to use objective criteria when deciding who will be laid off. ☐ True ☐ False

9. Workers are generally entitled to at least 60 days' advance notice of a layoff. ☐ True ☐ False

10. Before laying workers off, a company should try to cut costs in other ways. ☐ True ☐ False

Answers

1. Not necessarily. Cutting pay, hours, or both, can lead to legal problems, even if employees are fully on board. Before resorting to these cost-cutting measures, companies should consult with a lawyer.

2. It depends. Your company may have an obligation to tell employees of an impending layoff under the WARN Act. Even if it doesn't, employees will learn that layoffs are brewing. Rather than keeping it a secret, some companies choose to be more open about the possibility of layoffs, so employees know how serious the situation is and are more willing to cut costs in other ways.

3. False. Your layoff criteria (which departments will have to be cut by how many people, and how you will determine which employees to let go) should determine who goes. Although you can consider performance and other issues in deciding who is laid off, you shouldn't try to shoehorn problem employees on to the layoff list if they wouldn't be there otherwise. This could lead them to doubt the reasons you give for firing them, which can lead to a lawsuit. It could also lead other employees to question whether layoffs are really necessary, if your company appears to be using them just to "clean house."

4. False. Your company must pay nonexempt employees for every hour they work, even if you have told them not to work that time.

5. False. Although you might hold a group follow-up meeting to explain severance, continuing benefits, and so on, the initial layoff should be conducted individually and in person.

6. False. Studies show that most companies that downsize don't realize any increases in productivity or long-term gains in shareholder value. Also, the company will be losing workers in a layoff, so, to realize a net gain, the costs it saves will have to at least make up for the lost productivity, sales, and/ or other contributions of those workers.

7. True. A layoff should target the company's problem areas, not its problem employees. If the company is using layoffs as a way to get rid of certain workers, it might face a lawsuit claiming that the layoff was just an excuse for an illegal firing.

8. True. Although companies are allowed to consider subjective factors when deciding whom to lay off, the safest plan is to use objective criteria. This will make it harder for workers to argue that they were improperly targeted for layoffs.

9. True, if the layoff is covered by the WARN Act and no exception applies.

10. True. Workers are more likely to accept layoffs if they believe that the company is really trying to reduce expenses and that layoffs were used as a last resort.

State Layoff and Plant-Closing Laws

ALABAMA
Ala. Code § 25-3-5

When law applies: Substantial layoff or closing of any plant or industry

State assistance for employees: Commissioner of labor to provide seminars to unemployed or underemployed employees on legal rights regarding debts. To lessen the financial burden of closure or layoffs, commissioner may meet with management and with labor or other organizations, may facilitate communication with creditors, and may set up programs to provide financial assistance. No employer or employee group may be required to contribute to or participate in these programs.

ALASKA
Alaska Stat. § 23.15.635

State assistance for employees: Department of Labor offers employment and training programs to workers who are liable to be displaced because of reductions in workforce or job elimination.

CALIFORNIA
Cal. Lab. Code § 1401

When law applies: Mass layoff, relocation, or closing of any industrial or commercial facility with at least 75 employees

Notification requirements: Employer must give employees at least 60 days' advance notice in writing before mass layoff, relocation, or termination. Employer must also notify the Employment Development Department, the local workforce investment board, and the chief elected official of each city and county government within which the termination, relocation, or mass layoff occurs. Notice shall include the elements required by the federal WARN Act.

COLORADO
Colo. Rev. Stat. § 23-60-306

When law applies: Plant closings; workers displaced by technological changes

State assistance for employees: Workers who have lost their previous jobs because of plant closings are eligible for retraining for new jobs through customized training programs provided by the State Board for Community Colleges and Occupational Education.

CONNECTICUT
Conn. Gen. Stat. Ann. §§ 31-51n, 31-51o

When law applies: Permanent shutdown or relocation of facility out of state

Employers affected by requirements: Employers with 100 or more employees at any time during the previous 12-month period

Severance requirements: Employer must pay for existing group health insurance coverage for terminated employee and dependents for 120 days or until employee is eligible for other group coverage, whichever comes first.

Exceptions: Facility closure due to bankruptcy

DISTRICT OF COLUMBIA
D.C. Code Ann. §§ 32-101, 32-102

When law applies: When a new contractor takes over a service contract

Employers affected by requirements: Contractors and subcontractors who employ 25 or more nonprofessionals as food service, health service, or janitorial or building maintenance workers

Severance requirements:
- Within 10 days after a new contract is awarded, previous contractor must give new contractor names of all employees. New

State Layoff and Plant-Closing Laws (cont'd)

contractor must hire all employees who have worked for past 8 months for a 90-day transition period. After 90 days must give each employee a written performance evaluation and retain all employees whose performance is satisfactory.

- Contractor whose contract is not renewed and who is awarded a similar contract within 30 days must hire at least 50% of the employees from the former sites.

FLORIDA
Fla. Stat. Ann. §§ 288.972, 379.2352, 446.60

When law applies: Job loss or displacement due to industry changes

State assistance for employees:
- Department of Labor and Employment Security established Workforce Florida, which provides counseling, training, and placement services to displaced workers in the defense industry and local telecommunications exchange workers.
- State agencies must give priority hiring to anyone who loses full-time employment in the commercial saltwater fishing industry because of the constitutional amendment limiting the use of nets to harvest marine species.

HAWAII
Haw. Rev. Stat. §§ 394B-1 to 394B-13

When law applies: Permanent or partial closing of business; relocation of all or substantial portion of business operations out of state

State assistance for employees: Dislocated workers' program in Department of Labor and Industrial Relations provides assistance and training for workers who have lost their jobs or received a notice of termination.

Employers affected by requirements: Employers with 50 or more employees at any time during the previous 12-month period

Severance requirements: Employer must provide 4 weeks' dislocated worker allowance as a supplement to unemployment compensation; amount is the difference between the weekly former wage and the unemployment benefit. Employers who do not follow notice and severance requirements are liable to each employee for 3 months of compensation.

Notification requirements: Employer must provide each employee with written notice 60 days in advance of closing or relocation.

ILLINOIS
820 Ill. Comp. Stat. §§ 65/1 to 65/99

When law applies: Mass layoff, relocation, or employment loss

Employers affected by requirements: Any business enterprise that employs 75 or more full-time employees or 75 or more employees who in the aggregate work at least 4,000 hours per week (not counting overtime)

Notification requirements: Employer must give 60 days' written notice to affected employees and representatives of affected employees, and to both the Department of Commerce and Economic Opportunity and the chief elected official of each municipal and county government within which the employment loss, relocation, or mass layoff occurs.

Exceptions: Employer seeking capital in good faith; completion of explicitly temporary project; unforeseen circumstances; strike or lockout; physical calamity or war

Penalties: Up to 60 days of back pay and the value of benefits for that time; up to $500 per day

State Layoff and Plant-Closing Laws (cont'd)

civil penalty, unless employer pays the back pay within 3 weeks of announced layoffs; federal penalty payments count toward state penalty

KANSAS

Kan. Stat. Ann. §§ 44-603, 44-616

When law applies: Employers involved in manufacture, transportation, or preparation of food products or clothing; fuel mining or production; public utilities, or transportation must apply to state Secretary of Labor for approval before limiting or discontinuing business operations.

LOUISIANA

La. Rev. Stat. Ann. §§ 23:1842 to 23:1846

When law applies: Job loss related to state environmental protection laws

State assistance for employees: Workers who have lost jobs because employer has relocated to another state to avoid compliance with state environmental protection laws or instituted technological changes because of laws are eligible for services through the Displaced Worker Retraining Program administered by the Department of Workforce Development.

MAINE

Me. Rev. Stat. Ann. tit. 26, § 625-B

When law applies: Discontinuation or relocation of business operations at least 100 miles from original location

Employers affected by requirements: Employers with 100 or more employees at any time during the previous 12-month period

Severance requirements: Employer must give severance pay of one week for each year of employment to all employees who have worked for at least 3 years; pay due within one

regular pay period after employee's last full day of work.

Notification requirements: Employer must give employees at least 60 days' advance notice in writing before relocating a plant. Employer must also notify the director of the Bureau of Labor Standards and municipal officials where the plant is located. Within 7 days, if employer lays off 100 or more employees, employer must report to the director the expected duration of the layoff and if the layoff is definite or indefinite.

MARYLAND

Md. Code Ann. [Lab. & Empl.] §§ 11-301 to 11-304

When law applies: Shutdown of workplace or a portion of the operations that results in layoffs of at least 25% of workforce or 15 employees, whichever is greater, over any 3-month period

State assistance for employees: Department of Labor will provide on-site unemployment insurance bulk registration (when more than 25 workers are laid off), retraining, job placement, and job-finding services.

Employers affected by requirements: Employers with 50 or more employees who have been in business at least one year

Severance requirements: Employers are encouraged to follow Department of Labor voluntary guidelines for severance pay, continuation of benefits, and notification.

Notification requirements: 90 days whenever possible

Exceptions: Bankruptcy, seasonal factors common to industry, labor disputes, temporary workplaces, or construction sites

State Layoff and Plant-Closing Laws (cont'd)

MASSACHUSETTS

Mass. Gen. Laws ch. 149, §§ 179B, 182, 183; ch. 151A, §§ 71A to 71H

When law applies:
- Permanent cessation or reduction of business operations which results or will result in the permanent separation of at least 90% of the employees within 6 months
- Sale or transfer of ownership of a business with 50 or more employees

State assistance for employees:
- Reemployment assistance programs which provide counseling, placement, and training are available through the employment and training division of the Department of Workforce Development.
- Employees who have worked for a company for at least one year are eligible for up to 13 weeks of reemployment assistance benefits.

Employers affected by requirements:
- Employers receiving assistance from state business financing or development agencies
- Employers with 50 or more employees who sell or transfer control of a business

Severance requirements:
- Employers receiving state agency assistance must make a good-faith effort to provide 90 days' group health insurance coverage for employees and dependents, at the same payment terms as before plant closing.
- When a company with 50 or more employees is sold or changes hands, new owner must give severance pay of 2 weeks' compensation for every year of service to employees who have worked at least 3 years. Employees terminated within 2 years of the sale are due severance within one regular pay period after last day of work; employees terminated within one year of sale are due severance within 4 pay periods after the sale.

Notification requirements:
- Employers receiving state agency assistance are expected to provide 90 days' notice.
- Employers with 12 or more employees must notify the Director of Labor and Workforce Development when business changes location.
- New owner of business with 50 or more employees must provide written notice of rights to each employee and to any collective bargaining representative within 30 days of completion of sale.

MICHIGAN

Mich. Comp. Laws §§ 450.731 to 450.737

When law applies: Permanent shutdown of operations at any establishment with 25 or more employees

State assistance for employees: Department of Labor may study the feasibility of the employees establishing an employee-owned corporation to continue the business.

Notification requirements: Department of Labor encourages businesses that are closing or relocating to give notice as soon as possible to the Department, the employees and any organization representing them, and the community.

State Layoff and Plant-Closing Laws (cont'd)

MINNESOTA

Minn. Stat. Ann. §§ 116L.17, 116L.976

When law applies:

- Plant closing: Announced or actual permanent shutdown of a single site
- Substantial layoff: Permanent reduction in workforce (not due to plant closing) at a single site which results in job loss for at least 50 full-time employees during any 30-day period

Notification requirements: Employers are encouraged to give 60 days' notice to the Department of Trade and Economic Development. If federal WARN Act requires notice, then employer must report to state commissioner of employment and economic development the occupations of workers being terminated.

State assistance for employees: Department of Trade and Economic Development offers rapid response assistance to employees and businesses through the dislocated worker program. May include on-site emergency assistance, information about state and other agency resources, and help in setting up an employee-management committee.

MISSOURI

Mo. Rev. Stat. § 409.516(5)

When law applies: Any company making a business takeover offer

Notification requirements: Company making offer must file a registration statement with the state securities commission disclosing any plans to liquidate, merge, or consolidate the target company, sell its assets, or make any other major change to its business, corporate structure, management, or employment policies.

NEW HAMPSHIRE

N.H. Rev. Stat. Ann. § 421-A:4(IV)

When law applies: Any company making a business takeover offer

Notification requirements: Company making offer must file a registration statement with the secretary of state and with the target company disclosing any plans to liquidate, merge, or consolidate the target company, sell its assets, or make any other major change to its business, corporate structure, management, or employment policies.

NEW JERSEY

N.J. Stat. Ann. §§ 34:1B-30, 52:27H-95

When law applies: Potential plant closings

State assistance for employees: Department of Labor and other agencies mandated to assist workers who want to establish employee ownership plans to save jobs threatened by plant closure. If plant closure would cause significant employment loss to an economically distressed municipality, the commissioner of commerce may fund a profitability study of an employee stock ownership plan.

NEW YORK

N.Y. Lab. Law §§ 835 to 849; Pub. Auth. Law §§ 1836-a to 1836-g; Bus. Corp. Law § 1603(5)

When law applies:

- Plant closing: Permanent or temporary shutdown of a single site or one or more facilities or operating units within a single site which results in job loss for at least 25 full-time employees during any 30-day period. (If shutdown causes job losses at other sites, they also count toward the 25.)

State Layoff and Plant-Closing Laws (cont'd)

- Substantial layoff: Reduction in workforce (not due to shutdown) at a single site which results in job loss for at least 33% full-time and 50 part-time employees or 500 full-time employees during any 30-day period
- Any company making a business takeover offer

State assistance for employees:

- The Department of Labor, in coordination with the Department of Economic Development and the dislocated worker unit, provides rapid response services after a plant closure, including: on-site intervention within 48 hours; basic emergency readjustment services; information about retraining, unemployment insurance, and technical assistance.
- The Job Development Authority encourages employees of plants that are about to be closed or relocated to continue to operate them as employee-owned enterprises; state assistance is available.

Notification requirements: Company making offer must file a registration statement with the attorney general's New York City office and with the target company disclosing plans for plant closures or major changes in employment policies.

OHIO
Ohio Rev. Code Ann. §§ 122.13 to 122.136

When law applies: Permanent shutdown of operations at a business with at least 25 employees; relocation of all or substantial portion of operations at least 100 miles from original location

State assistance for employees: Department of Development has an employee ownership assistance program that provides technical assistance and counseling; will conduct a feasibility study for workers who want to establish employee ownership plans to continue running a business threatened by plant closure.

OKLAHOMA
Okla. Stat. Ann. tit. 71, § 453(F)(3)

When law applies: Any company making a business takeover offer

Notification requirements: Company making offer must file a registration statement with the state securities commission disclosing plans to close or relocate facilities or to make major changes in employment policies.

OREGON
Or. Rev. Stat. §§ 285A.510 to 285A.522, 657.335 to 657.340

When law applies

- Plant closing: Permanent or temporary shutdown of a single site or one or more facilities or operating units within a single site which results in job loss for at least 50 full-time employees during any 30-day period.
- Mass layoff: Reduction in workforce at a single site not due to shutdown which results in job loss for at least 33% of the workforce and 50 full-time employees, or for 500 full-time employees during any 30-day period

State assistance for employees: State assistance and professional technical training available to dislocated workers. Workers who are in training are entitled to unemployment compensation and related benefits.

Employers affected by requirements: Employers with 100 or more full-time employees

State Layoff and Plant-Closing Laws (cont'd)

Notification requirements: Employers must notify the Department of Community Colleges & Workforce Development of plant closings or mass layoffs.

PENNSYLVANIA

43 Pa. Cons. Stat. Ann. §§ 690a.1 to 690a.6; 70 PCSA §§ 74; 75(4)

When law applies:

- Current or projected plant closures
- Any company making a business takeover offer

Notification requirements: Company making offer must file a registration statement 20 days in advance with the state securities commission, the target company, and the collective bargaining agent. Must disclose plans for closing down the target company, making major changes in employment policies, or changing any collective bargaining agreements.

State assistance for employees: Workers dislocated by plant closures are eligible for customized job training program through the Department of Labor & Industry and are eligible for assistance to support them while in training.

RHODE ISLAND

R.I. Gen. Laws § 27-19.1-1

When law applies: Involuntary layoff; permanent reduction of workforce

Severance requirements: Employees and dependents are entitled to at least 18 months' continuation of health care coverage at own expense; premium rate must be the same as the one offered under the group plan. (Length of coverage cannot exceed time of continuous employment.)

SOUTH CAROLINA

S.C. Code Ann. § 41-1-40

Employers affected by requirements: Employers who require employees to give notice before quitting work

Notification requirements: Employers must give same amount of notice they require of employees or at least 2 weeks' warning. Notice must be in writing and posted in every room of the work building. Employers who do not comply are liable to every employee for any damages that result from failure to give notice.

TENNESSEE

Tenn. Code Ann. §§ 50-1-601 to 50-1-604

When law applies: Closing, modernization, relocation, or new management policy of a workplace or a portion of the operations that permanently or indefinitely lays off 50 or more employees during any three-month period

Employers affected by requirements: Employers with 50 to 99 full-time employees within the state

Notification requirements: Employer must first notify employees who will lose their jobs due to a reduction in operations and then notify the Commissioner of Labor and Workforce Development. Must give circumstances of closing and number of employees laid off. Toll-free telephone line established to encourage employer compliance.

Exceptions: Construction sites; seasonal factors common to industry

TEXAS

Tex. Gov't. Code Ann. §§ 2310.301 to 2310.308; Tex. Util. Code Ann. § 39.906

When law applies: Industry restructuring or plant or facility closing

State Layoff and Plant-Closing Laws (cont'd)

Employers affected by requirements: Private employers who contract with Department of Defense or whose business is directly affected by defense-related economic factors

State assistance for employees:
- Through defense readjustment projects, state provides funding to communities, programs, and businesses that assist or hire dislocated defense workers.
- Public Utility Commission allows employers to recover reasonable transition costs for severance, retraining, early retirement, outplacement, and related expenses for employees affected by electric utility industry restructuring.

UTAH

Utah Code Ann. § 67-1-12

When law applies: Defense industry layoffs

State assistance for employees: Workers in defense or defense-related jobs who are laid off may apply to the Office of Job Training for assistance in retraining or reeducation for job skills in demand.

WASHINGTON

Wash. Rev. Code Ann. §§ 50.04.075, 50.12.280, 50.20.042, 50.20.043, 50.70.030 to 50.70.050

When law applies: Employees who have been terminated or received a notice of termination and are unlikely to return to work at their principal occupations or previous industries

State assistance for employees: The Department of Employment Security offers special training and counseling programs for dislocated workers in aerospace, thermal electric generation, and forest products industries in addition to any regular unemployment compensation.

WISCONSIN

Wis. Stat. Ann. §§ 106.15, 109.07

When law applies:
- Business closing: Permanent or temporary shutdown of an employment site or of one or more facilities or operating units at a site or within one town that affects 25 or more employees
- Mass layoff: Reduction in workforce that is not the result of a business closing and that affects at least 25% or 25 employees, whichever is greater, or at least 500 employees
- Employees who have worked at least 6 of the previous 12 months and who work at least 20 hours/week

Employers affected by requirements: Employers with 50 or more employees in the state

Notification requirements: An employer who has decided upon a business closing or mass layoff in Wisconsin must give at least 60 days' written notice to:
- the Dislocated Worker Committee in the Department of Workforce Development
- every affected employee
- the employees' collective bargaining representative, and
- the highest official of the municipality where the business is located.

Employer must also include contact information for the local workforce development board. Employer who does not comply is liable to employees for pay and for the value of benefits employees would have received if closing or layoff did not take place, from the day that notice was required to the day notice was actually given or business closing or mass layoff occurred, whichever is earlier.

State Layoff and Plant-Closing Laws (cont'd)

WYOMING

Wyo. Stat. §§ 27-13-101 to 27-13-103

When law applies: Workers unemployed due to plant closings or in substantial plant layoffs

State assistance for employees: Department of Employment, in conjunction with the Department of Education, the University of Wyoming, and the Community College Commission, offers occupational transfer and retraining programs and services for displaced workers.

Departing Workers

Whether an employment relationship is good or bad, odds are it will end one day, and perhaps sooner than you think. Employment statistics show that the days of an individual staying with a company until retirement are long gone: According to a 2004 study by the U.S. Bureau of Labor Statistics, workers spend an average of only four years with a company before moving on.

Observing legal rules is especially important at the end of the employment relationship. Departing workers (especially those who are leaving involuntarily) may be unhappy, angry, or dissatisfied with the way they've been treated by your company. If you show respect to departing employees, and make sure you observe all of their legal rights, you have a much better chance of averting lawsuits and other problems.

In this chapter, we look at some common issues you'll face when workers depart, paying special attention to trouble spots. Regardless of why a worker leaves—whether he or she was fired, was laid off, or quit—you'll face many of the same issues as the employment relationship winds down. These issues include how to give references, how to extend health

Frequently Asked Questions About Departing Workers

Do we have to give references for every worker who leaves?

No. No law requires employers to give a reference for a former employee, just as no law prohibits telling the truth about a former employee. However, there are some steps you should take to make sure you don't create unnecessary legal problems when you provide a reference. (For more about this issue, see "References," below.)

What should we say to our remaining workers when an employee leaves?

It depends on why the employee is leaving. If the employee is separating on good terms, you can let other workers know where and when the employee is going. For employees who are fired, however, you should probably be less forthcoming. (See "What to Tell Coworkers When an Employee Leaves," below, for more information.)

Do we have to continue to pay a former employee's health insurance premiums?

No. For more than a year (from March 1, 2009 through the end of May 2010), a federal government subsidy paid about two-thirds of the cost of continuing health insurance for certain workers. Employers had to pay this portion initially, but could take a credit for it against their payroll taxes. However, the subsidy has expired. Now, former employees are once again required to pay the full premium to continue coverage.

Frequently Asked Questions About Departing Workers (cont'd)

Are we legally required to pay severance?

Probably not. Unless your company has led employees to believe that they are entitled to severance, there is no obligation to give it. (For more information, see "Severance," below.)

Is there anything we can do to protect the company from lawsuits by former employees?

Yes. You can ask employees to sign a release in which they agree not to sue the company over the termination. Some companies routinely ask employees to sign a release as a condition of receiving a severance package. (For more about this, see "Releases," below.)

Are all departing workers entitled to unemployment compensation?

No. The unemployment laws vary from state to state, but generally workers who quit for ordinary reasons or who lose their jobs because of gross misconduct are not entitled to receive benefits. Workers who are laid off, who quit for compelling reasons, or who are fired for conduct that isn't very serious can receive benefits. (For more information, see "Unemployment Benefits," below.)

---

benefits, whether to dispute unemployment benefits, and whether to give severance.

References

Whenever an employee leaves, your company will have to decide what to say to other employers who call for a reference. The decision is pretty straightforward if the employee left on good terms: You and the former employee can come up with a mutually agreeable statement to explain the departure. Or, you can simply tell the whole glowing truth to any prospective employer who calls for a reference. But if the employee was fired, you face a more difficult task.

Defamation

If you are not careful in your statements about former employees, your company might find itself defending a defamation lawsuit. And, because defamation is a personal injury claim that can be brought against individuals as well as organizations, you could even be sued personally for your comments.

To prove defamation, a former employee typically must show that company representatives intentionally damaged his or her reputation by making harmful statements about the employee that they knew to be false.

At first glance, it might seem like only the most spiteful manager would get caught in this trap. But, if you make an unflattering statement that you don't absolutely know to be true, it could happen to you. Let's face it: Most reasons for firing make the employee look bad. And managers often cannot prove what they strongly believe to be true: that an employee is stealing from the company, is incompetent, or lied about job qualifications, for example. A manager who makes such statements about a former employee could get into trouble. Your best policy is to say as little as possible and stick to facts you can prove.

Rules for Giving References

When a potential employer calls for a reference, you may feel trapped between wanting to tell the truth and fearing a lawsuit if you say anything unflattering. Unfortunately, this fear is not unfounded. The number of defamation lawsuits filed over negative references is growing all the time. And, even if a former employee can't successfully prove that you defamed him or her, your company and/or you will have to spend precious time and money fighting the allegation.

Here are some tips to help you avoid problems:

- **Warn a difficult employee that your reference won't be good.** Yes, the employee should know this already. But you can avoid problems at the outset by stating the obvious: "I cannot provide a positive reference for you."
- **Keep it brief.** Some companies adopt a policy of only giving out dates of employment, job title, and final salary to prospective employers. If your company

chooses to tell more, keep it to a minimum.
- **Stick to the facts.** Now is not the time to speculate about a former employee's bad qualities or to opine on the reasons for his or her failure to perform. Limit your comments to accurate, easily documented information.
- **Don't be spiteful.** Many states offer some protection for former employers called upon to provide a reference. These laws generally provide that your company will be shielded from defamation lawsuits as long as you provide information in good faith. This is a fairly nebulous legal standard, but it surely does not cover nasty or mean-spirited gripes.
- **Don't give false flattery.** If you had to fire a real bad egg (for example, a worker who was violent in the workplace or threatened coworkers), don't lie about it. You may choose to give only name, rank, and serial number, but, if you give a more expansive reference, don't hide the bad news. Your company could also end up in legal trouble for failing to warn the new employer about these serious problems.
- **Designate one person to give references.** Choose one trusted person in the company to be responsible for all references, and tell employees to direct inquiries to that person. Make sure that your company keeps a record of every request for a reference and every response, in case of later trouble. Some companies provide only written

Lessons From the Real World

Randi was a female student at a California middle school when she was called into the vice principal's office one day in 1992. Later, she claimed that the vice principal, Robert Gadams, sexually molested her while she was in his office.

As it turned out, the school hired Gadams after receiving positive recommendations from another school district where Gadams had worked. Even though supervisors in his former school district knew that Gadams had been accused of sexual misconduct and impropriety with students, it failed to mention these claims when the new middle school asked for a reference. In fact, the former district gave letters of recommendation for Gadams that contained unconditional praise.

One letter recommended Gadams "for an assistant principalship or equivalent position without reservation."

When Randi sued Gadams's previous school district, the district claimed that she had no legal grounds for suit. After all, it argued, it didn't have any sort of obligation to her, a student in a different district. The California Supreme Court disagreed. It said that Randi could sue because the school district had a duty to not misrepresent the facts when describing the character and qualifications of an employee to a prospective employer (in this case, the middle school that Randi attended).

Randi W. v. Muroc Joint Unified School District, et al., 14 Cal.4th 1066, 60 Cal.Rptr.2d 263 (1997).

---

references, to make sure they have proof of exactly what was said.

- **Insist on a written release.** To make absolutely sure your company is protected against lawsuits, require former employees to sign a release: an agreement that gives you permission to provide information to prospective employers (and promises not to sue over the information you provide).

What to Tell Coworkers When an Employee Leaves

Before a departing employee walks out the door, sit down and discuss what you will tell coworkers about the situation. If the employee is leaving on good terms, this decision should not be difficult. You'll probably want to thank the worker for his or her service, tell coworkers where the worker is going, and express high hopes for the worker's future.

You'll need to take extra steps if a worker is fired, however. Imagine how other employees will feel when they learn that a coworker—perhaps a friend—has been fired.

Not only will they want to know why that person was fired, but they may also start to fear for their own jobs. Rumors will circulate. Morale may drop. This is especially true if you're terminating a popular employee or someone who's been with the company for a number of years.

You may be tempted to say nothing to other workers about the termination. Although this instinct is understandable, it's not a good one. Employees are not going to ignore or forget about the termination, no matter how much they may have wanted the employee gone. Every employee secretly fears being fired, so it is unsettling at best when it happens to a coworker.

So what should you do? You can keep other workers informed, boost morale, and avoid any legal missteps by following these tips:

- **Call a meeting.** Consider calling a meeting with employees to announce the termination so you can acknowledge the event on behalf of the company and encourage workers to move past it.
- **Relay the facts.** At the meeting, tell them who has been terminated and as of what date. Do not explain why the employee was fired.
- **Keep it neutral.** Do not express anger or relief. Be professional and calm. Tell workers that you can't go into details because you must respect the fired employee's privacy.

Of course, this doesn't mean managers can never discuss the reasons for termination with anyone. If there is a compelling business need to tell an employee why a coworker was terminated (for example, an employee is taking on the terminated worker's projects and needs to know what the worker did wrong), then do it one on one, in a private and confidential setting. Instruct the employee not to reveal anything you say to anyone else in the organization.

Health Insurance

With the astronomical increases in the costs of medical care, health insurance has become a coveted—if not essential—employee benefit. The importance of health care coverage means that this will be one of the first issues a terminated employee will ask about.

Many companies offer to foot the bill for continued insurance coverage—at least for a while—as part of an employee's severance package. Often, this benefit helps give former workers peace of mind and makes them feel more kindly disposed toward a former employer. (See "Severance," below, for more about this issue.)

Warm fuzzies aside, there are also federal and state laws that may require employers to make continued coverage available to former employees.

Federal Law

A federal workplace law, the Consolidated Omnibus Budget Reconciliation Act (COBRA), 29 U.S.C. § 1162, applies to companies that have 20 or more employees and offer a group health care plan. Among other things, it requires companies to offer former employees the option of continuing their health care coverage for up to 18 months if they quit or are fired for any reason other than gross misconduct. Companies must also make this opportunity available to the employee's spouse and dependents.

From March 1, 2009 through May 31, 2010, employees who lost their jobs involuntarily were entitled to a partial subsidy of 65% of their COBRA premiums. The subsidy initially lasted for nine months, then was extended to 15 months. Initially, the employer had to pay the subsidized portion of the employee's premium, then claim a tax credit against its payroll tax obligations. However, the premium has not been renewed since its expiration (and, given the current climate of government cost cutting and belt tightening, commentators don't expect the issue to resurface any time soon).

Except for the brief period when the subsidy was in effect, the general rule is that former employees must pay the full cost of continuing coverage under COBRA, including both the employee's and the company's share of the premiums. To learn more about COBRA, go to www.dol.gov/dol/topic/health-plans/cobra.htm.

State Laws

Most states also have laws that give former employees the right to continue group health insurance after they leave a job. Your company must comply with both state and federal law. In other words, complying with COBRA may not get your company off the hook if state law requires more. State protections are generally more detailed and more generous to workers than COBRA. In addition, even small businesses (fewer than 20 employees) that escape COBRA may have to comply with state laws.

To learn more about your state's law, see "State Health Insurance Continuation Laws," at the end of this chapter.

Severance

Many employers assume they have to offer a severance package—some combination of money and continuing benefits—to fired employees. In most cases, however, a company is not legally required to pay employees severance. (A few states require some employers to pay a small amount of severance when they lay off a significant number of workers at one time; see "State Layoff and Plant-Closing Laws," in Chapter 13, for more information.)

The law requires a company to provide severance to former employees only if it led them to believe they would receive it by:

- signing a written contract agreeing to pay severance
- promising employees severance pay in an employee handbook or personnel policy
- historically paying severance to other employees in the same position, or
- verbally promising severance to the employee.

Even so, many employers routinely give severance packages to long-term employees, unless the employees are terminated for serious misconduct. Many employers do this to soften the blow of being fired or laid off and to buy a little insurance against lawsuits. A severance package may help sweeten the sour grapes workers feel about losing their jobs. As a general rule, a happier former employee is a less litigious former employee.

If your company decides to pay severance, the most important rule is to be consistent. The amount of severance can vary depending on how long the employee has worked for the company and on the employee's job category. But be sure to treat employees equally. A company that is evenhanded and uniform in paying severance is less likely to face claims of discrimination (for example, that men received higher severance pay than women).

What to Include in a Severance Package

There are no hard-and-fast rules about what constitutes a severance package. The idea is to ease the burden on the soon-to-be-jobless employee. You might consider including any or all of the following benefits:

- **Pay.** Realistically, this is what is most important to employees. Many employers pay a set amount—a week or two of salary—for every year of employment.
- **Insurance benefits.** Some employers offer to pay for continuation of insurance coverage for a period of time after an employee is fired. Although COBRA requires most employers to offer their employees the opportunity to continue their health insurance, it does not require employers to foot the whole bill (or any of it, in some circumstances). (For more about COBRA, see "Health

Insurance," above.) An employer may also want to continue other benefits, such as life or disability insurance.

- **Uncontested unemployment compensation.** Fired employees can apply for unemployment benefits if they were fired for reasons other than serious misconduct. After an employee applies for benefits, the employer has the opportunity to contest the employee's claim. By agreeing not to contest an employee's claim, a company makes it more likely that the employee will receive benefits. (For more information about how unemployment works, see "Unemployment Benefits," below.)
- **Outplacement services.** Outplacement programs help employees find new jobs. They may offer counseling on career goals and job skills, tips on résumé writing, leads for potential jobs, practice interview sessions, and help in negotiating with potential employers.
- **References.** You might agree to come up with a mutually agreeable letter of reference for an employee to use in job hunting. But proceed with caution here: Giving references carries with it some possible risks. (For more about this issue, see "References," above.)
- **Other benefits.** Certain benefits or items may be particularly important to a departing employee. If possible, have an honest discussion to find out what the worker would like in a severance package. You might want to consider allowing the employee to keep advances or money paid for moving expenses,

giving the employee equipment such as a cell phone or computer, or releasing an employee from contractual obligations, like a covenant not to compete.

As you can see, severance means more than money. If you think creatively and communicate with the employee, you should be able to come up with some valuable benefits that won't break the bank.

Releases

Firing or laying off a worker is never pleasant. But sometimes, it's actually risky. Perhaps the employee complains a lot or stirs up trouble in the workplace. Or maybe you have made some mistakes in your management of the employee and have reason for concern if a judge or jury later reviews your decisions.

Checklist: Collecting Company Property

Before a departing worker walks out the door for the last time, you'll need to disable the employee's passwords and security codes so the employee will no longer have access to the company's computers, telephone system, and workplace. You'll also need to get back any company property in the employee's possession, and it's much easier to do this before the employee leaves than to try to track the employee (and the property) down later. Here are some of the things you may need to collect:

☐ company car

☐ keys and security cards that allow access to the workplace

☐ company credit card (you should also call the credit card issuer to cancel the account)

☐ computer password

☐ long-distance calling card (you should also call the provider to cancel the account)

☐ confidential files, client lists, manuals, and other company documents

☐ laptop computer, and

☐ cell phone.

Either way, if your company is worried about a lawsuit, you might want to ask the employee to sign a release: an agreement not to sue the company in exchange for receiving certain benefits. Some employers routinely ask employees to sign a release as a condition of receiving a severance package. Others ask for releases only from employees who might have a legitimate legal claim against the company or who seem especially motivated to sue.

Because some states have specific requirements about what language must go into a release, you should consult an attorney for help in crafting a legal agreement that will meet your needs. Here are some general considerations to keep in mind:

- **Give the employee something in exchange for the release.** You are asking the employee to waive the right to sue the company, and that right is worth something. This means that if your company offers severance packages to employees who don't sign releases, it will have to give something extra to employees who do sign. Specify the additional benefits in the release.
- **Be clear about the rights the employee is waiving.** The release might state that the employee is waiving any right to sue for claims arising out of the employment relationship, including the termination of that relationship. In any case, make sure the agreement is specific enough to prevent employees from later claiming that they didn't know what rights they were giving up.

- **Give the employee plenty of time to decide whether to sign.** It is reasonable for an employee to take a week or two to decide whether to give up the right to sue. You might even suggest that the employee consult with a lawyer to review the agreement.
- **Avoid any hint of coercion.** An employee must sign the release voluntarily or courts will not enforce it. Don't threaten or talk tough with employees to convince them to sign; a release that gets thrown out of court won't do your company much good.
- **Special rules apply to older workers.** If the employee is 40 years of age or older, a federal law—the Older Workers' Benefit Protection Act (OWBPA)—dictates what language must be included in a release. Among other things, these employees must have a longer period of time to review the release; be able to revoke the agreement (change their minds) for a limited time after they sign; and be advised, in writing, to consult with an attorney.

Unemployment Benefits

Not everyone who's out of work is entitled to unemployment benefits. There are a couple of factors that dictate whether a former employee will receive unemployment: the circumstances of the employee's departure and whether his or her former employer decides to contest the employee's claim. This means your company has a lot of power over whether the worker will receive unemployment benefits.

Employee Eligibility

Employees are eligible for unemployment benefits only if they are out of work through no fault of their own. This rule works differently depending on whether the employee quit, was laid off, or was fired.

If an employee quits. An employee who quits or resigns from a job will be eligible for benefits only if he or she did so for what is called "good cause." A good reason for quitting a job is not necessarily good cause. The law requires the reason to be "compelling": that is, the worker would have suffered some sort of harm or injury by staying. Put another way, the reason must be the sort that would have made any reasonable person leave.

For example, leaving a job because it doesn't offer opportunities for career advancement is a good reason, but it won't make a worker eligible for unemployment benefits. Similarly, simple job dissatisfaction is a good reason that does not amount to good cause.

If an employee leaves the job because of intolerable working conditions (such as being sexually harassed) or because he or she was offered the opportunity to quit in lieu of being fired, most states would allow the worker to collect unemployment. Similarly, leaving a job because it poses a serious threat to the worker's health or safety is usually good cause.

If an employee is laid off. An employee who loses a job through a layoff or reduction in workforce is eligible for benefits.

If an employee is fired. Fired employees can claim unemployment benefits if they were terminated because of financial cutbacks or because they were not a good fit for the job for which they were hired. They can also receive benefits if the employer had a good reason to fire but the infractions were relatively minor, unintentional, or isolated.

In most states, however, an employee who is fired for misconduct will not be able to receive unemployment benefits. Although you may think that any action that leads to termination should constitute misconduct, the unemployment laws don't look at it that way. Not all actions that result in termination are serious enough to qualify as misconduct and justify denying benefits to the terminated worker.

What qualifies as misconduct? Generally speaking, an employee engages in misconduct by willfully doing something that substantially injures the company's interests. Revealing trade secrets or sexually harassing coworkers is misconduct; simple inefficiency or an unpleasant personality is not. Other common types of misconduct include extreme insubordination, chronic tardiness, numerous unexcused absences, intoxication on the job, and dishonesty.

Common actions that often result in firing—but do not constitute misconduct—are poor performance because of lack of skills, good faith errors in judgment, off-work conduct that does not have an impact on the employer's interests, and poor relations with coworkers.

It is important to remember that what qualifies as misconduct is a matter of interpretation and degree. Annoying one coworker might not be misconduct, but intentionally engaging in actions that anger an entire department even after repeated warnings might be.

Should Your Company Contest the Claim?

Your state's unemployment office—not your company—will ultimately decide whether the former employee can receive unemployment benefits. You do, however, have the option of contesting the employee's application, and that option gives your company a great deal of power. In California, for example, the unemployment board presumes that a terminated employee did not engage in misconduct unless the employer contests the claim. Thus, in California, terminated employees who claim unemployment benefits receive them unless the former employer intervenes.

Remember, there is no reason—and there are no grounds—to contest an unemployment claim if the employee was laid off. There are also no grounds to contest the claim if the employee did not engage in misconduct but was fired for sloppy work, carelessness, poor judgment, or inability to learn new skills, for instance.

Even if an employee does engage in misconduct, your company might want to give up its right to contest an unemployment insurance claim as part of a severance package. This is especially true if the fired employee seems likely to sue. (See "Severance," above, for more about severance packages and unemployment insurance.)

Your company should contest a claim only if it has grounds to do so (because the employee engaged in serious misconduct or quit without a compelling reason). And even then, your company should also have a good, practical reason to contest. Employers typically fight unemployment claims for one of two reasons:

- They are concerned that their unemployment insurance rates may increase. After all, the employer—not the employee—pays for unemployment insurance. The amount the employer pays is often based in part on the number of claims made against the employer by former employees.
- They are concerned that the employee plans to file a wrongful termination action. The unemployment application process can be a valuable time to discover the employee's side of the story, and it can also provide an excellent opportunity for gathering evidence, both from the employee and from witnesses.

If your company plans to contest an unemployment compensation claim, proceed with extreme caution. These battles not only cost time and money, but they also ensure that the former employee will become an enemy. The employee might even file a wrongful termination lawsuit that otherwise could have been avoided. If the fired worker has friends who remain on the job, they too may doubt and distrust your company's tactics.

Before making any decisions, you might want to do some research by contacting your state's unemployment office for specific information about the law in your state. This office can tell you what effect a successful claim will have on your company's rates. If it's relatively small, backing off might be a good idea.

Anatomy of an Unemployment Compensation Claim

Although the unemployment compensation system varies in each state, some general principles apply in most cases. An unemployment claim will typically proceed through the steps described below.

Step 1: **Claim filing.** The process starts when the former employee files a claim with the state unemployment program. Your company receives written notice of the claim and can file a written objection.

Step 2: **Eligibility determination.** The state agency makes an initial determination of whether the former employee is eligible to get unemployment benefits. Usually there's no hearing at this stage.

Step 3: **Hearing.** Your company or the former employee can appeal the initial eligibility decision and have a hearing before a referee: a hearing officer who is on the staff of the state agency. Normally conducted in a private room at the unemployment office, this is the most important step in the process. At the hearing, the company and the former employee each has an opportunity to speak. In addition, you are entitled to have a lawyer there and to present witnesses and any relevant written records, such as employee evaluations or warning letters.

Step 4: **Administrative appeal.** Either your company or the employee can appeal the referee's decision to an administrative agency, such as a board of review.

Step 5: **Judicial appeal.** Either side can appeal to the state court system, but this is rare.

Legal Dos and Don'ts: Departing Workers

Do:

- **Fight fair.** As a practical matter, it makes sense to contest an unemployment claim only in limited circumstances, such as when you know the employee plans to file a lawsuit (your company can use the information you gather at the unemployment hearing to help build a defense). Otherwise, let it go: Pursuing a vendetta against a former employee will only take up time and money. It might even convince the employee to sue.

- **Negotiate creatively.** If you can offer a fired or laid-off worker something—anything—to ease the pain of losing a job, you will reduce the risk of a lawsuit. You don't have to break the bank to offer a meaningful severance package; the employee may want something that you hadn't considered, such as keeping a company laptop.

- **Show respect for departing employees.** Even if an employee leaves on bad terms, you shouldn't trash the employee to other workers or prospective employers. Bad-mouthing a former employee can lead to defamation lawsuits, and it will give remaining workers a sour taste of what they might expect should they ever leave the company.

Don't:

- **Ask every employee who leaves to sign a release.** There's a big downside to using releases: Some employees who otherwise wouldn't consider a lawsuit might start thinking about it when faced with a document that asks them to give up their legal rights. Reserve releases for employees whom you suspect might sue or situations in which your company's conduct has been questionable.

- **Play favorites.** You might be tempted to treat some departing workers better than others. However, treating workers differently can lead to resentment and legal problems. Make sure you have legitimate, business-related reasons for your actions.

- **Make life difficult for terminated employees.** If you treat former employees fairly, they are much less likely to sue your company. Remember this simple rule when deciding whether to contest an unemployment claim, give an angry reference, or deny a fired employee a simple benefit or two, such as paying for a couple of months of continued health insurance.

Test Your Knowledge

Questions

1. Your company can be sued for giving an honest but negative reference about a former employee, if the reference prevents the employee from getting another job.   ☐ True   ☐ False

2. The best reference policy is to say only positive things, even if a former employee was truly dreadful.   ☐ True   ☐ False

3. Managers should not go into detail when telling workers that an employee has been terminated.   ☐ True   ☐ False

4. Companies must continue to pay for health insurance for former employees for up to 18 months.   ☐ True   ☐ False

5. Employers are legally required to pay one week of severance for every year an employee has worked for the company.   ☐ True   ☐ False

6. A company may have to pay severance to a fired employee if it has always paid severance to employees who held that position in the past.   ☐ True   ☐ False

7. A company can refuse to pay an employee severance unless he or she signs a release agreeing not to sue the company.   ☐ True   ☐ False

8. A release is valid only if the employee has talked to a lawyer before signing it.   ☐ True   ☐ False

9. Employees who are fired cannot collect unemployment benefits.   ☐ True   ☐ False

10. Companies should always contest unemployment claims.   ☐ True   ☐ False

Answers

1. False. To sue for defamation, an employee must be able to prove that your statements were false. As long as you are honest and aren't motivated by malice or ill will toward the employee, a defamation lawsuit will fail.

2. False. If you give a detailed reference (that is, you go beyond name, salary, and position) for an employee who was dangerous, violent, or otherwise posed a risk to others but you omit that information, the prospective employer may have a legal claim against you if that employee goes on to cause harm. If you choose to be expansive, you must give the bad news as well as the good.

3. True. The safest course is simply to say that the employee has been terminated and explain who will be responsible for that employee's projects going forward.

4. False. Although some companies are required to allow departing employees to continue their health insurance benefits, the company is not required to foot the bill.

5. False. Except for the few states that require employers who conduct mass layoffs to pay a small amount of severance, employers are not legally required to pay severance unless they led employees to believe that they would receive it.

6. True. If your company has always paid severance to employees who are fired from certain positions, an employee could argue that this is company policy, and that your failure to adhere to it constitutes a breach of contract or discrimination.

7. It depends on your company's severance policies. If employees at your company are already entitled to receive severance, you cannot require them to sign a release to get it. If, however, an employee is not entitled to receive severance, you can condition a severance package on the employee's agreement not to sue.

8. False. In some circumstances—for example, if your company is firing an older worker or your state's law requires it—you may have to advise workers of their right to talk to a lawyer before signing a release. However, if the worker decides not to heed this advice, the release will still be valid.

9. False. A worker who is fired for serious misconduct is probably not entitled to benefits, but workers who are fired for poor performance or poor fit generally are.

10. False. In fact, there are very few situations when it makes sense to contest an unemployment claim. Fighting an employee's effort to collect unemployment will take time and money. It could also convince the employee to try to get money out of your company through a lawsuit.

State Health Insurance Continuation Laws

ALABAMA
Ala. Code § 27-55-3(4)

Special Situations: 18 months for subjects of domestic abuse who have lost coverage they had under abuser's insurance and who do not qualify for COBRA

ARIZONA
Ariz. Rev. Stat. §§ 20-1377, 20-1408

Employers affected: All employers who offer group disability insurance

Length of coverage for dependents: Insurer must either continue coverage for dependents or convert to individual policy upon death of covered employee or divorce. Coverage must be the same unless the insured chooses a lesser plan.

Qualifying event: Death of an employee; change in marital status

Time employer has to notify employee of continuation rights: No provisions for employer. Insurance policy must include notice of conversion privilege. Clerk of court must provide notice to anyone filing for divorce that dependent spouse entitled to convert health insurance coverage.

Time employee has to apply: 31 days after termination of existing coverage

ARKANSAS
Ark. Code Ann. §§ 23-86-114 to 23-86-116

Employers affected: All employers who offer group health insurance

Eligible employees: Continuously insured for previous 3 months

Length of coverage for employee: 120 days

Length of coverage for dependents: 120 days

Qualifying event: Termination of employment; death of insured employee; change in insured's marital status

Time employee has to apply: 10 days

CALIFORNIA
Cal. Health & Safety Code §§ 1373.6, 1373.621; Cal. Ins. Code §§ 10128.50 to 10128.59

Employers affected: Employers who offer group health insurance and have 2 to 19 employees

Eligible employees: All covered employees are eligible

Length of coverage for employee: 36 months

Length of coverage for dependents: 36 months

Qualifying event: Termination of employment; reduction in hours; death of employee; change in marital status

Time employer has to notify employee of continuation rights: 15 days

Time employee has to apply: 31 days after group plan ends; 30 days after COBRA or Cal-COBRA ends (63 days if converting to an individual plan)

Special situations: Employee who is at least 60 years old and has worked for employer for previous 5 years may continue benefits for self and spouse beyond COBRA or Cal-COBRA limits (also applies to COBRA employers). Employee who began receiving COBRA coverage on or after 1/1/03 and whose COBRA coverage is for less than 36 months may use Cal-COBRA to bring total coverage up to 36 months.

COLORADO
Colo. Rev. Stat. § 10-16-108

Employers affected: All employers who offer group health insurance

Eligible employees: Employees continuously insured for previous 6 months

Length of coverage for employee: 18 months

Length of coverage for dependents: 18 months

Qualifying event: Termination of employment; reduction in hours; death of employee; change in marital status

State Health Insurance Continuation Laws (cont'd)

Time employer has to notify employee of continuation rights: Within 10 days of termination

Time employee has to apply: 30 days after termination; 60 days if employer fails to give notice

CONNECTICUT

Conn. Gen. Stat. Ann. §§ 38a-538, 38a-554; 31-51o

Employers affected: All employers who offer group health insurance

Eligible employees: Full-time employees or employees who have either worked or expect to work twenty hours a week for at least 26 weeks in a 12-month period

Length of coverage for employee: 30 months, or until eligible for Social Security benefits

Length of coverage for dependents: 30 months, or until eligible for Social Security benefits; 36 months in case of employee's death or divorce

Qualifying event: Layoff; reduction in hours; termination of employment; death of employee; change in marital status

Time employer has to notify employee of continuation rights: 14 days

Time employee has to apply: 60 days

Special situations: When facility closes or relocates, employer must pay for insurance for employee and dependents for 120 days or until employee is eligible for other group coverage, whichever comes first (does not affect employee's right to conventional continuation coverage which begins when 120-day period end).

DISTRICT OF COLUMBIA

D.C. Code Ann. §§ 32-731 to 32-732

Employers affected: Employers with fewer than 20 employees

Eligible employees: All covered employees are eligible

Length of coverage for employee: three months or for the period of time during which the employee is eligible for ARRA subsidy

Length of coverage for dependents: three months or for the period of time during which the employee is eligible for ARRA subsidy

Qualifying event: Any reason employee or dependent becomes ineligible for coverage

Time employer has to notify employee of continuation rights: Within 15 days of termination of coverage

Time employee has to apply: 45 days after termination of coverage

FLORIDA

Fla. Stat. Ann. § 627.6692

Employers affected: Employers with fewer than 20 employees

Eligible employees: Full-time (25 or more hours per week) employees covered by employer's health insurance plan

Length of coverage for employee: 18 months

Length of coverage for dependents: 18 months

Qualifying event: Layoff; reduction in hours; termination of employment; death of employee; change in marital status

Time employer has to notify employee of continuation rights: Carrier notifies within 14 days of learning of qualifying event (employer is responsible for notifying carrier).

Time employee has to apply: 30 days from receipt of carrier's notice

State Health Insurance Continuation Laws (cont'd)

GEORGIA

Ga. Code Ann. §§ 33-24-21.1 to 33-24-21.2

Employers affected: All employers who offer group health insurance

Eligible employees: Employees continuously insured for previous 6 months

Length of coverage for employee: three months plus any part of the month remaining at termination; 9 months if eligible for ARRA subsidy

Length of coverage for dependents: three months plus any part of the month remaining at termination; 9 months if eligible for ARRA subsidy

Qualifying event: Termination of employment (except for cause)

Special situations: Employee, spouse, or former spouse, who is 60 years old and who has been covered for previous 6 months may continue coverage until eligible for Medicare. (Applies to companies with more than 20 employees; does not apply when employee quits for reasons other than health.)

HAWAII

Haw. Rev. Stat. §§ 393-11, 393-15

Employers affected: All employers required to offer health insurance (those paying a regular employee a monthly wage at least 86.67 times state hourly minimum—about $542)

Length of coverage for employee: If employee is hospitalized or prevented from working by sickness, employer must pay insurance premiums for 3 months or for as long employer continues to pay wages, whichever is longer.

Qualifying event: Employee is hospitalized or prevented by sickness from working.

ILLINOIS

215 Ill. Comp. Stat. §§ 5/367e, 5/367.2, 5/367.2-5

Employers affected: All employers who offer group health insurance

Eligible employees: Employees continuously insured for previous 3 months

Length of coverage for employee: 12 months for policies issued, delivered, amended, or renewed after 6/18/2009. This requirement doesn't apply to employees eligible for ARRA subsidy.

Length of coverage for dependents: nine months (see "Special situations")

Qualifying event: Termination of employment; reduction in hours; death of employee; divorce

Time employer has to notify employee of continuation rights: 10 days

Time employee has to apply: 30 days after termination or reduction in hours or receiving notice from employer, whichever is later, but not more than 60 days from termination or reduction in hours

Special situations: Upon death or divorce, 2 years' coverage for spouse under 55 and eligible dependents who were on employee's plan; until eligible for Medicare or other group coverage for spouse over 55 and eligible dependents who were on employee's plan. A dependent child who has reached plan age limit or who was not already covered by plan, is also entitled to 2 years' continuation coverage.

IOWA

Iowa Code §§ 509B.3, 509B.5

Employers affected: All employers who offer group health insurance

Eligible employees: Employees continuously insured for previous 3 months

State Health Insurance Continuation Laws (cont'd)

Length of coverage for employee: nine months

Length of coverage for dependents: nine months

Qualifying event: Any reason employee or dependent becomes ineligible for coverage

Time employer has to notify employee of continuation rights: 10 days after termination of coverage

Time employee has to apply: 10 days after termination of coverage or receiving notice from employer, whichever is later, but no more than 31 days from termination of coverage

KANSAS

Kan. Stat. Ann. § 40-2209(i)

Employers affected: All employers who offer group health insurance

Eligible employees: Employees continuously insured for previous 3 months

Length of coverage for employee: 18 months

Length of coverage for dependents: 18 months

Qualifying event: Any reason employee or dependent becomes ineligible for coverage

Time employee has to apply: 31 days from termination of coverage

KENTUCKY

Ky. Rev. Stat. Ann. § 304.18-110

Employers affected: All employers who offer group health insurance

Eligible employees: Employees continuously insured for previous 3 months

Length of coverage for employee: 18 months

Length of coverage for dependents: 18 months

Qualifying event: Any reason employee or dependent becomes ineligible for coverage

Time employer has to notify employee of continuation rights: Employer must notify insurer as soon as employee's coverage ends; insurer then notifies employee

Time employee has to apply: 31 days from receipt of insurer's notice, but no more than 90 days after termination of group coverage

LOUISIANA

La. Rev. Stat. Ann. §§ 22:1045, 22:1046

Employers affected: All employers who offer group health insurance and have fewer than 20 employees

Eligible employees: Employees continuously insured for previous 3 months

Length of coverage for employee: 12 months

Length of coverage for dependents: 12 months

Qualifying event: Termination of employment.

Time employee has to apply: Must apply and submit payment before group coverage ends

Special situations: Surviving spouse who is 50 or older may have coverage until remarriage or eligibility for Medicare or other insurance

MAINE

Me. Rev. Stat. Ann. tit. 24-A, § 2809-A

Employers affected: All employers who offer group health insurance

Eligible employees: Employees continuously insured for previous 3 months

Length of coverage for employee: One year (either group or individual coverage at discretion of insurer)

Length of coverage for dependents: One year (either group or individual coverage at discretion of insurer); upon death of insured, continuation only if original plan provided for coverage

Qualifying event: Termination of employment

Time employee has to apply: 90 days from termination of group coverage

State Health Insurance Continuation Laws (cont'd)

Special situations: Temporary layoff or work-related injury or disease: Employee and employee's dependents entitled to one year group or individual continuation coverage; (must have been continuously insured for previous 6 months; must apply within 31 days from termination of coverage)

MARYLAND

Md. Code Ann., [Ins.] §§ 15-407 to 15-410

Employers affected: All employers who offer group health insurance

Eligible employees: Employees continuously insured for previous 3 months

Length of coverage for employee: 18 months

Length of coverage for dependents: 18 months upon death of employee; upon change in marital status, 18 months or until spouse remarries or becomes eligible for other coverage

Qualifying event: Involuntary termination of employment; death of employee; change in marital status

Time employer has to notify employee of continuation rights: Must notify insurer within 14 days of receiving employee's continuation request

Time employee has to apply: 45 days from termination of coverage. Employee begins application process by requesting an election of continuation notification form from employer.

MASSACHUSETTS

Mass. Gen. Laws ch. 175, §§ 110G, 110I; ch. 176J, § 9

Employers affected: All employers who offer group health insurance and have fewer than 20 employees

Eligible employees: All covered employees are eligible

Length of coverage for employee: 18 months; 29 months if disabled

Length of coverage for dependents: 18 months upon termination or reduction in hours; 29 months if disabled; 36 months on divorce, death of employee, employee's eligibility for Medicare, or employer's bankruptcy

Qualifying event: Involuntary layoff; death of insured employee

Time employer has to notify employee of continuation rights: When employee becomes eligible for continuation benefits

Time employee has to apply: 60 days

Special situations: Termination due to plant closing: 90 days' coverage for employee and dependents, at the same payment terms as before closing

MINNESOTA

Minn. Stat. Ann. § 62A.17

Employers affected: All employers who offer group health insurance and have 2 or more employees

Eligible employees: All covered employees are eligible

Length of coverage for employee: 18 months; indefinitely if employee becomes totally disabled while employed

Length of coverage for dependents: 18 months for current spouse; divorced or widowed spouse can continue until eligible for Medicare or other group health insurance. Upon divorce, dependent children can continue until they no longer qualify as dependents under plan. Upon death of employee, spouse and/or dependent children can continue for 36 months.

Qualifying event: Termination of employment; reduction in hours

State Health Insurance Continuation Laws (cont'd)

Time employer has to notify employee of continuation rights: Within 14 days of termination of coverage

Time employee has to apply: 60 days from termination of coverage or receipt of employer's notice, whichever is later

Special benefits: Additional subsidy available to those eligible for ARRA subsidy, if insured meets income limits

MISSISSIPPI

Miss. Code Ann. § 83-9-51

Employers affected: All employers who offer group health insurance and have fewer than 20 employees

Eligible employees: Employees continuously insured for previous 3 months

Length of coverage for employee: 12 months

Length of coverage for dependents: 12 months

Qualifying event: Termination of employment; divorce; employee's death; employee's eligiblity for Medicare; loss of dependent status

Time employer has to notify employee of continuation rights: Insurer must notify former or deceased employee's dependent child or divorced spouse of option to continue insurance within 14 days of their becoming ineligible for coverage on employee's policy.

Time employee has to apply: Employee must apply and submit payment before group coverage ends; dependents or former spouse must elect continuation coverage within 30 days of receiving insurer's notice.

MISSOURI

Mo. Rev. Stat. § 376.428

Employers affected: All employers who offer group health insurance and are not subject to COBRA

Eligible employees: All employees

Length of coverage for employee: 18 months

Length of coverage for dependents: 18 months if eligible due to termination or reduction in hours; 36 months if eligible due to death or divorce

Qualifying event: Termination of employment; death of employee; divorce; reduction in hours

Time employer has to notify employee of continuation rights: Same rules as COBRA

Time employee has to apply: Same rules as COBRA

MONTANA

Mont. Code Ann. §§ 33-22-506 to 33-22-507

Employers affected: All employers who offer group disability insurance

Eligible employees: All employees

Length of coverage for employee: One year (with employer's consent)

Qualifying event: Reduction in hours

Special situations: Insurer may not discontinue benefits to child with disabilities after child exceeds age limit for dependent status.

NEBRASKA

Neb. Rev. Stat. §§ 44-1640 and following, 44-7406

Employers affected: Employers not subject to federal COBRA laws

Eligible employees: All covered employees

Length of coverage for employee: six months

Length of coverage for dependents: One year upon death of insured employee. Subjects of domestic abuse who have lost coverage under abuser's plan and who do not qualify for COBRA may have 18 months' coverage (applies to all employers).

State Health Insurance Continuation Laws (cont'd)

Qualifying event: Involuntary termination of employment (layoff due to labor dispute not considered involuntary)

Time employer has to notify employee of continuation rights: Within 10 days of termination of employment must send notice by certified mail

Time employee has to apply: 10 days from receipt of employer's notice

NEVADA
Nev. Rev. Stat. Ann. §§ 689B.245 and following, 689B.0345

Employers affected: Employers with fewer than 20 employees

Eligible employees: Employees continuously insured for previous 12 months

Length of coverage for employee: 18 months

Length of coverage for dependents: 36 months; insurer cannot terminate coverage for disabled dependent child who is too old to qualify as a dependent under the plan.

Qualifying event: Involuntary termination of employment; involuntary reduction in hours; death of employee; divorce or legal separation; loss of dependent status; employee's eligibility for Medicare

Time employer has to notify employee of continuation rights: 14 days after receiving notice of employee's eligibility

Time employee has to apply: Must notify employer within 60 days of becoming eligible for continuation coverage; must apply within 60 days after receiving employer's notice

Special situations: While employee is on leave without pay due to disability, 12 months for employee and dependents (applies to all employers)

NEW HAMPSHIRE
N.H. Rev. Stat. Ann. §§ 415:18(VII)(g), (VII)(a)

Employers affected: Employers with 2 to 19 employees

Eligible employees: All insured employees are eligible

Length of coverage for employee: 18 months; 29 months if disabled at termination or during first 60 days of continuation coverage

Length of coverage for dependents: 18 months; 29 months if disabled at termination or during first 60 days of continuation coverage; 36 months upon death of employee, divorce or legal separation, loss of dependent status, or employee's eligibility for Medicare

Qualifying event: Any reason employee or dependent becomes ineligible for coverage

Time employer has to notify employee of continuation rights: Within 15 days of termination of coverage

Time employee has to apply: Within 31 days of termination of coverage

Special situations: Layoff or termination due to strike: 6 months' coverage with option to extend for an additional 12 months. Surviving, divorced, or legally separated spouse who is 55 or older may continue benefits available until eligible for Medicare or another employer-based group insurance.

NEW JERSEY
N.J. Stat. Ann. §§ 17B:27-51.12, 17B:27A-27

Employers affected: Employers with 2 to 50 employees

Eligible employees: Employed full time (25 or more hours)

State Health Insurance Continuation Laws (cont'd)

Length of coverage for employee: 18 months; 29 months if disabled at termination or during first 60 days of continuation coverage

Length of coverage for dependents: 18 months; 29 months if disabled at termination or during first 60 days of continuation coverage; 36 months upon death of employee, divorce or legal separation, loss of dependent status, or employee's eligibility for Medicare

Qualifying event: Termination of employment; reduction in hours; change in marital status; death

Time employer has to notify employee of continuation rights: At time of qualifying event, employer or carrier notifies employee.

Time employee has to apply: Within 30 days of qualifying event

Special benefits: Coverage must be identical to that offered to current employees.

Special situations: Total disability: employee who has been insured for previous 3 months and employee's dependents, entitled to continuation coverage that includes all benefits offered by group policy (applies to all employers)

NEW MEXICO
N.M. Stat. Ann. § 59A-18-16

Employers affected: All employers who offer group health insurance

Eligible employees: All insured employees are eligible

Length of coverage for employee: Six months

Length of coverage for dependents: May continue group coverage or convert to individual policies upon death of covered employee or divorce or legal separation

Qualifying event: Termination of employment

Time employer has to notify employee of continuation rights: Insurer or employer gives written notice at time of termination.

Time employee has to apply: 30 days after receiving notice

NEW YORK
N.Y. Ins. Law §§ 3221(f), 3221(m)

Employers affected: All employers who offer group health insurance and have fewer than 20 employees

Eligible employees: All covered employees are eligible.

Length of coverage for employee: 36 months

Length of coverage for dependents: 36 months

Qualifying event: Termination of employment; death of employee; divorce or legal separation; loss of dependent status; employee's eligibility for Medicare

Time employee has to apply: 60 days after termination or receipt of notice, whichever is later

NORTH CAROLINA
N.C. Gen. Stat. §§ 58-53-5 to 58-53-40

Employers affected: All employers who offer group health insurance

Eligible employees: Employees continuously insured for previous 3 months

Length of coverage for employee: 18 months

Length of coverage for dependents: 18 months

Qualifying event: Termination of employment

Time employer has to notify employee of continuation rights: Employer has option of notifying employee as part of the exit process.

Time employee has to apply: 60 days

State Health Insurance Continuation Laws (cont'd)

NORTH DAKOTA

N.D. Cent. Code §§ 26.1-36-23, 26.1-36-23.1

Employers affected: All employers who offer group health insurance

Eligible employees: Employees continuously insured for previous 3 months

Length of coverage for employee: 39 weeks

Length of coverage for dependents: 39 weeks; 36 months if required by divorce or annulment decree

Qualifying event: Termination of employment

Time employee has to apply: Within 10 days of termination or of receiving notice of continuation rights, whichever is later, but no more than 31 days from termination

OHIO

Ohio Rev. Code Ann. §§ 3923.38, 1751.53

Employers affected: All employers who offer group health insurance

Eligible employees: Employees continuously insured for previous 3 months who were involuntarily terminated for reasons other than gross misconduct on the part of the employee

Length of coverage for employee: 12 months

Length of coverage for dependents: 12 months

Qualifying event: Involuntary termination of employment

Time employer has to notify employee of continuation rights: At termination of employment

Time employee has to apply: Whichever is earlier: 31 days after coverage terminates; 10 days after coverage terminates if employer notified employee of continuation rights prior to termination; 10 days after employer notified employee of continuation rights, if notice was given after coverage terminated

OKLAHOMA

Okla. Stat. Ann. tit. 36, § 4509

Employers affected: All employers who offer group health insurance

Eligible employees: Employees insured for at least 6 months; (all other employees and their dependents entitled to 30 days' continuation coverage)

Length of coverage for employee: 63 days for basic coverage; 6 months for major medical at the same premium rate prior to termination of coverage (only for losses or conditions that began while group policy in effect)

Length of coverage for dependents: 63 days for basic coverage; 6 months for major medical at the same premium rate prior to termination of coverage (only for losses or conditions that began while group policy in effect)

Qualifying event: Any reason coverage terminates

Special benefits: Includes maternity care for pregnancy begun while group policy was in effect

OREGON

Or. Rev. Stat. §§ 743.600 to 743.610

Employers affected: Employers not subject to federal COBRA laws

Eligible employees: Employees continuously insured for previous 3 months

Length of coverage for employee: 9 months

Length of coverage for dependents: 9 months

Qualifying event: Termination of employment

Time employee has to apply: 10 days after termination or after receiving notice of continuation rights, whichever is later, but not more than 31 days

State Health Insurance Continuation Laws (cont'd)

Special situations: Surviving, divorced, or legally separated spouse who is 55 or older and dependent children entitled to continuation coverage until spouse remarries or is eligible for other coverage; must include dental, vision, or prescription drug benefits, if they were offered in original plan (applies to employers with 20 or more employees)

PENNSYLVANIA

Pa. Stat. 40 P.S. § 764j

Employers affected: Employers that offer group health insurance and have 2 to 19 employees

Eligible employees: Employees continuously insured for at least 3 months

Length of coverage for employee: 9 months

Length of coverage for dependents: 9 months

Qualifying event: Termination of employment; reduction in hours; death of employee; change in marital status; employer's bankruptcy

Time employer has to notify employee of continuation rights: 30 days after qualifying event

Time employee has to apply: 30 days after receiving notice

RHODE ISLAND

R.I. Gen. Laws §§ 27-19.1-1, 27-20.4-1 to 27-20-4-2

Employers affected: All employers who offer group health insurance

Eligible employees: All insured employees are eligible

Length of coverage for employee: 18 months (but not longer than continuous employment); cannot be required to pay more than one month premium at a time

Length of coverage for dependents: 18 months (but not longer than continuous employment);

cannot be required to pay more than one month premium at a time

Qualifying event: Involuntary termination of employment; death of employee; change in marital status; permanent reduction in workforce; employer's going out of business

Time employer has to notify employee of continuation rights: Employers must post a conspicuous notice of employee continuation rights.

Time employee has to apply: 30 days from termination of coverage

Special situations: If right to receiving continuing health insurance is stated in the divorce judgment, divorced spouse has right to continue coverage as long as employee remains covered or until divorced spouse remarries or becomes eligible for other group insurance. If covered employee remarries, divorced spouse must be given right to purchase an individual policy from same insurer.

SOUTH CAROLINA

S.C. Code Ann. § 38-71-770

Employers affected: All employers who offer group health insurance

Eligible employees: Employees continuously insured for previous 6 months

Length of coverage for employee: Six months (in addition to part of month remaining at termination)

Length of coverage for dependents: Six months (in addition to part of month remaining at termination)

Qualifying event: Any reason employee or dependent becomes ineligible for coverage

Time employer has to notify employee of continuation rights: At time of termination

State Health Insurance Continuation Laws (cont'd)

must clearly and meaningfully advise employee of continuation rights

SOUTH DAKOTA

S.D. Codified Laws Ann. §§ 58-18-7.5, 58-18-7.12; 58-18C-1

Employers affected: All employers who offer group health insurance

Eligible employees: All covered employees

Length of coverage for employee: 18 months; 29 months if disabled at termination or during first 60 days of continuation coverage

Length of coverage for dependents: 18 months; 29 months if disabled at termination or during first 60 days of continuation coverage; 36 months upon death of employee, divorce or legal separation, loss of dependent status, or employee's eligibility for Medicare

Qualifying event: Termination of employment; death of employee; divorce or legal separation; loss of dependent status; employee's eligibility for Medicare

Special situations: When employer goes out of business: 12 months' continuation coverage available to all employees. Employer must notify employees within 10 days of termination of benefits; employees must apply within 60 days of receipt of employer's notice to or within 90 days of termination of benefits if no notice given.

TENNESSEE

Tenn. Code Ann. § 56-7-2312

Employers affected: All employers who offer group health insurance

Eligible employees: Employees continuously insured for previous 3 months

Length of coverage for employee: Three months (in addition to part of month remaining at termination)

Length of coverage for dependents: Three months (in addition to part of month remaining at termination); 15 months upon death of employee or divorce

Qualifying event: Termination of employment; death of employee; change in marital status

Special situations: Employee or dependent who is pregnant at time of termination entitled to continuation benefits for 6 months following the end of pregnancy

TEXAS

Tex. Ins. Code Ann. Art. §§ 1251.252 to 1251.255

Employers affected: All employers who offer group health insurance

Eligible employees: Employees continuously insured for previous 3 months

Length of coverage for employee: Nine months; for employees eligible for COBRA, 6 months after COBRA coverage ends

Length of coverage for dependents: Nine months; for employees eligible for COBRA, 6 months after COBRA coverage ends

Qualifying event: Termination of employment (except for cause); employee leaves for health reasons

Time employee has to apply: 60 days from termination of coverage or receiving notice of continuation rights from employer or insurer, whichever is later

Special situations: Layoff due to a labor dispute: employee entitled to continuation benefits for duration of dispute, but no longer than 6 months

State Health Insurance Continuation Laws (cont'd)

UTAH

Utah Code Ann. § 31A-22-722

Employers affected: All employers who offer group health insurance

Eligible employees: Employees continuously insured for previous 3 months

Length of coverage for employee: 12 months

Length of coverage for dependents: 12 months

Qualifying event: Termination of employment; retirement; death; divorce; reduction in hours; sabbatical; disability

Time employer has to notify employee of continuation rights: In writing within 30 days of termination of coverage

Time employee has to apply: Within 30 days of receiving employer's notice of continuation rights

VERMONT

Vt. Stat. Ann. tit. 8, §§ 4090a to 4090c

Employers affected: All employers who offer group health insurance and have fewer than 20 employees

Eligible employees: All covered employees are eligible.

Length of coverage for employee: 18 months

Length of coverage for dependents: 18 months

Qualifying event: Termination of employment; reduction in hours; death of employee; change of marital status; loss of dependent status

Time employer has to notify employee of continuation rights: Within 30 days of qualifying event

Time employee has to apply: Within 60 days of receiving notice following the occurrence of a qualifying event

VIRGINIA

Va. Code Ann. §§ 38.2-3541 to 38.2-3452; 38.2-3416

Employers affected: All employers who offer group health insurance

Eligible employees: Employees continuously insured for previous 3 months

Length of coverage for employee: 90 days; 9 months if involuntarily terminated during any period when ARRA subsidy is available

Length of coverage for dependents: 90 days; 9 months if coverage lost due to involuntary termination of employee during any period when ARRA subsidy is available

Qualifying event: Any reason employee or dependent becomes ineligible for coverage; for 9-month coverage provision: involuntary termination of employment

Time employer has to notify employee of continuation rights: 15 days from termination of coverage; 30 days if eligible for ARRA subsidy.

Time employee has to apply: Must apply for continuation and pay entire 90-day premium before termination of coverage; 60 days if eligible for ARRA subsidy

Special situations: Employee may convert to an individual policy instead of applying for continuation coverage (must apply within 31 days of termination of coverage).

WASHINGTON

Wash. Rev. Code Ann. §§ 48.21.075, 48.21.250, 48.21.260

Employers affected: All employers who offer and pay for group health insurance

Eligible employees: Insured employees on strike

Length of coverage for employee: Six months if employee goes on strike

State Health Insurance Continuation Laws (cont'd)

Length of coverage for dependents: Six months if employee goes on strike

Qualifying event: Any reason employee or dependent becomes ineligible for coverage

Time employee has to apply: 31 days after the date the employee's group coverage terminates or 31 days after the date the employee receives notice of termination of coverage, whichever is later

Special situations: Former employees may continue benefits for a period of time agreed upon with the employer. At the end of that time, the employee may then convert to an individual policy unless terminated for misconduct—in that case, employee's spouse and dependents may convert, but not employee.

WEST VIRGINIA
W.Va. Code §§ 33-16-2, 33-16-3(e)

Employers affected: Employers providing insurance for at least 2 employees

Eligible employees: All employees are eligible

Length of coverage for employee: 18 months in case of involuntary layoff

Qualifying event: Involuntary layoff

WISCONSIN
Wis. Stat. Ann. § 632.897

Employers affected: All employers who offer group health insurance

Eligible employees: Employees continuously insured for previous 3 months

Length of coverage for employee: 18 months (or longer at insurer's option)

Length of coverage for dependents: 18 months (or longer at insurer's option)

Qualifying event: Any reason employee or dependent becomes ineligible for coverage

Time employer has to notify employee of continuation rights: Five days from termination of coverage

Time employee has to apply: 30 days after receiving employer's notice

WYOMING
Wyo. Stat. § 26-19-113

Employers affected: Employers not subject to federal COBRA laws

Eligible employees: Employees continuously insured for previous 3 months

Length of coverage for employee: 12 months

Length of coverage for dependents: 12 months

Time employee has to apply: 31 days from termination of coverage

Resources

Federal Agencies

This section includes contact information for the federal agencies that enforce the laws covered in this book. You can find more information on each agency's authority, enforcement powers, and resources for employers in the chapter that covers the law the agency administers.

Department of Health and Human Services

Administration for Children & Families (ACF)
Office of Child Support Enforcement
370 L'Enfant Promenade SW
Washington, DC 20447
Phone: 202-401-9323
www.acf.hhs.gov
The ACF enforces PRWORA.

Department of Justice

Civil Rights Division
Office of the Special Counsel for Immigration-Related Unfair Employment Practices (OSC)
950 Pennsylvania Avenue, NW
Washington, DC 20530
Phone: 202-616-5594
Employer Hotline: 800-255-8155
TDD: 800-237-2515
www.justice.gov/crt/about/osc
The OSC enforces the antidiscrimination provisions of IRCA.

Department of Labor

Employee Benefits Security Administration (EBSA)

Frances Perkins Building
200 Constitution Avenue, NW
Washington, DC 20210
Phone: 866-444-EBSA (3272)
www.dol.gov/ebsa
The EBSA shares enforcement responsibility for COBRA with the IRS.

Employment and Training Administration (DOLETA)

Office of National Response
200 Constitution Avenue, NW
Room N-5422
Washington, DC 20210
Phone: 877-872-5627
www.doleta.gov/layoff
DOLETA issued the regulations interpreting WARN, and has some explanatory resources available.

Occupational Safety and Health Administration (OSHA)

200 Constitution Avenue, NW
Washington, DC 20210
Phone: 800-321-OSHA
TTY: 877-889-5627
www.osha.gov
OSHA enforces the OSH Act and the whistleblower provisions of Sarbanes-Oxley (SOX).

Veterans Employment and Training Service (VETS)

200 Constitution Avenue, Room S-1325
Washington, DC 20210

Phone: 202-693-4701
www.dol.gov/vets
The VETS enforces USERRA.

Wage and Hour Division (WHD)

Employment Standards Administration
200 Constitution Avenue, NW
Washington, DC 20210
Phone: 866-487-9243
TTY: 877-889-5627
www.dol.gov/whd
The WHD enforces the EPPA, FLSA, and FMLA.

Equal Employment Opportunity Commission (EEOC)

131 Elm Street, NW
Washington, DC 20507
Phone: 202-663-4900 or 800-669-4000
TTY: 202-663-4494 or 800-669-6820
www.eeoc.gov
The EEOC enforces the ADA, ADEA, EPA, OWBPA, PDA, and Title VII.

Federal Trade Commission (FTC)

600 Pennsylvania Avenue
Washington, DC 20580
Phone: 202-326-2222 or 877-382-4357
TTY: 866-653-4261
www.ftc.gov
The FTC enforces the FCRA.

Internal Revenue Service (IRS)

U.S. Treasury Department
1500 Pennsylvania Avenue, NW
Washington, DC 20220
Phone: 800-829-4933 (for businesses)

TDD: 800-829-4059
www.irs.gov
The IRS shares enforcement responsibility for COBRA with the EBSA.

National Labor Relations Board (NLRB)

1099 14th Street, NW
Washington, DC 20570
Phone: 866-667-6572
TTY: 866-315-NLRB (866-315-6572)
www.nlrb.gov
The NLRB enforces the NLRA.

Securities and Exchange Commission (SEC)

100 F Street, NE
Washington, DC 20549
Phone: 202-942-8088
TTY: 202-551-6020
www.sec.gov
The SEC enforces the complaint procedures provision of Sarbanes-Oxley (SOX).

U.S. Citizenship and Immigration Services (USCIS)

Office of Business Liaison
111 Massachusetts Avenue, NW
Washington, DC 20539
Phone: 800-357-2099
TDD: 800-767-1833
www.uscis.gov
The USCIS enforces the employment verification provisions of IRCA.

State Agencies

State Labor Departments

Note: Phone numbers listed are for each department's headquarters. Check the website for regional office locations and numbers.

State Labor Departments

ALABAMA
Department of Industrial Relations
Montgomery, AL
334-242-8990
http://dir.alabama.gov

ALASKA
Department of Labor and Workforce
  Development
Juneau, AK
907-465-2700
www.labor.state.ak.us

ARIZONA
Industrial Commission
Phoenix, AZ
602-542-4515
www.ica.state.az.us

ARKANSAS
Department of Labor
Little Rock, AR
501-682-4500
www.arkansas.gov/labor

CALIFORNIA
Department of Industrial Relations
San Francisco, CA
415-703-5070
www.dir.ca.gov

COLORADO
Department of Labor and Employment
Denver, CO
303-318-8000
www.colorado.gov/CDLE

CONNECTICUT
Labor Department
Wethersfield, CT
860-263-6000
www.ctdol.state.ct.us

DELAWARE
Department of Labor
Wilmington, DE
302-761-8000
www.delawareworks.com

DISTRICT OF COLUMBIA
Department of Employment Services
Washington, DC
202-724-7000
www.does.ci.washington.dc.us

FLORIDA
Agency for Workforce Innovation
Tallahassee, FL
850-245-7105
www.floridajobs.org

GEORGIA
Department of Labor
Atlanta, GA
404-232-7300
www.dol.state.ga.us

HAWAII
Department of Labor and Industrial
  Relations
Honolulu, HI
808-586-8842
www.hawaii.gov/labor

State Labor Departments (cont'd)

IDAHO
Department of Labor
Boise, ID
208-332-3570
http://labor.idaho.gov

ILLINOIS
Department of Labor
Chicago, IL
312-793-2800
www.state.il.us/agency/idol

INDIANA
Department of Labor
Indianapolis, IN
317-232-2655
www.in.gov/dol

IOWA
Labor Services Division
Des Moines, IA
515-281-5387
www.iowaworkforce.org/labor

KANSAS
Department of Labor
Topeka, KS
785-296-5000
www.dol.ks.gov

KENTUCKY
Department of Labor
Frankfort, KY
502-564-3070
www.labor.ky.gov

LOUISIANA
Department of Labor
Baton Rouge, LA
225-342-3111
www.ldol.state.la.us

MAINE
Department of Labor
Augusta, ME
207-623-7900
www.state.me.us/labor

MARYLAND
Division of Labor and Industry
Baltimore, MD
410-767-2241
www.dllr.state.md.us/labor

MASSACHUSETTS
Department of Labor
Boston, MA
617-626-7100
www.mass.gov/dol

MICHIGAN
Department of Labor and Economic Growth
Lansing, MI
517-373-1820
www.michigan.gov/dleg

MINNESOTA
Department of Labor and Industry
St. Paul, MN
800-342-5354
651-284-5005
www.dli.mn.gov

State Labor Departments (cont'd)

MISSISSIPPI
Department of Employment Security
Jackson, MS
601-321-6000
www.mdes.ms.gov

MISSOURI
Department of Labor and Industrial Relations
Jefferson City, MO
573-751-4091
www.labor.mo.gov

MONTANA
Department of Labor and Industry
Helena, MT
406-444-2840
www.mt.gov

NEBRASKA
Department of Labor
Lincoln, NE
402-471-9000
www.dol.nebraska.gov

NEVADA
Office of the Labor Commissioner
Las Vegas, NV
702-486-2650
www.laborcommissioner.com

NEW HAMPSHIRE
Department of Labor
Concord, NH
603-271-3176
www.labor.state.nh.us

NEW JERSEY
Department of Labor and Workforce
    Development
Trenton, NJ
609-292-7060
http://lwd.state.nj.us/labor

NEW MEXICO
Department of Workforce Solutions
Albuquerque, NM
505-841-4000
www.dws.state.nm.us

NEW YORK
Department of Labor
Albany, NY
518-457-9000
888-469-7365
www.labor.ny.gov/home

NORTH CAROLINA
Department of Labor
Raleigh, NC
919-807-2796
800-625-2267
www.nclabor.com

NORTH DAKOTA
Department of Labor
Bismarck, ND
701-328-2660
www.nd.gov/labor

State Labor Departments (cont'd)

OHIO
Division of Labor and Worker Safety
Reynoldsburg, OH
614-644-2450
www.com.ohio.gov/laws

OKLAHOMA
Department of Labor
Oklahoma City, OK
405-521-6100
www.ok.gov/odol

OREGON
Bureau of Labor and Industries
Portland, OR
971-673-0761
www.oregon.gov/boli

PENNSYLVANIA
Department of Labor and Industry
Harrisburg, PA
717-787-1116
www.dli.state.pa.us

RHODE ISLAND
Department of Labor and Training
Cranston, RI
401-462-8000
www.dlt.state.ri.us

SOUTH CAROLINA
Department of Labor, Licensing, and Regulation
Columbia, SC
803-896-4300
www.llr.state.sc.us/labor

SOUTH DAKOTA
Department of Labor
Pierre, SD
605-773-3101
http://dol.sd.gov

TENNESSEE
Department of Labor and Workforce
    Development
Nashville, TN
615-741-6642
www.state.tn.us/labor-wfd

TEXAS
Texas Workforce Commission
Austin, TX
800-832-2829 (employees)
800-832-9394 (employers)
www.twc.state.tx.us

UTAH
Labor Commission
Salt Lake City, UT
801-530-6800
www.laborcommission.utah.gov

VERMONT
Department of Labor
Montpelier, VT
802-828-4000
www.labor.vermont.gov

VIRGINIA
Department of Labor and Industry
Richmond, VA
804-371-2327
www.doli.virginia.gov

State Labor Departments (cont'd)

WASHINGTON
Department of Labor and Industries
Tumwater, WA
360-902-5800
800-547-8367
www.lni.wa.gov

WEST VIRGINIA
Division of Labor
Charleston, WV
304-558-7890
www.wvlabor.com

WISCONSIN
Department of Workforce Development
Madison, WI
608-266-3131
www.dwd.state.wi.us

WYOMING
Department of Employment
Cheyenne, WY
307-777-7672
http://doe.wyo.gov

State Agencies That Enforce Laws Prohibiting Discrimination in Employment

Note: Phone numbers listed are for each department's headquarters. Check the website for regional office locations and numbers.

State Agencies That Enforce Laws Prohibiting Discrimination in Employment

ALABAMA
EEOC District Office
Birmingham, AL
205-212-2105
800-669-4000
http://eeoc.gov/field/birmingham/index.cfm

ALASKA
Commission for Human Rights
Anchorage, AK
907-274-4692
800-478-4692
http://humanrights.alaska.gov

ARIZONA
Civil Rights Division
Phoenix, AZ
602-542-5263
877-491-5742
www.azag.gov/civil_rights/index.html

ARKANSAS
Equal Employment Opportunity Commission
Little Rock, AR
800-669-4000
www.eeoc.gov/field/littlerock/index.cfm

CALIFORNIA
Department of Fair Employment and Housing
Sacramento District Office
Sacramento, CA
916-478-7200
800-884-1684
www.dfeh.ca.gov

COLORADO
Civil Rights Division
Denver, CO
303-894-2997
800-262-4845
www.dora.state.co.us/Civil-Rights

CONNECTICUT
Commission on Human Rights and Opportunities
Hartford, CT
860-541-3400
800-477-5737
www.ct.gov/chro/site

DELAWARE
Office of Labor Law Enforcement
Division of Industrial Affairs
Wilmington, DE
302-761-8200
www.delawareworks.com/industrialaffairs/welcome.shtml

DISTRICT OF COLUMBIA
Office of Human Rights
Washington, DC
202-727-4559
http://ohr.dc.gov/ohr/site/default.asp

FLORIDA
Commission on Human Relations
Tallahassee, FL
850-488-7082
800-342-8170
http://fchr.state.fl.us

GEORGIA
Atlanta District Office
U.S. Equal Employment Opportunity Commission
Atlanta, GA
800-669-4000
www.eeoc.gov/field/atlanta

HAWAII
Hawai'i Civil Rights Commission
Honolulu, HI
808-586-8636 (Oahu only)
www.hawaii.gov/labor/hcrc

State Agencies That Enforce Laws Prohibiting Discrimination in Employment (cont'd)

IDAHO
Idaho Commission on Human Rights
Boise, ID
208-334-2873
888-269-7025
http://humanrights.idaho.gov

ILLINOIS
Department of Human Rights
Chicago, IL
312-814-6200
www.state.il.us/dhr

INDIANA
Civil Rights Commission
Indianapolis, IN
317-232-2600
800-628-2909
www.in.gov/icrc

IOWA
Iowa Civil Rights Commission
Des Moines, IA
515-281-4121
800-457-4416
www.state.ia.us/government/crc

KANSAS
Human Rights Commission
Topeka, KS
785-296-3206
www.khrc.net

KENTUCKY
Human Rights Commission
Louisville, KY
502-595-4024
800-292-5566
www.kchr.ky.gov

LOUISIANA
Commission on Human Rights
Baton Rouge, LA
225-342-6969
http://gov.louisiana.gov/HumanRights/
humanrightshome.htm

MAINE
Human Rights Commission
Augusta, ME
207-624-6290
www.maine.gov/mhrc

MARYLAND
Commission on Human Relations
Baltimore, MD
410-767-8600
800-637-6247 (in-state only)
www.mchr.state.md.us

MASSACHUSETTS
Commission Against Discrimination
Boston, MA
617-994-6000
www.mass.gov/mcad

MICHIGAN
Department of Civil Rights
Detroit, MI
313-456-3700
www.michigan.gov/mdcr

MINNESOTA
Department of Human Rights
St. Paul, MN
651-296-5663
800-657-3704
www.humanrights.state.mn.us

State Agencies That Enforce Laws Prohibiting Discrimination in Employment (cont'd)

MISSISSIPPI
Department of Employment Security
Jackson, MS
601-321-6000
www.mdes.ms.gov

MISSOURI
Commission on Human Rights
Jefferson City, MO
573-751-3325
877-781-4236
www.labor.mo.gov

MONTANA
Human Rights Bureau
Employment Relations Division
Department of Labor and Industry
Helena, MT
406-444-2884
800-542-0807
http://erd.dli.mt.gov/human-rights-bureau.html

NEBRASKA
Equal Opportunity Commission
Lincoln, NE
402-471-2024
800-642-6112
www.neoc.ne.gov

NEVADA
Equal Rights Commission
Reno, NV
775-823-6690
www.detr.state.nv.us/nerc.htm

NEW HAMPSHIRE
Commission for Human Rights
Concord, NH
603-271-2767
www.nh.gov/hrc

NEW JERSEY
Division on Civil Rights
Newark, NJ
609-292-4605
www.nj.gov/oag/dcr/index.html

NEW MEXICO
Human Rights Bureau
Santa Fe, NM
505-827-6838
800-566-9471
www.dws.state.nm.us/new/Labor-Relations/
    humrights.html

NEW YORK
Division of Human Rights
Bronx, NY
718-741-8400
www.dhr.state.ny.us

NORTH CAROLINA
Employment Discrimination Bureau
Department of Labor
Raleigh, NC
919-807-2796
800-NC-LABOR
www.nclabor.com/edb/edb.htm

NORTH DAKOTA
Human Rights Division
Department of Labor
Bismarck, ND
701-328-2660
800-582-8032
www.nd.gov/labor/human-rights/index.html

State Agencies That Enforce Laws Prohibiting Discrimination in Employment (cont'd)

OHIO
Civil Rights Commission
Columbus, OH
614-466-5928
888-278-7101
www.crc.ohio.gov

OKLAHOMA
Human Rights Commission
Oklahoma City, OK
405-521-2360
888-456-2558
www.ok.gov/ohrc

OREGON
Civil Rights Division
Bureau of Labor and Industries
Portland, OR
971-673-0764
www.oregon.gov/BOLI/CRD

PENNSYLVANIA
Human Relations Commission
Harrisburg, PA
717-787-4410
717-787-9784
www.phrc.state.pa.us

RHODE ISLAND
Commission for Human Rights
Providence, RI
401-222-2661
www.richr.state.ri.us/frames.html

SOUTH CAROLINA
Human Affairs Commission
Columbia, SC
803-737-7800
800-521-0725
www.state.sc.us/schac

SOUTH DAKOTA
Division of Human Rights
Pierre, SD
605-773-4493
www.state.sd.us/dol/boards/hr

TENNESSEE
Human Rights Commission
Knoxville, TN
865-594-6500
800-251-3589
www.tennessee.gov/humanrights

TEXAS
Commission on Human Rights
Austin, TX
512-463-2642
www.twc.state.tx.us/customers/jsemp/
jsempsubcrd.html

UTAH
Antidiscrimination and Labor Division
Labor Commission
Salt Lake City, UT
801-530-6801
800-222-1238
www.laborcommission.utah.gov/
AntidiscriminationandLabor/
employmentdiscrimination.html

VERMONT
Attorney General's Office
Civil Rights Division
Montpelier, VT
802-828-3171
www.atg.state.vt.us

State Agencies That Enforce Laws Prohibiting Discrimination in Employment (cont'd)

VIRGINIA
Council on Human Rights
Richmond, VA
804-225-2292
http://chr.vipnet.org

WASHINGTON
Human Rights Commission
Seattle, WA
206-464-6500
800-233-3247
www.hum.wa.gov

WEST VIRGINIA
Human Rights Commission
Charleston, WV
304-558-2616
888-676-5546
www.wvf.state.wv.us/wvhrc

WISCONSIN
Equal Rights Division
Madison, WI
608-266-6860
http://dwd.wisconsin.gov/er

WYOMING
Department of Employment
Cheyenne, WY
307-777-7261
http://doe.wyo.gov/Pages

Index

⚖ NOLO   *Keep Up to Date*

1 Go to Nolo.com/newsletters to sign up for free newsletters and discounts on Nolo products.

- **Nolo's Special Offer.** A monthly newsletter with the biggest Nolo discounts around.

- **Landlord's Quarterly.** Deals and free tips for landlords and property managers.

2 Don't forget to check for updates. Find this book at **Nolo.com** and click "Legal Updates."

Let Us Hear From You

3 Register your Nolo product and give us your feedback at Nolo.com/book-registration.

- Once you've registered, you qualify for technical support if you have any trouble with a download or CD (though most folks don't).

- We'll send you a coupon for 15% off your next Nolo.com order!

ELBA6

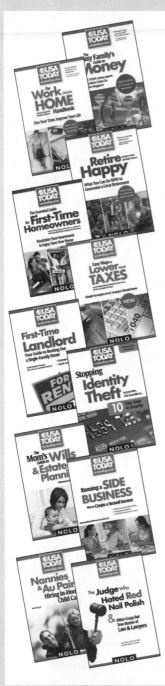

⚖️ NOLO *Online Legal Forms*

Nolo offers a large library of legal solutions and forms, created by Nolo's in-house legal staff. These reliable documents can be prepared in minutes.

Create a Document

- **Incorporation.** Incorporate your business in any state.
- **LLC Formations.** Gain asset protection and pass-through tax status in any state.
- **Wills.** Nolo has helped people make over 2 million wills. Is it time to make or revise yours?
- **Living Trust (avoid probate).** Plan now to save your family the cost, delays, and hassle of probate.
- **Trademark.** Protect the name of your business or product.
- **Provisional Patent.** Preserve your rights under patent law and claim "patent pending" status.

Download a Legal Form

Nolo.com has hundreds of top quality legal forms available for download—bills of sale, promissory notes, nondisclosure agreements, LLC operating agreements, corporate minutes, commercial lease and sublease, motor vehicle bill of sale, consignment agreements and many, many more.

Review Your Documents

Many lawyers in Nolo's consumer-friendly lawyer directory will review Nolo documents for a very reasonable fee. Check their detailed profiles at **Nolo.com/lawyers**.